Israel Smith Clare

The World's History Illuminated - Vol. 04

Israel Smith Clare

The World's History Illuminated - Vol. 04

ISBN/EAN: 9783744651530

Printed in Europe, USA, Canada, Australia, Japan

Cover: Foto ©ninafisch / pixelio.de

More available books at **www.hansebooks.com**

STATUE OF COLUMBUS, GENOA, ITALY

THE WORLD'S HISTORY
ILLUMINATED

CONTAINING A RECORD OF THE HUMAN RACE FROM THE EARLIEST HISTORICAL PERIOD TO THE PRESENT TIME. EMBRACING A GENERAL SURVEY OF THE PROGRESS OF MANKIND IN NATIONAL AND SOCIAL LIFE, CIVIL GOVERNMENT, RELIGION, LITERATURE, SCIENCE AND ART

COMPLETE IN EIGHT VOLUMES

Compiled, Arranged and Written by...... ISRAEL SMITH CLARE Author of "THE WORLD'S HISTORY ILLUMINATED," and "COMPLETE HISTORICAL COMPENDIUM."

REVIEWED, VERIFIED AND ENDORSED BY THE PROFESSORS OF HISTORY IN FIVE AMERICAN UNIVERSITIES, WITH AN INTRODUCTION ON THE EDUCATIONAL VALUE OF HISTORICAL STUDY

By MOSES COIT TYLER, A.M., L.H.D.

PROFESSOR OF AMERICAN HISTORY IN CORNELL UNIVERSITY.

"NOT TO KNOW WHAT HAPPENED BEFORE WE WERE BORN IS TO REMAIN ALWAYS A CHILD; FOR WHAT WERE THE LIFE OF MAN DID WE NOT COMBINE PRESENT EVENTS WITH THE RECOLLECTIONS OF PAST AGES?"—*CICERO.*

Volume IV.—Mediæval History

ILLUMINATED WITH MAPS, PORTRAITS AND VIEWS.

ST. LOUIS
WESTERN NEWSPAPER SYNDICATE

COPYRIGHT, 1897,

BY

R. S. PEALE AND J. A. HILL.

TABLE OF CONTENTS.

PART II.—MEDIÆVAL HISTORY.—VOL. IV.

CHAPTER I. THE DARK AGES.

SECTION I.

CHARACTER OF MEDIÆVAL HISTORY, . . . 1179

New Races in Europe.—Mediæval and Modern History.—The Dark Ages.—The Middle Ages.—Character of the Mediæval Period.

SECTION II.

THE NEW RACES IN EUROPE, ... 1180–1185

The Aryan Races in Europe.—Greeks and Latins.—Celts, Teutons and Slavonians.—Civilization of the Barbarians by the Romans.—The Amalgamation of the Latin and Teutonic Races.—Visigoths.— Sueves.— Heruli. — Vandals. — Burgundians. — Lombards.— Alemanni. — Thuringians.—Franks. — Saxons. — Northmen. — Turanian Races in Europe.—Laps, Fins and Basques.—Avars, Bulgarians and Hungarians.—Mongols and Ottoman Turks.—Semitic Races.—Saracens and Moors.—Rise of Modern Languages.

SECTION III.

THE VISIGOTHIC KINGDOM IN SPAIN, . 1186–1190

Migration of the Visigoths to Spain.—Adolphus.—Sigeric.— Wallia. — Theodoric I. — Thorsimund.—Theodoric II.—Euric.—Alaric II.—Gensaleic.—Theodoric the Ostrogoth.—Amalaric.—Theudis.—Theudisdel. — Agilan. — Athanagild. — Leuva I.—Leovigild. — Recared I. — Leuva II. — Witeric.—Gundemar.— Sisebert.— Recared II.— Swintila.—Sisenand.—Chintila.—Tulga.—Chindaswind.—Receswind.—Wamba.—Ervigius.—Egica.—Witiza.—Roderic.—Saracen Conquest of Spain.

SECTION IV.

THE OSTROGOTHIC KINGDOM IN ITALY, 1190–1194

Italy under Odoacer.—Ostrogothic Conquest of Italy.—Theodoric.—Athalaric.—Theodatus.—Vitiges.—Wars with the Eastern Empire.—Invasion of Italy by Belisarius.—Siege of Rome by Vitiges.—Capture of Ravenna by Belisarius.—Totila.—His Capture of Rome.—Belisarius in Italy.—Totila's Second Capture of Rome.—Victories of Narses in Italy.—Teias.—His Defeat and Death.—German Invasion of Italy.—Italy Annexed to the Eastern Empire.—The Exarchs of Ravenna.

SECTION V.

THE LOMBARD KINGDOM IN ITALY, . . 1194–1198

The Lombard Migration to the Danube.—Audoin. — Alboin. — Lombard Migration to Italy.—Cleph.—Autharis.—Agilulf.—The Iron Crown of Lombardy.— Adaluald. — Arinald.— Rotharis.—Roduald.--Aribert I.—Berthariht and Godebert.—Grimvald.—Bertharit.—Cunibert.—Luitbert.— Raginbert.— Aribert II.—Ansprand.—Luidprand.—Wars with the Exarchs of Ravenna and with the Pope. — Hildebrand. — Rachis. — Astolph. — War with the Pope and Pepin the Little, King of the Franks.—Pepin's Invasion of Italy.—Beginning of the Pope's Temporal Power.—Desiderius.—Conquest of the Lombard Kingdom by Charlemagne.

SECTION VI.

THE FRANKS IN GAUL, ... 1198–1206

Wars of the Franks with the Romans in Gaul.—Ripuarian Franks.—Salian Franks.—Pharamond.—Clodian. — Merovéus. — Childeric. — Clovis. — His Conquest of Northern Gaul.—His Christian Wife Clotilda.—His Victory over the Alemanni in the Battle of Zülpich.—His Conversion to Christianity.—His Alliance with the Church.—His Conquest of the Bretons of Armorica.—His Victory over the Burgundians.—His Victory over the Visigoths near Poitiers.—His Repulse at Arles.—His Annexation of Aquitaine.—Embassy from the Eastern Emperor Anastasius to Clovis.—Extent of the Frank Kingdom.—Character of the Government of Clovis.—His Religion.—His Codes of Laws.—Murders of Other Frankish Kings.—Death of Clovis.—His Sons and Successors.—Theodoric.—Clodomir.—Childebert.—Clotaire.—Their Quarrels.—War with the Burgundians.—Clotilda.—Murder of her Sons by Clotaire.—Theodebert.—War with the Visigoths of Spain.—Theodebert's Conquest of Northern Italy.— Theodebald. — Chramnè War with the Bretons.—Clotaire's Four Sons.—Charibert, Gontram, Chilperic, Sigebert.—Quarrels and Crimes of Brunehaut and Fredegonda.—Childebert II.—Clotaire II.—Dagobert I.—His Canonization.—His Successors, Rois-Fainéants. — Mayors of the Palace.—Pepin d' Heristal.—His Successes over the Other German Tribes.—Conversion of the Germans to Christianity.—Plectrude and Dagobert III.—Charles Martel.—His Victories over the Saxons, Frisians and Burgundians.—His Great Victory over the Saracens at Tours.—Its Results.—Carloman and Pepin the Little.—Chilperic III.—St. Boniface, or Winfried.—Carloman's Retirement.—Deposition of Chilperic III., the Last Merovingian King, by Pepin the Little, who thus Founded the Carlovingian Dynasty.

SECTION VII.

THE ANGLES AND SAXONS IN BRITAIN, 1206–1218

Britain under the Romans.—The Scots and Picts.—Their Inroads.—Helplessness of the Britons.—Migration of the Angles and Saxons to Britain.—Their Conquest of Britain.—The Anglo-Saxon

TABLE OF CONTENTS.

Heptarchy.—The Three Saxon Kingdoms.—The Three Angle Kingdoms.—Anglo-Saxon Religion.—Origin of the Names of the Days of the Week.—The Names of the Months.—Anglo-Saxon Government.—Conversion of the Anglo-Saxons to Christianity.—The Monk Austin, or Augustine.—Wars Among the Anglo-Saxon Kingdoms in Britain.—Founding of the Kingdom of England by Egbert —Condition of the Anglo-Saxons.—The Monasteries.—The Venerable Bede.—Cædmon the Poet.—The Irish Missionaries.—Gildas the Wise.—The Witenagemote.—Counties, or Shires.—Earls and Aldermen.—Sheriffs.—Earls, Thanes, Churls and Serfs.—Household Serfs and Villains.—Officers of the King's Household.—Criminal Laws of the Anglo-Saxons.—Modes of Trial.—The Ordeal.—Table of the Anglo-Saxon Heptarchy.—Tables of the Sovereigns of the Barbarian Monarchies.

SECTION VIII.

THE EASTERN ROMAN EMPIRE, ... 1219-1242

The Eastern Empire under Arcadius.—Theodosius II.—Invasion of the Empire by the Huns.—The Empress Pulcheria.—Marcian.—Leo I.—Zeno.—Anastasius I.—Justin I.—Accession of Justinian.—War with Persia.—Factions at Constantinople.—The Nika Riots.—Conquest of the Vandal Kingdom in Africa by Belisarius.—Wars with the Ostrogoths in Italy.—Conquest of the Ostrogoths by Belisarius.—Belisarius Sent against the New Persians.—Justinian's Ungrateful Treatment of Belisarius.—The Long War War between the Eastern Roman and New Persian Empires.—Revolts in Africa and Italy.—The Revolt of the Ostrogoths in Italy.—Victories of Belisarius over the Ostrogoths.—Recall of Belisarius.—Conquest of the Ostrogoths by Narses.—The Exarchate of Ravenna.—The Gepidæ and the Lombards.—Slavonians and Bulgarians.—Avars and Turks—Victories of Belisarius over the Bulgarians and Slavonians.—Justinian's Ingratitude to Belisarius.—Cathedral of St. Sophia.—Rampart of Gog and Magog.—The Civil Law.—Silk Manufacture.—Justin II.—Tiberius.—Maurice.—War with the Franks.—War with Persia.—Phocas.—Heraclius.—War with Persia.—Persian Conquest of Syria, Palestine and Egypt.—Persian Invasion of Asia Minor.—Victories of Heraclius in Persia.—Saracen Conquest of Syria and Palestine.—Constantine III. and Heracleonas.—Constans II.—Constantine IV.—First Siege of Constantinople by the Saracens.—Justinian II.—Leontius and Absimarus.—Justinian II. Restored.—Philippicus.—Anastasius II.—Theodosius III.—Leo III., the Isaurian.—Iconoduli and Iconoclasts.—War of Iconoclasm.—Constantine V., Copronymus.—His Persecution of the Iconoduli.—Leo IV.—Constantine VI.—Irene.—Nicephorus.—Stauracius.—Michael I.—Leo V., the Armenian.—Bulgarian Ravages.—Michael II., the Armorian.—Theophilus.—Michael III., the Drunkard.—End of the Iconoclastic War.—Separation of the Greek and Roman Catholic Churches.—Basil I.—His Victories over the Saracens.—The Basilica—Leo VI., the Philosopher, and Alexander.—Constantine VII., Porphyrogenitus.—Romanus I., Leucapenus.—Christopher. — Stephen. — Constantine VIII.—Constantine VII. Restored.—Romanus II.—Nicephorus II., Phocas.—John I., Zimisces.—His victories over the Saracens and the Russians.—Basil II. and Constantine IX.—War with the Bulgarians.—Romanus III. and Argyropulus.—Michael IV., the Paphlagonian. — Michael V., Caliphates.—Constantine X., Monomachus and Zoë.—Theodora and Michael VI., Stratiotes.—Isaac Comnenus.—Constantine XI.—Eudocia.—Romanus IV., Diogenes.—His Defeat and Capture by the Seljuk Turks.—His Release and Dethronement.—Michael VII., Parapinaces.—Nicephorus III.—A Large part of Asia Minor Ceded to the Seljuk Turks.—Alexis I., Comnenus. — Calamities of the Empire.—Empire of the Seljuk Turks.—The First Crusade.—John II.—Manuel I.—Wars with the Seljuk Turks, the Hungarians, and the Normans of Sicily.—Decline of the Eastern Empire.—Adventures of Andronicus — Alexis II.—Andronicus.—His Cruelty.—Isaac Angelus.—Fate of Andronicus.—Alexis III.—Rival Claimants.—Decline of the Eastern Empire.—Its Reduced Dominions.

SECTION IX.

NEW PERSIAN EMPIRE OF THE SASSANIDÆ, ... 1242-1348

Victories of Arsaces XXX., the Last Parthian King, over the Romans—Condition of Persia under the Parthian Dominion.—Revolt of the Persians under Artaxerxes.—Defeat and Death of Arsaces XXX. of Parthia at Hormuz.—End of the Parthian Empire.—Founding of the New Persian Empire of the Sassanidæ.—Restoration of Zoroastrianism and the Magi.—Extension of the New Persian Empire.—Maxims of Artaxerxes I.—His Zeal for Zoroastrianism.—His War with Chosröes of Armenia.—His War with the Romans.—Renewal of the War with Armenia.—Government of Artaxerxes I.—His Dying Speech.—Revival of Persian Art.—Sculptures of Artaxerxes I.—Coins.—Bas-Reliefs.—Zoroastrianism and Magism.—Religious Reforms of Artaxerxes I.—Publication of the Zend-Avesta.—Powers Conferred on the Magi.—Sapor I.—War with Hatra.—War with Rome.—Captivity of the Roman Emperor Valerian.—Sapor's Ravages in Syria and Asia Minor.—His War with Odenatus of Palmyra.—Sapor's Great Works. — Bas-Reliefs and Rock-Inscriptions. — Great Dyke at Shuster. — Sapor's Coins.—Revival of Zoroastrianism.—Manis, or Manes, and his Religion. — His Ertang.—Character of Sapor I.—Character of his Successors.—Hormisdas I.—Varahran I.—His Persecution of the Manichæans and the Christians.—His Alliance with Zenobia of Palmyra.—His Wars in the East.—War with the Romans—Varahran III.—Civil War between Narses and Hormisdas.—Triumph of Narses.—His War with Tiridates of Armenia.—His War with the Romans.—Hormisdas II.—His Character and Works.—His Court of Justice.—Afghan Civilization.—Anecdote of Prince Hormisdas.—His Murder by the Nobles.—Sapor II. Proclaimed King before his Birth.—His Lifelong Reign of Seventy Years.—His Victories over the Neighboring Nations.—His Cruelties.—His Cruel Persecution of his Christian Subjects.—His War with the Romans.—Civil and Religious War in Armenia.—Renewal of the War with Rome.—First Siege of Nisibis. — Armenian Affairs. — Second Siege of Nisibis.—Battle of Singara.—Third Siege of Nisibis.—Invasion of Persia by the Massagetæ.—Alliance of Rome and Armenia.—Eastern Wars of Sapor II.—Peace Negotiations between Persia and Rome.—Renewal of Hostilities.—Siege and Capture of Amida by the New Persians.—Of Singara.—Of Bezabde.—Sapor's Repulse at Virta.—Roman Repulse at Bezabde.—Invasion of the New Persian Empire by the Roman Emperor Julian the Apostate.—Capture of Anathan.—Siege and Capture of Perisabor.—Of Maogamalcha.—Julian's March to Coché.—His Victory There.—His Sudden Retreat.—Sapor's Pursuit.—Battle of Maranga.—Battle of Samarah and Death of Julian the Apos-

TABLE OF CONTENTS.

tate.—Continued Retreat of the Romans.—Peace of Dura.—Triumph of Sapor II.—Hostile Attitude of Armenia toward Rome.—Arsaces, King of Armenia, Seized and Blinded by Sapor II.—Armenian Resistance to Sapor II.—Sapor's Conquest of Iberia.—His Siege and Capture of Artogerassa.—Armenia's Patriotic Stand.—Division of Iberia.—War with the Roman Emperor Valens.—Death of Sapor II.—His Coins.—Artaxerxes II.—His Amiable Character.—Armenia Made Tributary to Persia.—War between Persia and Armenia.—Sapor III.—Division of Armenia between Rome and Persia.—Sculptured Memorial of Sapor III. at Kermanshah.—Coins of Artaxerxes II. and Sapor III.—Character of Sapor III.—Varahran IV.—Revolt of Chosroës of Armenia.—His Imprisonment and Deposition.—Character of Varahran IV.—Isdigerd I.—His Character and Peaceful Reign.—His Guardianship of the Roman Prince Theodosius.—His Successive Persecutions of the Christians and the Magians.—Isdigerd's Persecution of the Armenians.—Coins of Isdigerd I.—His Character.—Legend Concerning his Death.—Disputed Succession.—Varahran V.—His Persecution of the Christians.—War with the Eastern Roman Empire.—Siege of Theodosiopolis.—A Single Combat.—Peace.—His Conciliatory Policy toward Armenia.—Religious War in Armenia.—Persarmenia Absorbed by Persia.—Beginning of Wars with the Ephthalites.—Defeats of the Ephthalites.—Peace.—Coins of Varahran V.—His Character.—His Death.—Isdigerd II.—Short War with the Eastern Roman Empire.—War with the Ephthalites.—Forcible Effort to Force Zoroastrianism on the Armenians.—Revolt of the Armenians and Iberians.—War with the Ephthalites.—Coins of Isdigerd II.—His Character.—Hormisdas III.—His Usurpation and Overthrow.—Perozes.—War with Albania.—Era of Prosperity.—Drought and Failure of Crops.—Efficient Measures of Perozes.—Wars with the Ephthalites.—Persecution of the Armenian Christians.—Armenian Revolt.—War with the Ephthalites.—Death of Perozes.—His Character.—His Coins.—Balas.—Peace with the Ephthalites.—Pacification of Armenia.—Character of Balas.—His Coins.—Kobad's First Reign.—War with the Khazars.—Mazdak and his Religious Movement.—Kobad's Conversion to the New Religion. — Disorders. — Deposition of Kobad.—Zamasp.—His Overthrow.—His Coins.—Kobad's Second Reign.—Mazdakism Checked.—War with the Eastern Roman Empire. — Siege and Capture of Amida by the New Persians.—Peace.—War with the Ephthalites.—Kobad's Four Sons.—Plot of the Mazdakites.—Massacre of the Mazdakites.—Persecution of the Christians of Iberia.—Iberian Revolt.—Its Suppression by the New Persians.—War with the Eastern Roman Empire.—First Campaigns of Belisarius.—Persian Alliance with Alamundarus.—Kobad's Death.—His Character.—His Coins.—Khosrou Nushirvan.—Opposition to His Accession.—His Cruel Persecution of the Mazdakites.—The "Endless Peace."—Renewal of the War with the Eastern Roman Empire.—Khosrou Nushirvan's Invasion of Syria.—His Siege and Capture of Antioch.—Peace with the Romans.—Khosrou's Spoils.—Renewal of the War with the Eastern Roman Empire.—Khosrou's New City of Antioch, on the Tigris.—Revolt of Lazica against the Romans.—It Becomes a Persian Province.—Campaigns of Belisarius and Khosrou Nushirvan.—Five Years' Truce.—Revolt of Lazica against the New Persians.—It again Becomes a Roman Province.—The Lazic War.—Sieges of Petra.—Its Capture by the Romans.—Second Five Years' Truce.—Continuance of the Lazic War.—Alienation of Lazica from the Romans.— Renewal of its Alliance with the Romans. — Siege of Phasis. — Defeat of the New Persians.—Third Five Years' Truce.—Peace with the Romans.—Khosrou Nushirvan's War with the Ephthalites.—Abyssinian Conquest of Arabia Felix, or Yemen.—New Persian Conquest of Yemen.—Khosrou Nushirvan's Wars with the Turks.—Dizabul, the Turkish Khan.—His Alliance with the Eastern Roman Empire.—Renewal of the War between the New Persian and Eastern Roman Empires.—Persian Invasion of Syria.—Khosrou Nushirvan's Siege and Capture of Daras.—A Year's Truce.—Three Years' Truce.—Renewal of the War. — Negotiations. — Death of Khosrou Nushirvan.—His Vigorous Administration.—His Reforms.—His Patronage of Science and Learning.—His Toleration of Christianity.—His Unhappy Domestic Relations.—His Character.—His Coins.—Hormisdas IV.—His Wars with the Eastern Roman Empire.—His Tyranny.—Invasions of the New Persian Empire by the Arabs, Khazars and Turks.—Bahram's Victory over the Turks.—His Defeat by the Romans.—His Quarrel with his King.—His Revolt.—Overthrow and Murder of Hormisdas IV. — His Character. — His Coins. — Khosrou Parviz.—His Difficult Situation.—Bahram's Threatening Attitude.—Flight of Khosrou Parviz to the Romans.—He is Aided by the Eastern Roman Emperor Maurice.—Bahram's Short Reign. — Bahram's Victory. — His Defeat. — His Flight to the Turks. — His Coins. — Second Reign of Khosrou Parviz. — His Situation at his Restoration.—Fate of his Uncles.—Of Bahram.—His Partial Conversion to Christianity.—His Christian Wife, Shirin.—His Immense Harem.—His Wars with the Ephthalites and Turks.—His Friendly Relations with the Emperor Maurice.—His War with the Eastern Roman Emperors Phocas and Heraclius.—Persian Invasion and Conquest of Syria.—Capture of Antioch, Damascus and Jerusalem. — Massacre of Jerusalem. — The "True Cross" Carried to Ctesiphon.—Persian Invasion and Conquest of Egypt.—Capture of Alexandria.—Persian Invasion of Asia Minor.—Siege and Capture of Chalcedon and Ancyra.—Conquest of the Island of Rhodes.—Great Extent of the New Persian Empire.—Approach of the Avars to Constantinople.—Desperate Straits of the Emperor Heraclius.—His Intended Flight to Carthage Prevented by the Populace of Constantinople.—His Desperate Resolution.—His Invasion of Persia.—His Victories in Persia.—The Persians Defeated in Asia Minor.—Attack of the Avars on Constantinople Repulsed.—Continued Victories of Heraclius in Persia.—He Plunders the Persian Palaces.—His Retreat.—Tyranny and Cruelty of Khosrou Parviz.—His Overthrow and Murder by his Son and Successor, Siröes.—Character of Khosrou Parviz.—His Splendid Palaces.—His Vast Number of Animals.—His Nine Seals of Office.—His Moral Defects.—His Esteem for his Christian Wife.—His Coins.—Siröes.—Peace with the Eastern Roman Empire.—Popularity of Siröes at his Accession.—His Massacre of his Brothers and Half Brothers.—His Remorse and Death.—His Coins.—Artaxerxes III.—Revolt of Shahr-Barz.—His Alliance with Heraclius.—His Usurpation of the Persian Throne.—His Overthrow and Murder by his Troops.—Purandocht.—Azermidocht. — Insignificant Kings.—Isdigerd III.—Mohammed and the Arabs.—The Mohammedan Conquest of Persia.—Flight and Assassination of Isdigerd III.—Persia under the Saracen Dominion.—Character of Isdigerd III.—His Coins.—New Persian Civilization. — Architecture.—Palaces of Khosrou Parviz.—Statue of

Sapor I.—Bas-Reliefs of Sapor I.—Other Bas-Reliefs.—Bas-Reliefs of Khosrou Nushirvan.—Of Khosrou Parviz.—Zoroastrianism and Magism under the New Persians.—The Magi.—Court of the Sassanidæ.—Seven Ranks of Courtiers.—The Royal Harem.—The Great Officials.—Persepolis, the Early Capital.—Ctesiphon, the Later Capital.—Dastagherd.—Costume of the Sassanidæ.—Their Armor.—Their Pastimes.—Hunting.—Musical Instruments.—New Persian Warfare.—Elephant Corps.—Cavalry.—Archers.—Ordinary Infantry.—Great National Standard.—The Higher Classes.—All Classes Free from Oppression, Except the Highest.—Justice Honestly Administered.—The King's Tribunal.—The Highest Class Oppressed.—Table of the Kings of Persia.

SECTION X.

ISLAM'S RISE AND THE SARACEN EMPIRE, ... 1348–1420

Geography of Arabia.—Shiekhs.—The Arabs a Semitic Race.—Their Nomadic Character.—The Horse and Camel.—Arabia Before Mohammed.—Cities.—Commerce.—The Kaaba.—Mecca.—Its Antiquity.—Yatreb, or Medina.—Literature.—Science.—Ancient Arabian Religions.—Mohammed.—His Birth.—His Descent.—His Youth.—Omens.—His Caravan Journeys.—His Marriage with Kadijah.—His Religious Meditation.—Visions of Angels.—Revelations.—Mohammed's First Converts.—His Relatives and Protectors.—The Cardinal Doctrine of his Creed.—His Adopted Children.—His Early Proselytes.—Ali.—Abu Taleb.—Abu Bekr.—Mohammed's Open Avowal of his Mission.—His Slow Progress at First.—Opposition of the Koreish.—Conversion of the Koreish.—Persecution of Mohammed's Followers.—Omar's Conversion.—The Hashamites.—Mohammed's Mission to Taif.—His Faith.—Mohammed's Preaching.—Pilgrims from Yatreb.—Mohammed's Celebrated Dream.—The Hegira.—Mohammed's Progress.—His Degeneracy.—The Holy War.—Battle of Bedr.—Battle of Ohud.—Mohammed's Fanaticism.—Persecution of Jews.—Battles with Syrians, Jews and the Koreish.—Mohammed's Capture of Mecca.—His Letters to the Emperor Heraclius of Constantinople and King Khosrou Parviz of Persia.—Mohammed's Conquest of Arabia.—Spread of Islam.—Mohammed's First Foreign War.—Invasion of Syria.—Forced Entrance into Mecca.—Conversion of the Meccans.—Mohammed the Ruling Sovereign of Arabia.—The Year of Embassies.—Mohammed's Household.—His Last Days.—His Death.—Grief of his Followers.—His Character.—The Koran.—Its Teachings.—Its Descriptions of the Resurrection, the Judgment, Hell and Paradise.—Abu Bekr, the First Khalif.—Khaled, the Sword of God.—Moslem Zeal.—Saracen Invasion of the Eastern Roman and the New Persian Empires.—Conquest of Hira and Obolla by Khaled.—Abu Obeidah's Invasion of Syria.—Arab Victories.—Capture of Bosrah.—Battles of Aiznadin and Yermuk.—Capture of Damascus.—Death of Abu Bekr.—His Character.—Omar, the Next Khalif.—His Simple Life.—Capture of Emesa and Baalbec.—Siege and Capture of Jerusalem.—Omar's Entry into Jerusalem.—Capture of Aleppo and Antioch.—Conquest of Syria.—Renewal of Hostilities with the New Persians.—Arab Victories in Irak.—Abu Obeidah's Defeat and Death.—Battle of El Boweib.—Arab Demands Rejected by Isdigerd III.—Battle of Cadesia.—Great Persian Defeat.—Flight of Isdigerd III.—Capture of Ctesiphon by the Arabs.—Their Spoils of Conquest.—Battle of Jalula.—Continued Flight of Isdigerd III.—More Arab Victories.—Conquest of Persian Provinces.—Recall of Sa'ad.—Battle of Nehavend.—End of the New Persian Empire.—Assassination of Isdigerd III.—Mohammedan Persecution of the Magi.—Amru's Invasion of Egypt.—Capture of Pelusium, Memphis and Alexandria.—Destruction of the Alexandrian Library.—Conquest of Egypt.—Assassination of Omar.—His Character.—Othman, the Third Khalif.—Saracen Invasion of Asia Minor and Armenia.—Conquest of Cyprus and Rhodes.—Civil War.—Assassination of Othman.—Ali, the Fourth Khalif.—Revolts against him.—Battle of Khoraiba.—Moawiyah's Revolt.—His Usurpation of the Khalifate.—Sunnites and Shyites.—Renewal of the Civil War.—Assassination of Ali.—His Character.—Moawiyah, the First of the Ommiyades.—Damascus Made the Saracen Capital.—Internal Tranquillity Restored.—Invasion of North Africa.—Founding of Kairwan.—First Siege of Constantinople by the Saracens.—Greek Fire.—The Khalif Yezid.—Hossein's Revolt.—His Overthrow and Death.—The Day of Hossein.—Extension of the Saracen Dominion and of Islam.—Saracen Conquest of North Africa.—Conversion of the Moors.—Saracen Invasion of Spain.—Battle of Xeres de la Frontera.—Conquest of Spain.—Spain Becomes Arab.—Second Siege of Constantinople by the Saracens.—Saracen Invasion of France.—Battle of Tours.—Results of the Saracen Defeat.—Spain under the Saracen Dominion.—Great Extent of the Saracen Empire.—The Khalif's Habits.—Saracen Energy.—The Khalifs and the People.—Overthrow of the Ommiyades.—Accession of the Abbássides.—Abul Abbas al Saffah.—Massacre of the Ommiyades.—Separation of Spain from the Khalifate.—Al Mansur.—Bagdad Founded and Made the Saracen Capital.—Splendor of the Court of the Khalifs at Bagdad.—Al Mohdi.—Musa.—Haroun al Raschid.—His Great Reign.—His Invasion of the Eastern Roman Empire.—Yahia, the Grand Vizier.—His Sons.—Massacre of the Barmecides.—Splendor of Haroun al Raschad's Reign.—His Death.—Al Mamoun and Al Amin.—Civil War and Overthrow of Al Amin.—Al Mamoun's Brilliant Reign.—His Patronage of Literature.—Conquest of Crete.—Saracen Invasions of Sicily.—Saracen Ravages on the Italian Coast.—Saracen Progress in Science and Literature.—Influence of Saracen Civilization on Christian Europe.—College at Bagdad.—Mohammedan Colleges and Libraries.—Astronomy.—Medicine.—Chemistry.—Translations from Greek Writers.—Philosophy.—Astrology.—The Arabian Nights.—Arts and Manufactures.—Architecture.—Rebellions, Civil Wars and Religious Dissensions.—Al Motassem.—Al Moktador.—Decline of the Saracen Empire.—The Khalifs of Bagdad and Cordova.—Mohammedan Sects.—The Two Khalifates.—Dismemberment of the Khalifates.—The New Mohammedan Kingdoms.—Turkish Mercenaries.—Ascendency of the Turks.—Decay of the Khalifate of Bagdad.—Mohammedan Spain.—Egypt under Saracen Dominion.—New Arab Kingdom in North Africa.—The Khalifate of Cairo.—The Three Khalifates.—The Seljuk Turks.—End of the Khalifate of Bagdad.—Great Characters.—Tabari and Macoudi.—Averrhoes.—Achmet.—Geber.—Avicenna.—Abulfeda.—Table of the Saracen Khalifs.

SECTION XI.

THE SARACEN KINGDOM OF CORDOVA, 1421–1430

Spain after the Saracen Conquest.—Introduction of Arabian Customs and Manners.—The Emirs under the Ommiyades.—Condition of Spain.—

TABLE OF CONTENTS.

Spain Becomes Independent under Abderrahman I.—Beginning of the Kingdom of Cordova.—Reign of Abderrahman I.—His Great Works.—The Great Mosque at Cordova.—Transplanting of the Palm-Tree.—The Christian Kingdom of Asturias.—Character of Abderrahman I.—Hixem the Good.—Alhakem the Cruel.—The Spanish March.—Character of Alhakem the Cruel.—His Expensive Guard.—Rebellion.—Its Cruel Suppression.—Alhakem's Remorse.—Abderrahman II.—Spain Ravaged by the Northmen.—Mohammed I.—Almondhir.—Abdalla.—Abderrahman III., the First Khalif of Cordova.—His Extermination of Rebels.—Conquest of the African Kingdom of Fez.—Cultivation of the Arts of Peace.—Character of Abderrahman III.—The Palace and City of Azhara.—Sublime Justice of Abderrahman III.—His Brilliant Reign.—Wealth, Power and Prosperity of the Khalifate of Cordova.—Manufactures.—Agriculture.—Commerce.—Palaces and Gardens.—Libraries and Academies.—Science and Literature.—The Physicians of Cordova.—Alhakem II.—His Character.—His Fondness for Literature.—His Library.—Hixem II.—The Regent Al Mansur.—Weak Character of Hixem II.—Rivals and Usurpers.—Dismemberment of the Khalifate of Cordova.—Hixem III., the Last Khalif of Cordova.—His Character.—Revolts.—His Forced Abdication.—End of the Dynasty of the Ommiyades and of the Khalifate of Cordova.—Cause of Its Ruin.—Spain During the Next Two Centuries.—The Almoravides and the Almohades.—Petty Mohammedan Kingdoms in Spain.—Extent of the Kingdom of Cordova.—Intermarriages of Moors and Christian Spaniards.—Moorish Agriculture and Manufactures.—Splendor of Cordova.—Its Beautiful Gardens.—Moorish Manners and Customs.—Dress.—Women.—Moorish Government.—Treatment of Christians and Jews.

SECTION XII.

EGYPT UNDER THE FATIMITES . . . 1430-1432

Rise of the Arab Kingdom of the Fatimites in Northern Africa under Mohammed al Mehdi.—Conquest of Egypt by Muezzedin.—Cairo Founded.—The Fatimite Khalifs.—Al Hakem.—His Persecution of the Jews and the Christians.—His New Religion.—Persecution of Mohammedans.—Al Hakem's Cruelty and Tyranny.—Assassination of Al Hakem.—Flight of Hamza.—The Sect of the Druses in Syria.—Weakness of the Later Fatimite Khalifs.—Their Grand Viziers.—Adhed.—Contests for Power.—The Grand Vizier Shiracouh.—Saladin.—End of the Fatimite Khalifate.—Saladin Becomes Sultan of Egypt and Syria.—Dismemberment of his Dominions after his Death.—Malek Sala and the Mamelukes.—Egypt under the Mamelukes.

SECTION XIII.

THE WESTERN EMPIRE RESTORED, . 1432-1452

Pepin the Little, the First Carlovingian King of the Franks.—His Compact with Pope Zachary.—The Pope and the Frankish Sovereign.—Pepin's Aid to the Popes against the Lombards.—St. Boniface, or Winfried.—Conversion of the Germans.—Pepin's Wars with the Saracens in the South.—His Reduction of Aquitaine.—His Death.—Charles and Carloman.—Their Mutual Jealousy.—Carloman's Death.—Charlemagne, or Charles the Great, Sole Sovereign of the Franks.—Charlemagne's Character.—His Greatness.—Attitude of the Lombard King Desiderius.—Charlemagne's First War with the Saxons.—His Conquest of the Lombard Kingdom in Northern Italy.—His Second War with the Saxons.—His War with the Saracens of Spain.—Battle of Roncesvalles and Death of Roland.—The Spanish March.—Charlemagne's Third and Fourth Wars with the Saxons.—Margravate of Brandenburg.—Thassilo, Duke of Bavaria.—The Eastern Margravate.—Charlemagne's Conquest of the Avars—His Second Marriage.—Plot against Charlemagne.—Charlemagne Crowned at Rome, as Emperor of the West.—Separation of the Greek and Roman Catholic Churches.—Charlemagne's Treaty with the Eastern Emperor Nicephorus I.—Revolt of the Saxons.—Their Final Conquest by Charlemagne.—Beginning of the Ravages of the Northmen.—Extent of Charlemagne's Empire.—His Capital, Aix la Chapelle.—Organization of his Empire.—Extension of Christianity and Revival of Civilization.—Charlemagne's Government.—His Capitularies or Laws.—Dukes and Counts.—The Marks on the Borders of Germany.—Brandenburg, Austria, and Carinthia.—Administration of Justice.—Missi Dominici.—Charlemagne's Friendship for the Church.—His Efforts to Improve the Morals of the Clergy.—His Fondness for Learning and Learned Men.—His Encouragement of the Arts, Agriculture, Commerce and Literature.—His Studious Habits.—The Anglo-Saxon Monk, Alcuin.—Charlemagne's System of Education.—Monastic Schools.—Charlemagne's Personal Appearance.—His Simple Habits.—His German Character.—His Private Character.—His Will.—His Eldest Son's Death.—Charlemagne's Last Days.—His Death.—His Tomb.—End of the Carlovingian Glory.—Louis le Debonnaire.—His Weak Reign.—His Sons.—Bernard's Revolt.—His Punishment and Death.—Louis le Debonnaire's Remorse.—His Second Marriage.—His Son Charles the Bald.—Revolt of His Other Sons.—Their Triumph and Insolence.—Their Father's Actions Produce a Second Rebellion.—They are Aided by the Pope.—The Loyal Bishops of France.—Louis le Debonnaire's Humiliating Surrender.—His Dethronement.—Bishop Ebbo's Iniquitous Scheme.—Louis le Debonnaire's Forced Penance and Written Confession.—His Imprisonment.—Louis le Debonnaire Restored by a Popular Revolution.—His Imbecility and Subserviency to the Pope.—New Division of His Dominions.—Revolt of his Son Louis.—Death of Louis le Debonnaire.—Quarrels of his Sons.—Battle of Fontenay.—Partition Treaty of Verdun.

SECTION XIV.

THE NEW CARLOVINGIAN KINGDOMS, . 1452-1463

Kingdoms of Italy, Germany and France.—Lorraine, Burgundy and Provence.—Weakness of the Carlovingian Kings of France, Germany and Italy.—Ravages of the Northmen.—Extent of Lothaire's Kingdom of Italy, Burgundy and Lorraine.—Germany under Louis the German.—France under Charles the Bald.—Languages of the Various Carlovingian Kingdoms.—The Saracens in Sicily and Southern Italy.—Defense of Rome by Pope Leo IV.—The Leonine City.—Lothaire's Death.—His Sons and Successors.—League Against the Saracens in Southern Italy.—Capture of Bari.—Revival of the Greek Power in Southern Italy.—Continued Ravages of the Northmen in Germany.—Louis the German's Wars with the Slavonians and with Charles the Bald of France.—France under Charles the Bald.—Distracted Condition of the Kingdom.—Ravages of the Northmen.—Their First Capture and Plunder of Paris.—Their Second Capture of Paris and Massacre of the Inhabitants.—Their Third Attack on Paris and Repulse.—Suffering of France from the Ravages of the North-

TABLE OF CONTENTS.

men.—Lothaire II. of Lorraine and Pope Nicholas the Great.—Lorraine Divided between France and Germany.—Charles the Bald's Quarrel with Pope Adrian II.—His Reconciliation with the Pope.—Charles the Bald Crowned Emperor.—War Between Charles the Bald and Louis the German.—Death of Louis the German.—His Sons.—Renewal of the Saracen Ravages in Southern Italy.—Charles the Bald Goes to the Aid of Pope John VIII.—Death of Charles the Bald.—The Pope Forced to Pay Tribute to the Saracens.—Establishment of the Feudal System.—Beginning of the French Nation and Language.—Charles the Fat Becomes Sole King of Germany.—Louis the Stammerer, King of France.—Louis III. and Carloman.—Founding of the Second Kingdom of Burgundy by Boso.—Charles the Fat of Germany Makes Himself King of Italy.—He is also Made King of France.—His Disgraceful Peace with the Northmen.—The Northmen Under Rollo Ravage France and Besiege Paris.—Brave Defense of Paris by Count Eudes.—Dethronement of Charles the Fat.—Arnulf Elected King of Germany.—Eudes Made King of France.—Italy Contested Between the Dukes of Friuli and Spoleto.—Insanity and Death of Charles the Fat.—Arnulf's Victory Over the Northmen at Louvain.—He Calls in the Aid of the Magyars, or Hungarians.—Their Settlement in the Valleys of the Theiss and the Danube.—Guido, Duke of Spoleto, Becomes King of Italy and Emperor.—Arnulf Crowned Emperor.—Beranger, Duke of Friuli, Makes Himself King of Italy.—Arnulf's Death.—Louis the Child, King of Germany.—Germany Ravaged by the Hungarians.—End of the Carlovingian Dynasty in Germany.—Italy Ravaged by the Hungarians and the Saracens.—Defeat of the Saracens by Pope John XII.—Italy Distracted by Frequent Revolutions.—France Divided Between Eudes and Charles the Simple.—Charles the Simple Becomes King of All France.—Settlement of the Northmen Under Duke Rollo in France.—Beginning of the Duchy of Normandy.—Weakness and Incapacity of Charles the Simple.—His Dethronement.—Robert Becomes King of France.—His Victory and Death at Soissons.—Duke Rodolph, of Burgundy, Made King of France.—Captivity and Death of Charles the Simple.—Hugh the Great, Count of Paris.—Louis d'Outremer, King of France.—Power of Hugh the Great, Count of Paris.—Civil War Between Louis d'Outremer and Hugh the Great.—Captivity and Death of Louis d'Outremer.—Lothaire, King of France.—Count Hugh the Great and St. Bruno.—Hugh Capet, Count of Paris.—Lorraine Seized by Otho the Great of Germany.—Lothaire's Invasion of Germany.—Invasion of France by Otho II. of Germany.—His Defeat by Lothaire.—Peace.—Louis le Fainéant, the Last Carlovingian King of France.—Hugh Capet Elected King of France.—Table of the Carlovingian Sovereigns.

SECTION XV.

THE NORTHMEN AND THEIR RELIGION, 1463-1487

Geography of Scandinavia.—Its Two Peninsulas.—The Scandinavians, or Northmen, an Aryan Race.—Ancient Scandinavia.—The Cimbri and Teutons.—The Jutes.—Comparison of the Baltic and Mediterranean Seas.—The Aryan Migration to Europe.—Freedom of the North and Civilization of the South of Europe.—Christianity.—The Danes and Normans in Other Parts of Europe.—Old Northern Ideas Still Retained.—Days of Week.—Legislative Bodies.—Jury Trials.—Teutonic Civilization Developed in Scandinavia.—Classes of Scandinavian Society.—Patriarchal Institutions.—Respect for Women.—Skalds.—Old Norse Language.—Maritime Hardihood.—Their Raids.—Vikings.—Sagas.—Character of a Viking.—Their Highest Ambition.—Feasting.—Kempe.—Hioroll and Half.—Gunnar and Regnald.—Berserker.—Halfdan and Hartben.—Arngrim's Sons.—Beginning of the Raids of the Northmen.—Ragnar Lodbrog.—Raids of the Northmen in Germany and France.—Their Settlement of Normandy.—The Danes in England and Ireland.—Danish and Norman Conquests of England.—Raids of the Northmen in Spain, Italy and Greece.—Settlement of the Normans in Southern Italy.—Robert Guiscard.—Harald Fairhair Founds Norway.—Gorm the Old Founds Denmark.—Kurik Founds the Russian Empire.—Iceland and Greenland Discovered by Northmen.—The Coasts of Labrador, Nova Scotia and New England Discovered by Northmen Five Centuries before Christopher Columbus.—Central Idea of the Scandinavian Religion.—Dualism and War in the Natural World.—Courage the Chief Virtue.—Valhalla, or Paradise.—Resemblance of the Scandinavian Religion to Zoroastrianism.—The Icelandic Republic.—Eddas and Sagas.—The Völuspa.—Song of Hyndla.—The Havamal.—Odin's Song of Runes.—Heimskringla.—Cosmogony of the Eddas.—Legends of the Gods and Valhalla.—The Death of Baldur the Good.—Adventures of Thor.—Battle between the Gods and the Giants.—Restitution of All Things.—The Gods.—Odin.—Thor.—Baldur.—Njörd.—Frey and Frigga.—Tyr.—Bragi.—Heimdall.—Æsir.—Vidar.—Vali.—Ullur.—Forseti.—Loki and his Progeny.—The Goddesses.—Scandinavian Worship.—Three Great Festivals.—Scandinavian Courage.—Priests and Soothsayers.—Magic and Charms.—Remains of the Scandinavian Religion.—Sacrifices.—Conversion of the Goths.—Bishop Ulfilas.—Slowness of the Conversion of the Scandinavians to Christianity.—Mission in Denmark.—St. Ansgar in Sweden.—The Swedish Diet Allows Christianity to be Preached.—Harald Bluetooth, King of Denmark.—Apostacy of his Son, Sweyn.—Canute the Great—Hakon the Good, King of Norway.—His Successors.—Olaf the Saint Cruelly Enforces Christianity in Norway.—The All-Thing of Iceland Adopts Christianity.—Scandinavian Development of Christian Life.

SECTION XVI.

DUCHY OF NORMANDY, ... 1487-1492

Character of the Nations that Invaded Southern Europe.—Rollo's Invasion of France during the Reign of Charles the Simple.—His Settlement in France.—Founding of the Duchy of Normandy.—Reign of Rollo, or Robert I.—Bretagne, or Brittany, the Ancient Armorica.—Flight of Britons to Brittany.—Resistance of the Bretons to Duke Robert I., of Normandy.—His Conquest of Brittany.—Government of Duke Robert I.—Tranquillity of Normandy During his Reign.—His Abdication—William Long-sword.—His Aid to Foreign Princes.—His Assassination.—Richard the Fearless.—His Captivity in Paris.—His Wars with Louis d'Outremer, King of France.—Richard the Good.—Events of his Reign.—Richard III.—Robert the Devil.—His Pilgrimage to the Holy Land.—William II., the Conqueror of England.—Norman Adventurers in Southern Italy.—William Iron-arm.—Norman Victory Over the Forces of Pope Leo IX.—Robert Guiscard.—His Victories Over the Greeks and the Saracens in Southern Italy and Sicily.—Conquest of Sicily by Count Roger I.—Robert Guiscard's Invasion of the Eastern Empire.—His Capture of Durazzo.—Kingdom of Naples and Sicily Founded by Roger II.— William III., the Last Norman King of Naples and Sicily.—Table of the Dukes of Normandy.

SECTION XVII.

DANES AND NORMANS IN ENGLAND, . 1497-1520

Founding of the Kingdom of England by Egbert.—Incursions of the Danes.—Reign of Ethelwolf.—Inroads of the Danes.—Prince Alfred.—Reigns of Ethelbert, Ethelbald and Ethelred I.—Continued Raids of the Danes.—Accession of Alfred the Great.—His Struggle with the Danes.—His Great Defeat.—His Desperate Situation.—His Seclusion.—His Victory Over the Danes.—His Benevolence.—Defeat of the Danes.—Alfred's Visit to the Danish Camp in Disguise.—His Great Victory Over the Danes.—He Grants Lands to the Danes.—His Power and Glory.—Danish and Saxon England.—The Anglo-Danes.—Civilization and the Arts of Peace.—Education.—Schools Founded by Alfred the Great.—Oxford University.—Alfred's Literary Works.—His Learning.—The Anglo-Saxon Chronicle.—Alfred's Favorite Works.—His Version of the Psalms, the Gospels and the Lord's Prayer.—His Studious Habits.—His Measurement of Time.—His Code of Laws.—Counties or Shires.—Tithings and Hundreds.—Effective Police Regulations.—Renewal of Danish Incursions.—Foreign Artisans.—English Goldsmiths.—Blacksmiths.—Alfred the Founder of English Institutions.—His Death.—His Greatness and Character.—The Witenagemote.—Meaning of Saxon Names.—Reign of Edward the Elder.—Renewal of Danish Invasions.—Athelstan's Great Reign.—Stratagem of the Danish Prince Aulaff.—The Long Battle.—Reign of Edmund I.—Revolts of the Danes Settled in England.—Their Defeat.—Assassination of Edmund I.—Reign of Edred.—St. Dunstan and the Monks.—Reign of Edwy—His Quarrel with St. Dunstan and Archbishop Odo.—Murder of Elgiva.—Reign of Edgar the Peaceable.—St. Dunstan and the Monks.—Edgar's Good Reign.—St. Dunstan Made Archbishop of Canterbury.—His Ambition and Arrogance.—Wales Rid of Wolves.—Edgar's Fleet.—Edgar's Victories Over the Welsh, Scots and Irish.—The Three Earldoms of Yorkshire, Northumberland and Lothian.—Rise of Edinburgh.—Reign and Assassination of Edward the Martyr.—Reign of Ethelred the Unready.—His Wicked Mother, Elfrida.—Her Remorse.—Renewal of the Danish Inroads.—Danegelt.—Massacre of the Danes in England.—Invasion and Conquest of England by Sweyn, King of Denmark.—Canute the Great of Denmark and Edmund Ironside.—Canute the Great, Sole King of England.—His Good and Wise Reign.—His Conversion to Christianity.—His "King's English."—His Stature and Appearance.—His Poetry.—His Rebuke of his Courtiers.—His Four Kingdoms, England, Denmark, Sweden and Norway.—Reigns of Harold Harefoot and Hardicanute.—Restoration of the Saxon Dynasty.—Reign of Edward the Confessor.—His Preference for Normandy.—His Norman Favorites.—Hostility between Them and the English.—Banishment of Earl Godwin.—Arrogance of the Norman Party.—Visit of Duke William II. of Normandy.—Earl Godwin's Revolt.—The Witenagemote Sustains Him.—Outlawry and Flight of the Norman Bishops, Priests and Knights.—Godwin's Son and Successor, Harold.—English Invasion of Scotland.—The Succession to the English Throne.—Harold's Ministry.—His Capture and Release by the Normans.—His Agreement with Duke William II. of Normandy.—His Subsequent Influence.—Tostig's Oppression in Northumberland Causes a Revolt.—Edwin and Morcar.—Death of Edward the Confessor.—His Popularity.—King's Evil.—Canonization of Edward the Confessor.—His Tomb in Westminster Abbey.—The Coronation Chair.—Coronation of King Harold II.—His Victory Over His Brother Tostig and King Harald Hardrada of Norway at Stamford Bridge.—Invasion of England by Duke William II. of Normandy.—Battle of Hastings and Defeat and Death of Harold.—William the Conqueror Crowned King of England.—The Whole Fate of England Changed by the Norman Conquest.—English Social Life.—Peaceful and Orderly Habits.—The English Women.—Houses.—Dress.—Feasts.—Illiteracy.—Gleemen.—Backgammon.—Relations Between the Nobles and the Common People.

SECTION XVIII.

RISE OF THE GERMANO-ROMAN EMPIRE, 1520-1546

Germany Made an Elective Monarchy.—Reign of Conrad I. of Franconia.—Accession of Henry the Fowler, the First of the Saxon Kings of Germany.—Hungarian Inroads.—Nine Years' Truce with the Hungarians.—Seizure of Lorraine by Henry the Fowler.—His Wars with the Slavonians.—He Reduces Bohemia to Vassalage.—Conquers the Wends.—Renewal of the Hungarian Raids.—Their Defeat by Henry the Fowler at Merseburg.—Invasion of Germany by the Danes.—They are Driven Back by Henry the Fowler, Who Wrests Holstein from Them.—Henry's Reorganization of the German Armies—His Fortification of the German Towns.—Rapid Growth of the German Towns in Population and Importance.—Rise of the Burghers.—Otho the Great, King of Germany.—His Coronation.—Prince Henry's Rebellion.—Otho the Great Secures the Duchies of Bavaria, Lorraine and Suabia to His Family.—Power of Otho the Great.—His Alliance with Louis d'Outremer of France Against Duke William Long-sword of Normandy and Count Hugh the Great of Paris.—His War with the Danes.—Mark of Schleswig.—Otho Reduces Denmark and Poland to Vassalage.—Spread of Christianity in Northern Germany.—Marriage of Otho the Great with Queen Adelaide of Lombardy —His Conquest of Lombardy.—Renewal of Hungarian Incursions.—Their Power Destroyed by the Victory of Otho the Great at Lechfeld.—Otho the Great Crowned Emperor at Rome.—The Holy Roman Empire of the German Nation.—Otho's Quarrel with Pope John XII.—Deposition of John XII —Popes Leo VIII. and John XIII.—Otho's War with the Eastern Emperor.—Otho II., King of Germany and Emperor.—He Subdues the Revolts of His Vassals.—His Invasion of France.—Convulsions in Italy.—Defeat of Otho II. in Southern Italy.—Otho III., King of Germany.—His Character.—He is Crowned Emperor.—He Makes Gerbert Pope Sylvester II.—Henry II., the Saint, of Bavaria, the Last of the Saxon Kings of Germany.—Revolt of the Duke of Poland Subdued.—Henry II., King of Italy.—Crowned Emperor.—Conrad II., of Franconia, the First of Four Successive Frankish Kings of Germany.—His Able Reign.—Crowned King of Italy and Emperor.—Becomes King of Burgundy.—Suppresses Revolts of Bohemia and Poland.—Subdues Several Slavonic Tribes.—Hungarian Invasion Defeated.—The Fiefs of the Empire Made Hereditary.—Henry III., King of Germany and Burgundy.—A Powerful Sovereign.—Extends His Suzerainty Over Bohemia, Poland and Hungary.—His Great Duchies.—He Abolishes Private Wars.—Corruption of the Church.—Simony and the Marriage of the Clergy.—Henry III. Seeks to Make the Popes His Dependents.—Three Rival

Popes.—Henry III. Raises a German Bishop to the Papacy.—Vices of Pope Benedict IX.—The Monk Hildebrand.—Good Rule of Pope Gregory VI.—Henry III. Crowned Emperor.—Gregory VI. and Hildebrand Driven into Exile.—Reforms of Pope Leo IX.—Henry III. Reduces the King of Hungary to Homage.—Henry IV., King of Germany.—Troubles of the Regency.—Oppression of the Saxons by Henry IV.—He Suppresses the Revolt of the Saxons.—Rise and Development of the Papal Power.—Hildebrand Becomes Pope Gregory VII.—His Quarrel with Henry IV.—Beginning of the War of Investitures.—Excommunication of Henry IV. —His Reverses.—His Journey to Canossa.—His Humiliation by the Pope.—Rudolf of Suabia a Rival Emperor.—Henry IV. Proclaims Guibert Antipope.—Defeat and Death of Rudolf of Suabia. —Capture of Rome by Henry IV.—His Coronation as Emperor.—Recapture of Rome by the Norman Duke, Robert Guiscard, Hildebrand's Ally.—Hildebrand's Death.—His Character.—His Policy Continued by His Successors.—Prince Henry's Rebellion Against Henry IV.—Death of Henry IV.— Henry V., King of Germany.—His Quarrel with Pope Paschall II.—He is Crowned Emperor.—The Concordat of Worms.—Lothaire of Saxony, King of Germany and Emperor.

SECTION XIX.

EMPIRE OF THE SELJUK TURKS, ... 1546-1551

Origin of the Seljuk Turks.—Conquests and Elevation of Togrul.—Victories and Death of Alp Arslan.—Administration of Nizam ul Mulk.—Glory of Malek Shah's Reign.—Anecdote of His Flatterers. —Disgrace and Assassination of Nizam ul Mulk.—Accession of Sultan Sanjar.—His Misfortunes and Death.—Decline of the Seljuk Turkish Empire.—Togrul III.— Tokush.— Mohammed.— Jellal ud Deen.—End of the Seljuk Turkish Empire.

SECTION XX.

PERSIA AND THE GHIZNIVIDE EMPIRE, . 1551-1557

Persia under the Saracen Dominion.—Rise of Yakoob ben Leis.—The Samanees and the Dilamees.—Origin of the Ghiznivide Dynasty.—Rise of Mahmoud of Ghiznee.—His Conquests in India.—Decline and Fall of the Ghiznivide Empire.

CHAPTER II.—MEDIÆVAL CIVILIZATION.

SECTION I.

THE FEUDAL SYSTEM AND CHIVALRY, 1558-1561

Origin of the Feudal System.—Division of Lands Among the Barbarians.—Castles of the King and Barons. —Allotment of the Lands. — Feuds, or Fiefs.—Vassals and Lord-Paramount.—Conditions of the Allotment.—Sub-Fiefs.—Fiefs and Titles Become Hereditary.—Origin of Chivalry.—Devotion to the Cause of the Weak and Oppressed.—Virtues Requisite for Knighthood.—Education of a Knight.—Ceremonies of Admission to Knighthood.—Dress and Arms of a Knight.—Knights-Errant.—Tournaments.—Good Effects of Chivalry on European Civilization.

SECTION II.

PAPACY, HIERARCHY AND MONACHISM, 1561-1564

The Papal Power.—Hildebrand.—Interdict and Excommunication.—The Power and Influence of the Clergy.—Origin of Monachism, or Monasticism.—Life of Solitude and Religious Devotion.—The Benedictine Monks.—The Augustinian Monks and Other Monastic Orders.—The Franciscan and Dominican Monks.—Monastic Vows.—Nuns and Nunneries—Relations of Monachism to the Papacy.
—Beneficial Influence of Monachism on Civilization and the Manners of the Age.

SECTION III.

MEDIÆVAL LEARNING AND LITERATURE, 1565-1566

Mediæval European Civilization.—Great Names of the Dark Ages.—Mediæval European Universities.—Abelard and the Scholastic Philosophy.—The Schoolmen.—Thomas Aquinas.—Duns Scotus. —Anselm.—Peter Lombard.—Roger Bacon.—Albertus Magnus.—The Mystics.—Thomas à Kempis and his Imitation of Christ.—Rise of Modern European Languages.—Mediæval Italian Literature.—Dante, Petrarch and Boccaccio.—English Literature of the Time of Edward III.—Mandeville, Chaucer, Gower, Langland and Wickliffe.—French Mediæval Historians, Froissart and Comines.—Minnesingers, Meistersingers and Troubadours.—Epic Poems.

SECTION IV.

TOWNS, COMMERCE AND SOCIAL LIFE, . 1566-1567

Increase of European Wealth and Power.—Growth of Towns.—Flemish Woolen Manufacture. —English Commerce.—Italian Commerce.—Silk Manufacture.—The Jews and Moneyed Institutions. —Social Condition of the People.

CHAPTER III.—THE CRUSADES.

SECTION I.

THE FIRST CRUSADE, ... 1568-1573

Christian Pilgrimages to Jerusalem.—Outrages upon the Pilgrims.—Preaching of Peter the Hermit.—Enthusiasm of the People of Europe.—Pope Urban II. and the Council of Clermont —The First Band of Crusaders, under Peter the Hermit and Walter the Penniless.—Fate of Other Disorderly Bands.—The Great Army under Godfrey of Bouillon.—The Other Chief Leaders.—Siege and Capture of Antioch by the Crusaders.—Their Cruelties.—Great Christian Victory at Antioch.—Siege and Capture of Jerusalem by the Crusaders.—Massacre of Mohammedans.—Founding of the Christian Kingdom of Jerusalem.—Founding of the Knights of St. John and the Knights-Templars.

SECTION II.

SECOND AND THIRD CRUSADES, . . . 1573-1575

Loss of Christian Fortresses in Palestine. — Preaching of St. Bernard.—Second Crusade.—Expeditions of Conrad III. of Germany and Louis VII. of France.—Conquest of Palestine and Capture of Jerusalem by Saladin, Sultan of Egypt.—Third Crusade.—Expeditions to the Holy Land.—Frederick Barbarossa's Victory at Iconium.—His Accidental Death.—Siege and Capture of Acre by Richard the Lion-hearted and Philip Augustus.—Quarrel Between Richard the Lion-hearted and Philip Augustus.—Arrogance and Cruelty of Richard the Lion-hearted.—His Insult to the German Banner at Acre.—Richard's Captivity in Germany.—His Ransom and Release.

SECTION III.

THE LAST FOUR CRUSADES, ... 1575-1578

Fourth Crusade.—Expedition of French and Italian Knights under Count Baldwin of Flanders.—Storming of Constantinople by the Crusaders.—Temporary Subversion of the Greek Empire.—A New Roman or Latin Empire.—Fifth Crusade.—Separate Bands of Crusaders.—The Child's Crusade.—Expedition of King Andrew II. of Hungary. Expedition of Frederick II. of Germany to Palestine.—His Treaty with Malek Kamel.—Ravages of the Korasmians in Palestine.—Capture and Massacre of Jerusalem.—Sixth Crusade.—Expedition of St. Louis to Egypt.—His Captivity.—His Ransom and Release.—Seventh Crusade.—Expedition of St. Louis to Tunis.—His Death.—Exploits of Prince Edward of England in the Holy Land.—Siege and Capture of Acre by the Turks.—Loss of the Holy Land to the Christians.—Losses of the Christians and Mohammedans During the Two Centuries of the Crusades.

SECTION IV.

RESULTS OF THE CRUSADERS, ... 1578-1581

Influence of the Crusades on Chivalry.—The Knights of St. John.—The Knights-Templars.—The Teutonic Knights.—Influence of the Crusades on the Feudal System.—Diffusion of Knowledge. —Development of Commerce—The Old Man of the Mountain and the Assassins.

SECTION V.

CRUSADE AGAINST THE ALBIGENSES, ... 1581-1586

Influence of the Crusades on the Church.—Crusade against the Albigenses, in the South of France.—Their Creed.—Action of Pope Innocent III.—Defeat of Count Raymond VI. of Toulouse by the Crusaders.—Massacre of the Albigenses.—Desolation of Languedoc.—Campaign of Louis VIII. of France against the Albigenses.—Capture of Avignon.—Conquest of the Albigenses.—Languedoc Annexed to the Possessions of the French Crown.

MAPS IN VOLUME IV.

New Persian Empire of the Sassanidæ............ 1171	Anglo-Saxon and Celtic Kingdoms in the British
Europe, A. D. 500 .... 1174, 1175	Isles... 1494, 1495
Europe, A. D. 800 .... 1434, 1435	Scotland during the Saxon Period................. 1496
Britain under the Saxons............................ 1493	Europe, A. D. 1000................................ 1522, 1523

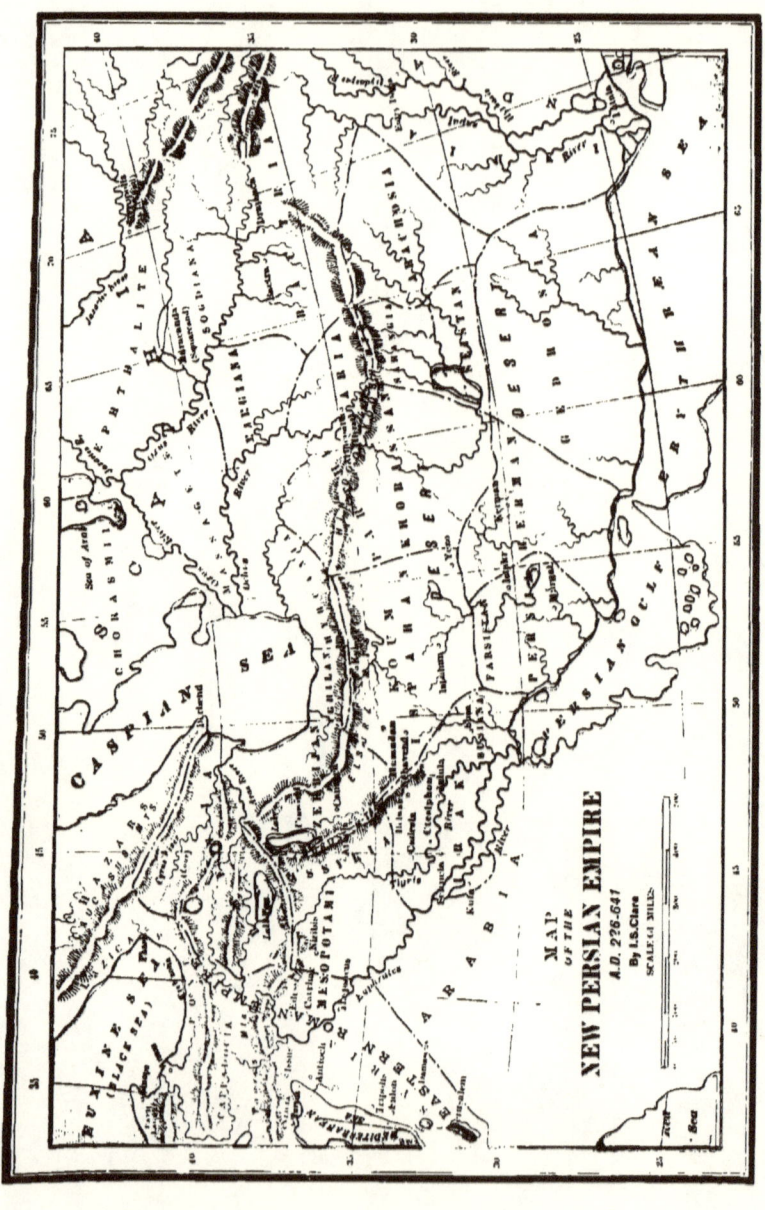

PART SECOND.

MEDIÆVAL HISTORY.

CHAPTER I.

THE DARK AGES.

SECTION I.—CHARACTER OF MEDIÆVAL HISTORY.

NCIENT history, as we have already seen, ended with the fall of the Western Roman Empire; and new races and a new civilization appeared upon the scene to take the places of the old and worn-out actors in the great drama of the world's history. Ancient history was confined wholly to Asia, Northern Africa, and Southern and Western Europe. With the fall of the Western Roman Empire the historical field becomes enlarged. New nations come into view; and the main interest of the historical narrative is transferred to the continent of Europe, which at the time under consideration was divided among four great divisions of the Aryan branch of the Caucasian race—the Græco-Latins, the Celts, the Teutons or Germans, and the Slavs or Slavonians. The Græco-Latins alone belong to ancient history. The Celts, Teutons and Slavs only appear in mediæval and modern history.

Modern writers usually divide the era since the fall of the Western Roman Empire into two portions—*Mediæval History*, embracing the period of a thousand years from the fall of the Western Roman Empire to the Discovery of America; and *Modern History*, comprising the epoch from the Discovery of America to the present time. The first six centuries of Mediæval History are generally termed the *Dark Ages*, and the last four centuries are more properly called the *Middle Ages*. The chief events of the Dark Ages were the migrations of the Northern or Teutonic nations; the rise, progress and fall of the Saracen Empire; the revival of the Western Roman Empire; and the rise of Feudalism and Chivalry. The Middle Ages are marked by greater activity of the tendencies to order and civilization. During this latter period the various European tribes settle into nations, the last vestiges of the migratory impulse expending themselves in pilgrimages and crusades. Languages are developed and improved. Chivalry refines the manners of the warrior, but itself declines, feudal chieftains becoming subject to consolidated monarchies. Learning is diffused, and industry acquires a considerable portion of its proper dignity and importance.

Until recently the character of the mediæval period was not correctly understood. Ancient civilization was regarded as having perished with the extinction of the Western Roman Empire, and the world was considered as having relapsed into barbarism. But the great fact is that European civilization survived the breaking up of the dominion of Rome, and was taken up and carried forward to a more perfect development by the great Teutonic portion of the Aryan branch of the Caucasian race. Thus this epoch, apparently so full of darkness and chaos, was in reality a germinating and developing season, during which European civilization was being shaped, and during which it was gaining strength for the distinguished part it was to play in the great drama of modern history.

SECTION II.—THE NEW RACES IN EUROPE.

THE Græco-Latins, Celts, Teutons and Slavs all belonged to the great Aryan, or Indo-European branch of the Caucasian race, to which the Hindoos, Medes and Persians also belonged. The home of the prehistoric Aryans—the ancestors of all the Indo-European nations —was in Central Asia, in the region of the ancient Bactria, the modern Balk, in Southern Turkestan. The Aryan migration westward into Europe occurred in prehistoric times, probably as far back as three thousand years before Christ.

The evidence of language shows us that the Celts migrated first and established themselves in Central Europe; but after a time they were pressed into Western Europe by the Teutons, whereupon they settled in Spain, Gaul and the British Isles. The Teutons thus occupied Central and Eastern Europe. The Latin and Hellenic nations occupied respectively the two great peninsulas of Southern Europe—Italy and Greece. The Slavonians—the last of the Aryan nations to enter Europe—overspread the vast steppes of Eastern Europe.

The original civilization of ancient Europe was confined to the two great peninsulas of Southern Europe—Greece and Italy—where a favored portion of the Aryan branch of the Caucasian race attained a social organization and a high state of development in culture; while their kinsmen—the Celts, Teutons and Slavonians—still continued in an undeveloped condition, without written language or literature, or the useful or fine arts, or the different appliances of civilization. All of Europe outside of Greece and Italy was a world of barbarians before the rise of the Roman power.

The Greeks exerted no influence whatever in civilizing the barbarians, that work being wholly performed by the Romans. The Celts were the first of the barbarian nations to come in contact with the Romans. We have observed that the Gauls of Cisalpine Gaul (Northern Italy), who were Celts, were reduced under the dominion of the Roman Republic, and that they obtained the Roman franchise at the hands of Julius Cæsar. The same great conqueror reduced the vast Celtic population of Transalpine Gaul (now France) under the Roman dominion, and these people were eventually invested with Roman citizenship. The same was the case with the Celtiberians of Spain. The Celts of Britain were likewise clothed with the rights of Roman citizens. The result of the contact of the Celtic populations of Spain, Gaul and Britain with the Romans was that they had become thoroughly Latinized and Christianized before the dissolution of the Western Roman Empire.

The leading Germanic or Teutonic tribes were the Goths, the Vandals, the Burgundians, the Franks, the Lombards, the Saxons, the Angles and the Scandinavians. The last played no part in history until the ninth and tenth centuries, when they appeared as Normans and Danes.

The primitive home of the Goths was in Scandinavia, in that part of modern Sweden still known as Gothland. But the roving spirit so natural to barbarism prompted them to seek homes beyond their native swamps and forests. They began their migrations about A. D. 200; soon after which they appeared in Central Europe in three great divisions—Visigoths (West Goths), Ostrogoths (East Goths), and Gepidæ (Laggards.) The Goths were the first of the Teutonic nations to embrace Christianity. A considerable time before the fall of the Western Roman Empire they had been converted to Arian Christianity.

We have observed how, in the closing period of ancient history, the Northern barbarians, in their southern and western migrations, overran and overthrew the Western Roman Empire and occupied its various provinces. Glancing at the settlement of

Page—Byzantinian Emperor.

Byzantinian Warrior and Major-Domo.

Servant—Byzantinian Empress and Princess.

Deacon—Byzantinian Bishop—Levite.

BYZANTINE EMPIRE.

the Teutonic tribes at the period when Odoacer subverted the empire of the Cæsars, we find the Germanic race already predominant in Europe, and the Germanic tribes beginning to press the Celtic nations within more circumscribed limits.

The Teutons had no influence upon the progress of history until the series of events connected with the overthrow of the Roman dominion in Western Europe. At that period the Germanic or Teutonic race commenced to play its mighty part in the great drama of the world's history. From its home in Central and Northern Europe the great Teutonic race began immediately, upon the overthrow of the Western Roman Empire, to absorb and shape the destiny and character of nearly the whole European continent; and the development of European civilization during the six centuries of the Dark Ages is mainly connected with the wonderful growth and expansion of the Germanic race.

The amalgamation of the Teutonic or Germanic tribes of the North with the Latin and Celtic races of the South and West of Europe produced modern society; and mediæval history is the history of the blending of Teutonic or Germanic barbarians with the Latin and Celtic elements. Modern society derives its ingredients from this commingling of these two ancient societies—the love of personal liberty and the feeling of independence from the barbarians, and the forms of an old civilization from the Romans.

We will now proceed to an account of the settlements of the Teutonic or Germanic tribes at the time of the downfall of the Western Roman Empire. The *Visigothic* kingdom under Euric embraced all of Spain and that part of Gaul south of the Loire and west of the Rhone; and its capital, Arles, was considered the center of Western civilization. The *Sueves* in North-western Spain were tributary to Euric. The *Heruli*, the German tribe under Odoacer, who put an end to the Western Empire, held Italy, but were soon conquered by the *Ostrogoths*, who at this time occupied the region between the Danube and the Adriatic. The *Gepidæ*, also a Gothic tribe, as we have seen, possessed the region of the modern Roumania and Eastern Hungary.

The *Vandals*, besides their original homes south and east of the Baltic, were now masters of Northern Africa, with Corsica, Sardinia and the Balearic Isles. The *Burgundians* occupied the valley of the Rhone and the country about the Swiss lakes, the region called *Burgundy*, whose ruler was a powerful rival of the French kings for a thousand years.

The *Lombards*, or *Longobards* (men with long beards) originally occupied Jutland, whence they migrated to the banks of the Elbe, and afterwards to the region between the Danube and the Vistula, where they were settled at the time of the fall of the Western Roman Empire. A century later they migrated to Northern Italy, where they occupied the region since called *Lombardy*.

The *Alemanni* held Southern Germany, with Alsace and Northern Switzerland. The *Thuringians* were settled between the head-waters of the Danube and those of the Elbe. The *Franks* or *Freemen*, who originally occupied Belgium and the region of the Lower Rhine, overran Gaul soon after the fall of the Western Roman Empire, expelling the Visigoths from the South and conquering the Burgundians in the South-east; and the name of *France* was given to their new country (from *Francia*, the land of the Franks). The modern French are the descendants of the Latinized Gauls and their Frankish conquerors.

The *Saxons* (knife-men, from *Sachs*), originally occupied the region of the modern Holstein; but about the time of the downfall of the Roman dominion in Western Europe they had overspread the whole of Northern Germany from the Rhine to the Baltic. Two of the leading Saxon tribes were the Angles and the Jutes; the first occupying the region of the modern Schleswig, and the latter the peninsula of Jutland. The Saxons had never come in contact with the Romans, and were therefore unaffected by Roman influences. They were still pagans and worshipers of Odin and Thor. Their piratical craft had carried terror along the entire coast of Europe for a century. Many of the Saxons were at this period settled among the wooded inlets in the North of Gaul; while roving bands of Saxons, Angles and Jutes had settled in Britain and thus laid the foundations of *England* (Angleland) and the English language. The modern English are the descendants of the savage Angles, Saxons and Jutes, who thus migrated to and conquered Britain in the fifth century of the Christian era.

The Scandinavians, under the name of *Northmen* or *Norsemen*, or *Normans* and *Danes*, began their piratical voyages in the ninth century, and ravaged and plundered Germany, France, England and Ireland, establishing themselves in Northern Russia late in the ninth century; in that province of North-western France to which they gave the name of *Normandy* late in the tenth century: and in Southern Italy about the middle of the eleventh century, while bands of Normans even terrorized the Eastern Roman, or Greek Empire, spreading alarm even to the walls of Constantinople. For two centuries the Normans, under the name of Danes, ravaged Anglo-Saxon England, which they finally conquered early in the tenth century; and in the latter half of the same century the Normans of France conquered the same country, thus entirely changing its destiny.

Such were the settlements of the Germanic or Teutonic tribes at the time of the overthrow of the Western Roman Empire. Colonies of Britons, who had been driven from their native island by the conquering and freebooting Angles and Saxons, had crossed the British Channel and were at this time mingled with their Celtic kinsmen in the North-west of Gaul, in that portion of France afterwards known as Brittany, or Bretagne. Hibernia (now Ireland), Caledonia (now Scotland) and Cambria (now Wales) were inhabited by the original unconquered Celtic tribes—ancestors of the modern Irish, Highland Scotch and Welsh.

In the vast steppes of Eastern Europe, beyond the Elbe, was the fourth and last division of the Aryan branch of the Caucasian race in Europe—the Slavs or Slavonians —ancestors of the modern Russians, Poles, Bohemians, Servians, Bosnians, Bulgarians, Illyrians and Croatians. The Slavonians were a pastoral people, more numerous but less powerful than the Teutons. They did not play any important part in history until near the close of the Dark Ages. The woes to which they were subjected during the long wars of mediæval times are sadly suggested by the word *slave*, borrowed from the proper noun *Slave*, or *Slav*. Such Slavonic tribes as the Servians, Bosnians and Croatians migrated during the seventh century from their original seats north of the Carpathian mountains into the countries south of the Middle Danube bearing their respective names.

In the South-east of Europe, the Eastern Roman, or Greek Empire embraced nearly the region comprised by the modern Turkish dominion, and was inhabited by the original Greek races and the Macedonians, Thracians and Illyrians.

Thus Europe has in all historical times been almost wholly in possession of four great divisions of the Aryan branch of the Caucasian race—the Græco-Latins, the Celts, the Teutons and the Slavonians. Still there were some remnants of the primitive or prehistoric inhabitants of primeval Europe; such as the *Laps* and *Fins* of the frozen, marshy regions of the extreme North of Europe, and the *Basques* of Northern Spain— representatives of the Turanian branch of the Mongolian race.

There were some remnants of the fierce Huns—also belonging to the Turanian branch of the Mongolian race—who had overrun and terrorized Europe for almost a century during the period preceding the fall of the Western Roman Empire. These remnants of the Huns, called *Avars*, finally settled in the hills and vales of what is now Hungary. The *Bulgarians*, also a Turanian people, migrated in two divisions from their homes near the Caspian Sea—one founding the kingdom of *Great* or *White Bulgaria* on the Volga river; and the other passing in the fifth century to the west, where they established the kingdom of *Black Bulgaria* in the region between the Carpathians and the Balkans. They were driven south of the Danube, into the region of the modern Bulgaria, in the ninth century by the Magyars; and in that country they mingled with the original Slavonian inhabitants, who then took the name of *Bulgarians*, and from these the modern Bulgarians are descended.

About the middle of the ninth century the wild nomadic *Magyars*, or *Hungarians* —also belonging to the Turanian branch of the Mongolian race—migrated from the Ural mountains to the valleys of the Theiss and the Middle Danube, where they laid the foundations of modern Hungary, driving out the Avars and Bulgarians. These were all of the Turanian nations that entered Europe during the Dark Ages. In the thirteenth century the *Mongols*, or *Moguls*, conquered Russia, where they remained two and a half centuries. The *Ottoman Turks*, the last Turanian people who entered Europe, late in the Middle Ages established their dominion on the ruins of the Eastern Roman, or Greek Empire.

Early in the eighth century the Mohammedan *Saracens* and *Moors*, mingled Semites and Hamites, overran and conquered Spain, in the southern part of which they remained until the end of the Middle Ages. In the ninth, tenth and eleventh centuries they ravaged Sicily and Southern Italy. The enlightened and cultured Saracens of Spain exerted great influence upon Christian Europe during the Dark and Middle Ages.

The establishment of the Teutonic race in the Celtic and Latin countries of Western and Southern Europe gave rise to new languages. At the time when the Northern barbarians established themselves in Italy and the provinces of the Western Roman Empire, Latin had become the common speech of Gaul and Spain, as well as of Italy. The old Celtic language of Gaul and the Celtiberian of Spain only lingered in a few remote places, so that a corrupt Latin was the prevailing speech in those two countries of Western Europe. As the Teutonic settlers were far outnumbered by the native populations, they were obliged to acquire the Latin in order to communicate with the people among whom they had established themselves; but in learning it they still further corrupted it, thus giving rise to corrupt Latin dialects, which by the close of the Dark Ages, had developed into the modern Italian, French, Spanish and Portuguese.

In Britain the Angles, Saxons and Jutes did not mingle with the Celtic Britons; so that the language of Anglo-Saxon England was purely Teutonic or Germanic, and thus remained until England was conquered by the French-speaking Normans near the close of the Dark Ages. From that time the Anglo-Saxon language of England began to be modified; so that toward the close of the Middle Ages the *English* language took shape, in consequence of the introduction of many Norman-French words, and the mingling together of the Anglo-Saxon and Norman-French.

The new nations of purely Teutonic or Germanic origin which arose in Germany and Scandinavia were entirely unaffected in their speech by Latin influences, so that the languages of those countries remained purely Teutonic. Such are the modern German, Dutch, Danish, Swedish and Norwegian. The Slavonic languages—chief among which are the modern Russian and Polish—are entirely different from the Germanic and Latin languages.

While the new languages arose among the Germanic and Latin nations, the pure Latin language of ancient Rome continued to be the learned and written language among those nations during the whole of the Dark and Middle Ages; so that scholars and writers throughout the whole of Teutonic and Latin Europe exclusively used that pure ancient classical tongue during the entire mediæval period. The ancient Latin has remained a learned language to the present time, though no longer a spoken tongue, and therefore ever since classed as a *dead language*.

SECTION III.—THE VISIGOTHIC KINGDOM OF SPAIN.

THE Visigoths first made their appearance in Spain in A. D. 411; that province having been offered to them by the Emperor Honorious, who thus bribed them to retire from Italy. After establishing their dominion in Southern Gaul, they burst through the passes of the Pyrenees, under the leadership of their king, ADOLPHUS, and founded a kingdom in Spain; which for two years had been ravaged with fire and sword by the Sueves under Hermeric, the Alans under Atace, and the Vandals under Gunderic, who had entered the country in A. D. 409. The Sueves had established themselves in Gallicia, in the North-west of Spain; the Alans in Lusitania, in the West; and the Vandals in Bætica, in the South.

After establishing themselves in the Northeast of Spain, the Visigoths undertook several expeditions against the Vandals. Adolphus, who had married Placidia, the sister of the Emperor Honorius, considered it best to become the ally of the Romans. By this course he incurred the hostility of his chieftains, who despised the Romans; and Adolphus was assassinated within a year after he had entered Spain. His successor, SIGERIC, was a brutal ruffian; and was speedily put to death by his subjects, who had become thoroughly disgusted with his cruelty.

The next Visigothic king was WALLIA, who proved himself a worthy sovereign. He undertook an expedition against the Roman possessions in Africa, but his fleet was wrecked in a storm. This disaster induced Constantius, the Roman commander in Gaul, to march in the direction of the Pyrenees. Wallia made ready to oppose him; but a conflict was averted by the surrender, by Wallia, of Placidia, the widow of Adolphus, to Constantius, who was deeply enamored of her. When Constantius had married Placidia, Wallia entered into an alliance with the Romans against the Vandals, Alans and Sueves (A. D. 417).

The Vandals were driven from the territories which they had occupied, and were obliged to seek refuge among the Sueves in Gallicia. The Alans in Lusitania were almost exterminated, and the remnant of that nation was absorbed by the Vandals; so that the Alans then disappeared entirely from the history of Spain. The Sueves averted a similar fate by placing themselves under Roman protection; and Wallia, who was unprepared to engage in war with Rome, permitted them to remain in undisturbed possession of their territories. The Emperor Honorius regarded Wallia as his ally, and rewarded him by bestowing upon him a part of Southern Gaul, from Toulouse to the Mediterranean. Wallia immediately repaired to his new dominions; and thenceforth until the reign of Euric, the Visigothic kings remained in Southern Gaul, while still regarding Spain as a portion of their dominions.

THEODORIC I. succeeded Wallia, who died about A. D. 420. During this reign the Vandals made war upon the Sueves, who had received them with kindness during the reign of Wallia. The Sueves were driven into the mountains of Asturias in the North of the peninsula, and there they successfully defended themselves against the attacks of the Vandals. The Vandals then abandoned Asturias and fought their way southward to their former homes in Bætica, where they maintained themselves against all the efforts of the Roman generals to dislodge them. They gave their territory in Southern Spain the name of *Vandalusia*, which in the course of time became corrupted into *Andalusia*.

As the Vandals had command of the sea, their fleets were able to terrorize the coast of Spain and the islands of the Mediterranean. In A. D. 429 they crossed over into Africa, which they conquered from the Romans in

A. D. 439, after a war of ten years, thus laying the foundations of a kingdom which lasted a century; as already related. The Sueves then issued from their mountain retreats in Asturias and soon recovered Gallicia. They steadily extended their dominions, and in A. D. 438 they pushed their conquests into the South of Spain, routing the Romans on the banks of the Xenil, and seizing Merida and Seville; and for the next ten years Richilan, the Suevic king, governed this vast realm with a strong hand.

In the meantime Theódoric I., the reigning Visigothic king, had been humbling the Roman power in the South of Gaul. After achieving this result, he was about to take the field against the Sueves in Spain, when he was called to take part in the struggle against the Huns under Attila, and was slain in the great battle of Châlons, as already related.

Theódoric I. was succeeded by his son, THORSIMUND, who was murdered within a year by his two brothers, the elder of whom became his successor under the name of THEODORIC II. This new king subdued the Sueves; but when he was obliged to return to his dominions in Southern Gaul, his army was cut to pieces by the people of Leon, in revenge for the excesses which it had committed. Spain then quickly fell into a condition of anarchy, and the people experienced great sufferings. The condition of affairs in Gaul prevented Theódoric's return to Spain. He had just restored tranquillity to his Gallic dominions, and was about to return to Spain, when he was assassinated by his brother EURIC, who then became his successor (A. D. 466).

Euric was a great monarch. He conquered the Sueves, restored the Visigothic dominion over Andalusia, and reduced all of Central and North-eastern Spain under his dominion. He allowed the Sueves to retain possession of Gallicia, with a part of the territory of modern Leon and Portugal, under their own sovereigns; but made the Suevic monarch his vassal. For the next century the Sueves peacefully submitted to the Visigothic rule.

Euric next drove the Romans from Spain, wresting from them Tarraco (now Tarragona), their last stronghold in the country, and made himself master of the whole Spanish peninsula; after which he enlarged his dominions in the South of Gaul at the expense of the Romans and the Burgundians, and forced Odoacer, the Herulian King of Italy, to relinquish to him all the Roman possessions in Gaul south of the Loire and in the valley of the Rhone.

Thenceforth the Visigoths considered Gaul and Spain as their proper dominion. Euric made Arles his capital; and that city was then regarded as the center of Western civilization, being the chosen seat of learning and refinement in Europe; while the Visigothic monarch was the most powerful and enlightened of European sovereigns, his preëminence being acknowledged even by the Persians through their embassies. Euric is rightly considered the founder of the Visigothic kingdom in Spain. His predecessors had ruled Gaul, but had only a feeble hold on Spain. Euric firmly established his dominion in the peninsula, and gave Spain its first code of laws. He tarnished his memory by his violent persecutions of the orthodox Catholics, to whom he, as an Arian, was bitterly opposed.

Euric died at Arles in A. D. 483, and was succeeded by his son ALARIC II., who was a weak monarch, and reigned twenty-three years. During the latter portion of his reign, Alaric II. became involved in a war with Clovis, King of the Franks, who had conquered Northern Gaul, and who now wrested most of Southern Gaul from the Visigothic sovereign. Alaric II. died A. D. 506, leaving a son who was too young to wield the helm of state.

The Visigoths accordingly placed GENSALEIC, the brother of Alaric II., upon the throne. The new sovereign was hard pressed by the Franks and the Burgundians, who besieged him in Carcassonne. Theódoric, the powerful King of the Ostrogoths, the father-in-law of Alaric II., now made war on both the Frankish and Visigothic kings, regarding the latter as having unlawfully usurped the throne which rightfully belonged to his nephew, the grand-son of the Ostrogothic monarch. After forcing Clovis, King of the Franks, to make peace, and defeating Gensaleic and putting him to death, Theódoric the Ostrogoth disregarded his grandson's rights by making himself King of Spain, entrusting the government of that country to Theudis, one of his ablest generals. Theódoric established justice and order in Spain, and protected the orthodox Catholics, though he was himself an Arian.

Four years before his death, Theódoric the Ostrogoth resigned the crown of Spain to his grandson AMÁLARIC, who made Seville his capital, thus becoming the first Gothic King of Spain who established his residence in that country. Amálaric relinquished his Gallic territory between the Rhone and the Alps to Athálaric, the successor of Theódoric as King of the Ostrogoths. He married Clotilda, the daughter of Clovis, King of the Franks; but as this princess was a Catholic, she brought only trouble to her Arian husband. Their quarrels over their religious opinions were so violent that Amálaric treated his wife with such indignity that she appealed for protection to her brother, Childebert I., one of the sons and successors of Clovis. Childebert accordingly invaded Spain, defeated and killed Amálaric in a great battle in Catalonia, and returned to France laden with the plunder of the Arian churches (A. D. 531).

THEUDIS, who had governed Spain for Theódoric the Ostrogoth, now received the Visigothic crown. He was obliged to relinquish his possessions in Gaul, but successfully defended Spain against the attacks of the Frankish kings. He was a wise and able sovereign, and his name was long cherished by the Visigothic nation. He was assassinated in A. D. 548, and was succeeded by THEUDISDEL, who had been one of his generals; but this monarch so misgoverned his subjects that they murdered him the next year (A. D. 549). The next king, AGILAN, had a troubled reign of five years, as the southern portion of Spain refused to recognize him as king; and he was defeated and slain in A. D. 554.

ATHANAGILD, the rebel leader, then ascended the throne of Spain. He had called in the forces of the Eastern Roman Emperor, Justinian, to aid him in his revolt. He now demanded that they should retire from the country; but they refused to leave, and established themselves in the province of Carthagena, from which they made frequent incursions into the neighboring provinces. Athanagild was unable to expel them, and they retained possession of the places which they had seized until in the progress of time they became absorbed in the Visigothic nation. During this reign the Sueves, who had been converted to Arian Christianity a century before, adopted the orthodox Catholic faith (A. D. 560). Athanagild died in A. D. 567, after a peaceful and beneficent reign of fourteen years.

The next king, LIUVA I., died after a reign of three years (A. D. 570), and was succeeded by his brother LEOVIGILD, who was one of the greatest of the Visigothic kings. He drove the troops of the Eastern Roman Empire out of Granada, and suppressed several revolts against his authority, firmly establishing his power throughout Spain after ten years of constant effort. In A. D. 582 he associated his oldest son, Ermenigild, with himself in the government, and secured for him as his bride the Frankish princess Ingunda, who was a Catholic and converted her husband to that religious faith. Soon afterward Ermenigild rebelled against his father, but was subdued after a desperate struggle; and was pardoned, but deprived of his royal dignity. He soon revolted a second time, but was again reduced to submission, and was this time put to death at his father's order. The Catholic Church has always considered him a martyr for his religion, and has canonized him.

Upon the death of Ermenigild, the Frankish monarch, the brother of his widow, took up arms to avenge him; and the Sueves renounced their allegiance and joined the Franks. Aided by his second son, Recared,

Leovigild drove back the Franks and reduced the Sueves to submission. He put an end to the Suevic kingdom by annexing the Suevic territories to the possessions of the Visigothic crown. Leovigild violently persecuted his Catholic subjects, and plundered their churches, surrounding himself with a brilliant court by means of the wealth which he thus amassed. He did much for the improvement of his dominions, and is the first Visigothic monarch represented in the ancient coins with the royal crown upon his head.

Leovigild died in A. D. 587, and his son and successor, RECARED I., was promptly acknowledged throughout the entire Spanish peninsula. Recared was converted from Arianism to Catholicism in A. D. 589, and the whole Visigothic nation followed his example. This result ended the religious dissensions in Spain, and contributed much to the amalgamation of the Visigoths, the Latins and the Celtic Spaniards into one Spanish nationality, with a predominance of the Latin element. Recared I. defeated the efforts of the Franks to invade Spain, conquered the Basques, and chastised the Eastern Roman imperialists, whom he confined to their fortresses on the coast. Recared I. was a liberal and enlightened monarch, and his reign was highly beneficial to his subjects.

Recared I. died in A. D. 601, and his three immediate successors, whose reigns were uneventful, were LIUVA II., from A. D. 601 to A. D. 603; WITERIC, from A. D. 603 to A. D. 610; and GUNDEMAR, from A. D. 610 to A. D. 612. SISEBERT, who reigned from A. D. 612 to A. D. 621, achieved signal victories over the Basques, wrested many fortresses from the Eastern Roman imperialists, and persecuted the Jews. The next king, RECARED II., reigned only three months during A. D. 621. SWINTILA, who reigned from A. D. 621 to A. D. 631, reduced all the fortresses of the Eastern Roman imperialists, thus putting an end to their influence in Spain.

The next four reigns, which were uneventful, were those of SISENAND, from A. D. 631 to A. D. 636; CHINTILA, from A. D. 636 to A. D. 640; TULGA, from A. D. 640 to A. D. 642; and CHINDASWIND, from A. D. 642 to A. D. 649. RECESWIND, who reigned from A. D. 649 to A. D. 672, was a firm and vigorous sovereign, marking his reign by the promptness and energy with which he suppressed all opposition to his government, and by the enactment of a law requiring future Visigothic monarchs to transmit their wealth to their *successors on the throne*, and not to their children.

Upon Receswind's death in A. D. 672, the Visigothic electors chose the virtuous WAMBA to the throne. His virtues and wisdom were well known to the entire Visigothic nation. For a long time he declined to accept the crown, but was finally forced to yield to the decision of the electors by the threat of being put to death if he persisted in his refusal. Revolts broke out in various parts of Spain soon after Wamba's accession in A. D. 673; but the new sovereign suppressed these outbreaks with promptness and firmness, forcing the rebels to beg for mercy. He banished from his kingdom all the Jews who refused baptism, thus forcing many to be formally baptized in order to escape exile, but left them highly exasperated against him. He defeated the Saracens, who had conquered all Northern Africa, in an attempt to invade Spain.

Wamba was rigidly just and incorruptible in the exercise of his sovereign power, uniting moderation with firmness, and he possessed the devoted affection of his subjects. He was attacked with a sudden illness on the 14th of October, A. D. 680, and quickly fell into a comatose state. His attendants believed him to be dead, and made preparation for his funeral, according to the custom of the times, by shaving his head and enveloping him in a penitential habit. Being thus transformed from a layman into a member of the monastic order, he was rendered incapable of wearing the crown. Within twenty-four hours he regained consciousness; but as his fate had been irrevocably decided, he was forced to retire into a monastery, where he died some years later.

Wamba's successor was ERVIGIUS, a nephew of King Chindaswind. After an uneventful reign, he died A. D. 687 and was succeeded by EGICA, Wamba's brother, whose reign was memorable mainly for the severe laws against the Jews, who were suspected of instigating the Saracens of Northern Africa to invade Spain. Ergica was succeeded by his son, WITIZA, in A. D. 701. The first portion of Witiza's reign seems to have been just and prosperous, but he ultimately degenerated into a cruel and lustful tyrant. His cruelties finally caused a rebellion against him under the leadership of Roderic, a powerful noble. Witiza's reign ended in A. D. 709; and RODERIC, who became his successor, was the last Gothic king.

Roderic seems to have been no better than his predecessor. He soon aroused against himself a powerful opposition. Witiza's relatives, headed by Count Julian, refused to recognize his authority. Some writers tell us that Count Julian was governor of the fortresses of Tangier and Ceuta, on the African coast opposite Gibraltar. King Roderic having dishonored the Lady Florinda, Count Julian's only daughter, her father determined to revenge himself upon the Visigothic monarch, and accordingly invited the Saracens to invade Spain, at the same time putting them in possession of the African fortresses commanding the entrance to that European peninsula. Other authorities deny the story of Florinda, and assert that Count Julian was solely influenced, in making his offer to the Saracens, by his loyalty to the dynasty of Witiza and his animosity to King Roderic, whom he considered a usurper. At any rate, Count Julian placed the African fortresses in the possession of the Saracen general Muza, evidently not calculating upon the ultimate consequences of his action.

Muza acted very cautiously even after he had obtained possession of the African fortresses. But after becoming fully satisfied that the outward splendor of the Visigothic kingdom merely concealed an internal rottenness, he made preparations for the invasion of Spain. On the 30th of April, 711, a formidable Saracen and Moorish army under Tarik, an able and experienced general, effected a landing at Gibraltar, which received its name from him, *Gibraltar* meaning *Gibal-Tarik*, or mountain of Tarik. After overcoming the first resistance of the Visigoths, Tarik advanced northward with great rapidity, and defeated King Roderic in the great battle of Xeres de la Frontera, on the Guadalete not far from Cadiz; Roderic himself being drowned in the Guadalete after the battle (A. D. 711). This decisive conflict put an end to the Visigothic monarchy in Spain, which had lasted three centuries (A. D. 411-711). The Saracens gradually conquered the whole of Spain except the mountainous districts of Asturias, Cantabria and Navarre in the North, into which the Christians under King Pelayo retired.

SECTION IV.—THE OSTROGOTHIC KINGDOM IN ITALY.

PON the ruins of the Western Roman Empire, as already related, the German tribe of the Heruli under Odoacer erected the Kingdom of Italy in A. D. 476. Odoacer fixed his capital at Ravenna, and distributed the lands of Italy among his followers, making the peasants who lived upon the lands their slaves. He, however, allowed the old Roman laws and institutions to remain, and retained the Roman magistrates in their offices.

Odoacer was the first barbarian monarch who reigned over Italy, and was worthy of the high honor to which he had been called. He restored the Consulship of the West within seven years after his accession. He compelled the barbarians of Gaul and Germany to respect the Italian frontiers, and devoted himself to the restoration of tran-

THE CATHEDRAL OF S. APOLLINARE NUOVA, RAVENNA.

quillity and good government to his subjects. Notwithstanding his exertions, misery and desolation prevailed all over Italy. The population of the country was reduced by famine and pestilence, and the means of subsistence were diminishing in the same proportion. Under the Roman Empire the tributary harvests of Egypt and Africa furnished Italy with an inexhaustible source of food; but these were now withdrawn, and there was no way of supplying the deficiency. After reigning over Italy seventeen years, Odoacer was forced to give way before the superior genius of Theódoric the Ostrogoth; and the Kingdom of the Heruli in Italy ended in A. D. 493.

THEODORIC was born in A. D. 455, and had been carefully educated in the arts of war at Constantinople, where he had resided as a hostage. He disdained the more peaceful part of the Greek training, and was unacquainted with the art of writing to the very end of his life. Theódoric became King of the Ostrogoths upon the death of his father in A. D. 476. The Ostrogoths then occupied the region between the Danube and the Adriatic, where they proved themselves dangerous neighbors to the Eastern Roman Emperor, who sought to rid himself of them by agreeing to Theódoric's proposal to march against Odoacer and to restore Italy to the Roman dominion.

The Emperor with great prudence left it doubtful whether the Ostrogothic conqueror of Italy was to govern that country as his vassal or his ally. Theódoric's reputation attracted an immense host to his standard, from the neighboring nations no less than from his Ostrogothic countrymen, at whose head he marched for Italy in A. D. 489. The march occurred in midwinter, and the Ostrogoths took their families and all their movable possessions with them. They endured numerous hardships, but at length the Ostrogothic host poured over the Julian Alps and entered Italy. Odoacer was defeated in three battles and shut up in the impregnable fortress of Ravenna, his capital, where he was besieged for three years, at the end of which time peace was made through the intervention of the Bishop of Ravenna, Odoacer and Theódoric agreeing to divide the dominion of Italy between them (A. D. 493). Theódoric either murdered his rival soon afterward, or caused his death at a riotous banquet, in total violation of his plighted word.

By the murder of Odoacer the Kingdom of the Heruli in Italy came to an end, and Theódoric the Ostrogoth thus became sole King of Italy, establishing his capital at Ravenna. He divided one-third of the lands of Italy among his soldiers. He employed the original inhabitants of Italy in agriculture and commerce, while to his Ostrogothic followers he assigned the duty of defending the state. Like Odoacer, Theódoric allowed the ancient Roman laws and institutions to remain, and encouraged agriculture, manufactures and commerce; and Italy enjoyed great prosperity under his dominion, becoming the most peaceful and flourishing country in the world.

The Ostrogothic kingdom under Theódoric extended far beyond the limits of Italy to the north, east and west. During the minority of his grandson Amálaric, the King of the Visigothic monarchy in Gaul and Spain, Theódoric governed his kingdom wisely and well. As soon as the other barbarians of the West were satisfied that Theódoric did not intend to include them in his conquests, they universally recognized the Ostrogothic monarch as the leading sovereign of the West, and sought his alliance and mediation.

Though Theódoric was himself an Arian, he protected his Catholic subjects, thus tolerating all forms of religious belief in his dominions. The fanatical mob burned the shops and dwellings of the Jews in several cities, but the king compelled them to restore the destroyed buildings. This exact justice brought down upon Theódoric the wrath of the Catholics, and he became convinced that his efforts in behalf of his subjects had not been sufficient to overcome their prejudice against him as an Arian.

Jealous of so powerful a vassal, the Eastern Roman Emperor, Anastasius, attacked

Theódoric's dominions from the direction of the Danube, but was defeated by the Ostrogothic monarch at the head of an inferior force. In order to atone for this humiliation, the Emperor sent an expedition to plunder the coasts of Apulia and Calabria. The imperial forces won some indecisive successes, but Theódoric's firmness and energy forced them to retreat, thus in a short time bringing about an honorable peace.

Theódoric's last years presented a striking contrast with the beginning of his reign. The ingratitude of his subjects made him suspicious and cruel. He caused Boëthius, the most celebrated and learned Roman of his time, to be put to death on the charge of plotting to restore the Eastern Roman Emperor's authority; and the execution of Symmachus, his venerable father-in-law, followed soon afterward. The death of Theódoric, which occurred in A. D. 526, was hastened by remorse for these crimes. Theódoric did not appear to have desired a union of the Ostrogoths and the Romans, and did not even claim the title of King of Italy, but merely called himself King of the Ostrogoths.

Theódoric was succeeded on the throne of the Ostrogoths by his grandson ATHÁLARIC. As the new sovereign was a boy of ten years, his mother, Amalasontha, Theódoric's daughter, was made regent and was aided by the wise counsels of her minister, Cassiodórus. Her son did not profit by her care and instruction, but abandoned himself to riotous living and all kinds of excesses. When his mother punished him he appealed to his countrymen to sustain him, and the queen-regent was forced to relinquish her authority to him; but he died soon afterward, at the age of sixteen years, from the effects of intemperance. In violation of the Gothic law and custom, his mother, Amalasontha, then sought to recover her power by marrying her cousin THEODATUS and making him king; but Theódatus, refusing to be ruled by a woman, caused his wife to be strangled in her bath (A. D. 535).

Justinian, the illustrious Emperor of the East, had been eagerly watching for a pretext to restore Italy to the Roman dominion, and now undertook to avenge Amalasontha, preparing to send an army under his illustrious general, Belisarius, into the Italian peninsula. Belisarius conquered Sicily late in A. D. 535, and in the spring of the following year he passed over into the mainland of Italy. The main strength of the Ostrogoths was in the North of Italy, and the Greek influence was sufficiently strong in the South to make its conquest by the forces of the Eastern Empire a very easy task. Belisarius was hailed as a deliverer by the Southern Italians, but the barbarian garrison in Naples made a stand against him. The city was taken by surprise, and its fall placed Apulia and Calabria under the dominion of the Eastern Empire. Belisarius marched northward and entered Rome, which joyfully opened its gates to him (A. D. 536).

VITIGES, the Ostrogothic king who succeeded Theódatus, assembled a powerful Ostrogothic army and besieged Rome, which Belisarius gallantly defended with an inferior force for over a year. During this siege the sepulcher of the Emperor Adrian, now known as the Castle of St. Angelo, was used as a fortress for the first time. The Ostrogoths suffered heavy losses in their assaults upon Rome, thirty thousand having fallen in the main attack; and Vitiges was obliged to retire to Ravenna with his shattered army, thus leaving Belisarius master of Italy. This renowned general might have easily subdued all Italy had he not been frustrated by the dissensions of the Roman leaders. Valuable time was thus lost, and the Ostrogoths were given a breathing spell before the final struggle.

Ten thousand Burgundians, allies of the Ostrogothic king, took and destroyed Milan, which had revolted from Vitiges in A. D. 538. In the following spring the Frankish king, Theódebert, the grandson of Clovis, crossed the Alps with one hundred thousand Franks, defeated the armies of both the Eastern Roman Empire and the Ostrogoths near Pavia, and ravaged Liguria and Æmilia until he was obliged to return to his own

THE OSTROGOTHIC KINGDOM IN ITALY.

country in consequence of losses from disease and the intemperance of his troops.

Belisarius now devoted himself to the task of completing the conquest of Italy. He besieged Vitiges in Ravenna, and reduced that impregnable stronghold by famine. Weary of their king, the Ostrogoths proposed to surrender the city to the imperial general, if he would make himself king. Belisarius pretended to accept the proposal, but when he obtained possession of Ravenna he threw off the mask, declaring that he held the city only as the servant of the Eastern Emperor.

Only Pavia, which was garrisoned by ten thousand Ostrogoths, made a defense; and these warriors, in accordance with Gothic custom, raised TOTILA, the nephew of Vitiges, upon a shield, thus hailing him as king. Before Belisarius was able to undertake any movement against this stronghold, he was recalled to Constantinople by the Emperor Justinian, who had grown jealous of the fame of his celebrated general. Totila immediately sought to recover all that Vitiges had lost. Many Italian cities which had welcomed Belisarius as a deliverer had been so sorely oppressed by the officials of the Eastern Emperor that they now gladly opened their gates to Totila. The Ostrogoths took Rome in A. D. 546 and carried its Senators into captivity, whereupon its population scattered. Totila, by his noble character, gained friends on every side, and it appeared that he was on the point of restoring the Ostrogothic kingdom in all its former strength.

Such rapid and marked success forced the Emperor Justinian to restore Belisarius to the imperial command in Italy; but Justinian, unable to overcome his jealousy of his great general, sent him to Italy without troops, and delayed those which were ordered to follow him. Belisarius soon perceived that he must depend largely upon his own resources, without much encouragement or assistance from his imperial master. He accordingly crossed from Italy to the shores of Epirus, where he succeeded by extraordinary exertions in assembling a

small army, with which he started for Italy sailing to the mouth of the Tiber.

Belisarius arrived at Rome in time to witness the capture of the city by Totila; and, though he did not have a sufficient force to avert this disaster, he prevented Totila from destroying the city, firmly but temperately remonstrating against so violent a proceeding. When Totila departed for Southern Italy, Belisarius, at the head of a thousand cavalry, seized the deserted city and erected the imperial standard upon the Capitol, thus inducing the scattered inhabitants to return. The fortifications of Rome were repaired, and Totila was repulsed with heavy loss in his efforts to retake the city in A. D. 547.

Belisarius, still hampered by Justinian's jealousy, was unable to follow up his success. The disobedience and cowardice of his own officers defeated his movements in Southern Italy. As he found it impossible to effect anything against such odds, he sought and obtained permission to return to Constantinople in A. D. 548. Totila again took Rome in A. D. 549, overran Italy, conquered Sicily, Sardinia and Corsica, and invaded Greece. These successes of Totila caused the Pope to head a deputation to the Emperor Justinian, imploring his assistance against the Ostrogothic king. Justinian accordingly sent a large army to Italy under the eunuch Narses, a favorite of the Emperor and a man of great talents. Narses was entrusted with absolute power for the prosecution of the war, and was liberally supported by his imperial master. He soon proved himself a great general like Belisarius, regaining the territory which the imperialists had lost. He defeated and killed Totila in a great battle near Tagina, which gave him possession of Rome (A. D. 552), that city having changed masters for the fifth time during Justinian's reign.

TEIAS, Totila's successor and the last Ostrogothic King of Italy, sought the assistance of the Franks. Before he could be able to obtain this aid, he was defeated and killed at Cumæ in A. D. 553. In the following autumn an army of seventy-five thousand Germans crossed the Alps and ravaged Italy as far as the extreme southern point of the peninsula, but were defeated with terrible slaughter by Narses at Casilínum, on the Vulturnus.

The defeat and death of Teias put an end to the Ostrogothic kingdom in Italy, which had existed sixty years (A. D. 493-553). Italy then became a province of the Eastern Roman Empire, the Emperor Justinian erecting the conquered country into the Exarchate of Ravenna. The Emperor's governors, called *Exarchs*, ruled the whole peninsula from their capital, Ravenna. Narses, the conqueror of the Ostrogoths, was the first and greatest of the Exarchs, and ruled Italy from A. D. 554 to A. D. 568. The Ostrogoths either migrated from Italy in quest of new homes, or were absorbed into the mass of the Italian nation, and their history ceased thenceforth.

SECTION V.—THE LOMBARD KINGDOM IN ITALY.

THE overthrow of the Ostrogothic power in Italy produced a result which the Emperor Justinian had not foreseen. During the reign of Theódoric and the regency of his daughter Amalasontha, the Ostrogoths had effectually guarded the great barrier of the Upper Danube against the Gepidæ, who, since the time of Attila, had occupied the country on the opposite side of the Danube, the region now embraced by Hungary and Transylvania. The necessities of the Ostrogoths in Italy had forced them to evacuate Pannonia and Noricum to defend their Italian possessions against the arms of the Eastern Roman Empire.

The evacuated territories were immediately occupied by the Gepidæ, who, unsatisfied with these acquisitions, threatened to burst into Italy. To frustrate this design the Emperor Justinian called in the Lombards, or Longobards (Long Beards), who had migrated from the eastern banks of the Elbe southward to the Upper Danube. The Lombard king, AUDOIN, accepting the Emperor's invitation, accordingly moved into Pannonia with his troops, and commenced a war of thirty years with the Gepidæ. Upon Audoin's death, his son, ALBOIN, became King of the Lombards. Alboin was distinguished for his savage bravery. Finding the Gepidæ too powerful to be conquered by his own nation, he entered into an alliance with the Avars, or Huns, and thus brought about the extermination of the Gepidæ. Alboin killed Cunimund, the King of the Gepidæ, and married his daughter, the beautiful Rosamond (A. D. 566). The Avars obtained the lands of the Gepidæ as a reward for their assistance to the Lombards, and the latter were obliged to seek new homes. As the way to Italy stood open to them they determined to migrate into that country. Narses having been degraded and removed from the Exarchate of Ravenna, the Emperor Justinian had no general capable of staying the progress of these fierce warriors from the north.

Alboin crossed the Julian Alps in A. D. 568, and soon came into possession of Italy as far south as Ravenna and Rome. Only Pavia made any resistance, and withstood a three years' siege, but was taken by Alboin in A. D. 571, and became the capital of the Lombard kingdom in Italy, which was divided into thirty duchies. The region in Northern Italy still called *Lombardy* received its name from this rude and fierce German tribe. The Lombards treated the conquered people with harshness, and deprived them of their possessions; but they also commenced to devote themselves to the cultivation of their newly-acquired lands, and began to make some progress in civilization.

Alboin lived to enjoy his triumph but two years. He was assassinated by a band of conspirators in A. D. 573, at the instigation

THE LOMBARD KINGDOM IN ITALY.

of his wife, the beautiful Rosamond, in revenge for compelling her, during a festival, to drink from the goblet which had been fashioned from the skull of her father, Cunimund, the King of the Gepidæ, whom Alboin had killed in battle seven years before, as already related. Rosamond and her lover, the latter of whom was the leading assassin, fled to the court of the Exarch of Ravenna. Longinus, the Exarch, became enamored of the beautiful queen, and offered to marry her. For the purpose of accepting the Exarch's offer, Rosamond endeavored to poison her lover, Helmichis. Discovering her treachery, Helmichis compelled her to drink also of the fatal cup; and she expired a few moments after her lover.

Upon the assassination of Alboin, the Lombard chiefs chose CLEPH, or CLEPHO, the one of their number who was the most distinguished for his bravery, for their sovereign. He was assassinated in A. D. 574, and the Lombard kingdom had no regular government for the next ten years. Each Lombard chieftain seized a city for himself, and some of them endeavored to invade the territories of the German tribes north of the Alps. The people of Rome solicited aid of the Emperor Tiberius, who, unable to assist them, bribed Chilperic, the Frankish monarch, to invade Italy and drive out the Lombards. Thereupon the Lombards bestowed their crown upon AUTHARIS, the son of Cleph, who defeated the Franks and forced them to return to their own country. Autharis also withstood two other Frankish invasions. The last of these invasions was led by Childebert, whom the Eastern Emperor Maurice had encouraged to it. Autharis thoroughly baffled the Frankish sovereign by his prudence and superior generalship, avoiding a conflict and allowing the summer heat to frustrate his adversary. The triumphant Lombard monarch extended his dominion to the southern extremity of Italy, where he founded the great duchy of Benevento.

Autharis established a perfectly feudal monarchy among the Lombards, assigning to the dukes their duchies in perpetuity, on condition of their giving one moiety of their revenue to support the royal dignity. The dukes could not be deprived of their possessions except for high-treason, but held power only at the sovereign's will. Although a similar system appears to have been in force among the Franks almost from the very origin of their monarchy, feudal law first received a complete form among the Lombards; and the rules concerning the succession, acquisition and investiture of fiefs among other nations were mostly derived from the Lombard code.

Upon the death of Autharis, in A. D. 590, his widow, Theodolinda, was entrusted by the Lombard nation with the choice of his successor. She bestowed the crown on AGILULF, Duke of Turin, whom she married, and who reigned until A. D. 615. She converted her husband and many of his subjects from the Arian to the Catholic faith, and was rewarded by Pope Gregory the Great with the famous *Iron Crown of Lombardy*, which was said to have been forged from one of the nails of the True Cross, and which is still preserved in the cathedral of Milan.

Italy was now divided between the Exarch of Ravenna and the Lombard king. The Exarch ruled over all the country east of the Apennines from the Po to Ancona, along with Rome and the country between Terracina and Civita Vecchia, the duchy of Naples, the islands of Sicily, Sardinia and Corsica, and the territories of the young republic of Venice. The duchy of Naples soon became virtually independent, though it still acknowledged a nominal allegiance to the Eastern Emperor. The Lombard kingdom embraced Northern Italy and the two great duchies of Spoletum and Beneventum.

The Lombards held themselves aloof from the Italians, whose weakness they despised, though they treated them with justice. Nevertheless the long-bearded barbarians from the north had already made some progress in civilization. The Lombard kingdom in Italy was more peaceful and prosperous than any other which had been formed from the fragments of the Western Roman Empire. The code of laws framed by the Lombard king Rotharis, who reigned from A. D. 636 to A. D. 652, is considered the best of the barbarian codes.

Under ADALUALD, Agilulf's son and successor, who ascended the Lombard throne in A. D. 615, the triumph of the orthodox Catholic faith was completed, and this circumstance greatly tended to reconcile the Italians to the Lombard supremacy. Nevertheless, the Arian party was sufficiently powerful to elevate ARIUALD to the throne, but both rivals died without issue, and the general assembly of the Lombards chose ROTHARIS for their sovereign (A. D. 636). Rotharis was an Arian, but won the affections of all his subjects by the wise code of laws which he framed, as stated. Rotharis also wrested some important places from the Exarch of Ravenna and reduced the dominion of the Eastern Empire in Italy to so low a condition that it simply existed upon the sufferance of the Lombards.

On the death of Rotharis in A. D. 652, a scene of weakness and confusion followed, which lasted ten years; RODUALD being raised to the Lombard throne in A. D. 652, ARIBERT I. in A. D. 653, and both BERTHARIT and GODEBERT in A. D. 661. This period of dissension and weakness ended with the accession of GRIMVALD, Duke of Benevento, in A. D. 662. Grimvald was soon involved in a war with the Franks, who invaded Italy, but were totally defeated. No sooner had the Lombard sovereign repelled this Frankish invasion than the Eastern Emperor Constans made his appearance in Italy at the head of a formidable army and besieged Benevento; but the imperialists encountered so fierce a resistance from the garrison that they were soon obliged to retreat, and, being overtaken on their march, were routed with terrific slaughter. The Emperor Constans fled to Sicily with the shattered remnant of his forces, and was murdered in a bath by some of his own servants. Grimvald died shortly after his triumph, in A. D. 672, universally lamented by his subjects.

Grimvald's death was followed by a series of obscure and uninteresting revolutions which deluged Italy with blood, and during which six sovereigns were successively elevated to the throne—BERTHARIT in A. D. 671, CUNIBERT in A. D. 686, LUITBERT in A. D. 700, RAGIMBERT in A. D. 701, ARIBERT II. in A. D. 701, and ANSPRAND in A. D. 711.

The prosperity of the Lombards was once more restored upon the accession of LUIDPRAND to the throne in A. D 711. Luidprand framed several wise laws, rectified the evils which had crept into the administration of justice during the recent disturbances, and won the favor of the nobles who had opposed his elevation to the throne by his judicious display of courage and prudence. Nevertheless he was actuated by his ambition to undertake the thorough conquest of all Italy, taking advantage of the troubles caused by the edicts of the Eastern Emperor Leo III. for the destruction of images. Luidprand invaded the territories of the Exarchate and took Ravenna itself; but his success aroused the jealousy of Pope Gregory II., who, though delighted with the chastisement of the Iconoclasts, or image-breakers, was not pleased with the growth of the Lombard power. The Lombards began to invade the Roman territory, whereupon the Pope entered into an alliance with the Venetians, whom he instigated to aid the Exarch in recovering Ravenna.

The Italians everywhere supported the Pope against the Emperor, who had aroused the most determined hostility of the Italians by his championship of Iconoclasm. Still the Pope hesitated to renounce his allegiance to the Emperor, as he needed an ally against the Lombards, who were pressing him very hard. Instead of manifesting any gratitude to Pope Gregory II. for his intervention in the Emperor's favor in the war with the Lombards, Leo III. sent emissaries to arrest the Pope, who was only saved from imprisonment by the prompt interference of the Lombard king.

Incensed at the Emperor's violent zeal

THE LOMBARD KINGDOM IN ITALY.

against images, the Italians broke out into open revolt against Leo III., and several cities voluntarily submitted to the Lombard monarch, who pretended an extravagant zeal for the orthodox Catholic faith. But the Pope dreaded Luidprand and sought the protection of Charles Martel, the Duke of the Franks, against the Eastern Emperor, who displayed an equal hostility to the Lombards and the Pope. Italy was thus distracted with religious and political dissensions.

Pope Gregory II. died in the midst of his negotiations with the Frankish ruler; but his successor, Gregory III., continued the struggle with unabated vigor. Ravenna was then taken from the Exarch, who afterwards fled; and Italy was forever lost to the Eastern Roman Empire, only the Pope and the Lombard king remaining to dispute its sovereignty. As Luidprand was seeking to force Pope Gregory III. to submission, the Pope was under the necessity of appealing to Charles Martel, the leader of the Franks, for aid, as his predecessor had done. The Pope offered the Frankish chieftain the sovereignty of the Roman people as a reward for his intervention. Charles Martel prepared to accept the Pope's offer, but died before he was able to do so (A. D. 741).

Upon the death of Luidprand, in A. D. 743, the Lombards chose HILDEBRAND for their king. RACHIS was chosen as Hildebrand's successor in A. D. 744, and was succeeded by ASTOLPH in A. D. 749. During Astolph's reign the Lombard kingdom reached the zenith of its greatness. Astolph conquered the Exarchate of Ravenna and changed it into a new dukedom; after which he led his forces against Rome, which was practically ruled by the Pope, though nominally subject to the Eastern Emperor. Alarmed at the danger which menaced him, Pope Stephen II. applied first to the Eastern Emperor Constantine V. for aid; but finding that the Emperor manifested little concern for Italy, the Pope appealed to Pepin the Little, the son of Charles Martel and the first Carlovingian King of the Franks, whom Pope Zachary had declared king.

Pope Stephen II. crossed the Alps to solicit the Frankish monarch's protection, and was received by Pepin with the highest reverence. In the autumn of A. D. 754 Pepin led a formidable army into Italy and besieged Astolph, the Lombard king, in Pavia, his capital, and compelled him to purchase peace by ceding to the Pope the places which he had seized in the Roman dukedom, along with the Exarchate of Ravenna and the marches of Ancona. As soon as Pepin retired from Italy the Lombard king renewed the war, encamped before Rome, and demanded the Pope's surrender as the condition of sparing the city. In response to the Pope's appeal, Pepin again crossed the Alps into Italy and reduced the Lombards to such desperate extremities that Astolph was obliged to purchase peace by relinquishing all his conquests, including the Exarchate of Ravenna and the Pentapolis.

Pepin declared that he undertook the war for the glory of St. Peter, and bestowed the whole of the restored territory upon the Pope, thus laying the foundations of the Pope's temporal power, which continued until 1871. The district thus conferred upon the Pope included Ravenna, Rimini and twenty-three other cities, and comprised the Exarchate and the Pentapolis, which were subsequently known as the *States of the Church*, or the *Papal States;* but the Pope was not yet an independent sovereign, as money was still coined and justice administered in the name of the Frankish king, and even the election of the Pope was subject to his revision.

The Lombard king Astolph secretly resolved to renew the war with the Pope at the first favorable opportunity; but before his preparations were completed he was killed by a fall from his horse, and the Lombard kingdom was distracted by a disputed succession. By the Pope's assistance, DESIDERIUS succeeded in establishing himself upon the Lombard throne; but as he was afterwards exposed to the Pope's jealousy, he endeavored to secure himself by giving his daughters in marriage to Pepin's sons and successors, Charles and Carloman.

The alliance between the Lombard monarch and the Frankish sovereigns did not last very long. Charles divorced his wife; whereupon Desiderius sought revenge by endeavoring to induce the Pope to anoint Carloman's children Kings of the Franks. Pope Adrian I. steadily refused the Lombard king's request; whereupon Desiderius invaded the Papal territories, laid waste the country and menaced Rome. The Pope, being unable to make any effective resistance, placed himself under the protection of Charles, or Charlemagne (Charles the Great). This great Frankish king accordingly crossed the Alps into Italy at the head of a powerful army in A. D. 774; took Pavia, the Lombard capital, after a siege of two months; made Desiderius a prisoner; and thus put an end to the Lombard kingdom, which had been the great power in Italy for two centuries (A. D. 571-774). Desiderius and his family were sent to France, where they died in obscurity, Desiderius himself ending his days in a cloister. Charlemagne, as conqueror, received the Iron Crown of Lombardy.

A few years later Arigiso, the Lombard Duke of Benevento, who had married the daughter of Desiderius, headed a league of the enemies of the Pope and the Frankish king. Charlemagne entered Italy in A. D. 781 to protect the Pope, and promptly reduced the members of the hostile league to submission.

SECTION VI.—THE FRANKS IN GAUL.

ONE of the most important of the Germanic tribes were the Franks, or *Freemen*, so called because of their determination to be free. The history of these people for several centuries is the history of France and Germany. They subdued Gaul and their own kinsmen, and laid the foundations of the kingdoms of Germany and France. They commenced their attacks upon the Roman dominions on the west bank of the Rhine in the third century of the Christian era; and, notwithstanding their frequent repulses, their persistent efforts were eventually rewarded with perfect success. By the latter portion of the fifth century they had subjugated the entire region between the Middle Rhine and the Meuse, and had established their capital at Cologne. These were the Ripuarian Franks.

The Lower Rhine was held by the Salian Franks, who were mainly descended from the Sicambri, whom the Emperor Tiberius had settled there. These people only submitted to the Roman dominion with great reluctance, and were ever on the eager watch for an opportunity to recover their independence. They were severely chastised by the Emperor Julian the Apostate, but he permitted them to retain the lands which they had seized west of the Rhine, and which extended west of the Meuse. By the beginning of the fifth century they had become so formidable that they refused any longer to recognize the supremacy of Rome, though they still furnished mercenary soldiers to the Roman army

At this time the Salian Franks were governed by their own kings. Among their legendary monarchs at this period was PHARAMOND, who is said to have died in A. D. 428. His reputed successor was CLODION, celebrated for the beauty of his hair. He extended the limits of his kingdom westward to the Somme. He entered into an alliance with the Romans, and gave them important assistance in their efforts against Attila, King of the Huns, in A. D. 451. The institutions of this Frankish kingdom were similar to those of the other German tribes. Clodion's successor was MEROWIG, as he is called in German (meaning *eminent warrior*), and whose name has been Latinized as *Merovéus*. He is regarded as the founder of the famous *Merovingian* dynasty. Merowig, or Merovéus, was succeeded by his son, CHILDERIC (meaning *bold in combat*), who reigned during the latter half of the fifth century of the Christian era, and had his capital at Tournay. Childeric was a great king and a brave warrior, and assisted the Romans against the Visigoths. This connection with Rome prepared the way for the events which soon followed. Childeric was a slave to his passions. An insult which he offered to the wife of one of his officers caused a revolt, which led to the dethronement of Childeric. Count Egidius, or Giles, was then proclaimed king. After an exile of eight years, Childeric was restored; and the remainder of his reign seems to have been tranquil.

Upon Childeric's death, in A. D. 481, his son CHLODWIG (meaning *famous warrior*), who is better known by his Latin name, *Clovis*, or *Ludovicus*, which is equivalent to the modern German *Ludwig*, the modern Italian *Ludovico* and the English *Lewis*. Clovis was but fifteen years of age when he became King of the Salian Franks. His kingdom at the time of his accession embraced only the island of the Batavians and the ancient dioceses of Tournay and Arras, and he had no more than five thousand warriors. His wonderful talents soon extended his influence over the kindred Frankish tribes, which were settled along the Scheldt, the Meuse, the Moselle and the Lower Rhine, and which were ruled by independent kings and attracted many warriors to his standard.

The ardor of his youth, along with the circumstances of his position, urged him on to a career of conquest; as the fertility of the Belgic soil, the purity of its waters and its atmosphere, constantly attracted fresh hordes to the Lower Rhine, who endeavored to cast their lot with the subjects of Clovis. Finding it thus necessary to enlarge his dominions, Clovis invaded the Roman province in Belgic Gaul. He defeated Syágrius, the son of his father's rival, Egidius, in a decisive battle near Soissons, in A. D. 486. The vanquished Syágrius fled to the Visigoths in the South of Gaul, to seek an asylum among that people; but the Visigothic nation had lost much of its martial spirit, and King Alaric II. sent the fugitive general bound to Clovis, who beheaded him.

Clovis had now become the most powerful monarch of his time, and the neighboring princes eagerly sought his alliance. In A. D. 493 he married Chlodohilde, (meaning *brilliant and noble*), who is better known as Clotilda, and who was the niece of the King of the Burgundians. Clotilda was a Christian, who had been educated in the orthodox Catholic faith, though reared in an Arian court. She labored earnestly and diligently to convert her husband to Christianity, and particularly urged him when his crown and his life were jeopardized by an invasion of the Alemanni.

Clovis for a time refused to embrace his wife's religion, but allowed their eldest child to be baptized. The great decisive battle in the war against the Alemanni was fought at Tolbiac, or Zülpich, near Cologne, in A. D. 496. It was a stubbornly contested struggle, and for some time the result of the conflict was doubtful. In this crisis Clovis raised his hands toward heaven, invoking "the God of Clotilda," and vowing that if that God would give him the victory he would embrace the Christian faith and receive Christian baptism. He triumphed in the battle, and when it ended he accepted Christianity; and on Christmas day (A. D. 496) he was baptized with great pomp and splendor, along with three thousand of his subjects, by St. Remi, Bishop of Rheims, in the great cathedral in that historic city. Clovis gave the bishop, as a fee, all the land he could ride around while the king slept after dinner—a gift exceedingly characteristic of a conqueror who felt that he could acquire new dominions whenever he awoke. The *sacred phial* filled with oil for the consecration of the king has been preserved to the present day, and the superstitious people of the time of Clovis believed that the phial and sacred oil were brought from heaven by a dove. The Kings of France have ever since been called "Most Christian King," and have been solemnly crowned in the great cathedral of Rheims.

By embracing Christianity of the orthodox Catholic faith, Clovis obtained the firm support of that Church; and the alliance was of great service to the interests of both parties. In the advancing power of Clovis, the Church found an instrument which might humble the power of the Arian Visigoths and Burgundians for persecution, and unite the whole country in dutiful submission to the Bishop of Rome; while Clovis gained in the Church an ally having the complete confidence of the people whose land he designed to conquer, and ready to proclaim him as the chosen of Heaven, whose scepter would be the surest guaranty of a nation's prosperity and greatness. Neither the Frankish monarch nor the Church could have succeeded without the support of the other, but both together were irresistible.

The results of the alliance between Clovis and the Church were soon manifest. In A. D. 497 the Bretons of Armorica (afterward called Brittany or Bretagne) entered into a treaty with Clovis by which they acknowledged themselves his tributaries. This treaty extended the frontiers of the Frankish dominions southward to the Loire. In A. D. 500 Clovis won a decisive victory over the Burgundians, and forced their king, Gondobald, to acknowledge himself a tributary of the Frankish monarch. This triumph of Clovis put an end to the glory and greatness of the Burgundian kingdom, which was not, however, definitely annexed to the Frankish dominion until the succeeding generation.

Encouraged by the conquest of the Burgundians, Clovis undertook the reduction of the Visigothic kingdom south of the Loire. The civil government of this portion of ancient Gaul was mainly exercised by the clergy, who now rallied to the support of the Frankish king as the champion of the orthodox Catholic faith. The Romanized Gallic subjects of Alaric II., the Visigothic monarch, longed for the victory of the Franks, and made very little resistance to them. Clovis advanced in the direction of the ancient Genabum, the modern Orleans, and crossed the Loire, everywhere spreading the terror of his name. After entering Aquitania, he pillagd the houses, laid waste the fields and plundered the temples; in the language of a contemporary historian, "leaving nothing to the wretched inhabitants but the soil, which the Franks could not take away."

Clovis defeated the Visigoths in the decisive battle of Voillé, near Poitiers, in A. D. 507, himself killing the Visigothic king, Alaric II.; after which the victorious Frankish monarch overran the country between the Loire and the Garonne, passing the winter at Bordeaux. The next spring Clovis endeavored to drive the Visigoths beyond the Pyrenees; but Theódoric, the great Ostrogothic King of Italy, sent an army to the aid of his Visigothic kinsman, thus compelling the Frankish king to pause. Clovis met with a decisive repulse before Arles, the Visigothic capital, and left the Visigoths in possession of a small part of their territory known as the province of Septimania, of which the capital was Narbo, or Narbonne. The remainder of the Visigothic territory in Gaul was permanently annexed to the Frankish dominion.

Upon returning to Tours, Clovis received an embassy from the Eastern Roman Emperor Anastasius, who congratulated him and invested him with the titles and insignia of Consul and Patrician. This was practically very little gain to the Frankish sovereign, who was absolute master of most of Gaul; but its moral influence was considerable, as this action of the Eastern Emperor caused the Romanized Gallic subjects of Clovis to regard the Frankish monarch as the legitimate successor to all the rights and privileges of the Roman Cæsars.

Thus the kingdom which Clovis established extended from the Rhine to the Pyrenees, and from the Alps to the Atlantic; comprising the whole of ancient Gaul and Roman Germany, or modern France and Belgium with the neighboring Dutch and German territory west of the Rhine. Al-

CLOVIS RECOVERING THE SACRED VASE.

though the conquering king had everywhere met with submission from the various Romanized Celts of Gaul, his nominal subjects closed upon his rear. Neither was Clovis absolute over his own Frankish soldiers, his army being composed of freemen, who disdained to submit to despotic power. They gave their sovereign no more than his share of the booty; as is shown by a curious anecdote related by Gregory of Tours, an eminent French historian of the sixth century, in his *History of the Franks*, in the following words:

"About this time the army of Clovis pillaged a great number of churches and houses. His soldiers had taken away, from one of the cathedrals, a vase of surprising size and beauty. The bishop of the diocese sent a messenger to reclaim it. To this man, the king said: 'Follow me to Soissons, where the plunder will be shared, and should chance give me the vase, I will do what your prelate requires.' When they reached Soissons they went to the place where the plunder was piled, and the king said: 'I entreat you, my brave warriors, to give me this vase in addition to my share.' Upon this, a presumptuous soldier exclaimed: 'You shall have nothing but the portion assigned you by lot.'"

Gregory of Tours also says: "After this, Clotaire and Childebert, sons of Clovis, formed the design of marching against the Burgundians. Their brother, Theódoric, was unwilling to engage in the expedition, but the Franks who followed him said unanimously: 'If you will not join your brothers, we will quit you, and choose another leader.'"

The religion of Clovis never restrained him in the course of ambition, as he seized every opportunity for the extension of his dominions either by fraud or violence. During the Dark Ages it was believed that all crimes might be atoned for by the erection of churches and the support of monasteries. The priests, blinded by this liberality to themselves, ignored many of these acts of cruelty and treachery in their histories. In order to secure his own authority, Clovis caused the heads of many of his relatives to be shaved, and afterwards he put them to death, lest time should renew their long hair, the emblem of royalty. Clovis may be regarded as the original founder of the French monarchy, as he reunited the Frankish and Romanized Gallic elements into one nation.

Though Clovis was so cruel, he was a wise monarch, and established several just and humane codes. One of these codes was the *Ripuarian*, derived from the Ripuarian Franks. Another Code was the *Salic Law*, derived from the Salian Franks. One of the provisions of the Salic Law has ever since remained in force—that which excludes females from the throne of France. The wives of the Kings of France have always been called *queens;* but, from the time of Clovis to the very last French monarchy, there has never been a sole reigning *Queen* of France.

During his last years Clovis rid himself of rivals by deliberately murdering the other Frankish chiefs, some of whom were his Merovingian kinsmen; thus showing that the religion of Christ had no influence in restraining his savage disposition. Clovis finally made Paris the capital of his kingdom, and died in that city in A. D. 511, leaving his dominions to his four sons— THEODORIC (meaning *brave among the people*), CHILDEBERT (meaning *brilliant warrior*), CLODOMIR (meaning *celebrated chief*), and CLOTAIRE (meaning *celebrated and excellent*).

All the sons of Clovis established their capitals north of the Loire, which is conclusive evidence of the insecurity of the tenure by which the conquests made by Clovis south of that great river were thus far held. Theódoric, the eldest son, took for his share the eastern provinces between the Meuse and the Rhine, along with the districts of Auvergne, Limousin and Quercy; and his capital was Metz. Clodomir held sway over the Orleannais, Anjou, Maine and Touraine; with his capital at Orleans. Childebert reigned over the Isle de France and Armorica, his kingdom thus extending from Paris and Rouen on the east to Rennes, Vannes and Nantes on the west; and had Paris for his capital. Clotaire, the youngest son, held dominion over the ancient country of the Salian Franks, along with the maritime district extending from the Somme to the mouth of the Meuse, together with some territory in the Cevennes and on the Upper Garonne; and had Soissons for his capital.

The dominions of the four brothers thus intersected each other in the most confusing manner; and it was frequently necessary for one sovereign to cross another's dominions in order to reach the remote portions of his territories, thus giving rise to many disputes, and none of the brothers was disposed to lived peaceably with the others. Theódoric, though a fierce and violent sovereign, gave his subjects a wise and excellent code of laws, and strenuously endeavored to establish Christianity wherever paganism had previously existed.

Theódoric and Clodomir engaged in a war with Gundumir, King of the Burgundians; and Clodomir was killed in a great battle near Vienne in A. D. 522, but Theódoric won a decisive victory and annexed the Burgundian kingdom to his own dominions. Gundumir means *pacific and great*. Gregory of Tours gives the following account of this war: "The brothers joined their forces at Veserancia, a place situated in the territory of the city of Vienne, and gave battle to Gundumir. The Burgundian having taken to flight with his army, Clodomir pursued him, and when he was at a distance from his friends, the Burgundians, imitating the signals of the Franks, exclaimed: 'Come this way, we are thine.' He believed them, and spurred his horse into the midst of the enemy. They surrounded him, cut off his head, and fixing it on a pike, displayed it to their pursuers."

Clotilda took the guardianship of her infant grandchildren, but the decided preference which she exhibited for Clodomir's three sons aroused the resentment of Childebert, King of Paris, who secretly proposed to his youngest brother, Clotaire, King of Soissons, that they should obtain possession of the persons of the young princes, shave their heads, and divide their possessions. Clotaire eagerly united in the scheme, and put the two eldest of his nephews to death. The third was saved by faithful servants, and cut off his own hair and thereafter lived a life of celibacy in a monastery. Shaving the head was the form of dethroning a monarch at this period; and among the early Franks the crown of hair was as much an emblem of royalty as a crown of gold.

Gregory of Tours gives the following interesting account of this transaction: "Clotaire readily adopted his brother's project and came to Paris. Childebert had already spread a report that he and his brother had agreed to invest their nephews with royalty, and they sent a messenger to Clotilda, then residing in the same city, who said: 'Send your grandchildren, that they may be raised to the throne.' She, joyous, and knowing nothing of the plot, after having made the children eat and drink, sent them to their uncles, saying: 'Go, children, I will believe that my son is not lost, when I see you on the throne.' When the children came to their uncles, they were taken and separated from their servants and governors. Then they shut them up apart, the children in one place, and the attendants in another. When this was done, Childebert and Clotaire sent Arcadius, one of their officers, to the queen, with a scissors and a drawn sword. When he came into her presence, showing her these, he said: 'Thy sons, our lords, desire to know thy pleasure, gracious queen, respecting the manner in which they should treat the children. Order either their hair or their throats to be cut.' Astounded by these words, and enraged at beholding the scissors and the naked sword, the queen gave vent to her wrath, and, scarcely knowing what she said, so troubled was her mind, imprudently replied: 'If they are not to reign like their father, I would rather see them dead than shaven.' Then Arcadius returned promptly to those who sent him, and said: 'You may persevere; the queen approves what you have begun, and her will is, that you complete your project.' Immediately Clotaire, taking the eldest of the children by the arm, threw him on the ground, and stabbing him under the shoulder, put him cruelly to death. His brother, terrified at the scene, threw himself at the feet of Childebert, and kissing his knees, exclaimed: 'Help me, my good father, let me not be murdered like my poor brother.' Then Childebert, melting into tears, said to Clotaire: 'Oh! I entreat you, my very dear brother, have the kindness to spare this child's life; if you consent to spare him, I will give you whatever you may demand.' But Clotaire, overwhelming him with reproaches, said: 'Thrust the child away, or you shall die in his stead, for you were the first to urge me to this deed, though you now shrink from its completion.' Then Childebert, alarmed, pushed the child over to Clotaire, who struck his dagger into the boy's side, and slew him on the body of his brother. Afterward they murdered the servants and tutors. When they were dead, Clotaire mounted his horse, without showing any compunction for the murder of his nephews, and retired with Childebert to the suburbs. The queen, Clotilda, having placed the bodies on a bier, conducted them, with litanies, sacred songs and profound grief, to the church of St. Peter's, where they were buried together. One was ten years old, and the other six. The third son, named Clodoald, was saved by the interference of some brave men, called *barons*. Renouncing his earthly kingdom, he became a clerk, and, persisting in good works, finally received priest's orders. The two kings shared among them the inheritance of Clodomir."

Ten years after the murder of Clodomir's sons, Theódoric died, and was succeeded by his son THEODEBERT (meaning *very brilliant among the people*), who called himself King of Austrasia (Eastern kingdom). His uncles, Childebert and Clotaire, endeavored to deprive him of his dominions; but, as they were daunted by the display of his power, they turned their arms against Spain, laid waste Aragon, Biscay and Catalonia, stormed Pampeluna, besieged Saragossa, and were only induced to withdraw from the country by a present of the tunic of St. Vincent, a relic which was highly prized in that superstitious age.

Theódebert's fame extended to Constantinople. The Emperor Justinian sought to gain his friendship by ceding to him the nominal claims of the Eastern Empire over Provence; but Theódebert formed an alliance with Totila, the reigning king of the Ostrogoths in Italy, the Emperor's enemy. The Austrasian king crossed the Alps into Italy at the head of a formidable army and speedily conquered the greater portion of Northern Italy. After Theódebert's return to his dominions, the army which he left behind him in Italy suffered some reverses; and Justinian's exorbitant vanity induced him to issue a medal on which he styled himself "Conqueror of the Franks." This arrogance so enraged Theódebert that he made preparations to lead an army through Hungary into Thrace and attack Justinian in his capital; but this bold design was thwarted by Theódebert's sudden death in A. D. 548, he being killed by the fall of a tree while hunting the wild buffalo—a dangerous sport to which he was most passionately addicted.

Theódebert was succeeded as King of Austrasia by THEODEBALD (meaning *vigorous above all*), who died after a glorious reign of seven years (A. D. 555). Childebert soon followed him to the grave, so that Clotaire obtained sole but not quiet possession of Austrasia and Neustria—the former being the country between the Rhine, the Meuse and the Moselle; and the latter the region between the Meuse, the Loire and the ocean. Aquitaine, or the country south of the Loire, was at this time independent of Frankish sway. Clotaire's own son, Chramnè (meaning *warlike*), headed a revolt of the turbulent Bretons, but he was defeated, and suffered a cruel death with his whole family by order of his father. The old chroniclers tell us that Clotaire died the next year (A. D. 561) at Compeigne, on the anniversary of his son's death, and at the exact hour one year after the shocking tragedy.

Gregory of Tours gives the following account of this defeat of the Bretons: "The two armies having come to an engagement, the Count of the Bretons ran away, and was slain in flight; after which Hram (Chramnè) began to fly toward the ships he had prepared on the sea; but, while he was endeavoring to save his wife and children, he was overtaken by his father's army, made prisoner and bound. When the news was brought to Clotaire, he ordered that the prince, together with his wife and daughters, should be burned. They shut them up in a poor hut, where Hram, extended on a bench, was strangled. They then set fire to the house, and it was consumed with all its inmates."

Clotaire's four sons—CHARIBERT (meaning *glorious in the army*), GONTRAM (meaning *generous man*), CHILPERIC (meaning *brave in combat*), and SIGEBERT (meaning *glorious conqueror*)—divided his dominions among them. Sigebert, King of Austrasia, married Brunilda, or Brunehaut; and Chilperic, King of Neustria, married Galeswintha—both women being sisters, the daughters of Athanagild, the reigning Visigothic King of Spain. Brunehaut was a woman of great beauty and accomplishments, but of violent passions. Galeswintha was the younger sister, and was murdered by Chilperic soon after their marriage, at the instigation of his low-born mistress, Fredegonda, whom he then married. Brunehaut became the bitter enemy of Fredegonda; and, though she accepted the settlement of the quarrel, she was thenceforth determined upon revenge on her sister's murderers.

The turbulent period which followed was chiefly remarkable for the crimes of Brunehaut and Fredegonda. The mutual jealousy between these two ambitious and unprincipled women was aggravated by Brunehaut's desire for revenge and by Fredegonda's difficulty of maintaining her dignity when she was changed from the mistress to the wife of Chilperic. During the period over which their mutual resentments spread, it is difficult to distinguish anything but murders and assassinations.

The personal quarrels between these two infamous women was further aggravated by the rivalry between the Kingdoms of Austrasia and Neustria; the Frankish or German population almost entirely prevailing in Austrasia, and the Romanized Gallic population being very largely predominant in Neustria. Fredegonda, who abandoned herself to a life of crime, caused the assassination of Sigebert, and to escape punishment she also procured the murder of her husband, Chilperic. She also caused Chilperic's two sons to be murdered, being enraged at Merovèe (meaning *eminent warrior*), who had married Brunehaut.

Sigebert was succeeded as King of Austrasia by CHILDEBERT II., who also inherited the kingdom of his uncle Gontram, who died A. D. 593. The widowed Brunehaut continued to rule in Austrasia as the guardian of her son. She was almost as wicked as Fredegonda. She enjoyed the friendship of Pope Gregory the Great and other good and learned men, and was the patroness and protector of Christianity and learning, notwithstanding her infamous crimes.

Brunehaut and her son, Childebert II., maintained a long and sanguinary war with Fredegonda and her young son, CLOTAIRE II., King of Neustria. Childebert II. died young, leaving two children to divide his distracted dominions ; both of whom were murdered by Brunehaut, whose animosity they had aroused by remonstrating against her crimes. Brunehaut endeavored to crush the power of the Austrian nobles; but they proved too powerful for her, and, with the aid of the forces of Neustria and Burgundy, they finally defeated her, took her prisoner and delivered her to Clotaire II., who, in revenge and punishment for her enmity to his mother and himself, exhibited her for three days, mounted on a camel, to the derision of his army, subjected her to the most cruel tortures, and finally fastened her to the tail of a wild horse, which tore the wretched queen to pieces before the eyes of the soldiers.

All the Frankish dominions were now united under Clotaire II., who reigned as

THE DEATH OF BRUNEHAUT

sole king from A. D. 613 to A. D. 628. Clotaire II. published a code of laws, which enjoys some reputation; but his administration lacked vigor, and the ambitious nobles made encroachments on the royal power. On the death of Clotaire II., in A. D. 628, his son DAGOBERT I. (meaning *brilliant as the day*) became King of the Franks. Dagobert I. made Paris the capital of his dominions, which extended from the Weser to the Pyrenees, and from the Atlantic Ocean to the frontiers of Bohemia, thus embracing all of France and most of Germany. Although the Merovingian dynasty reached its greatest extent of dominion under Dagobert I., that king had the mortification to see the royal authority enfeebled by the increasing power of the Mayors of the Palace. He died A. D. 638, after a weak and dissolute reign; but, singularly enough, he was canonized as a saint.

The cause of the canonization of Dagobert I. singularly illustrates the superstitions of the age. Audoald, Bishop of Poitiers, while on an embassy to Sicily, according to his own statement, was miraculously informed of the king's death by a holy hermit named John, who said: "While I was asleep last night, an old man with a long beard bade me get up and pray for the soul of King Dagobert, who was on the point of death. I arose, and looking through the window of my hermitage, I saw, in the middle of the sea, a host of devils carrying the king's soul to hell. The unfortunate soul, grievously tormented, invoked the aid of St. Martin, St. Maurice and St. Denis. At his cries, the spirits of these holy martyrs descended from heaven, in the midst of thunders and lightnings, delivered the king's soul and bore it up with them through the air, singing the canticle of David, '*O Lord, how happy is the man that thou hast chosen.*'" Audoald related this to the king's chancellor on his return to France; and the chancellor entered the relation of the affair in the archives of the kingdom, and enrolled Dagobert I. among the saints.

The Merovingian successors of Dagobert I. were weak and insignificant, being mere phantoms of royalty. They were called "Rois-fainéants" (Do-nothing kings)—a designation fully expressing their character for the next century. The real power in the kingdom was exercised by the bishops and nobles, and particularly by the king's minister, the Mayor of the Palace. The Mayor of the Palace was a noble chosen by his order to be the king's adviser in peace and the commander of the royal army in war, for the purpose of aiding the nobles in their efforts for the restriction of the royal power.

Under the feeble Merovingian kings who succeeded Dagobert I., the Mayors of the Palace were the real sovereigns of France. One of the greatest of these rulers was the famous Pepin d' Heristal, grandson of Pepin of Landen. After becoming the real ruler of half the kingdom as Duke of Austrasia, and suffering some reverses, Pepin d' Heristal vanquished the Neustrian nobility in the decisive battle of Testry in A. D. 687; and thus having inflicted the death-blow upon Merovingian royalty, he made the office of Mayor of the Palace hereditary in his family, and made himself master of France, which he governed for twenty-seven years with great vigor, prudence and success.

The victory of Pepin d' Heristal was also important in another sense, as it established the supremacy of the Teutonic or Germanic element over the Latin-Celtic element in Gaul. Pepin assumed the title of *Duke of the Franks*. The Merovingian king, "the long-haired shadow of royalty," was shown to the people once a year at the Champ de Mars (Field of March); but was kept in a kind of mild captivity at other times.

Pepin d' Heristal passed the remaining portion of the seventh century and the first years of the eighth in reëstablishing the old Frankish supremacy in Germany; forcing the Frisians, the Saxons, the Alemanni, the Suabians, the Thuringians and the Bavarians to acknowledge the Frankish dominion. These successes led to the introduction of Christianity among the German tribes; as bands of monks, mostly Anglo-Saxon from Britain, followed in the rear of the Frankish armies, and converted multitudes of the pagan Germans to Christianity. One of these Anglo-Saxon monks, St. Willibrord, was consecrated Archbishop of the Frisians by Pope Sergius I. in A. D. 696.

Pepin d' Heristal died in December, A. D. 714. After his death his widow, Pleêtrude, endeavored to govern the Frankish kingdom as regent for her infant grandson, DAGOBERT III.; but was opposed by the Austrasian nobles led by Charles Martel, an illegitimate son of Pepin, and was finally forced to yield. Charles Martel, as Mayor of the Palace, then came into undisputed possession of his father's authority and dominions (A. D. 719), and ruled with wisdom and vigor for twenty-three years.

Charles Martel's many victories over the Saxons, the Frisians and the Burgundians rendered his name illustrious, but the greatest of all his exploits was his brilliant triumph over the Saracen invaders of France. In accordance with a deliberate plan of conquest, the Saracens of Spain crossed the Pyrenees and overran the Frankish dominions as far north as the Loire. Charles Martel led his Christian Franks against them and inflicted upon them so overwhelming a defeat near Tours in A. D. 732 that the remnants of their immense host fled southward, thus freeing Christian Europe from the danger of Mohammedan conquest. Charles Martel followed up his victory; but was unable to drive the Saracens entirely from France, as they lingered in Septimania, in the extreme South of France, until A. D. 759, when they were driven back into Spain by Pepin the Little, the son and successor of Charles Martel.

By his great victory over the Saracens, Charles Martel acquired the extensive district of Aquitaine, south of the Loire, under its own rulers. Like his father, Charles Martel did not assume the royal title, but ruled as Duke of the Franks. Upon the death of King THIERRY IV., in A. D. 737, Charles Martel felt his power so firmly established that he neglected appointing a successor to the deceased monarch, and the Merovingian throne remained without even a figure-head.

The valiant Charles Martel died in A. D. 741, leaving the Frankish dominions to his two sons, Carloman and Pepin the Little; Carloman receiving Austrasia and the Frankish territories in Germany, and Pepin obtaining Neustria, Burgundy and Provence. Carloman and Pepin sought out the last of the Merovingian dynasty and proclaimed him King of the Franks under the name of CHILPERIC III. With the assistance of St. Boniface, or Winfried, the Anglo-Saxon missionary, who was about this time consecrated Archbishop of Mayence, Carloman and Pepin effected many reforms in the Church and won the hearty support of the priesthood by their liberal concessions. In A. D. 747 Carloman relinquished his share in the government to his brother and became a Benedictine monk. Finally, in A. D. 752, Pepin, with the sanction of the Pope and the support of the nobles, dethroned the feeble Chilperic III., the last Merovingian king, condemned him to the seclusion of a cloister, and made himself King of the Franks; thus founding the famous *Carlovingian* dynasty, which governed France and Germany for several centuries.

SECTION VII.—THE ANGLES AND SAXONS IN BRITAIN.

BRITAIN, under the Roman dominion, had become civilized and Christianized, but enfeebled and utterly helpless. Roads and bridges were built, which have survived to this day the ravages of time. Under the pavements of London, York and Chester are the remains of cities more finely built and more richly ornamented than those which have risen upon their ruins. But with the increase of commerce and luxury, Britain was slowly losing

THE ANGLES AND SAXONS IN BRITAIN.

her strength. Her young men were drafted into the Roman armies and shed their life-blood upon Italian or Asiatic battle-fields. The few remaining at home were corrupted by the pleasures, more than they were ennobled by the arts, of civilized life. The perfect peace and order maintained in Britain by the presence of Roman legions did not educate the Britons how to defend or govern themselves.

Early in the fourth century a change occurred in the northern portion of the island of Britain, which now for the first time began to be called *Scotland*. The Scots, a fierce and savage tribe, crossed from their original home in Ireland, and established themselves in that portion of modern Scotland known as Argyleshire, soon reducing the native Caledonians under their supremacy. The Caledonians were thenceforth known as *Picts*. The walls of Adrian, Antoninus Pius and Septimius Severus were no barriers against the Scots, who swarmed into Roman Britain and spread their destructive ravages over its fertile harvest-fields.

When the Roman Emperors were obliged to recall their legions from Britain in order to defend their continental dominions against the inroads of the Northern barbarians, the Picts and Scots embraced the opportunity to renew their incursions into the southern part of the island. In A. D. 368 they penetrated as far southward as London, but were driven back by Theodosius, the father of the great Roman Emperor of that name. In A. D. 396 they again ravaged Roman Britain, but were beaten back by Stilicho, the valiant general under the Emperor Honorius.

As the Western Roman Empire itself was now tottering to its ruin under the attacks of the Northern or Germanic barbarians, the Emperor Honorius was obliged to withdraw the Roman legions from Britain for the defense of Gaul; and the Britons, utterly helpless, were exposed to the destructive ravages of the Saxon pirates from Germany and the Picts and Scots of Caledonia. In A. D. 418 the Emperor Honorius responded to the appeals of the Britons for help by sending the Roman legions back into Britain. The Picts and Scots were driven back into Caledonia, and the Romans repaired the fortresses of Britain and instructed the Pritons in the manufacture and use of arms for their own defense.

The Romans then withdrew from Britain forever, leaving the helpless natives once more to the mercy of the Saxon pirates from the east and the Scots and Picts from the north, while the Britons were further weakened by dissensions among themselves. The national party under Vortigern desired a return to the old Celtic customs which had prevailed among the Britons before the Roman conquest, while the Roman party headed by Ambrosius upheld the law and order which Britain had derived from its recent Roman rulers.

The Roman party in Britain again appealed for Roman aid against the inroads of the Picts and Scots, writing a piteous letter to Aëtius, the Roman commander in Gaul, as follows: "To Aëtius, thrice Consul. The Groans of the Britons. The barbarians drive us into the sea; the sea throws us back upon the barbarians; and we have only the hard choice of perishing by the sword or by the waves." But Aëtius was unable to afford any aid to the Britons, as the necessities of his struggle with Attila the Hun required the presence of all his available forces in Gaul for the defense of that Roman province.

The national party in Britain had recourse to the piratical Saxons from the North of Germany. These pagan barbarians had already made themselves masters of lands on the coasts of the present Yorkshire and Durhamshire, but they were still glad to obtain a settlement on the fertile plains of Kent. In A. D. 448 three ship-loads of Jutes, a Saxon tribe from the peninsula of Jutland, which derived its name from them, came to the assistance of Vortigern, the British prince, and were led by two brother-chieftains named Hengist and Horsa. These Jutes received the isle of Thanet, then separated from the mainland by a wide channel, as a reward for their assistance. Sixteen more vessels laden with Jutes followed the first band under Hengist and Horsa, and after landing in Kent they defeated and drove back the invading Scots, receiving from the grateful Britons fertile lands in Kent as a reward for this victory.

No sooner had the Jutes assisted the Britons in driving back the Picts and Scots than they coveted the beautiful island of Britain for themselves. They accordingly turned their victorious arms against the helpless Britons. Swarms of Angles and Saxons from the region of the modern Schleswig-Holstein—kindred Teutonic tribes with the Jutes—were continually arriving in Britain, to follow the example of their kinsmen. The Anglo-Saxon invaders fell mercilessly upon the defenseless Britons and defeated them in many battles, in one of which the Jutish leader Horsa was killed. Hengist then became leader of the Anglo-Saxon hordes, and assumed the title of King of Kent in A. D. 457, thus founding the first Germanic or Teutonic kingdom in what is now England.

Forced to fight in defense of their homes and their firesides, the Britons gradually recovered their ancient valor. The struggle lasted a century and a half, from the first invasion of the Jutes under Hengist and Horsa in A. D. 448, to the battle of Chester in A. D. 607, which established the supremacy of the Anglo-Saxon invaders. The districts still occupied by the native Britons were severed from one another, and were therefore no longer able to act in concert; and the lingering struggle ceased to have a national character. Beaten on every side and pursued with fire and sword, the helpless Britons were either exterminated or forced to seek a safe retreat among the mountain fastnesses of Wales and Cornwall, while many fled across the British Channel and settled in that part of Western France which received from them the name of *Brittany* or *Bretagne*. The present inhabitants of Wales, Cornwall and Britanny are the descendants of these ancient Celtic Britons, who fled from their homes before the conquering arms of the barbarous Anglo-Saxon invaders from Germany.

In the mountain fastnesses of Wales, the Britons, animated by a burning love of liberty, maintained an unbroken war of six centuries against the whole power of England; and in that country their descendants, the modern Welsh, now live—a hardy, vigorous race, who have for the last eight centuries shared with the English, the descendants of their Anglo-Saxon conquerors, the blessings of a common country.

The most renowned of the valiant British heroes who struggled against the Anglo-Saxon conquest was the celebrated King Arthur, the chief of one of the British tribes in the West of the island; but so much of fable and romance has been interwoven with the story of this British patriot and his sixty "Knights of the Round Table" that all we really know about that renowned prince is that he lived and bravely defended his country against its Germanic invaders and conquerors.

Each of the conquering Anglo-Saxon chieftains seized for himself what he had conquered; and in the course of a century seven or eight Germanic kingdoms arose in Britain, and these are commonly known as the *Anglo-Saxon Heptarchy*. The first of these Teutonic kingdoms was *Cantia*, or Kent, founded by the Jutes under Hengist in A. D. 457; embracing the region of the present county of Kent, and having Canterbury for its capital.

The three Saxon kingdoms were *Sussex*, or South Saxony; *Essex*, or East Saxony; and *Wessex*, or West Saxony. Sussex was founded by the Saxon chief Ella in A. D. 490, and comprised the district included in the present counties of Surrey and Sussex; and had Chichester for its capital. Wessex was founded by Cerdic in A. D. 519, and included the territory of the present counties of Hampshire, Berkshire, Wiltshire, Dorsetshire, Somersetshire and the eastern part of Devonshire; and its capital was Winchester. Essex was founded by Ercewin in A. D. 527, and embraced the country included in the present counties of Essex,

THE ANGLES AND SAXONS IN BRITAIN.

Middlesex and part of Hertfordshire; and its capital was London.

The three Angle or Engle kingdoms were *Northumbria*, or Northumberland (the land north of the Humber); *East Anglia*, or East Engle; and *Mercia*, or Myrcna (Marchmen, or people on the march or frontier). Northumbria was founded by Ida in A. D. 547, and embraced the present counties of Yorkshire, Durham and Northumberland, along with the south-eastern part of Scotland, comprising the present counties of Roxburghshire, Selkirkshire, Berwickshire, East Lothian or Haddingtonshire, Mid Lothian or Edinburghshire, and West Lothian or Linlithgowshire; and its capital was York. Northumbria was frequently divided into the two kingdoms of Bernicia and Deira—the former north of the Tyne, and the latter south of that river.

East Anglia was founded by Uffa in A. D. 575, and embraced the present counties of Norfolk (Northfolk), Suffolk (Southfolk) and Cambridgeshire; and its capital was Dunwich, on the coast of Norfolk. Mercia was founded by Cridda in A. D. 582, and comprised the present midland counties of Chester or Cheshire, Derbyshire, Nottinghamshire, Lincolnshire, Leicestershire, Rutland, Northamptonshire, Huntingdonshire, the western half of Hertfordshire, Bucks or Buckinghamshire, Oxfordshire, all of Gloucestershire east of the Severn, Warwickshire, Worcestershire, Herefordshire, Shropshire or Salop, and Staffordshire; and its capital was Tamworth, in Staffordshire.

The present counties of Lancaster or Lancashire, Westmoreland and Cumberland, along with South-western Scotland, embracing the present counties of Dumfriesshire, Kirkcudbrightshire, Wigtonshire, Ayrshire, Renfrewshire, Lanarkshire and Peeblesshire, formed the Celtic or Scottish kingdom of Strathclyde. The present county of Cornwall, all of Devonshire except that portion east of the river Ex, all of Gloucestershire west of the Severn, and all of Monmouthshire, along with the whole of Wales, was occupied by the Britons. The celebrated King Arthur's kingdom was chiefly in

3—4.-U. H.

Somersetshire, where was his capital, Camelot, or Cadbury.

While Britain was thus yielding to the Anglo-Saxon conquest, Ireland remained the peaceful abode of piety and learning. Scholars fled from the tumults of Britain and continental Europe in quest of a quiet retreat at Armagh or Durrow, to add to the fame of the Irish universities at those two places, then celebrated throughout Western Europe. Irish missionaries preached the Gospel in the British Isles, in Italy, Switzerland and Eastern France. St. Columba, an Irish refugee, founded the monastery of Iona; and Aidan, one of its monks, founded the yet more celebrated bishopric and seminary at Lindisfarne, which sent missionaries into all the heathen kingdoms. Cuthbert, the Apostle of the Lowlands, from his mission-station at Melrose, traveled over bogs and moors and rough mountain sides, preaching the religion of Christ to the pagan peasants of Scotland and Northumberland.

The Britons had become Christians long before the Anglo-Saxon invasion. The Anglo-Saxons were pagans and worshipers of Odin, or Woden, and Thor, and so continued for a century after their conquest of Britain. Roman law, the Latin and Celtic languages, and Christianity disappeared in the path of the Germanic conquerors; and the pagan religion and customs of the Teutonic tribes, along with their language, prevailed instead.

Like other barbarous nations, the Anglo-Saxons made the future existence a realization of their highest ideal of the present life; and, like the other Germanic tribes, they filled Valhalla, their heaven, with scenes of war, where happy Saxons would live forever, passing the days in the slaughter of their enemies, and the nights in sitting with Odin drinking beer from the skulls of their slaughtered foes; the cowards who died a natural death away from the battlefield being excluded from this paradise.

From the chief of the Germanic deities the names of the seven days of the week have been derived. The idol which represented the sun was the chief object of Anglo-Saxon adoration, and is described like the bust of a man with outstretched arms having a burning wheel before his breast. The first day of the week was especially dedicated to his worship, and was called *Sun's daeg;* whence our word *Sunday.* The idol of the moon was designed to represent a woman, attired in a short coat and a hood with two long ears, and the moon which she held in her hand designated the quality. The idol of the moon was worshiped on the second day of the week, and was called *Moon's daeg;* whence our word *Monday.*

Tuisca was at first deified as the father and ruler of the Teutonic race, but in the progress of time he was worshiped as the son of the earth; and he is represented standing on a pedestal as an old venerable sage, clothed with the skin of an animal, holding a scepter in his right hand. As this god was particularly worshiped on the third day of the week, that day was called *Tuisca's daeg;* whence our word *Tuesday.*

Odin, or Woden, the war-god, was the supreme deity of all the Germanic or Teutonic nations. He was a very ancient hero, supposed to have emigrated from the East in an unknown age and from an unknown land. His exploits constituted the leading portion of the mythological creed of the Scandinavian nations, and his achievements were magnified beyond all credibility. Woden was represented in a bold and martial attitude, clad in armor, with a broad sword uplifted in his right hand. As he was especially worshiped on the fourth day of the week, that day was called *Woden's daeg;* whence our word *Wednesday.*

Thor, the god of storms and thunder, was the eldest and the bravest of the sons of Odin, or Woden, and his wife, Freya, or Frigga; and was, next to his parents, regarded as the greatest of the Germanic or Teutonic deities. Thor is represented as sitting on a throne, with a golden crown upon his head, adorned with a circle in front, wherein were set twelve bright burnished gold stars, and with a regal scepter in his right hand. As he was particularly worshiped on the fifth day of the week, that day was named *Thor's daeg;* whence our word *Thursday.*

Freya, or Frigga, the wife of Odin, or Woden, was, next to that supreme god, the most highly revered divinity among the Germanic nations; and in the most ancient times she was the same as the goddess Hertha, or Earth. Frigga is represented with a drawn sword in her right hand and a bow in her left. As the sixth day of the week was especially devoted to her adoration, that day was designated as *Frigga's daeg;* whence our word *Friday.*

The god Seater was represented by an idol standing on a pedestal, whereon was placed a perch, on the sharp prickled back of which he stood, his head being uncovered and his visage lean. He held up a wheel in his left hand and a pail of water in his right, and in this water were fruits and flowers. He was dressed in a long coat, girded with linen. As the seventh and last day of the week was especially consecrated to the worship of Seater, that day was called *Seater's daeg;* whence our word *Saturday.*

The Anglo-Saxon names of the months were singularly descriptive of the seasons. The first month—which we call January, from the Roman god Janus—was called by the Saxons *Aefter Yula,* or after Christmas. The second month—which we call February—was named by the Saxons *Sol Monath,* because of the returning of the sun. The third month—which we call March, after Mars, the Roman God of war—was designated by the Saxons as *Rethe Monath,* meaning *rugged month.* The fourth month—which we call April—was named by the Saxons *Easter Monath,* from a Saxon goddess whose name we preserve to this day. The fifth month—which is known to us as May—was styled by the Saxons *Trimilchi,* because the cows were then milked thrice a day. The sixth month—which we call June, after the Roman goddess Juno—was known to the Saxons as *Sere Monath,* meaning *dry month.* The seventh month—named by us July, after Julius Cæsar—was designated by the Saxons as *Mæd Monath,* because the meads were then in bloom. The eighth month—called by us August, after Augustus Cæsar—was known to the Saxons as *Woed Monath*, because of the luxuriance of weeds. The ninth month—which we call September, from the Latin word *septem*, meaning *seven*, because it was the seventh month of the Roman year—was known to the Saxons as *Hæfest Monath*, meaning *harvest month*. The tenth month—which we call October, from the Latin word *octo*, meaning *eight*, because it was the eighth month of the Roman year—was known to the Saxons by the name *Winter Fyllish*, because winter approached with the full moon of that month. The eleventh month—which we call November, from the Latin word *novem*, meaning *nine*, because it was the ninth month of the Roman year —was known to the Saxons under the appellation of *Blot Monath*, because of the blood of cattle slain that month and stored for winter provision. The twelfth and last month of the year—which we call December, from the Latin word *decem*, meaning *ten*, because it was the tenth month of the Roman year—was known to the Saxons under the designation of *Midwinter Monath*, whose meaning it is unnecessary to explain.

Each of the Anglo-Saxon tribes had a royal family regarded as being descended from Odin, or Woden, their chief god; and from this family the king was chosen by the votes of all the freemen, in accordance with the German customs described by Tacitus. The custom of strict hereditary succession was entirely unknown to these barbarous Teutonic tribes. No king's son could claim his father's crown until the votes of the nation had duly conferred it upon him; and if he was young, or his valor was not yet proven, his father's brother was generally chosen instead. The seven or eight Germanic kingdoms in Britain sometimes acknowledged a common head known as the *Bretwalda* (Wielder of Britain), whose authority in this island somewhat resembled that of the Emperor on the European continent over the various nations owning allegiance to Rome. Mercia and Northumbria for a while struggled for the supremacy, but Wessex gained it at last, as we shall presently see.

Ethelbert, the fourth King of Kent, was the third of the Bretwaldas, and the first Christian king in Anglo-Saxon England. He married the Frankish princess Bertha, daughter of Charibert; and his relations with her countrymen introduced many civilizing influences into his kingdom. His subjects were the first of the English people to enjoy the benefits of a written code of laws; and his long reign of fifty years was productive of honor to himself and blessings to his kingdom, but its most important event was the introduction of Christianity.

The "Venerable Bede," the celebrated Anglo-Saxon church historian, who is our chief authority for early English history, informs us as to what led to the introduction of Christianity into Anglo-Saxon Britain. Several years previous a good Christian priest visited the slave market of Rome, where he saw three beautiful children exposed for sale. Their faces attracted his attention, and he inquired where they were from. Being told that they were Angles, he quickly replied: "Not *Angles*, but *angels*. They ought to be made fellow-heirs of the angels in heaven. But of what tribe of Angles are they?" "Of Deira," was the reply. Thereupon the good priest exclaimed: "*Deira*! then they are called from the wrath of God to his mercy! And what is the name of their king?" "Ælla," was the response. Then the priest exclaimed: "Ælla. *Ælla!* then *Alleluia* shall be sung in his land."

Besides being pleased with his puns, this good man was excited by true missionary zeal, and he obtained the Pope's sanction to start instantly to England to preach the Gospel of Christ in that distant heathen land; but his flock in Rome would not let him go, and on the death of Pope Pelagius II. he was elected Pope with the title of Gregory I. and is known in history as Gregory the Great. Still remembering his desire for the conversion of the heathen Anglo-Saxons in Britain, the new Pope commissioned the Benedictine monk, St. Augustine, or Austin, and forty other monks of Rome to go to that remote island and preach the religion of the crucified Jesus to its benighted pagan population (A. D. 596).

When these missionaries reached France, whose people had already been converted to Christianity, they heard such dreadful accounts of the savage manners of the Anglo-Saxons that they were afraid to proceed to England, and they sent Augustine back to Rome to ask the Pope's sanction to relinquish the enterprise. But Gregory the Great exhorted them to persevere, and advised them to take some of the Franks with them as interpreters, because the language of the Franks and that of the Anglo-Saxons were almost identical. Augustine and his band of monks proceeded on their mission and found the danger less than they had anticipated.

Bertha, the wife of King Ethelbert of Kent, was already a Christian; and through her influence Ethelbert received the good missionaries with kindness and gave them a cordial hearing. After hearing what they had to say, he told them that he could not, without due deliberation, abandon the religion of his ancestors; but, as they had come so far on a friendly errand, they might remain in peace and exert themselves to their best to convert his subjects. The monks at once entered upon their missionary task, and their labors were crowned with perfect success, as King Ethelbert and many of his subjects were soon converted.

Augustine baptized the king and ten thousand of his subjects on Christmas day, A. D. 597; and was soon afterwards made the first Archbishop of Canterbury, being at the same time endowed by Pope Gregory the Great with authority over all the churches yet to be founded in Anglo-Saxon Britain. Augustine introduced the Roman liturgy in Latin, which was then an unknown tongue in England, though understood in other parts of Europe. Canterbury Cathedral, founded by Augustine, is still the mother church or metropolitan of all England.

The new religion was soon embraced by the people of Essex, and a Bishop of London was consecrated, and churches were erected in that city, respectively to St. Peter and St. Paul, on the sites still occupied by those great historic edifices, Westminster Abbey and St. Paul's Cathedral.

A daughter of Ethelbert and Bertha became the bride of King Edwin of Deira, and had the honor of introducing the Christian religion into that remote northern Angle kingdom. Edwin was baptized at York, his capital; and on the site thus consecrated arose a church which was the humble predecessor of that grand and stately edifice, the famous cathedral now known as York Minster. Paulinus, who had accompanied the young queen of King Edwin of Deira in her journey from Kent, became the first Archbishop of York. Ever since that period the Archbishops of Canterbury and York have been at the head of the ecclesiastical establishment of England, the Archbishop of Canterbury being styled the *Primate.*

The Christians of Wales and Cornwall, being the conquered Britons, refused obedience either to a Pope at Rome or to a Primate at Canterbury; but their independent spirit was punished by a massacre of two hundred of their priests. Churches and monasteries were in a short time scattered throughout England, and the fierce superstitions of Germanic paganism yielded to the purer and gentler faith of the great Nazarene.

Christianity made rapid progress in England during the seventh century. For a while Kent relapsed into paganism in consequence of the apostasy of Eadbald, who married his mother-in-law—a union forbidden by the Church. By the exertions of Laurentius, Augustine's successor, Eadbald was brought back into the Church, and all his subjects with him; he having first renounced his marriage with his mother-in-law.

At first Northumbria held the ascendency among the Anglo-Saxon kingdoms. Then Mercia obtained the supremacy under King

THE ANGLES AND SAXONS IN BRITAIN.

Offa, who reigned from A. D. 757 to A. D. 796. He was the friend and ally of Charlemagne, at whose request he sent Alcuin, a Saxon clergyman renowned for his learning, to the court of the great Frankish monarch, ing from the Wye to the Dee, to protect the Saxon colonists against the attacks of the Britons. But Offa was cruel and treacherous, and his glory was clouded by crime. He caused the East Anglian king who was

YORK MINSTER.

whose most trusted friend and counselor he was for many years, and whom he instructed in the sciences.

Offa achieved great victories over the Britons in Wales, and erected a vast mound of earth still known as Offa's Dyke, extending a guest at his court to be murdered, and seized his kingdom by violence (A. D. 792). Like many other monarchs of that time, Offa sought to relieve his conscience by liberal gifts to the Church. He bestowed one-tenth of all his goods on the clergy, and followed the example of King Ina in Wessex by imposing a tax of a penny on every household in his dominions, in order to support an English college at Rome. He did not find it so easy a matter to recall what he had granted, and the Pope's claim for "Peter's Pence" continued to be enforced almost a thousand years after the first imposition of the tax.

In the wars between the Germanic kingdoms in England resulting from their constant feuds and jealousies, all the Anglo-Saxon royal families became extinct, except one. The sole remaining dynasty was that of Cerdic, the founder of Wessex; and it was at this time represented only by Brihtric, the reigning sovereign of that kingdom, and Egbert, his young cousin, whom many regarded as having a better claim to the crown. Perceiving that he had incurred the enmity of Brihtric, Egbert retired to continental Europe, passing his years of exile and probation in studying the arts of war and government with the greatest warrior and statesman then living—the great King of the Franks, who afterwards came to be known as Charlemagne, or Charles the Great, the first sovereign of the newly-restored Western Empire.

Brihtric's wife was Eadburga, daughter of Offa, a woman notorious even in that dark age for her crimes and misfortunes. She had determined to poison a nobleman who was her husband's friend, but the poison was accidentally taken by the king. Eadburga fled in a passion of shame and remorse, and Egbert was called to the throne of Wessex by the people in A. D. 802. Egbert now put in practice the lessons which he had learned in Charlemagne's camp and court, devoting himself to the vigorous government of his dominions and the conquest of the Britons of Cornwall and Wales.

After Egbert had thus spent twenty-five years, the King of Mercia invaded Wessex, thus bringing on a series of wars which made Egbert over-lord of almost the entire island. Kent, Sussex and East Anglia, which had been unwilling tributaries of Mercia, gladly transferred their allegiance to the wisest and best of Englishmen of that day; and their example was followed by Northumbria, while Mercia was conquered by Egbert. Thus the Heptarchy ended in a united English monarchy within four centuries of the first Germanic invasion of Britain. Thus was founded the Kingdom of *Angle-land*, or *England*, in the year A. D. 827; and Egbert was thus the first king who reigned over the entire country. Nevertheless, Egbert's immediate dominion still ended at the Thames, and he still styled himself, as before, "King of the West Saxons." It was his great-grandson, Edward the Elder, who first assumed the title of "King of the English."

In the meantime the Anglo-Saxons had lost much of their original ferocity, and their customs and institutions had become more civilized. Our knowledge of them is rather obscure; as none except the clergy made any pretensions to learning, and few of these were able to do more than read their prayer-books and write their names, while there were many even among the high clergy who were unable to do this. There are deeds yet in existence, made by lord-bishops, which are signed by some other persons in their names, because the lord-bishops could not write their own names.

The monasteries were the only schools during the period of the Heptarchy. They were not as gloomy as the Benedictine institutions which St. Dunstan afterwards introduced into the country; but were more like great families assembled under a single roof, in a collection of adjoining buildings, for study and devotion. Bede—usually called the "Venerable Bede"—the first great English scholar and the father of English learning, passed his long life in instructing the monks of Jarrow and the boys sent there by their parents to be taught. He put into familiar Latin text-books all that was then known in Western Europe, of science, literature and the rules of music, for the benefit of his pupils. His most famous work is his *Ecclesiastical History of the English Nation*, written in Latin. He died just when he had completed a translation of the Gospel of St. John into his own Anglo-Saxon tongue.

The abbess Hilda, a woman of royal birth, had charge of a seminary of bishops and priests, and also a convent of nuns, on the high cliffs of Whitby, commanding a view of the ocean. She was so celebrated for her wisdom that kings sought her advice in matters of state. Her monastery is also famous as the home of Cædmon, the distinguished Anglo-Saxon poet, who was simply a poor cowherd. The Anglo-Saxons had a great taste for music and the rough verses which recounted the heroic deeds of their warlike ancestors on sea and land. After their evening meals it was their custom to pass the harp from hand to hand, so that each might have his turn in singing for the entertainment of the rest. Cædmon the cowherd was unable to sing, and was therefore in the habit of slipping away when the harp was passed to him.

One night when Cædmon had taken refuge in the stables, he is said to have seen a heavenly vision which said: "Sing, Cædmon, come sing to me." Cædmon replied: "I can not sing." To this the vision responded: "However that may be, you shall sing to me." Thereupon Cædmon murmured: "What shall I sing?" Then the vision answered: "The beginning of created things." The extravagant story is told that a noble song of the Creation then flowed from Cædmon's lips. He is said to have awoke and to have found that new power had been given him. The abbess Hilda and brethren then bade the poet relinquish his humble toil and enter their order; and he is said to have passed the remainder of his life in rehearsing in Saxon verse the entire sacred history as recorded in the Bible.

The zeal of the Irish missionaries had the effect of making the North of England superior to the other portions of the island in means of education. The first English library was kept in the cathedral of York, and there was the celebrated school under the charge of Archbishop Egbert, and afterwards of Alcuin, the friend and tutor of Charlemagne, the illustrious Frankish monarch.

Our sources concerning the early history of the Anglo-Saxons and their social condition are the writings of Gildas, the earliest Saxon historian, and the great ecclesiastical historian, the Venerable Bede. Gildas lived in the sixth century, and was so much admired by his countrymen as to be called by them "Gildas the Wise." The Venerable Bede lived in the seventh century, and his fame spread all over Europe, although he was but a simple monk. The Pope courted his society, and sought his counsel in the administration of the affairs of the Church.

From these sources we are able to learn that the Anglo-Saxons were governed by kings, whose powers were very much restricted and controlled by a great council called *Witenagemote*, or "Assembly of the Wise Men," consisting of the great nobles, the Ealdormen or Earls, all freemen who possessed a certain portion of land, and, after the introduction of Christianity, the bishops and abbots. All of these were, of right, members of this great national assembly. This council assembled regularly at Christmas, Easter and Whitsuntide, and on special occasions when summoned. At the death of the king, this great national council was convened to elect his successor, who was taken from the royal family, though not always the next in line. Thus the crown was elective, but the choice was generally restricted to one family.

Before the Germanic tribes had settled into highly organized nations, every freeman was entitled to appear in arms at the council of his chief; and the affairs of the entire people were transacted in the March or May fields, under the open canopy of heaven. In continental Europe these martial assemblies were superseded by diets, in which the clergy participated; while in England these same kind of assemblies were succeeded by the assemblies of the *Witenagemote*, or "Meeting of the Wise." Although, in strict law, every freeman had the right to be present at the Witenagemote, the difficulties of travel and communication rendered the presence of all freemen impossible; and the assembly came to consist principally of bishops, abbots and ealdormen.

Under the Romans, Britain was divided into colonies and governments; but the Anglo-Saxons parcelled the country out into *counties*, or *shires*. The government of a shire was entrusted to an *Earl*, or *Ealdorman*, whence the present terms *earl* and *alderman*. The earl usually exercised this government by his deputy, who was called the *shire-reeve*, or *sheriff*, meaning *guardian of a shire*.

The Anglo-Saxons consisted of four ranks or orders—*Earls, Thanes, Churls* and *Serfs*. Originally all high offices were reserved for men of noble blood. The earls acted as judges and rulers in their respective shires. The ealdormen, or chief rulers in cities and villages, were chosen from among the earls; and every churl was required to choose some earl as his lord and protector. The "lordless man" was an outlaw.

The churls embraced the great mass of the freemen, and were chiefly employed in husbandry, whence a husbandman and a churl came to be synonymous terms. A churl could raise himself in rank in various ways. Agricultural success might furnish him with the means of obtaining the requisite amount of land, with buildings essential to the dignity. If a churl acquired sufficient learning and became a priest, he was considered a thane. If he was successful in trade or in war, he was elevated to the same rank. The only professions of a freeman were agriculture, commerce, arms or the church. In this way the rank of thanes gradually grew up between the earls and the churls, and these thanes were ennobled by services rendered to the king or the state.

The serfs, or slaves, were the lowest class among the Anglo-Saxons, and composed about two-thirds of the inhabitants. An Englishman could only become a serf by crime or voluntary sale. Parents sometimes sold their own children, and any person over thirteen years of age might sell himself. The Church constantly antagonized the institution of serfdom, and several good bishops set the example of emancipating the serfs found by them on the lands attached to their sees. The clergy made great exertions to improve the condition of the serfs and to secure the rights which their influence had procured for them. In spite of all these efforts, the greater portion of the common people remained in abject slavery during the whole Anglo-Saxon period of English history.

There were two kinds of serfs among the Anglo-Saxons—*household serfs*, who lived in the family and discharged the ordinary duties of domestic servants; and *rustic serfs*, or *villains*, who were attached to particular estates and transferred with the soil. The villains were so called because they dwelt in the villages belonging to their masters, and performed all the servile labors required upon the land.

We now come to the officers of the king's household. The first in dignity was the Mayor of the Palace, who was always a prince of the royal family. The second in rank was the priest, who sat at the royal table to bless the meat and to chaunt the Lord's Prayer. The third was the steward, who had a variety of perquisites, and was entitled to a large portion of every barrel of good ale and every cask of mead. The fourth was the judge, who was distinguished for his learning and by his long beard. The last, and perhaps the most useful, of these officials of the royal household was the king's feet-bearer, who was a young gentleman that was assigned the duty of sitting on the floor and holding the king's feet in his bosom while the king sat at table, to keep the feet warm and comfortable.

The criminal laws of the Anglo-Saxons were very mild, and every crime might be compensated for in money. The value of a man's life or limb depended upon his rank or office, and a price was fixed accordingly, which was to be paid by the person who. should deprive him of either. The Anglo-Saxons had singular modes of proving crimes. They did not do this by the evidence of witnesses, but referred the decision to the "Judgment of God," as they called it. One of the methods of doing this was by the *ordeal*, and was practiced by boiling water or a red-hot iron.

The water or iron was consecrated by many prayers and fastings, and the accused individual then took up with his naked hand a stone sunk in the boiling water, or carried the heated iron to a certain distance. After this the hand was wrapped up, and the covering was sealed for three days. If no marks of burning or scalding appeared at the end of these three days the accused person was declared innocent, but if there were marks he was pronounced guilty. Another mode of performing the ordeal of hot iron was by making the person who was to be tried walk blindfolded over nine hot plowshares placed at certain distances. If he was able to do this without being burned he was acquitted; if not, he was found guilty.

The whole fiery ordeal was conducted under the direction of the priests, and the ceremony was performed in a church. No person except the priest and the accused were admitted until the iron was heated, when twelve friends of the accused and twelve of the accuser were allowed to enter, and were ranged along the wall on each side of the church, at a respectful distance. After the iron was taken from the fire several prayers were said, and many forms were gone through, all of which took considerable time if the priest was indulgent. It was always remarked that no good friend of the Church ever suffered the slightest injury from the ordeal; but if any one who had wronged the Church appealed to this method of trial he was sure to burn his fingers or his feet, and so lose his cause.

THE ANGLO-SAXON HEPTARCHY.

KINGDOMS.	FOUNDED BY	BEGAN.	ENDED.	CAPITALS.
Kent, or Cantia.	Hengist.	A. D. 457	A. D. 823	Canterbury.
Sussex, or South Saxony.	Ella.	490	600	Chichester.
Wessex, or West Saxony.	Cerdic.	519	1066	Winchester.
Essex, or East Saxony.	Ercewin.	527	746	London.
Northumberland.	Ida.	547	792	York.
East Anglia.	Uffa.	575	783	Dunwich.
Mercia.	Cridda.	582	847	Tamworth.

SOVEREIGNS OF THE BARBARIAN MONARCHIES.

VANDAL KINGS IN SPAIN.			
A. D. 409	GUNDERIC.	A. D. 425	GENSERIC (passed into Africa in 529).

SUEVIC KINGS IN SPAIN.			
A. D. 409	HERMANRIC.	A. D. 550	CARRIARIC.
438	RECHILA.	559	THEODOMIR.
448	RECHIARIUS.	569	MIR.
457	MALDRAS.	582	EBORIC.
460	FRUMARIUS.	583	ANDECA.
464	REMISMUND.	584	Visigothic conquest of Sueves.

VANDAL KINGS OF AFRICA.			
A. D. 429	GENSERIC.	A. D. 523	HILDERIC.
477	HUNNERIC.	531	GELIMER.
484	GUNDAMUND.	533	Byzantine conquest of Africa.
496	THRASIMUND.		

MEDIÆVAL HISTORY.—DARK AGES.

VISIGOTHIC KINGS OF SPAIN.

A. D.		A. D.	
411	ADOLPHUS, or ATAULFUS.	601	LEUVA II.
415	SIGERIC.	603	WITERIC.
415	WALLIA.	610	GUNDEMAR.
420	THEODORIC I.	612	SISEBERT.
451	THORSIMUND.	621	RECARED II.
452	THEODORIC II.	621	SWINTILA.
466	EURIC.	631	SISENAND.
483	ALARIC II.	636	CHINTILA.
506	GENSALEIC.	640	TULGA.
511	THEODORIC III.	642	CHINDASWIND.
522	AMALARIC.	649	RECESWIND.
531	THEUDIS.	672	WAMBA.
548	THEUDISDEL.	680	ERVIGIUS.
549	AGILAN.	687	EGICA.
554	ATHANAGILD.	701	WITIZA.
567	LEUVA I.	709	RODERIC, or RODRIGO.
570	LEOVIGILD.	712	Saracen conquest of Spain.
587	RECARED I.		

OSTROGOTHIC KINGS OF ITALY.

A. D.		A. D.	
493	THEODORIC.	540	THEODEBALD.
526	ATHALARIC.	541	TOTILA.
534	THEODATUS.	552	TEIAS.
536	VITIGES.	553	Byzantine conquest of Italy.

LOMBARD KINGS OF NORTHERN ITALY.

A. D.		A. D.	
571	ALBOIN.	686	CUNIBERT.
573	CLEPH, or CLEPHO.	700	LUITBERT.
574	AUTHARIS.	701	RAGIMBERT.
590	AGILULF.	701	ARIBERT II.
615	ADALUALD.	711	ANSPRAND.
625	ARIUALD.	711	LUIDPRAND.
636	ROTHARIS.	743	HILDEBRAND.
652	RODUALD.	744	RACHIS.
653	ARIBERT I.	751	ASTOLPH.
661	BERTHARIT and GODEBERT.	756	DESIDERIUS.
662	GRIMVALD.	774	Charlemagne's conquest of the Lombards.
672	BERTHARIT.		

MEROVINGIAN KINGS OF THE FRANKS.

		A. D.	
Dates uncertain.	PHARAMOND.	613	CLOTAIRE II. sole king.
	CLODION.	628	DAGOBERT I., the Great.
	MEROVEUS.	638	CLOVIS II. } Jointly.
	CHILDERIC I.		SIGEBERT II.
A. D. 481	CLOVIS.	656	CLOTAIRE III.
511	THEODORIC, or THIERRY I. } Kingdom divided.	670	CHILDERIC II.
	CHILDEBERT I.	670	THIERRY III.
	CLODOMIR.	674	DAGOBERT II.
	CLOTAIRE I.	691	CLOVIS III. } Pepin d' Heristal, Mayor of the Palace.
534	THEODEBERT I.	695	CHILDEBERT III.,
548	THEODEBALD.		the Just.
558	CLOTAIRE I. sole king.	711	DAGOBERT III. } Charles Martel, Mayor of the Palace.
561	CHARIBERT. } Kingdom divided.	715	CHILPERIC II. (deposed),
	GONTRAM.	717	CLOTAIRE IV.
	CHILPERIC I.	720	CHILPERIC II. restored
	SIGEBERT I.	720	THIERRY IV.
575	CHILDEBERT II.	737	An interregnum.
584	CLOTAIRE II.	742	CHILPERIC III., the Stupid (deposed in 751 by Pepin the Little, son of Charles Martel).
596	THIERRY II. } Jointly.		
	THEODEBERT II.		

SECTION VIII.—THE EASTERN ROMAN EMPIRE.

WHILE the Western Roman Empire was rapidly falling to pieces, the Eastern Roman, or Greek Empire, with its capital at Constantinople, had become firmly and securely established as an independent and separate monarchy under ARCADIUS, the elder son of Theodosius the Great, and his successors. The Eastern Emperor assumed and obstinately retained the vain and finally fictitious title of "Emperor of the Romans," along with the hereditary appellations of Cæsar and Augustus. The form of government was an absolute monarchy; the name of the Roman Republic, which had for so long a time preserved a faint tradition of freedom, being restricted to the Latin provinces; while the Eastern Emperors measured their greatness by the servile obedience of their subjects.

The Eastern Empire extended from the Adriatic on the west to the Tigris on the east, and the entire interval of twenty-five days' navigation separating the extreme cold of Scythia from the torrid heat of Ethiopia was included inside the limits of the Eastern Emperor's dominions. The populous provinces of the Empire were seats of art and learning, of luxury and wealth; and the inhabitants of those provinces, who had adopted the Greek language and manners, considered themselves the most civilized and enlightened portion of mankind. Constantinople became the permanent capital of the Eastern Empire, and rapidly grew in wealth and greatness, and continued to defy the hostile efforts of the barbarians for ages.

The reign of Arcadius was chiefly marked by the struggles of unworthy favorites to gain power; and the renowned St. Chrysostom, "the golden-mouthed orator" and one of the Fathers of the Greek Church, flourished, and was sent into exile and death in a foreign land for having ventured to rebuke the profligacy of the Empress Eudoxia.

Arcadius was succeeded by his son THE-ODOSIUS II., who was only seven years old; and during this sovereign's minority the Empire was ably governed by his sister Pulcheria, as the Emperor was but a mere cipher in the government. The last years of the reign of Theodosius II. were disturbed by the invasion of the Eastern Empire by the Huns under Attila, who made their appearance in the Empire in A. D. 441, and ravaged the whole peninsula between the Danube and the Adriatic for nine years, destroying seventy cities of the Empire and so devastating the open country that Attila was justified in boasting that the grass never grew where his horse trod. Theodosius II. at length bribed the Huns to withdraw from the Empire, by paying them six thousand pounds of gold, and by promising them an annual tribute of twenty-one hundred pounds of the same precious metal (A. D. 450).

Theodosius II. was drowned near Constantinople in A. D. 450; whereupon his sister, the regent PULCHERIA, was proclaimed Empress. As a measure of prudence, she contracted a nominal marriage with Marcian, a Senator about sixty years of age, who was invested with the imperial dignity. After the death of Pulcheria, in A. D. 453, MARCIAN remained on the throne until his own death in A. 457.

The next Emperor was LEO I., the Thracian, a military Tribune, whom the Patrician Aspar, the most powerful of the Eastern Emperor's subjects, elevated to the imperial throne. Leo I. interfered in the concerns of the Western Empire in A. D. 467, appointing Anthemius Emperor of the West. Leo I. again intervened in the affairs of the Western Empire in A. D. 474, in order to secure the Western throne for Julius Nepos. Leo I. and his son LEO II. died A. D. 474, and was succeeded by his son-in-law, ZENO, the Isaurian, who reigned seventeen years. Upon ZENO's death, in A. D. 491, ANASTASIUS I., an aged domestic of the palace, became Emperor of the East, married Zeno's widow, and also reigned seventeen years.

Upon the death of Anastasius, in A. D. 518, JUSTIN I., originally a Dacian peasant, who had risen to eminence by his virtues and abilities, was raised to the imperial throne by the unanimous approval of the army. He had traveled on foot to Constantinople during the reign of Leo I., enlisted in the imperial guards, and so distinguished himself by his strength and valor during the succeeding reigns that he was gradually promoted to the command of the household guards. Upon the death of Anastasius, the eunuch Amantius, desirous of securing the imperial throne for one of his creatures, furnished Justin with a vast sum of money to bribe the guards; but Justin appropriated this money to the purchase of votes for himself, and thus was raised to the imperial dignity (A. D. 518). Justin I. was wholly ignorant himself, and was therefore fully sensible of the value of education. He was sixty-eight years of age when he ascended the throne, and reigned nine years. During the last year of his reign he associated his nephew Justinian with him in the Empire, having adopted him as his heir, and having had him instructed in all the learning of the times.

Upon the death of Justin I., in A. D. 527, JUSTINIAN became sole Emperor, being then forty-five years of age; and he reigned almost thirty-nine years (A. D. 527-565). Just before his accession Justinian had fixed a permanent stigma upon his name by marrying Theodora, a woman of low birth and infamous character, whose vices had disgusted even so licentious a capital as Constantinople. This infamous woman soon acquired an unlimited influence over her husband, and maintained that influence unimpaired until her death in the twenty-fourth year of her marriage and the twenty-second of her husband's reign.

The first five years of Justinian's reign were passed in an unprofitable and expensive war with the New Persian Empire of the Sassanidæ. At the end of that time a treaty was concluded with Persia, and was styled "the Endless Peace," but we shall see further on that it was merely a short suspension of hostilities.

Among the most singular and disgraceful follies of the Eastern Empire were the factions of the circus, which resulted from the colors worn by the charioteers who competed for the prize of swiftness. The *White* and the *Red* were the most ancient of these factions, but the *Blue* and the *Green* were the most remarkable for their inveterate hostility. All these factions obtained a legal existence, and the Byzantines willingly jeopardized life and fortune in behalf of their favorite color.

The Emperor Justinian was a partisan of the Blues; and his favor toward them provoked the hostility of the Greens, and gave rise to a series of disturbances at the close of the war with Persia just alluded to, known as the "Nika riots," which almost laid Constantinople in ashes (A. D. 532). The first outbreak occurred in the circus. Justinian ordered the rioters to be secured, whereupon both factions instantly turned against the Emperor. The soldiers were called out, but they were unable to contend against the citizens in the narrow streets. The barbarian mercenaries were assailed from the tops of the houses; but they flung fire-brands in revenge, thus kindling a terrible conflagration, which destroyed many public and private edifices, including the great cathedral of St. Sophia. Thirty thousand persons perished in the tumult, and for five days Constantinople was in the hands of a lawless mob. Hypatius, a nephew of Anastasius, was proclaimed Emperor; and Justinian was about to retire from Constantinople, but was persuaded to remain and suppress the riot, by the Empress Theodora, whose firmness, along with the skillful disposition of Belisarius, who commanded the imperial troops, alone quelled the outbreak and saved the throne to Justinian. Justinian now contrived to revive the former hostility between the Blues and the Greens, and the Blues declared for the Emperor, while a strong body of veterans marched to the Hippodrome, or race-course, which was closed for several years, and the games were suppressed, in punishment for the disturbances.

After securing his power at home, the Emperor Justinian undertook to extend his dominion over the countries formerly included within the Roman Empire. His first expedition was against the Vandal kingdom in Northern Africa. The Vandal throne had been usurped by Gelimer, whose success was mainly attributable to the support which he received from the Arian clergy. Gelimer's usurpation induced Justinian to undertake the conquest of the Vandals, who had been weakened by a century of African life. In this war Justinian appeared both as the friend of an allied sovereign and as the protector of the orthodox Catholic faith.

Justinian assigned the command of the imperial forces to Belisarius, the greatest general of his time and one of the ablest of any age. This illustrious commander had risen by the force of his own genius from the humble condition of a peasant. A large fleet was assembled in the harbor of Constantinople to transport the imperial army to Africa (A. D. 533). After being blessed by the Patriarch of Constantinople, the imperial armament set sail; and, after a prosperous voyage, Belisarius effected a landing on the African coast without opposition.

After landing in Africa, Belisarius at once marched upon Carthage, defeated the Vandals on the march, and easily obtained possession of the city. Although Gelimer, the Vandal king, had thus lost his capital, he made one more effort to save his kingdom, but failed, his army being irretrievably ruined, while he himself was closely besieged in the castle in which he sought refuge. After suffering the most dreadful extremities of famine, the unfortunate Vandal king was obliged to surrender unconditionally, and was carried a captive to Constantinople, where he was led at the head of a train of captives in the triumphal procession of Belisarius. The fallen monarch exhibited no sorrow for his overthrow, but found consolation in Solomon's reflection on the instability of human greatness, frequently repeating: "Vanity of vanities, saith the preacher, all is vanity." Thus Northern Africa, with Sardinia, Corsica and the smaller islands of the Western Mediterranean, was recovered to the Roman dominion; and the whole conquered kingdom was erected into the *Exarchate of Africa*.

The conquest of the Vandal kingdom in Africa by the imperial forces was followed by the subjugation of the Ostrogothic kingdom in Italy. Justinian found a pretext for attacking the Ostrogothic dominion in the murder of Amalasontha, the wife of the Ostrogothic king, Theódatus, by her revengeful husband. An imperial armament under Belisarius sailed from Constantinople to Sicily and easily conquered that important island (A. D. 535).

In great terror, Theódatus sought to avert the threatening danger by declaring himself a vassal of the Emperor Justinian; but when he was informed of the defeat of two imperial generals in Dalmatia by the Ostrogothic forces, he suddenly arose from the extreme of despair to the height of presumption, and renounced his allegiance to the Byzantine Emperor. Belisarius soon made his appearance to chastise the Ostrogothic king's perfidy, and transported his army across from Sicily to the mainland of Italy, effecting a landing at Rhegium (now Reggio). The Byzantine forces speedily subdued the greater portion of Southern Italy, including the important city of Naples; while Theódatus, secure within the walls of Rome, made no effort to protect his subjects in that part of the peninsula.

At length the Ostrogoths, disgusted with their sovereign's incapacity, removed him from the throne and chose Vitiges for their monarch instead. But Vitiges was obliged to begin his reign by abandoning Rome, and Belisarius at once took possession of that city without encountering any opposition (A. D. 537). During the following winter the Ostrogoths were assembled from all quarters to make a final effort to save their dominion in Italy. A formidable

Ostrogothic army, animated by a dauntless spirit, was soon collected, and Vitiges besieged Rome. Belisarius concentrated his troops in the "Eternal City," which he defended with great skill and bravery; but the inhabitants soon suffered the horrors of famine and became anxious for a capitulation. A conspiracy was organized under the sanction of Pope Sylverius to betray the city to the Ostrogoths, but this plot was disclosed by means of an intercepted letter. Thereupon Belisarius sent Pope Sylverius into banishment and directed the bishops to elect a new Pope; but, before a synod could be assembled for the purpose, the imperial general's wife, the infamous Antonína, sold the Holy See to Vigilius for a bribe of two hundred pounds of gold.

Soon afterward reinforcements arrived for the Byzantine army, and the Ostrogoths were obliged to raise the siege of Rome, after they had lost one-third of their army before the walls of the city. Belisarius pursued the retreating foe to the marshes of their own capital, Ravenna, which he was only prevented from capturing by the jealousy of the Emperor Justinian, who had assigned the eunuch Narses to the independent command of a large portion of the imperial army. The Ostrogoths profited by the animosity between the two Byzantine generals by rallying their strength; and ten thousand Burgundians, who had been sent to invade Italy by order of Theódebert, King of the Franks, had stormed and sacked Milan. Soon afterward Theódebert himself passed the Alps at the head of one hundred thousand men. The Franks stormed Genoa and ravaged Liguria, but their excesses brought pestilence into their camp and thousands of them perished, and Theódebert's increasing distresses caused him to come to terms with the Emperor Justinian. When Belisarius was relieved from this pressing danger he laid siege to Ravenna, which he forced to capitulate, thus overthrowing the Ostrogothic power in Italy (A. D. 539).

Belisarius returned in triumph to Constantinople, leading the captive Vitiges, the fallen Ostrogothic king, with him. Vitiges was treated with remarkable generosity by the Emperor Justinian, who allowed the captive king to pass the remainder of his days in affluence in Constantinople. The victorious Byzantine general was soon sent to take the field against the New Persians, the "Endless Peace" not having proved as lasting as had been anticipated. The greatest of the New Persian kings, Khosrou Nushirvan, broke the treaty in A. D. 540, invaded Syria, burned Antioch and devastated Asia Minor. Belisarius was sent against him, and in two campaigns (A. D. 541-542) forced him, without striking a blow, to retreat to his own dominions.

Belisarius was then sent back to Italy by the ungrateful Justinian, who was jealous of the glory and fame of his illustrious general; whereupon the New Persians were again successful and vanquished a Byzantine army of thirty thousand men. Repenting of his ingratitude, Justinian restored Belisarius to his command in the East; and by that illustrious general's judicious exertions Khosrou Nushirvan was compelled to retreat across the Euphrates, carrying with him, however, a vast amount of spoils.

The next enterprise of the Persian king was the conquest of the Caucasian districts inhabited by the Lazi, the Colchians and other semi-barbarous tribes, which the Byzantines endeavored to prevent, thus giving rise to the exhausting and wearisome Lazic war, which uselessly wasted the strength of both empires. In consequence of the war with Persia, Justinian concluded a treaty with the Abyssinians, whose king had conquered most of Arabia, expecting by his means to open a naval communication with China and India; but this design was frustrated by the Abyssinian king's reluctance to engage in a doubtful struggle with Persia.

The war between the Eastern Roman and New Persian Empires went on in a desultory manner until A. D. 561, when the advancing age of both Justinian and Khosrou Nushirvan inclined them to agree to a peaceful settlement. Justinian purchased this peace by agreeing to pay an annual tribute of thirty thousand pieces of gold. Thus, after a war of twenty-one years (A. D. 540–561), the frontiers of the two empires remained unchanged.

The provinces of Africa and Italy, which the valor of Belisarius had won for the Byzantine Empire, were almost lost to it by the incapacity and tyranny of his successors, whose weakness encouraged the Moors to rise in arms. Though these barbarians were finally subdued, the African province was reduced from a fertile and populous country into a wild and silent desert. The revolt of the Ostrogoths in Italy under their valiant king, Totila, in A. D. 541, was still more dangerous, as Totila in a very short time recovered most of Italy. After the Byzantine generals had been successively defeated, Justinian sent Belisarius to the scene of his former glory, but neglected to furnish the hero with adequate forces, thus enabling Totila to take Rome almost in sight of the imperial army.

The famous city was soon afterward recovered by Belisarius, who won some successes over the Ostrogothic king; but finding himself unsupported by the Emperor, the illustrious Byzantine general asked permission to return to Constantinople, and he departed from Italy in disgrace, not so much on account of his failure as because he had allowed his infamous wife, Antonina, to extort plunder from those he was sent to defend (A. D. 548). Soon after the departure of Belisarius from Italy, Totila again made himself master of Rome; but the maritime cities of Italy resisted his attacks and supported the imperial interests until the eunuch Narses was sent into the peninsula (A. D. 552).

The Emperor Justinian granted a sufficient supply of the munitions of war to Narses, who unexpectedly proved himself a great general like Belisarius; while the allies were entreated to send contingents, and mercenaries were hired from the leading barbarous tribes. Thus supplied, the Emperor's favorite eagerly sought to bring the Ostrogoths to an engagement; but Totila exhibited no less ardor for the conflict, and the hostile armies soon encountered each other in the vicinity of Rome. In the very beginning of the battle the Ostrogothic cavalry, hurried forward by their impetuosity, advanced beyond their infantry so far that they were surrounded and cut to pieces before they were able to obtain aid. While hastening with a chosen body of troops to remedy this disorder, Totila was struck to the ground mortally wounded, and his followers instantly fled in confusion. Rome opened its gates to the victorious imperialists; but the Byzantine forces, particularly the barbarian mercenaries, treated the renowned city more cruelly than the Ostrogoths had done, inflicting upon the citizens the mingled horror of lust, rapine and murder. The bravest of the Ostrogoths retired beyond the Po after their defeat, and chose Teias for their king. The war was then renewed; but in a furious battle lasting two full days Teias was slain, and the Ostrogothic power in Italy was irretrievably ruined.

Narses had scarcely time to recover from the fatigues of this campaign when he was called to repel an invasion of the Franks and the Alemanni, whom he routed with terrific slaughter; after which he returned to Rome and gratified its citizens by the semblance of a triumph. Thus Italy was reduced to the condition of a province of the Eastern Roman Empire, under the name of the *Exarchate of Ravenna;* and the first and greatest of the Exarchs of Ravenna was the eunuch Narses himself, the conqueror of the Ostrogoths. For fifteen years Narses governed the whole Italian peninsula with wisdom and firmness.

In the meantime, while the conquests of Belisarius and Narses were restoring Africa and Italy to the imperial dominion, barbarian hordes were ravaging the north-eastern frontiers of the Byzantine Empire with impunity. As Justinian was unable or unwilling to meet the Gepidæ in the field, he entered into an alliance with the Lombards, who had just cast off the yoke of the Heruli, and gave them settlements in Pannonia. The Empire was protected from the invasions of both the Lombards and the Gepidæ by a forty years' war between those two barbarous hordes; but it was still exposed to the destructive inroads of the barbarian Slavonians and Bulgarians, who annually purchased a passage through the territories of the Gepidæ and extended their ravages as far as Southern Greece.

Commotions in the far East of Europe at this time made Europeans acquainted with new and formidable races of barbarians, such as the Avars and the Turks. From an unknown age the Avars, a Mongolian nation, possessed the mountains and deserts bordering on Lake Baikal, in North-eastern Asia; whence they advanced southward under a monarch named Tulun, extending their dominion eastward to the Sea of Japan. The conquering sovereign assumed the title of Khakan or Chagan—a name still used on the coins of the Sultan of Turkey. But the prosperity of the Avars was of short duration, as they were assailed by rival tribes from the north, and were at the same time harassed by civil wars.

While the Avars were thus distressed, they were attacked by a new horde of barbarians, whom the Chinese writers call Thiukhiu, but who are known to Europeans as the Turks. The Turks overthrew the Avars and utterly broke up their power; but the name of the Avars was adopted by a new Mongolian nation called Oigurs, or Varchonites, who, after being defeated by the Turks, migrated westward into Europe by the route of the Volga. They chose the false title of Avars because the name of the Avars, or Huns, was still formidable, and they retained the name on account of the terror which they observed that it inspired.

The Turks first appeared in history as the slaves of the original Avars. They inhabited the region about the great Altai mountains, and belonged to the Turanian branch of the Mongolian race. They were engaged in working the mines and in attending the forges of those rich mineral districts. They possessed great skill in forging iron armor and weapons, and so prided themselves upon the excellence of their manufactures that when they became lords of Eastern Asia their Khakans annually forged a piece of iron in the presence of the heads of the nation.

Under the leadership of Thumen, the Turks asserted their independence and enslaved their former masters. Their progress was so rapid that during the reigns of Thumen and his successor, Dizabul, their dominion extended from the Volga to the Sea of Japan. Thus they were brought to the frontiers of the Eastern Roman and New Persian Empires, and they engaged in commercial relations with both, in consequence of their occupation of the countries through which the silk trade was carried.

Justinian received the Avars who fled to the Caucasus before the conquering Turks with great liberality, and encouraged them to invade the territories of the Bulgarians and Slavonians. Within ten years the Avars destroyed many tribes, reduced the remainder to tribute and service, and extended their camps as far west as the Elbe. Justinian afterwards renounced the friendship of the Avars for the more powerful alliance of the Turks; but the Avars were able, during his successor's reign, to conquer the present territories of Hungary, Roumania and European Turkey, and found the kingdom of the Chagans, which lasted two hundred and thirty years.

In his old age the Emperor Justinian had recourse to the services of his aged general, Belisarius, to drive away the barbarian Bulgarians and Slavonians, who had invaded the Byzantine Empire from the north and approached the gates of Constantinople. At the head of a small but valiant band, Belisarius gained a decisive victory and repelled the barbarians, but the intrigues of the courtiers prevented him from improving his advantages. The Bulgarians were induced to return to the north of the Danube by the payment of a large ransom for their captives; and Justinian claimed the gratitude of his subjects for accelerating the retreat of the barbarians by his threat of placing armed vessels in the Danube.

This was the last campaign of the renowned Belisarius. The applauses with which the populace greeted the old hero again excited Justinian's jealousy. The ungrateful Emperor, charging his faithful servant with treason and with aspiring to the imperial throne, caused the illustrious general who had conquered two kingdoms to be imprisoned in his own house and his possessions to be confiscated. The innocence of Belisarius being afterward proven, he was released and his fortune and honors were restored to him; but grief and resentment at the unjust and harsh treatment which he had received hastened his death three months after the Emperor's tardy act of justice, and eight months before the death of Justinian (A. D. 565). The common story that the eyes of Belisarius had been put out, and that in his old age he was often seen blind and led by a child, begging alms in the streets of Constantinople to support his living, is not fully authenticated.

Justinian's reign was distinguished by the number and grandeur of his public buildings, among which the most celebrated was the famous cathedral of St. Sophia, which the Emperor esteemed as rivaling the glories of Solomon's Temple. More substantial monuments of his time existed in the numerous fortifications which guarded the frontiers of the Empire, but which revealed its weakness rather than its strength. The Danube was defended by more than eighty fortresses, and long walls protected the friendly Goths from their barbarous northern neighbors; while the "Rampart of Gog and Magog," extending from the Euxine, or Black Sea, to the Caspian, and erected at the joint expense of the Eastern Roman and New Persian Empires, served for the protection of both against the barbarous hordes which overran the region north of the Euxine and the Caucasus. Beyond the Euphrates the eastern frontier of the Byzantine dominion was defended against the New Persians by the three fortresses of Amida, Edessa and Dara.

Justinian suppressed the schools of Athens and abolished the Consulate, which had degenerated from an august dignity into a mere useless and costly show. The great-

est glory of Justinian's reign was his celebrated compilation of the Roman laws, known as the *Civil Law*, as comprised in his three great works—the *Code*, the *Pandects* and the *Institutes*—which were digested by his illustrious minister Tribonian and the eminent lawyers selected for that purpose.

In the early part of his reign Justinian directed his attention to the state of the law in his dominions, and entertained the useful design of digesting into a uniform code the vast mass of laws, rules and judicial maxims which the various interests of the Romans and the Byzantines, their advance in civilization, and the inconstancy of their rulers, had produced during a period of thirteen centuries. The Emperor observed that the numerous ordinances caused confusion and disorder, and that the many inconsistent decisions and regulations produced a labyrinth in which justice was misdirected and iniquity found avenues of escape. In other words, the Roman laws had become so numerous and conflicting as to cause endless confusion. The mere word of an Emperor had acquired the force of a decree, and as such it had become a law binding upon all subsequent times. It required the devotion of a lifetime to become acquainted with these laws, and no private fortune was sufficient to obtain copies of all. Consequently the administration of justice was hampered, even where the judges were pure and desirous of discharging their duties with impartiality.

The execution of Justinian's great plan was worthy of the design. Tribonian, a lawyer of great renown, but also an interested flatterer and a corrupt judge, was appointed at the head of a commission of ten eminent lawyers to arrange the *Code*. Tribonian, being accustomed to sell justice, altered, perverted or suppressed many excellent laws. He frequently persuaded the Emperor to destroy, by means of supplementary edicts called *Novels*, the principles of right which had been previously established in the Code and Pandects.

Justinian began with the Code. In an edict dated February 3d, A. D. 528, and addressed to the Senate of Constantinople, he declared his determination to collect into a single volume all the laws in the three previous Codes of Gregory, Hermogenianus and Theodosius, and also the laws that had been published since the framing of the Theodosian Code. The commission of ten eminent lawyers headed by Tribonian was assigned the execution of this task. They were allowed to suppress repetitions, to remove contradictory or obsolete laws, to add whatever was essential for exactness or explanation, and to unite under one head what was spread over a great variety of laws.

The work of the commission progressed so rapidly that in little over a year the new Code, which contained in twelve books all the laws of the Roman Emperors since the accession of Adrian, was completed. Justinian affixed the imperial seal to the new Code in A. D. 529, and transmitted it, with a suitable edict, to Mennas, the Prætorian Prefect. In this edict Justinian congratulated himself and the Empire on having found commissioners who were possessed of such zeal, knowledge and probity. He gave the Code the force of law, ordaining that it should be cited in courts of justice, and ordered the Prætorian Prefect to publish it throughout the Empire.

The collection of the scattered monuments of ancient jurisprudence was found to be a more difficult task. Justinian intrusted this work also to Tribonian, authorizing him to nominate his fellow commissioners. Tribonian selected one of the magistrates who had already assisted in the framing of the Code, along with four professors of jurisprudence and eleven advocates of eminent legal reputation. These seventeen commissioners were instructed to search out, collect, and arrange in proper order, all that was really useful in the books of the jurisconsults who had been empowered to frame or interpret laws by preceding Emperors. The seventeen commissioners were permitted, as in the case of the Code, to change, add or omit, and to fix doubtful cases by exact definitions. The Emperor recommended them, in settling any point, to pay no regard to the number or the reputation of the jurisconsults who had given opinions on the subject, but to be guided wholly by reason and equity.

Their collection was to be arranged in fifty books, with all the matter systematically placed under their respective titles, and was named the *Digest*, because of its orderly classification, or the *Pandects*, on account of its containing all of ancient jurisprudence. The fifty books of the Pandects were divided into four hundred and twenty-three titles, containing nine thousand one hundred and twenty-three laws, each marked with the name of its author.

But the commissioners appear to have done their work with more zeal than exactness. The Emperor himself did not expect the task to be completed in less than ten years. It was necessary to examine with care more than two thousand volumes; to discuss, compare, and arrange in order, a multitude of decisions; to reform some of them, to reverse others, and to classify the whole. But Tribonian was well aware that in enterprises which engage the vanity of princes the delay between the design and the execution is borne very impatiently, and he therefore hurried on the work with such haste that it was finished in three years.

On the 16th of December, A. D. 533, Justinian clothed this collection—the *Digest*, or *Pandects*—with the authority of law, by a constitution of state, which he addressed to the Senate of Constantinople and to all his subjects. In this edict the Emperor stated that the vast chaos of ancient decisions had been reduced to a twentieth part, without omitting anything essential; so that the order and conciseness of this body of jurisprudence, and the facility with which it could be learned, left no excuse for negligence or ignorance. Justinian asserted that though some errors may have found their way into such an immense work, their number was very small; and he declared, with too much haste, that it contained none of those inconsistent decisions known to lawyers as *antinomies*. If any point should be found deficient and obscure, he declared that recourse should be had to the Imperial authority, which alone possessed the power of supplying or intrepreting the laws. In order to prevent the recurrence of the ancient confusion by diversity of sentiments, the Emperor forbade all commentary, allowing the laws to be only translated into Greek, with the addition of titles and paratitles, or, in other words, summaries of their contents.

Justinian forbade the use of abbreviations in transcribing the laws, asserting that the copy in which a contraction was found should be considered to be of no authority, and that the transcriber should be punished for forgery. All other laws were declared to be abrogated, and were even forbidden to be cited in the tribunals; while the judges were ordered to conform to the Pandects in everything from the day of the edict. The Emperor enjoined the three Prætorian Prefects to publish the Pandects in their respective jurisdictions, and closed by saying that he was desirous of having this beneficent revolution effected during his third Consulate, so that a year which heaven blessed by a peace with Persia and the conquest of Africa should be signalized by the completion of this great collection of Roman laws, as a holy and august temple, in which justice should pronounce her oracles.

While the commissioners were at work upon the Pandects, the Emperor ordered Tribonian and two eminent professors to prepare an elementary work on jurisprudence in four books, as an introduction to the study of the law. This—called the *Institutes*—was the most valuable portion of Justinian's legislation, and was completed and published a little before the Digest.

Thus the whole system of ancient jurisprudence was simplified, reduced to its essentials, and arranged in the Institutes, the Pandects and the Code of Justinian. But, after their publication, the Emperor published more than two hundred supplementary edicts; and when the great compilations began to be used in the courts of law several errors and imperfections came to light, as might reasonably be expected in a work of such vast proportions, executed with unnecessary haste. Justinian therefore appointed a new commission to revise the Code; and the result was a second edition, which obtained the Emperor's sanction by an edict issued on the 16th of November, A. D. 534, abrogating the former imperfect Code.

The Emperor expressly reserved to himself the right to add subsequently but separately such constitutions as he might deem necessary. These were termed *Novels;* and they limited, extended, and in some instances repealed, the Code. This inconsistency has led to the suspicion that Justinian and Tribonian were occasionally guided by interest and favor, rather than by reason and equity. There were one hundred and sixty-eight of these Novels, but only ninety-eight had the force of law, and these were arranged into a volume in the last year of Justinian's reign.

Justinian's legislation was superseded in the East by the *Basilica*, or Greek codes of later Emperors. Illyria was the only province in the West which received Justinian's legislation until the overthrow of the Ostrogothic kingdom in Italy afforded an opportunity to introduce it into that country; but the Code was superseded by the laws of the Lombards when those people became masters of Ravenna. After Charlemagne had overthrown the Lombard kingdom in Italy, he vainly searched that country for a copy of Justinian's legislation; and it remained concealed until the twelfth century, when a copy of the Pandects was discovered in consequence of the capture of Amalfi by the troops of the German Emperor Lothaire II., and was presented by him to the citizens of Pisa, who had assisted his troops in this expedition. At a subsequent period a copy of the Code was found at Ravenna, and the Novels discovered in various parts of Italy were arranged in a collection.

Justinian was thus not so much a framer of new laws as a restorer and a simplifier of the old ones. In the Institutes the elementary principles of the law were discussed. The Code was a condensation of all the en-

MEDIÆVAL HISTORY.—DARK AGES.

Incipit lib᷑ VII

☩ DEVSVTRVCTVETQVIMADMODVM
QVISVTATVRFRVATVR ☩
Paulus libᵒ tertio ad uitellium usus fru
ctus est ius alienis rebus utendi fruendi
salua rerum substantia.
Celsus libᵒ 8ᵒ ᵉᵗ tauo deciᵒ odices topiuᵃ·;
est enim ususfructus ius in corpore quo su
blato et ipsum tolli necesse est
Gaius libᵒ secundo rerum cottidianarum
uel aureorum omnium praediorum iure
legati potest constitui usus fructus ut
heres iubeatur dare alicui usum fructuᵐ
Dare autem intellegi tur si induxe ri t in
fundum legatarium eumue ᶠᵃ tiat uput
fruier t sue res tamen toli t eomsi qui s u-
li tus um fructum constitue re a tionib.
et stipulationibus idem prope pote st con
stiti tali te cmu sus fructus non tantum ᵢₙ fu-
do et aedibus uerum etiam in servis et iu
mentis ce teris quepe Busneta men i num
ue psuᵐ inutiles essent prop ria etate se-
per abs cedenteus ufructup lacuit cepti
modis extinguili sumfructum et proprᵢᵤₘ
tateper reptiqui Busautem modis ususfrᵤₛ
ctus et constitui tetfini tupis de᷈rmodis
etiam nudus ususs olete tcon s titue tpi
u ipi·

FRAGMENTS FROM THE PANDECTS OF JUSTINIAN.

(Fac-simile. 5-7 of original size.)

Manuscript from the VII Century. In the library of the Medici (Laurentiana) at Florence. The tinted letters are written in red ink in the Original.

This MSS., one of the most precious in the world, contains the Pandects, a considerable portion of the Roman law, compiled from decisions of the older jurists, by order of Justinian, who ordered its codification. The MSS. contains two volumes, is written on white parchment, bound in the most elegant manner in purple silk, ornamented with clasps and silver locks, and preserved in a magnificent case. The MSS. was written in Constantinople, and got to Amalfi (lower Italy) in unknown times. When in the year 1134, Amalfi got into the possession of Emperor Lothaire II., he presented the copy to his confederates, the Pisans. Pisa fell into the power of the Florentines in the year 1406; since which time the MSS. has remained in Florence.

TRANSCRIPTION.

Incipit liber VII.

R(ubrica) De usufructu et quemadmodum quis utatur fruatur. R(ubrica).

Now follows the text of the law:

Paulus libro tertio ad Vitellium : Ususfructus est jus alienis rebus utendi, fruendi, salva rerum substantia.
Celsus 1) libro octavo decimo digestorum : Est enim ususfructus jus in corpore, quo sublato et ipsum tolli necesse est.
Gaius libro secundo rerum cottidianarum vel aureorum : Omnium praediorum jure legati potest constitui ususfructus, ut heres jubeatur dare alicui, usumfructu (m). Dare autem intelligitur, si induxerit in fundum legatarium, eumve patiatur utifrui. Et sine 2) testamento autem si quis velit usumfructum constituere, pactionibus 3) et stipulationibus id efficere potest. Constitit autem ususfructus non tantum in fundo et aedibus, verum etiam in servis et jumentis ceterisque rebus. Ne tamen in universum inutiles essent propriaetates semper abscedente 4) usufructu, placuit certis modis extingui usumfructum et proprietatem reverti. Quibus autem modis ususfructus et constitui et finitur, iisdem modis etiam nudus usus solet et constitui et finiri.

1. The names of the cited jurists are written in red (shown by light face letters in this reproduction). 2. The copyist wrote u instead of n, and corrected himself. 3. Another correction: The copyist wrote rationibus. 4. After absce crossed out n.

actments of the Roman Emperors since Adrian. The Pandects, or Digest, consisted of a compilation of all the precedents and decisions of the wisest and most learned Roman judges since the framing of the Laws of the Twelve Tables, a thousand years before. These works were declared to be the legitimate system of civil jurisprudence, and no others were admitted in the tribunals of the Empire. Schools were established at Constantinople, Rome, and Beyreut in Syria, for the more perfect extension of this system throughout the Empire.

Such was the origin of the celebrated Civil Law, which has immortalized the memory of Justinian, and which has ever since formed the basis of legislation in all the European countries except England. This famous code is highly respected in England and the United States, and is frequently quoted in the courts of both of these English-speaking nations.

Justinian's reign is also celebrated for the introduction of the silk manufacture into Europe. Silk had been known as an article of commerce, and had been extensively used in the West long before the silk-worm was brought to Constantinople. Before the reign of Justinian no one had contemplated such an enterprise. Only by long and painful journeys through the perilous and difficult wilds of Central Asia was procured this valuable article of merchandise, which the advance of wealth and luxury rendered almost indispensable to the civilized nations of Europe, Asia and Africa surrounding the Mediterranean.

In the early ages the Assyrians and the Medes had long enjoyed a monopoly of this commerce, and for this reason garments made of silk were generally called "Median robes" by the ancient writers. The Assyrians and the Medes were succeeded in the silk traffic by the Persians, who considered this trade of great importance, and neglected nothing that could keep it exclusively in their hands. The Persians sold silk to the Greek and Syrian merchants who transported the precious article into the Western countries.

As the article passed a number of hands, it was of course scarce and costly. During Justinian's reign the Byzantines, or, as they still called themselves, the Romans, were anxious to be freed from their dependence upon the Persians for the supply of this precious article. They endeavored to lower the price of silk by purchasing the article from other Asiatic nations, and by making exertions to open a direct communication with the country which produced it; but their ignorance of geography was a great obstacle in the way of their success. They had vague ideas concerning the location of the region which produced this desirable commodity. They had an obscure notion that it was some part of India or some very distant land of Eastern Asia.

The Byzantine writers have informed us that the silk-producing country was Serica, which is considered the same as China, where silk is still more abundantly produced than in any other country in the world. The very name *Seres* seems to have been derived from this precious commodity; as *Se*, or as it pronounced in the provincial dialects, *Seer*, is the Chinese name for the silk-worm. We likewise find the Sinæ identified with the Seres by the ancient geographers, and we are aware that *Sin* or *Chin* has always been the name assigned to China by the nations of Western Asia. In the history of Roman commerce during the age of the Antonines, we have mentioned that a Roman embassy was at that period sent to China. As an evidence of the commercial relations between this ancient empire of Eastern Asia and the Western nations, we find that the Chinese histories contain a tolerably accurate account of the political annals of the Persian and Parthian Empires.

The silk was imported from China in packages, which caravans of merchants transported across the entire continent of Asia, from China to the sea-coast of Syria, in a journey of two hundred and forty-three days. The Persians, who supplied the Romans with silk, generally made their purchases from the Sogdians on the banks of the Oxus; and their traffic was subject to interruption by the White Huns and the Turks, who successively conquered the industrious Sogdians. But the obstacles to travel between Maracanda (now Samarcand), the Sogdian capital, and Shensi, the nearest Chinese province, led to repeated attempts to open a new and less dangerous route, which, however, resulted in failure. From the time that the enterprising Sogdians passed the Jaxartes, they had to contend with the dangers and difficulties of the intervening deserts, and also against the wandering hordes who have always regarded the citizen and the traveler as proper objects of lawful rapine.

As an evidence of the enormous expense of the magnificent spectacles with which Julius Cæsar sought to dazzle and conciliate the Roman populace, it is recorded that he decorated the actors in his various pageants with a profusion of silk dresses, which the Italians viewed with wonder and admiration. Because of the difficulties of transportation, the immense area of desert which the caravans were obliged to traverse, and perhaps the limited supply of silk in China itself, this precious article commanded a very high price in Rome, and was frequently sold for its weight in gold. Silk dresses were considered too expensive and delicate for men, and were only worn by ladies of distinguished rank and opulence.

In the commencement of the reign of Tiberius, a law was passed enacting that "no man should disgrace himself by wearing a silk dress." This may have been a religious as well as a sumptuary ordinance, as several Oriental religious bodies, particularly the Mohammedans, regard silk as unclean because it is the excretion of a worm. All the Mohammedan doctors of the Sunnite sect have decided that a person who wears a garment made entirely of silk can not offer up the daily prayers which the Koran enjoins.

The profligate and sensual Heliogábalus was the first of the Roman Emperors to wear a garment wholly of silk; and his example had the effect of making the custom of wearing silk general among the wealthy citizens of Rome and the provinces in a very short time. The price of the precious article may also have diminished in consequence of its beginning to be imported by the maritime route through Alexandria, instead of by caravans through the arid deserts of Tartary and Turkestan. Chinese histories inform us that an ambassador from one of the Antonines visited China for the purpose of concluding a commercial treaty —a circumstance highly probable from the fact that Oriental commodities became abundant and cheap in Rome during and after the reigns of their dynasty. Ammianus Marcellinus informs us that silk was generally worn even by the lower classes of Romans in his time, about A. D. 370.

During the long series of wars that ensued between the dynasty of the Sassanidæ in Persia, who considered themselves the legitimate heirs of Cyrus the Great, and the Byzantine Emperors, who desired to be regarded as the rightful successors of Alexander the Great, the command of the Arabian Sea gave the Persians a decided advantage over the Egyptian merchants, who were under the necessity of importing Oriental commodities by the tedious and perilous navigation of the Red Sea. Until the introduction of steam navigation, the Red Sea, or *Yam Suph*, "the Sea of Weeds," as the Orientals call it, was universally dreaded by voyagers. The Arabs significantly named the strait at its entrance *Bab-el-Mandeb*, or "the Gate of Tears;" and Eastern sailors have a common saying that "Yam Suph is a double-locked sea; there are six months in the year that you can not get into it, and six more that you can not get out of it."

But the New Persians were not content with this natural superiority; as they had it in their power to molest or cut off the caravans, which, for the purpose of procuring a supply of silk for the Eastern Roman Empire, traveled by land to China through the northern provinces of the New Persian Empire. The New Persians accordingly imposed such oppressive transit duties on foreign merchants that the Byzantines were obliged to relinquish this branch of commerce and to purchase their silk from the New Persians and the Sogdians. Both these latter peoples, with the rapacity usual with monopolists, raised the price of silk to such an exorbitant height that the Greek manufacturers, whose looms were dependent upon the supply of this raw material, were deprived of employment and almost ruined.

The Emperor Justinian was anxious to obtain a full and certain supply of the precious commodity, which had now become indispensable, and was also solicitous to relieve the commerce of his subjects from the exactions of his foreign enemies. He accordingly endeavored, by means of his ally, the Christian king of Abyssinia, to wrest some part of the silk-trade from the New Persians. He was unsuccessful in this effort; but, contrary to all expectation, by an unforeseen circumstance, he attained his great object of procuring for his subjects an abundant supply of silk, independent alike of ships and caravans.

Two Persian monks who had been employed as Christian missionaries by some of the churches which had been established in India pursued their evangelical duties until they had penetrated into the distant land of the Seres, or Chinese, in A. D. 551. There they observed the labors of the silk-worm, the manner in which this insect was fed on the mulberry-leaf, the care bestowed upon it in the several periods of insect transformation, and the attention requisite to obtain perfect cocoons. The mere possession of the insects would have been useless without such knowledge, as the time that passes while the caterpillar is undergoing its changes varies according to the temperature and the quantity of nourishment which is supplied to it. The health of the insect and the subsequent perfection of the silk depends upon the manner in which these changes are made, and upon the intervals between the successive moultings of the skin, which occur before the insect attains its full growth.

According to Chinese calculation, the same number of insects which would produce twenty-five ounces of silk if they had attained the full size in twenty-three or twenty-four days, would produce but twenty ounces if their growth occupied twenty-eight days, and but ten ounces if their development occupied forty days. Therefore, for the purpose of accelerating their growth, the Chinese supply the silk-worms with fresh food every half hour during the first day of their existence, and then gradually reduce the number of meals as the worms grow older. The substance on which the silk-worm feeds is the leaf of the mulberry-tree, and no other insect will partake of the same food, thus ensuring a certain supply for this valuable worm.

After acquainting themselves with these facts concerning the silk-worm, the Christian missionary monks hastened to Constantinople and disclosed their newly-acquired information to the Emperor Justinian. Encouraged by his liberal promises, these monks undertook to bring a sufficient number of silk-worms to the Byzantine capital. They returned to China and finally accomplished the object of their mission by obtaining an adequate supply of the eggs of the silk-worm, concealing them in a hollow cane. After they had returned to Constantinople, the eggs were hatched by the artificial heat of a dunghill, under the direction of the monks, and the worms were fed on the leaves of the wild mulberry-tree. Such care was bestowed upon the insects that they rapidly multiplied and worked in the same manner as in China.

Justinian first endeavored to monopolize this source of profit, but the rapid increase of the worms opened the silk-trade. The conquest of Sogdiana by the Turks, who descended from the Altai mountains in the last half of the sixth century, was a circumstance in favor of the speedy success of the Byzantines in the manufacture of silk. The conquered Sogdians had found the demand for silk rapidly diminishing—a circumstance which they ascribed to the commercial jealousy of the New Persians. They complained of their losses to the Turkish Khakan, their new master, who thereupon sent ambassadors to Persia to form a commercial treaty with the famous New Persian king, Khosrou Nushirvan.

It was clearly unwise policy to strengthen the power of the new Turkish state which had arisen beyond the Oxus; and Khosrou Nushirvan was also anxious to open a direct communication with China by way of the Persian Gulf. He purchased all the goods of the Sogdians and cast them into the flames, in order to show his contempt for the offers of that commercial people. The Turkish Khakan then sent ambassadors to the Emperor Justin II., Justinian's successor; and these ambassadors arrived at Constantinople in A. D. 571, after a toilsome journey, just twenty years after the silk-worm had been introduced into the Byzantine capital.

To their utter astonishment, these ambassadors found that the Byzantines manufactured their own silk, and that they had become so skilled in the art that their manufactures already rivaled those of the Chinese. Thenceforth the Sogdian silk-trade declined, and it was completely ruined about the middle of the ninth century, when a fanatical rebel in China murdered the foreign merchants, and cut down the mulberry-trees in order to destroy the silk that enticed foreigners to the Celestial Empire.

For almost six centuries the Byzantines were the only Europeans who possessed the silk-worm. At length Roger I., one of the Norman kings of Sicily, became involved in a war with the Byzantine Empire, captured some persons who were skilled in the production and manufacture of silk, and established factories at Palermo, which rapidly acquired celebrity. From Sicily the silk trade spread into Italy, Spain and France; but in most of these countries the silk manufacture was for a long time considered more important than the production of the raw material.

The present prosperity of France in the silk trade is owing to the patriotic efforts of King Henry IV., who established extensive nurseries of mulberry plants and distributed them gratuitously to all who desired establishing plantations. King James I. of England sought to introduce the production of raw silk, as a trade, into that country; and since his time the effort has been frequently repeated, but only with partial success. Similar experiments in Ireland have not yet answered the expectations of those who projected them.

Upon Justinian's death in November, A. D. 565, his nephew JUSTIN II. became Emperor. The reign of Justin II. was uneventful; and, disabled by disease, he appointed, at his wife Sophia's suggestion, Tiberius, the captain of the guards, as his successor, in A. D. 574. TIBERIUS faithfully administered the government until the death of Justin II. in A. D. 578, when he became sole Emperor.

The Empress Sophia had expected to marry Tiberius upon her husband's death and to continue her reign in this new character; but Tiberius, upon his accession as sole sovereign, proclaimed as Empress his secret but lawfully-married wife, Anastasia. He conferred honors and riches upon Sophia, in order to atone for her disappointment; but, while Sophia apparently accepted these offerings with pleasure, she secretly plotted for the overthrow of Tiberius; and the Emperor, upon discovering her plot, reduced her to a private station.

Tiberius reigned only four years, during which he gained the affections of his subjects by his many virtues. Upon his death, in A. D. 582, he was succeeded by MAURICE, whom he had selected as his heir, and who was worthy of the exalted honor conferred upon him. Soon after the accession of Maurice, Pope Pelagius II. appealed to him to deliver Italy from the Lombards. As the Emperor was unable to accomplish this result himself, he invited the Franks to act as his substitutes.

The Franks endeavored to act upon the Emperor's invitation, and accordingly made several invasions of Italy. The last of these Frankish expeditions was the one under Childebert II., the grandson of the great Clovis. Childebert II. failed in two expeditions into Italy, but was more successful in a third. As the Byzantines failed to render the Frankish king any substantial assistance, his expeditions degenerated into mere forays. The attention of the Emperor Maurice was chiefly directed to the East. Another war broke out between the Eastern Roman and New Persian Empires in A. D. 572, in the seventh year of the reign of Justin II., and lasted seven years with varied success. Upon Khosrou Nushirvan's death, in A. D. 579, his son, Hormisdas IV., became his successor. The latter's tyranny led to a rebellion of his subjects. About the same time the Byzantines made great gains on the frontiers of Mesopotamia and Assyria, while four hundred thousand Turks invaded the New Persian Empire from the line of the Oxus.

In this crisis Persia was saved by a hero named Varanes, or Bahram, who was victorious over both the Byzantines and the Turks, and was proclaimed King of Persia by his triumphant troops. Thereupon the Persian nobles deposed Hormisdas IV., put out his eyes, and elevated his son Khosrou Parviz to the Persian throne. Varanes refused to acknowledge Khosrou Parviz as king, and reduced him to such desperate straits that he fled to the Byzantine lines and threw himself upon the generosity of the Emperor Maurice, who espoused his cause. A Byzantine army entered Persia, drove out the usurper, and reëstablished Khosrou Parviz on the Persian throne. In gratitude for this service, Khosrou Parviz maintained the most friendly relations with the Eastern Roman Empire until the death of the Emperor Maurice.

Maurice gained some substantial successes over the Avars in the latter part of his reign. He sought to improve the discipline of his army, thus provoking a sedition which ended in the elevation of PHOCAS to the imperial throne and the murder of Maurice and his five sons at Chalcedon in A. D. 602. Phocas was an ignorant ruffian, whose tyranny soon disgusted his subjects. Heraclíus, the Exarch of Africa, threw off his allegiance to Phocas, and sent his son, the younger Heraclíus, to Constantinople with a strong fleet to seize the imperial throne. Phocas was put to death, and the younger HERACLIUS was proclaimed Emperor, A. D. 610.

At the beginning of his reign the Emperor Heraclíus was obliged to defend his dominions against the Persian king, Khosrou Parviz, who, under the plea of avenging the death of Maurice, overran the whole of Syria, Egypt and Africa as far west as Tripoli. The triumphant Persian monarch took Antioch, Damascus, Jerusalem and other Eastern cities of the Byzantine Empire by storm in A. D. 614, gave over Jerusalem to violence, burned the Holy Sepulcher and the stately churches erected by Constantine the Great, plundered the Holy City of its wealth, and transported the Patriarch and the "*true cross*" to Persia.

The victorious Persian king massacred ninety thousand Christians, and completed the conquest of Egypt in A. D. 616. In the meantime a Persian army marched through Asia Minor to the Bosphorus and took Chalcedon, and maintained a Persian camp within sight of Constantinople for ten years. The Persian arms appeared invincible, and Khosrou Parviz seemed about to revive the power and glory of his illustrious ancestors, Cyrus the Great and Daríus Hystaspes.

During all this time the Emperor Heraclíus remained in his capital, abandoned to slothfulness and pleasure; making little effort to retain his dominions, and seeming unconcerned regarding their fate. At length when everything appeared lost, Heraclíus suddenly cast off his weakness and assumed a heroic spirit. He borrowed the consecrated wealth of the churches under a solemn vow to restore it with usury, and collected an army and a fleet, with which he sailed to the Cilician coast, where he landed his troops and occupied Issus, at which place he was attacked by the Persians, and there gained a brilliant victory in A. D. 622, on the very spot where Alexander the Great had defeated Daríus Codomannus almost a thousand years before.

In the course of the next three years (A.

D. 623–625) the Emperor Heraclíus led a second expedition against Khosrou Parviz, penetrated into the heart of the New Persian Empire, and forced the Persian monarch to withdraw his troops from the Nile and the Bosphorus for the defense of Persia itself. The Persian king incited the Avars to attack Constantinople, but they were defeated with frightful slaughter in A. D. 626. The successes of Heraclius induced many of the Eastern tribes to join his standard, and the Emperor again marched into the interior of the New Persian Empire in A. D. 627. The Persians were completely routed in a decisive battle upon the site of the buried city of Nineveh, and for the first time the Assyrian cities and palaces were open to the Romans. Though reduced to despair, Khosrou Parviz refused to solicit peace.

As Khosrou Parviz was now an old man, he endeavored to secure the Persian crown to his favorite son, Merdaza; but another son, Siroës, headed a conspiracy against his father and seized him, put Khosrou's other eighteen sons to death in their father's presence, and cast the aged king himself into a dungeon, where he died on the fifth day of his captivity, A. D. 628. With Khosrou Parviz ended the glory of the New Persian Empire, and Siroës lived only eight months to enjoy the fruits of his unnatural crimes. For four years after the death of Siroës, nine pretenders to the Persian crown plunged the country into anarchy and bloodshed; and after a miserable existence of eight years more, the New Persian Empire fell a prey to the conquering arms of the Saracen Khalifs.

The remaining portion of the reign of Heraclíus was important only for the loss of Syria, Palestine and the other far eastern provinces of the Byzantine Empire, which were quickly overrun by the Saracens, never to be recovered for the Eastern Empire. The great exertions of Heraclíus against the New Persians had exhausted the Greek Empire, which was thus in no condition to make a successful stand against such new and vigorous foes as the Saracens. Besides this, the clergy, who proved themselves inexorable creditors, received most of the public funds in a usurious return of the loan which they made to Heraclíus for the preservation of the Empire.

Upon the death of Heraclíus, in A. D. 641, his sons, CONSTANTINE III. and HERACLEONAS, succeeded to the sovereignty of the Eastern Roman Empire. Constantine III. died soon afterward, supposed to have been poisoned by his stepmother, who, with her son, Heracleonas, was mutilated and exiled. Thereupon CONSTANS II., the eldest son of Constantine III., was made Emperor at the age of eleven (A. D. 641). Constans II. caused his brother Theodosius to be put to death, in order to insure his succession; but remorse for this crime drove him into exile in A. D. 662, and he was murdered in Sicily in A. D. 668.

Constans II. was now succeeded by his brother CONSTANTINE IV., who shared the imperial dignity with his two brothers, but kept the real power in his own hands. His brothers were deprived of their new titles, in consequence of having conspired against him. During the reign of Constantine IV. the Saracens conquered most of Western Asia, and advanced to the Bosphorus and laid siege to Constantinople in A. D. 668. The siege lasted seven years; but the city was successfully defended by means of the newly-discovered Greek fire, as the assailants were utterly unable to stand before this formidable agent.

Constantine IV. died in A. D. 685, and was succeeded by his son JUSTINIAN II., who outraged his subjects by his cruelties, and was deprived of his nose and driven into exile among the Tartars in A. D. 695. LEONTIUS and ABSIMARUS reigned as Emperors for the next ten years (A. D. 695–705). The Khan of Tartary gave his sister in marriage to the exiled Justinian II. She was baptized as a Christian and assumed the name of Theodora. Her brother, the Khan, was won over to the enemies of Justinian II., and agreed to deliver the exiled Emperor into their power; but Theodora discovered the plot and secured her husband's escape. Justinian II. fled to the camp of the Bulgarian king, who became his ally and agreed to aid him in an attempt to recover his throne.

Justinian II. recovered the imperial throne in A. D. 704, by the assistance of the Bulgarian king Terbelis; and passed the next seven years in revenging himself upon his enemies. His infamous cruelties rendered him so odious to his subjects that they deposed him and put him to death in A. D. 711, and made PHILIPPICUS Emperor. Philippicus was murdered in A. D. 713, whereupon ANASTASIUS II. was elevated to the imperial throne. Anastasius II. was dethroned in A. D. 716, and was succeeded by THEODOSIUS III. In A. D. 717 Theodosius III. was forced to give way to his able and powerful rival, LEO III., the Isaurian.

Leo III. was the first Greek Emperor belonging to the Isauric dynasty, and was called "the Second Founder of the Eastern Empire." He commenced his reign with a gallant defense of Constantinople against the Saracens. As he was himself an Armenian, he intrusted the most important offices of state and court to Armenians, on whom he could rely; and although Greek was the language of the court, the church and the people, the government was generally administered by Asiatics. Leo III. revived and reinvigorated the Eastern Empire, and his wise reforms gave it a new career of greatness and prosperity. His vigilant execution of the laws gave peace and security to all classes of his subjects, and Constantinople became the center of commerce.

The worship and use of pictures and images had been gradually adopted by the Christian Church, and Leo III, who had conceived a fierce hatred of the practice, attempted to put down image-worship, thus giving rise to a struggle between two parties —*Iconoduli*, who favored images, and *Iconoclasts*, who opposed them. This struggle—which shook the Eastern Empire for over a century, and plunged Christendom into commotion—ended in the triumph of the image worshipers, and finally led to the separation of the Eastern, or Greek, and the Western, or Latin Churches.

In the eleventh year of his reign (A. D. 726), the Emperor Leo III. issued an edict forbidding image-worship, thus beginning the bitter "War of Iconoclasm." Soon afterward Leo III. issued a second decree, ordering all the images to be destroyed and the walls of the churches to be whitewashed. These measures were fiercely resisted throughout the Empire, but the Emperor's authority prevailed in the East. The Western, or Latin, Church refused compliance with the Emperor's edicts, and the Pope constituted himself the champion of image-worship.

Leo III. died A. D. 741, after a reign of twenty-four years, and was succeeded by his son, CONSTANTINE V., surnamed Coprónymus, because of his pollution of the baptismal font. The war against images was continued with great animosity during his reign. The image-worshipers rose against Constantine Coprónymus and drove him from the imperial throne, but he afterwards recovered his crown and punished the rebellion by a severer and more violent persecution. A council of the Christian Church at Constantinople, in A. D. 754, formally condemned image-worship as idolatrous, forbidding the use and worship of images.

Aside from his persecution of the image-worshippers, Constantine Coprónymus seems to have been a wise and able sovereign. He vigorously defended the Asiatic provinces of the Empire against the Saracens, redeemed several thousand captives from foreign slavery, and settled new colonies along the depopulated coast of Thrace. His abilities were even admitted by the ecclesiastics whose antipathy toward him was most deadly.

Constantine Coprónymus died A. D. 775, and was succeeded by his son, LEO IV., a weak prince, who willingly relinquished the imperial power to his Athenian wife, Irene; while his infant son, CONSTANTINE VI., then only five years of age, was crowned Emperor and associated in the government. Leo IV. died five years later (A. D. 780), leaving his wife regent for her son. Irene was an ardent partisan of the image-worshipers and zealously espoused their cause. A general council of the Christian Church at Nice, in Asia Minor, in A. D. 787, declared image-worship conformable to the Scriptures and reason, thus reversing the decree of the Council of Constantinople in A. D. 754.

During the childhood of Constantine VI., his mother, Irene, showed herself to be a prudent and able ruler, and also a careful and judicious mother. But as the Emperor approached manhood he became impatient of her control and abandoned himself to the influence of favorites of his own age, who were ambitious of sharing his powers as well as his pleasures. The contest between the mother and the son which followed placed each alternately in possession of the imperial throne. The Empress IRENE finally triumphed, put out her son's eyes, and reigned alone in external splendor, regardless of the reproaches of her conscience and the denunciations of her subjects (A. D. 797-802).

Irene's reign was ended in A. D. 802 by a rebellion. The Empress was exiled to Lesbos; and the great Treasurer, NICEPHORUS, the rebel leader, became Emperor, and reigned nine years. His experience as Treasurer enabled him to increase the revenue by taxation, and he was not apparently guilty of more crimes than were common to the Eastern monarchs of his time. A few years before his reign (A. D. 800) the final separation between Eastern and Western Christendom was brought about by the revival of the Western Empire under Charlemagne—a result which Nicephorus was unable to prevent. In the second year of his reign Nicephorus entered into a treaty with Charlemagne defining the boundaries of the Eastern and Western Empires. Nicephorus was decisively defeated by the Saracen Khalif Haroun al Raschid in A. D. 805; and in A. D. 811 he was defeated and killed in a war with the Bulgarians.

Nicephorus was succeeded by his son STAURACIUS, who reigned only two months, when he was forced to relinquish the imperial crown to his brother-in-law, Michael Rhangabe, who became the Emperor MICHAEL I. Michael's troops, who were disgusted with his peaceful and unwarlike disposition, forced him to resign the imperial crown in A. D. 813; whereupon he retired to a monastery, although he was supported by the citizens and clergy of Constantinople.

Leo the Armenian, the rebel leader against Michael I., then ascended the imperial throne as LEO V. He was one of the best of the Byzantine Emperors. As he had been reared a soldier, he cared little for theological controversies, and pursued a policy regarding image-worship which gained for him from churchmen the title of "the Chameleon." During the reign of Leo V. the Bulgarians perpetrated great outrages in the European provinces of the Greek Empire, ravaging the country to the gates of Constantinople, and taking fifty thousand captives in one expedition alone. These Christian slaves became so many missionaries of their religion in the land to which they were carried into captivity, and converted thousands of Bulgarians to Christianity. Near the end of the ninth century the Bulgarian king Bogoris embraced the religion of Christ.

Michael the Armorian was one of the most trusted friends of the Emperor Leo V. at the beginning of his reign, but Michael soon began to conspire against his sovereign and benefactor, who conferred riches and honors upon him. Michael was frequently detected and pardoned, but continued his plotting until he was finally condemned to death. In order to save his life, his adherents rose in revolt against Leo V. and put him to death in A. D. 820.

Michael the Armorian was then brought from his dungeon with his limbs still fettered, and was elevated to the imperial throne with the title of MICHAEL II. He reigned nine years, during which the Eastern Empire entered upon a great career of commercial prosperity, in the midst of its far advance in political decline. The Empire had a monopoly of the Mediterranean trade; while a large and profitable commerce between Europe and Asia flowed through Constantinople and enriched its inhabitants, notwithstanding the fact that the Saracens had become masters of Crete and of some of the other islands of the Mediterranean. Michael II. died A. D. 829, and was succeeded by his son THEOPHILUS, an able sovereign, but whose reign was clouded by misfortune. Theophilus attempted to recover the provinces which the Saracens had wrested from the Eastern Empire, but was finally defeated. He exhausted his enormous revenues in adorning Constantinople, instead of applying them to the fortification of the frontiers of the Empire. Theophilus was an Iconoclast and fiercely opposed image-worship.

Theophilus died A. D. 842, leaving his wife, Theodora, regent for their son, who succeeded him as MICHAEL III. Theodora restored the images amid the rejoicings of her subjects, thus putting an end to the "Iconoclastic War," which had lasted more than a century, and which had finally caused the separation of the Eastern, or Greek, and the Western, or Latin Churches. Michael III. was five years of age at the time of his father's death, and his mother Theodora held the regency thirteen years. She then prudently relinquished the government to her son and retired to private life, having for some time perceived that her influence was waning, and that her son was becoming impatient of her rule.

After becoming sole ruler of the Empire, Michael III. demonstrated his unfitness to govern. He was a brutal, drunken tyrant, and is known as "Michael the Drunkard." He had no regard for the sacredness of religion or the dignity of his own exalted station. He was as contemptible as he was odious, and so disgusted his subjects that they longed to be rid of him. Michael the Drunkard was finally murdered in his sleep, in A. D. 867, in the thirtieth year of his age, by Basil, one of his own officers, who is said to have been a Slavonian.

BASIL I., the assassin and successor of Michael the Drunkard, claimed to be a descendant of Alexander the Great, and for this reason the dynasty founded by him is called the Macedonian dynasty. Basil I. gained great successes over the Saracens, carrying his victorious arms as far as the Euphrates, and crushed the republic of the Paulicians, but he lacked the talents and the spirit of a warrior. He is mainly celebrated for his legislation. A revision of Justinian's whole system of jurisprudence was rendered necessary by the change of language and manners. The voluminous mass of the Institutes, Pandects, Code and Novels of Justinian was digested in the Greek idiom under forty titles; and the *Basilica*, which Basil's son and grandson completed and improved, owed their origin to the native genius of the founder of their dynasty.

The treaty with Charlemagne assigned the cities of Southern Italy to the Eastern Empire. In A. D. 878 the Saracens captured Syracuse and extended their dominion over the whole of Sicily. They afterwards firmly established themselves in Southern Italy, thus diminishing the Greek Emperor's power.

Upon the death of Basil I., in A. D. 886, his sons, LEO VI. and ALEXANDER, were both invested with the imperial dignity; but the elder of these two brothers, Leo VI., surnamed "the Philosopher," was the real sovereign, because, as Gibbons sarcastically remarks, "the son of Basil was less ignorant than the greater part of his contemporaries in church and state." The reign of Leo the philosopher was clouded by calamities; one of the greatest of which was the capture of Thessalonica, the second city of the Eastern Empire, by the Saracens, who massacred all its inhabitants except twenty-two thousand youth, whom they sold into slavery. Leo the Philosopher won the hostility of the Church by contracting a fourth marriage, this time with Zoë, who had borne him a son —a marriage not recognized by the Greek Church as lawful.

Leo the Philosoper died A. D. 911, after a reign of twenty-five years, and was succeeded by his son, CONSTANTINE VII., surnamed Porphyrogenítus, meaning "Born of the Purple." He was but five years of age when his father died. During his minority the government was administered by his uncle Alexander, and by his mother Zoë after Alexander's death, and by other regents.

In A. D. 919 ROMANUS I., surnamed Leucapenus, the leading general of the Byzantine army, usurped the imperial government, assuming the titles of Cæsar and Augustus, and associating his three sons successively with him in the Empire; and for twenty-five years the lawful Emperor was degraded to the lowest rank of this imperial college. CHRISTOPHER, one of these, ruled from A. D. 920 to A. D. 928, and STEPHEN and CONSTANTINE VIII. from A. D. 928 to A. D. 944.

Upon the expulsion of these usurpers, in the year A. D. 945. Constantine VII. assumed the sole administration, and reigned alone almost fifteen years (A. D. 945–959). His mild and benevolent disposition won the affections of his subjects. He wrote several scientific and historical works, and rendered valuable service to literature by causing a number of precious manuscripts to be preserved.

Constantine Porphyrogenitus died A. D. 959, and was succeeded by his son, ROMANUS II., whose reign was rendered memorable by the exploits of his general, Nicephorus Phocas, who recovered the island of Crete from the Saracens and won other important successes over them. After a reign of four years, Romanus II. was poisoned by his wife, Theophano, who married the victorious general, Nicephorus Phocas, who then ascended the imperial throne as NICEPHORUS II., assuming the title of Augustus, without degrading the infant Emperors Basil II. and Constantine IX., the sons of Romanus II. and Theophano (A. D. 963).

Nicephorus Phocas reigned vigorously and successfully for six years, steadily resisting the Saracens and maintaining his frontiers unbroken against their assaults. His reign marked the beginning of the most vigorous period of the Eastern Roman Empire before its final division—a period which continued until about A. D. 1025. Nicephorus Phocas was murdered in A. D. 969 by his nephew, John Zimisces, who succeeded him on the imperial throne as the guardian of the youthful Emperors Basil II. and Constantine IX., assuming the title of JOHN I.

John Zimisces had been one of the lovers of the Empress Theophano during her last husband's life, and she hoped to share the imperial throne with her paramour; but John discarded her, at the relentless command of the Patriarch of Constantinople, and dismissed her to a private station. John showed himself an able and energetic ruler. He won many victories over the Saracens in the East, recovered Antioch and other cities which they had taken, and made the Euphrates once more the eastern boundary of the Byzantine Empire. John likewise gained decisive successes over the Norman rulers of Russia, who were annoying the frontiers of the Eastern Empire; decisively defeating the Russian forces at Presthlava, in Bulgaria, in A. D. 971, and forcing them to solicit peace. By the terms of the treaty, the Russians ceded to the Emperor John I. the Kingdom of Bulgaria, which they had recently conquered, thus once again making the Danube the northern boundary of the Greek Empire.

Upon the death of John I., in A. D. 976, the two legitimate Emperors, BASIL II. and CONSTANTINE IX., ascended the imperial throne. Basil II. was a man of genius and energy, but Constantine IX. was a weak and effeminate prince. Basil II. soon made himself the real ruler of the Empire, which attained the height of its military greatness under him. He waged a vigorous war against the Bulgarians and the other Slavonic tribes of the Balkan peninsula for almost forty years. The Bulgarians were thoroughly subdued; but the victorious Emperor tarnished his triumph by cruelly putting out the eyes of fifteen thousand of his prisoners, whom he sent back to their king, who died in consequence of grief and rage at the sight.

Basil II. died in A. D. 1025, after a reign

of almost half a century, passing away "amid the blessings of the clergy and the curses of the people." Constantine IX. reigned alone three years longer, and died in A. D. 1028, after having borne the title of Augustus for sixty-six years, but doing nothing in all that time to deserve the honor.

Basil II. left no children, and Constantine IX. had only three daughters. As there were no male heirs, the Byzantine throne was for almost thirty years in the possession of the infamous favorites of the Empresses Zoë and Theodora, the daughters of Constantine IX. These rulers were ROMANUS III. and ARGYROPULUS (A. D. 1028-1034), MICHAEL IV., the Paphlagonian (A. D. 1034-1041), MICHAEL V., Caláphates (A. D. 1041-1042), CONSTANTINE X., MONOMACHUS and ZOE (A. D. 1042-1054), THEODORA (A. D. 1054-1056), and MICHAEL VI., Stratíotes (A. D. 1056-1057). The only important events during this period were the outbreaks of the citizens of Constantinople, who were enraged by the weakness and licentiousness of these corrupt rulers.

In A. D. 1057 the Byzantine army elevated ISAAC COMNENUS, a general of noble birth, to the imperial throne. This Emperor reigned only two years, abdicating the throne in A. D. 1059, on account of failing health. As his brother, John Comnenus, refused the imperial crown, CONSTANTINE XI., who belonged to a different family, was raised to the Byzantine throne. Constantine XI. died in A. D. 1067, after a reign of eight years, leaving the government in the hands of his widow, the Empress EUDOCIA, who married Romanus Diogenes, who then became the Emperor ROMANUS IV., and reigned with honor and dignity for four years.

In the meantime the Seljuk Turks, who had adopted the Mohammedan religion, had become masters of the Saracen dominions in Asia, and began to press heavily upon the remaining provinces of the Eastern Roman Empire. It was this peril which mainly caused the Empress Eudocia to marry Romanus Diogenes, who was an able and experienced soldier. He exerted himself to preserve the integrity of his Asiatic provinces, with his slender resources, but invincible courage. He drove the Turks beyond the Euphrates in three hard-fought campaigns. He endeavored to recover Armenia from them in a fourth campaign, in A. D. 1071; but was defeated and taken prisoner by the Turkish Sultan, Alp Arslan, "the Valiant Lion." The captive Emperor was released upon promising to pay a heavy ransom and an annual tribute; but when he returned to Constantinople he found that his subjects had dethroned him upon hearing of his captivity, and had forced the Empress Eudocia to retire to a convent. Romanus Diogenes was defeated and slain in an attempt to recover the imperial crown.

Romanus Diogenes was succeeded by MICHAEL VII., Parapinaces, who reigned from A. D. 1071 to A. D. 1078. The next Emperor was NICEPHORUS III., whose accession was disputed in Asia by another Nicephorus. The Emperor Nicephorus III. called the Turks to his assistance and defeated his rival, but obtained his triumph by sacrificing his Asiatic provinces, which thus came into the possession of the Seljuk Turks. A few years afterward Nicephorus III. was able to extend the eastern limits of the Byzantine Empire to Nicomedía, in Asia Minor, about sixty miles from Constantinople; but the old Greek provinces beyond that frontier remained in the possession of the Turks, with the sole exception of Trebizond, at the south-eastern extremity of the Euxine, or Black Sea, which, on account of its strong natural fortifications, remained in the possession of the Greek Emperor.

Nicephorus III. was deposed in A. D. 1081, whereupon Alexis Comnenus, son of John Comnenus, was elevated to the imperial throne under the title of ALEXIS I. This Emperor ascended the Byzantine throne at a time of great misfortune, and "every calamity that can afflict a declining empire was accumulated on his reign by the justice of Heaven and the vices of his predecessors." The Seljuk Turks had overrun all Western Asia from Persia to the Hellespont, while

Norman adventurers invaded the Greek Empire on the west, and new Slavonic hordes of barbarians poured across the Danube on the north.

While the Eastern Roman Empire was thus assailed by foreign foes on sea and land, the imperial palace was distracted with secret treason and conspiracy. Suddenly the banner of the Crusades was displayed by the Latins from the West of Europe; and in the great and protracted struggle between the Cross and the Crescent—between Christendom and Islam—Constantinople was almost swept away.

In this momentous crisis, the Emperor Alexis I. conducted the helm of state with skill and wisdom. Says Gibbon: "In the tempest Alexis steered the imperial vessel with dexterity and courage. At the head of his armies he was bold in action, skillful in stratagem, patient of fatigue, ready to improve his advantages, and rising from his defeats with inexhaustible vigor. The discipline of the camp was revived, and a new generation of men and soldiers was created by the example and the precepts of their leader. In his intercourse with the Latins, Alexis was patient and artful; his discerning eye pervaded the new system of an unknown world, and with superior policy he balanced the interests and passions of the champions of the First Crusade. In a long reign of thirty-seven years he subdued and pardoned the envy of his equals; the laws of public and private order were restored; the arts of science and wealth were cultivated; the limits of the Empire were enlarged in Europe and Asia; and the Comnenian scepter was transmitted to his children of the third and fourth generation."

The Emperor Alexis I. died in A. D. 1118, and was succeded by his eldest son, JOHN II. John II. acquired the title of "the Handsome," in derision on account of his insignificant stature and his harsh, swarthy features; but his keen-witted subjects retained the surname in gratitude and admiration for his noble qualities. He was a wise and liberal sovereign, and by his military vigor he recovered some of the former Greek territory conquered by the Seljuk Turks, whom he drove from the maritime provinces of Asia. As John II. was feared by his nobles and beloved by his subjects, he was never obliged to punish or pardon his personal enemies.

Upon the death of John II., in A. D. 1143, his youngest surviving son, MANUEL I., became Emperor. The reign of Manuel I. lasted thirty-seven years, and was a period of almost constant war. The Seljuk Turks were driven beyond Mount Taurus in Asia Minor; while the Hungarians, or Magyars, and other barbarous hordes north of the Danube were obliged to respect the frontiers of the Eastern Roman Empire. Manuel I. was more of a knight-errant than a good monarch or a great general, but for some time he made the power of the Greek Empire respected and feared. The fleets of the Norman King of Sicily several times ravaged the coasts of Greece, and Manuel I. was under the necessity of repelling these attacks and of retaliating by assailing the Normans in Sicily. Manuel I. was at length defeated by the Turks in a great battle in the province of Pisidia, in Asia Minor, but escaped through the victorious Sultan's generosity. After this defeat the Byzantine Empire again declined.

Manuel's relative, Andronícus, the younger son of Isaac Comnenus, one of the sons of the Emperor Alexis I., was a remarkable person, whose adventures were most extraordinary. Andronícus is said to have been brave, eloquent, accomplished, of singular grace and beauty, and temperate in an extraordinary degree, "with a heart to resolve, a head to contrive, and a hand to execute." The sister of the Empress became his spouse without the sanction of the legal authority.

In punishment for an attempt to assassinate the Emperor Manuel I., Andronícus was imprisoned twelve years. He finally discovered a part of the prison wall where the bricks could be removed and replaced so as not to change their usual appearance. Adjoining this wall was a recess, in which a person might be concealed, but beyond which he was unable to go. Andronícus removed the bricks, and, after passing into the recess, replaced them so as to excite no suspicion. As he was not seen in his cell the next day, he was believed to have made his escape; and his spouse, who was suspected of having assisted him, was sent to take his place in the prison. In the dead of night she imagined seeing a specter. Her husband appeared before her. She recognized him. They shared their provisions until they had been together a sufficient time to devise an ingenious plan of escape. This plan succeeded. Andronícus fled to the Danube, whence, after many perils, he made his way to Russia, where he rendered such important service to the Greek Emperor that he obtained his pardon, and was thus enabled to return to Constantinople.

Andronícus again fell under the Emperor Manuel's displeasure, and was consequently banished to Cilicia, in Asia Minor, but was intrusted with a military command. In that country his romantic amours had the effect of bringing him into new difficulties, and he undertook a pilgrimage to Jerusalem to escape the consequences of his conduct. He was plunged into a deeper sea of troubles in consequence of new adventures with the queen-dowager of Jerusalem, and a price was set upon his head. He fled from Jerusalem to Damascus, thence to Bagdad and Persia, and at length settled among the Turks in Asia Minor—the inveterate enemies of his country.

At the head of a band of outlaws, Andronícus made predatory incursions into the Greek Empire, and became distinguished as a bandit throughout the East. The Emperor Manuel's attempt to capture him failed, but his wife and two children were taken and sent to Constantinople. At length he obtained his pardon by manifestations of penitence. He prostrated himself at the foot of Manuel's throne, and was sent into exile at the eastern extremity of the Euxine, or Black Sea.

Manuel I. died in A. D. 1181, leaving the imperial crown to his infant son ALEXIS II., who reigned two years in the midst of a civil war at Constantinople. The friends of

Andronícus encouraged his ambition with high hopes. Andronícus collected an army and marched to Constantinople, where he assumed the guardianship of Manuel's infant son, the Emperor Alexis II. This unfortunate child and his mother were soon disposed of, the mother being cast into the sea, and the child being strangled with a bowstring. After surveying the murdered infant's body, Andronícus rudely struck it with his foot, saying: "Thy father was a knave, thy mother a harlot, and thyself a fool."

ANDRONICUS thus ascended the Byzantine throne A. D. 1183. He was an able but cruel sovereign, and in him was fully verified the ancient proverb: "Bloodthirsty is the man who returns from banishment to power." The common fate of such as had incurred his displeasure were poison, the knife, the sea and the flames. Alexis Angelus, who was marked as a victim, slew the executioner who approached him, in a moment of despair, and fled to the cathedral of St. Sophia, where a sorrowful multitude assembled, whose lamentations soon gave way to curses, and whose curses were quickly followed by threats. At dawn the next day the Byzantine capital rose in insurrection, and in the general clamor ISAAC ANGELUS was raised to the imperial throne (A. D. 1185).

Andronícus was absent at the time on one of the islands in the Propontis (now Sea of Marmora). He hastened to Constantinople, which he found filled with tumult; the palace being deserted and himself being forsaken by all mankind. He endeavored to escape by sea, but his galley was overtaken, and he was brought in chains before the new Emperor. Andronícus was set astride a camel and conducted through the city, subjected to the blows and the insults of the populace, after which he was hung alive by the feet between the pillars that supported the figures of a wolf and a sow. All the citizens whom he had deprived of a father, a husband or a friend, were allowed to execute vengeance. As a poor compensation for their losses, his teeth, hair, an eye and a hand were torn from him. All the exclamations that he uttered were: "Lord, have mercy upon me; why will you bruise a broken reed?" Finally two furious Italians ended his prolonged agony by plunging their swords into his body.

Isaac Angelus, the successor of Andronicus, reigned ten years (A. D. 1185-1195), and was a prince of generous disposition and effeminate manners; but was driven from the imperial throne and deprived of his eyes by his own brother Alexis, who then became the Emperor ALEXIS III. (A. D. 1195). A son of Isaac Angelus, also named Alexis, fled from Constantinople and found refuge in Western Europe, where he sought to induce the great powers to aid him in his efforts to recover his father's throne, spending about nine years in these fruitless efforts, and despairing of accomplishing anything, when his labors were suddenly and unexpectedly crowned with success, as we shall afterwards see in the account of the Fourth Crusade.

The struggles of the various claimants of the Byzantine throne weakened the Greek, or Eastern Roman Empire, and prepared it for the first great period in its fall. The decline of the Empire, which commenced with the death of Manuel I. and the quarrels of his successors, continued during the closing years of the twelfth and the first years of the thirteenth century. Having thus traced the history of the Byzantine Empire from its origin, through the Dark Ages, to the temporary substitution of a Latin for a Greek dynasty at Constantinople—a period embracing a little over eight centuries—we will give the remainder of the history of the Eastern Empire in subsequent portions of this volume.

This Empire—which under Justinian had extended from the Alps and the Danube to the Euphrates and the great African desert, embracing Italy and all of Europe south of the Danube, Asia Minor, Syria, Palestine, Egypt and all of Northern Africa—was now reduced to comparatively small dimensions, comprising only that part of Southeastern Europe south of the Balkan mountains, included in Thrace, Macedonia, Greece and Illyricum, along with the western and part of the northern coasts of Asia Minor, included in the ancient provinces of Caria, Lydia, Mysia, Bithynia and Paphlagonia.

SECTION IX.—NEW PERSIAN EMPIRE OF THE SASSANIDÆ.

ALREADY we have seen that the New Persian Empire of the Sassanidæ arose on the ruins of the Parthian Empire of the Arsacidæ. The Persians had for a long time been discontented with the Parthian dominion. Although the last Parthian king, Arsaces XXX., had defeated the Romans, the Parthian Empire was distracted with the claims of rival pretenders who contended with Arsaces XXX. for the Parthian crown. Two branches of the family of the Arsacidæ—both of them settled in Bactria—were at feud with the reigning Parthian monarch; and these offended relatives carried their animosity to such extremes as to regard submission to a foreign ruler preferable to subjection to the ruling head of their dynasty. The success of Arsaces XXX., in his war with the Romans, had no effect upon his domestic foes.

This condition of affairs encouraged the Persians to cast off their allegiance to the Parthians and to recover their independence. In the original arrangements of the Parthian Empire, the Persians had been treated with a certain degree of favor, being permitted to retain their native kings—a concession naturally involving the continuance of the nation's laws, customs and traditions. Their religion had not been persecuted, and had even attracted a considerable degree of favor with the Parthian court in the early times of the Parthian dominion. But it appears that in the latter period of the Parthian supremacy the national privileges of the Persians had been diminished, while their prejudices were wantonly shocked.

At that time the tributary King of Persia under the Parthian dominion was Artaxerxes, or Ardeshir Bábigan, as the native Persian historians call him, the son of Sassan, who claimed descent from the ancient dynasty of Cyrus the Great. Encouraged by dissensions in the Parthian kingdom, Artaxerxes, or Ardeshir Bábigan, rose in arms against his suzerain, the Parthian king, Arsaces XXX., in A. D. 220, or perhaps a little later; and was soon successful in establishing the independence of Persia proper, the modern province of Fars, or Farsistan. He then turned his victorious arms eastward against the ancient province of Carmania, the modern Kerman, and reduced it; after which he proceeded to overrun Media. The Parthian monarch then marched against his rebellious vassal, but was defeated three times, and finally killed in the great battle of Hormuz, A. D. 226. ARTAXERXES was saluted on the field with the title of *Shah in Shah*, or *King of Kings*—a title ever since assumed by the Persian kings.

The sons of Arsaces XXX. continued the struggle against the Persians, and were assisted by Chosroës, King of Armenia; but the Persians were everywhere victorious, and the old Parthian Empire of the Arsacidæ gave place to the New Persian Empire of the Sassanidæ, after a struggle of a few years. After Artaxerxes had been thus left in possession of the new Persian monarchy, he proceeded to consolidate his empire, and restored the ancient religion of Zoroaster and the authority of the Magi. The dynasty which he founded—called the Sassanidæ, from his father, Sassan—occupied the Persian throne for more than four centuries and consisted of twenty-nine kings.

Artaxerxes took advantage of the impression made by his great triumph to enlarge the New Persian Empire, extending it to the Euphrates on the west and to the Kingdom of Kharasm on the north. His fame spread in all directions, and all the petty states in the vicinity of his empire proffered submission, while the greatest monarchs from Orient to Occident courted his friendship. He was one of the wisest sovereigns that Persia ever had. The revolution which he effected in his country's condition was truly wonderful. He formed a well-consolidated empire out of the scattered fragments of the Parthian monarchy, which had been for centuries in a distracted condition. The name *Parthia*, given by Western writers to the empire east of the Euphrates for almost five centuries, ceased upon the elevation of Artaxerxes to the throne; and the empire which he founded was recognized by the title *Persia*.

Persian writers have preserved sayings of Artaxerxes which exhibit his goodness and wisdom, such as the following: "There can be no power without an army; no army without money; no money without agriculture; and no agriculture without justice." It was one of his common sayings that "a ferocious lion was better than an unjust king; but an unjust king was not as bad as a long war." He was likewise in the habit of saying that "kings should never use the sword when the cane would answer"—a fine lesson to tyrannical sovereigns, whom it was designed to teach that they should never take away life when the offense will admit of a milder punishment.

One of the characteristic features of the reign of Artaxerxes was his zeal to uphold the ancient Zoroastrian religion, which the Parthian monarchs had neglected or degraded. This zeal was as much attributable to policy as to piety. He summoned a great assembly of *mobuds* and Magi from every portion of his dominions to aid him in his religious reform—a circumstance still considered as most important in the creed of Zoroaster. The testamentary advice which Artaxerxes addressed to his son, as recorded by Firdusi, the renowned Persian poet of the eleventh century, exhibits his views of religion and of the duties of a sovereign in a very favorable light. Artaxerxes caused the Zend-Avesta to be published.

Artaxerxes was involved in a war with Chosroës of Armenia, who was on friendly terms with Rome, and might count on a Roman contingent and the assistance of the Bactrian Arsacidæ. Chosroës took the Parthian Arsacidæ under his protection, giving them a refuge in Armenia, and also negotiated with Bactria and Rome, made arrangements with the barbarians on his northern frontier to assist him, and led a large army into the New Persian Empire on the northwest and achieved some successes, thus establishing the independence of Armenia and checking the advance of the New Persians in Western Asia.

Axtaxerxes next entered upon a series of negotiations with Rome, the result of which was a final rupture between the New Persian and Roman Empires. Artaxerxes was not satisfied with the monarchy which he had built up in five or six years; but longed for the glorious times of Cyrus the Great and Darius Hystaspes, when all Western Asia from the shores of the Ægean to the valley of the Indus, and parts of Europe and Africa, acknowledged the dominion of the Persian monarch. Artaxerxes considered the territories ruled by these princes as his own right by inheritance, and Herodian and Dio Cassius tell us that he boldly proclaimed these views. His emissaries everywhere declared that their sovereign claimed the dominion of Asia as far westward as the Ægean and the Propontis. It was his duty and his mission to recover the pristine Persian Empire. What Cyrus the Great had conquered, what the Persians had held from that time until the overthrow of Darius Codomannus by Alexander the Great, belonged to Artaxerxes by indefeasible right, and he was about to take possession thereof.

The Persian army at once crossed the Tigris and overran the entire Roman province of Mesopotamia. The youthful Roman Emperor, Alexander Severus, at once sent an embassy to Artaxerxes, counseling him to be satisfied with what belonged to him and not seek to revolutionize Asia. Artaxerxes replied by an embassy in which he ostentatiously displayed the wealth and magnificence of Persia, and demanded the immediate acceptance of his terms, ordering the Romans and their Emperor to give up all of Syria and the rest of Western Asia, and to allow the Persians to exercise dominion over all Asia Minor, because "these countries belonged to Persia by right of inheritance."

Alexander Severus was so incensed at the insolence of these demands that he stripped the Persian ambassadors of their magnificent apparel, treated them as prisoners of war, and settled them as agricultural colonists in Phrygia. He instantly raised an army and led it against the Persian king, crossing the Euphrates into Mesopotamia, in A. D. 232, and recovered that province. A Roman force traversed Armenia and overran and ravaged Media; but another Roman detachment which crossed Mesopotamia and threatened to invade Persia proper was cut to pieces by a countless Persian host under King Artaxerxes himself—a defeat characterized by Herodian as "the greatest calamity which had ever befallen the Romans."

The Roman forces at once retreated to the west side of the Euphrates into Syria; but Artaxerxes, finding Rome more powerful than he had imagined, abandoned his grand ideas of conquest and dispersed his army. Peace was thereupon made between the Roman and New Persian Empires on the general principle of a return to the *status quo ante bellum*, or a restitution of the old boundaries between the Roman and Parthian Empires.

Not feeling perfectly at ease so long as an Arsacid reigned in Armenia, Artaxerxes renewed the war with that country immediately upon the conclusion of peace with Rome. Chosroës, the Armenian king, defended himself so successfully that the Persian monarch summoned an assembly of all the vassal kings, governors and commandants throughout his Empire, and promised a rich reward to any one who would assassinate the Armenian king. His offers were accepted by Anak, a Bactrian noble of Arsacid blood, who accordingly undertook the assassination of his own relative, the Armenian monarch. Anak, with his wife, his children, his brother, and a train of attendants, pretended to seek refuge in Armenia from the threatened vengeance of the Persian monarch, who caused his troops to pursue him as a deserter and a rebel to the very frontiers of Armenia.

Chosroës, not suspecting any evil design, received the pretended exiles with favor and discussed with them his designs for the conquest of Persia. After sheltering them during the autumn and winter he asked them to accompany him in his campaign the next spring. Anak at once arranged a meeting between himself, his brother and the Armenian king, without attendants, on the pretext of discussing the plan of campaign; and at this meeting he and his brother treacherously murdered the unsuspecting Chosroës with their swords. The Armenians rose in arms and seized the bridges and practicable outlets of their capital, and the assassins were drowned in an attempt to escape by swimming the river Araxes. The Persian armies at once entered Armenia and easily reduced the country to submission, notwithstanding that the Armenians were aided by a Roman contingent. Thus Armenia lost its independence and became an integral portion of the New Persian Empire of the Sassanidæ.

Artaxerxes governed his dominions either through native vassal kings or through Persian satraps. Like the old Achæmenian dynasty, he kept the armed force under his control by the appointment of generals or commandants distinct from the satraps. Unlike the Parthian monarchs, he did not intrust the defense or tranquillity of his dominions to a mere militia; but maintained a standing army on a war footing, regularly paid and disciplined.

His chief endeavors were to administer strict justice. Daily reports were made to him concerning all that occurred in his capital and in every province of his Empire, and he was acquainted with even the private actions of his subjects. He earnestly desired that all well-disposed persons should feel absolutely secure in their lives, their property and their honor. He severely punished crimes, even making entire families suffer for the misdeeds of one of their members.

Artaxerxes was an absolute monarch, like all Oriental sovereigns, having entire power of life and death over his subjects, and deciding all matters according to his own will and pleasure. But like most Oriental despots, he took the advice of counselors. In his foreign relations he consulted with the vassal kings, the satraps and the commandants. In religious affairs he counseled with the Magi.

In his "testament," or "dying speech," which he addressed to his son Sapor, he said: "Never forget, that, as a king, you are at once the protector of religion and of your country. Consider the altar and the throne as inseparable. They must always sustain each other. A sovereign without religion is a tyrant, and a people who have none may be deemed the most monstrous of all societies. Religion may exist without a state, but a state cannot exist without religion, and it is by holy laws that a political association can alone be bound. You should be to your people an example of piety and of virtue, but without pride or ostentation. * * * * * Remember, my son, that it is the prosperity or adversity of the ruler which forms the happiness or misery of his subjects, and that the fate of the nation depends on the conduct of the individual who fills the throne. The world is exposed to constant vicissitudes. Learn, therefore, to meet the frowns of fortune with courage and fortitude, and to receive her smiles with moderation and wisdom. To sum up all—may your administration be such as to bring, at a future day, the blessings of those whom God has confided to our parental care upon both your memory and mine!"

The Arabian writer Maçoudi and Tabari say that Artaxerxes near the end of his life appointed his favorite son Sapor regent and relinquished to him the government, at the same time appointing him his successor. Artaxerxes placed Sapor's effigy on one of his later coins, and in a bas-relief at Takht-i-Bostan he is represented as investing Sapor with the royal diadem. The coins of Artaxerxes present five different types.

On the accession of Artaxerxes there was immediately a revival of Persian art, which under the Parthians had sunk to its lowest ebb; and the coins of Artaxerxes, compared with those of the later Parthian kings, at once show a renaissance. The head is well cut; the features have individuality and expression, and the epigraph is sufficiently legible. The sculpture of Artaxerxes is still more surprising. He represents himself as receiving the Persian diadem from the hands of Ahura-Mazda, both he and the god being mounted upon chargers of a stout breed spiritedly portrayed; while Arsaces XXX., the last Parthian king, lies prostrate under the feet of the steed of Artaxerxes; and under the feet of Ahura-Mazda is the form of Angra-Mainyus, also prostrate, and apparently dead.

The coins of Artaxerxes and of the Sassanian Kings of Persia are based partly upon Roman and partly upon Parthian models. Artaxerxes found current in the countries which he overran and conquered a gold and a silver coinage, coming from different sources and possessing no common measure. As he retained what he found already existing, the New Persian monetary system had an anomalous character.

The bas-relief of Artaxerxes already alluded to is accompanied by two bilingual inscriptions, which possess much antiquarian and some historical interest. These inscriptions proved the continued use of the Greek character and language by the Sassanian kings; while they also show the character of the native language and letters which the New Persians used when they suddenly came into notice as the ruling people of Western Asia; and they inform us of the relationship of Artaxerxes to Babek, or Papak, of the rank of Babek, and of the religious sympathies of the Sassanians.

The bas-reliefs and their inscriptions show us that the New Persians under the early Sassanian kings exhibited their great theological personages in sculptured forms, and reveal to us the actual forms then regarded as appropriate to Ahura-Mazda (Ormazd) and Angra-Mainyus (Ahriman). These inscriptions also show that the Sassanian sovereigns, from the very beginning of their monarchy, claimed a qualified divinity for themselves, assuming the title of *Bag*, or *Alha*, meaning "god," and, according to the Greek version of their legends, the corresponding name of *Zeus*.

At the very beginning of his reign Artaxerxes addressed himself to the task of substituting the ancestral Persian religion in the place of the Parthian idolatry. This religion —as already observed in the history of the ancient Medes and Persians—was a combination of Dualism with a qualified creature-worship, and a special reverence for the elements —earth, air, fire and water. In other words, it was a combination of Zoroastrianism and Magism. We refer the reader to our account of the ancient Medes and Persians for a description of this religion.

Artaxerxes found the Magi depressed by the systematic action of the later Parthian kings, who had virtually abandoned the Zoroastrian religion and had become mere idolators. He found the fire-altars in ruins, the sacred flame extinguished, and the most essential of the Magian ceremonies and practices disregarded. He found idolatry established in every portion of his dominions except in Persia proper. Temples of the sun abounded, where images of Mithra were the object of worship, and the Mithraic cult was carried out with a variety of imposing ceremonies. Similar temples to the moon existed in many places, and the images of the Arsacidæ were associated with those of the sun and moon gods in the sanctuaries dedicated to them.

Zoroaster's precepts were forgotten. Though the sacred compositions bearing that illustrious sage's name, and which had been transmitted from a remote antiquity, were still preserved in the memory of the faithful few who clung to the old creed, if not in a written form, yet they had ceased to be considered by the great mass of Western Asiatics as binding upon their consciences. In Western Asia were mixed up a score of contradictory creeds, old and new, rational and irrational; the most prominent being Sabaism, or star-worship, Magism, Zoroastrianism, Greek polytheism, teraphim-worship, Chaldee mysticism, Judaism and Christianity.

Artaxerxes undertook to bring order out of this confusion—to establish an absolute uniformity of religion in the place of this extreme diversity. He suppressed idolatry by a general destruction of the images. He raised the Magian hierarchy to a rank of honor and dignity which they had not enjoyed even under the later Achæmenidæ, securing them in a condition of pecuniary independence by assigning them lands and allowing their title to claim a tithe of all the possessions of the faithful. He caused the sacred fire to be rekindled on the altars where it was extinguished, and assigned to certain bodies of priests the charge of maintaining the fire in each locality.

Artaxerxes next proceeded to publish the Zend-Avesta, by collecting Zoroaster's supposed precepts into a volume, for the purpose of establishing a standard of orthodoxy whereto he might require all to conform. He found the Zoroastrians themselves divided into a number of sects, among which he established uniformity by means of a general council, which was attended by Magi from every portion of the New Persian Empire, and which settled what was to be considered the true Zoroastrian faith. Oriental writers tell us that forty thousand, or eighty thousand, Magi, after assembling, reduced themselves to four thousand, to four hundred, to forty, and finally to seven, the most highly respected for their piety and learning. There was one of these seven, a young but holy priest named Ardâ-Viraf, who was recognized as preëminent by the universal consent of his brethren.

Says Milman, in his *History of Christianity*, concerning this priest: "Having passed through the strictest ablutions, and drunk a powerful opiate, he was covered with a white linen and laid to sleep. Watched by seven of the nobles, including the king, he slept for seven days and nights; and, on his reawaking, the whole nation listened with believing wonder to his exposition of the faith of Ormazd, which was carefully written down by an attendant scribe for the benefit of posterity."

Thus was brought about the authoritative issue of the Zend-Avesta, which the learned of Europe have now possessed for almost half a century, and which the labors of Spiegel have in our own day made accessible to the general reader. Though the Zend-Avesta may contain fragments of a very ancient literature, it assumed its present shape in the time of the first of the Sassanidæ, and was perhaps first collected from the mouths of the Zoroastrian priests and published by Ardâ-Viraf. Certain additions may have been made to it since; but Max Müller tells us that "their number was small," and that we "have no reason to doubt that the text of the Avesta, in the days of Ardâ-Viraf, was on the whole exactly the same as at present."

The religious system of the New Persian Empire is thus completely shown to us. After settling the true text of the Zend-Avesta, its interpretation was to be agreed upon. Though the language of this sacred volume was pure Persian, it was of so archaic a type that none but the most learned of the Magi were able to understand it, and it was a dead letter to the common people and even to the ordinary priest. Artaxerxes appears to have recognized the necessity of accompanying the Zend text with a translation and a commentary in the Pehlevi, or Huzvaresh, the Persian language of his own time. Such a translation and commentary exist, and their earlier parts date back to the time of Artaxerxes, who may be credited with the desire to make the Zend-Avesta "understood of the people."

In order to secure uniformity of belief, it was also necessary to give very extensive powers to the Magian priesthood, the keepers and interpreters of the Zend-Avesta. The Magian hierarchy was therefore associated with the Persian king in the civil government and administration. It was declared that the altar and the throne were inseparable and must always sustain each other. The Magi were constituted the great national council of Persia; and while they supported the crown, the crown upheld them against all impugners and enforced their decisions by pains and penalties. Persecution was adopted and asserted as a principle of action without any disguise. An edict of Artaxerxes closed all places of worship except the temples of the fire-worshipers. Christians and Jews, Greeks, Parthians and Arabs, submissively allowed their sanctuaries to be closed; and the non-Zoroastrians of the New Persian Empire—the votaries of foreign religions—were soon estimated at the small number of eighty thousand.

Upon the death of Artaxerxes, in A. D. 240, his son, SAPOR I., or SHAHPUHRI I., became King of Persia. The Persian historians tell us that Sapor's mother was a daughter of Artabanus, or Arsaces XXX., the last Parthian monarch; Artaxerxes having married her after he had conquered her father. The series of wars in which Sapor I. engaged show his active and energetic character. At the beginning of his reign Armenia revolted and attempted to regain its independence, but was reduced to submission.

At the same time Manizen, King of Hatra, or El Hadhr, declared himself independent, and even assumed dominion over the entire region between the Euphrates and the Tigris, the Jezireh of the Arabian geographers. The city of Hatra was betrayed into Sapor's hands by Manizen's daughter, who thus turned against her father and treacherously betrayed him into the power of the Persian king upon the latter's promise to marry her; but, instead of fulfilling his part of the bargain, Sapor delivered the traitress into the hands of the executioner, to suffer the death which she merited on account of her treacherous and unnatural conduct.

These two minor successes encouraged Sapor I. to resume his father's bold projects and to engage in a war with Rome. He crossed the Tigris and invaded the Roman province of Mesopotamia, where he attacked the strong and important city of Nisibis, which he reduced by breaching its walls after it had made a prolonged resistance. Sapor then crossed the Euphrates and invaded the Roman province of Syria, where he surprised and took the rich and luxurious city of Antioch. The Romans under Timesitheus defeated the New Persian invaders in a series of engagements, recovered Antioch, crossed the Euphrates, retook Carrhæ, defeated the Persian king near Resaina (Ras-el-Ain), recovered Nisibis, and again planted the Roman standards on the banks of the Tigris. Sapor I. hastily evacuated most of his conquests and retired across the Euphrates and the Tigris, pursued by the Romans, who garrisoned the various towns of Mesopotamia, and even menaced the great city of Ctesiphon; but a treaty of peace was made between the Roman and New Persian Empires in A. D. 244, Armenia being left to the Persians, while Mesopotamia was restored to the Romans.

In the meantime Bactria revolted from the dominion of the Sassanidæ and recovered its independence, at the same time entering into an alliance with Rome. Sapor I. provoked a second war with Rome by again invading Mesopotamia in A. D. 258, carrying all before him, becoming master of Nisibis, Carrhæ and Edessa, and crossing the Euphrates into Syria and surprising Antioch while that city was occupied in the enjoyment of theatrical and other representations.

The aged Roman Emperor Valerian hastened to the protection of his more eastern provinces, and at first achieved some successes, retaking Antioch and making that city his headquarters during the campaign. But the tide soon turned in favor of the New Persians. Through the treachery of his lieutenant, the Prætorian Prefect, Macrianus, the Emperor Valerian was brought into a difficult position, and the Roman army in Mesopotamia was betrayed into a situation whence escape was impossible, and where its capitulation was but a question of time. A bold attempt to force a way through the Persian lines utterly failed, after which famine and pestilence commenced their work in the Roman camp.

The Emperor Valerian vainly sent envoys to solicit peace and offered to purchase his escape by the payment of an immense sum in gold. Sapor, confident of victory, rejected the overture, and, when the aged Emperor was in the greatest extremity, invited him to a conference, where he treacherously made him a prisoner; whereupon the Roman army surrendered or dispersed. While rival Emperors distracted the Roman world with their dissensions, Sapor invested Miriades, or Cyríades, an obscure citizen of Antioch, with the imperial purple.

Sapor's victory at Edessa exposed the whole of Roman Asia to attack, and the Persian king at once crossed the Euphrates in force and took Antioch a third time. Sapor then overran the Roman provinces of Cilicia and Cappadocia, capturing the famous city of Tarsus, and also taking Cæsaréa Mázaca, which was bravely defended by its governor, Demosthenes, and only captured through the treachery of some of its citizens, Demosthenes escaping by cutting his way through the victorious Persian host.

Sapor ravaged Asia Minor with fire and sword, marking his course everywhere by ruin and devastation, by smoking towns, ravaged fields and heaps of slain; filling the ravines and valleys of Cappadocia with dead bodies, and leading his cavalry across them. He depopulated Antioch, killing or carrying off into slavery nearly the entire population. He suffered his prisoners in numerous instances to perish from hunger, and drove them to water once a day like beasts; thus proving himself a merciless scourge, and an avenger bent on spreading the terror of his name, rather than a conqueror seeking to enlarge his empire. During this plundering expedition Sapor I. met with but one check. His attack upon Emesa (now Hems) was repulsed by the inhabitants led by the High Priest.

When Sapor advanced into Syria he received an embassy from Odenatus, a Syrian or Arab chief, who occupied a position of semi-independence at Palmyra, which had recently become a flourishing commercial city in the midst of the Syrian desert. Odenatus sent a long train of camels laden with presents, consisting partly of rare and precious merchandise, to the King of Persia, imploring him to accept them, and claiming his favorable regard because he had hitherto refrained from hostile acts against the New Persians. Sapor was offended at the tone of this communication, because it was not sufficiently humble to please him. He tore the letter to pieces and trampled it under his feet, exclaiming: "Who is this Odenatus, and of what country, that he ventures thus to address his lord? Let him now, if he would lighten his punishment, come here and fall prostrate before me with his hands tied behind his back. Should he refuse, let him be well assured that I will destroy himself, his race and his land." At the same time he ordered his servants to cast the costly presents of the Palmyrene prince into the Euphrates.

This arrogant and insolent conduct of Sapor I. naturally changed Odenatus from a willing friend into a hostile enemy. The Palmyrene prince, however, remained aloof from the contest until the Persian army commenced its retreat toward the Euphrates, when he collected an army of Syrians and Arabs and harassed the retreating Persian host, cutting off their stragglers and capturing much of their spoil, even taking a part of the Great King's seraglio. The retreating Persians only escaped across the Euphrates with considerable difficulty and loss. On their retreat through Mesopotamia the Persians purchased the neutrality of the people of Edessa by relinquishing to them all the coined money that they had carried off in their raid through Syria, after which their retreat was unmolested, and Sapor returned safely to Persia with most of his army, taking with him his imperial captive.

The writers nearest to Sapor's time tell us that the captive Roman Emperor Valerian grew old in his captivity, and that he was kept in the condition of a slave. Authors of the next generation say that he was exposed to the constant gaze of the multitude, fettered, and clad in the imperial purple, and that whenever Sapor mounted his horse he placed his foot upon his illustrious prisoner's neck. Others say that when Valerian died, about A. D. 265 or 266, his body was flayed and his skin stuffed, and dyed in scarlet and hung up in a Persian temple as a precious trophy, exposed to the view of Roman envoys on their visits to the Great King's court. As the writers of Sapor's own time say nothing of these atrocities, and as Sapor's inscriptions and bas-reliefs do not record anything of the kind, Gibbon's skepticism concerning them may be well founded. The bas-reliefs simply represent Valerian in an humble attitude but not fettered, simply bending his knees in the Great King's presence.

Odenatus of Palmyra resolved upon wresting Mesopotamia from the New Persians, who had held possession of that province as a prize of their victory over Valerian. After a short contest with the Romans under Macrianus and his son Quietus, Odenatus again took the field against the New Persians about A. D. 263, crossed the Euphrates into Mesopotamia, took Carrhæ and Nisibis, defeated Sapor and some of his sons in a battle, drove the whole Persian army into confusion to the gates of Ctesiphon, the Western capital of the New Persian Empire, and besieged that city. Contingents for the relief of the beleaguered capital flocked from all portions of the New Persian Empire; and Odenatus was defeated in several engagements and forced to retreat, but he succeeded in carrying off a vast amount of booty and prisoners, among whom were several satraps. Odenatus also retained possession of Mesopotamia, which remained a portion of the Palmyrene kingdom until the capture of Zenobia, the widow of Odenatus, by the Roman Emperor Aurelian in A. D. 273.

The successes of Odenatus in A. D. 263 were followed by a long period of tranquillity; as that ambitious prince appears to have been satisfied with holding dominion over the region from the Tigris to the Mediterranean, and with the titles of *Augustus*, which he received from the Roman Emperor Gallienus, and *King of Kings*, which he assumed upon his coins. He did not press upon Sapor any further, nor did the Roman Emperor make any serious effort to recover his father's person or avenge his defeat upon the New Persians.

Odenatus was murdered by a kinsman a few years after his great successes; and his widow, Zenobia, who styled herself *Queen of the East*, defeated a Roman expedition under Heraclianus, and governed her kingdom with masculine vigor. The enmity which sprung up between Rome and Palmyra at the time of Zenobia's accession secured Persia from any attack on the part of either.

Relieved from any further necessity of defending his dominions by arms, Sapor employed his remaining years in constructing great works, especially in the erection and ornamentation of a new capital named Shahpur, the ruins of which yet exist near Kazerun, in the province of Fars, and which commemorate the name and afford some indication of the grandeur of the second sovereign of the New Persian Empire. Among these ruins are the remains of buildings and a number of bas-reliefs and rock inscriptions, some of which were the work of Sapor I.

In one of the most remarkable of these works the Persian king is represented on horseback, wearing the crown usually seen upon his coins, and holding by the hand a figure clothed in a tunic, believed to be Miriades, whom he presented to the captured Romans as their sovereign. The kneeling figure of a chieftain, believed to be Valerian, is the foremost to do him homage, and behind this figure are seventeen persons in a double line, apparently representing the different corps of the Roman army. All these persons are on foot; and, in contrast with them, ten guards on horseback are ar-

NEW PERSIAN EMPIRE OF THE SASSANIDÆ.

ranged behind Sapor I., representing his irresistible cavalry.

Another bas-relief at the same place represents a general view of Sapor's triumph on his return to Persia with the captive Valerian. In this bas-relief fifty-seven guards are ranged behind the king, while thirty-three tribute-bearers are in front, having an elephant and a chariot with them. In the center is a group of seven figures, comprising Sapor, who is represented on horseback in his usual costume; Valerian, who is represented under the horse's feet; Miriades, who stands by Sapor's side; three principal tribute-bearers in front of the main figure; and a figure of Victory which floats in the sky.

Tradition also assigns the great dyke at Shuster to Sapor I. This important work is a dam across the river Karun, constructed of cut stones, cemented by lime and fastened together by iron clamps. This dyke is twenty feet wide and about twelve hundred feet long. The whole is a solid mass except in the center, where two small arches have been formed in order to enable a portion of the stream to flow in its natural bed. The greater part of the water is directed eastward into a canal cut for it; and the town of Shuster is thus protected by a water barrier, whereby its position becomes one of immense strength. According to tradition Sapor I. used his power over the captive Valerian to procure Roman engineers for this work; and the great dam is yet called the *Bund-i-Kaisar*, or "Dam of Cæsar," by the inhabitants of the neighboring country.

Sapor I. also erected memorials to himself at Haji-abad, Nakhsh-i-Rajab and Nakhsh-i-Rustam, near Persepolis, and also at Darabgerd, in South-eastern Persia, and other places; most of which yet exist and have been described by different travelers. At Nakhsh-i-Rustam, Valerian is seen in one tablet making his submission, while the glories of Sapor's court are represented in another. In some instances inscriptions accompany the sculptures; one being, like that of Artaxerxes, bilingual, Greek and Persian. Sapor, in the main, follows the phrases of his father, Artaxerxes, but claims a more extensive dominion. Artaxerxes is content to rule over Ariana, or Iran, only while his famous son calls himself lord both of the Aryans and the non-Aryans, or of Iran and Turan. From this it has been inferred that Sapor I. held some Scythic tribes under his dominion.

Sapor's coins resemble those of Artaxerxes in general type, but may be distinguished from them, first by the head-dress, which is either a cap terminating in the head of an eagle, or a mural crown surmounted by an inflated ball; and, secondly, by the emblem on the reverse, which is almost always a fire-altar between two supporters.

The legends on Sapor's coins show that he was a zealous Zoroastrian. His faith was exposed to considerable trial, as there never was a time of greater religious ferment in the East, or a crisis which more shook men's beliefs in ancestral creeds. The absurd idolatry which had generally been prevalent throughout Western Asia for two thousand years—a nature-worship which gave the sanction of religion to the gratification of men's lowest propensities—was shaken to its foundations; and everywhere men were striving after something higher, nobler and truer than had satisfied previous generations for twenty centuries.

The sudden revival of Zoroastrianism, after it had been depressed and nearly forgotten for five centuries, was one result of this stir of men's minds. Another result was the rapid progress of Christianity, which in the course of the third century spread over large parts of the East, taking deep root in Armenia and obtaining some hold in Babylonia, Bactria, and probably even India. Judaism, which for a long time had a footing in Mesopotamia, and which, after the time of the Roman Emperor Adrian, may be considered as having had its headquarters at Babylon, also exhibited signs of life and change, assuming a new form in the schools wherein was compiled the vast and strange work called *the Babylonian Talmud*.

Mani, or Manes, who was born in Persia

about A. D. 240, grew to manhood during the reign of Sapor I., exposed to the influences of the various religions just alluded to, studying the different systems of belief which he found established in Western Asia—the Cabalism of the Babylonian Jews, the Dualism of the Magi, the mysterious doctrines of the Christians, and even the Buddhism of India. He first inclined toward Christianity, and is said to have been admitted to priest's orders and to have ministered to a congregation; but he afterwards aimed at the formation of a new religious creed, which should combine all that was best in the religious systems with which he was acquainted, and omit all that was objectionable or superfluous.

Manes adopted the Dualism of the Zoroastrians, the metempsychosis of India, the angelism and demonism of the Talmud, and the Trinitarianism of the Gospel of Christ. He indentified Christ with Mithra, and assigned Him Mithra's abode in the sun. He assumed to be the Paraclete promised by Christ, who should guide men into all truth; and claimed that his *Ertang*, a sacred book illustrated by pictures of his own painting, should supersede the New Testament. Soon after making these pretensions Manes was expelled from the Christian Church, and was obliged to carry his teaching elsewhere. He then addressed himself to Sapor, who was at first disposed to show him some favor; but when the king discovered what the new teacher's doctrines actually were, Manes was proscribed or threatened with penalties, and was thus obliged to retire to a foreign land.

Thus Sapor I. maintained the Zoroastrian faith in its purity, not allowing himself to be imposed upon by the new teacher's specious eloquence, but ultimately rejecting the strange amalgamation offered by Manes. Though the morality of the Manichæans was pure, and though their religion is by some considered as a kind of Christianity, there were very few points in which it was an improvement upon Zoroastrianism. Its characteristic features were its pronounced and decided Dualism; its questionable Trinitarianism; its teaching regarding Christ, which destroyed the doctrines of the incarnation and the atonement; and its *Ertang*, which was a poor substitute for the Jewish and Christian Scriptures. Its morality was deeply penetrated with asceticism, and was therefore a wrong type and inferior to that preached by Zoroaster. It was well for the progress of Christianity in the East that Sapor rejected the creed of Manes, as the general currency of the debased amalgam would have checked the advance of the purer faith of Christ.

Sapor I. was one of the most remarkable of the Sassanidæ. He was inferior to his father in military talent, but as a statesman he was one of the foremost of the New Persian kings. He maintained Persia's power in the West, and perhaps extended his dominion in the East. He united works of utility with the construction of memorials having only a sentimental and æsthetic value. He liberally patronized art, and is believed to have encouraged foreign as well as native talent. He decided to maintain unimpaired the religious system transmitted to him from his ancestors. He is represented as having been a man of remarkable beauty, of great personal courage, and of a noble and princely liberality. The Orientals also tell us that "he only desired wealth that he might use it for good and great purposes."

Sapor I. died in A. D. 271, after a reign of thirty-one years (A. D. 240-271). Artaxerxes I. and Sapor I.—the first and second sovereigns of the New Persian Empire—were men of mark and renown. Their successors for several generations were comparatively feeble and insignificant. The first burst of vigor and freshness usually attending the advent of a new race to power in the East, or the recovery by an old one of its former position, had passed away; and was followed, as so frequently occurs, by reaction and exhaustion, the monarchs becoming luxurious and inert, while the people readily submitted to a policy the principle of which was " Rest and be thankful." The short reigns of the New Persian kings during this period tended to keep matters in this condition; four monarchs successively occupying the throne within twenty-two years. Sapor I. was succeeded by his son, HORMISDAS I.—also called HORMISDATES I., or HORMUZ I.—who reigned but one year and ten days (A. D. 271-272), during which Mani, who fled from Sapor, returned to Persia and was received with respect and favor. Hormisdas I. received him kindly, permitted him to propagate his doctrines, and even assigned him a castle named Arabion for a residence, whence he spread his views among the Christians of Mesopotamia, and soon founded the sect of the Manichæans, or Manichees, which gave the Christian Church much trouble for several centuries. Some writers tell us that Hormisdas I. founded the city of Ram-Hormuz, in the province of Carmania, now Kerman.

Upon the death of Hormisdas I., in A. D. 272, VARAHRAN I., or VARARANES I., became his successor. Varahran I. reigned only three years (A. D. 272-275); and the Persian historians tell us that he was a mild and amiable ruler, but the little that is known of him does not corroborate this testimony. It is said that he flayed Mani alive, stuffed his skin with straw, and suspended it over the gate of the great city of Shahpur. He followed up this atrocity by persecuting the disciples of Mani, who had organized a hierarchy consisting of twelve apostles, seventy-two bishops, and a numerous priesthood, and whose sect was widely established at the time of his execution. Varahran I. handed such of the Manichæans whom he was able to seize over to the tender mercies of the Magi, who put many of them to death. Many Christians at the same time perished, as the Magian priesthood devoted all heretics to a common destruction.

Varahran I. became the ally of Zenobia, the Queen of the East, the widow and successor of Odenatus of Palmyra. This illustrous queen maintained a position inimical to both Rome and Persia; but when the Roman Emperor Aurelian took the field against her, she made overtures to the New Persians, which were received with favor by the Persian monarch, who sent troops to her assistance. But Varahran I. allowed Zenobia to be defeated and made a captive without making a determined effort to save her, though he continued his alliance with her to the end. After Zenobia's overthrow, Varahran I. sent an embassy to the victorious Aurelian, deprecating his anger and seeking to propitiate him by costly presents, among which were an exceedingly brilliant purple robe from Cashmere and a splendid Persian chariot. The Roman Emperor accepted these gifts and granted the Persian monarch terms of peace. In Aurelian's triumph at Rome, in A. D. 274, the Persian envoys bore the presents with which their sovereign appeased the wrath of the Roman Emperor.

But in A. D. 275 Aurelian declared war against the New Persians and marched for the East with a large army, but was assassinated near Byzantium. Varahran I. died the same year, and was succeeded on the Persian throne by his young son, VARAHRAN II., who is said to have ruled tyrannically at first, and to have disgusted all his principal nobles, who conspired against his life. The chief of the Magians interposed, and so alarmed the king that he acknowledged himself wrong and promised an entire change of policy, whereupon the nobles returned to their allegiance. Varahran II. thereafter ruled with such wisdom and moderation as to gain popularity with all classes of his subjects.

Varahran II. engaged in a war with the Segestani, or Sacastani, the inhabitants of Segestan, or Seistan, a people of Scythic origin, and soon reduced them to subjection; after which he engaged in a long and indecisive war with some native tribes of Afghanistan. In A. D. 283 he became involved in hostilities with the Roman Emperor Carus, who crossed the Euphrates and quickly overran Mesopotamia, while Persia was distracted by a civil war and most of her forces were engaged in the struggle with the Afghan tribes. The Roman writers tell us that the Romans recovered Mesopotamia, ravaged the whole tract between the Euphrates and the Tigris, and easily took the two great cities of Seleucia and Ctesiphon. Persia proper was saved from Roman invasion by the sudden death of the Emperor Carus during a thunderstorm in A. D. 283, whereupon the Romans retreated and made peace with the Persian king.

In A. D. 286 the celebrated Roman Emperor Diocletian provoked a war with Persia by espousing the cause of Tiridates, son of Chosroës, and directed his efforts to the establishment of that Arsacid prince as a Roman tributary on his father's throne. Varahran II. was unable to offer any effectual resistance. Armenia had at this time been a Persian province for almost half a century, but it had not been conciliated or united with the rest of the New Persian Empire. The Armenian people had been distrusted and oppressed. The Armenian nobles had been deprived of employment, while a heavy tribute had been imposed upon their country, and a religious revolution had been violently effected.

Accordingly when Tiridates, supported by a Roman contingent, appeared upon the Armenian frontiers, the whole Armenian population welcomed him with transports of joy and loyalty. All the Armenian nobles flocked to his standard, and instantly acknowledged him as their king, while the Armenian people received him with acclamations. A native Arsacid prince received the support of all Armenians, who enthusiastically engaged in a war of independence. The fact that Tiridates was but a puppet in the hands of the Roman Emperor, and that Armenia was simply changing foreign masters, was lost sight óf.

Tiridates was at first successful; defeating two Persian armies in the open field, driving the Persian garrisons out of the more important Armenian towns, and becoming undisputed master of the country. He even invaded the other Persian provinces, particularly Assyria, and won signal victories on recognized Persian territory. The native Armenian writers tell us that Tiridates performed most extraordinary personal exploits; defeating singly a corps of giants, and routing on foot a large Persian detachment mounted on elephants. Though these statements are highly exaggerated, Tiridates was complete master of the Armenian highland within a year of his invasion, and was in a position to carry his victorious arms beyond the Armenian frontiers.

Varahran II. died in A. D. 292, after a reign of seventeen years, leaving the Persian crown to his elder son, VARAHRAN III., who was of an amiable temper but a feeble constitution. He was with difficulty persuaded to accept the throne, and anticipated an early death from the very first. According to the best authorities his reign lasted but four months.

Upon the death of Varahran III., in A. D. 292, two brothers, Narses and Hormisdas, contended for the Persian crown. Narses was from the very first preferred by the Persians, and Hormisdas relied chiefly for success upon the arms of foreign barbarians. As Hormisdas was beaten in conflicts in which Persians fought against Persians, he called the wild hordes of the North to his aid—Gelli from the shores of the Caspian, Scyths from the Oxus or the regions beyond, and Russians, who were now mentioned for the first time by a classical writer. Hormisdas failed in his efforts and is no more heard of, while NARSES was firmly established on the Persian throne.

In A. D. 296 Narses made war on Tiridates of Armenia, who had made constant raids into Persian territory, sometimes even as far south as Ctesiphon. Unable to resist the invading arms of Narses, Tiridates sought refuge in flight, thus leaving Armenia in the hands of the Persians, and a second time placed himself under the protection of Rome. The Roman Emperor Diocletian made war on the Persian king in A. D. 296, and sent an army under his son-in-law Galerius to reinstate Tiridates on the Armenian throne and to punish Narses.

Narses having invaded the Roman province of Mesopotamia, Galerius attempted to expel him, but, after two indecisive battles, he was defeated most disastrously near Carrhæ, near the very site of the disastrous defeat and death of Crassus by the Parthians three and a half centuries before. Both Galerius and Tiridates of Armenia escaped from the field, Tiridates swimming the Euphrates in safety. The vanquished Galerius hastened toward Antioch to rejoin his father-in-law, the Emperor Diocletian, who was so offended that he refused to speak to his unfortunate son-in-law or to listen to his explanations and apologies until he had followed him a mile on foot.

Galerius importuned Diocletian for an opportunity to redeem the past and recover his lost laurels, and the Emperor finally acceded to his wishes. Accordingly Galerius led a Roman army of twenty-five thousand men into Armenia in A. D. 297, and defeated Narses, making many illustrious Persians prisoners, and also taking captive the wives, sisters and many of the children of the Persian monarch, and obtaining possession of his military chest. Narses was wounded, and his army was totally destroyed.

The Persian king sent Apharban as an envoy to the camp of Galerius to solicit peace. Apharban implored for moderation and clemency, but Galerius reminded him of the barbarous treatment of Valerian and dismissed the envoy. After congratulating Galerius upon his victory, Diocletian sent Sicorius Probus as an envoy to the Persian king in Media to offer peace. Narses received the Roman envoy with all honor, but detained him until he had collected a large army, merely for the purpose of securing better terms by the display of force. The Persian king was surprised at the moderation of the Roman demands; and peace was accordingly concluded, the Tigris being recognized as the boundary between the Roman and New Persian Empires, and Persia yielding to Rome the protectorate over Iberia, along the western shore of the Caspian, including the right of giving investiture to the Iberian kings.

Narses abdicated the Persian throne in A. D. 301, and was succeeded by his son HORMISDAS II., whose reign lasted but eight years (A. D. 301-309). Hormisdas II. had a pleasing personal appearance, and was able to control his naturally harsh temper. His reign was one of absolute peace, and he devoted himself to the welfare of his subjects. He displayed a remarkable taste for building. In his journeys through his dominions, he was followed by an army of masons who rebuilt the ruined towns and villages, repairing dilapidated homesteads and cottages with the same care as the public edifices. Some writers tell us that Hormisdas II. founded several new towns in Susiana, or Khusistan; while others say that he built the important city of Hormuz, or Ram-Hormuz, in the province of Kerman; but others state that this city was founded by Hormisdas I.

Hormisdas II. established a new Court of Justice for the express purpose of listening to the complaints of the poor and weak against oppression and extortion by the rich and powerful; the Judges being required to redress such wrongs and to punish the oppressors. To strengthen the authority of this court and secure impartial sentences, the king himself frequently presided over it, hearing causes and pronouncing judgments in person. Thus the most powerful and influential nobles were made to feel that they could not offend without being subjected to proper punishment, while the weakest and poorest of the people were encouraged to come forward and make complaint if they had suffered injury.

It is said that, among his other wives, Hormisdas II. married a daughter of the King of Cabul. From the first to the fourth century Afghanistan seems to have been governed by princes of Scythian descent and of considerable wealth and power. Kadphises, Kanerki, Kenorano, Ooerki and Baraoro had the principal seat of their empire in the region about Cabul and Jellalabad, from which center they exercised an extensive dominion. Their extensive gold coinage shows them to have been monarchs of vast wealth, while their use of the Greek letters and language indicates a certain degree of civilization.

The reigning King of Cabul is said to have sent his daughter to her husband's court in Persia with a wardrobe and ornaments of the utmost magnificence and costliness.

Hormisdas II. had a son named Hormisdas, who grew to manhood during his father's reign. This prince was regarded as the heir-apparent, but was no favorite with the Persian nobles, who openly and publicly insulted him during the celebration of the king's birthday, which was always the greatest yearly festival in Persia. All the nobles, being invited to the banquet, came and took their respective places. The prince arrived late, bringing with him a quantity of game, the produce of the morning's chase. The nobles, in direct violation of the rules of etiquette, did not rise from their seats and did not take the slightest notice of the prince's arrival—an indignity which naturally aroused his resentment. In the heat of the moment, the prince loudly exclaimed that "those who had insulted him should one day suffer for it—their fate should be the fate of Marsyas." This threat was at first only understood by one chieftain, who explained to his fellows that according to the Greek myth Marsyas was flayed alive—a punishment common in Persia. The nobles, fearing that the prince intended to carry out his threat, became thoroughly alienated from him and resolved that he should never reign, laying up the dread threat in their memory and patiently waiting for the moment when the throne would become vacant.

These nobles did not have to wait very long. King Hormisdas II. died within a few years (A. D. 309), whereupon the nobles rose in insurrection, seized prince Hormisdas and cast him into a dungeon, intending that he should remain there for the rest of his life. They themselves assumed the direction of public affairs, and as prince Hormisdas was the only son of his father, one of whose widows was about to become a mother, they proclaimed the unborn infant King of Persia. The short interregnum of a few months was ended when this widow of Hormisdas II. fortunately gave birth to a boy, thus ending the difficulties of the succession.

All classes of Persians readily acquiesced in the rule of the infant king, who received the name of SAPOR II.

The reign of Sapor II. lasted about seventy years. He was born in A. D. 309, and died in A. D. 379. He thus reigned almost three-quarters of a century; and was contemporary with the Roman Emperors Galerius, Constantine the Great, Constantius II. and Constans, Julian the Apostate, Jovian, Valentinian I. and Valens, Gratian and Theodosius the Great, and Valentinian II. This long reign may be divided into two periods. The first period, embracing a space of twenty-eight years, from A. D. 309 to A. D. 337, comprised the sixteen years of Sapor's minority and the twelve years during which he waged successful wars with the Arabs. The second period was the time of his wars with the Romans.

During Sapor's minority the neighboring nations attacked and ravaged the New Persian Empire with impunity. The Arabs made constant raids into Babylonia, Khusistan, and the neighboring regions; desolating these provinces and carrying the horrors of war into the very heart of the empire. The Arab tribes of Beni-Ayar and Abdul-Kaïs, dwelling along the southern shores of the Persian Gulf, took the lead in these inroads; inflicting terrible sufferings on the inhabitants of the provinces which they invaded. About the same time a Mesopotamian chief named Tayer, or Thair, attacked Ctesiphon, took that western capital of the New Persian Empire by storm, and made captive a sister or aunt of King Sapor II.

The nobles who directed the Persian government during the king's minority were incapable of checking these incursions, and for sixteen years the marauding bands had the advantage. Persia was gradually becoming weaker, more impoverished, and more unable to recover herself. It is said that the young king displayed extraordinary discretion and intelligence; diligently training himself in all manly exercises, and preparing himself mentally and physically for the important duties of his station.

When Sapor II. attained the age of sixteen his minority ceased, but at a later age than Oriental ideas require; and he asserted his manhood, placed himself at the head of his army, and took the entire direction of civil and military affairs into his own hands.

Thenceforth the fortunes of Persia rose. After repelling and chastising the marauding bands on Persian territory, Sapor II. assumed the offensive. He collected a fleet, placed his troops on board, and conveyed them to the city of El Katif, an important town on the southern coast of the Persian Gulf, where he disembarked and proceeded to ravage the neighboring region with fire and sword. In this and a long series of expeditions he devastated the whole region of the Hejer; gaining many victories over the Arab tribes, such as the Temanites, the Beni-Waïel, the Abdul Kaïs, and others who had taken a prominent part in raids into Persian territory.

Sapor's military genius and his valor were everywhere conspicuous, but he tarnished his triumphs by the most inhuman cruelties. Exasperated by the sufferings of his countrymen for so many years, he massacred the greater portion of every tribe that he conquered; and the captives who escaped death had their shoulders pierced, and in the wound was inserted a string or thong by which they were dragged into captivity. These atrocities were approved by the age and by the nation; and the king who ordered them was saluted with the title of *Dhoulactaf*, or "Lord of the Shoulders," by his admiring subjects.

At the same time Sapor II. sanctioned cruelties almost as great toward his Christian subjects. His Zoroastrian zeal was so great that he felt it his duty to check the progress of Christianity in his dominions. Soon after attaining his majority he issued severe edicts against the Christians, and when they sought the Roman Emperor's protection he punished their disloyalty by imposing an additional oppressive tax. When Symeon, Archbishop of Seleucia, complained of this additional burden in an offensive manner, Sapor retaliated by closing the Christian Churches, confiscating the ecclesiastical property, and putting the complainants to death.

When the Roman Emperor Constantine the Great, who had assumed the character of a sort of general protector of the Christians throughout the world, heard of these persecutions of the Christian subjects of the Persian king, he remonstrated with Sapor II., but to no purpose. Sapor II. had resolved to renew the struggle which had been ended so unfavorably by his grandfather, Narses, forty years before. Making Constantine's interference in Persian affairs and his encouragement of the Persian monarch's Christian subjects a ground of complaint, Sapor II. began to threaten hostilities. Some negotiations followed, but both sides resolved upon war. Constantine's death in A. D. 337 dispelled the last chance of peace, as his great military fame had caused the Persian monarch to hesitate; but upon hearing of the great Emperor's death Sapor instantly commenced hostilities.

Prince Hormisdas, Sapor's elder brother and the rightful heir to the Persian throne, had, after a long imprisonment, contrived, with his wife's help, to escape from his dungeon, and had fled for refuge to Constantine's court as early as A. D. 323. The refugee prince had been received by Constantine with every mark of distinction and honor, and had been given a maintenance suited to his rank, also enjoying other favors. Fear that Constantine might create dissensions among the Persians by setting up prince Hormisdas as a pretender to the Persian crown may have caused Sapor's hesitation to engage in war with the Roman Empire during Constantine's reign.

The division of the Roman Empire among three Emperors after Constantine's death, and the outburst of licentiousness and violence among the Roman soldiery in the imperial capital and in the Eastern Roman provinces, gave Sapor II. high hopes of success; while the distracted condition of Armenia was also such as to encourage the Persian king. Though King Tiridates of Armenia had persecuted his Christian subjects in the early part of his reign, he had been afterwards converted to Christianity by Gregory the Illuminator; after which he enforced Christianity upon his subjects by fire and sword, thus giving rise to a sanguinary civil and religious war.

A large portion of the Armenians had been firmly attached to the old national idolatry, and had offered a determined resistance to the forced establishment of Christianity by their king. Armenian nobles, priests and people fought desperately in defense of their temples, images and altars; and though the king's persistent will bore down all opposition, a discontented faction arose in Armenia and from time to time resisted its sovereign, being tempted all the while to ally itself with any foreign power from which it might hope for the reëstablishment of the old national religion. After the death of Tiridates, Armenia had fallen under the government of weak monarchs, and Persia had recovered the portion of Media Atropatênê ceded to Armenia by the treaty between Narses and the Roman Emperor Galerius. Sapor, therefore, could reasonably expect to find friends among the Armenians themselves in case he attempted to restore Persian influence over the Armenian highland.

Sapor's forces crossed the Roman frontier soon after Constantine's death; and, after a forty years' peace between them, the two great powers of the world again engaged in a sanguinary contest. After paying the last honors to his illustrious father's remains, the Roman Emperor Constantius II. hastened to the eastern Roman frontier, where he at once applied himself to the task of strengthening the numbers and discipline of his poorly-armed, poorly-provided and mutinous army.

In the meantime Sapor II. set the Arabs and Armenians in motion; exciting the pagan party in Armenia to revolt, to deliver their king, Tiranus, into his power, and to make raids into the Roman territory, while the Arabs ravaged the Roman provinces of Mesopotamia and Syria. Sapor II. himself won moderate successes during the first year of the war (A. D. 337). Constantius II. gained some advantages; restoring the direction of affairs in Armenia to the party friendly to Rome, winning some of the Mesopotamian Arabs from the Persian to the Roman side, and even erecting forts in Persian territory on the east side of the Tigris.

The next year (A. D. 338) Sapor II., resolved upon recovering Mesopotamia, overran and ravaged that Roman province, plundering the crops, driving off the cattle, and burning the villages and homesteads. He laid siege to the strongly fortified city of Nîsibis, the Nazibîna of the Assyrians, and the most important town of Mesopotamia under the Romans. After a gallant defense by the Roman garrison and the inhabitants, who were sustained by the prayers and exhortations of its Christian bishop, St. James, the Persian king was repulsed with heavy loss and forced to raise the siege, which had lasted two months.

The war between Persia and Rome languished for some years after the siege of Nîsibis. The Persians constantly defeated Constantius II. in the open field, but continually failed in their sieges of the Roman fortified posts. To the end of A. D. 340 Sapor II. had made no permanent gain, had struck no decisive blow, but occupied almost the same position as at the beginning of the war. But affairs changed in the year A. D. 341.

After making Tiranus, the Armenian king, captive, Sapor II. tried to make himself master of Armenia, and even endeavored to set up one of his own relatives as king; but his attempt failed on account of the indomitable spirit of the Armenians and their attachment to their Arsacid princes, and tended to throw Armenia into the arms of Rome. Sapor, after some time, convinced of the folly of his policy, endeavored to conciliate the Armenians. He even offered to replace Tiranus on the Armenian throne; but as Tiranus had been blinded by his captors, and therefore could not exercise royal power, according to Oriental notions, he declined the proffered honor, and suggested the substitution of his son Arsaces, who was also a prisoner in Persia, like himself. Sapor II. willingly consented; and Arsaces was released from captivity, whereupon he returned to his own country, and was installed as King of Armenia by the Persians, with the good will of the natives, who were satisfied so long as they had an Arsacid prince on their throne. By this arrangement Armenia became the ally of Persia, and so remained for many years during Sapor's struggle with Rome.

Thus Sapor II. had a friendly sovereign on the Armenian throne, whom he had bound to his cause by oaths, establishing his influence over Armenia and the region northward to the Caucasus. As he still longed to drive the Romans from Mesopotamia, he besieged Nísibis a second time, in A. D. 346; but after a vigorous siege of three months, he was again repulsed and forced to retire with heavy loss, thus losing much of his military prestige.

In A. D. 348 Sapor II. called out the whole military force of his empire and increased it by large bodies of allies and mercenaries; and towards the middle of summer he crossed the Tigris by three bridges and invaded Central Mesopotamia with a large and efficient army. The Roman army under the Emperor Constantius II. was in the vicinity of the town of Síngara, the modern Sinjar. The Roman Emperor acted on the defensive.

Sapor established a fortified camp along the skirts of the Sinjar hills, which he occupied with his archers. His troops then advanced and challenged the Romans to battle —a challenge accepted by the Romans. The battle began about noon, but the Persians soon hastily retreated to their fortified camp, where their cavalry and the flower of their archers were posted. The Persian cavalry charged, but were easily defeated by the Roman legionaries, who, flushed with success, burst into the Persian camp, in spite of the efforts of their leader to check their ardor. The Romans massacred a small detachment within the ramparts, and dispersed among the tents, some in quest of plunder, others only to find some means to quench their raging thirst. In the meantime the sun had set, and night was rapidly approaching.

The Romans, sure of victory, gave way to sleep and feasting. But Sapor II. now saw his opportunity. His light troops on the neighboring hills advanced and surrounded the camp. The Persians, fresh and eager, fought under cover of the darkness, while the fires of the camp showed them the Romans, who were fatigued, sleepy and drunken. The carnage was frightful, the Roman legionaries being overwhelmed with showers of Persian darts and arrows. As flight was impossible, most of the Roman soldiers perished where they stood. In their desperation, the Roman legionaries took an atrocious revenge. Turning their fury upon Sapor's son, whom they had taken prisoner during the day, they beat the innocent youth with whips, wounded him with the points of their weapons, and finally killed him with countless blows.

Sapor neglected to follow up his victory; but in A. D. 350 he made his third and most desperate effort to take Nísibis. He collected a large army and reinforced it by a body of Indian allies, who brought a large troop of elephants with them. He led this army across the Tigris early in the summer, took several fortified posts, and marched northward and commenced the third siege of Nísibis. Count Lucilianus, the Roman commander, defended the place by various subtle stratagems; but the bishop, St. James, roused the enthusiasm of the inhabitants by his exhortations, counsels and prayers.

After battering the walls with his rams and sapping them with mines, Sapor, seeing that the river Mygdonius (now the Jerujer), swollen by the melting snows in the Mons Masius, had overflowed its banks and inundated the plain around Nísibis, embanked the lower part of the plain to prevent the water from running off, thus forming a deep lake around the city, the water gradually creeping up the walls until it had almost reached the battlements. After creating this artificial sea, the Persian king quickly collected or constructed a fleet, on board of which he placed his military engines, and launched the ships upon the waters, thus attacking the walls of the town at great advantage.

The Roman garrison made a determined resistance, setting the engines on fire with torches, and lifting the Persian ships from the water by means of cranes or shattering them with huge stones which they discharged from their balistæ; but still no impression was made. Finally an unforseen circumstance reduced the besieged to the most imminent peril, and almost caused the capture of Nísibis. The inundation was prevented from running off by the mounds of the Persians, thus pressing with constantly increasing force against the defenses of the city, until one part of the wall was unable to withstand the tremendous weight of the water which bore upon it, and suddenly gave way for about one hundred and fifty feet, thus opening a breach through which the Persians were about to enter the town, Sapor taking up his position on an eminence, while his troops rushed to the assault. First came the heavy Persian cavalry and the horse-archers; then the elephants bearing iron towers on their backs, accompanied by heavy-armed infantry.

The Persian assault ended in failure, as usual. The horses became quickly entangled in the ooze and mud which the subsiding waters had left behind. The elephants were not equal to these difficulties, and sank in the swamp as soon as they were wounded, never to rise again. Sapor hastily ordered the assailing column to retreat and to seek shelter in the Persian camp, while he also ordered his light archers to the front; and these were formed into divisions which were to act as reliefs, and were ordered to shower an incessant storm of arrows into the breach made by the waters, for the purpose of preventing the Romans from restoring the ruined wall.

The firmness and activity of the Roman garrison and the inhabitants foiled Sapor's undertaking. While the heavy-armed troops stood in the breach defending themselves against the shower of arrows as best they could, the unarmed inhabitants erected a new wall in their rear, and by the next morning this wall was six feet high. This evidence of his enemies' resolution and resource thoroughly convinced Sapor of the hopelessness of his enterprise. After some delay he raised the siege, which had lasted three months and cost him twenty thousand men, and retired.

Sapor II. was called away from the siege of Nísibis by an invasion of his dominions by the Massagetæ, a nomadic Scythian tribe, whose seat was in the low flat sandy region east of the Caspian, and whose whole life, like that of other Scythian tribes, was spent in war and plunder. Though the Oxus was the nominal boundary of the New Persian Empire on the north-east, the Turanian and Scythian nomads were practically dominant over the entire desert to the foot of the Hyrcanian and Parthian hills, and made constant plundering forays into the fertile region south and east of the desert. Occasionally some bolder chieftain made a deeper inroad and a more sustained attack than usual, spreading consternation around, and terrifying the reigning court for its safety.

The Massagetæ made such an attack towards the autumn of A. D. 350. These people are considered as of Turkoman or Tartar blood, akin to the Usbegs and other Turanian tribes still occupying the sandy steppe. Sapor II. regarded the crisis so serious as to require his personal presence; and thus, while the Roman Emperor was recalled from Mesopotamia to the West of Europe to contend against two rival pretenders to the imperial throne, the Persian king was summoned to his north-eastern frontier to repel a Scythian invasion. War-ridden Mesopotamia was now given a breathing-spell to recover from the ruin and desolation which had overwhelmed it; while the rivalry between Rome and Persia was transferred from the battlefield to the cabinet, and the Roman Emperor found in diplomatic triumphs a compensation for his ill success in the field.

Soon after the close of the first war between Sapor II. and Constantius II., circuuustances once more placed Armenia under Roman influence. Arsaces, whom Sapor II. had placed upon the Armenian throne in A. D. 341, upon the notion that he would govern Armenia in the Persian interest, soon began to chafe under the obligations which Sapor had put upon him, and desired to be a real and independent sovereign, and not a mere vassal monarch. In the interval between A. D. 351 and 359, while the Persian king was engaged in his war with the invading Massagetæ, Arsaces sent envoys to Constantinople requesting the Emperor Constantius II. to give a member of the imperial house in marriage to him.

Constantius II. gladly accepted this proposal, and sent Olympias, the lately betrothed bride of his own brother Constans, to Armenia, where she was welcomed by Arsaces, who made her his chief wife, thus provoking the jealousy and aversion of his previous chief queen, Pharandzem, a native Armenian. This engagement naturally led to a formal alliance between Rome and Armenia—an alliance which Sapor II. vainly endeavored to disturb, and which continued unimpaired to A. D. 359, when another war broke out between the Roman and New Persian Empires.

Sapor's Eastern wars, of which very little is known, occupied him for seven years (A. D. 350-357), and were generally successful. The Eastern enemies of the Persian king were the Chionites and the Gelani, and perhaps the Euseni and the Vertæ. The Chionites are supposed to be the Hiung Nu or Huns. The seat of these wars was east of the Caspian, and Persian influence and power was extended over this region.

While Sapor II. was thus engaged in the far East, he received a letter from the officer whom he had left in charge of his western frontier, informing him that the Romans very much desired a more settled and formal peace than the precarious truce which Mesopotamia had been permitted to enjoy for the last five or six years. Two great Roman officials, Cassianus, Duke of Mesopotamia, and Musonianus, Prætorian Prefect, had considered the time favorable for ending the provisional truce in Mesopotamia by a definite peace, as Sapor II. was engaged in a bloody and difficult war at the eastern extremity of his dominions, while the Emperor Constantius II. was fully occupied with the troubles occasioned by the barbarian inroads into the more western Roman provinces.

Accordingly these two Roman officials had opened negotiations with Tamsapor, the Persian satrap of Adiabêné, suggesting to him that he should sound his sovereign on the subject of concluding peace with Rome. Tamsapor seems to have misunderstood the character of these overtures, or to have misrepresented them to Sapor II. In his dispatch he represented the Emperor Constantius II. as moving in the matter and as humbly imploring the Persian monarch to grant him conditions. The message happened to reach Sapor II. just as he had come to terms with his eastern foes and had succeeded in making them his allies. Elated by his success and considering the Roman overture as a simple acknowledgment of weakness, the Persian king gave it a most haughty reply. His letter was conveyed to the Roman Emperor at Sirmium, in Pannonia, by an ambassador named Narses, and was couched in the following terms :

"Sapor, king of kings, brother of the sun and the moon, and companion of the stars, sends salutation to his brother, Constantius Cæsar. It glads me to see that thou art at last returned to the right way, and art ready to do what is just and fair, having learned by experience that inordinate greed is ofttimes punished by defeat and disaster. As then the voice of truth ought to speak with all openness, and the more illustrious of mankind should make their words mirror their thoughts, I will briefly declare to thee what I propose, not forgetting that I have often said the same things before. Your own authors are witness that the entire tract within the river Strymon and the borders of Macedon was once held by my ancestors; if I required you to restore all this, it would not ill become me (excuse the boast), inasmuch as I excel in virtue and in the splendor of my achievements the whole line of our ancient monarchs. But as moderation delights me, and has always been the rule of my conduct—wherefore from my youth up I have had no occasion to repent of any action—I will be content to receive Mesopotamia and Armenia, which were fraudulently extorted from my grandfather. We Persians have never admitted the principle, which you proclaim with such effrontery, that success in war is always glorious, whether it be the fruit of courage or trickery. In conclusion, if you will take the advice of one who speaks for your good, sacrifice a small tract of territory, one always in dispute and causing continual bloodshed, in order that you may rule the remainder securely. Physicians, remember, often cut and burn, and even amputate portions of the body, that the patient may have the healthy use of what is left to him; and there are animals which, understanding why the hunters chase them, deprive themselves of the thing coveted, to live thenceforth without fear. I warn you, that, if my ambassador returns in vain, I will take the field against you, so soon as the winter is past, with all my forces, confiding in my good fortune and in the fairness of the conditions which I have now offered."

The Persian ambassador, Narses, endeavored by his conciliating manners to atone for his sovereign's rudeness; but the Emperor Constantius II. replied in a dignified and calm tone, as follows: "The Roman Emperor, victorious by land and sea, saluted his brother, King Sapor. His lieutenant in Mesopotamia had meant well in opening a negotiation with a Persian governor; but he had acted without orders, and could not bind his master. Nevertheless, he (Constantius) would not disclaim what had been done, since he did not object to a peace, provided it was fair and honorable. But to ask the master of the whole Roman world to surrender territories which he had successfully defended when he ruled only over the provinces of the East was plainly indecent and absurd. He must add that the employment of threats was futile, and too common an artifice; more especially as the Persians themselves must know that Rome always defended herself when attacked, and that, if occasionally she was vanquished in battle, yet she never failed to have the advantage in the event of every war."

The three Roman envoys intrusted with the delivery of this reply to the Persian king were Prosper, a count of the Empire; Spectacus, a Tribune and notary; and Eustathius, an orator and philosopher, a pupil of the famous Neo-Platonist, Iamblichus, and a friend of St. Basil. The Roman Emperor was most anxious for peace on account of the threatened war with the Alemanni. But the Persian king was bent on war, and had concluded arrangements with the Eastern tribes, so long his enemies, by which they agreed to join his standard with all their forces in the following spring. Sapor was acquainted with the perilous position of Constantius II. in the West, and of the dangers with which he was constantly menaced from external foes.

Antonínus, a Roman official, had recently taken refuge with the Persian king from the claims of pretended creditors, and had been received into high favor because of the information which he was able to communicate concerning the Roman forces. Antonínus was ennobled by Sapor and assigned a place at the Persian royal table. He thus gained great influence over the Persian king, and stimulated him by alternately reproaching him with his past awkwardness, and reminding him of the prospect of easy victory over Rome in the future. He stated that the Roman Emperor, with most of his troops and treasures, was detained in the regions bordering on the Danube, and that the Eastern Roman provinces were left almost unprotected. He exaggerated his own abilities, and exhorted the Persian king to bestir himself and to have confidence in his good fortune. He advised the Persian monarch to flank the strongholds of Mesopotamia and march across that province into the rich and unprotected Syria, which had not been invaded for almost a century.

The views of Antonínus were adopted, but were practically overruled by the circumstances of the situation. A Roman army occupied Mesopotamia and advanced to the Tigris, laying waste the country as the Persians advanced, destroying the forage, relinquishing the indefensible towns to the Persians, and fortifying the Euphrates with castles, military engines and palisades. The swell of the Euphrates prevented the Persians fording the river at the usual point of passage into Syria. By the advice of Antonínus, Sapor marched to the Upper Euphrates, defeated the Romans near Amida, now Diarbekr, and took two castles which defended the town.

Amida was an important town from very ancient times, and had been fortified by the Emperor Constantius II., who repaired its walls and towers. It was defended by a garrison of seven Roman legions, and some horse-archers, composed of foreigners. Sapor, hoping to terrify the town into submission by his mere appearance, rode up to the gates with a small body of troops, expecting the gates to be opened to him; but the brave garrison showered their darts and arrows upon him, directing them against his person, which was conspicuous by its ornaments. One of the Roman weapons passed through his dress and almost wounded him.

Sapor was then induced by his followers to withdraw and leave Grumbates, King of the Chionites, to continue the assault. The next day Grumbates assailed the walls with a body of select troops, but was repulsed with heavy loss; his only son, a promising youth, being killed by his side by a dart from a Roman balista. The death of this prince spread dismay and mourning through the Persian camp, but it was now a point of honor to take a town which had injured one of the Great King's allies, and Grumbates was promised that Amida should be made the funeral pile of his lost son.

Amida was then regularly invested and besieged. Each of the allied nations in the Persian army was assigned its place. The Chionites, burning with a desire for revenge, were on the east. The Vertæ were on the south. The Albanians, warriors from the region west of the Caspian, were on the north. The Segestans, regarded as the bravest soldiers of all, were on the west. A continuous line of Persians, five ranks wide, surrounded the city and supported the foreign auxiliaries. The whole besieging army was estimated at a hundred thousand men; while the besieged, both the garrison and non-combatants, numbered less than thirty thousand.

After a day's pause, Grumbates gave the signal for the assault by hurling a bloody spear into the space before the walls, in the style of a Roman *fetialis*. Thereupon a cloud of darts and arrows were showered upon the besieged, doing considerable damage; while the garrison was also galled with discharges from the Roman military engines which the Persians had captured at Síngara. The vigorous resistance of the garrison, and the heavy losses of the besiegers during the two days' assault, caused the adoption of the slow process of a regular siege. Trenches were opened before the walls, along which the troops advanced under cover of hurdles towards the ditch, which they proceeded to fill up in places. Mounds were then thrown up against the walls, and movable towers were constructed and brought into play, guarded externally with iron, and each mounting a balista.

Sabinianus, the new Roman Prefect of the East, jealous of his subordinate, Ursicínus, rejected the latter's advice to harass the rear of the Persians and attack their convoys. He was old and rich, and both disinclined to and unfit for military enterprise. He said he had positive orders from the imperial court to act on the defensive, and not to imperil his troops by employing them in hazardous adventures. He declared that Amida must not expect relief from him. Ursicínus was obliged to submit to this decision, but chafed terribly under it. His messengers carried the dispiriting tidings to the devoted city. Sabinianus had orders to keep Ursicínus unemployed.

The brave garrison, thus left to its own

resources, made occasional sallies upon the besiegers' works; and on one occasion two Gaulish legions, which had been banished to the East for supporting Magnentius, penetrated into the heart of the besieging camp by night, and imperiled King Sapor's person; but these legions were repulsed with the loss of one-sixth of their number. The losses of both sides were terrific, and a truce of three days followed.

The besieged city soon suffered the horrors of pestilence, while desertion and treachery were also added to the garrison's difficulties. A native of Amida went over to the Persians and informed them that on the southern side of the city a neglected staircase led up from the margin of the Tigris through underground corridors to one of the principal bastians; and under his guidance seventy archers of the Persian guard, picked men, ascended the dark passage at dead of night, occupied the tower, and at dawn the next morning they displayed a scarlet flag, as a sign to their countrymen that a part of the wall was taken. The Persians instantly made an assault; but the garrison recaptured the tower by extraordinary efforts before its occupants could receive any support, and then directed their battering-rams and missiles against the assailing Persian columns, inflicting heavy losses upon them and soon compelling them to return hastily to their camp. The Vertæ, who maintained the siege on the south side of the city, chiefly suffered from this useless attempt.

Having spent seventy days in the siege of Amida, without making any progress in the reduction of the city, Sapor determined on a last effort. He had erected towers higher than the walls, and from these towers missiles were discharged upon the garrison. He had brought his mounds in places to a level with the ramparts, and had forced the garrison to raise mounds within the walls for defense. Having resolved to press the assault day after day, his battering-rams, his infantry and his elephants were all employed; and the garrison were allowed no rest. He personally directed the operations and participated in the supreme struggle, exposing his life and losing many of his attendants.

After a conflict of three days, one of the inner mounds, raised by the garrison behind their wall, gave way suddenly, involving its defenders in its fall, and also filling up the entire space between the wall and the mound raised outside by the Persians. The Persians instantly occupied the way thus made into the town, and speedily put an end to all resistance. Some of the besieged fled; and all who remained, armed and unarmed, regardless of age or sex, were barbarously massacred by the victorious Persians.

Thus Amida fell into the hands of the Persians after a siege of seventy-three days. Sapor was exasperated by the prolonged resistance of the garrison and by the losses which he had sustained in the siege, thirty thousand of his best soldiers having perished, and the son of his principal ally having been among the slain. He therefore allowed his infuriated soldiery to massacre and pillage with impunity. All his captives who belonged to the five provinces beyond the Tigris, claimed by Sapor as his own, but ceded to Rome by his grandfather, were slaughtered in cold blood. Count Ælian, the commander of the brave Roman garrison, was barbarously crucified. Many other Romans of high rank were manacled, and were carried into captivity or slavery into Persia.

The campaign of A. D. 359 ended with this costly victory, and Sapor retired across the Tigris without leaving any garrisons in Mesopotamia. He prepared for the next year's campaign, accumulating stores of all kinds during the winter; and in the spring of A. D. 360 he again invaded the Roman province of Mesopotamia with a larger and better-organized army than the one with which he took Amida the year before. The Roman garrison in Síngara having refused to surrender, the Persian king attacked that city by scaling parties with ladders, and by battering parties which shook the walls with the ram.

The garrison kept the scalers at bay by a constant discharge of stones and darts from their balistæ, arrows from their bows, and leaden balls from their slings. They met the assaults of the battering-ram by efforts to fire the wooden covering which protected it and those who worked it. The besiegers finally discovered a weak point in the defenses of the town—a tower so recently built that the mortar in which the stones were laid was still moist, and which therefore crumbled before the blows of a strong and heavy battering-ram, and soon fell to the ground. The Persians entered the town through the gap and soon put an end to all resistance.

In consequence of this easy victory, Sapor forbade any further bloodshed, and ordered that as many as possible of the garrison and inhabitants should be taken alive. He revived the favorite policy of the most ancient Oriental sovereigns by transporting his captives to the extreme eastern parts of his empire, where he might employ them in defending his frontier against the Scythians and the Indians.

After the capture of Síngara, Sapor marched northward and attacked the strong fort of Bezabde, on the east bank of the Tigris, the chief city of the province of Zabdicêné. This place was highly valued by the Romans, who fortified it partially with a double wall, and defended it with three legions and a large body of Kurdish archers. Sapor reconnoitered the place and recklessly exposed his life. He sent a flag of truce to demand a surrender, sending some prisoners of high rank taken at Síngara, along with the messengers, to prevent his convoys being fired upon by the enemy. This device succeeded, but the garrison determined to resist to the last. All the known resources of attack and defense were again brought into play; and after a long siege the wall was breached, the city was taken, and its garrison was indiscriminately massacred. Sapor carefully repaired the defenses of Bezabde, provisioned it abundantly, and garrisoned it with some of his best troops.

After the capture of Bezabde the Persian king took many lesser strongholds, which offered little resistance. Near the end of the year (A. D. 360) he attacked the strong fortress of Virta, on the Tigris, but failed to persuade or force the garrison to surrender; and, after considerable loss, the Persian king reluctantly relinquished the siege and returned to his own country.

In the meantime the Roman Emperor Constantius II. proceeded to the East; and when Bezabde refused to surrender, he laid siege to that strong fortress, but his repeated assaults failed to reduce the place, and the bold sallies of the garrison destroyed the Roman works. The Emperor was finally obliged to relinquish the siege, whereupon he retired across the Euphrates and went into winter quarters at Antioch.

The successes of Sapor II. in the campaigns of A. D. 359 and 360—his captures of Amida, Síngara and Bezabde, and the repulse of Constantius II. before the last-named city—tended to shake the fidelity of the Roman vassal kings, Arsaces of Armenia and Meribanes of Iberia. Therefore Constantius II. sent emissaries to these tributary monarchs, and sought to secure their fidelity by bestowing upon them valuable gifts. The Roman Emperor succeeded so far as to prevent any revolt of these dependent sovereigns, who remained nominally subject to Rome.

Both the Persian and Roman monarchs were inactive during the year A. D. 361; and Constantius II. died near the close of the year, whereupon Julian the Apostate became sovereign of the vast Roman Empire. Sapor II. found Julian a far abler antagonist than Constantius II. had been. Julian assigned the legions he had collected for the campaign of A. D. 362 to two generals, Victor, a distinguished Roman, and Prince Hormisdas, the Persian refugee, who safely led the legions to Antioch, where the new Emperor himself arrived during the summer. By the advice of his counselors, Julian deferred the campaign until the next year, and passed the winter of A. D. 362-3 in collecting ships, military stores and engines of war.

During Julian's stay at Antioch he received an embassy from King Sapor II., who made overtures of peace. The new Roman Emperor treated the Persian envoys with great haughtiness and rudeness; tearing their sovereign's autograph letter to pieces before their faces, and responding with a contemptuous smile that "there was no occasion for an exchange of thought between him and the Persian king by messengers, since he intended very shortly to treat with him in person." After receiving this rebuff, the Persian envoys returned to their sovereign and informed him that he must prepare to resist a serious invasion.

About the same time the Roman Emperor received offers of assistance from the independent or semi-independent princes and chieftains of the regions bordering on Mesopotamia; but Julian rejected these overtures, saying that it was for Rome rather to give aid to her allies than to receive assistance from them. He, however, had taken a strong body of Gothic auxiliaries into his service, and had called upon the neighboring Arab tribes to fulfil their promise to lend him troops, but he afterwards allowed these brave nomads to become disaffected.

Early in A. D. 363 Julian addressed a letter to Arsaces, King of Armenia, ordering him to levy a considerable army and to be ready to execute such commands as he would shortly receive. The haughty and offensive character of this letter affronted Arsaces, who desired to remain neutral in the war, as he was under obligations to both Rome and Persia, and felt no interest in the standing quarrel between them, while it was for his advantage to have them evenly balanced. The Armenian people, the most educated of whom were now strongly attached to the Christian religion, supported their king in his course; as they hated Julian the Apostate, who had renounced Christianity and become a pagan, and who had intimated his design of sweeping the religion of Christ from the face of the earth. Moses of Chorênê, the great Armenian historian, stated that Julian the Apostate offered an open insult to the Armenian religion.

Julian's own troops numbered almost a hundred thousand, while Armenia and the Arabs were expected to furnish considerable forces. In the spring of A. D. 363 Julian marched from Antioch hastily to the Euphrates, crossed the river at Hierapolis by a bridge of boats, and proceeded to Carrhæ, the Haran of Abraham's time. He then divided his army; sending a force under Procopius, his relative, and Sebastian, Duke of Egypt, to Armenia, to join the Armenian king in invading and ravaging Media, and then to join him at Ctesiphon; and with the main body of his army he marched from Carrhæ down the Euphrates valley to Callinícus, or Nicephorium, where the Arab chiefs made their submission and presented the Emperor with a golden crown, and where his fleet of eleven hundred vessels made its appearance.

Thence the Roman Emperor marched to Circésium; whence he proceeded to invade the Persian territory, placing his cavalry under the command of Prince Hormisdas, the Persian refugee, and some of his select legions under the command of Nevitta, and retaining the main body under his own direction; while a flying corps of fifteen hundred men proceeded in advance as a reconnoitering party, and the rear was covered by a detachment under Secundínus, Duke of Osrhoëne, Dagalaiphus and Victor.

Julian crossed the Khabour in April by a bridge of boats, which he immediately broke up, and marched along the Euphrates, supported by his fleet. At Zaitha, where Gordian was murdered and buried, the Emperor encouraged his soldiers by an eloquent speech, recounting the past Roman successes, and promising an easy victory over the Persian king. He then marched to Anathan, the modern Anah, a strong fortress on an island in the Euphrates, garrisoned by a Persian force. After failing to surprise the place by a night attack, Julian caused Prince Hormisdas to persuade the garrison to surrender the fort and place themselves under his mercy. Julian burned Anathan and sent his prisoners to Syria, settling them in the territory of Chalcis, near Antioch.

Thilutha, another strong fortress, on an island eight miles below Anathan, was held by a Persian garrison. Feeling unable to take it, Julian sought to persuade the garrison to surrender. The garrison rejected his overtures, but promised to remain neutral and not to molest his advance so long as they were not attacked. Julian left Thilutha unassailed and marched on, allowing other towns also to assume a neutral position, and thus permitting the Euphrates route to remain practically in Persian hands.

The ancient town of Diacira, or Hit, on the west side of the Euphrates, was well provided with stores and provisions, but was deserted by its male inhabitants, and the women were massacred by the Romans. At Zaragardia, or Ozogardana, was a stone pedestal known to the natives as "Trajan's Tribunal," in memory of that great Roman Emperor's expedition against the Parthians a century and a half before.

When the Roman army thus arrived on the fertile alluvium of Babylonia, the Persians changed their passive attitude and began an active system of perpetual warfare; placing a Surena, or general of the first rank, in the field, at the head of a strong body of cavalry, and accompanied by an Arab sheikh called Malik, or King Rodosaces. The Persians retreated as Julian advanced; but continually delayed his progress by harassing his army, cutting off stragglers, and threatening every unsupported detachment.

On one occasion Prince Hormisdas was almost made a prisoner to the Surena. On another occasion the Persian force, after allowing the Roman vanguard to proceed unmolested, suddenly appeared on the southern bank of one of the great canals connecting the Tigris and the Euphrates, and sought to prevent Julian's main army from crossing the canal. But the Roman Emperor detached troops under Victor to make a long circuit, cross the canal far to the east, recall Lucilianus with the vanguard, and then attack the Surena's troops in the rear; and he thus finally overcame the resistance in his front and got across the canal.

Julian continued his march along the Euphrates, and soon came to the city of Perisabor (now Firuz-Shapur), almost as important as Ctesiphon. As the inhabitants refused all terms, and insulted Prince Hormisdas, who was sent to treat with them, by reproaching him as a deserter and a traitor, the Roman Emperor resolved to besiege the town to force it to surrender. Perisabor was surrounded with a double wall, and was situated on an island formed by the Euphrates, a canal, and a trench connecting the canal with the river. The citadel, on the north, commanding the Euphrates, was particularly strong; and the garrison was large, brave and confident. But the walls were partly composed of brick laid in bitumen, and were thus weak, so that the Romans easily shattered one of the corner towers with the battering-ram, thus gaining an entrance into the city.

The real struggle now commenced. The brave garrison retreated into the citadel, which was of imposing height, and from which they galled the Romans who had entered the town with an incessant shower of arrows, darts and stones. As the ordinary catapults and balistæ of the Romans could not avail against such a storm descending from such a height, Julian attempted to burst open one of the gates on the second day of the siege. Accompanied by a small band, who formed a roof over his head with their shields, and by a few sappers with their implements, the Roman Emperor approached the gate-tower, and made his troops begin their operations. As the doors were found to be protected by fastenings, too strong to make any immediate impression upon them, and as the alarmed garrison kept up a furious discharge of missiles on the bold assailants, the Emperor was obliged to relinquish the daring effort and to retire.

Julian then constructed a movable tower like the *Helepolis* invented by Demetrius Poliorcétes seven centuries before, thus placing the assailants on a level with the garrison even on the highest ramparts. The garrison, feeling that they could not resist the new machine, anticipated its use by surrendering. The Roman Emperor consented to spare their lives, and allowed them to retire and join their countrymen, each man taking with him a spare garment and some money. The victorious Romans obtained possession of the corn, arms and other valuables found within the walls of the city. The Emperor distributed among his troops whatever was serviceable, while that which was useless was cast into the Euphrates or burned.

Julian continued his march along the Euphrates, while the dashes of the Persian cavalry caused him some sensible losses. He finally came to the point where the *Nahr-Malcha*, or "Royal River," the principal canal connecting the Euphrates with the Tigris, branched off from the Euphrates and ran almost directly east to the vicinity of Ctesiphon. The canal was navigable by the Roman ships, and the Emperor therefore directed his march eastward along the canal, following the route taken by Septimius Sevérus in his expedition against the Parthians, a century and a half before. As the Persians flooded the country with water and disputed his advance at every favorable point, his progress was slow and difficult; but by felling the palms which grew so abundantly in this famous region, and forming them into rafts supported by inflated skins, Julian was able to pass the inundated region.

When the Roman Emperor approached within about eleven miles from Ctesiphon, his progress was obstructed by the fortress of Maogamalcha, or Besuchis, erected to protect the western capital of the new Persian Empire, and being strongly fortified, commanded by a strong citadel, and held by a large and brave garrison. As a part of the garrison made a sally against the Roman army, Julian laid siege to the town. All the usual arts of attack and defense were employed for several days; while the garrison used blazing balls of bitumen, which they shot from their high towers against the besiegers and their works. The Emperor Julian continued assailing the walls and gates with his battering-rams; while he also caused his men to construct a mine, which was carried under both of the walls of the city, thus enabling him to introduce suddenly a body of troops into the heart of the city, and all resistance was at an end.

Thus fell the strong fortress of Maogamalcha, which had just boasted of being impregnable and had laughed to scorn the vain efforts of the Roman Emperor. The triumphant Romans sacked and pillaged right and left, and massacred the entire population, without distinction of age or sex. The commandant of the fortress was executed on a trivial charge; and a miserable remnant of the populace which had concealed itself in caves and cellars was hunted out, smoke and fire being employed to drive the fugitives from their hiding-places, or to cause them to perish in their darksome dens by suffocation.

Only the river Tigris was now between the Roman army and the great city of Ctesiphon, which had for centuries been successively a capital of the Parthian and New Persian Empires. It had been in later Parthian times perhaps the sole capital of the great empire of the Arsacidæ. It was also the western capital of the Sassanidæ; being secondary only to Persepolis, or Istakr, the ordinary residence of the New Persian court. In the vicinity of Ctesiphon were various royal hunting-seats, surrounded by shady gardens and adorned with paintings and bas-reliefs; while near these were parks or "paradises," containing the game kept for the monarch's sport, including lions, wild-boars and fierce bears.

As Julian advanced, these pleasure-grounds successively fell into his possession; and the rude Roman soldiery trampled the flowers and shrubs under foot, destroyed the wild beasts, and burned the residences. The Roman army spread ruin and desolation over a most fertile district, after drawing abundant supplies from it in their advance, leaving only behind them a blackened, wasted, and almost uninhabited region. One of Sapor's sons made a reconnoissance in force, but retired when he saw the strength of the Roman advanced guard.

Julian had now arrived at the western suburb of Ctesiphon, the suburb which was formerly the great city of Seleucia, but which was at this time called Coché. Some country people whom he had seized showed him the line of the canal which his great predecessors, Trajan and Septimius Sevérus, had cut from the Nahr-Malcha to a point on the Tigris above Ctesiphon. The Persians had erected a strong dam with sluices on the Nahr-Malcha where the short canal began, by this means turning a part of the water into the Roman cutting. Julian caused the cutting to be cleared out and the dam to be torn down, whereupon the main body of the stream flowed into the old channel, which filled rapidly and was discovered to be navigable by the largest Roman vessels. Thus the Roman fleet was brought into the Tigris above Coché, and the Roman army advancing with it encamped on the west bank of the river.

The Persians now appeared in force to dispute the passage of the Tigris. Along the east bank of the river, which was naturally higher at this point than the west bank, and which was also crowned by a wall built originally to fence in one of the royal parks, dense masses of the Persian cavalry and infantry could be seen; the cavalry encased in glittering armor, and the infantry protected by huge wattled shields. Vast forms of elephants could be seen behind these troops, and were regarded with extreme dread by the legionaries.

When night had fully set in, Julian divided his fleet into parts and embarked his army upon it, and gave the signal for the passage, against the dissuasions of his officers. Five ships, each conveying eighty soldiers, led the way, and safely reached the opposite shore, where the Persians showered burning darts upon them, soon setting the two foremost on fire. The rest of the Roman fleet wavered at this sight; but Julian, with remarkable presence of mind, exclaimed aloud: "Our men have crossed and are masters of the bank; that fire is the signal which I bade them make if they were victorious."

The crews were so encouraged that they plied their oars vigorously, thus rapidly impelling the other vessels across the stream. At the same time some of the Roman soldiers who had not been put on board were so impatient to aid their comrades that they plunged into the stream and swam across supported by their shields. The impetuosity of the Romans soon put an end to all resistance on the part of the Persians. The half-burned vessels were saved, the flames were extinguished, and the men on board were rescued from their perilous position; while the Roman troops safely landed, fought their way up the bank against a storm of missiles, and drew up in good order upon its summit.

At dawn the next day Julian led his troops against the Persians and engaged in a hand-to-hand struggle from morning until noon, when the Persians fled. Their leaders—Tigranes, Narseus and the Surena—were the first to leave the field and take refuge within the defenses of Ctesiphon. The entire Persian army then abandoned its camp and baggage, and rushed across the plain in the wildest confusion to the nearest of the gates of Ctesiphon; being closely pursued by the victorious Romans to the very walls of the city. The Roman general Victor, who was wounded, recalled his men as they were about to rush into the open gateway; and the Persians closed the gate upon them.

Thus the entire Persian army was defeated by one-third of the Roman army under the Emperor Julian. The vanquished Persians left twenty-five hundred men dead upon the field, while the triumphant Romans lost only about seventy-five. The Romans came into possession of rich spoil; as they found couches and tables of massive silver in the abandoned camp, and a profusion of gold and silver ornaments and trappings and apparel of great magnificence on the bodies of the slain Persian soldiers and horses. The lands and houses in the vicinity of Ctesiphon also furnished a welcome supply of provisions to the almost famished Roman soldiers.

As the Romans had not yet seen the great Persian army which Sapor had collected for the relief of his western capital, Julian called a council of war, which pronounced the siege of Ctesiphon too hazardous an enterprise, and dissuaded the Emperor from undertaking it, as the heat of summer had arrived and the malaria of autumn was not far off; and as the supplies brought by the Roman fleet were exhausted, Julian decided upon a retreat and caused all his vessels but twelve to be burned, these twelve to serve as pontoons.

As the route along the Euphrates and the Nahr-Malcha had been exhausted of its supplies and its forage, and its towns and villages desolated, Julian ordered the retreat through the fertile country along the east bank of the Tigris, and the army to spread over the productive region to obtain ample supplies. The march was to be directed on the rich Roman province of Cordyênê (now Kurdistan), about two hundred and fifty miles north of Ctesiphon.

The retreat began June 16, A. D. 363. No sooner had the Roman army been set in motion than an ominous cloud of dust on the southern horizon appeared, and grew larger as the day advanced. Julian at once knew that the Persians were in full pursuit. He therefore called in his stragglers, massed his troops, and pitched his camp in a strong position. At dawn the earliest rays of the sun were reflected from the polished breastplates and cuirasses of the Persians, who had drawn up during the night at no great distance from the Roman army. The Persian and Arabian cavalry vigorously attacked the Romans, and especially threatened their baggage, but were repulsed by the firmness and valor of the Roman infantry.

Julian after a while was enabled to resume his retreat; but his enemies surrounded him, some keeping in advance of his army, or hanging on his flanks, destroyed the corn and forage so much needed by his troops, while others pressing upon his rear retarded his march and occasionly caused him some loss. The Roman army was closely pursued by dense masses of Persian troops, by the heavy Persian cavalry clad in steel panoplies and armed with long spears, by large bodies of Persian archers, and even by a powerful corps of elephants. The Persian army which thus pressed heavily upon the Roman rearguard was commanded by Meranes and two of Sapor's sons.

Julian was obliged to confront his pursuers and give them battle at Maranga. The Persians advanced in two lines, the first composed of the mailed horsemen and the archers intermixed, the second of the elephants. Julian arranged his army in the form of a crescent to receive the attack; but as the Persians advanced into the hollow space, he suddenly and hastily led his troops forward, and engaged the Persians in close combat before their archers had time to discharge their arrows. After a long and bloody conflict the Persians broke and fled, covering their retreat with clouds of arrows which they discharged at the victorious foe. The Romans were unable to pursue very far because of the weight of their arms and the fiery heat of the summer sun, and Julian recalled them to protect his camp, and rested for some days to care for the wounded.

The Persian troops destroyed or carried off all the forage and provisions, and wasted the country through which the Roman army was obliged to retire. The Roman troops were already suffering from hunger, and the Emperor's firmness gave way to melancholy forebodings, and he saw visions and omens portending disaster and death. While he was studying a favorite philosopher during the dead of night in the silence of his tent, he imagined that he saw the Genius of the State, with veiled head and cornucopia, stealing away slowly and sadly through the hangings. Soon afterward, when he had just gone forth into the open air to perform some averting sacrifices, the fall of a shooting star appeared to him a direct threat from Mars, he having recently quarreled with that god. The soothsayers who were consulted counseled abstinence from all military movements, but the exigencies of the situation caused their advice to be disregarded on this occasion. The continuance of the retreat was rendered necessary by the want of supplies, and for the final extrication of the Roman army from the perils surrounding it.

At dawn on June 26, A. D. 363, the Roman army struck its tents and resumed its retreat across the wasted plain along the east side of the Tigris. Near Samarah the Roman rearguard was violently assailed by the Persians, and when Julian hastened to its relief he was informed that the van was also attacked and was already in difficulties. While the Emperor was hurrying to the front, the right center of his army suffered the brunt of the Persian attack; and he was dismayed at finding himself entangled amid the masses of Persian cavalry and elephants, which had thrown his column into confusion. He had been unable to don his complete armor, because of the suddenness of the appearance of the Persians; and as he fought without a breastplate, and, aided by his light-armed troops, repulsed the Persians, falling on them from behind and striking the backs of their horses and elephants, the javelin of a Persian horseman grazed the flesh of his arm and lodged in his right side, penetrating through the ribs to the liver.

Julian grasped the weapon and vainly endeavored to draw it forth, as the sharp steel cut his fingers, and the pain and loss of blood caused him to fall fainting from his steed. His guards carried him to the camp, where the surgeons at once pronounced the wound fatal. When the Roman soldiery heard the sad news they struck their shields with their spears and rushed upon their enemies with incredible ardor and reckless valor, determined on vengeance. But the Persians resisted obstinately until the darkness of night put an end to the conflict. Both armies lost heavily. Among the Roman slain was Anatolius, Master of the Officers. The Persian generals Meranes and Nohodares and about fifty satraps and great nobles also perished.

The wounded Julian died in his tent towards midnight on the day of the battle, whereupon his army proclaimed Jovian Emperor. A Roman deserter informed the Persian king that the new Emperor was slothful and effeminate, thus giving a fresh impulse to the pursuit; and the Persian army engaged in disputing the Roman retreat was reinforced by a strong force of cavalry, while Sapor himself pressed forward with all haste, resolved to hurl his main force on the rear of the retreating foe.

On the day of his elevation to the imperial dignity Jovian proceeded to lead his army over the open plain, where the Persians were assembled in great force, ready to dispute with him every inch of ground. Their cavalry and elephants again assailed the Roman right wing, throwing the renowned Roman corps of the Jovians and Herculians into disorder, and driving them across the plain in headlong flight and with heavy loss; but when the fleeing Romans reached a hill, their baggage train repulsed the Persian cavalry and elephants. The elephants, wounded by the javelins hurled down upon them, and maddened by the pain, turned upon their own side, roaring frightfully, and carried confusion into the ranks of the Persian cavalry, which thus broke and fled. Many of the frantic beasts were killed by their own riders or by the Persians on whom they were trampling, while others fell by the blows of the enemy. The frightful carnage ended with the Persian repulse and the resumption of the Roman retreat. Just before night the Roman army arrived at Samarah, a fort on the Tigris, and quietly encamped in its vicinity during the night.

The Roman retreat now continued for four days along the east bank of the Tigris, constantly harassed by the Persians, who pressed on the retreating columns but avoided fighting at close quarters. On one occasion they even attacked the Roman camp and insulted the legions with their cries; after which they forced their way through the Prætorian gate, and had almost penetrated to the Emperor's tent when they were met and defeated by the legionaries. The Arabs, who had deserted the Romans and joined the Persians, because they were offended at Julian, who had refused to contribute to their subsidies, were particularly troublesome, and pursued the Romans with a hostility intensified by indignation and resentment.

When the Romans reached Dura, a small town on the Tigris, about eighteen miles north of Samarah, they entreated the Emperor Jovian to permit them to swim across the river. His refusal led to mutinous threats, and he was obliged to allow five hundred Gauls and Sarmatians, who were expert swimmers, to make the attempt, which succeeded beyond his hopes. A part of the Roman army crossed at night and surprised the Persians on the west bank of the river. Jovian proceeded to collect timber, brushwood and skins to construct rafts to transport the remainder of his troops, many of whom were unable to swim.

This movement of his enemy caused no little solicitude to the Persian king, who saw that the foe which he had considered as almost a certain prey was about to escape from him. As his troops could not swim the Tigris; as he had no boats and as the country about Dura could not supply any; and as the erection of a bridge would consume sufficient time to place the Roman army beyond his reach, he opened negotiations with the enemy, who were still in a perilous position, as they could not embark and cross the river without suffering tremendous loss from the pursuing Persians, and as they were still two hundred miles from the Roman territory.

Accordingly Sapor sent the Surena and another great Persian noble as envoys to the Roman camp at Dura to make overtures of peace. The envoys said that the Great King would mercifully allow the Roman army to escape if the Cæsar would accept the terms of peace required, which terms would be explained to any envoys whom the Roman Emperor might authorize to discuss them with the Persian plenipotentiaries. Jovian and his council gladly availed themselves of the offer, and appointed the general Arinthæus and the Prefect Sallust to confer with King Sapor's ambassadors and to ascertain what conditions of peace would be granted. These terms were very humiliating to Roman pride, and great efforts were made to induce the Persian king to relent, but Sapor remained inexorable; and after four days of negotiation the Roman Emperor and his council were obliged to accept their adversary's terms.

The treaty stipulated first, that the five provinces east of the Tigris which had been ceded to Rome by Narses, the grandfather of Sapor II., after his defeat by Galerius, were to be restored to Persia with their fortifications, their inhabitants, and all that they contained of value, the Roman population in the territory to be allowed to withdraw; secondly, that three places in Eastern Mesopotamia—Nísibis, Síngara, and a fort called "the camp of the Moors"—were also to be ceded to Persia, the inhabitants to be allowed to retire with their movables; thirdly, that all connection between Rome and Armenia was to be dissolved, Arsaces to be left to his own resources, and Rome to be precluded from affording him any assistance in any quarrel which might arise between him and Persia. Peace for thirty years was concluded on these conditions; and oaths were interchanged for its faithful observance; while also hostages were given and received on both sides, to be retained until after the execution of the stipulations of the treaty. To the honor and credit of both parties, the treaty was faithfully observed, and all its stipulations were honestly and speedily executed.

Thus the second period of the great struggle between Rome and Persia ended in a triumph for the Persian king; Rome being obliged to relinquish all what she had gained in the first period, and even to cede some of the territory which she had occupied at the beginning of hostilities. Thus Nísibis —the great stronghold of Eastern Mesopotamia, and so long the bulwark of Roman power in the East, having been in Rome's possession for two centuries, and having been repeatedly attacked by Parthia and Persia, and only once taken but soon recovered—was now surrendered to the victorious Persian monarch, thus dealing a fatal blow to Roman prestige in the East, and exposing the whole eastern frontier of the

Roman dominion to attack, making Amida and Carrhæ, and even Antioch itself tremble. This fear proved groundless, as the Roman possessions in the East were not further reduced by the New Persians for two centuries; but Roman influence in Western Asia steadily declined from the time of this humiliating treaty, and Persia was thenceforth considered the greatest power in these regions.

King Sapor II. exhibited great ability and sagacity during his long war with the Emperors Constantius II., Julian the Apostate and Jovian. He knew when to assume the offensive and when to take the defensive; when to press on the enemy and when to hold himself in reserve and let the enemy follow his own devices. He rightly perceived the importance of Nísibis from the very first, and resolutely persisted in his determination to acquire possession, until he ultimately succeeded. He might have appeared rash and presumptuous when he threw down the gauntlet to Rome in A. D. 337, but the event justified him. In a war which lasted twenty-seven years, he fought many pitched battles with the Romans, and did not suffer a single defeat. He proved an abler general than Constantius II. and Jovian, and not inferior to Julian the Apostate. By his courage, perseverance and promptness, he brought the long contest to a triumphant close; restoring Persia to a higher position in A. D. 363 than she had held even under his illustrious predecessors, Artaxerxes I. and Sapor I., the first two monarchs of the Sassanian dynasty. He fully deserves the title of "the Great," which historians with general consent have assigned him; as he was without doubt among the greatest of the Sassanidæ, and may with propriety be ranked above all his predecessors, and above all his successors but one.

The attitude assumed by Armenia soon after Julian the Apostate began his invasion contributed largely to Sapor's triumph in his war with Julian and Jovian. The Roman generals Procopius and Sebastian, whom Julian had sent into Armenia, were joined

8—8.-U. H.

by the Armenian army under King Arsaces; and the allies invaded Media and ravaged the fertile district of Chiliacomus, or "the district of a Thousand Villages," with fire and sword. The refusal of the Armenians to advance any further caused the defeat of Julian's plans. Moses of Chôrené, the Armenian historian, informs us that 7 ætus, the Armenian general, was ꝑ ᷣ ated in his conduct by his repugnance to aid the apostate Roman Emperor who had renounced the Christian faith.

The Roman generals who were thus deserted differed as to the proper course to pursue, and a policy of inaction was the natural result. When Julian on his march to Ctesiphon heard of the defection of the Armenians, he sent a letter to Arsaces, complaining of his general's conduct, and threatening to exact a heavy contribution on his return from his Persian campaign if the offense of Zuræus was not punished. Arsaces was very much alarmed at the message, and hastened to acquit himself of complicity in the conduct of Zuræus by executing him and his entire family, but did not lend the aid of fresh troops to the Roman Emperor. Supposing himself thus secured against Julian's anger, the Armenian king indulged his love of ease and his dislike for the Roman alliance by remaining wholly passive during the remainder of the war.

Notwithstanding the hostile attitude of Arsaces towards Rome, the Persian king was so little satisfied with the Armenian monarch that he determined to invade Armenia at once and deprive Arsaces of his crown. As Rome had relinquished her protectorate over Armenia by the recent treaty with Persia, and had bound herself not to interfere in any quarrel between Armenia and Persia, Sapor II. resolved to embrace the opportunity thus afforded to subject Armenia to his sway, using intrigue and violence to attain that end. By intriguing with some of the Armenian satraps, and making armed raids into the territories of others, he so harassed the country that most of the satraps after some time went over to his side, and represented to Arsaces that submission to Persia was the only course left open to him. In order to obtain possession of Armenia, Sapor II. addressed a letter to Arsaces in the following terms: "Sapor, the offspring of Ormazd, comrade of the sun, king of kings, sends greeting to his dear brother, Arsaces, King of Armenia, whom he holds in affectionate remembrance. It has come to our knowledge that thou hast approved thyself our faithful friend, since not only didst thou decline to invade Persia with Cæsar, but when he took a contingent from thee thou didst send messengers and withdraw it. Moreover, we have not forgotten how thou actedst at the first, when thou didst prevent him from passing through thy territories, as he wished. Our soldiers, indeed, who quitted their post, sought to cast on thee the blame due to their own cowardice. But we have not listened to them. Their leader we punished with death, and to thy realm, I swear by Mithra, we have done no hurt. Arrange matters then so that thou mayest come to us with all speed, and consult with us concerning our common advantage. Then thou canst return home."

On receiving this missive, Arsaces at once left Armenia and hastened to Sapor's court in Persia, where he was instantly seized and blinded; after which he was fettered with silver chains, according to a common practice of the Persians with distinguished prisoners, and was strictly confined in a place called "the Castle of Oblivion." But the Armenian people did not at once submit because their king was removed. A national party in Armenia rose in revolt under Pharandzem, the wife of Arsaces, and Bab, or Para, his son, who shut themselves up in the strong fortress of Artogerassa (Ardakers), and there offered a determined resistance to the Persian king. Sapor entrusted the conduct of the siege to two renegade Armenians, Cylaces and Artabannes, and also sought to extend his influence over the neighboring country of Iberia, which was closely connected with Armenia and generally followed its fortunes.

Iberia was then governed by a king named Sauromaces, who had received his investiture from Rome, and was therefore likely to uphold Roman interests. The Persian king invaded Iberia, drove Sauromaces from his kingdom, and bestowed the Iberian crown on Aspacures. Sapor II. then retired to his own country, leaving the complete subjection of Armenia to be accomplished by his officers, Cylaces and Artabannes, or, as the Armenian historians call them, Zig and Garen.

Cylaces and Artabannes vigorously besieged Artogerassa, and strongly urged the garrison to submit; but when they entered within the walls to negotiate, they were won over to the national side, and joined in planning a treacherous attack on the besieging army, which was surprised at night and forced to raise the siege. Para at once left the town and threw himself upon the protection of the Eastern Roman Emperor Valens, who permitted him to reside in kingly state at Neocæsaréa; but he soon afterwards returned to Armenia by the advice of Cylaces and Artabannes, and was hailed as king by the national party, Rome secretly countenancing his proceedings.

Therefore the Persian king led a large army into Armenia, drove Para and his counselors, Cylaces and Artabannes, to the mountains, besieged and took Artogerassa, captured the queen Pharandzem and the treasure of Arsaces, and finally induced Para to come to terms and send him the heads of the two arch-traitors, Cylaces and Artabannes. Notwithstanding the treaty of Jovian with Sapor II., Rome now came to Armenia's assistance.

The Armenians and Iberians, with a burning love of liberty and independence, were particularly hostile to Persia, the power from which they had most to fear. As Christian nations, they had at this time additional reason for sympathy with Rome and for hatred of the Persians. The patriotic party in both Armenia and Iberia were thus violently opposed to the extension of Sapor's dominion over them, and spurned the artifices by which he endeavored to persuade them that they still enjoyed freedom and autonomy.

At the same time Rome was under the sway of Emperors who had no hand in making the disgraceful peace with the Persian king in A. D. 363, and who had no overmastering feeling of honor or religious obligation concerning treaties "with barbarians," and were getting ready to fly in the face of the treaty, and to interfere effectually to check the progress of Persia in Northwestern Asia, regarding Rome's interest as the highest law.

Rome first interfered in Iberia, sending the Duke Terentius into that country with twelve legions towards the end of A. D. 370 to place Sauromaces, the old Roman feudatory, upon the Iberian throne. Terentius marched into Iberia from Lazica, which bordered it on the north, and easily conquered the country as far as the river Cyrus, where Aspacures, Sapor's vassal king, proposed a division of Iberia between himself and Sauromaces, the tract north of the Cyrus to be assigned to Sauromaces, and that south of the river to himself. Terentius agreed to this arrangement, and Iberia was accordingly divided between the rival claimants.

Upon hearing of this transaction King Sapor II. was intensely excited. He complained bitterly of the division of Iberia without his consent and even without his knowledge, and that the spirit, if not the letter, of his treaty with the Emperor Jovian had been violated by that Emperor's successor, as Rome had by that treaty relinquished Iberia along with Armenia. The Count Arinthæus had also been sent with a Roman army to assist the Armenians if the Persian king molested them.

King Sapor II. vainly appealed for the faithful observance of the Treaty of Dura in A. D. 363. Rome dismissed his ambassadors with contempt and adhered to her policy. Sapor II. accordingly prepared for war, and collected a large army from his subjects and from his allies to punish Rome for her unfaithfulness. The Eastern Roman Emperor Valens prepared to resist the threatened Persian invasion, and sent a large army to the East under Count Trajan and Vadomair, ex-king of the Alemanni. The Emperor Valens, however, pretended to feel so much regard for the Treaty of Dura that he ordered his generals not to begin hostilities, but to wait until they were attacked.

They did not have to wait long; as the Persian king led a large army of native cavalry and archers, supported by many foreign auxiliaries, into the Roman territory in the East, and attacked the Romans near Vagabanta. The Roman commander ordered his troops to retire, which they did under a shower of Persian arrows, until several of them were wounded, when they felt that they could truly declare that the Persians were responsible for the rupture of the peace. The Romans then advanced and defeated the Persians in a short action, inflicting a severe loss upon their enemies.

After a guerrilla warfare in which the advantage was alternately with the Persians and the Romans, the commanders on both sides negotiated a truce, which allowed King Sapor II. to retire to Ctesiphon, while the Emperor Valens went into winter quarters at Antioch. After an alternation of negotiations and hostilities during the interval between A. D. 371 and 376, a treaty of peace was concluded in the last-named year, which gave tranquillity to the East during the remaining three years of Sapor's reign.

The reign of Sapor II., which began with his birth in A. D. 309, ended with his death in A. D. 379; thus embracing his whole life of seventy years. Notwithstanding the length and brilliancy of his reign, he left behind him neither any inscriptions nor any sculptured memorials; and the only material evidences of his reign are his numerous coins. The earliest have on the reverse the fire-altar, with two priests or guards looking towards the altar, and with the flame rising from the altar in the usual way. The head on the obverse is archaic in type, and very much resembles that of Sapor I. In many cases the crown has that "cheek piece" attached to it which is otherwise confined to the first three of the Sassanian kings. These coins are the best from an artistic standpoint, and very much resemble those of Sapor I.; but are distinguishable from them, first, by the guards looking towards the altar instead of away from it; and, secondly, by the greater abundance of pearls about the monarch's person. The coins of the second period lack the "cheek piece" and have on the reverse the fire-altar without supporters; while they are inferior to those of the first period in artistic merit, but much superior to those of the third. These last display a marked degeneracy, and are particularly distinguished by having a human head in the middle of the flames that rise from the altar; while in other respects, except their inferior artistic merit, they much resemble the early coins. The ordinary legends upon the coins are not remarkable, but in some instances the king takes the new and expressive epithet of *Toham*, "the strong."

The glorious reign of Sapor II., under which the New Persian Empire had reached the highest point whereto it had thus far attained, was followed by a time which offered a most thorough contrast to that remarkable reign. Sapor II. had lived and reigned seventy years, but the reigns of his next three successors together amounted to only twenty years. Sapor II. had been engaged in constant wars, had spread the terror of the Persian arms on every side, and reigned more gloriously than any of his predecessors. His immediate successors were pacific and unenterprising. They were almost unknown to their neighbors, and were among the least distinguished of the Sassanidæ. This was more especially the case with the two immediate successors of Sapor II.—Artaxerxes II. and Sapor III.—who reigned respectively four and five years, and whose annals during this period are almost a blank.

ARTAXERXES II. is called by some of the ancient writers a brother of Sapor II., but the Armenian writers call him Sapor's son. He succeeded to the Persian throne upon Sapor's death in A. D. 379, and died near Ctesiphon in A. D. 383. He was characterized by kindness and amiability, and is known to the Persians as *Nikoukar*, "the Beneficent," and to the Arabs as *Al Djemil*, "the Virtuous." According to the *Modjmel-al-Tewarikh*, he took no taxes from his subjects during the four years of his reign, thus securing their affection and gratitude.

Artaxerxes II. received overtures from the Armenians soon after his accession, and for a time those turbulent mountaineers recognized him as their sovereign. After the murder of Bab, or Para, the Romans placed Varaztad, or Pharasdates, an Arsacid prince, but no relative of the recent Arsacid kings, on the Armenian throne; while they assigned the real direction of Armenian affairs to an Armenian noble named Moushegh, one of the illustrious family of the Mamigonians. Moushegh governed Armenia with vigor; but was suspected of maintaining over-friendly relations with the Eastern Roman Emperor Valens, and of designing to undermine and supplant his sovereign, who finally caused him to be executed, having been influenced to the act by his counselors.

Thereupon Moushegh's brother Manuel excited a rebellion against King Varaztad, defeated him in battle and drove him from his kingdom. Manuel then surrounded the princess Zermanducht, widow of King Para, and her two young sons, Arsaces and Valarsaces, with royal pomp, conferring the title of king on the two princes, but retaining the real government himself. Manuel then sent an embassy with letters and rich gifts to King Artaxerxes II., offering to acknowledge the Persian King lord-paramount of Armenia, in return for his protection, and promising unshaken fidelity.

The terms were accordingly arranged. Armenia was to pay a fixed tribute to Persia; to receive a Persian garrison of ten thousand men and to provide liberally for their maintenance; to allow a Persian satrap to share with Manuel the government of Armenia, and to supply his court and table with all that was necessary. Arsaces and Valarsaces and their mother Zermanducht were to be allowed royal honors; Armenia was to be protected against invasion; and Manuel was to be maintained in his office of *Sparapet*, or *generalissimo* of the Armenian forces. A few years later Meroujan, an Armenian noble, jealous of Manuel's power and prosperity, made Manuel believe that the Persian commandant in Armenia intended to send him a prisoner to Persia or put him to death. Manuel, in great alarm, thereupon attacked and massacred the ten thousand Persians in Armenia, only permitting their commander to escape. War then followed between Persia and Armenia, but Manuel repulsed several Persian invasions and maintained the independence and integrity of Armenia until his death in A. D. 383.

SAPOR III., the brother and successor of Artaxerxes II., became King of Persia in A. D. 383. He attacked the warlike Arab tribe of Yad in their own country, and thus received the title of "the Warlike." One party in Armenia called on Rome for help, while the other party solicited the aid of Persia. But as neither Rome nor Persia desired to renew the old contest concerning Armenia, those two great powers concluded a treaty; and in A. D. 384 the Roman Emperor Theodosius the Great received in Constantinople the envoys from the court of Persepolis and concluded a treaty with them, providing for the partition of Armenia between Rome and Persia, annexing the outlying Armenian districts to their own territories, and dividing the remainder of the country into two unequal parts, the smaller and more western portion being conferred upon the young King Arsaces and placed under the protection of Rome, while the more eastern and larger portion was bestowed on an Arsacid named Chosroës, a Christian, who received the title of king, and one of the sisters of King Sapor III. of Persia as a bride. The friendly relations thus established remained undisturbed for thirty-six years (A. D. 384-420).

A sculptured memorial of Sapor III. is still seen in the vicinity of Kermanshah, consisting of two very similar figures, looking towards each other, and standing in an arched frame. On each side of the figures are inscriptions in the old Pehlevi character, by which the individuals represented with the second and third Sapor can be identified. The coins of Artaxerxes II. and Sapor III. have little about them that is remarkable, and exhibit the marks of decline, but the legends upon them are in the usual style of royal epigraphs.

Sapor III. was a man of simple tastes, and was more fond of the freedom and ease of a life under tents than the magnificence and dreary etiquette of the court. On one occasion, while he was encamping, a violent hurricane fell with full force on the royal encampment, blowing down the tent, the main tent-pole striking the king in a vital part, thus causing his death (A. D. 388).

Sapor III. was succeeded by VARAHRAN IV., who is called his brother by some authorities, and his son by others. Oriental writers call this king "Varahran Kermanshah," or "Varahran, King of Carmania." Agathias tells us that during the lifetime of his father he was made governor of Kerman, or Carmania, thus obtaining the title of Varahran Kerman-shah; and this statement is confirmed by this king's seal before he ascended the throne—a curious relic which is still preserved, and which contains his portrait and an inscription, which, translated into English, reads: "Varahran, King of Kerman, son of Ormazd-worshipping divine Sapor, King of the Kings of Iran and Turan, heaven-descended of the race of gods." Another seal of Varahran IV., belonging to him after he became King of Persia, contains his full-length portrait, and exhibits him as trampling under foot a prostrate figure.

On the death of Arsaces of Western Armenia in A. D. 386, Rome absorbed his territories into her Empire, placing the new province under a count. About A. D. 390 Chosroës of Eastern Armenia became dissatisfied with his position as a vassal king under Persia, and entered into relations with Rome which greatly displeased the Persian king. Chosroës obtained from the Roman Emperor Theodosius the Great his appointment as Count of Armenia, thus uniting both Roman and Persian Armenia under his government.

Chosroës then trenched on the rights of the Persian king as lord-paramount; and when Varahran IV. addressed him a remonstrance, Chosroës replied in insulting terms, renounced Varahran's authority, and placed the whole of the Armenian kingdom under the suzerainty and protection of Rome. As the Roman Emperor Theodosius the Great refused to receive the submission which Chosroës tendered to him, the unfortunate Armenian prince was obliged to surrender himself to Varahran IV., who imprisoned him in the Castle of Oblivion, and placed his own brother, Varahran-Sapor, upon the Armenian throne.

Some native Persian authorities represent Varahran IV. as mild in temper and irreproachable in conduct. Others say that he was a hard man, and so neglectful of his duties as even not to read the petitions or complaints addressed to him. His death was the result of a mutiny of his troops, who surrounded him and shot their arrows at him. One well-aimed arrow struck him in a vital part, causing his instant death. Thus perished in A. D. 399, the third son of the great Sapor II., after a reign of eleven years.

Varahran IV. was succeeded by his son ISDIGERD I., or IZDIKERTI I., who is said to have been prudent and moderate at his accession—a character which he sought to confirm by uttering high-sounding moral sentiments. His reign was peaceful, and the Roman Empire had split into two separate sovereignties. When Isdigerd I. had reigned nine years he is said to have received a compliment of an unusual character from the Eastern Roman Emperor Arcadius, who committed his son Theodosius, a boy of tender age, to the guardianship of the Persian king. Arcadius solemnly appealed to the magnanimity of Isdigerd, exhorting him to defend with all his force, and guide with his best wisdom, the young prince and his dominion. One writer says that Arcadius also bequeathed a thousand pounds of pure gold to the Persian king, requesting him to accept the bequest as a token of his good will.

When the Emperor Arcadius died and his will was opened, Isdigerd I. was informed of its contents, and at once accepted the guardianship of the young prince, addressing a letter to the Senate of Constantinople, in which he announced his determination to punish any attempt against his ward with the utmost rigor. The Persian monarch selected a learned eunuch of his own court, named Antíochus, as a guide and instructor for the youthful prince, and sent him to Constantinople, where he was the constant companion of the youthful Theodosius for several years. Even after the death or expulsion of Antíochus, in consequence of the intrigues of Pulcheria, the elder sister of Theodosius, the King of Persia remained faithful to his charge. During his whole reign, Isdigerd I. maintained peace and friendship with the Romans.

During the first part of his reign, Isdigerd I. seemed inclined to favor the Christians, and even contemplated accepting Christian baptism and entering the Christian Church. The eunuch Antíochus, his representative at Constantinople, openly wrote in favor of the persecuted Christians; and the encouragement thus given from high quarters rapidly increased the number of professing Christians in the New Persian Empire. The Persian Christians had long been allowed their own bishops, though they had been oppressed; and Isdigerd I. is said to have listened approvingly to the teachings of two of these Christian bishops—Marutha, Bishop of Mesopotamia, and Abdaäs, Bishop of Ctesiphon.

Convinced of the truth of Christianity, but unfortunately not acting in accordance with its loving spirit, Isdigerd I. began a persecution of the Magians and their most powerful adherents; thus causing himself to be detested by his subjects, and attaching to his name such epithets as *Al-Khasha*, "the Harsh," and *Al-Athim*, "the Wicked." But this persecution soon ceased. The excessive zeal of Bishop Abdaäs eventually produced a reaction, and Isdigerd I. deserted the cause of the Christians and joined the Zoroastrian and Magian party. Abdaäs had ventured to burn down the great Fire Temple of Ctesiphon, and had then refused to rebuild it. Isdigerd I. authorized the Magian hierarchy to retaliate by a general destruction of the Christian churches throughout the New Persian Empire, and by the arrest and punishment of all avowed Christians.

A terrible massacre of the Christians in Persia followed during five years. Some of these Christians, in their eagerness for the earthly glory and the heavenly rewards of martyrdom, boldly proclaimed themselves members of the persecuted sect. Others, with less courage or less inclination to self-assertion, sought rather to conceal their creed; but these latter were carefully sought out, alike in the towns and in the country districts, and upon conviction were mercilessly put to death. The victims were subjected to various kinds of cruel sufferings, and most of them expired from torture. Thus Isdigerd I. alternately persecuted the two religious creeds which divided the great mass of his subjects; and by thus giving both Zoroastrians and Christians reason to hate him, he deserved and received a unanimity of execration which has very seldom been the lot of persecuting sovereigns.

Isdigerd I. also sanctioned an effort to extirpate Christianity in the dependent country of Armenia. Varahran-Sapor, the successor of Chosröes, had governed Armenia quietly and peaceably for twenty-one years. Dying in A. D. 412 he left behind him but one son, Artases, then but ten years of age. Isaac, the Metropolitan of Armenia, proceeded to the court of Ctesiphon and petitioned Isdigerd to replace on the Armenian throne the prince who had been deposed twenty years before, and who was still a prisoner on parole in the Castle of Oblivion —Chosroës. Isdigerd I. granted the request; and Chosroës was released from confinement and restored to the throne from which Varahran IV. had expelled him in A. D. 391, but he survived his restoration but one year.

Upon the death of Chosroës in A. D. 413, Isdigerd I. appointed his own son Sapor to the viceroyalty of Armenia, forcing the reluctant Armenians to acknowledge him as their sovereign. Prince Sapor was instructed to ingratiate himself with the Armenian nobles by inviting them to visit him, by feasting them, making them presents, holding friendly intercourse with them, hunting with them; and was ordered to use such influence as he might obtain to convert the Armenian chiefs from Christianity to Zoroastrianism. The young prince seems to have done the best he could; but the Armenians were obstinate, resisted his blandishments and continued Christians, in spite of all his efforts. Sapor ruled over Armenia from A. D. 414 to 418, and then, upon hearing of the ill health of his father, he returned to the Persian court to press his claims to the succession.

The coins of Isdigerd I. are numerous and possess some interesting features, but are not remarkable for their artistic merit. They seem to have been issued from the same mint, and all have a head of the same type—that of a middle-aged man, with a short beard, and hair gathered behind in a cluster of curls. The distinguishing mark is the head-dress, having the usual inflated ball above a fragment of the old mural crown, and also having a crescent in front. The reverse has the usual fire-altar with supporters, and is rudely executed. The ordinary legend on the obverse is, translated into English, "The Ormazd-worshipping divine most peaceful Isdigerd, King of the Kings of Iran;" and on the reverse is, "The most peaceful Isdigerd."

Oriental writers tell us that Isdigerd I. had by nature an excellent disposition, and that at the time of his accession he was generally considered eminently wise, prudent and virtuous; but after he became king his conduct disappointed all hopes. These writers say that he was then violent, cruel and pleasure-seeking; that he broke all human and divine laws; that he plundered the rich, oppressed the poor, despised learning, did not reward those who did him a service, and suspected everybody. They likewise say that he wandered about his vast dominions continually, to make all his subjects suffer equally, but not to benefit any of them. The Western authors represent his character as quite in contrast with the above. They praise his magnanimity and his virtue, his peaceful temper, his faithful guardianship of the young Byzantine prince Theodosius, and even his exemplary piety. His alternate persecutions of Zoroastrians and Christians show that religious tolerance was at least none of his virtues; though Mr. Malcolm, a modern British writer, has tried to make it appear that he was a wise and tolerant prince, whose very mildness and indulgence offended the bigots of his own country and caused them to do their utmost to blacken his memory and to represent his character in the most odious light.

There is a curious legend concerning the death of Isdigerd I., which occurred in A. D. 420. It is said that while he was still in the full vigor of manhood, a horse of rare beauty, without bridle or caparison, came of its own accord and stopped before the gate of the king's palace. When Isdigerd was informed of this, he ordered that the strange steed should be saddled and bridled, and prepared to mount the animal. But the horse reared and kicked, so that no one could come near, until the king himself approached, when the beast entirely changed its conduct, appeared gentle and docile, stood perfectly still, and allowed both saddle and bridle to be put on. But the crupper required some arrangement, and Isdigerd proceeded with the fullest confidence to complete his task, when the horse suddenly lashed out with one of his hind legs, inflicting upon the king a blow which killed him on the spot; after which the animal sped off, released itself of it accouterments, and galloped away to be seen no more. Mr. Malcolm simply tells us that "Isdigerd died from the kick of a horse." The Persians of Isdigerd's time considered the occurrence as an answer to their prayers, and looked upon the wild steed as an angel sent by God.

Isdigerd's death was followed by a disputed succession. His son Varahran, whom he had named as his heir, seems to have been absent from the capital at the time of his father's death; while his other son, Sapor, who had been the Persian viceroy of Armenia from A. D. 414 to 418, was present at court and determined on pressing his claims. The Oriental writers all tell us that Varahran had been educated among the Arab tribes dependent upon Persia, who now occupied most of Mesopotamia; that his training had made him more of an Arab than a Persian; and that he was believed to have inherited the violence, the pride and the cruelty of his father. His countrymen had therefore resolved that he should never reign; nor were they disposed to support the pretensions of Sapor, who had not been a very successful viceroy of Armenia, and whose recent desertion of his proper post for the advancement of his own private interests was a public crime meriting punishment rather than reward. As Armenia had actually revolted and driven out the Persian garrison, and had become a prey to rapine and disorder, it is not surprising that Sapor's hopes and schemes were ended by his own murder soon after his father's death.

The Persian nobles and the principal Magi formally enthroned a prince named Chosroës, a descendant of Artaxerxes I., but only remotely related to Isdegerd I. But Prince Varahran persuaded the Arabs to espouse his cause, led a large army against Ctesiphon, and prevailed upon Chosroës, the nobles and the Magi to submit to him. The people readily acquiesced in this change of masters; and Chosroës descended into a private station, while VARAHRAN V., son of Isdigerd I., became King of Persia (A. D. 420).

Varahran V. immediately threw himself into the hands of the Magian priesthood and resumed the persecution of the Christians inaugurated by his father. Various kinds of tortures were employed against the followers of Christ, and in a short time many of the persecuted sect left the Persian dominions and placed themselves under Roman protection. The Persian king instructed his ambassadors to the court of Constantinople to require the surrender of the Persian Christian refugees; and when the Eastern

NEW PERSIAN EMPIRE OF THE SASSANIDÆ.

Roman Emperor Theodosius II., to his honor, indignantly rejected the insolent demand, the Persian ambassadors were ordered by their sovereign to protest against the Emperor's decision and to threaten him with the Persian monarch's vengeance.

The relations of the New Persian and Eastern Roman Empires at this time were not very friendly. The Persians had recently commenced to work their gold mines and had hired experienced Roman miners, whose services they found so valuable that they would not permit them to return to their homes when their term of service had expired. The Persians were also accused of mistreating the Roman merchants who traded in the Persian dominions, and of having actually robbed them of their merchandise. The Eastern Romans made no counter-claims, simply refusing to accede to the Persian demand for the extradition of the Persian Christian fugitives; but their moderation was not appreciated by the Persian king.

When Varahran V. heard that the Eastern Roman Emperor would not restore the Persian Christian refugees, he declared the peace at an end and immediately prepared for war; but the Romans had anticipated his decision, and took the field before the Persians were ready. An Eastern Roman army under Ardaburius marched through Armenia into the fertile Persian province of Arzanêné, where he defeated the Persian army under Narses. As the Roman commander was about to plunder Arzanêné, he suddenly heard that his antagonist was on the point of invading the Eastern Roman province of Mesopotamia, which was then perfectly defenseless.

Ardaburius thereupon hastened to the defense of Mosopotamia, and was in time to prevent the threatened Persian invasion. Narses then threw himself into the fortress of Nísibis, where he stood on the defensive. As Ardaburius did not feel himself strong enough to invest the fortified city, the two commanders remained inactive for some time, watching each other.

The Greek writer Socrates tells us that during this period of inactivity the Persian general sent a challenge to the Roman, inviting him to fix the time and place for a trial of strength between the two armies. Ardaburius prudently declined, saying that the Romans were not accustomed to fighting battles when their enemies wished, but when it suited themselves. When he was reinforced he invaded Persian Mesopotamia and besieged Narses in Nísibis.

The danger to Nísibis—that dearly won and highly prized possession—so alarmed Varahran V. that he took the field in person, enlisting on his side the services of the Arabs under their great sheikh, Al-Amundarus, or Moundsir, and collecting a strong body of elephants. When the Persian king advanced to the relief of the beleaguered city, the Roman commander burned his siege machinery and raised the siege and fled. Soon afterwards the Arab allies of Varahran V. were seized with a sudden panic, rushed in headlong flight to the Euphrates, threw themselves into the river, and a hundred thousand of them perished in the stream.

The next year (A. D. 421) the Persian king besieged the strong city of Theodosiopolis, which had been built near the sources of the Euphrates by the reigning Eastern Roman Emperor, Theodosius II., for the defense of Roman Armenia, and which was defended by strong walls, lofty towers and a deep ditch, while hidden channels conducted an unfailing supply of water into the heart of the town, and the large public granaries were usually well supplied with provisions.

King Varahran V. besieged Theodosiopolis for more than a month and employed all the means of capture then known to the military art; but the defense was ably conducted by Eunomius, the bishop of the city, who was resolved to do his utmost to prevent a non-Christian and persecuting monarch from lording it over his see. Eunomius animated the garrison and took part personally in the defense, even on one occasion discharging a stone from a balista with his own hand, and thus killing a prince who had insulted the Christian religion. The death of this prince is said to have caused Varahran V. to raise the siege and to retire.

It is said that the Emperor Theodosius II. appointed the Patrician Procopius to an independant command, and sent him with a detachment against the Persian king. Just as the armies were about to engage in battle, Varahran V. proposed to decide the war by a single combat. Procopius assented; and a warrior was selected from each side, the Persians choosing Ardazanes as their champion, while the Romans presented Areobindus the Goth, Count of the Fœderati. In the combat which followed, the Persian champion charged his antagonist with his spear; but the nimble Goth avoided the thrust by leaning on one side, after which he entangled Ardazanes in a net, and then killed him with his sword. The Persian king accepted the result as decisive of the war, and abstained from any further hostilities. Areobindus received the thanks of the Emperor Theodosius II. for his victory, and was rewarded with the Consulate twelve years later.

In the meantime the Romans were successful in other quarters. In Mesopotamia, Ardaburius had enticed the Persian army into an ambuscade, where he destroyed it with seven of its generals. Vitianus had exterminated the remnant of the Arabs not drowned in the Euphrates. The Persians were everywhere defeated.

Early in A. D. 422 Maximus, a Roman envoy, appeared in the Persian king's camp, and, when brought into the presence of Varahran V., stated that he was authorized by the Roman commanders to open negotiations, but had no communication with the Eastern Roman Emperor, who resided at so great a distance that he had not heard of the war, and who was so powerful that even if he did know of it he would consider it of small account.

As Varahran V. was tired of the war and was short of provisions, he was disposed to entertain the proposals of the Roman envoy; but the famous Persian corps of the *Immortals* took a different view and requested to be granted an opportunity to attack the Romans unawares, while they supposed negotiations to be in progress. The Greek writer Socrates states that the Persian king consented, and that the Immortals attacked the Romans, who were at first in some danger, but were finally saved by the unexpected arrival of a reinforcement, when the Immortals were defeated and all slain. King Varahran V. then made peace with Rome through the instrumentality of the envoy Maximus, consenting that Rome might furnish an asylum to the Persian Christians, and that all persecutions of Christians throughout the New Persian Empire should cease thenceforth.

The well-judged charity of an admirable Christian prelate accompanied the formal conclusion of peace. Acacius, Bishop of Amida, pitying the condition of the Persian prisoners captured by the Romans during their raid into Arzanênê, and who were being carried off into slavery, interposed to save them; and used all the gold and silver plate that he could find in the churches of his diocese in ransoming seven thousand captives, whose wants he most tenderly supplied, and whom he sent to King Varahran V.

Persian Armenia had no sovereign since Varahran's brother Sapor had withdrawn from that country in A. D. 418, and had fallen into a condition of complete anarchy and wretchedness; no taxes being collected; the roads being unsafe; the strong robbing and oppressing the weak at their pleasure. Isaac, the Armenian Patriarch, and other Christian bishops, had abandoned their sees and taken refuge in Roman Armenia, where they were received with favor by Anatolius, the Roman Prefect of the East. The Persian king's fear that his portion of Armenia might also fall to Rome hastened the conclusion of peace.

After making peace with Rome, Varahran V. conciliated the Armenian nobles by conferring the royal dignity of Persian Armenia upon an Arsacid prince named Artases, whom he required to assume the illustrious name of Artaxerxes, and to whom he assigned the entire government of the country (A. D. 422). But the bad personal character of Artaxerxes and the caprice of the Armenian nobles caused the Armenians six years later to request Varahran V. to absorb Persian Armenia into the New Persian Empire and to place the new province under the government of a Persian satrap (A. D. 428).

Isaac, the Armenian Patriarch, resisted this movement with all his might, as he maintained that the rule of a Christian, however lax he might be, was preferable to that of a heathen, however virtuous. But the Armenian nobles were resolute, and the opposition of Isaac only had the result of involving him in his sovereign's fall. The nobles appealed to the Persian king; and Varahran V., in solemn state, listened to the charges made against Artaxerxes by his subjects, and heard his answer to the charges. The Great King then gave his decision; pronouncing Artaxerxes to have forfeited the Armenian crown, deposing him, confiscating his property, and imprisoning him. The Armenian kingdom was declared to be at an end, and Persarmenia was absorbed into the New Persian Empire and placed under the administration of a Persian satrap. The Patriarch Isaac was degraded from his office and kept a prisoner in Persia; but was released some years later, when he was permitted to return to Armenia, and to resume his episcopal functions under certain restrictions.

During the reign of Varahran V. began the wars of the Persians with the Ephthalites, a people living on the north-eastern frontier of the New Persian Empire—wars which lasted about a century and a half. During the fifth and sixth centuries of the Christian era the Ephthalites occupied the regions east of the Caspian Sea, particularly those regions beyond the Oxus river. They were generally considered as belonging to the Scythic or Finno-Turkish population which as early as B. C. 200 had become powerful in that region. Such Greek writers as Procopius, Theóphanes and Cosmas designated them as *White Huns;* but it is admitted that they were entirely distinct from the Huns under Attila who invaded Europe. The description of the physical character and habits of the Ephthalites left to us by Procopius is utterly inconsistent with the view that they were really Huns. The Ephthalites were light-complexioned, while the Huns were swarthy. The Ephthalites were not ill-looking, whereas the Huns were hideous. The Ephthalites were an agricultural people, whereas the Huns were nomads. The Ephthalites had excellent laws, and were somewhat civilized, but the Huns were savages. The Ephthalites probably belonged to the Thibetan or Turkish stock, which has always been in advance of the Finnic, and has exhibited a greater talent for political organization and social progress.

It is said that the war of Varahran V. with the Ephthalites began with an invasion of the New Persian Empire by the Ephthalite Khakan, or Khan, who crossed the Oxus with a large army and ravaged some of the most fertile provinces of Persia with fire and sword. The rich oasis of Merv, the ancient Margiana, was overrun by these invaders, who are said by the Arab writer Maçoudi and others to have crossed the Elburz mountain range into the Persian province of Khorassan, and to have proceeded westward to Rei, or Rhages.

The Persian court was terribly alarmed upon receiving tidings of the Ephthalite invasion. Varahran V. was urged to collect his forces instantly and to encounter the new and strange enemy; but he pretended absolute indifference, saying that Ahura-Mazda would preserve the Empire, that he himself was going to hunt in Azerbijan, or Media Atropatêné, and that his brother Narses could conduct the government in his absence.

All Persia was thrown into consternation; and it was believed that Varahran V. had lost his senses, and that the only prudent course was to send an embassy to the Ephthalite Khakan and make a treaty with him by which Persia should acknowledge his suzerainty and agree to pay him tribute. Accordingly Persian ambassadors were sent to the invaders, who were satisfied with the offers of submission and remained in the position which they had taken up, waiting for the tribute and keeping slack guard, as they thought that they had nothing to fear. But during all this time King Varahran V. was preparing to attack the invaders unawares. He had started for Azerbijan with a small force of select warriors, and collected additional troops from Armenia. He proceeded along the mountain line through Taberistan, Hyrcania and Nissa, or Nishapur; marching only by night and cautiously masking his movements, thus reaching the vicinity of Merv unobserved. He then planned and successfully executed a night attack upon the invaders; attacking them suddenly in the dark, alarming them with strange noises and assailing them most vigorously, thus putting their entire army to flight. The Khan himself was killed, and the fleeing host of the Ephthalites was pursued by the victorious Persians to the banks of the Oxus. The entire camp equipage of the vanquished invaders became the spoil of the victors; and Khâtoun, the great Khan's wife, was taken captive. The plunder was of immense value, and included the royal diadem of the Khan with its rich setting of pearls.

The Persian king then followed up his victory by sending one of his generals with a large force across the Oxus, while he attacked the Ephthalites in their own country and defeated them in a second battle with frightful carnage. The Ephthalites begged for peace, which the triumphant Varahran V. granted them; while he also erected a column to mark the boundary of the New Persian Empire in that region, and appointed his brother Narses satrap of Khorassan, ordering him to fix his residence at Balkh, the ancient Bactria, and to prevent the Ephthalites and other Tartar races from making raids across the Oxus. These precautions were successful, as there were no more hostilities in that region during the remainder of the reign of Varahran V.

The coins of Varahran V. are mainly remarkable for their rude and coarse workmanship, and for the number of mints from which they were issued. The mint-marks include Ctesiphon, Ecbatana, Ispahan, Arbéla, Ledan, Nehavend, Assyria, Khuzistan, Media and Kerman, or Carmania. The usual legend upon the reverse is "Varahran" with a mint-mark. The head-dress has the mural crown in front and behind, but between these are a crescent and a circle. The reverse shows the usual fire-altar, with guards or attendants watching it. The king's head is seen in the flame upon the altar.

Oriental writers tell us that Varahran V. was one of the best of the Sassanidæ. He carefully administered justice among his many subjects, remitted arrears of taxes, bestowed pensions upon scientific and literary men, encouraged agriculture, and was extremely liberal in relieving poverty and distress. His faults were his over-generosity and his over-fondness of amusement, particularly of the chase. The Orientals conferred upon him the nickname of "Bahram-Gur," which marks his predilection for hunting by giving him the name of the animal which was the special object of his pursuit. He was almost as fond of dancing and of games. Still his inclination for pastime did not interefere with his public duties. Persia is said to have been in a most flourishing condition during the reign of Varahran V. He was an active, brave, energetic and sagacious sovereign, as the great acts of his reign clearly demonstrate. He does not appear to have appreciated art, but he encouraged learning, and exerted himself to his utmost to advance science.

Varahran V. died in A. D. 440, after a reign of twenty years. The Persian writers state that he was engaged in the hunt of the wild ass, when his horse came suddenly upon a deep pool, or spring of water, and either plunged into it or threw the king into it, Varahran sinking and being never seen thereafter. This incident is supposed to have occurred in a valley between Ispahan and Shiraz. In that same valley in 1810 an English soldier lost his life through bathing in the spring which tradition declared to be the one which proved fatal to King Varahran V. This coincidence has caused a story which would perhaps otherwise have been considered wholly romantic and mythical to be generally accepted as true.

Upon the death of Varahran V., in A. D. 420, his son, ISDIGERD II., became King of Persia. His first act was to declare war against the Eastern Roman Empire, whose forces were then concentrated in the vicinity of Nisibis. Isdigerd II. invaded the Roman territory to anticipate a Roman invasion of his own dominions. His army was composed partly of his own subjects, and partly of foreign auxiliaries, such as Arabs, Tzani, Isaurians and Ephthalites. With this force he made a sudden irruption into the Roman territory when the imperial officers were totally unprepared for it; but storms of rain and hail hindered the advance of the Persian invaders, and gave the Roman generals a breathing spell, during which they collected an army.

The Eastern Roman Emperor Theodosius II. was so anxious for peace that he ordered Count Anatolius, the Roman Prefect of the East, to conclude a peace. A truce of a year was then made, and this was followed by a permanent treaty. Anatolius went alone and on foot to the Persian camp, in order to place himself wholly in the power of King Isdigerd II.—an act which is said to have so impressed the Persian king that he immediately consented to a peace on the terms suggested by Anatolius, one condition being that neither the Persians nor the Romans should erect any new fortified post in the vicinity of the other's territory.

The Ephthalites were again making trouble on the north-eastern frontier of the New Persian Empire, and King Isdigerd II. undertook a long war against them and conducted it with great resolution and perseverance. Leaving the administration of affairs in the capital to his vizier, Mihr-Narses, the Persian king established his own residence at Nishapur, in the mountain region between the Persian and Khorasmian deserts, whence he conducted a campaign against the restless Ephthalites regularly every year from A. D. 443 to 451. In the last-named year he crossed the Oxus, attacked the Ephthalites in their own country, utterly defeated them, drove their sovereign from the cultivated part of the country, and forced him to seek refuge in the desert.

Isdigerd II. next undertook to forcibly convert Armenia from Christinity to Zoroastrianism. The religious differences which had separated the Armenians from the Persians ever since Armenia had made Christianity the religion of the state and nation was a source of weakness to Persia in her wars with Rome. Armenia was always naturally on the Roman side, as a religious sympathy united it with the court of Constantinople, and a religious difference tended to detach it from the court of Ctesiphon.

During the war between Isdigerd II. and the Emperor Theodosius II. the former was obliged to send an army into Persarmenia on account of Roman intrigues in that country. The Persians knew that so long as Armenia remained Christian and Persia continued Zoroastrian the two countries could never maintain friendly relations with each other. Persia would always have a traitor in her camp; and in any time of trouble—especially in any trouble with Rome—might expect this part of her territory to desert to the enemy. It is no wonder that Persian statesmen were anxious to end so unsatisfactory a condition of affairs, and to find some means whereby Armenia might be made a real friend instead of a concealed enemy of Persia.

King Isdigerd II. therefore undertook to convert the Armenians to the Zoroastrian religion. In the early part of his reign he hoped to accomplish this by persuasion, and sent his vizier, Mihr-Narses, into the country with orders to employ all possible peaceful means—gifts, blandishments, promises, threats, removal of malignant chiefs—to induce the Armenians to change their religion. Mihr-Narses exerted himself to his utmost, but signally failed. He carried off the Christian leaders of Armenia, Iberia and Albania, telling them that the Persian king required their services against the Tartars, and forced them with their followers to take part in the Persian war against the Ephthalites. He intrusted Armenia to the charge of the Margrave, Vasag, a native Armenian prince who was well disposed toward the Persian cause, instructing him to bring about the change of religion by a conciliatory policy.

But the Armenians were obstinate, and were not moved by threats, promises or persuasions. A manifesto was vainly issued, painting the religion of Zoroaster in the brightest colors and requiring every Armenian to conform to it. It was in vain that arrests were made and punishments threatened. The Armenians were not affected by argument or menace, and no progress was made toward the desired conversion.

In A. D. 540 the Armenians induced their Patriarch, Joseph, to hold a great assembly, at which they declared by acclamation that they were Christians and would remain thus, whatever it might cost them. The Persian king thereupon summoned to his presence the principal Armenian chiefs—Vasag the Margrave, the *Sparapet* or commander-in-chief, Vartan the Mamigonian, Prince Vazten of Iberia, and King Vatché of Albania —and then threatened them with instant death if they did not at once renounce Christianity and profess Zoroastrianism. The chiefs yielded to this threat and declared themselves converts, whereupon Isdigerd II. sent them back to their respective countries, with orders to force a similar change of religion on their fellow-countrymen.

Thereupon the Armenians and Iberians openly revolted. Vartan the Mamigonian repented of his weakness, abjured his new creed, resumed his former profession of Christianity, made his peace with Joseph, the Armenian Patriarch, called his people to arms, and soon raised an army of a hundred thousand men. Three Armenian armies were formed, to act separately under different generals—one watching Azerbijan, or Media Atropatêné, whence the principal attack of the Persians was expected; another, under Vartan, proceeding to the relief of Albania, where efforts were also made to fasten Zoroastrianism on the people; the third, under Vasag the Margrave occupying a central position in Armenia, ready to move wherever danger should threaten.

The Armenian rebels also attempted to induce the Eastern Roman Emperor Marcian to espouse their cause and afford them military aid; but Marcian declined to interfere, as he was then in danger of conquest by Attila the Hun. Thus Armenia had to face the Persians single-handed; and Vasag deserted to the enemy, carrying his army with him, thus dividing Armenia against itself and ruining the cause of the Christian party. When the Persians entered the field half of Armenia was ranged on their side; and the victory was already decided in their favor, although a long and bloody struggle followed. After much desultory warfare, a great battle was fought in A. D. 455 or 456, in which the Armenian Christians were defeated by the Persians and their Armenian allies, Vartan and his brother being among the slain. All further resistance was hopeless; the Patriarch Joseph and other Armenian bishops were carried off to Persia and martyred; and the religion of Zoroaster was enforced upon the Armenian nation. All Armenians accepted Zoroastrianism, except a few who took refuge in the Eastern Roman dominions or fled to the mountain fastnesses of Kurdistan.

About the time of the close of the Armenian war of religion King Isdigerd II. was again involved in a war with the Ephthalites, who had again crossed the Oxus and invaded the province of Khorassan in force. The Persian king drove the Ephthalites from his dominions; but when he retaliated by invading their country, they lured him and his army into an ambuscade, where they inflicted a severe defeat upon him, thus compelling him to retreat to his own dominions. This occurred near the end of Isdigerd's reign.

The coins of Isdigerd II. are almost similar to those of his father, Varahran V., differing only in the legend and in the fact that the mural crown of Isdigerd is complete. The legend on Isdigerd's coins is,

NEW PERSIAN EMPIRE OF THE SASSANIDÆ. 1287

translated, as follows: "Ormazd-worshiping great Isdigerd," or "Isdigerd the Great." The coins are not numerous and have only three mint-marks, which are interpreted to mean "Khuzistan," "Ctesiphon" and "Nehavend."

Isdigerd II. was an able, resolute and couragous sovereign. His subjects called him "the Clement," but his policy in religious matters showed anything but clemency. He was a bitter and successful persecutor of the Christian religion, which he entirely stamped out for his time, both in his own proper dominions and in the newly-acquired province of Armenia. When less violent means failed, he did not scruple to use the extremest and severest coercion. Being a bigoted Zoroastrian, he was determined to have religious uniformity all over his dominions; and he secured such uniformity at the cost of crushing a Christian people, and so alienating them as to make it certain that they would cast off the Persian yoke entirely at the first convenient opportunity. Isdigerd II. died in A. D. 457, after a reign of seventeen years; and his younger son, HORMISDAS III., seized the Persian throne, owing his elevation largely to the partiality of his father, who preferred his younger son above his elder. Isdigerd II. had made his elder son, Perozes, satrap of the remote province of Seistan, thus removing him from court, while he retained Hormisdas about his own person. The advantage thus secured to Hormisdas enabled him to usurp the throne when his father died; and Perozes was obliged to flee from the Persian dominions and place himself under the protection of the Ephthalite Khan, Khush-newâz, who ruled in the valley of the Oxus, over Bactria, Tokaristan, Badakshan and other neighboring districts. The Ephthalite Khan received the refugee Persian prince favorably, and finally agreed to afford him military aid against his brother.

Hormisdas III., though bearing the epithet of *Ferzan*, "the Wise," was soon at variance with his subjects, many of whom gathered at the court which his brother was permitted to maintain in Taleqan, one of the Ephthalite cities. With the support of these Persian refugees and an Ephthalite contingent, Perozes advanced against his brother. His army was commanded by Raham, or Ram, a noble of the Mihran family, and attacked the forces of Hormisdas III., defeated them, and made Hormisdas himself a prisoner. The vanquished king's troops then deserted in a body to his victorious brother (A. D. 459).

Thereupon PEROZES was acknowledged king by the whole Persian people, after he had lived in exile for more than two years (A. D. 457-459). Perozes then left Taleqan and established his court at Ctesiphon, or Al Modian, which had by this time become the principal capital of the New Persian Empire. The Armenian writers say that Raham caused Hormisdas III. to be put to death after defeating him; but the native Persian historian, Mirkhond, states that the triumphant Perozes forgave his brother for having usurped the Persian throne, and amiably spared his life.

The short civil war between the princely brothers cost Persia a province. Vatché, King of Albania, or Aghouank, took advantage of this civil war to cast off his allegiance to Persia, and succeeded in making himself independent. As soon as Perozes became King of Persia he made war on Vatché to recover Albania, though Vatché was his sister's son; and with the aid of his Ephthalite allies, and of a body of Alans whom he had taken into his service, Perozes vanquished the revolted Albanians and thoroughly subdued the rebellious province.

An era of prosperity for Persia now ensued. King Perozes ruled with moderation and justice. He dismissed his Ephthalite allies with presents that amply satisfied them, and lived and reigned for five years in peace and honor. But in the fifth year of his reign the prosperity of Persia was suddenly interrupted by a terrible drought, which produced the most frightful consequences. The crops failed; the earth became parched and burnt up; smiling districts were changed into wildernesses; fountains and brooks ceased to flow; the wells had no water; and, it is said, even the great rivers Tigris and Oxus ran entirely dry. Vegetation wholly ceased; the beasts of the field and the fowls of the air perished; not a bird was to be seen throughout the whole Persian dominion; the wild animals and the reptiles entirely disappeared.

This dreadful calamity afflicted Persia for seven years; but owing to the wisdom and beneficence of King Perozes, it is said that not one person, or, according to another account, but one, perished from hunger. Perozes began by issuing general orders that the rich should come to the relief of the poor. He required the governors of towns and the headmen of villages to see that food was furnished to such as were in want; and threatened that for each poor man who died from starvation in a town or village, he would put a rich man to death. After the drought had continued two years he refused to take any revenue from his subjects, remitting taxes of all kinds, whether they were money imposts or contributions in kind. In the fourth year of this terrible calamity he distributed money from his own treasury to those in need. He also imported corn from Greece and India, from the valley of the Oxus and from Abyssinia, thus obtaining ample supplies to furnish adequate sustenance to all his subjects. In consequence of these measures of the king, the famine caused no mortality among the poorer classes, and no Persian subject was obliged to leave his country to escape the pressure of this affliction.

Such are the Oriental accounts of the great famine which afflicted Persia during the early part of the reign of Perozes; but as he then engaged in a great war with the Ephthalites, who had aided him to obtain his crown, and as his ambassadors to the Greek or Eastern Roman court then requested a subsidy for his military preparations, and not food supplies, it seems probable that the accounts of the famine are largely exaggerated.

A contemporary Greek authority states that the cause of the war of Perozes against the Ephthalites was the refusal of those people to pay their customary tribute to Persia. Perozes resolved to enforce his claims, and led an army against the Ephthalites, but was defeated in his first operations. After some time he concluded to end the war, but determined to take a secret revenge upon his enemy by means of an occult insult. He proposed to the Khan, Khush-newâz, to conclude a treaty of peace and to strengthen the agreement by a marriage alliance, Khush-newâz to take one of the Persian king's daughters as a wife, thus uniting the interests of the two reigning families. Khush-newâz accepted this proposal, and readily espoused the young Persian princess who was sent to his court in attire suitable to her rank.

But the Ephthalite Khan soon found that he had been deceived. The Persian king had not sent his daughter, but one of his female slaves; and the royal race of the Ephthalite sovereigns had been disgraced by a matrimonial union with a person of a servile condition. Khush-newâz was rightly indignant, but he dissembled his feelings, and resolved to retaliate by a trick of his own. He wrote to Perozes that he intended to make war on a neighboring tribe, and that he wanted experienced officers to conduct the military operations. The Persian king, unsuspicious of any deception, readily granted this request, and sent three hundred of his principal officers to Khush-newâz, who instantly put some of them to death, mutilated the remainder, and commanded them to return to their sovereign and inform him that the Khan of the Ephthalites now felt that he had adequately avenged the trick of which he had been made the victim by the Persian monarch.

When Perozes received this message he renewed the war, marched toward the country of the Ephthalites, and established his headquarters in Hyrcania, at the city of Gurgân. He was accompanied by Eusebius, a Greek, an ambassador from the Eastern Roman Emperor Zeno, who brought to Constantinople the following account of the campaign.

When Perozes invaded the Ephthalite country and engaged the enemy, the latter pretended to be seized with a panic and instantly fled. They retreated to a mountain-region, where a broad and good road led into a wide plain, surrounded on every side by wooded hills, steep and in places precipitous. There the mass of the Ephthalite troops were cunningly concealed amid the foliage of the woods, while a small number remained visible and allured the Persian army into the ambuscade, the unsuspecting Persians only perceiving their peril when they observed the road by which they had entered occupied by the troops from the hills. The Persian officers then only knew that they had been cleverly entrapped, but all seemed afraid to inform their king that he had been deceived by a stratagem. They therefore requested Eusebius to inform Perozes of his perilous situation, and to exhort him to try to save himself by counsel and not by any desperate act.

Eusebius thereupon employed the Oriental method of apologue, relating to Perozes how a lion in pursuing a goat got himself into difficulties, from which all his strength was not able to extricate him. Perozes caught his meaning, comprehended the situation, desisted from the pursuit, and prepared to offer battle where he stood. But the Ephthalite monarch did not wish to push matters to extremities. He sent an embassy to Perozes, offering to release him from his perilous position and allow him and his army a safe return to Persia, if he would swear a perpetual peace with the Ephthalites and do homage to himself as his lord and master by prostration before him. Perozes felt that his only choice was to accept these humiliating terms. Instructed by the Magi, he made the required prostration at the moment of sunrise, with his face turned toward the east, thinking thus to escape the humiliation of abasing himself before a mortal by the mental reservation that the intention of his act was to adore the great Persian divinity. He then swore to the peace, and was permitted to return with his whole army to Persia.

3—9.—U. H.

Soon after this disgraceful peace, serious troubles again broke out in Armenia. Perozes followed his father's policy, incessantly persecuting the Christians of his northern provinces, especially those of Armenia, Georgia and Albania. His measures were so severe that many of the Armenians fled from their country and placed themselves under the protection of the Eastern Roman Emperor, becoming his subjects and entering into his service. Persian officials and apostate natives governed Armenia, treating the Christian inhabitants with extreme rudeness, insolence and injustice. They particularly oppressed the few noble Armenian families who adhered to the religion of Christ and who had not expatriated themselves. The most important of these were the Mamigonians, who had long been renowned in Armenian history, and who were then the chief of the Armenian nobility.

The renegade Armenians sought to discredit this noble family with the Persians; and Vahan, son of Hemaïag, the head of the family, was obliged to repeatedly visit the Persian court to refute the charges of his enemies and counteract their calumnies. He successfully vindicated himself, and was received into high favor by King Perozes; in consequence of which treatment he became a religious apostate, formally abjuring the Christian religion, for which he had defended himself firmly against all the blasts of persecution, and professing himself a Zoroastrian; thus turning his back upon all his past professions and record, merely to please his sovereign.

When the triumph of the anti-Christian party in Armenia thus seemed secured, a reaction began. The perfidious Vahan became subject to remorse, returned secretly to his old religious creed, and longed for an opportunity to wipe out the shame of his apostasy by imperilling his life for the Christian cause. The desired opportunity presented itself in A. D. 481, when King Perozes was defeated by the barbarous Krushans, who then occupied the low tract along the western coast of the Caspian Sea, from

Asterabad to Derbend. Iberia at once revolted, killed its Zoroastrian king, Vazken, and placed a Christian king, Vakhtang, upon the Iberian throne. The Persian satrap of Armenia, who received orders to suppress the Iberian rebellion, marched with all the troops that he could muster into Iberia, thus leaving the Armenians free to follow their own devices.

A rising instantly occurred; and all the efforts of Vahan, who doubted Armenia's power to cope with Persia, were not capable of restraining the popular enthusiasm of the Armenian Christians, who rushed to arms with the determination to be free. The Persians and their Armenian supporters fled from the country. The Christian party besieged and took Artáxata, the Armenian capital, and were completely victorious. After making themselves masters of all Persarmenia, they proceeded to establish a national government, with Sahag the Bagratide as king and Vahan the Mamigonian as *Sparapet*, or commander-in-chief. Upon hearing of these events, Ader-Veshnasp, the Persian satrap, returned to Armenia from Iberia with a small army of Medes, Atropatenians and Cadusians; but was utterly defeated and slain by Vasag, Vahan's brother, on the river Araxes (A. D. 481).

In A. D. 482 the Persians vigorously endeavored to recover their lost ground by sending an army under Ader-Nerseh against Armenia, and another under Mihran into Iberia. Ader-Nerseh was defeated by the Armenians under Vahan and King Sahag in the plain of Ardaz. Mihran soon overmatched the Iberian king, Vakhtang, who was obliged to apply to Armenia for aid. The Armenians who came to Vakhtang's assistance were ill rewarded for their generosity, as the Iberian king plotted to make his peace with Persia by treacherously betraying his allies into the power of their enemies; and the Armenians, thus obliged to fight at a great disadvantage, were severely defeated. Sahag, the Armenian king, and Vasag, Vahan's brother, were slain; and Vahan escaped with a few followers to the highlands of Daïk, on the frontiers of the Roman and Iberian territory. There he was hunted upon the mountains by Mihran; but when the Persian general was summoned by his sovereign to take the field against the Koushans of the low Caspian region, Vahan recovered possession of all Armenia in a few weeks.

In A. D. 483 the Persians made another desperate effort to crush the Armenian revolt, sending an army under Hazaravougd into Armenia early in the spring. Vahan was for some time besieged in the city of Dovin, but finally escaped, and renewed the guerrilla warfare in which he was so skillful. The Persians recovered most of Armenia, and Vahan was repeatedly driven across the border and obliged to seek refuge in Roman Armenia, whither he was pursued by the Persian general, and where he was for some time in constant peril, from which he was only saved when Hazaravougd was ordered by his king to direct his efforts to suppress the revolt in Iberia, and was succeeded in the government of Armenia by Sapor, a newly-appointed satrap.

Hazaravougd succeeded in restoring Persian authority in Iberia, and the Iberian king, Vakhtang, fled to Colchis. Sapor vainly attempted to procure Vahan's assassination by two of his officers, whose wives were Roman prisoners; after which he led a formidable army against Vahan, but was surprised and defeated with great loss and his army was dispersed. A second battle resulted as disastrously, and the demoralized Persian army was compelled to retreat; while Vahan assumed the offensive, established himself in Dovin, and again rallied the great mass of the Armenian nation to his side. The breaking out of another war between the Persians and the Ephthalites caused a pause in the Armenian struggle, and resulted in putting Armenian affairs on a new footing.

Some years after his disgraceful treaty with the Ephthalites, Perozes determined to renew the war with that people to atone for his humiliation by a great and signal victory. The Chief Mobed and the king's other counselors vainly opposed this design and sought to dissuade him, as did also his great general, Bahram ; while his soldiers also displayed reluctance to fight. Perozes could not be turned from his resolution; and collected an army of a hundred thousand men and five hundred elephants, and then took the field against the Ephthalites, leaving the government in the hands of Balas, or Palash, his son or brother.

Some Oriental writers tell us that Perozes sought by a curious subterfuge to free himself from the charge of having broken his treaty with the Ephthalite Khan. By that treaty the Persian king had sworn never to march his forces past a certain pillar which Khush-newâz, the Ephthalite sovereign, had erected to mark the boundary line between the Persian and Ephthalite dominions. Perozes persuaded himself that he would sufficiently observe his engagement if he kept his letter ; and he therefore lowered the pillar and placed it on a number of chariots attached together and drawn by a train of fifty elephants in front of his army. In this way he never "passed beyond" the pillar which he had sworn not to pass, no matter how far he invaded the Ephthalite country. In his own opinion he kept his vow, but not in the judgment of his advisers. By the mouth of the Chief Mobed, the Magian priesthood disclaimed this wretched casuistry and exposed its fallacy.

On hearing of the design of Perozes, the Ephthalite monarch prepared to meet his attack by stratagem. He had established his camp near Balkh, the ancient Bactria, where he dug a deep and wide trench in front of his whole position; and after filling this trench with water, he covered it carefully with boughs of trees, reeds and earth, so that it could not be distinguished from the general surface of the plain on which he was encamped. When the Persians arrived in his front he held a parley with Perozes, reproaching him with ingratitude and breach of faith, and offering to renew the peace.

When Perozes scornfully refused, the Ephthalite sovereign hung the broken treaty on the point of a lance, paraded it in front of the Persian army, and exhorted the Persian troops to avoid the vengeance which was certain to overtake the perjured by deserting their doomed sovereign. Tabari tells us that one-half of the Persian army then retired, and that Khush-newâz then sent a part of his army across the trench with orders to challenge the Persians to battle, and when the conflict commenced, to flee hastily, and to return within the trench by the sound passage and unite themselves with the main army.

As had been expected, the whole Persian host pursued the fleeing Ephthalites and came unawares upon the concealed trench and plunged into it, becoming inextricably entangled and being easily destroyed. King Perozes, several of his sons, and most of his army, perished. Firuz-docht, his daughter, along with the Chief Mobed and many of the rank and file, were made prisoners. The victorious Ephthalites took a vast booty, among which, Procopius and Tabari tell us, were an ear-ring, and an amulet which King Perozes carried as a bracelet. Khush-newâz did not stain his triumph by any cruelties, but treated his captives with kindness, and searched for the body of the Persian king, which, after being found, was honorably interred.

Thus perished King Perozes in A. D. 483, after a reign of twenty-six years, according to Tabari and Mirkhond. He was a brave monarch and fully merited the epithet of *Al Merdaneh*, "the Courageous," which his subjects bestowed upon him. But his bravery amounted to rashness, and he was not possessed of any other military quality. He did not possess the sagacity to form a good plan of campaign, nor the ability to conduct a battle. He was personally unsuccessful in all the wars in which he engaged, and his generals won the only triumphs which attended his arms. He obtained a reputation for humanity and justice in his civil administration; and, if the Oriental accounts of his conduct during the great famine are correct, his wisdom and benevolence had no parallels among Oriental monarchs. His conduct toward Khush-newâz was the great blot which tarnished his fair fame.

There are numerous coins of Perozes, and they are distinguished usually by having a wing in front of the crown and another behind it. They bear the legend, *Kadi-Piruzi*, or *Mazdisn Kadi Piruzi*, "King Perozes," or "the Ormazd-worshiping King Perozes." The king's ear-ring is a triple pendant. The reverse has the usual fire-altar and supporters, and also a star and a crescent on each side of the altar-flame. The mints named are those of Persepolis, Ispahan, Rhages, Nehavend, Darabgherd, Zadracarta, Nissa, Behistun, Khuzistan, Media, Kerman, Azerbijan, Rasht, Baiza, Modaīn, Merv, Shiz, Iran, Yez and others. The general character of the coinage is rude and coarse, and the reverse of the coins especially exhibit signs of degeneracy. There is also a cup or vase of antique and elegant form assigned to the reign of Perozes, engraved with a hunting-scene.

Perozes was succeeded by a king called BALAS by the Greeks, and PALASH by the Arabs and the later Persians, but whose real name seems to have been VALAKHESH, or VOLAGASES. The native Persian writers call him the son of Perozes, while the Greeks and the contemporary Armenians represent him as the brother of Perozes.

The new king immediately sent Sukhra, or Sufrai, the satrap of Seistan, to defend the north-eastern frontier against the victorious Ephthalites. Sukhra led a large army to the menaced frontier, and alarmed Khushnewâz by a display of his skill in archery; after which he entered into negotiations with the Ephthalite sovereign and obtained the release of Firuz-docht, of the Grand Mobed and of the other important prisoners, along with the restoration of a considerable part of the captured booty. But the Persian general was probably compelled to accept some humiliating conditions on his sovereign's part, as Procopius informs us that Persia became subject to the Ephthalites and paid them tribute for two years.

Balas next devoted his attention to the pacification of Armenia. He first appointed Nikhor, a Persian, Marzpan, or governor of Armenia. Nikhor, who was a man of justice and moderation, proposed to Vahan, the Armenian prince, who was then master of most of Armenia, that they should discuss amicably the terms upon which the Armenian people would be satisfied to resume their old position of dependence upon Persia. Vahan declared that he and his partisans were willing to lay down their arms on the conditions that the existing fire-altars in Armenia should be destroyed, and no others erected in that country; that the Armenians should be allowed the full exercise of the Christian religion, and no Armenians should in the future be bribed or tempted to declare themselves disciples of Zoroaster; that if converts were made from Christianity to Zoroastrianism, no places should be assigned to them; and that the Persian king should personally administer the government of Armenia, and not by viceroy or governor.

Nikhor agreed to these terms; and, after an exchange of hostages, Vahan visited the Persian camp and arranged with Nikhor for a solemn ratification of peace on the aforesaid conditions. An edict of toleration was issued, and it was formally declared that "every one should be at liberty to adhere to his own religion, and that no one should be driven to apostatize." Upon these terms Vahan and Nikhor concluded peace; but before King Balas had ratified the treaty, Zareh, a son of Perozes, laid claim to the Persian crown, and, being supported by a large body of the Persian people, involved the country in civil war.

Nikhor, the Persian governor of Armenia, was one of the officers appointed to suppress Zareh's rebellion. By suggesting to Vahan that it would strengthen the Armenian claims to afford effective aid to Balas, Nikhor induced the Armenian leader to send a formidable force of cavalry commanded by his own nephew, Gregory. By the valor of this Armenian contingent, Zareh was defeated, and was pursued in his flight to the mountains, taken prisoner and slain. Soon afterward Kobad, another son of Perozes, claimed the Persian crown, but met with no success, and was obliged to leave Persia and place himself under the protection of the Ephthalites. Balas then directed his attention to the complete pacification of Armenia. He summoned Vahan to his court, received him with the highest honors, listened attentively to his representations, and finally accepted the terms formulated by Vahan. He then appointed Antegan governor of Armenia. This man was a worthy successor of Nikhor—"mild, prudent and equitable." To show his confidence in Vahan, King Balas appointed him *Sparapet*, or commander-in chief. After Antegan had governed Armenia for a few months, he recommended to his sovereign that the wisest course would be to intrust Vahan with the government of Armenia.

The Persian king accordingly recalled Antegan and appointed Vahan to the governorship of Armenia; while Vahan's brother, Vart, was assigned to the office of Sparapet. Christianity was then formally established as the state religion of Armenia. The fire-altars were destroyed; the churches were reclaimed and purified; and the Christian hierarchy was restored to its former position and powers. Almost the entire Armenian nation was reconverted to the Christian religion, the apostate Armenians abjuring Zoroastrianism. Armenia and Iberia were pacified, and the two provinces which had been so long a cause of weakness to Persia soon became the main sources of Persian strength and prosperity.

Balas was a wise and just sovereign, mild in his temper, averse to war, and conciliatory. His internal administration gave general satisfaction to his subjects. He protected and relieved the poor, extended cultivation, and punished governors who permitted any men in their respective provinces to fall into poverty. His prudence and moderation ended the chronic Armenian difficulty and made Armenia a loyal province of the New Persian Empire.

The coins assigned to Balas have on the obverse the head of a king with the usual mural crown surmounted by a crescent and an inflated ball. The beard is short and curled, while the hair falls behind the head in curls. The ear-ring ornamenting the ear has a double pendant. Flames issue from the left shoulder. The full legend upon the coins is *Hur Kadi Valakâshi*, "Volagases, the Fire King." The reverse has the usual fire-altar, but with the king's head in the flames, and with the star and the crescent on each side. It usually bears the legend "*Valakâshi*," with a mint-mark. The mints named are those of Iran, Kerman, Ispahan, Nissa, Leden, Shiz, Zadracarta and several others.

Soon after the pacification of Armenia, Balas died (A. D. 487), after a reign of four years, without appointing a successor. When Kobad fled to the Ephthalites, on his failure to seize the Persian crown, he was welcomed; and when Balas withheld his tribute, three years later, Khush-newâz furnished Kobad with an army with which he returned to the Persian capital. KOBAD'S first reign lasted eleven years (A. D. 487-498), and during its early portion he intrusted the administration of public affairs to Sukhra, or Sufrai, his father's chief minister. Sufrai's son, Zer-Mihr, had faithfully adhered to Kobad throughout his exile, and Kobad magnanimously forgave Sufrai for opposing his ambition and using his power against him.

Sufrai accordingly governed Persia for some years, having the civil administration wholly in his hands, while the army obeyed him. Kobad therefore grew jealous of his minister, and sought to deprive him of his quasi-legal authority and to assert his own right to direct public affairs. He therefore called in the aid of an officer named Sapor, who quarrelled with Sufrai and imprisoned him, putting him to death several days afterward. Sapor then became Kobad's prime minister, and also *Sipehbed*, or commander-in-chief. Kobad allowed the whole administration to fall into Sapor's hands.

During Kobad's first reign Persia was engaged in a war with the Khazars, who then occupied the steppes between the Volga and the Don, whence they made raids through the passes of the Caucasus into the fertile Persian provinces of Iberia, Albania and Armenia. The Khazars were at this time a race of fierce and terrible barbarians, nomadic in their habits, ruthless in their wars, cruel and uncivilized in their customs, and a fearful scourge to the regions which they overran and desolated. Kobad led a hundred thousand men against them, defeated them in a battle, destroyed most of their army, and returned to his capital with a vast booty. Tabari tells us that Kobad built the town of Amid on the Armenian frontier to check the inroads of the Khazars.

Soon after returning in triumph from his Khazar campaign, Kobad was involved in difficulties which finally lost him his crown. Mazdak, a Persian and an Archimagus, or High Priest of the Zoroastrian religion, announced himself as a reformer of Zoroastrianism early in Kobad's reign, and commenced making proselytes to the new doctrines which he declared himself commissioned to reveal. He asserted that all men were, by God's providence, born equal; that none brought any property into the world, nor any right to possess more than another; that property and marriage were mere human inventions, contrary to God's will, which required an equal division of the good things of this world among all, and which forbade the appropriation of particular women by individual men; that in communities based upon property and marriage, men might lawfully vindicate their natural rights by taking their fair share of the good things wrongfully appropriated by their fellows; and that adultery, incest, theft, etc., were not really crimes, but neccessary steps towards the reëstablishment of the laws of nature in such societies.

Besides these communistic views, the Magian reformer added tenets from the Brahmans of India, or from some other Oriental ascetics; such as the sacredness of animal life, the necessity of abstaining from animal food, except milk, cheese or eggs, and also the propriety of simplicity in dress and the need of abstemiousness and devotion. He thus appeared as a religious enthusiast preaching a doctrine of moral laxity and self-indulgence, simply from a conviction of duty, and not from any base or selfish motive. It is not surprising that the new teacher's doctrines were embraced with ardor by large classes of Persians—by the young of all ranks, by the lovers of pleasure, and by the great bulk of the lower orders. But it naturally excites our wonder that the king himself was among the proselytes to the new religion which leveled him with his subjects. Mazdak claimed to authenticate his mission by the possession and exhibition of miraculous powers. He imposed on Kobad's weak mind by a clever device.

He excavated a cave below the fire-altar on which he was accustomed to offering, and contrived to pass a tube from the cavern to the upper surface of the altar, where the sacred flame was maintained perpetually. He then placed a confederate in the cavern and invited Kobad to attend, and in the king's presence he appeared to converse with the fire itself, which the Persians regarded as the symbol and embodiment of divinity. The king accepted the pretended miracle as conclusive evidence of the divine authority of the new teacher, and thenceforth was his zealous supporter and disciple.

Disorders followed the king's conversion to the new creed. The followers of Mazdak were not satisfied with establishing community of property and of women among themselves, but claimed the right to plunder the rich at their pleasure, and to carry off the inmates of the most illustrious harems for the gratification of their own passions. The Mobeds vainly declared that the new creed was false and monstrous, and that it ought not to be tolerated for an hour. Mazdak's disciples had the king's support—a protection which secured them perfect impunity. They grew bolder and more numerous daily. Persia became too narrow a field for their ambition, and they sought to diffuse their doctrines into the neighboring countries.

Traces of their doctrine were to be found in the remote West of Christendom; and the Armenian historians tell us that they so pressed their doctrines upon the Armenian people that an insurrection broke out, and Persia was threatened with the loss of one of her most valued dependencies by intolerance. Vahan the Mamigonian had been superseded in the government of Armenia by another Marzpan, who was resolved upon forcing the Armenians to adopt the new creed. Vahan again appeared as his country's champion, took up arms to defend the Christian faith, and sought to induce the Eastern Roman Emperor Anastasius I. to accept the sovereignty of Persarmenia, along with the duty of protecting it against the Persians. Anastasius hesitated, but a revolution in Persia itself rescued the unfortunate Armenians.

The Mobeds and the chief nobles in Persia had vainly protested against the diffusion of the new religion and the patronage which it received from the Persian court. Finally an appeal was made to the Chief Mobed, who was requested to devise a remedy for the existing evils, which were now regarded as beyond endurance. The Chief Mobed decided that the only effectual remedy, under the circumstances, was the deposition of the sovereign, through whose culpable connivance the disorders had reached their height. This decision was generally sustained. The Persian nobles unanimously agreed to depose Kobad and to place his brother Zamasp upon the throne. Zamasp was noted for his love of justice and for the mildness of his disposition. After making the requisite arrangements they rose in unanimous rebellion, arrested Kobad and imprisoned him in the "Castle of Oblivion," and proclaimed ZAMASP and crowned him King of Persia with all the usual formalities.

An effort to inflict a fatal blow on the new religion by seizing and executing Mazdak failed. The seizure and imprisonment of Mazdak roused his followers, who broke open his prison doors and released him. The government did not possess sufficient strength to enforce its intended policy of coercion; and Mazdak was permitted to live in retirement unmolested, and to augment the number of his followers.

Zamasp's reign lasted almost three years, from A. D. 498 to 501. The Persian army urged him to put Kobad to death, but he hesitated to adopt so extreme a course, and preferred to retain his rival in imprisonment. The "Castle of Oblivion" was considered a safe place, but the ex-king soon effected his escape from prison through the assistance of his wife. He took refuge with the Ephthalites, and sought to induce the Great Khan to espouse his cause and furnish him with an army. Khush-newâz received the royal fugitive with every mark of honor, betrothed him to one of his daughters, and placed an army of thirty thousand men at his disposal.

Kobad returned to Persia with this force and offered battle to Zamasp, who declined the conflict, as he had not secured the popularity of his subjects, and as he knew that a large party desired his brother's return to the throne. Therefore when Kobad reached the vicinity of the Persian capital with the thirty thousand Ephthalites and a strong force of Persian supporters, Zamasp abdicated the throne in favor of his brother and voluntarily retired to private life. Procopius tells us that the restored Kobad blinded his brother's eyes; but Mirkhond says that Zamasp was pardoned, and that his brother even bestowed marks of affection and favor upon him.

Zamasp's coins have the usul inflated ball and mural crown, but have a crescent instead of the front limb of the crown. The ends of the diadem appear over the two shoulders. There is a star on each side of the head and a crescent over each shoulder. There are three stars with crescents outside the encircling ring, or "pearl border." The reverse has the usual fire-altar, with a star and a crescent on each side of the flame. The legend is either *Zamasp*, or *Bag Zamasp*, "Zamaspes," or "the divine Zamaspes."

KOBAD'S second reign lasted from A. D. 501 to 531, thus embracing a period of thirty years. He reigned contemporaneously with the Eastern Roman Emperors Anastasius I., Justin I. and Justinian I., and with Theodoric, the Ostrogothic King of Italy; while such eminent characters as Cassiodórus, Boëthius, Symmachus, Procopius and Belisarius flourished at the same time. We get little of this part of his history from the Oriental writers; while the Byzantine authors give us copious accounts of his transactions with the Eastern Roman Emperors, and also some interesting notices of other matters which engaged his attention.

Procopius, the eminent rhetorician and secretary of Belisarius, who was born about the time of Kobad's restoration to the Persian throne, and who became secretary to the great Byzantine general four years before Kobad's death, gives ample details of the principal events. Concerning this writer, Gibbon says: "His facts are collected from the personal experience and free conversation of a soldier, a statesman and a traveler; his style continually aspires, and often attains, to the merit of strength and elegance; his reflections, more especially in the speeches, which he too frequently inserts, contain a rich fund of political knowledge; and the historian, excited by the generous ambition of pleasing and instructing posterity, appears to disdain the prejudices of the people and the flattery of courts."

Though still holding fast to the views of the communistic prophet Mazdak, and not ashamed to confess himself an adherent of that creed, the restored Kobad, as a king, gave no support to the partisans of the religion in any extreme or violent measures. As a result the new doctrine languished. Mazdak escaped persecution and continued to propagate his views, but the progress of the new opinions was practically checked. As these opinions no longer commanded royal advocacy, they no longer endangered the state. Though they still fermented among the masses, they were now the harmless speculations of a certain number of enthusiasts who no longer ventured to carry their theories into practice.

About a year after his restoration to the Persian throne, Kobad's relations with the Eastern Roman Empire became troubled, and after some futile negotiations hostilities again commenced. By the terms of the peace between Isdigerd II. and Theodosius II., concluded in A. D. 442, the Romans agreed to pay an annual contribution towards the expenses of a fortified post which the two powers undertook to maintain in the pass of Derbend, between the spurs of the Caucasus and the Caspian. This fortress, known as Juroipach, or Biraparach, commanded the usual passage by which the Northern hordes were accustomed to issue from their vast arid steppes upon the rich and populous regions of the South for the purpose of plundering raids, if not of actual conquests.

As these barbarian incursions threatened alike the Eastern Roman and the New Persian dominions, it was felt that the two empires both had an interest in preventing them. The original treaty stipulated that both powers should contribute equally, alike to the erection and to the maintenance of the fortress; but the entire burden fell upon the Persians, as the Romans were too much occupied in other wars. The Persians occasionally demanded from the Romans the payment of their share of the expenses, but as these efforts were ineffectual the debt accumulated.

When Kobad lacked money to reward sufficiently his Ephthalite allies, he sent an embassy to the Emperor Anastasius to demand a peremptory remittance. Procopius says that Anastasius absolutely declined to make any payment; while Theóphanes says that he declared himself willing to loan his "Persian brother" a sum of money on receiving the usual acknowledgment, but refused an advance on any other conditions. Kobad instantly declared war, and the sixty years' peace between the Eastern Roman and New Persian Empires was broken. The war began by a sudden Persian invasion of Roman Armenia; and Theodosiopolis, after a short siege, was surrendered to the invaders by its commandant, Constantine; after which most of Roman Armenia was overrun and ravaged. Kobad led his army from Armenia into Roman Mesopotamia, and laid siege to Amida about the beginning of winter.

Amida was only defended by a small force under the philosopher Alypius; but the resolution of the inhabitants, and particularly of the monks, was great. All Kobad's efforts to take the town met with a determined resistance. At first he hoped to effect a breach in the defenses by means of the battering-ram; but the besieged employed the usual means of destroying his engines, and where these failed the walls were so thick and strong that the Persian battering-rams could make no serious impression upon them. Kobad next raised an immense mound near the wall for the purpose of commanding the town, driving the defenders from the battlements, and then taking the city by escalade; but his mound was undermined by the enemy, and finally fell with a terrible crash, involving hundreds in its ruin.

It is said that Kobad, despairing of success, was then about to raise the siege and to retire with his army; but that the taunts and insults of the besieged, or his confidence in the prophecies of the Magi, who saw an omen of victory in the grossest of all the insults, induced him to alter his intention and to continue the siege. Soon afterward one of his soldiers discovered the outlet of a drain or sewer in the wall, imperfectly blocked up with rubbish, which he removed during the night, thus finding himself able to pass through the wall into the beleaguered town.

This soldier revealed his discovery to Kobad, who the next night sent a few picked men through the drain to seize the nearest tower, which was slackly guarded by some sleepy monks, who had been keeping festival the previous day. Kobad brought most of his army with scaling-ladders to the adjoining part of the wall; and by his presence, exhortations and threats, forced them to make their way into the town. The inhabitants strenuously resisted, but were overpowered by superior numbers, and the carnage in the streets was terrific.

Finally a venerable priest, appalled at the indiscriminate massacre, boldly addressed the Persian king, telling him that it was no kingly act to slaughter captives. The angry monarch asked: "Why, then, did you choose to fight?" The priest answered: "It was God's doing; He willed that thou shouldest owe the conquest of Amida, not to our weakness, but to thy own valor." Kobad was so pleased with this flattery that he stopped the shedding of blood, but he allowed the sack of the town to continue. The whole city was pillaged, and most of the inhabitants were carried into slavery.

The siege of Amida lasted eighty days, during the latter part of A. D. 502 and the beginning of 503. The Emperor Anastasius had sent a considerable force to the relief of this frontier town. This force was under four commanders—Areobindus, grandson of the Gothic officer of the same name who had distinguished himself in the Persian war of Theodosius II.; Celer, captain of the imperial guard; Patricius, the Phrygian; and Hypatius, one of the Emperor's nephews. This divided force arrived too late to save Amida and accomplished nothing.

Kobad left a small force to garrison Amida, carried off all of his rich booty to his city of Nísibis, and placed most of his army in a good position on the frontier. The Romans invaded the Persian territory, but Areobindus retreated when Kobad advanced, allowing the enemy to capture his camp and stories; while Patricius and Hypatius destroyed Kobad's advance guard of eight hundred men almost to a man, but these Roman divisions were afterwards surprised on the banks of a stream while some of the men were bathing and others were breakfasting, and were completely cut to pieces by Kobad, scarcely any except the generals escaping.

But in A. D. 503, when fortune was wholly on the side of the Persians, Kobad was obliged to leave to others the conduct of the war against the Romans, being called to the defense of his north-eastern frontier by an Ephthalite invasion; and thenceforth the Romans had the advantage. In A. D. 504 the Roman division under Celer invaded Arzanênê, destroyed a number of forts, and ravaged the whole province with fire and sword. Celer then marched southward and threatened Nísibis. Towards winter Patricius and Hypatius besieged Amida; and, after failing in several assaults on the town, they turned the siege into a blockade, entrapped Glones, the commander of the Persian garrison, by a stratagem, and reduced the garrison to such distress that they could not have held out much longer.

At this point a Persian ambassador of high rank arrived from King Kobad, authorized to conclude peace with the Romans, and instructed to declare his sovereign's willingness to relinquish all his conquests, including Amida, on the payment of a considerable sum of money. The Roman generals gladly consented, and handed the Persians a thousand pounds of gold, receiving in exchange the captured city and territory. A treaty was signed by which the Romans and Persians agreed to remain at peace and respect each other's dominions for seven years.

Kobad was occupied ten years in the Ephthalite war which compelled him to make peace with the Emperor Anastasius I. During this period the Romans profitted by Persia's difficulties by establishing strongly fortified posts upon their Persian frontier. Anastasius restored Theodosiopolis and greatly strengthened its defenses, and also erected an entirely new fortress at Daras, on the southern skirts of the Mons Masius, within twelve miles of Nísibis, at the edge of the great plain of Mesopotamia. This place was not merely a fort, but a city, containing churches, baths, porticos, large granaries and extensive cisterns. This place was a standing menace to Persia, and its erection was in direct violation of the treaty between Isdigerd II. and Theodosius II., which both nations regarded as still in force.

It is not surprising that, as soon as his Ephthalite war was over, Kobad made formal complaint at Constantinople of the violation of the treaty (A. D. 517). Anastasius met the charge by a mixture of bluster and professions of friendship, and when this method proved ineffectual he bribed the Persian ambassadors with a large sum of money. After the death of Anastasius, in A. D. 518, Kobad entered into negotiations with the new Emperor, Justin I.

But Justin I., soon after his accession, sent an embassy with rich gifts to the Hunnic chief, Ziligdes, or Zilgibis, and concluded a treaty with him by which the Hun bound himself to aid the Romans against the Persians. Soon afterwards a Lazic prince named Tzath, a vassal of Persia, went to Constantinople and expressed a desire to become a Christian and a vassal of the Eastern Roman Emperor. The Emperor Justin I. warmly welcomed the Lazic prince, had him baptized, married him to a Byzantine lady of high rank, and sent him back to Lazica adorned with a diadem and robes that sufficiently indicated his position as a vassal of the Eastern Roman Emperor.

Neither Kobad nor Justin I. desired a rupture, both being advanced in years and both having domestic troubles on hand, while Kobad was especially anxious about his succession. He had four sons—Kaöses, Zames, Phthasuarsas and Chosroës. Kaöses, the eldest prince, did not please him. His affections were centered on his fourth son, Chosroës, and he desired to secure his crown to his favorite child. Procopius and other Byzantine writers tell us that Kobad made a strange proposal to the Emperor Justin I., asking him to adopt Chosroës, so that that prince might have Roman assistance against his countrymen if his right of succession should be disputed; but the Eastern Roman Emperor declined the proposal.

Persia again became distracted with religious troubles about the year A. D. 523. Mazdak's followers, who had thus far been protected by Kobad, and who had lived in peace and multiplied throughout the Persian dominions, had been content with the toleration which they had enjoyed for almost a quarter of a century, and thus created no disturbance. But as Kobad was growing old, and as Phthasuarsas, who had little chance for the succession, was the only one of all Kobad's sons that embraced their doctrines, they began to feel that their position was insecure. Their happiness, their very safety, thus depended upon a single life.

They therefore resolved to anticipate the natural course of events by promising Phthasuarsas to obtain by their prayers his father's abdication and his own appointment as his successor, and asked the prince to pledge himself to establish their religion as that of the state when he became king. Phthasuarsas consented; but when the Mazdakites proceeded to arrange their plans Kobad suspected that a conspiracy was on foot to deprive him of his crown. In the East it is an offense even to speculate on the king's death, and Kobad construed the intrigues of the Mazdakites as a dangerous plot against himself. Resolved at once to nip the scheme in the bud, he invited the Mazdakites to a solemn assembly, pretending that he would there confer the royal dignity on Phthasuarsas, and caused his army to surround and massacre the entire unarmed multitude.

Kobad was now confronted with troubles in Iberia. Pursuing the intolerant policy of his predecessors, he had ordered Gurgenes, the Iberian king, to renounce Christianity and to profess Zoroastrianism. The Persian king had particularly demanded that the Iberian custom of burying the dead should be relinquished, and that the Persian practice of exposing corpses to be devoured by dogs and birds of prey should supersede the Christian rite of sepulture.

Gurgenes was too sincerely attached to the Christian faith to entertain these propositions for a moment. He immediately cast off the Persian yoke, and by declaring himself a vassal of the Eastern Roman Emperor he obtained a promise from Justin I. to stand by the Iberian cause. The Emperor Justin I., instead of sending his own armies to that remote and inhospitable region, attempted to engage the Tartars of the Crimea in his service against the Persians; but only a small Crimean force was raised and sent to aid Gurgenes.

A large Persian army under Boës now entered Iberia; whereupon Gurgenes fled from Iberia into Lazica, where he was able to maintain himself through the difficult nature of the ground, the support of the natives and the aid of the Romans. But the Persians again became masters of Iberia, and even entered Lazica and occupied some forts commanding the passes between Lazica and Iberia.

The Romans retaliated on the Persians by invading Persarmenia and Mesopotamia. In this campaign the renowned and unfortunate Belisarius, the greatest general of that age, first held a command and commenced his experience as a military leader. He had hitherto been a mere guardsman, and was still a mere youth; and, as he was on this occasion hampered by a colleague, he did not win any laurels in this campaign. A Persian army under Narses and Aratius defended Persarmenia, and defeated the Romans under Belisarius and Sittas. At the same time Licelarius, a Thracian in the Roman service, made an irruption into the Persian territory about Nísibis, but soon hastily retreated. Thereupon the Emperor Justin I. recalled Licelarius, and intrusted Belisarius with the conduct of the war in Mesopotamia.

The Emperor Justin I. died in A. D. 527, and was succeeded by his nephew Justinian I., the greatest of all the Eastern Roman Emperors. Justinian restored and strengthened the frontier city of Martyropolis, on the Nymphius; and early in A. D. 528 he ordered Belisarius to build a new fort at Mindon, on the Persian frontier, a little to the left of Nísibis. After Belisarius had begun work on the new fort, a Persian army of thirty thousand men under Xerxes, son of Kobad, and Perozes, the Mihran, attacked the Roman workmen, and afterwards defeated Belisarius, after he had been strengthened by reinforcements from Syria, and forced him to seek safety in flight. The unfinished fort was then leveled with the ground, and the Mihran returned to Persia with many important prisoners.

The Emperor Justinian I. now conferred upon Belisarius the title of *General of the East.* Thereupon Belisarius assembled an army of twenty-five thousand men at Daras, consisting of Romans and allies, the latter being mainly Massagetæ. He was soon confronted by a Persian army of forty thousand men under Perozes the Mihran, who sent an insolent message to Belisarius, asking him to have his bath prepared for the morrow, as he would need that kind of refreshment after taking Daras.

Belisarius so disposed his troops in front of Daras that his centre and his flanks would be protected by a deep ditch, outside of which there would be no room for his cavalry to act. After reconnoitering the position, Perozes hastily sent to Nísibis for ten thousand more troops, and passed the day in some insignificant single combats and a cavalry demonstration against the Roman left wing.

The Persian reinforcement arrived the next morning; and after some exchange of messages with Belisarius, Perozes placed his infantry in the center and his cavalry upon each wing, as the Romans had also done, and arranged his infantry so that one-half should from time to time relieve the other half, after which he assailed the Romans with a shower of darts and arrows. The Romans replied with their missile weapons; but the Persians had the advantage of numbers, and were protected by huge wattled shields, while they were also more accustomed to this style of warfare than the Romans. The Romans continued their resistance; and when the missile weapons on both sides became exhausted, and a closer fight began along the entire line with swords and spears, the Romans fought to more advantage. But the Romans were routed by the Cadiseni, or Cadusians, under Pituazes, who were hastily pursuing their enemies when they were charged on their right flank and thrown into disorder by the Massagetic cavalry under Suníeas and Aigan and by three hundred Heruli under Pharas. Three thousand were killed on the Persian side, and the rest were driven back upon the main army, which still fought gallantly. The Romans then occupied their former position.

Then the Persian corps of the Immortals and other troops furiously charged the Roman right and forced it to a hasty retreat, but the pursuing Persian column was cut in two by an impetuous charge of the barbarian cavalry in the Roman army, thus deciding the battle in favor of the Romans. Those Persians who advanced farthest were completely surrounded and slain. The fall of the standard-bearer of Baresmanes, the commander of the Persian left, increased the general confusion; and the Persian column vainly attempted an orderly retreat. The Romans attacked it in front and on both flanks, and a frightful carnage ensued. Baresmanes was slain by Suníeas, the Massa-Goth; whereupon the entire Persian army broke and fled, leaving five thousand dead, among whom were many of the Immortals.

In the meantime the Persian army under Mermeroës in the Armenian highlands was twice defeated by the Roman forces only half as large under Sittas and Dorothéus, once in Persarmenia and again in Roman Armenia. These Roman victories led to desertions to the Roman side.

After vainly attempting to negotiate peace with the Romans, the Persians entered into an alliance with Alamándarus, a powerful Arab shiekh, who had long been a bitter enemy of the Romans, and who for half a century had ravaged the eastern provinces of the Eastern Roman Empire with impunity, from his safe desert retreat. He had two years before ravaged Upper Syria with fire and sword, had burned the suburbs of Chalcis, and threatened the rich and luxurious Antioch. He apparently owed a nominal allegiance to Persia, though practically independent, and made his expeditions when and where he saw fit.

In A. D. 531 Alamándarus offered to unite with Persia in a joint expedition, and suggested a new plan of campaign. He proposed that the Persians should invade the country beyond the Euphrates and attack and sack Antioch. Kobad resolved to act upon the plan thus suggested, and sent a force of fifteen thousand cavalry under Azarethes, whom he ordered to take Alamándarus for a guide, and to make a joint expedition with the Arab shiekh across the Euphrates for the purpose of taking and pillaging Antioch.

The allied Persian and Arabian army crossed the Euphrates below Circésium, and moved up the west bank of the river as far as the latitude of Antioch, when they marched westward and arrived at Gabbula, the modern Jabul, on the northern shore of the salt lake now known as Sabakhah, where they were surprised to learn that Belisarius had become informed of their design. The great Roman general had at once left Daras, and proceeded by forced marches to the defense of Syria with an army of twenty thousand men, composed of Romans, Isaurians, Lycaonians and Arabs. Belisarius established his headquarters at Chalcis, between Gabbula and Antioch; thus thwarting the design of the invaders, who then retreated from Syria with the plunder of the towns which they had sacked in their advance.

Belisarius was obliged by the eagerness of his troops, against his own better judgment, to attack the retreating foe on the banks of the Euphrates, nearly opposite Callinícus, on Easter Eve, April 19, A. D. 531. The Roman infantry firmly held their ground; but his Arab allies and the Isaurian and Lycaonian cavalry, who had been most eager for the fray, almost instantly fled from the field. As the Roman right was thus left exposed, Belisarius made his troops turn their faces to the enemy and their backs to the Euphrates, and in this position to resist the foe until night, when he was able to transport his troops in boats across the river. Thus the Persian raid into Syria had failed of its main object, and Kobad reproached Azarethes for uselessly sacrificing so many lives.

Another Persian army was sent into Mesopotamia, where Sittas now commanded the Roman forces, Belisarius having been hastily summoned to Constantinople to take the field against the Vandals in Africa. As this Persian army was unopposed, it invaded Sophêné and besieged the Roman fortress of Martyropolis, which was ill provisioned, and whose walls were out of repair. The fortress was saved from capture by a report spread by Sittas that the Huns were about to make a diversion as Roman allies. The Persian commanders were paralyzed by fear of being caught between two fires, and before they were undeceived they received tidings of the death of King Kobad and the accession of his son Chosroës to the Persian throne. Thereupon Chanaranges, the leading Persian commander, retired into the Persian territory with his army, thus yielding to the representations made by Sittas that a treaty of peace was now probable.

Kobad died of paralysis on the 13th of September, A. D. 531, after an illness of but five days. Before his death he had expressed to his chief minister, Mebodes, his earnest desire for the succession of his son Chosroës to the throne, and by the advice of Mebodes he bequeathed the crown to Chosroës by a will duly executed. He was eighty-two years of age at the time of his death. His long life was extremely eventful, and he was a monarch possessing the qualities of activity, perseverance, fertility of resource and general military capacity. But he was also cruel and fickle; he disgraced his ministers and generals for slight causes; he smothered his religious convictions from considerations of policy; and for the purpose of gratifying a favoritism he hazarded subjecting Persia to the horrors of civil war. He simply preferred Chosroës because of his beauty, and because he was the son of Kobad's best-loved wife, rather than for any good qualities; and Chosroës inherited the Persian dominions because he was his father's darling, and not because he had as yet shown any capacity for government.

Kobad's numerous coins resemble those of Zamasp in their general appearance, but do not have so many stars and crescents. The legend on the obverse is either *Kavât* or *Kavât afzui*, "Kobad," or "May Kobad be increased." The reverse exhibits the regnal year, ranging from eleven to forty-three, along with a mint-mark.

Thus began the reign of CHOSROES I., or KHOSROU NUSHIRVAN—usually considered the greatest of the Sassanidæ. His accession was disputed. Kaöses, Kobad's eldest son, considering himself entitled to the Persian crown by right of birth, assumed the insignia of royalty upon his father's death, and claimed to be acknowledged as sovereign. But Mebodes, the Grand Vizier, interposed by asserting a constitutional axiom that no one had the right to take the Persian crown until the assembly of the Persian nobles had assigned it to him. Kaöses, who fancied that he could count on the good will of the nobles, acquiesced; and, the assembly being convened, his claims were submitted to it. Thereupon Mebodes presented Kobad's "testament," or dying statement, which he had hitherto concealed, and submitting it to them, exhorted them to accept for their king the brave prince designated by a brave and successful father. The eloquence and authority of Mebodes prevailed; the claims of Kaöses and of at least one other son of Kobad were ignored; and, in accordance with his father's will, Chosroës was proclaimed the lawful King of Persia.

But a party among the nobles were dissatisfied with the decision of the majority, and dreaded the restlessness of Chosroës. As Zames, Kobad's second son, whom they would have supported, was legally incapacitated from reigning by having lost one eye, the discontented nobles formed a plot for the elevation of a son of Zames, a boy named after his illustrious grandfather Kobad, on whose behalf Zames would naturally be regent. Zames came into the plot very readily, and was supported by several of his brothers and by Chosroës's maternal uncle, the Aspebed. Chosroës discovered the conspiracy in time to prevent its success, and took prompt and effectual measures for its suppression. By his orders, Zames, Kaöses, and all of Kobad's other sons were seized, and were condemned to death, as were also their entire male offspring. The Aspebed and the other nobles found to have been accessory to the conspiracy were also executed.

The only prince who escaped was the intended puppet king, Kobad, who was saved through the compassion of the Persian who had the custody of him, and who passed many years in concealment, after which he became a refugee at the court of Constantinople, where he was kindly treated by the Emperor Justinian I.

After thus securing himself on the throne against the claims of pretenders, Chosroës I., or Khosrou Nushirvan, proceeded to repress the disorders, punish the crimes and compel the abject submission of his subjects. The first to suffer from the oppressive weight of his resentment were the heresiarch Mazdak, who had escaped the persecution instituted by Kobad in his later years, the sect of the Mazdakites, which was still strong and vigorous, in spite of Kobad's persecution. The new king's determination to make his will the law was attested by the corpses of a hundred thousand martyrs blackening upon gibbets. Mebodes also suffered capital punishment, because he hesitated to instantly obey an order sent him by the stern monarch, whose judgment on recent offenses was not affected by gratitude for past favors. Nor did Chanaranges, the nobleman who saved the young prince Kobad, escape his sovereign's vengeance because of his military services. This general—who had conquered twelve nations—was betrayed by an unworthy son, and was treacherously entrapped and put to death because of a single humane act which had not in any manner injured or imperiled the jealous monarch.

Khosrou Nushirvan's fame rests mainly upon his military exploits and successes. After ascending the Persian throne, he very readily assented to the Emperor Justinian's overtures for peace, and a truce was concluded early in A. D. 532. This truce was soon followed by a treaty—called "the Endless Peace"—by which the Eastern Roman and New Persian Empires agreed to the following conditions: 1. Rome was to pay to Persia eleven thousand pounds of gold toward the maintenance of the defenses of the Caucasus, the actual defense being undertaken by Persia; 2. Daras was to remain a fortified post, but was not to be made the Roman headquarters in Mesopotamia, which were to be fixed at Constantia; 3. Rome was to restore to Persia the district of Pharangium and the castle of Bolon, which she had recently taken, while Persia was to surrender the forts which she had captured in Lazica; 4. Rome and Persia were to be friends and allies, and were to assist each other whenever required with supplies of men and money. Thus was ended the thirty years' war, which, beginning with Kobad's attack on the Emperor Anastasius I. in A. D. 502, was terminated in A. D. 532, and was ratified by the Emperor Justinian I. the next year.

The "Endless Peace" was of short duration. The military prestige which the Eastern Roman Empire gained by the conquest of the Vandal kingdom in Africa and the Ostrogothic kingdom in Italy alarmed the Persian king and aroused his jealousy. Khosrou Nushirvan first vented his envy in insolent demands for a share of the Roman spoils, which Justinian I. prudently humored. But the repeated Roman victories induced the Persian monarch to listen to the applications for aid which were made to him by Vitiges, the Ostrogothic king, and by Bassaces, an Armenian chieftain; both of whom sent embassies to Chosroës I. in A. D. 539, urging him to declare war against the Eastern Roman Emperor for his own security before it was too late. These ambassadors asserted that the Emperor Justinian I. aimed at universal dominion, and that Persia was the only power in the world that was able to check his aggressions and frustrate his ambitious designs. In response to these appeals, Khosrou Nushirvan openly declared war against the Emperor Justinian I. and made an attack in force on the eastern provinces of the Eastern Roman Empire.

Khosrou Nushirvan crossed the Lower Euphrates with his army and invaded the rich Roman province of Syria. The small town of Surôn resisted him, and the Persian king determined to take a signal revenge in order to terrify the other Syrian towns into submission. After losing their commandant, the garrison offered to surrender; but Chosroës insisted on entering forcibly at one of the gates, and then treated the city as though he had taken it by storm, pillaged the houses, massacred many of the inhabitants, enslaved the others, and reduced the city to ashes. He afterwards allowed the neighboring Christian Bishop of Sergiopolis to ransom the twelve thousand unfortunate captives for the modest sum of two hundred pounds of gold.

The Persian monarch then led his army to Hierapolis, whose inhabitants he allowed to ransom their city for two thousand pounds of silver. Procopius tells us that Chosroës now offered to evacuate the Roman territory for a thousand pounds of gold; but the Romans were not yet reduced so low as to purchase peace, and they therefore rejected the terms offered by the Persian king through Megas, Bishop of Berhœa (now Aleppo), which Chosroës reached after a four days' march. As the defenses of this town were weak, Chosroës here demanded a ransom twice as large as that which he had received from the Hierapolites, and was only induced to relent by the tears and entreaties of the good bishop, who finally convinced the Persian king that the Berhœans were unable to pay so large a sum, and induced him to accept the half of it. A few days later Chosroës reached the suburbs of Antioch, "the Queen of the East," the richest and most magnificent of Oriental cities, which the Persians now besieged for the first time in three centuries.

Fourteen years before this siege, Antioch had suffered from a terrible calamity; the entire city having been ruined by a succession of earthquakes, beginning in October, A. D. 525, and ending in August, A. D. 526. For a time all was havoc and disorder. A part of the city had been buried by a landslide, and nearly every house in the remaining portion had been overthrown. But Justinian's liberality, the spirit of the inhabitants and the efforts of the governor, had effaced these disasters; and when the Persians appeared before Antioch the city was grander and more magnificent than ever before. But the defenses were imperfect, especially the citadel; while the garrison was also weak, and the commandants lacked sufficient military talent for the defense of the city.

Justinian had originally sent his nephew Germanus to defend Antioch, and assigned Buzes, who had gained some distinction in the Armenian war, to the general command of the Roman forces in the East during the absence of Belisarius in Italy; but Germanus soon retired into Cilicia, while Buzes disappeared no one knew where. Theoctistus and Molatzes hastened from Lebanon with six thousand Roman troops to the relief of the feeble garrison of Antioch. The Persian king with the flower of his army assailed the citadel, after ordering his less trusty troops to attack the lower town in various places. The Persians soon reduced the garrison to great distress.

Cramped for room upon the walls, the Romans had erected wooden stages between the towers, and hung them out by means of ropes. One of these stages gave way in the rush and tumult. The ropes broke, and the beams fell with a crash to the ground, carrying many of the garrison with them. The great noise produced by the fall caused a general impression that the wall itself had fallen. The towers and battlements were deserted, and the Roman soldiers rushed to the gates and commenced leaving the town; while the Persians took advantage of the panic to advance their scaling ladders, to mount the walls, and to obtain possession of the citadel. Thus Antioch was taken by the Persians. Khosrou Nushirvan allowed the Roman soldiers to retire; but he caused the Antiochene youth, who still resisted, to be massacred, and, after plundering the churches, and carrying off the works of art, the marbles, bronzes, tablets and pictures, which adorned the city, he reduced Antioch to ashes.

Khosrou Nushirvan improved his opportunity by concluding an advantageous peace. Justinian's ambassadors had long been pressing him to come to terms with the Eastern Roman Emperor. He now agreed to retire from Syria with his army on condition that the Romans should pay him five thousand pounds of gold as an indemnity for his expenses in the war, and that they should also contract to pay him five hundred pounds of gold annually toward the expense of maintaining the Caspian Gates and keeping out the Huns. He agreed to abstain from further hostile acts while Justinian was consulted on these proposals, and even to commence at once to withdraw his army, if hostages were given to him. Justinian's ambassadors readily assented to these terms, and it was agreed that a truce should be observed until the Great King received the Emperor's answer.

But the Persian monarch did not intend to leave the Syrian cities without a ransom. After visiting Seleucia, the port of Antioch at the mouth of the Orontes, bathing in the blue waters of the Mediterranean, and offering sacrifice to the setting sun upon the shore, he proceeded to Apaméa, a city on the middle Orontes, which was famed for its wealth, and especially for possessing a fragment of the "true cross," enshrined in a case which had been enriched with the most costly gold and jewels by the pious zeal of the faithful. He carried away all the valuables of the sacred treasury, along with the "true cross"—the relic which the Apaméans prized as the most important of their possessions. But as he coveted only the case, and not its contents, he readily restored the "true cross" in answer to the entreaties of the bishop and the inhabitants.

Chosroës then returned to Antioch, witnessed the games of the amphitheater and secured victory to the *green* champions because Justinian favored the *blue*; after which he began his return march to Persia, visiting Chalcis on his way to the Euphrates, and compelling the Chalcidians to pay a ransom of two hundred pounds of gold and to agree to deliver to him the Roman garrison of the town, but they avoided this last condition. The Persian army then marched to Obbane, on the Euphrates, and crossed the river by a bridge of boats.

NEW PERSIAN EMPIRE OF THE SASSANIDÆ.

Chosroës thus entered Roman Mesopotamia, and increased his spoil by plundering the cities of Edessa, Constantia and Daras, which purchased their safety by ransoms. Procopius says that although Chosroës had already received a communication from Justinian accepting the terms arranged with the Roman envoys at Antioch, he laid siege to Daras, which was defended by two walls, the inner one being sixty feet high and having towers a hundred feet high. After investing the city, Chosroës endeavored to enter inside the defenses by means of a mine; but his design was betrayed, and the Romans met him with a counter-mine, thus utterly frustrating his plan. The Persian king then retired, upon receiving a contribution of a thousand pounds of silver as a ransom for the city.

Upon hearing of the fines levied upon Apaméa, Chalcis, Edessa, Constantia and Daras, the Emperor Justinian renounced the recently concluded peace, throwing the blame of the rupture on the bad faith of Chosroës. The Persian king passed the winter in building and beautifying the new Persian city of Antioch, on the Tigris, in the vicinity of Ctesiphon; assigning it as a residence to his Syrian captives, for whose use he constructed public baths and a spacious hippodrome, where the entertainments with which they had been familiar from their youth were reproduced by Syrian artists. The new city was exempt from the jurisdiction of Persian satraps, and was directly governed by the Great King, who supplied it with corn gratuitously, and allowed it to become an inviolable asylum for all such Greek slaves as should seek refuge therein and be acknowledged by the inhabitants as their kinsmen. Thus a model of Greek civilization was brought into close contact with the Persian court.

In A. D. 541 the people of Lazica, in the Caucasus, revolted against their Roman masters, who encroached upon the rights of their dependents, seized and fortified a strong post called Petra, on the Euxine coast, appointed a commandant with authority equal to that of the Lazic king, and established
3—10—U. H.

a commercial monopoly which severely oppressed the poorer class of the Lazi. In the winter of A. D. 540-541 the Lazic ambassadors visited the Persian court, where they exposed the grievances of their countrymen, and besought Chosroës to become their suzerain and to extend to them the protection of his government. Lazica was a remote country, possessing but few attractions. It was poor and unproductive; and its inhabitants were dependent upon the neighboring countries for some of the necessaries and all the conveniences of life, having nothing to export but timber, skins and slaves.

The Persian king accepted the offer without hesitation. Lazica—the ancient Colchis, and the modern Mingrelia and Imeritia—bordered upon the Black Sea, which the Persian dominions did not yet touch. Chosroës perceived that if he possessed this tract he might launch a fleet on the Euxine, command its commerce, threaten or ravage its shores, and even sail against Constantinople and besiege the Eastern Roman Emperor in his capital. Khosrou Nushirvan, pretending to be called into Iberia to defend that country against a threatened invasion of the Huns, led a large Persian army into the heart of Lazica, the Lazic envoys leading the way; and after receiving the submission of Gubazes, the Lazic king, he pressed on to the coast and besieged Petra, which was defended by a Roman garrison. The garrison made a gallant defense and repulsed a number of Persian assaults, but capitulated after losing their commandant, Johannes, and after one of the principal towers had fallen. After thus obtaining possession of Petra the Persians strengthened its defenses, and Lazica became a Persian province for the time.

In A. D. 541 Belisarius led the Roman forces in Mesopotamia from Daras into the Persian territory, and repulsed a sally from the garrison of Nisibis; after which he captured the fort of Sisauranôn, taking eight hundred Persian cavalry prisoners and sending them to Constantinople, whence they were sent to Italy, where they served in the

Roman army against the Ostrogoths. Owing to the selfish conduct of Arethas, the Arab chief, who was to coöperate with Belisarius, the Roman general was obliged to retreat by his discontented troops, after the summer heat had decimated his army. Soon afterwards Belisarius was summoned to Constantinople by the Emperor Justinian.

In A. D. 542 Khosrou Nushirvan invaded the Roman province of Commagêné, whereupon Justinian sent Belisarius to the East a second time. Belisarius drove the Persian king from Roman Mesopotamia, but Chosroës in his retreat destroyed the ungarrisoned city of Callinícus and enslaved its inhabitants.

In A. D. 543 Khosrou Nushirvan led a Persian army into Azerbijan, because of the desertion of the Persian cause by the Roman Armenians; but hastily retreated after the pestilence had broken out in his army, and after the failure of his negotiations with the Roman officers who opposed him. As Belisarius had been sent to oppose the Ostrogoths in Italy, the Roman army in the East, numbering thirty thousand men, was commanded by fifteen generals, who invaded Persarmenia, but were defeated and routed at Anglon by the Persians under Nabedes, who pursued the fleeing Roman hosts, taking many prisoners, arms, animals and camp equipments. Narses fell on the Roman side.

In A. D. 544 Chosroës invaded Roman Mesopotamia and besieged Edessa; but was forced to raise the siege after failing in many desperate assaults, and to retire into his own dominions, after extorting five hundred pounds of gold from Martínus, the commandant of the garrison, and after great losses of men, of stores and of prestige.

In A. D. 545 Chosroës listened to the peace proposals made to him by the Emperor Justinian's ambassadors. There had been constant negotiations during the war; but thus far Khosrou Nushirvan had only trifled with his adversary, simply discussing the proposals without any serious purpose. But, now, after five years of incessant hostilities, in which he had gained much glory and little profit, he desired a rest.

Justinian's envoys visited Chosroës at Ctesiphon and informed him of their sovereign's desire for peace. The Persian monarch proposed a truce for five years, during which the two great powers might consider and discuss the causes of the quarrel and eventually arrive at a good understanding. The weakness of the Eastern Roman Empire is fully demonstrated by the fact that Justinian accepted his antagonist's proposal and was even willing to pay for the boon thus granted him. Khosrou Nushirvan received the services of a Greek physician and two thousand pounds of gold as the price of the five years' truce.

The Persian king seems to have observed the five years' truce more faithfully than did the Eastern Roman Emperor. The Arab sheikh, Alamándarus, though a vassal of Persia, considered it his right to pursue his quarrel with his natural enemy, Arethas, the Arab sheikh who acknowledged the suzerainty of the Eastern Roman Emperor, notwithstanding the truce; but the Romans did not even accuse Chosroës of instigating the proceeding of Alamándarus; and the war between the vassals continued without involving either of the two lords-paramount in the quarrel, so that neither side could complain on this score. But in the fourth year of the truce, the Romans violated its stipulations by accepting an alliance with the Lazi and sending eight thousand troops to aid them against the Persians.

The Lazi very soon repented of their rash and hasty action in submitting to Persia; finding that they had gained nothing by changing masters, while in some respects they had lost. The general system of the Persian administration was as arbitrary and oppressive as the Roman. Lazic commerce disappeared under Persian sway, and the Lazi could find no market for their products nor obtain the commodities which they needed. The Lazi, being zealous and devout Christians and possessed of a spirit of intolerance, detested the Persian customs and manners introduced into their country.

After holding Lazica for a few years, Khosrou Nushirvan became convinced that

Persia could not retain that remote country unless the disaffected population were removed and replaced by faithful subjects. Procopius tells us that the Persian monarch therefore intended to deport the entire Lazic nation and to settle the country with Persian colonies. As a preliminary step, Chosroës suggested to Phabrizus, his lieutenant in Lazica, that he should contrive the assassination of Gubazes, the Lazic king, whom he looked upon as an obstacle to the scheme. Phabrizus failed in his attempt to execute this design, and the Lazi at once revolted from Persia and threw themselves into the arms of the Eastern Roman Emperor, who took them under his protection, notwithstanding the existing treaty.

Thus the Lazic war was renewed, and it lasted nine years, from A. D. 549 to 557. Procopius and Agathias relate that Khosrou Nushirvan was resolved upon holding Lazica for the purpose of constructing a great naval station and arsenal at the mouth of the Phasis, from which his fleets might issue to command the commerce of the Black Sea or ravage its shores. The Romans began the war by attacking Petra, the great center of the Persian power in Lazica. This town, strongly situated on a craggy rock projecting into the Black Sea, had been carefully fortified by Justinian before Lazica passed into the Persian king's possession, and its defenses had afterwards been strengthened by the Persians. It was adequately provisioned and was garrisoned by fifteen hundred men.

A Roman force of eight thousand men under Dagisthæus besieged Petra, and by their incessant assaults they reduced the garrison to less than five hundred men. After being baffled in one effort to effect a breach, Dagisthæus contrived another, but threw away his chance of destroying the wall and entering the town by bargaining with the Emperor for a specific reward in case he captured the place. While waiting for his messenger to bring a reply, a Persian army of thirty thousand men under Mermeroës forced the passes from Iberia into Lazica, and descended the valley of the Phasis. Dagisthæus retired in great alarm, and Petra was relieved and revictualed. The walls were hastily repaired with sandbags, and the town received a new garrison of three thousand men. As Mermeroës then found difficulty in obtaining supplies for his large army, he retired into Persarmenia, leaving only five thousand men in Lazica besides the garrison of Petra. The Romans and Lazi soon afterwards surprised and defeated this small Persian force, killing or making prisoners almost the entire number.

In A. D. 550 the Persian general Chorianes with a large army of Persians and Alans appeared in Lazica. The allied Romans and Lazi under Dagisthæus and Gubazes encountered this new Persian army on the Hippis; and, though the Lazi were at first routed by the Persian cavalry, the Roman infantry finally carried the day after a severe battle, routing the Persian cavalry, who instantly fled after losing their general, Chorianes, who was killed by a chance arrow. The Romans and Lazi captured the Persian camp after a short conflict, and massacred most of the Persians found there, only a few escaping from Lazica to their own country.

Bessas, who superseded Dagisthæus in the Roman command, began a second siege of Petra soon afterward. The Persians had built a new wall of great height and solidity upon a framework of wood in the place which Dagisthæus had so nearly breached. The Persians had also filled up the Roman mines with gravel; and had collected a great quantity of offensive and defensive arms, a stock of flour and salted meat sufficient to support the garrison of three thousand men for five years, and a store of vinegar and of the pulse from which it was made.

The Roman general began the siege by attacking the defenses by means of a mine; but just as his mine was completed, the new wall with its framework of wood sank quietly into the excavation, without being disturbed in any of its parts, and enough still remaining above the surface to offer an effectual bar to the assailants. At the suggestion of his Hunnic allies, Bessas constructed three battering-rams so light that each could be carried on the shoulders of forty men. These rams would have battered down the wall, had not the garrison showered upon them from the walls lighted casks of sulphur, bitumen and naphtha; the last of which was known to the Greeks of Colchis as "Medea's oil."

The Roman general gallantly led a scaling party to another part of the walls, which he mounted at the head of his men, but he fell to the ground. About the same time the Romans had entered the town in two other places; one band having scaled the almost inaccessible rocks; and the other having effected its entrance after a severe struggle with the Persians at a gap in the piece of wall which sank into the Roman mine, the Persians having become dismayed when the wooden structure from which they fought had been lighted by the wind blowing back the fire which they showered upon the Roman battering-rams.

Thus the Romans captured Petra, the great Lazic fortress, after one of the most memorable defenses in history. Of the Persian garrison of three thousand men, seven hundred were killed during the siege. One thousand and seventy were slain in the last assault. Of the seven hundred and thirty who were taken prisoners, all but eighteen were wounded. The remaining five hundred defended themselves in the citadel, where they resisted to the last, refusing all terms of capitulation, until they all perished by sword and fire.

The siege of Petra had lasted far into the winter and had ended early in A. D. 551. In the spring of that year a large Persian cavalry force under Mermeroës, supported by eight elephants, marched to the coast to relieve Petra; but arrived too late, as the Romans had already taken the town and completely destroyed it. Mermeroës easily restored Persian authority over almost all of Lazica; and the Romans dared not meet him in the field, though they repulsed his attack on Archæopolis, the only important place in Lazica remaining subject to the Eastern Roman Empire. The Lazic king, Gubazes, and his followers had to hide themselves in the mountain recesses. Mermeroës quartered his troops on the upper Phasis, mainly about Kutaïs and its vicinity, and strengthened his hold upon the country by building or capturing forts. He even extended the Persian dominion beyond Lazica into Scymnia and Suania. But the Romans still tenaciously held certain tracts; and Gubazes remained faithful to his allies in their extremity, maintaining a guerrilla war, and hoping for the best at some future time.

In the meantime fresh negotiations were in progress at Constantinople. Isdigunas, the Persian ambassador at the Byzantine court, was an able and skillful diplomat. Accusing the Emperor Justinian of various violations of the five years' truce, he demanded the payment of two thousand six hundred pounds of gold, expressing his sovereign's willingness to conclude a new truce of five years on these terms, to begin with the payment of the money. The truce was only to apply to the settled portions of the two empires, while Lazica and the Arab country were to be excluded from its operation. Justinian assented to these conditions, notwithstanding the opposition of many of his subjects, who felt humiliated by the repeated payments of money to Persia, which placed the Eastern Roman Empire almost in the position of a Persian tributary.

Thus the Lazic war continued during the second five years' truce (A. D. 551-556). This struggle was renewed with vigor in the spring of A. D. 553, when the Persians under Mermeroës advanced from Kutaïs against Telephis, a strong fort garrisoned by the Romans. After expelling the commandant of the garrison, Martínus, by stratagem, the Persian general pressed forward against the enemy, who fled before him from Ollaria; finally driving them to the coast and cooping them up in "the Island," a small tract near the mouth of the Phasis, between that stream and the Docônus. On returning he reinforced a garrison which he had established at Onoguris, in the vicinity of Archæopolis, for the purpose of annoying and weakening that important station.

The fatigues of war hastened Mermeroës to his death during the winter of A. D. 553-554. He was succeeded in his command by Nachoragan, under whom the Persian cause was entirely ruined in the course of two years. But in the meantime the Roman influence over the Lazi was shaken by a most serious quarrel between Gubazes, the Lazic king, and some of the leading Roman commanders—a quarrel involving consequences fatal to the Lazi and the Romans. Gubazes had complained to the Emperor Justinian of the negligence and incompetency of the Roman commanders, who retaliated by accusing him of intending desertion to the Persian cause, and who had obtained the Emperor's consent to have him arrested, forcibly if he resisted. The Roman officers then quarrelled with the Lazic king, and killed him with their swords when he refused to do as they required.

This outrage naturally alienated the Lazi from the Roman cause, and they manifested an inclination to throw themselves wholly into the arms of Persia. The Romans were so dispirited at the attitude of their allies, and so at variance among themselves, that they became thoroughly demoralized; and Agathias says that an army of fifty thousand Romans at this time was routed by about four thousand Persians, allowing their camp to be taken and plundered. During this time the Persian general, Nachoragan, remained inactive in Iberia, simply sending messengers to announce his near approach and to encourage and animate his party.

When the Lazi found that the Persians made no effort to take advantage of their alienation from the Romans, and that the Romans still held possession of most of Lazica, they concluded that it would be impolitic to desert their natural allies because of a single outrage, and agreed to renew their close alliance with the Romans on condition that the murderers of Gubazes should be punished, and that his brother, Tzathes, should be appointed king in his place. The Emperor Justinian readily consented to this, and in the year A. D. 555 the Lazi were again in hearty accord with their Roman protectors.

After thus missing his opportunity, the Persian general Nachoragan led an army of sixty thousand men from Iberia into Lazica, in the region about Kutais, and prepared for a vigorous prosecution of the war. The bulk of the Roman forces under Martinus and Justin occupied the region on the lower Thasis, known as "the Island;" while a Roman detachment under Babas held the more central post of Archæopolis. After losing about two thousand men in the vicinity of Archæopolis, Nachoragan attacked the important post of Phasis, at the mouth of the river. The town was defended on the south side by an outer palisade, a wide ditch protected by sharp stakes and full of water, and an inner wooden bulwark of considerable height. The river Phasis guarded the town on the north, where a Roman fleet was stationed which aided the garrison at both ends of their line. Soldiers manned the yards of the ships, from which boats were hung containing slingers, archers, and even workers of catapults, who discharged their missiles from an elevation exceeding that of the towers.

An obstinate struggle ensued, in which the Persians had the advantage of numbers. They soon filled up a part of the ditch; but the Roman commander, Martinus, contrived to send a false report to Nachoragan that a Roman reinforcement from Constantinople was approaching, thus causing the Persian general to divide his army by sending half of them to confront the supposed Roman reinforcement. The Persian general then renewed the assault, but Martinus secretly sent five thousand Roman troops under Justin a short distance from the town. This detachment suddenly returned while the conflict was in progress at the wall; and the Persians, supposing it to be the arrival of the reported Roman reinforcement, were seized with a general panic, and made a hasty flight. The Roman garrison in Phasis made a general sally, and the Persians were routed with terrible carnage, losing almost one-fourth of their army. Nachoragan retired to Kutais, and soon afterwards went into winter quarters in Iberia, leaving Vaphrizes in command of the Persian troops in Lazica.

Nachoragan's failure convinced Khosrou Nushirvan of the hopelessness of annexing Lazica, and in the spring of A. D. 556 he sent an ambassador to Constantinople; and, after the negotiations had continued almost a year, a truce was agreed upon, which was to extend to Lazica as well as to the other dominions of the two great sovereigns. Each party was to retain all the territory, cities and castles which it possessed in Lazica. After a truce of five years, a treaty of peace was concluded in A. D. 562, by the ambassadors of the two powers, after a lengthy conference on the Mesopotamian frontier, between Daras and Nísibis.

The following were the terms of the treaty: 1. The Persians were to evacuate Lazica and to relinquish it to the Romans. 2. The Romans were to pay thirty thousand pieces of gold, the amount due for the first seven years to be paid in advance. 3. The Christians in Persia were guaranteed freedom of worship, but were forbidden to make proselytes from the disciples of Zoroaster. 4. Commercial intercourse was to be allowed between the two empires, but the merchants were restricted to the use of certain roads and certain emporia. 5. Diplomatic intercourse was to be entirely free, and the goods of ambassadors were to be exempt from duty. 6. Daras was to remain a Roman fortified town, but neither nation was to erect any new fortresses upon the frontier, and Daras itself was not to be made the headquarters of the Roman Prefect of the East, or to be occupied by a needlessly large garrison. 7. Courts of Arbitration were to settle all disputes arising between the two empires. 8. The allies of the two nations were to be included in the treaty, and to participate in its benefits and obligations. 9. Persia was to undertake the sole charge of maintaining the Caspian Gates against the Huns and the Alans. 10. The peace was for fifty years.

During the five years' truce which preceded this fifty years' peace between the New Persian and Eastern Roman Empires, Khosrou Nushirvan invaded the country of the Ephthalites, and, with the aid of the Great Kahn of the Turks, inflicted a crushing defeat upon the Ephthalites, who had so long been one of Persia's most formidable enemies. Tabari tells us that the Persian monarch actually killed the Ephthalite Khan, ravaged his territory and pillaged his treasures. About the same time Khosrou Nushirvan also prosecuted a war against the Khazars, whose country he overran and wasted with fire and sword, massacring thousands of the inhabitants.

The vast and sterile peninsula of Arabia has from time immemorial been the home of almost countless tribes, living independently of one another, each under its own shiekh or chief, in wild and unrestrained freedom. Very seldom have native Arab princes acquired any widely extended dominion over the scattered population; and foreign powers have still more rarely exercised authority for any length of time over the freedom-loving descendants of Ishmael.

But about the beginning of the sixth century of the Christian era the Abyssinians of Axum, a Christian people, "raised above the ordinary level of African barbarism" by their religion and by their constant intercourse with the Romans, succeeded in acquiring dominion over a large part of Yemen, or Arabia Felix, and at first governed it from their African capital, but afterwards by means of viceroys, who acknowledged but little more than a nominal allegiance to the Negus of Abyssinia. Abraha, an Abyssinian of high rank, was sent by the Negus to restore the Abyssinian dominion over Yemen when it was shaken by a general revolt. Abraha conquered the country, assumed its crown, established Abyssinians in all the chief cities, built many churches, especially a very magnificent one at Sana, and at his death transmitted his kingdom to his eldest son, Yaksoum.

Thus an important Christian kingdom was established in the great south-western peninsula of Asia; and the Emperor Justinian was naturally gratified at beholding the development of a power in that remote quarter which was sure to side with the Eastern Roman Empire against Persia in case the rivalry of these two great powers of the civilized world should extend into that region. Justinian had hailed the original Abyssinian conquest of Yemen with the highest satisfaction, and had entered into amicable relations with the Abyssinians of Axum and their colonists in Yemen.

Khosrou Nushirvan, on the contrary, had viewed the growth of the Abyssinian power in South-western Arabia with the gravest alarm; and he now resolved upon a counter movement, to drive the presumptuous Abyssinians from Asiatic soil, and to extend Persian influence over the whole of Arabia and thus confront the Eastern Roman Empire along its entire eastern boundary. Chosroë's expedition into Yemen was facilitated by an application which he received from a native of that part of Arabia.

Saïf, the son of Dsu-Yezm, who was a descendant of the race of the old Homerite kings who had been conquered by the Abyssinians, grew up at Abraha's court in the belief that that monarch, who had married his mother, was his father, and not his stepfather. After being undeceived by an insult offered him by Masrouq, the true son of Abraha and the successor of Yaksoum, Saïf became a refugee at the Persian king's court, and importuned Chosroës to espouse his quarrel and restore him to the throne of his ancestors. He asserted that the Homerite population of Yemen were groaning under the oppressive yoke of the Abyssinians, and that they only waited for an opportunity to free themselves. He declared that a few thousand Persian soldiers would be sufficient; that they might be sent by sea to the port of Aden, near the mouth of the Red Sea, where the Homerites would join them in large numbers; and that the combined forces might then engage in battle with the Abyssinians and exterminate them or expel them from Arabia.

Khosrou Nushirvan accordingly sent an expedition by sea against the Abyssinians of Yemen. After assembling his ships in the Persian Gulf and embarking a certain number of Persian troops on board of them, his flotilla proceeded, under the conduct of Saïf, first down the Persian Gulf, and then along the southern coast of Arabia to Aden. The arrival of the Persian flotilla and troops encouraged the Homerites to revolt against their Abyssinian oppressors, whom they drove from Arabian soil. The native race recovered its supremacy; and Saïf, the descendant of the old Homerite kings, was established on the throne of his ancestors as the vassal or viceroy of the Persian king. After a short reign, Saïf was murdered by his bodyguard; whereupon Chosroës conferred the government of Yemen upon a Persian officer bearing the title of Marzpan, like the other Persian provincial governors; so that the Homerites in the end simply gained a change of masters by their revolt.

Tabari and Mirkhond state that Khosrou Nushirvan also sent an expedition by sea against some part of Hindoostan, and that he received a cession of territory from an Indian sovereign; but the ceded provinces appear to have belonged to Persia previously, as Tabari states that Serendib (now Ceylon) was the residence of the Indian monarch alluded to, and that the ceded provinces were those previously ceded to Bahramgur.

Khosrou Nushirvan seems to have been engaged in a war on his north-eastern frontier about this period. The Turks had been recently becoming more powerful and approaching the confines of the New Persian Empire; having extended their dominion over the great Ephthalite kingdom by force of arms and by the treachery of the Ephthalite chieftain, Katulphus; while they had also received the submission of the Sogdians and of other tribes of the Transoxianian region previously held in subjection by the Ephthalites.

About the close of A. D. 567 Dizabul, the Turkish Khan, sent ambassadors to the great Persian monarch with proposals for the establishment of free commercial intercourse between the Turks and the Persians, and even the conclusion of a treaty of friendship and alliance between the two nations. Chosroës suspected the motive for the overture, but was afraid to openly reject it. He desired to discourage intercourse between his own subjects and the Turks; but his only modes of effecting his purpose were burning the Turkish merchandise offered to him after he had purchased it, and poisoning the Turkish ambassadors and having it reported that they had fallen victims to the climate.

This outrage on the part of Khosrou Nushirvan exasperated the Turkish Khan and created a deep and bitter hostility between the Turks and the Persians. The Turkish Khan at once sent an embassy to Constantinople to offer to the Eastern Roman Emperor the friendship which the great Persian king had thus scorned. This Turkish embassy reached the Byzantine court early in A. D. 568, and was graciously received by the Emperor Justin II., Justinian's nephew and successor. A treaty of alliance was concluded between the Eastern Roman Empire and the Turks; and a Roman embassy empowered to ratify the treaty visited the Turkish court in the Altai mountains in A. D. 569, and strengthened the bonds of friendship between the high contracting powers.

In the meantime Dizabul, the Turkish Khan, confident in his own strength, had resolved upon an expedition into the Persian dominions. He was accompanied on a portion of his march by Zemarchus, the Eastern Roman Emperor's ambassador, who witnessed his insulting treatment of a Persian envoy sent by Chosroës to meet him and deprecate his attack. Mirkhond says that the Great Khan of the Turks invaded the Persian territory in force, occupied Shash, Ferghana, Samarcand, Bokhara, Kesh and Nesf; but when he heard that Prince Hormisdas, the Persian king's son, was advancing against him, he suddenly fled, evacuating all the territory that he had occupied, and retiring to the most remote part of Turkestan.

In A. D. 571 Turkish ambassadors again visited Constantinople and entreated the Emperor Justin II. to renounce the fifty years' peace with Persia and to join them in a grand attack on the common enemy of the Turks and the Eastern Roman Empire. Justin II. gave the Turkish ambassadors no definite reply, but renewed his alliance with Dizabul, the Turkish Khan, and seriously considered whether he should yield to the representations made to him by the Turkish envoys and renew the war terminated by Justinian nine years previously.

Many circumstances urged the Emperor Justin II. to a rupture with the Persian king. The payments to be made to Persia under the terms of the fifty years' peace appeared to him in the nature of tribute, which he regarded as an intolerable disgrace. He had already discontinued a subsidy allowed by Justinian to the Arabs under Persian rule, thus bringing on hostilities between the Arabs subject to Persia and those acknowledging the suzerainty of the Eastern Roman Emperor. The successes of Chosroës in South-western Arabia had aroused Justin's jealousy and secured to the Eastern Roman Empire an important ally in the great Christian kingdom of Abyssinia. The Turks of Central Asia had sought his friendship and had offered to unite with him if he went to war with the great Persian monarch. The proselyting zeal of the Persian governors in Armenia had again produced rebellion in that country, where the natives took up arms and raised the standard of independence. Above all, the Great King, who had warred so successfully with Justinian I. for twenty years, was now advanced in age and seemed to have exhibited signs of feebleness; as in his recent expeditions he had personally taken no part, but had intrusted the command of his troops to others, having assigned the expedition to Arabia to Saif, and the command against the Turks to his eldest son, Hormisdas.

All these circumstances induced the Emperor Justin II., in A. D. 572, to renounce the fifty years' peace made by Justinian I. with Khosrou Nushirvan ten years before, and to renew the war with that great Persian monarch. The Eastern Roman Emperor therefore at once dismissed the Persian envoy, Sebocthes, with contempt, absolutely refused to make the stipulated payment, announced his intention of receiving the Armenian insurgents under his protection, and forbade the Persian king to do them the slightest harm. Justin II. then appointed Marcian to the Prefecture of the East, and assigned him the conduct of the war with Persia which was now inevitable.

As soon as King Chosroës I. found his dominions thus menaced by the Eastern Roman Emperor, he personally took the field at once, notwithstanding his advanced age. He assigned the command of a flying column of six thousand men to Adarman, a skillful general, and himself marched against the Romans, who, under Marcian, had defeated a Persian force and were besieging Nisibis. He forced the Romans to raise the siege, and advanced as they retired, compelling them to seek refuge within the walls of Daras, which he at once invested with his main army.

In the meantime the detachment under Adarman crossed the Euphrates near Circésium and entered Syria, which he overran and ravaged with fire and sword. He burned the suburbs of Antioch, where he was repulsed; after which he invaded Cœle-Syria, took and destroyed Apaméa, crossed the Euphrates, and rejoined Chosroës before Daras. That renowned fortress made a gallant defense of five months, resisting the Persian king's army of one hundred thousand infantry and forty thousand cavalry; but was at last obliged to surrender, towards the end of A. D. 573, as it had received no relief, and was closely invested, while it was deprived of water by the diversion of its streams into new channels.

Thus the great Roman fortress in this section was taken by the Persians in the first year of Khosrou Nushirvan's war with the Emperor Justin II. Justin II., becoming alarmed at his own rashness and recognizing his own incapacity, chose Count Tiberius as his colleague and successor. The Persian king having sent an embassy to the Romans immediately after capturing Daras, Tiberius and the Empress Sophia took advantage of this to send an envoy with an autograph letter from the Empress herself. A truce for a year was accordingly agreed upon, the Romans being obliged to pay to Persia forty-five thousand aurei.

During the truce the Emperor Tiberius made immense efforts for a renewal of hostilities, collecting an army of one hundred and fifty thousand men from the banks of the Danube and the Rhine, and from Scythia, Pannonia, Mœsia, Illyricum and Isauria; and this army was placed under the command of a famous general named Justinian, the son of Germanus, and was concentrated upon the Persian frontier of the Eastern Roman Empire.

But still lacking confidence in his strength, Tiberius sent a second embassy to the Persian headquarters, early in A. D. 575, and solicited an extension of the truce. The Romans desired a short armistice only, but wished for a general suspension of hostilities between the two empires; while the Persians wanted a longer truce, but insisted that it should not extend to Armenia. The dispute continued until the expiration of the year's truce, and the Persians resumed hostilities and threatened Constantia before the Romans would yield. A truce for three years was finally agreed upon, but Armenia was exempt from its operation. The Romans were to pay to Persia thirty thousand aurei annually during the continuance of the truce.

As soon as the three years' truce was concluded, King Khosrou Nushirvan led the Persian army into Armenia proper, and crushing the revolt there, reëstablished the Persian authority throughout that entire region; after which he invaded the Roman province of Armenia Minor and even threatened Cappadocia. The Roman General Justinian there opposed the Persian king's progress; and Kurs, or Cursus, a Scythian leader in the Roman service, defeated the Persian rear-guard and captured the camp and the baggage. Soon afterward the Persian king surprised and destroyed a Roman camp during the night, and then took and burned the city of Melitêné (afterwards Malatiyeh); after which he retired across the Euphrates and returned to his own dominions on the approach of winter. The Roman general Justinian then invaded Persarmenia and plundered that country, even penetrating to the Caspian Sea and embarking upon its waters, and not returning to the Roman territory until the spring of the next year (A. D. 576).

In A. D. 576 the Romans were successful in Northern Armenia and Iberia, while King Chosroës I. again invaded the Roman province of Armenia Minor and engaged in an unsuccessful siege of Theodosiopolis. Thereupon negotiations for peace were resumed; but were broken off by the Persians upon the arrival of news that Tamchosro, a Persian general, had defeated the Roman army under Justinian, and that Armenia had returned to its allegiance to the Persian king.

Fruitless negotiations occupied the year A. D. 578, during which the two sovereigns made vast preparations. Hostilities were resumed by King Chosroës I. in the spring of A. D. 578, when the Persian generals Mebodes and Sapoës invaded and ravaged Roman Armenia and threatened Constantia and Theodosiopolis; while another Persian force under Tamchosro entered the Roman territory from Persarmenia and plundered the country about Amida (now Diarbekr).

The Roman general Maurice, Justinian's successor, at the same time invaded Persarmenia, destroying the forts and plundering the country. He also invaded Arzanêné, occupied its stronghold, Aphumôn, and carried off its ten thousand inhabitants; after which he entered Persian Mesopotamia, took Sīngara, and ravaged the entire province as far east as the Tigris with fire and sword. He even sent a body of skirmishers across the river into Cordyêné (now Kurdistan); and these marauders, commanded by Kurs the Scythian, spread devastation and ruin over a region untrod by the foot of a Roman soldier for more than two centuries.

Agathias says that King Khosrou Nushirvan was then enjoying the summer in the Kurdish hills, and saw from his residence the smoke of the hamlets fired by the Roman troops. He hastily fled from the danger and sought refuge within the walls of Ctesiphon, where he was soon afterwards seized with the illness which ended his eventful life and reign.

In the meantime Kurs recrossed the Tigris with his booty and rejoined Maurice, who retired into the Roman territory on the approach of winter, evacuating all his conquests excepting Arzanêné. The winter was passed in negotiations for peace. The Emperor desired to recover Daras, and was willing to withdraw the Roman forces from Persarmenia and Iberia if Daras were restored to him. While the Roman envoys authorized to propose these terms were on their way to the Persian court, early in the year A. D. 579, the aged King Chosroës I., or Khosrou Nushirvan, died in his palace at Ctesiphon, after a reign of forty-eight years.

The Oriental writers—especially Mirkhond, Tabari, Maçoudi and Asseman—represent the reign of Chosroës I., or Khosrou Nushirvan, as a period of improved domestic administration, as well as a time of great military activity. Chosroës I. found the New Persian Empire in a disorganized and ill-regulated condition, taxation arranged on a bad system, the people oppressed by unjust and tyrannical governors, the military service a prey to the most scandalous abuses, religious fanaticism rampant, class arrayed against class, extortion and wrong connived at, crime unpunished, agriculture languishing, and the masses throughout almost the entire Persian dominion sullen and discontented.

Chosroës I. determined from the very beginning to carry out a series of reforms—to secure the administration of even-handed justice, to arrange the finances on a better footing, to encourage agriculture, to relieve the poor and the distressed, to abolish the abuses that destroyed the efficiency of the army, and to curb the fanaticism that was sapping the vitality of the Persian nation. We have already related how he effected the

NEW PERSIAN EMPIRE OF THE SASSANIDÆ.

last-named object by his wholesale destruction of the followers of Mazdak.

Until the reign of Khosrou Nushirvan the New Persian Empire had been divided into a number of provinces, the satraps or governors of which held their offices directly under the Persian crown. It was no easy task for the sovereign to exercise an adequate supervision over so many rulers, many of whom were remote from the court, and all of whom were united by a tie of common interest. Chosroës I. conceived the plan of forming four great governments, and assigning them to the charge of four individuals in whom he had confidence, whose duty should be to watch the conduct of the provincial satraps, to control them, direct them, or report their misconduct to the crown. The four great governments were those of the East, the West, the North and the South. The East comprised Khorassan, Kerman and Seistan. The West embraced Mesopotamia, Assyria, and Babylonia, or Irak. The North included Armenia, Azerbijan, Ghilan, Koum and Ispahan. The South consisted of Fars, or Persia proper, and Ahwaz.

The great monarch did not, however, put a blind trust in his instruments. He made occasional tours of inspection through his dominions, visiting each province in turn and inquiring into the condition of the inhabitants. He continually employed an army of inspectors and spies—the "Kings Eyes" and the "King's Ears"—who reported to him from every portion of the New Persian Empire the sufferings or complaints of the oppressed, and the sins of omission and commission on the part of those in authority. On the occurrence of any particularly suspicious circumstance, he appointed extraordinary commissions of inquiry, which proceeded to the suspected quarter, took evidence, and made a careful report of all wrongs and malpractices that they discovered.

When the guilt of the incriminated persons or parties was established they received swift and signal punishment. We have noticed the harsh sentences which Chosroës passed on those whose offenses were aimed at his own person and dignity. Where only the interests of his subjects were involved, an equal severity appears in his judgments. Mirkhond states that on one occasion he executed about eighty collectors of taxes on the report of a commission charging them with extortion.

Chosroës I. is said to have introduced a new arrangement of the taxation. Hitherto all lands paid a certain proportion of their produce to the state, the proportion varying from one-tenth to one-half, according to the estimated richness of the soil. This had the tendency to discourage all improved cultivation, because the state might absorb the entire profit of any increased outlay; and also to cramp and check the liberty of the cultivators in various ways, because the produce could not be touched until the revenue official made his appearance and carried off the share of the crop which he was authorized to take.

Chosroës I. substituted a land-tax for the proportionate payments in kind; and thus at once set the cultivator at liberty with respect to harvesting his crops, and allowed him the sole advantage of any increased production which might be secured by better methods of farming his land. His tax consisted partly of a money payment and partly of a payment in kind; but both payments were fixed and invariable, each measure of ground being rated in the king's books at one *dirhem* and one measure of the produce. Uncultivated land, and land lying fallow at the time, were exempt; and thus the plan involved an annual survey and an annual registration of all cultivators with the quantity of land under cultivation held by each and the nature of the crop or crops to be grown by them.

The system was very complicated; but, though it may have pressed somewhat severely upon the poorer and less productive soils, it was a vast improvement upon the previously prevailing practice, which had all the disadvantages of the modern tithe system, aggravated by the high rates exacted, and by the certainty that in any disputed case the subject would have had a poor chance of establishing his right against the crown. It is no wonder that when the Saracens conquered Persia they maintained the land system of Khosrou Nushirvan unaltered, regarding it as not readily admitting of much improvement.

Chosroës I. also introduced into Persia various other imposts. The fruit trees were everywhere counted, and a small payment was required for each. Maçoudi gives the following as the rate of payment: "Four palms of Fars, one *dirhem;* six common palms, the same; six olives, the same; each vine, eight *dirhems*." The personality of the citizens was valued, and a graduated property-tax was established, which did not exceed the moderate sum of forty-eight *dir hems* (equal to about one hundred and seventy-three dollars in United States money) in the case of the most opulent. Jews and Christians were required to pay a poll-tax.

Liberal exemptions were made from all these burdens on account of age or sex; no male over fifty years of age or under twenty, and no female, being required to pay anything. A tax table was published in each province, town and village, in which each citizen or alien could see opposite his name the amount which would be exacted from him, with the ground upon which it was regarded as due. Payments were required by installments at the end of every four months. For the purpose of preventing unfair extortion by the collectors of revenue, Chosroës I., by the advice of the Grand Mobed, authorized the Magian priesthood everywhere to exercise a supervision over the collectors of taxes, and to hinder them from exacting more than the legal rate. The priests were only too glad to discharge this popular function.

Chosroës I. also reformed the administration of the army. Under the system previously existing Chosroës found the resources of the state lavishly wasted, thus weakening the efficiency and equipment of the army. No security was taken that the soldiers were in possession of their proper accouterments, or that they could discharge the duties appropriate to their several grades. Persons having no horse and unable to ride appeared before the paymaster, claiming the pay of cavalry soldiers. Some calling themselves soldiers were unfamiliar with the use of any weapon. Others claimed pay for higher grades of the service than those to which they actually belonged. Those drawing the pay of cuirassiers had no coat of mail. Those professing themselves archers were wholly incompetent to draw the bow.

Tabari states that the fixed rate of pay for soldiers varied between a hundred *dirhems* a year and four thousand, and persons entitled only to the lowest rate often received an amount almost equal to the highest. Thus the public treasury was robbed by unfair claims and unfounded pretenses, while artifice and false seeming were encouraged, and the army was reduced to such a condition that no reliance could be placed upon it.

To remedy these evils, Chosroës I. appointed a single paymaster-general and insisted on his carefully inspecting and reviewing each body of troops before he was permitted to draw its pay. Each man was required to appear before him fully equipped and to show his proficiency with his weapon or weapons. Cavalry soldiers were required to bring their horses and to show their mastery over the animals by putting them through their paces, mounting and dismounting, and performing the other usual exercises. If any clumsiness or any deficiency in the equipment were noticed, the pay was to be withheld until the defect observed had been removed. Special care was to be taken that no one drew the pay of a class superior to that to which he actually belonged.

Mirkhond and Tabari relate a curious anecdote in connection with these military reforms. When Babek, the new paymaster, was about to hold his first review, he issued an order requiring that all persons belonging to the army then present in the capital should appear before him on a certain day. The troops made their appearance; but Babek dismissed them on the ground that

NEW PERSIAN EMPIRE OF THE SASSANIDÆ. 1317

a certain person whose presence was indispensable had not appeared. Another day was appointed with a similar result, except that on this occasion Babek plainly intimated that it was the king whom he expected to attend.

Thereupon, when a third summons was issued, Chosroës took care to be present, and made his appearance fully equipped for battle, as he himself thought. But the critical eye of the reviewing officer detected an omission, which he declined to overlook—the king had neglected to bring two extra bow-strings with him. Chosroës was required to return to the palace and remedy the defect, after which he was permitted to pass muster, and was then summoned to receive his pay.

Babek affected to consider seriously what the king's pay ought to be, and decided that it ought not to exceed that of any other individual in the army. In the presence of all, he then gave the king, or commander-in-chief, four thousand and one *dirhems*, which Chosroës carried home. In this way two important principles were believed to be established—that no defect of equipment whatsoever should be overlooked in any officer, however high in rank, and that none should draw more than four thousand *dirhems* (equal to five hundred and fifty dollars of United States money) from the public treasury.

An essential element in Zoroaster's religious system was the encouragement of agriculture; and King Khosrou Nushirvan, in devoting his attention to it, was performing a religious duty, as well as increasing the resources of the state. Tabari tells us that the king earnestly desired to bring into cultivation all the soil that was capable of it; and for this purpose he issued edicts commanding the reclamation of the lands, while at the same time he advanced from the public treasury the money necessary for the seed-corn, the implements and the beasts, to all poor persons willing to carry out his orders. The infirm, those disabled by bodily defect, and others, were relieved from the king's private purse. Mendicancy was forbidden, and idleness was made punishable. Mirkhond and Tabari tell us that the lands forfeited by Mazdak's followers were distributed to necessitous cultivators. Mirkhond also informs us that the water system was carefully attended to, and that river and torrent courses were cleared of obstructions and straightened. The superfluous water of the rainy season was stored, and meted out with a wise economy to the tillers of the soil, in the spring and summer.

Tabari states that King Khosrou Nushirvan encouraged and compelled marriage, in order to increase the population of Persia. All marriageable females were required to provide themselves with husbands. If they neglected this duty, the government interfered, and united them with unmarried men of their own class. These latter received an adequate dowry from the public treasury; and if any children resulted from the union, their education and establishment in life were undertaken by the state. Another of Chosroës's methods of increasing the population was the settlement of his foreign captives within his own dominions. The most important instance of this policy was the Greek settlement called *Rumia* (Rome), which Chosroës established near Ctesiphon, after his capture of Antioch in A. D. 540.

Unlike many other Oriental sovereigns, King Chosroës I. displayed no narrow and unworthy jealousy of foreigners. His mind soared above all such petty prejudice. He encouraged the visits of all foreigners except the barbarous Turks, readily received them at his court, and carefully provided for their safety. Mirkhond says that he kept the roads and bridges in perfect order throughout his empire, so as to facilitate locomotion; while guard-houses were built and garrisons maintained along the chief lines of the route for the express purpose of securing the safety of travelers. The result was that many Europeans visited Khosrou Nushirvan's court, and were hospitably treated, and invited, or even pressed, to prolong their visits.

King Chosroës I. also displayed his wisdom and enlightenment by studying philosophy and patronizing science and learning. Agathias says that in the beginning of his reign he gave a refuge at his court to seven Greek sages who were driven from their country by a persecuting edict issued by the Emperor Justinian I. One of these Greek refugees was Damascius of Syria, author of *De Principiis*, which has recently been found to display an intimate knowledge of some of the most obscure of the ancient Oriental religions, such as that of the Assyrians and Babylonians. Another of these Greek exiles was the eclectic philosopher, Simplicius of Cilicia, "the most acute and judicious of the interpreters of Aristotle."

Agathias says that King Chosroës I. gave this band of Greek philosophers a hospitable reception, entertained them at his table, and was unwilling to have them leave his court. They discovered that he was familiar with the writings of Plato and Aristotle, whose works he had caused to be translated into the Persian language. He discussed with these seven sages such questions as the origin of the world, its destructibility or indestructibility, and the derivation of all things from one First Cause or from more.

From Agathias we also learn that later in his reign Khosrou Nushirvan bestowed special favor upon a Greek sophist named Uranius, who became the Great King's instructor in Greek learning, and was presented by him with a large sum of money. Procopius tells us that Chosroës maintained the Greek physician, Tribunus, at his court for a year, and offered him any reward that he asked at his departure.

Khosrou Nushirvan also instituted a medical school at Gondi-Sapor, in the vicinity of Susa, which gradually became a university, wherein philosophy, rhetoric and poetry were likewise studied. He not only patronized Greek learning; but under his fostering care the history and jurisprudence of his native Persia were made special objects of study. The laws and maxims of Artaxerxes I., the founder of the New Persian Empire of the Sassanidæ, were brought forth from the obscurity which had hidden them for ages, and were republished and declared to be authoritative. At the same time the annals of the New Persian Empire were collected and arranged; and a *Shah-namch*, or "Book of the Kings," was composed, which is believed to have formed the basis of the great work of Firdusi, the illustrious Persian poet of the eleventh century. Even far-off Hindoostan was explored in quest of varied knowledge, "and contributed to the learning and civilization of the time the fables of Bidpai and the game of chess."

Though Khosrou Nushirvan fiercely persecuted Mazdak's followers, he admitted and practiced the principles of toleration to a certain extent. When he ascended the Persian throne he announced as a rule of his government that only the actions of men were subject to his authority, not their thoughts. He was therefore bound not to persecute any of his subjects for their opinions, and he punished the Mazdakites for their crimes rather than for their views. He displayed mildness and moderation towards his numerous Christian subjects. Mirkhond informs us that he married a Christian woman and permitted her the free exercise of her religion; and when one of his sons became a Christian, he inflicted no other punishment upon him than to confine him to the palace.

The number of Christians in the New Persian Empire was increased by the colonies which Chosroës I. introduced from other lands. He allowed his Christian subjects full religious toleration; permitting them to erect churches, choose bishops, and conduct Christian worship at their pleasure, and even allowing them to bury their dead, though such pollution was considered sacrilegious by the Zoroastrians. No unworthy observances of the state-religion were required of the Christians. But they were not permitted to make proselytes; and perhaps all Christian sects were not viewed with the same favor, as Chrosroës is accused of persecuting the Catholics and the Monophysites, and of compelling them to join the Nestorians, who constituted the prevailing Christian sect in the Persian dominions.

But while Chosroës disliked differences of

NEW PERSIAN EMPIRE OF THE SASSANIDÆ.

practice, he appears to have encouraged a freedom of religious discussion which must have tended to shake the hereditary faith of his subjects. A remarkable indication of his liberal and tolerant views was given when he made his first peace with the Eastern Roman Empire, when he most stoutly insisted upon the article securing freedom of opinion in their own country to the seven Greek sages who had found at his court a refuge from persecution in their hour of need.

Khosrou Nushirvan was unfortunate in his domestic relations. He appears to have lived always on excellent terms with his chief wife, the daughter of the Great Khan of the Turks; and his affection for her induced him to select the son whom she had borne him to succeed him on the Persian throne. But the wife who occupied the next place in his favor displeased him by her persistent refusal to renounce the Christian religion and adopt the Zoroastrian in its stead; and the quarrel between them was apparently intensified by the conduct of their son, Nushizad, who, when he arrived at an age of discretion, deliberately preferred his mother's religion to that of his father and of the Persian nation. Chosroës I. was naturally offended at this son's choice; but he restrained his anger within moderate bounds, and simply punished the young prince by forbidding him to leave the precincts of the palace.

Unfortunate consequences ensued. Nushizad in his confinement heard a rumor that his father, after starting for the war against the Romans in Syria, was stricken with illness, was unlikely to recover, was dead. A golden opportunity appeared to him, which it would be foolish in him not to improve. He therefore left his palace prison, circulated the report of his father's death, seized the public treasure and distributed it liberally among the soldiers in the capital, summoned the Christians throughout the Persian dominions to his aid, assumed the title and state of king, was acknowledged by the entire province of the South, and believed himself strong enough to assume the offensive and attempt the subjugation of Irak, or Babylonia. Such is the account of Mirkhond, and that of Procopius is much the same. In Irak the young prince was utterly defeated in a pitched battle by Phabrizus, one of his father's generals. Mirkhond says that Nushizad fell in the midst of the conflict, fatally wounded by a chance arrow. Procopius says that he was taken prisoner and brought to his father, who merely destroyed his hopes of ever reigning by cruelly disfiguring him, instead of punishing him with death.

It is the great glory of Khosrou Nushirvan that his subjects conferred on him the title of "*the Just.*" That epithet would seem to be unmerited according to modern ideas; and accordingly Gibbon has declared that he was actuated by mere ambition in his external policy, and that "in his domestic administration he deserved the appellation of a tyrant." True, the punishments inflicted by him were mostly severe, but they were not capricious nor uniform, nor without reference to the character of the offense. He punished with death such offenses as plotting against his crown or his person when the conspirators were of full age, treasonable correspondence with the enemy, violation of the sanctity of the harem, and the proselytism which was strictly forbidden by the laws. But when the rebel was a mere youth he was satisfied with inflicting a disfigurement. When the offense was less, he could imprison, or confine to a particular spot, or merely banish the offender from his presence.

Instances are recorded of his clemency. Mirkhond relates an anecdote illustrating this, as follows: On one occasion, Chosroës banished one of his attendants from court upon being displeased with him. The man absented himself; but on a certain day, when all subjects had the right of appearing before the king, he returned to the palace, and, resuming his former duties, waited upon the guests at the royal table. While he was thus occupied, he took an opportunity of secreting a plate of solid gold about his person, after which he left the guest-chamber and disappeared entirely. Chosroës had seen the entire proceeding, but took no notice, and simply remarked, when the plate was missed: "The man who took it will not bring it back, and the man who saw him will not tell." A year afterward the attendant appeared again on the same day; whereupon the king called him aside and said: "Is the first plate all gone that you have come again to get another?" The offender acknowledged his guilt and begged pardon, which was granted him. Chosroës also took him back into his service.

It is generally admitted that the administration of Khosrou Nushirvan was wise, and that Persia prospered under his government. His vigilance, his activity, his care for the poor, his efforts to prevent or check oppression, are notorious, and cannot be questioned. Nor can it be denied that he was brave, hardy, temperate, prudent and liberal. It may perhaps be open to doubt whether he possessed the softer virtues, compassion, kindness, a tender and loving heart. He appears to have been a good husband and a good father, not easily offended, and not unduly severe when offense was given him. His early severities against his brothers and their followers may be regarded as caused by the advice of others, and were perhaps justified by state policy. In his later years, when he was his own master, he punished rebellion in a milder manner.

Intellectually, the Persians, and even many of the Greeks, exalted Khosrou Nushirvan high above the ordinary Oriental level, representing him as capable of apprehending the most subtle arguments and the deepest problems of philosophy; but Agathias made a more moderate estimate of his mental abilities and attainments. To his credit, Chosroës I., although occupied in almost constant wars, and burdened also with the administration of a mighty empire, possessed a mind capable of considering intellectual problems and of enjoying and participating in their discussion. It cannot be denied that he possessed a quick, active intellect, and broad views seldom found in an Oriental monarch.

Great as Khosrou Nushirvan was in peace, he was still greater in war; and he chiefly distinguished himself and gained his greatest laurels in his wars, which occupied his entire reign of almost half a century, during which he triumphed over the armies of the Eastern Roman Empire, and over the Abyssinians, the Ephthalites and the Turks, and extended his empire on every side. He also pacified the discontented Armenians, crushed internal revolt, frustrated the most threatening combinations, and established Persia in a position which she had not occupied since the times of Darius Hystaspes more than a thousand years before, making her for the time the most powerful empire in the world.

The most remarkable of Khosrou Nushirvan's many coins have the king's head on the obverse, presenting the full face, and surmounted by a mural crown with a low cap. The beard is close, and the hair is arranged in masses on each side. There are two stars above the crown, and two crescents, one over each shoulder, with a star and a crescent on the dress in front of each shoulder. The king wears a necklace, from which hang three pendants. On the reverse these coins have a full-length figure of the king, standing to the front, with his two hands resting on the hilt of his straight sword, and its point placed between his feet. The crown resembles that on the obverse, and there is a star and a crescent on each side of the head. The legend on the obverse is *Khusludi afzun*, "May Chosroës increase." There are two legends on the reverse; the one on the left being *Khusludi*, with the regnal year. The one on the right has not yet been satisfactorily interpreted.

The more ordinary type on the coins of Chosroës I. differs very little from those of his father, Kobad, and those of his son, Hormisdas IV. The obverse has the king's head in profile, and the reverse has the usual fire-altar and supporters. In addition to the legends, these coins have three simple crescents in the margin of the obverse, instead of three crescents with stars.

A relic of Chosroës I., of great beauty,

has been transmitted to us. This is a cup composed of a number of small disks of colored glass, united by a gold setting, and having at the bottom a crystal, engraved with a figure of the king.

On the death of King Chosroës I., or Khosrou Nushirvan, in A. D. 579, his son HORMAZD, known to the Greek and Latin writers as HORMISDAS IV., became King of Persia. Hormazd was the eldest, or perhaps the only son borne to Chosroës I., by his chief wife, the Turkish princess, Fakim. His illustrious descent on both sides, with the express appointment of his father, caused Hormisdas IV. to be universally accepted as king; and he began his reign amid the plaudits and acclamations of his subjects, delighting them by declaring that he would follow in the footsteps of his illustrious father in all things—that he would pursue the same policy, maintain the same officers in power, and try to govern in all respects as his father had governed.

The Mobeds endeavored to persuade him to favor only the Zoroastrians and to persecute such of his subjects as were Jews and Christians; but Hormisdas IV. rejected their advice with the remark that, as there were certain to be varieties of soil in an extensive territory, so it was appropriate that a great empire should include men of various opinions and manners. In his tours through his empire he permitted no injury to the lands and gardens along the route, and severely punished all who disobeyed his orders. His good inclinations only lasted during the time that he had the counsel and support of Abu-zurd-mihir, one of his father's best advisers; but when the infirmities of age obliged this venerated sage to retire from court, the king fell under other influences, and soon degenerated into a cruel tyrant.

Hormisdas IV. was engaged in wars with the Eastern Roman Emperors Tiberius and Maurice, who pressed upon Persia with increased force, confidently hoping to recover their lost laurels. As soon as Tiberius heard of Khosrou Nushirvan's death, he endeavored to negotiate with that great

8—11.-U. H.

monarch's successor, offering to relinquish all claim on Armenia and to exchange Arzanênê, with its strong fortress, Aphumôn, for Daras; but Hormisdas IV. absolutely rejected his proposals, declaring that he would surrender nothing, and declining to make peace on any other terms than that the Eastern Roman Empire should resume her old system of paying to Persia an annual subsidy.

The war therefore continued; and the Emperor Maurice invaded the Persian dominions in the summer of A. D. 579, sending a force under Romanus, Theódoric and Martin, across the Tigris. This force ravaged Kurdistan, destroying the crops with impunity. In A. D. 580 Maurice, supposing he had secured the alliance of the Arab skeikh, Alamándarus, and having collected a fleet to convey his stores, marched from Circésium down the course of the Euphrates, to carry the war into Persian Mesopotamia and to capture Ctesiphon. He was disappointed in his hopes of taking the Persians unawares, as the Arab sheikh proved treacherous, and the Persian king had heard of his enemy's march and at once took measures to frustrate the designs of Maurice. A large Persian army under Adarman marched into Roman Mesopotamia and threatened the important city of Callinícus in the rear of the Roman army. Maurice was therefore obliged to burn his fleet and to retreat hastily into Roman Mesopotamia, where he defeated Adarman before Callinícus, driving him back into the Persian dominions.

After a futile effort at negotiation, in the spring of A. D. 581, the Persians again invaded the Roman territory and attacked the city of Constantia. Maurice hastened to its relief, and defeated the Persians in a great battle in the vicinity of the city; the Persian commander, Tamchosro, being killed. The triumphant Maurice returned to Constantinople, and became sole sovereign of the Eastern Roman Empire upon the death of Tiberius, who gave him his daughter in marriage.

Johannes, or Mustacon, whom the Emperor Maurice had left in the command of the Roman forces in the East, was defeated by the Persians at the junction of the Nymphius with the Tigris; after which he besieged Arbas, a strong fort on the Persian side of the Nymphius, while the Persian main army attacked Aphumôn, in the neighboring district of Arzanênê. The garrison of Arbas made signals of distress, whereupon the Persian army hastened to its relief; and Mustacon was again defeated at Arbas, and was obliged to cross the Nymphius into the Roman territory. The Emperor Maurice then removed the incompetent Mustacon, and appointed Philippicus, his brother-in-law, to the command of the Roman forces in the East.

In A. D. 584 and 585 Philippicus made plundering raids into the Persian territory on both sides of the Upper Tigris. Late in A. D. 585 the Persians made unsuccessful attacks on Monocartum and Martyropolis. After unsuccessful negotiations, in A. D. 586, Philippicus invaded Persian Armenia and defeated the Persians in a great battle near Solachon, after arousing the enthusiasm of his troops by carrying along their ranks a picture of Christ. He pursued the fleeing Persians to Daras, which refused to receive within its walls an army which had so disgraced itself. The Persian army retired farther inland; whereupon Philippicus invaded Arzanênê and besieged the stronghold of Chlomarôn, and sent detachments farther eastward.

The Persian general, after rallying his army and strengthening it by fresh recruits, hastened to the relief of Arzanênê. Philippicus, utterly surprised, was forced to raise the siege of Chlomarôn and to retreat in disorder. The Persians pursued him across the Nymphius, until he took refuge in the strong fortress of Amida. Disgusted and disgraced by his ill success, Philippicus assigned the direction of active operations to Heraclíus, but remained at headquarters to supervise the general movements.

Heraclíus at once led the Roman army into the Persian territory, devastated the country on both sides of the Tigris, and rejoined Philippicus before the winter. Through the jealousy of Philippicus, who, in A. D. 587, divided his command between Heraclíus and others, the Romans only reduced two fortresses. At the approach of winter Philippicus returned to Constantinople, leaving Heraclíus in command of the Roman army in the East.

Encouraged by the mutinous spirit of the Roman army, the Persians invaded the Roman territory early in A. D. 588 and threatened Constantia, which was, however, saved by Germanus. The mutinous spirit having been quelled later in the year, the Romans invaded Arzanênê, but were driven back into their own territory by the Persian general, Maruzas, who pursued them, but was defeated and killed near Martyropolis. The head of the slain Maruzas was cut off and sent as a trophy to the Emperor Maurice.

In A. D. 589 the Persians took Martyropolis, through the treachery of a petty Roman officer named Sittas. Philippicus vainly besieged the town twice. During the second siege the garrison was strongly reinforced by the Persian troops under Mebodes and Aphraates, who defeated Philippicus in a pitched battle and sent a large detachment to reinforce the garrison. Thereupon Philippicus was deprived of his command, and was succeeded by Comentiolus, with Heraclíus as his lieutenant.

The new Roman commanders invaded the Persian territory in force, ravaging the country about Nísibis; and, in a pitched battle at Sisarbanôn, near that city, in which Comentiolus was defeated and routed, Heraclíus finally defeated the whole Persian army, driving it from the field with the loss of its commander, who was slain in the thick of the fight. The next day the Persian camp was taken, with a rich booty and many standards. The remnant of the vanquished Persian army found refuge within the walls of Nísibis. Later in the year Comentiolus took Arbas from the Persians, after a short siege.

The Oriental writers tell us that Hormisdas IV. had gradually become a tyrant; oppressing the rich, under the plea of protecting the poor, and putting thirteen thousand of the higher classes to death, through jealousy or fear; thus completely alienating all the more powerful portion of the Persian nation. Aware of his unpopularity, the neighboring tribes and nations began a series of aggressions, plundered the frontier Persian provinces, defeated the Persian detachments sent against them under disaffected commanders, and everywhere reduced the New Persian Empire to the most imminent peril. The Arabs crossed the Euphrates and ravaged Mesopotamia; the Khazars invaded Armenia and Azerbijan; and the Great Khan of the Turks led his hordes across the Oxus, occupied Balkh and Herat, and was threatening to penetrate into the very heart of the New Persian Empire.

The advance of the Turks constituted the real danger to Persia. Hormisdas IV. selected a leader of great courage and experience, named Varahran, or Bahram, who had won distinction in the wars of Khosrou Nushirvan; placing the resources of the Empire at his disposal, and assigning to him the entire conduct of the war against the Turks. Mirkhond, Tabari and Maçoudi state that Bahram led only a small force of picked veterans against Balkh, and defeated the Great Khan of the Turks in a great battle, in which the Great Khan himself was slain. Bahram soon afterward defeated the Khan's son, whom he took prisoner and sent to King Hormisdas IV. Bahram also sent a vast booty to the Persian court.

In A. D. 589 Hormisdas IV. sent Bahram with an army into Colchis and Suania to renew the Lazic war. Bahram ravaged the province at his pleasure, but a Roman army soon hastened to its defense and defeated the Persians in a pitched battle on the Araxes. As soon as King Hormisdas IV. heard of Bahram's defeat, he sent a messenger to the Persian camp on the Araxes, who deprived the vanquished general of his command, and presented to him, on his sovereign's behalf, a distaff, some cotton, and a full set of female garments. Bahram was so incensed by this unmerited insult that he retorted with a letter, addressing the king as the "daughter" of Khosrou Nushirvan, and not as his son. Soon afterwards a second messenger from the court arrived at Bahram's camp, with orders to bring the recalcitrant commander home in chains. Thereupon Bahram openly revolted, caused the messenger to be trampled upon by an elephant, and induced his army to espouse his cause.

The news of Bahram's revolt was hailed with acclamations by the Persian provinces. The Persian army in Mesopotamia, stationed at Nisibis, joined in the revolt with that of Bahram in Albania; and the united force marched on Ctesiphon by way of Assyria, and took up a position on the Upper Zab river. King Hormisdas IV. sent an army under Pherochanes against the rebels; but Bahram's emissaries seduced the troops of Pherochanes from their allegiance, whereupon they murdered their commander and joined the other rebel forces. The insurgents then advanced nearer to the capital.

In the meantime King Hormisdas IV., distracted between hate and fear, suspecting every one and trusting no one, confined himself within the walls of the capital, where he continued the severities which had lost him the affections of his subjects. The Oriental writers state that the king suspected his son Chosroës of collusion with the rebels and drove him into exile, at the same time imprisoning his own brothers-in-law, Bindoës and Bostam, whom he feared would support their nephew. These violent measures precipitated the events which the king feared. A general revolt broke out in the palace. Bindoës and Bostam were released from prison, whereupon they placed themselves at the head of the malcontents, rushed into the presence-chamber, dragged the tyrant from his throne, deprived him of his diadem, and imprisoned him in the dungeon from which they had themselves escaped. The Oriental writers—Mirkhond, Tabari and Maçoudi—state that Hormisdas IV. was at once blinded, to disqualify him from thereafter reigning, and that he was soon afterwards assassinated in prison by Bindoës and Bostam.

The Greek and Oriental writers are unanimous in pronouncing Hormisdas IV. one of the worst kings that ever reigned over Persia. The fair promise of his early youth soon faded away; and during most of his reign he was a jealous and capricious tyrant, influenced by unworthy favorites, and stimulated to ever-increasing severities by his fears. His suspicions were aroused by any kind of eminence in others; and, besides the nobles and the illustrious, many philosophers and scientific men fell victims to his jealous tyranny. His treatment of Bahram was a folly and a crime—an act of base ingratitude, and a rash proceeding, whereof he had not considered the consequences. He was also indolent and effeminate. During his entire reign he did not relinquish the soft life of the palace; and he did not take the field in a single instance, either against his country's foes or his own. He deserved no pity for his miserable fate.

In the coins of Hormisdas IV. the head seems modeled on that of his father. The field of the coin is crowded with stars and crescents. The border also has stars and crescents, replacing the simple crescents of Chosroës I., and reproducing the combined stars and crescents of Zamasp. The legend on the obverse is *Auhramazdi afzud*, or sometimes *Auhramazi afzun*. On the reverse are the usual fire-altar and supporters, a regnal year and a mint-mark. The regnal years range from one to thirteen, and there are about thirty mint-marks.

Upon the deposition of Hormisdas IV., his eldest son, CHOSROES II., or KHOSROU PARVIZ, was proclaimed King of Persia. He was the last great Persian monarch belonging to the renowned dynasty of the Sassanidæ. The rebels at Ctesiphon, who perhaps acted with his connivance, and who calculated on his pardoning them for raising him to the Persian throne, declared him king without binding him by any conditions, and without negotiating with Bahram, who was still in arms a short distance away.

Chosroës II., or Khosrou Parviz, was suspected by most of his subjects of complicity in the murder of his father. The rebel Bahram—the greatest Persian general of the time—refused to recognize his authority and was arrayed against him. He had no established character to recommend him as yet. He had no merits to plead; and nothing to urge in his favor except that he was the eldest son of his father—the legitimate representative of the ancient line of the Sassanidæ. He had been placed upon the Persian throne by a revolution in a hasty and irregular manner. Nor is it certain that he went through the customary formality of asking the consent of the general assembly of the Persian nobles to his coronation; as Bahram stated that "the noble and respectable took no part in the vote, which was carried by the disorderly and low-born."

The new king's position was thus one of great difficulty, and perils surrounded him on every side. The most pressing danger, and the one which required to be at once confronted, was the threatening attitude of Bahram, who had advanced from Adiabênê to Holwan and occupied a strong position less than a hundred and fifty miles from the capital. The young king's security demanded the immediate conciliation or defeat of Bahram.

Chosroës II. first endeavored to try conciliation, by writing a letter to Bahram, inviting the great general to his court and offering him the second place in the empire if he would come in and make his submission. With the message, the king sent rich presents and offered that if the terms proposed were accepted they should be confirmed by an oath.

To the king's letter Bahram gave the following reply: "Bahram, friend of the gods, conqueror, illustrious, enemy of tyrants, general of the Persian host, wise, apt for command, god-fearing, without reproach, noble, fortunate, successful, venerable, thrifty, provident, gentle, humane, to Chosroës the son of Hormisdas (sends greeting). I have received the letter which you wrote with such little wisdom, but have rejected the presents which you sent with such excessive boldness. It had been better that you should have abstained from sending either, more especially considering the irregularity of your appointment, and the fact that the noble and respectable took no part in the vote, which was carried by the disorderly and low-born. If then it is your wish to escape your father's fate, strip off the diadem which you have assumed and deposit it in some holy place, quit the palace, and restore to their prisons the criminals whom you have set at liberty, and whom you had no right to release until they had undergone trial for their crimes. When you have done all this, come hither, and I will give you the government of a province. Be well advised, and so farewell. Else, be sure you will perish like your father."

King Khosrou Parviz, to his credit, was guilty of no hasty act or of no unworthy display of temper, in consequence of Bahram's insolent missive; but he restrained himself, and even made another effort at reconciliation. He still addressed Bahram as his friend, while striving to outdo him in the grandeur of his titles. He complimented the great general on his courage, and congratulated him upon his good health. The king said as follows: "There are certain expressions in the letter which I have received which I am sure do not speak my friend's real feelings. The amanuensis had evidently drunk more wine than he ought, and, being half asleep when he wrote, had put down things that were foolish and indeed monstrous. But I am not disturbed by them. I must decline, however, to send back to their prisons those whom I have released, since favors granted by royalty can not with propriety be withdrawn; and I must protest that in the ceremony of my coronation all due formalities were observed. As for stripping myself of my diadem, I am so far from contemplating it, that I look forward rather to extending my dominion over new worlds. As Bahram has invited me, I will certainly pay him a visit; but I will be obliged to come as a king, and if my persuasions do not produce submission I will have to compel it by force of arms. I hope that Bahram will be wise in time, and become my friend and helper."

Bahram did not reply to the king's second overture, and it became tolerably evident that the quarrel could only be settled by an appeal to arms. Chosroës II. therefore placed himself at the head of a body of troops and marched against his adversary, who was encamped on the Holwan river. Chosroës II., having no confidence in his soldiers, sought a personal interview with Bahram and renewed his offers of pardon and favor; but the conference only led to mutual recriminations, and at its close both sides resorted to arms. The two armies only skirmished for six days, as Chosroës II. used all his endeavors to avoid a regular battle; but on the seventh day Bahram surprised the young king by a night attack, threw his troops into confusion, and then persuaded them to desert the king and join the rebel side.

King Chosroës II. was compelled to flee. He fell back on Ctesiphon; but, as he despaired of making a successful defense, with the few troops that remained faithful to him, against Bahram's overwhelming force, he decided to evacuate the capital, to leave Persia, and to seek the protection of one of his neighbors. He is said to have been for a long time undecided as to whether he should seek refuge among the Turks, or the Arabs, or the Khazars of the Caucasus region, or in the Eastern Roman Empire. Some writers say that after he left Ctesiphon with his wives and children, his two uncles, and an escort of thirty men, he laid his reins on his horse's neck, leaving it to the animal's instinct to determine in what direction he should flee.

The sagacious beast proceeded toward the Euphrates; and when the fugitive king reached the banks of that river, he crossed the stream, followed up its course, and easily reached the well-known Roman station of Circésium, having been entirely unmolested in his retreat. As soon as Bahram was informed of the young king's flight, he sent four thousand cavalry to pursue and capture the royal fugitive. They failed through the action of Bindoës, who devoted himself to his nephew, and who, by deceiving the officer in command, enabled Chosroës II. to get so far in advance of his pursuers that the chase had to be abandoned; and the detachment returned to Ctesiphon with only Bindoës as a captive.

Probus, the Roman governor of Circésium, received the refugee Persian king with all possible honor, and the next day informed Comentiolus, the Roman Prefect of the East, then residing at Hierapolis, of what had transpired. At the same time Probus sent to Comentiolus a letter which the fugitive monarch had addressed to the Emperor Maurice, imploring his assistance against his enemies. Comentiolus approved what had been done, despatched a courier to carry the royal message to Constantinople, and soon afterwards, by direction of the imperial court, invited the illustrious refugee to take up his residence at Hierapolis, until the Eastern Roman Emperor should determine upon the course to be pursued.

After the letter of Chosroës II. had been read at Constantinople, a serious debate arose there as to the proper course to pursue. Some maintained that it was for the interest of the Eastern Roman Empire that the civil war in Persia should be prolonged, that Persia should be left to waste her strength and exhaust her resources in the domestic strife, at the end of which the Romans might easily conquer her. Others were less selfish and more far-sighted, and were in favor of supporting the fugitive Persian king in his efforts to recover his lost crown. The Emperor Maurice coincided with the views of the latter party and accepted their counsels.

Maurice accordingly replied to Chosroës II. that he accepted him as his guest and "son," espoused his cause, and would aid him with all the forces of the Eastern Roman Empire to recover the Persian throne. Maurice also sent the fugitive king some magnificent presents, and released the Persian prisoners confined at Constantinople, bidding them go with the envoys of Chosroës II. and resume the service of their sovereign. Soon afterward the Eastern Roman Emperor sent an army of seventy thousand men under Narses to support the claims of Chosroës II., and also advanced him a subsidy from the imperial treasury, equal in value to about five million dollars of United States money. But the refugee Persian king only obtained this aid by ceding to the Romans Persarmenia and Eastern Mesopotamia, with the strong towns of Martyropolis and Daras.

In the meantime BAHRAM had occupied Ctesiphon and proclaimed himself King of Persia, and had sent out messengers on every side to inform the Persian provinces of the change of kings. But when it was known that the Eastern Roman Emperor had espoused the cause of the dethroned Khosrou Parviz, the usurper Bahram found himself involved in difficulties. Conspiracy arose in his own court, and had to be suppressed by executions. Murmurs were heard in some of the more remote provinces. Armenia openly revolted, and declared for Chosroës II. It was also soon apparent that the loyalty of the Persian troops to Bahram was uncertain in many places; especially in Mesopotamia, which would have to bear the brunt of the attack when the Romans advanced.

To strengthen his hold on Mesopotamia, Bahram in midwinter sent two detachments commanded by officers upon whom he could rely, to occupy respectively Anatho and Nísibis, the two strongholds in the suspected region. Mir-aduris succeeded in entering and occupying Anatho. But before Zadesprates reached the vicinity of Nísibis, the garrison there deserted the usurper Bahram's cause and declared for Khosrou Parviz; and when Zadesprates approached to reconnoiter, he fell a victim to a stratagem, and was killed by an officer named Rosas. Soon afterwards Mir-aduris was slain by his own troops, who had caught the contagion of revolt, and his head was sent to Chosroës II.

Military operations began in the spring of A. D. 592. Chosroës II., besides his Roman and Persian supporters in Mesopotamia, had a second army in Azerbijan, raised by his uncles Bindoës and Bostam, which was reinforced by an Armenian contingent. Early in the spring Chosroës II. marched from Hierapolis, by way of Constantia, to Daras, and thence to the Tigris, across which he sent a detachment in the vicinity of the ruins of Nineveh. This detachment surprised and defeated Bryzacius, who commanded Bahram's forces in that region, in the night, taking Bryzacius himself prisoner.

The Greek writer, Theophylact, states that the captors of Bryzacius cut off his nose and his ears, and then sent him a prisoner to Chosroës II., who was overjoyed at the success. Chosroës II. instantly led his entire army across the Tigris, encamping for the night at Dinabadôn, where he entertained the Persian and Roman nobles at a banquet. In the height of the festivity the captive Bryzacius was brought in loaded with fetters, and was made sport of by the guests for a time, after which Chosroës II. gave a signal, whereupon the guards plunged their swords into the unfortunate captive's body, thus killing him in the presence of the banqueters. Chosroës II. then anointed his guests with perfumed ointment, crowned them with flowers, and bid them drink to his success in the civil war. Theophylact says: "The guests returned to their tents, delighted with the completeness of the entertainment, and told their friends how handsomely they had been treated, but the crown of all (they said) was the episode of Bryzacius."

The next day Khosrou Parviz advanced across the Greater Zab, and a week later he reached the Lesser Zab, where he and his Roman allies outmaneuvered Bahram. After seizing the fords of the Zab, and after five days of marching and countermarching, Chosroës II. effected a junction with his uncles Bindoës and Bostam. At the same time Mebodes, with a small Roman force, marched southward and occupied Seleucia and Ctesiphon without opposition, thus obtaining possession of the royal treasures, while he proclaimed Chosroës II. king and sent the most precious emblems of the Persian sovereignty to him in his camp.

In the plain country of Adiabênê, at the foot of the Zagros mountains, the first battle was fought between the armies of Khosrou Parviz and Bahram. In the army of Chosroës II. the Romans were in the center, the Persians on the right and the Armenians on the left. When the battle commenced, the Romans routed Bahram's center by a furious charge; whereupon Bahram retreated to a strong position on the slope of the hills, where he repulsed an attack of the Persians in Chosroës's army. The Romans under Narses came to the relief of Chosroës's routed troops; but the battle ended in an advantage for Bahram, who, however, evacuated his camp and retired to the fertile upland region.

Chosroës II. and his allies pursued Bahram to Canzaca, or Shiz; whereupon Bahram retreated to the Balarathus, where a second battle was fought, Bahram having in the meantime been reinforced by a number of elephants from the provinces bordering on India. All of Bahram's assaults upon the Roman lines were repulsed by Narses, who then charged in his turn and routed the whole of Bahram's forces, which fled in confusion from the field, six thousand of Bahram's troops deserting and allowing themselves to be made prisoners. Bahram himself fled with four thousand of his troops. His camp, with all its elegant furniture, and his wives and children, fell into the hands of the victors. The elephant corps still fought valiantly, but it was surrounded and compelled to surrender. The battle was entirely lost to Bahram, and the vanquished general fled for his life.

The triumphant Chosroës II. sent ten thousand men under his uncle Bostam in pursuit of the fugitives, who were overtaken; but the pursuers were repulsed, and they returned to Chosroës's camp. Bahram continued his flight, passed through Rei, or Rhages, and Damaghan, and finally reached the Oxus, where he placed himself under the protection of the Turks. After dismissing his Roman allies, the victorious Chosroës II. returned to Ctesiphon, after a year's absence, and was again seated on the throne of his ancestors.

Bahram's earlier coins have the mural crown, but no stars or crescents, his own head being among the flames of the fire-altar. His legends were *Varahran Chub,* "Bahram of the mace," or *Varahran, malkan malka, mazdisn, bagi, ramashtri,* "Bahram, King of Kings, Ormazd-worshiping, divine, peaceful." His later coins resemble those of Hormisdas IV., except in the legend on the obverse, which is *Varahran afzun,* or "Varahran greater." The regnal year and the mint-mark are on the reverse. The regnal year in every case is "one;" and the mint-marks are Zadracarta, Iran and Nihach.

The second reign of CHOSROES II., or KHOSROU PARVIZ, lasted almost thirty-seven years—from the summer of A. D. 591 to February, A. D. 628. From an external view, it is the most remarkable reign of the whole line of the Sassanians. At no other time did the New Persian Empire extend itself so far, or so distinguish itself by its military achievements, as in the twenty years included in the period from A. D. 602 to A. D. 622. It was seldom reduced so low as in the periods immediately before or immediately after these eventful twenty years, in the earlier and in the later portions of the reign whose central period was so glorious.

As Chosroës II. had achieved his triumph over Bahram by the assistance of the Eastern Roman Empire, he commenced his second reign amid the undisguised hostility of his subjects. He so greatly mistrusted their feelings towards him that he solicited and obtained from the Emperor Maurice the support of a Roman body-guard, to whom he intrusted the care of his person. Besides the odium always attaching in the minds of a spirited people to the sovereign imposed upon them by a foreign power, he was suspected of a crime of which no other Persian monarch had ever before been accounted guilty. He vainly protested his innocence. The popular belief held him an accomplice in the murder of his father, and branded the young prince with the horrible name of "parricide."

In order to clear himself of this imputation, he put to death the subordinate instruments by whom his father was actually deprived of his life; after which he instituted proceedings against his uncles Bindoës and Bostam, who had contrived the murder. So long as the success of his arms in the struggle with Bahram was doubtful, the young king had been glad to avail himself of the support of these two uncles, and to make use of their talents in his own interest. At one time in his flight he was indebted to the self-devotion of Bindoës for the preservation of his life; and both uncles had deserved his gratitude by their successful efforts to bring Armenia over to his cause and to raise a formidable army in that province. But the necessity of purging his own character made Chosroës II. forget the ties of consanguinity and gratitude.

He accordingly caused Bindoës, who resided at court, to be drowned in the Tigris. He recalled Bostam, whom he had appointed governor of Rei and Khorassan; but Bostam, who suspected his royal nephew's intentions, openly revolted, and proclaimed himself independent sovereign of the northern provinces, where he established his authority for some time. Tabari says that the young king caused Bostam's wife, Bahram's sister, to murder her husband, by promising to marry her.

In the meantime Bahram had been removed by similar intrigues. He had been a fugitive and an exile at the court of the Khan of the Turks, who had received him with honor and had given him his daughter in marriage. Chosroës II. was in constant fear that the great general would lead a Turkish horde into Persia to renew the struggle for the crown. The young king therefore sent an envoy into Turkestan, well supplied with valuable presents, instructing him to procure the death of Bahram. The envoy sounded the Turkish Kahn on the subject, but met with a rebuff: after which he succeeded by liberal gifts in inducing the Khatûn, the Khan's wife, to cause Bahram to be assassinated by one of her slaves, the exiled general being killed by means of a poisoned dagger.

NEW PERSIAN EMPIRE OF THE SASSANIDÆ. 1329

During his exile in the Eastern Roman Empire, Chosroes II. was impressed by what he saw and heard of the Christian religion. He professed a high veneration for the Virgin Mary, and adopted the then-customary practice of addressing his prayers and vows to the Christian saints and martyrs, who were practically the chief objects of the Oriental Christians' devotions. The exiled prince adopted Sergius, a martyr highly reverenced by the Christians of Osrhoêné and Mesopotamia, as a kind of patron-saint; and in times of difficulty he would vow some gift to the shrine of St. Sergius at Sergiopolis, providing the event corresponded to his wishes.

He is said on two occasions to have sent with his gift a letter explaining the circumstances of his vow and its fulfillment, and these letters have been transmitted to us in a Greek version. In one letter Chosroës II. ascribed the success of his arms on a certain occasion to the influence of the martyred St. Sergius; and in the other letter he attributed to that saint the credit of causing by his prayers Sira, or Shirin, the most beautiful and the best beloved of the young king's wives, to become a mother.

Sira appears to have been a Christian, and in marrying her Chosroës II. had violated the Persian laws, which forbade the Persian monarch to have a Christian wife. Sira had considerable influence over her husband, who allowed her to build many churches and monasteries about Ctesiphon. When she died, Chosroës II. caused her image to be perpetuated in sculpture; and Tabari tells that he sent statues of her to the Eastern Roman Emperor, to the Turkish Khan, and to different other potentates.

Mirkhond and Tabari state that Khosrou Parviz had an immense harem, or seraglio; his concubines numbering twelve thousand. The only one of his secondary wives whose name is known to us is Kurdiyeh, Bahram's sister and Bostam's widow, who murdered her first husband at Chosroës's suggestion.

The Armenian writers tell us that Chosroës II. intended to depopulate that part of Armenia which had not been ceded to the Romans, by making a general levy of all the males and marching them off to the East to fight the Ephthalites; but the design failed, as the Armenians carried everything before them, and under their native leader, Smbat, the Bagratunian, conquered Hyrcania and Taberistan, defeated the Koushans and the Ephthalites repeatedly, and even successfully encountered the Great Khan of the Turks, who supported his vassals with an army of three hundred thousand men. By Smbat's valor the Persian dominion was reestablished in the north-eastern mountain region, from Mount Demavend to the Hindoo Koosh; the Koushans, the Turks and the Ephthalites were held in check; and the barbarian tide which had threatened to engulf the New Persian Empire in that quarter was effectually resisted and rolled back.

Khosrou Parviz maintained the most amicable and intimate relations with the Eastern Roman Empire during the remaining eleven years of the Emperor Maurice's reign. Though he felt humiliated in accepting the terms on which alone Maurice was willing to aid him in recovering the Persian crown, after he had agreed to them he repressed every regret, made no effort to evade his obligations, refrained from all endeavors to undo by intrigue what he had done with his eyes open, however reluctantly.

Only once during these eleven years after the restoration of Chosroës II. did a momentary cloud threaten the peace between him and his imperial benefactor. In A. D. 600 some of the Arab tribes who were vassals of the Eastern Roman Empire made a raid across the Euphrates into the Persian territory, which they ravaged far and wide, after which they returned with their plunder to their desert homes. Khosrou Parviz was rightly incensed, but was pacified by the representations of Maurice's envoy, George.

The deposition and assassination of the virtuous and perhaps over-rigid Maurice in A. D. 662, and the usurpation of the imperial throne by his murderer, the centurion Phocas, aroused the indignation of the Persian king, who was angered upon hearing that his friend and benefactor, and his many sons and his brother, had been murdered. He was informed that one son had been sent by Maurice to implore the aid of the Persians, that this son had been overtaken and murdered by the usurper's emissaries; but it was also rumored that he safely reached Ctesiphon. Chosroës II. himself asserted that this prince, Theodosius, was at his court and that he intended to assert the young prince's right to the imperial throne.

Five months after his coronation, the usurper Phocas sent Lilius, the actual murderer of Maurice, as an envoy to Persia to announce his occupation of the imperial throne. Thereupon Khosrou Parviz resolved upon war, imprisoned the envoy, Lilius, declared his determination to avenge his dead benefactor's murder, and openly proclaimed war against the Eastern Roman Empire.

The war began the next year (A. D. 603). The Romans were then involved in civil war among themselves; as Narses, who commanded the Roman forces in the East ever since he restored Chosroës II. to the Persian throne, took the field against Phocas as soon as he heard of the murder of Maurice, seized Edessa and defied the armies of the usurper. Narses afterwards retreated to Hierapolis, whence, trusting to the promises of Domentziolus, he returned to Constantinople, where Phocas burned him to death.

In the meantime Germanus, the Roman commander at Daras, found himself unable to make head against Narses in Edessa, or against the Persian king, who led an army into Mesopotamia. Germanus was defeated by Chosroës II. near Daras, and was mortally wounded in the battle; after which he retired to Constantia, where he died eleven days later. The eunuch Leontius, the successor of Germanus, was defeated by Chosroës II. at Arxamûs, and many of his troops were made prisoners. Phocas then recalled Leontius, and appointed Domentziolus to the command. The war now languished for a short time.

In A. D. 605 Chosroës II. besieged Daras for nine months, finally capturing the stronghold, and thus striking a severe blow at Roman prestige. The Romans now suffered a long series of calamities. In A. D. 606 the Persian king took Tur-abdin, Hesen-Cephas, Mardin, Capher-tuta and Amida. In A. D. 607 he captured Carrhæ (the Haran of Abraham's time), Resaina, or Ras-el-ain, and Edessa, the capital of Osrhoëné; after which he advanced to the Euphrates, led his army across that river into Syria, and besieged and took Hierapolis, Kenneserin and Berhœa (now Aleppo) in several campaigns.

In the meantime another Persian army was operating in Roman Armenia, where it captured Satala and Theodosiopolis; after which it invaded Cappadocia and threatened the great city of Cæsaréa Mázaca, the principal Roman stronghold in that quarter. Marauding bands desolated the open country, spreading terror through the fertile regions of Phrygia and Galatia, which had escaped the horrors of war for centuries, and which were rich with the accumulated products of industry. Theóphanes states that some of the ravagers even penetrated as far westward as Chalcedon (now Scutari), on the Bosphorus, opposite Constantinople. In May, A. D. 611, the Persians again crossed the Euphrates, utterly destroyed the Roman army which defended Syria, and sacked the two great cities of Apaméa and Antioch.

In the meantime the cruel and incompetent reign and life of the Emperor Phocas had been ended by the double revolt of Heraclíus, Prefect of Egypt, and Gregory, his lieutenant; and Heraclíus ascended the throne of the Eastern Roman Empire. Although Heraclíus was a youth of promise, innocent of any connection with the murder of Maurice, and well disposed to avenge that dark deed, the Persian king, instead of adhering to his original statement that he took up arms to punish the murder of his friend and benefactor, and desisting from further hostilities after the death of Phocas, continued the war in spite of the change of

Emperors at Constantinople, and pushed his advantages to the very utmost.

In A. D. 611 Persian armies invaded Syria, defeated the Roman forces, and took Antioch and Apaméa. In A. D. 612 Chosroës II. again entered Cappodocia and captured Cæsaréa Mázaca. In A. D. 614 he sent his general, Shahr-Barz, into the region east of the Anti-Libanus mountains and took the ancient and celebrated city of Damascus. In A. D. 615 Shahr-Barz marched against Palestine, called the Jews to his assistance, and proclaimed a Holy War against the Christian "unbelievers," whom he threatened to enslave or exterminate. Twenty-six thousand Jews flocked to the Persian standard; and after occupying the Jordan valley and Galilee, the Persian general invested Jerusalem, which he captured after a siege of eighteen days, forcing his way into the Holy City and giving it over to plunder and rapine.

The cruel and fanatical hostility of the Jews had free reign. The Christian churches of Helena, of Constantine, of the Holy Sepulcher, of the Resurrection, and many others were laid in ashes or ruined; most of the Holy City was destroyed; the sacred treasuries were plundered; the relics were scattered or carried away; and thousands of the unfortunate inhabitants fell victims to the fanatical Jews and their Persian allies. This dreadful massacre lasted for some days; and the Armenian writers state that seventeen thousand persons were thus slaughtered, while the Greek writer Theóphanes places the number at *ninety* thousand, which is, however, improbable. Thirty-five thousand were taken prisoners, among whom was the aged Patriarch, Zacharias, who passed the remainder of his life in captivity in Persia. The Cross found by Helena, and believed to be the "True Cross," was also taken to Ctesiphon, where it was carefully preserved and duly venerated by the Christian wife of Khosrou Parviz.

In A. D. 616 the Persians under Shahr-Barz marched from Palestine into Egypt, which had not seen a foreign foe on its soil since the days of Julius Cæsar, six and a half centuries before. The Persian general surprised Pelusium, the key to Egypt, and pressed forward across the Delta and occupied the rich and luxurious city of Alexandria. John the Merciful, who was the Patriarch, and Nicétas the Patrician, who was the governor, had fled from the city before the Persians entered it, seeking refuge in Cyprus. After the capture of Alexandria, Egypt at once submitted to the Persians. Persian bands marched up the Nile valley to the Ethiopian frontier, and established the dominion of King Khosrou Parviz over the whole of Egypt—a land in which no Persian soldier had set foot since it had been wrested from King Daríus Codomannus by Alexander the Great, nine and a half centuries before.

In the meantime another Persian army, under Saina, or Shahên, marched from Cappadocia through Asia Minor to the shores of the Thracian Bosphorus, and besieged the strong city of Chalcedon, opposite Constantinople. Chalcedon made a vigorous defense; and the Emperor Heraclíus, anxious to save it from capture, had an interview with Shahên, at whose suggestion he sent three of his highest nobles as ambassadors to the Persian king, with an humble request for peace. The overture failed. King Chosroës II. imprisoned the Roman ambassadors and treated them cruelly. He also threatened Shahên with death for not bringing the Emperor Heraclíus in chains to the foot of his throne; and declared that he would grant no terms of peace—that the Eastern Roman Empire was his, and that Heraclíus must descend from his throne. Soon afterwards (A. D. 617) the Persians took Chalcedon, after a siege through the winter, and occupied this important stronghold, within a mile of Constantinople. In A. D. 620 the Persians also took Ancyra (now Angora), which had resisted for three years; and the island of Rhodes also submitted to the invaders.

Thus the Eastern Roman Empire had been deprived of all its dominions in Asia and Africa in the course of fifteen years; and the New Persian Empire was extended westward to the Ægean and the Nile, thus attaining the dimensions of the old Medo-Persian Empire. There were evidences of disorder and anarchy in the Provinces conquered from the Romans by the armies of Khosrou Parviz; but the Persians seem to have intended to retain, to govern, and to beautify the subjugated territory.

Eutychius informs us that when the Romans retired from Syria, the Jews resident in Tyre, numbering four thousand, plotted with their brethren of Jerusalem, Galilee, Damascus and Cyprus for a general massacre of the Tyrian Christians on a certain day. The conspiracy was discovered; and the Jews of Tyre were arrested and imprisoned by their fellow-citizens, who put the city in a state of defense. The twenty-six thousand foreign Jews, who came at the appointed time and attacked Tyre, were repulsed from the walls and defeated with terrible slaughter.

Khosrou Parviz augmented his revenue, thus indicating that he had established a settled government in the conquered provinces. The palace at Mashita, recently discovered by a traveler, is striking evidence that he looked upon his conquests as permanent acquisitions, and that he intended to retain them and to visit them occasionally.

The Emperor Heraclius was now well nigh driven to despair. Constantinople had been reduced to want by the loss of Egypt, and its tumultuous populace clamored for food. The Avars overran Thrace and continually approached nearer to the Byzantine capital. The glitter of the Persian arms could likewise be observed by the Emperor at any moment if he looked from his palace windows across the Bosphorus. There was no hope of relief or aid from any quarter. In the language of Gibbon, the Eastern Roman Empire was "reduced to the walls of Constantinople, with the remnant of Greece, Italy and Africa, and some maritime cities, from Tyre to Trebizond, of the Asiatic coast."

It is no wonder that under such circumstances the despondent Emperor resolved upon flight, and secretly made arrangements to transport himself and his treasures to the distant Carthage, where he might find refuge. After his ships, laden with their precious freight, had put to sea, and he was about to follow them, his intention became known or was suspected. Thereupon the populace of Constantinople arose; and the Patriarch, who espoused their cause, compelled the reluctant Emperor to accompany him to the church of St. Sophia and there swear that he would not desert the imperial city under any circumstances.

Thus frustrated in his design to escape from his perils by flight, Heraclius took a desperate resolution. Leaving Constantinople to its fate, and trusting its safety to the protection afforded by its walls and by the Bosphorus, he embarked with such troops as he was able to collect, and carried the war into the enemy's country. He had one advantage over his foe in possessing an adequate navy, and consequently having command of the sea and power to strike his blows unexpectedly in different quarters. When he revealed his design, it was not opposed, either by the Patriarch or by the people of Constantinople. He was permitted to coin the treasures of the various churches into money, to collect stores, to enroll troops, and to start on his expedition on Easter Monday, A. D. 622.

The fleet of Heraclius sailed southward, and, in spite of adverse gales, made a speedy and successful voyage through the Propontis, the Hellespont, the Ægean and the Cilician Strait, to the Gulf of Issus, in the angle between Asia Minor and Syria. He was soon confronted by the Persians under Shahr-Barz, the conqueror of Jerusalem and Egypt; and after various movements the Persian general was defeated in a battle in the mountain country towards the Armenian frontier—the first victory which the Romans had won since the death of Maurice. On the approach of winter Heraclius returned by sea to Constantinople.

The next year (A. D. 623) Heraclius, having in the meantime concluded an alliance with the Khan of the Khazars and other chiefs, embarked with five thousand men at

Constantinople, and sailed across the Black Sea to Trebizond and thence to Lazica, or Mingrelia, where he obtained contingents from his allies, which, with the reinforcements which he had collected from Trebizond and the other maritime towns, raised his army to one hundred and twenty thousand men. He led this force across the Araxes and invaded Armenia.

On hearing of this invasion, the Persian king advanced into Azerbijan with forty thousand men and occupied the strong city of Canzaca, whose site is believed to be marked by the ruins of Takht-i-Suleïman. Khosrou Parviz also ordered the armies under Shahr-Barz and Shahên to effect a junction and oppose any further advance of the Eastern Roman Emperor's army. But the two Persian generals were outstripped by the activity of Heraclius, who advanced from Armenia into Azerbijan and marched directly upon Canzaca. The advance-guard of Arabs in the Roman army actually surprised Chosroës's pickets, but the Persian king hastily evacuated Canzaca and retreated southward through Ardelan towards the Zagros mountains. Chosroës's army broke up and dispersed, upon beholding its sovereign flee. Heraclius pursued the fleeing Persian host, slaying all whom he captured; but his pursuit of Chosroës II. was unsuccessful, as the Persian king baffled his enemy by moving from place to place through the rough and difficult mountain region between Azerbijan and the Mesopotamian plain.

As Heraclius was far from his resources, he retreated across the Araxes on the approach of winter, and wintered in Albania. He was harassed in his retreat; as he had excited the fanaticism of the Persians wherever he went by destroying the Magian temples and extinguishing the sacred fire, which the Magian religion required to be kept constantly burning. He had likewise everywhere reduced the cities and villages to ashes, and carried away captive many thousands of the population. The exasperated Persians therefore hung upon his rear and impeded his march, though they were always defeated by Heraclius when they ventured upon a battle. Heraclius reached Albania safely, bringing with him fifty thousand captives, whom he, however, soon liberated, as it would have been difficult to feed and house them through the long and severe winter, and as it would have been disgraceful to sell or massacre them.

In A. D. 624 Khosrou Parviz assumed the offensive, and sent an army under Sarablagas into Albania before Heraclius had left his winter quarters, for the purpose of detaining him there. But Sarablagas, who feared his imperial antagonist, simply guarded the passes and occupied the high ground; and Heraclius finally outwitted him and entered Persia through the plains of the Araxes. As his auxiliaries, on whom he relied, were unwilling to advance farther southward, Heraclius was obliged to forego his wishes; while three Persian armies, commanded respectively by Shahr-Barz, Shahên and Sarablagas, closed in upon him. Heraclius feigned a disorderly flight, and thus drew on an attack from Shahr-Barz and Sarablagas, whom he easily repulsed. He then fell upon Shahên and utterly defeated him.

A way thus seemed opened for Heraclius into the very heart of Persia, and he again started off in quest of Khosrou Parviz; but his allies began to desert his standard and to return to their homes, and the defeated Persians rallied and impeded his march. He, however, won a third victory at a place called Salban by Theóphanes, where he surprised Shahr-Barz in the dead of night, massacred his wives, his officers, and the mass of the population, who fought from the flat roofs of the houses. The arms and equipage of Shahr-Barz were taken, and the general himself was almost captured. The remnant of the Persian army fled in disorder, and was relentlessly pursued by Heraclius until the arrival of the cold season, when he was obliged to retire into cantonments. The half-burned town of Salban afforded a welcome shelter to Heraclius's army during the snows and storms of an Armenian winter.

Early in the next spring the indefatigable Heraclíus led his army toward the Upper Tigris into Arzanêné, marched westward and recovered Martyropolis and Amida, which had been in possession of the New Persians for more than twenty years. He halted at Amida, and wrote to the Senate of Constantinople, informing them of his position and his victories.

Before the close of March the Persians under Shahr-Barz had once more taken the field in force, had occupied the usual passage of the Euphrates, and threatened the Emperor's line of retreat. As Shahr-Barz had broken the bridge over the Euphrates at that point, Heraclíus descended the stream to a certain ford, by which he crossed the river with his army, and hastened by way of Samosata and Germa-nicæa into Cilicia, where he was again in his own dominions.

Heraclíus took up a position on the right bank of the Sarus (now Syhun), in the immediate vicinity of the fortified bridge by which that river was crossed. Shahr-Barz pursued, and ranged his army along the left bank, placing the archers in the front line, and imperiling the Roman occupation of the bridge. But Heraclíus struck down a gigantic Persian with his own hand and flung him from the bridge into the river; after which he and a few of his men charged the Persian host in the plain, where a desperate conflict lasted until night, when Shahr-Barz retreated from Cilicia.

Heraclíus then crossed the Taurus into Cappadocia and marched to Sebaste (or Sivas), where he passed the winter. Theóphanes tells us that Khosrou Parviz was so exasperated at the bold invasion of the New Persian Empire by the Emperor Heraclíus that he revenged himself by seizing the treasures of the Christian churches in the Persian dominions and compelling orthodox Christians to embrace the Nestorian heresy.

The arrival of the twenty-fourth year of the war found the advantages on both sides about evenly balanced. The Persian king still held possession of Egypt, Syria and Asia Minor, and his troops still occupied Chalcedon, thus flaunting their banners within sight of Constantinople. But his hereditary dominion had been deeply penetrated by his enemy; his best generals had been defeated; his cities and palaces had been burned, and his favorite provinces had been desolated. Heraclíus had proved himself a most formidable foe.

Khosrou Parviz now endeavored to end the war by an effort, the success of which would have changed the history of the world. He enrolled a large number of foreigners and slaves as soldiers along with his Persians, entered into a close alliance with the Khan of the Avars, and organized two large armies. One of these Persian armies, under Shahên, was to watch the Emperor Heraclíus in Asia Minor; while the other, under Shahr-Barz, was to coöperate with the Avars in an effort to force Constantinople to surrender.

Heraclíus divided his own forces into three armies; sending one to assist in the defense of his capital, and leaving another under his brother Theodore to watch Shahên, while he himself led the third eastward to the distant province of Lazica. The Emperor again entered into an alliance with the Khazars, whose Khan, Ziebel, coveting the plunder of Tiflis, held an interview with the Heraclíus within sight of the Persian garrison of that town, adored his majesty, and received from the Emperor's hands the diadem that adorned his own brow.

The Khan of the Khazars was luxuriously entertained, and was presented with all the plate used in the banquet, with a royal robe and a pair of pearl ear-rings. He was also promised the Emperor's daughter in marriage. Thus dazzled and flattered, this barbarian chieftain readily concluded an alliance with the Eastern Roman Emperor and aided him with his arms. The allied Romans and Khazars then attacked Tiflis and reduced that town to great extremities, but a Persian force of a thousand men under Sarablagas forced·their way into the town and reinforced the garrison, whereupon the allies raised the siege and fled.

In the meantime Theodore engaged Shahên's army in Asia Minor, and defeated it with great slaughter, while a terriffic hailstorm was raging, and driving into the faces of the Persians. Khosrou Parviz was infuriated at this defeat, and his displeasure weighed so heavily upon the mind of Shahên that the latter soon after sickened and died. The angry sovereign ordered that the corpse of the dead general should be embalmed and sent to the court, in order that he might gratify his spleen by treating it with the grossest indignity.

The Persians also failed in their attack upon Constantinople. Shahr-Barz, then at Chalcedon, entered into negotiations with the Khan of the Avars, easily persuading him to assail the imperial capital. Thereupon a host of barbarians from the region north of the Danube—Avars, Slavs, Gepidæ, Bulgarians and others—advanced through the passes of the Hæmus into Thrace, destroying and devastating. The inhabitants fled before the invaders and sought refuge within the walls of Constantinople, which had been carefully strengthened in anticipation of the attack.

The barbarian hordes forced the outer works; but all their efforts, both by land and sea, were of no avail against the main defenses. They failed in their attempt to breach the wall; their siege engines were crushed by those of the Byzantines; a fleet of Slavonian canoes which endeavored to force an entrance by the Golden Horn was destroyed or driven ashore; and the towers with which they sought to overtop the walls were burned. Accordingly, after ten days of constantly repeated assaults, the Khan of the Avars perceived that he had undertaken an impossible task, and retired after burning his engines and siege-works. As the Persians under Shahr-Barz at Chalcedon had no ships, they were under the necessity of coöperating with the barbarians in their attack upon the Byzantine capital.

The war now neared its end, as the last hope of the Persians had failed; and as Constantinople was now safe, Heraclíus, with the assistance of the Khazars, was free to strike at Persia wherever he chose. In September, A. D. 627, he proceeded to Lazica with a large Roman army and a contingent of forty thousand Khazar cavalry, to surprise the Persians by a winter campaign. He rapidly marched through Armenia and Azerbijan without meeting an enemy that dared to dispute his progress, and suffered but a small loss from the guerrilla warfare of some bold mountaineers of those regions.

The Khazars refused to accompany Heraclíus farther south than Azerbijan. Notwithstanding their defection, the Emperor crossed the Zagros mountains into Assyria and menaced the royal cities of the Mesopotamian region; thus retaliating upon the Persian monarch for the Avar attack upon Constantinople of the previous year, which Chosroës II. had instigated. Chosroës II. had for the last twenty-four years established his court at Dastagherd, in the Mesopotamian plain, about seventy miles north of Ctesiphon.

In October of the same year (A. D. 627), Heraclíus refreshed his army by a week's rest at Chnæthas, in the low country near Arbéla; but his line of retreat was now threatened, and he was in danger of being placed between two fires, as Khosrou Parviz had collected a large army and sent it under Rhazates into Azerbijan. This Persian army, after reaching Canzaca, found itself in the rear of Heraclíus, between him and Lazica. The Emperor remained quiet for more than a month; and the Persian general, in accordance with his sovereign's orders to fight the Romans wherever he found them at all hazards, quickly pursued Heraclíus, and finally came up with him.

A battle occurred between the two armies in the open plain to the north of Nineveh, December 12th, A. D. 627. The conflict lasted from early morn until near midnight, and finally ended in the defeat of the Persians, Rhazates and their other commanders being slain, and the Persian chariots and twenty-eight standards being taken by the victorius Romans. During the night the Persians fell back upon their fortified camp, collected their baggage, and retired to a strong position at the foot of the mountains, where they were reinforced by a detachment sent to their aid by their king.

The Persians then approached Heraclíus once more, harassed his rear and impeded his movements. After his victory, the Emperor had resumed his march southward, had occupied Nineveh, recrossed the Greater Zab, advanced rapidly through Adiabêné to the Lesser Zab, seized its bridges by a forced march of forty-eight Roman miles, and conveyed his army safely to its left bank, where he pitched his camp at Yesdem, and allowed his troops another short rest for the purpose of keeping Christmas.

Upon hearing of the defeat and death of Rhazates, King Chosroës II. was extremely alarmed for his own safety. He hastily recalled Shahr-Barz from Chalcedon, and ordered the troops recently commanded by Rhazates to overtake the Romans, if possible, and interpose themselves between Heraclíus and Dastagherd; while he himself took up a strong position near that place with his own army and a number of elephants, there intending to await the Emperor's approach.

The king's army was protected by a broad and deep canal of the Baras-roth, or Barazrud, in his front, and further in his advance by the Torna, probably another canal. The defeated Persian army of Rhazates fell back from the line of the Torna; and as the victorious army of Heraclíus advanced, King Khosrou Parviz became dreadfully alarmed, and secretly fled from Dastagherd to Ctesiphon, where he crossed the Tigris to Guedeseer, or Seleucia, with his treasure and the best-loved of his wives and children.

The Persian army recently commanded by Rhazates rallied upon the line of the Nahrwan canal, three miles from Ctesiphon, where it was largely reinforced, though with a mere worthless mob of slaves and domestics. But this army made a formidable show, supported by its two hundred elephants. It had a deep and wide cutting in its front, and had destroyed all the bridges by which that cutting might have been crossed.

Heraclíus plundered the rich palace of Dastagherd and several less splendid royal residences, and on the 10th of January he encamped within twelve miles of the Nahrwan. The commander of the Armenian contingent, whom he sent forward to reconnoiter, informed him that the canal was impassable. The Emperor therefore thought it prudent to retreat at once, before the mountain passes would be closed by snow.

Like Julian the Apostate, Heraclíus therefore shrank from the idea of besieging Ctesiphon, after having come within sight of that famous Persian capital, and retraced his steps; but his retreat was not so disastrous as that of his great predecessor, as the defeat which he had inflicted on the Persian army under Rhazates paralyzed the energies of the Persians, who did not therefore molest his retreat. Heraclíus reached Canzaca on the 11th of March, A. D. 628, and there passed the rest of the winter.

Khosrou Parviz had escaped a great danger, but he had incurred a terrible disgrace by fleeing before the enemy without venturing to oppose his progress. He had seen one palace after another destroyed, and had lost the magnificent residence where he had held his court for the last twenty-four years. The victorious Romans had recovered three hundred standards, the trophies which Khosrou Parviz had won in the many victories of his early years. They had shown themselves able to penetrate into the heart of the New Persian Empire, and to withdraw without any loss.

Heraclíus was desirous of peace, and was ready to grant it on reasonable terms, such as the restoration of Egypt, Syria and Asia Minor to the Eastern Roman Empire. The Persians generally were tired of the long struggle, and would have hailed with joy almost any conditions of peace. But King Chosroës II. was obstinate, and did not know how to bear the frowns of fortune. Instead of bending his spirit, the disasters of the late campaign had simply exasperated him, and he vented upon his own subjects the ill humor provoked by the successes of the enemy.

Listening to a whispered slander, King

Chosroës II. ordered the execution of Shahr-Barz, thus mortally offending that great general, to whom the Romans communicated the despatch. The king imprisoned the officers who had been defeated by the Emperor Heraclíus, or had fled before that victorious invader. Tabari and Maçoudi tell us that the tyrannical monarch put many of the imprisoned officers to death, that he imprisoned his sons and forbade them to marry, and that he mutilated Merdanshah, governor of Zabulistan.

It is said that Chosroës II. was contemplating the setting aside of his son and legitimate successor, Siroës, in favor of a younger son, Merdasas, his offspring by his favorite Christian wife, Shirin; whereupon a rebellion broke out against his authority. Gurdanaspa, the commander of the Persian army at Ctesiphon, and twenty-two prominent nobles, among whom were two sons of Shahr-Barz, espoused the cause of Siroës, seized King Chosroës II., who meditated flight, and committed him to the "House of Darkness," a strong place where he kept his money.

There the imprisoned king was confined for four days, his jailors allowing him daily a morsel of bread and a small quantity of water. When he complained of hunger, they told him, by his son's orders, that he was welcome to satisfy his appetite by feasting upon his treasures. The officers whom he had confined were allowed free access to his prison, where they insulted him and spat upon him. Mardasas, the son whom he had preferred, and several of his other children, were brought into his presence and there murdered.

After suffering thus for four days, the unfortunate king was at last cruelly murdered by his son Siroës, on the fifth day from his arrest, February 28, A. D. 628. Heraclíus says that Siroës destroyed his father "by a most cruel death." Theóphanes informs us that Siroës killed his illustrious sire with arrows. Thus perished miserably the renowned Chosroës II., or Khosrou Parviz, after a memorable and brilliant, though finally a disastrous, reign of thirty-seven years (A. D. 591-628)—a tardy Nemesis overtaking the parricide.

3—12.-U. H.

The Oriental writers tell us that Khosrou Parviz was a sovereign whose character was at first admirable, but whose good disposition became gradually corrupted by the exercise of royal power. Says Mirkhond: "Parviz holds a distinguished rank among the Kings of Persia through the majesty and firmness of his government, the wisdom of his views and his intrepidity in carrying them out, the size of his army, the amount of his treasure, the flourishing condition of the provinces during his reign, the security of the highways, the prompt and exact obedience which he enforced, and his unalterable adherence to the plans which he once formed."

The Eastern writers all give Chosroës II. credit for a vigorous administration, a strong will, and a rare capacity for government. He may likewise be credited with a certain grandeur of soul, and power of appreciating the beautiful, not generally found to characterize the Sassanian kings. The architectural remains of Chosroës II., the descriptions given us of his treasures, his court, his seraglio, even his seals, surpasses all that is known of any other of the Sassanidæ.

The most remarkable feature of the palace at Canzaca was a domed edifice, the ceiling of which was ornamented with representations of the sun, moon and stars, while below was an image of the king, seated, and attended by messengers bearing wands of office. Machinery was attached, by which rain and thunder could be imitated. The treasures which the Romans found in the palace of Dastagherd have been mentioned. The Orientals say that the palace was supported on forty thousand columns of silver, adorned by thirty thousand rich hangings upon the walls, and also ornamented by a thousand globes suspended from the roof. Among other treasures of Koshrou Parviz, Tabari mentions a throne of gold, called *Takdis*, supported on feet which were rubies, a napkin which would not burn, and a crown embellished with a thousand pearls, each as large as an egg.

Tabari tells us that Chosroës II. had a thousand elephants; twelve thousand white camels; fifty thousand horses, mules and asses, of which eight thousand were kept for his own riding; and twelve thousand female domestics, many of whom were slaves. Maçoudi says that he had fifty thousand horses and eleven hundred elephants, whiter than snow; some of them eleven cubits high, and all accustomed to kneel at the sight of the king. Mirkhond says that he had twelve hundred elephants, twelve thousand camels and fifty thousand horses. Gibbon tells us that Khosrou Parviz had three thousand concubines. Mirkhond and Tabari say that he had twelve thousand.

Maçoudi says that Khosrou Parviz had nine seals of office. The first was a diamond ring with a ruby center, bearing the king's portrait, name and title. This seal was used for despatches and diplomas. The second seal, likewise a ring, was a carnelian set in gold, with the legend "*Khorassan Khureh;*" and was used for the state archives. The third seal was an onyx ring with the legend "*Celerity;*" and was used for letters sent by post. The fourth seal was a gold ring with a pink ruby, having the legend "*Riches are the source of prosperity;*" and was impressed upon letters of grace. The fifth seal was a red ruby, bearing the legend "*Khureh va Khorrem,*" or "Splendor and Prosperity;" and was impressed upon the chests wherein treasure was stored. The sixth seal, made of Chinese iron, bore the emblem of an eagle; and was used to seal letters addressed to foreign kings. The seventh seal was a bézoard, bearing a fly upon it; and was impressed upon meats, medicines and perfumes reserved for the king's use. The eighth seal was a pearl, bearing the emblem of a pig's head; and was impressed on persons condemned to death, and on death-warrants. The ninth seal was an iron ring, which the king took with him to the bath.

The employment of Byzantine sculptors and architects, as indicated by his works, imply an appreciation of artistic excellence uncommon among Orientals.

But the character of Khosrou Parviz was likewise stained by some serious moral defects. The murder of his father may have been a state necessity, and Parviz may not have ordered it, or may not have been accessory to it before the fact; but his ingratitude towards his uncles, Bindoës and Bostam, is utterly without excuse, and shows his cruelty, selfishness, and lack of natural affection, even in the earlier part of his reign.

He exhibited neither courage nor ability in war. All his chief military successes were due to his generals; and in his later years he appears never voluntarily to have exposed himself to danger. He followed the traditions of his race in suspecting and ill-treating his generals; but the insults which he offered to the dead body of Shahên, whose only fault was his defeat, were unusual and outrageous.

The accounts of his seraglio imply gross sensualism or extreme ostentation; but the Byzantine and Oriental writers all represent Chosroës II. as faithful to his favorite Christian wife, Shirin, to the last. The cruelties of his later years are entirely unpardonable; but his preference for Merdasas, his son by Shirin, as his successor—the act which cost him his throne and life—was simply a partiality for the son of a wife who deservedly possessed his affection.

The ordinary type of the many coins of Chosroës II. has on the obverse the king's head in profile, covered by a tiara, ornamented by a crescent and a star between two outstretched wings. The head is surrounded by a double pearl bordering, outside of which, in the margin, are three crescents and stars. The legend is *Khusrui afzud*, with a monogram of double meaning. The reverse has the usual fire-altar and supporters, inclosed by a triple pearl bordering. Four crescents and stars are in the margin outside the bordering. The legend is here only the regnal year and a mint-mark. Thirty-four mint-marks have been ascribed to Chosroës II.

A rarer type of this monarch's coins presents on the obverse the king's front face surmounted by a mural crown, having the star and crescent between outstretched wings at the top. The legend is *K'husrui malkan malka—afzud*, "Chosroës, King of Kings —increase (be his)." The reverse has a head like that of a woman, also fronting the spectator, and wearing a band encircled with pearls across the forehead, above which the hair gradually converges to a point.

SIROES—also called KOBAD II.—was proclaimed King of Persia on February 25th, A. D. 628, four days before the murder of his illustrious father. The Oriental writers tell us that he was very unwilling to put his father to death, and that he reluctantly consented to his execution when his nobles represented to him that it was a state necessity.

After his father's death, he at once made overtures of peace to the Emperor Heraclius, who was then wintering at Canzaca. Kobad II. addressed Heraclius as his brother and called him "most clement." He then declares that, having been raised to the Persian throne by God's special favor, he has resolved to do his best to serve the whole human race. He has therefore begun his reign by opening the prison-doors and restoring all who were detained in custody to their freedom. He also desired to live in peace and friendship with the Eastern Roman Emperor and his subjects, as well as with all neighboring kings and nations. He therefore has sent Phæak, one of his privy councilors, to express the love and friendship that he feels towards his brother, and to learn the terms upon which peace will be granted to him.

To this letter from Kobad II., the Emperor Heraclius sent a complimentary and favorable reply, expressing his willingness to bring the war to an end, and suggesting moderate and equitable terms of peace. The treaty was formulated by Eustathius, who accompanied Phæak to the Persian court, after Heraclius had royally entertained the ambassador for almost a week.

By this treaty the *status quo ante bellum* was restored. Persia was thus to restore Egypt, Palestine, Syria, Asia Minor and Western Mesopotamia to the Eastern Roman Empire, and to withdraw her troops from those provinces. Persia was also to release all the captives whom she had carried off from these conquered provinces, and likewise to return to the Romans the precious relic which had been taken from Jerusalem, and which was universally regarded as the veritable cross whereon Jesus Christ had been crucified—the famous "True Cross." The Romans having merely made raids, they had no conquests to restore to Persia. The Persians at once evacuated the Roman territories; and the wood of the "True Cross," which had been carefully preserved by Shirin, was restored. The next year (A. D. 629) the Emperor Heraclius made a grand pilgrimage to Jerusalem, and replaced the sacred relic in the shrine from which it had been taken.

Kobad II. was as popular on his coronation day as princes usually are on that occasion. His subjects rejoiced at the end of the war which had lasted a quarter of a century, and which had been a serious drain upon the Persian population, and had recently brought ruin and desolation upon the hearths and homes of thousands. The release of all prisoners had an appearance of liberality, and the remission of taxes was naturally a very popular measure. Kobad's careful administration of justice, and his mild treatment of the victims of his father's severities, also secured the regard of his subjects. He restored to their rank those whom Khosrou Parviz had degraded or imprisoned, and compensated them for their injuries by a liberal donation of money.

Thus far all seemed to promise well for the new reign, which bid fair to be tranquil and prosperous, though it had begun under unfavorable auspices. Only from one quarter was trouble threatened. Shahr-Barz, the great general, whose life Chosroës II. had attempted shortly before his own death, seems to have been dissatisfied with the terms on which Kobad II. had concluded peace with the Eastern Roman Empire. He held the government of the western Persian provinces, and commanded an army of sixty thousand men. Kobad II. treated him with distinguished favor, but the great general occupied such a position as to render him an object of fear and suspicion. For the time, however, Shahr-Barz remained quietly in his province, cultivating friendly relations with the Eastern Roman Emperor.

After Kobad II. had reigned but a few months he lost his character for justice and clemency by consenting to the massacre of all the other sons of Chosroës II., his own brothers or half brothers. Mirkhond says that Firuz, the chief minister of Kobad II., advised the deed; but no writer assigns any motive for this massacre, which almost extinguished the race of Sassan, and produced serious civil and dynastic troubles.

Kobad II. permitted his two sisters to live. These were still unmarried, and resided in the palace and had free access to their kingly brother. The eldest sister was Purandocht, and the younger was Azermidocht. These sisters bitterly grieved at the murder of their kindred, and rushed into the royal presence, reproaching the king in the following words: "Thy ambition has induced thee to kill thy father and thy brothers. Thou has accomplished thy purpose within the space of three or four months. Thou hast hoped thereby to preserve thy power forever. Even, however, if thou shouldst live long, thou must die at last. May God deprive thee of the enjoyment of this royalty!"

His sisters' words sank deep into the king's mind. He acknowledged their justice, burst into tears, and flung the royal crown upon the ground. He then sank into a deep melancholy, cared no more for the exercise of the royal power, and shortly afterwards died. The Orientals ascribe his death to his mental sufferings; but a Christian bishop —Eutychius, Patriarch of Alexandria—and the Arabian writers tell us that before Kobad II. had reigned many months he fell a victim to a plague in which several hundred thousand of his subjects also perished.

The coins of Kobad II. show that his reign lasted more than a year. He became King of Persia in February, A. D. 628, and seems to have died about July, A. D. 629. His coins very much resemble those of Chosroës II. and Artaxerxes III., but have no wings, and have the legend *Kavat-Firuz.* There is a single bordering of pearls on the obverse, and also on the reverse, but the king wears a double pearl necklace.

Kobad II. was succeeded on the Persian throne by his son, ARTAXERXES III., then a mere child. The nobles who proclaimed him king placed him under the direction of a governor or regent, to which office they appointed Mihr-Hasis, who had been the chief purveyor of Kobad II. Mihr-Hasis is said to have governed with justice and prudence, but he could not prevent the troubles and disorders so usual during the reign of a minor in the East.

Shahr-Barz considered the opportunity favorable for the gratification of his personal ambition and of avenging the wrong done him by Chosroës II., as the Persian throne was occupied by a mere boy and the posterity of Sassan was almost extinguished. As a preliminary step to revolt, he negotiated with the Emperor Heraclius, whose alliance and support he secured by promising him certain advantages.

Shahr-Barz met Heraclius at Heracléa, on the Propontis (now Sea of Marmora). Shahr-Barz undertook to complete the Persian evacuation of Egypt, Syria and Asia Minor, which he had delayed hitherto. He also promised to pay to Heraclius a large sum of money as indemnity for the injuries which the Persians had inflicted upon the Eastern Roman Empire during the late war, providing he succeeded in his rebellious design.

Heraclius conferred on Nicétas, the son of Shahr-Barz, the title of *Patrician;* consented to a marriage between Shahr-Barz's daughter, Niké, and his own son, Theodosius; and accepted Gregoria, the daughter of Nicétas, and grand-daughter of Shahr-Barz, as a wife for Constantine, the heir to the imperial throne. Heraclius is believed to have supplied Shahr-Barz with a body of troops to aid him in his revolt.

Shahr-Barz is said to have led an army of sixty thousand men against Ctesiphon, to have taken that Persian capital city, to have put to death Artaxerxes III., Mihr-Hasis and many of the nobles, and then to have seized the Persian throne. Thus began the reign of SHAHR-BARZ, which lasted less than two months.

During his brief reign, Shahr-Barz completed the Persian evacuation of the Roman provinces occupied by the armies of Chosroës II., and sent an expedition against the Khazars who had invaded Armenia, but this expedition was utterly cut to pieces by the barbarians. The Armenian writers say that Shahr-Barz married Purandocht, the eldest daughter of Chosroës II., with the view of securing his hold of the Persian crown; but this effort to conciliate his subjects failed in its design.

Before Shahr-Barz had reigned two months, his troops mutinied, and killed him with their swords in the open court before the palace. They then tied a cord to his feet and dragged his corpse through the streets of Ctesiphon, everywhere making the following proclamation: "Whoever, not being of the blood royal, seats himself upon the Persian throne, shall share the fate of Shahr-Barz." The mutineers then raised the princess PURANDOCHT to the royal dignity, so that the seat of Cyrus the Great was now for the first time occupied by a female.

The rule of a woman was insufficient to restrain the turbulent Persian nobles, and pretenders arose in all parts of the New Persian Empire. It is unknown whether Purandocht died a natural or a violent death, but she reigned less than two years, and was succeeded by her sister AZERMIDOCHT, who was murdered. The Persian crown passed quickly from one noble to another; and during the first five years after the death of Khosrou Parviz, it was worn by nine different sovereigns, most of whom reigned but a few months or a few days, and most of whose names were obscure. During these five years the Persian government was entirely unsettled, anarchy prevailing in all the Persian dominions, and the distracted kingdom being torn to pieces by the struggles of pretenders. In the language of Gibbon, "every province, and almost each city of Persia, was the scene of independence, of discord, and of bloodshed."

These internal commotions were finally ended in June, A. D. 632, by the elevation of a young prince, believed to be of the true blood of Sassan; and the entire Persian nation readily accepted this young sovereign, ISDIGERD III., better known as Yezdijird III. This young king was the son of Shahriar and the grandson of Khosrou Parviz. He had been banished from the court, and had been brought up in obscurity at Istakr, the ancient Persepolis, where he lived unnoticed until the age of fifteen, when his royal rank was discovered, and he was called from his retirement and invested with the sovereignty of Persia.

But the days of the New Persian Empire were numbered, and Isdigerd III. was the last of the famous dynasty of the Sassanidæ. While the Eastern Roman and New Persian Empires had reduced each other to the most deplorable weakness by their long and bloody wars, a new power had arisen in the neighboring desert country of Arabia, a country hitherto almost without any history and despised for its weakness. This new power was the dominion whose cornerstone was the new religion, called Islam, founded by Mohammed, the camel-driver of Mecca. His armed hosts, inspired by religious fanaticism, were irresistible and carried everything before them. Mohammed had secured the submission of the Persian governor of Yemen, and also of Al Mondar, or Alamúndarus, King of Bahrein, on the west coast of the Persian Gulf.

Isdigerd III. at once found himself menaced by the new power, which had already sent its conquering hosts into the Eastern Roman and New Persian Empires. Thus Persia was in imminent peril, and she lacked sufficient means to cope with this new foe, as she had been exhausted by her long foreign wars and her internal dissensions. The youthful and inexperienced Persian king was unable to withstand the Arab chiefs; though he made a heroic resistance for a score of years, in the midst of continual defeats, and only succumbed when the treachery of pretended friends and allies was added to the hostility of open foes.

The events of the Mohammedan conquest of Persia will be narrated in detail in our account of the rise of Islam and the Saracen Empire, and need not be related here. This conquest was effected after a succession of Persian disasters, such as Khaled's conquest of the vassal kingdom of Hira, on the west side of the Euphrates; the conquest of Obolla; the Arab invasion of Mesopotamia and the great Persian defeats in the bloody battles of El Boweib and Cadesia, in A. D. 636; the capture of Ctesiphon by the victorious Arabs and the flight of King Isdigerd III.; the Persian defeat at Jalula and the Arab conquest of Susiana and invasion of Persia proper; the final defeat of the Persians in the great battle of Nehavend, in A. D. 641, and the flight of Isdigerd III.; and the Arab conquest of the various Persian provinces.

King Isdigerd III. wandered about as a fugitive in the Eastern Persian provinces for ten years, and finally found refuge in the frontier Persian city of Merv. The Persian governor of Merv invited a neighboring Tartar chief to seize the fugitive Persian monarch. The Tartar chief accordingly entered Merv and took possession of that frontier Persian city. King Isdigerd III. fled from Merv on foot during the struggle between the Tartars and the inhabitants of the city. He reached a mill a few miles from Merv, and induced the miller to conceal him by the present of his elegant sword and belt; but the miller murdered the unfortunate king in his sleep, for the sake of getting possession of his valuable robes and other dress, and threw the corpse into the millstream. Thus King Isdigerd III., the last of the New Persian kings, was assassinated by one of his own subjects, like Darius Codomannus, the last of the Medo-Persian kings, a thousand years before.

In a few days the Persian governor of Merv began to suffer from the tyranny of the Tartars, and the inhabitants seized their arms and drove the invaders from the city. The sad fate of King Isdigerd III. soon became known. The treacherous miller fell a victim to the popular rage, and the remains of the murdered king were embalmed and sent to Istakr, the ancient Persepolis, to be entombed in the sepulcher of his illustrious ancestors.

The New Persian Empire of the Sassanidæ had lasted a little over four centuries (A. D. 226-651); and with its overthrow ended the religion of Zoroaster and the Magi, as a national faith. Persia and its provinces remained under the Saracen dominion for two centuries, during which the Persians embraced the Mohammedan religion.

Isdigerd III. was only fifteen years of age when he ascended the Persian throne, and thirty-four when he was murdered, in A. D. 651. In the language of Irving, "history lays no crimes to his charge." This can be said of very few of the Sassanidæ. Though persevering so long in the struggle against his fate, he seems to have been personally weak and of luxurious habits. He never led his armies in person, but intrusted the defense of his dominions entirely to his generals. He fled from one stronghold to another before the advance of the victorious Arabs, thus quitting Ctesiphon for Holwan, Holwan for Rei, and Rei for Merv; carrying the miserable pageant of au Oriental court with him in all his wanderings, and suffering his movements to be hampered and his resources to be crippled by four thousand useless retainers.

In the coins of Isdigerd III. the head much resembles that of Artaxerxes III. There is but one pe᠎ ᠎ bordering around it, and the usual sta᠎, and crescents are in the margin. Ther ᠎ is also a peculiar device in the margin, a᠎d also a legend translated as "Ormazd." The king's name is given as Iskart, or Iskarti. The numbers "nineteen" and "twenty" have been found among the regnal years marked on the reverse. Among the mint-marks are Azerbijan, Abiverd and Merv.

Having given the political history of the New Persian Empire, we will close this section by a brief sketch of New Persian civilization. Under the Parthian dominion architecture and the other arts had sunk to the lowest ebb in Persia and the other Parthian dependencies, as the Parthians preferred tents to buildings, and country life to city life. The Arab dynasty at Hatra, in Mesopotamia, ruling under the suzerainty of Parthia, had a palace; and this palace served as a model for Sassanian architecture. The early Sassanian palaces have almost entirely disappeared. The oldest that can be traced and described are those erected between A. D. 350 and 450. The main features are uniform and simple, the later edifices being simply enlargements of the earlier. The plan of the buildings is an oblong square. The main entrance is a lofty vaulted porch or arched hall. The buildings also contain square apartments, vaulted, with domes resting on pendatives. The many apartments open into one another without intervening passages; and towards the rear of the palace is a court, with apartments opening into it.

The exterior ornamentation of the Sassanian palaces was by pilasters, cornices, string-courses, and shallow arched recesses, with pilasters between them. The interior ornamentation was by pillars supporting transverse ribs, or by doorways and false windows, like the Persepolitan.

The elegant palaces at Serbistan, Firuzabad, Ctesiphon and Mashita are the best specimens of Sassanian architecture. The Serbistan palace has been assigned to Sapor II., about A. D. 350; and the Firuzabad palace to Isdigerd II., about A. D. 450. The third and grandest of the Sassanian palaces was that of Khosrou Nushirvan at Ctesiphon, known as the *Takht-i-K'hosrou*. The palace at Mashita was erected by Khosrou Parviz in the latter part of his reign, or between A. D. 614 and 627, and was far more elegantly ornamented. This last palace consisted of two distinct edifices, separated by a court-yard, in which was a fountain.

The ornamentation of the southern building of the Mashita palace is unparalleled by other Sassanian structures, and unsurpassed by the architecture of any other age or nation. On the outer wall, built of hard stone, are elegant sculptures of vegetable and animal forms, such as a bold pattern of zigzags and rosettes, and over the entire surface is a most delicate tracery of foliage, fruits and animals. Among the animals represented are lions, wild boars, buffaloes, panthers, lynxes and gazelles. The mythological symbolism of Assyria is represented on a panel of this palace wall by a winged lion. Among the birds shown amid the foliage are doves, parrots, partridges and peacocks. The zigzags and rosettes are ornamented with a patterning of large leaves; while the moulding below the zigzags, and the cornice or string-course above them, are covered with conventional designs.

The archivolte adorning the Takht-i-Bostan is also delicately ornamented, and its flowered panels are very elegant. Sassanian capitals are often of lovely design; being sometimes delicately diapered, sometimes worked with a pattern of conventional leaves and flowers, sometimes exhibiting the human form, or a flowery patterning, like that of the Takht-i-Bostan panels. The capitals are square.

The arch of Khosrou Parviz at Takht-i-Bostan, near Kermanshah, is an archway or grotto cut in the rock on the brink of a pool of clear water. The arch is twenty feet deep into the rock, thirty-four feet wide, and thirty-one feet high. The arch is elaborately ornamented, inside and outside. Externally the arch is surmounted by the archivolte, and in the spandrels on each side are flying figures of angels holding chaplets in one hand and cups or vases in the other. Between the figures is a crescent. The flowered panels are below the spandrels and the archivolte. The two sides and further end of the recess are decorated with bas-reliefs; those on the sides representing Khosrou Parviz engaged in the chase of the wild-boar and the stag; while those at the end are in two lines, the upper representing the king in his robes of state, receiving wreaths from ideal beings, and the lower showing him in his military costume, mounted on his favorite charger, Sheb-Diz, with his spear in his hand.

There is a mutilated colossal statue of Sapor I.—believed to have been originally about twenty feet high—cut out of the solid rock, in a natural grotto near the ruined city of Shahpur. This statue represented the king in peaceful attire, but with a long sword at his left side, wearing the mural crown seen on his bas-reliefs, and dressed in a tunic and trowsers. The hair, beard and mustache were neatly arranged. The right hand rested on the hip; the other touched the long straight sword.

Among the bas-reliefs of Sapor I. is one representing his triumph over the Roman Emperor Valerian, comprising four figures, three times life size. In this relief Sapor is represented on horseback; while the captive Valerian, on one knee and with outstretched arms, begs the conqueror's mercy. Another bas-relief of Sapor I. is seen on a rock surface at Shahpur; in which the king is represented mounted on horseback, and in his usual costume, with a dead Roman under his horse's feet, and holding another by the hand, while a third Roman is in front making his submission, followed by thirteen tribute-bearers bringing gold rings, shawls, bowls, etc., and leading a horse and an elephant. Thirteen mounted guardsmen are behind the king, fifty-six guardsmen to the left, and thirty-five tribute-bearers to the right. The entire tablet embraces ninety-five human and sixty-three animal figures, and a figure of Victory soaring in the sky.

The bas-reliefs of Varahran II., Varahran III., Narses and Sapor III. fall far below those of Sapor I. Varahran IV. (A. D. 388–399) encouraged artists. His gems were exquisitely cut and embodied in excellent designs. One of the bas-reliefs of Varahran IV. is at Nakhsh-i-Rustam, near Persepolis, and represents a mounted warrior, with the peculiar head-dress of Varahran IV., charging another at full speed, striking him with his spear, and bearing both horse and rider to the ground. A standard-bearer marches a little behind, and a dead warrior lies underneath the king's horse, which is clearing the obstacle in his bound. There is a similar bas-relief at Nakhsh-i-Rustam, being almost a duplicate of the former, but without the dead warrior. The head-dress of the Sassanian warrior in this figure consists of a cap, which spreads towards the top and breaks into three points, ending in large striped balls. His enemy wears a helmet crowned with a similar ball. The standard, in the form of a capital T, displays five balls, three rising from the cross-bar, and the other two hanging from it.

There is a bas-relief at Firuzabad showing the figures of five or six horsemen, one of whom is a warrior whose helmet ends in the head of a bird, and another one who wears a crown with a cap above, surmounted by a ball. The former of these pierces his spear into the latter, who falls to the ground, his horse tumbling also. At the right is a horse turning in falling.

There is also a bas-relief of Khosrou Nushirvan at Shahpur, seated on his throne, fronting to the spectator, with guards and attendants on one side, and soldiers bringing in prisoners, human heads, and booty on the other.

The bas-reliefs of Khosrou Parviz at Takht-i-Bostan consist of colossal figures and hunting-pieces. The king himself is represented as a mounted cavalier below the colossal figures, mounted on his war horse, Sheb-Diz. The hunting-pieces ornamenting the interior of the arched recess on each side are better. On the right is represented a stag hunt, in which the king and a dozen other mounted horsemen take part, aided by a dozen footmen and by a detachment mounted on nine elephants, three riders on each elephant. While the elephants are driving deer into enclosures, a band of twenty-six musicians on a platform delights the assembled sportsmen with a "concord of sweet sounds."

On the left side of the recess is represented a boar hunt, in which twelve elephants drive almost a hundred boars into an enclosure, while the king in a boat kills the game with his arrows. Two bands of harpers occupy boats on each side of the king's boat. Numerous reeds, ducks and fish are in the water about the boats. There is another boat with five figures clapping their hands, to drive the pigs towards the king. A more highly ornamented boat contains another figure of the king, discharging arrows, and his head being surrounded by a *nimbus*, or "glory."

We have already described Zoroastrianism and Magism, which was the religion of the New Persians, as well as of their ancient ancestors, the Medo-Persians. The Zoroastrianism of the New Persians was the most extreme kind of Dualism. We refer the reader to a former part of this work for an account of the ideas entertained with respect to the struggle between Ormazd, or Ahura-Mazda, and Ahriman, or Angra-Mainyus; of Mithra, Serosh, and the other lesser divinities, or genii; of the holy angels, the six Amshaspands, or Amesha-Spentas; of the six Daêvas, or wicked angels; of the fate of the righteous and of the wicked; of the religious duties of the Magi; of the sacred fire altars; of the Homa cermony and the animal sacrifices; and of the Zoroastrian forms of worship, consisting in singing hymns, in praises, prayers and thankgivings. As we have seen, agriculture was a part of religion, and moral and legal purity were required. The New Persians represented Ahura-Mazda and Angra-Mainyus, and the lesser deities and the angels, by sculptured forms; which was their nearest approach to idolatry, except the worship of the Assyro-Babylonian goddess Anaïtis, or Anahit. Ahura-Mazda was considered the special guardian of the New Persian kings, as He had been of their illustrious ancestors, the Medo-Persian kings.

Under the Sassanians, the Magi were entrusted with the whole control and direction of the Zoroastrian religion. At the head of this priestly tribe or caste was the *Tenpet*, "Head of the Religion," or *Movpetan Movpet*, "Head of the Chief Magi." He was called upon to conduct a revolution in times of difficulty and danger. The *Movpets*, or "Chief Magi," ranked next to the Tenpet. These were called *destoors*, or "rulers;" and under them were the large body of the ordinary Magi, dispersed throughout the empire, but especially congregated in the chief towns. We have mentioned the religious duties of the Magi, their costumes, etc., in a previous part of this work.

The court of the Sassanians, especially in the later period of the empire, was upon a scale of almost unparalleled magnificence and grandeur. The Great King wore beautifully embroidered robes, covered with hundreds of gems and pearls. The royal crown, too large to be worn, was suspended from the ceiling by a gold cord exactly over the head of the king when he sat in his throne-room, and is said to have been adorned with a thousand pearls each as large as an egg. The throne was of gold, and was supported on four feet, each formed of a single immense ruby. The large throne-room was ornamented with vast columns of silver, with hangings of elegant silk or brocade between them. On the vaulted roof were represented the sun, moon and stars, while globes of crystal or of burnished metal hung suspended from the roof.

There were seven ranks of courtiers. The first were the Ministers of the crown; the second were the *Mobeds*, or Chief Magi; the third were the *Hirbeds*, or Judges; the fourth were the four *Sipehbeds*, or commanders-in-chief; the fifth were the singers, the sixth the musicians, and the seventh the men of science. The king sat apart from all. Even the highest nobles could not approach nearer to him than thirty feet, unless summoned. He was separated from them by a low curtain, which was under the charge of an officer, who drew it only for those with whom the king desired to converse.

The king's harem, or seraglio, was an important part of his palace. The Sassanians practiced polygamy on the largest scale ever heard of, even surpassing David and Solomon. Khosrou Parviz is said by some Oriental authorities to have had three thousand concubines; while Tabari and Mirkhond say that he had twelve thousand. Twelve thousand additional females, chiefly slaves, attended upon these royal favorites, dressed them and obeyed their behests. Eunuchs were also employed in the palace, according to Oriental custom, and some of the early sculptures represent them as holding important offices. Each Sassanian king had one Sultana, or chief wife.

The king was usually attended by his parasol-bearer; his fan-bearer, a eunuch; the *Senekapan*, or Lord Chamberlain; the *Maypet*, or Chief Butler; the *Andertzapet*, or Master of the Wardrobe; the *Akhorapet*, or Master of the Horse; the *Taharhapet*, or Chief Cupbearer; the *Shahpan*, or Chief Falconer; and the *K'rhogpet*, or Master of the Workmen. Except the first two, all these officials presided over departments, and had many subordinates under them. Khosrou Parviz had thousands of grooms and stable-boys to attend fifty thousand horses, twelve hundred camels and twelve thousand elephants.

Other great officials were the *Vzourkhramanatar*, or Grand Keeper of the Royal Orders; the *Dprapet Ariats*, or Chief of the Scribes of Iran; the *Hazarapet dran Ariats*, or Chiliarch of the Gate of Iran; the *Hamarakar*, or Chief Cashier or Paymaster; and the *K'hohrdean dpir*, or Secretary of Council.

The Sassanian court generally resided at Ctesiphon, but in the earlier times sat at Persepolis, the ancient Persian capital, and near the end of the empire in the comparatively modern city of Dastagherd. The New Persian kings maintained many palaces, visiting them at their pleasure and residing there for a time. Besides the palaces already mentioned, there was a magnificent one at Canzaca. Khosrou Parviz built one near Takht-i-Bostan; and Sapor I. must have built one at Shahpur, where he set up most of his monuments.

The New Persian kings wore a long coat, partly open in front, and with close fitting sleeves reaching to the wrist; under which they wore a pair of loose trowsers descending to the feet. A belt or girdle encircled the waist. They wore patterned shoes, tied with long flowing ribbons. They sometimes wore a long cape or short cloak over the coat, and this was fastened across the breast with a brooch or strings, and flowed over the back and shoulders. The cloak was usually of light and flimsy material. The head-dress was a round cap.

The cap, the vest and the trowsers were richly ornamented with jewels. Every Sassanian king wore ear-rings, with one, two or three pendants. He also usually wore a collar or necklace around the neck, and this sometimes had two or more pendants in front. Sometimes a jewel hung from the point of the beard. The hair was worn long and elaborately curled, and hung down on each shoulder in many ringlets. When the king rode out in state, an attendant held the royal parasol over him.

In war the New Persian kings wore a coat of mail over the upper portion of the body, and this armor was composed of scales or links. The king wore three belts over this armor, one perhaps attached to his shield, another supporting his sword, and the third his quiver and probably his bowcase. The legs were protected by stiff embroidered trowsers, while the head was guarded by a helmet, and a vizor of chain mail hid all the face except the eyes. The head and fore-quarters of the royal charger were likewise covered with armor, which descended below the animal's knees in front, but did not extend back behind the rider. The king's shield was round, and carried on the left arm. His chief offensive weapon was a heavy spear, which he brandished in his right hand.

Hunting was one of the New Persian kings' favorite pastimes. The Sassanian remains represent the royal sportsmen engaged in the pursuit of the stag, the wild boar, the ibex, the antelope and the buffalo. In addition to these beasts of the chase, the classical writers mention the lion, the tiger, the wild ass and the bear. Lions, tigers, bears and wild asses were collected and kept in royal parks or paradises for purposes of sport. The king attacked the lion with sword or spear, and the tiger with arrows. Stags and wild boars were not kept in paradises, but were hunted in the marshes and woodlands by means of elephants, which drove the animals towards an inclosed space, where the king shot his arrows at them from a boat in the marsh or while on horseback riding at full speed. The sport was enlivened with music by bands of harpers and other musicians.

The musical instruments represented by the Sassanian sculptures are the harp, the horn, the drum, and the flute or pipe. The sculptures represent bands of musicians with these instruments. Hawking was also a pastime of the Sassanian kings, and the Head Falconer was an officer of the court. The kings also spent their leisure hours in games, and Khosrou Nushirvan introduced the game of chess from India.

The character of the warfare of the New Persians was very much like that of their ancestors, the Medo-Persians, though the war-chariot was almost out of use among the New Persians, while the elephant corps occupied the first position. The four arms of the service under the New Persians were the elephant corps, the horsemen, the archers, and the ordinary infantry. The elephant corps was recruited from India, and was commanded by the *Zendkapet*, or "Commander of the Indians." The New Persian cavalry was almost wholly of the heavy kind, armed and equipped; the horses being heavily armored about the head, neck and chest, while the rider's body was completely covered with a coat of mail as far as the hips, his head with a helmet, and his face with a vizor, which left only his eyes exposed. The cavalier carried a small round shield on his left arm, and was armed with a heavy spear, a sword, and a bow and arrows The New Persian cavalry often charged the Roman infantry with success, driving the legions from the battle-field.

The archers were the *élite* of the New Persian infantry. They used the same style of huge wattled shields as the Medo-Persians and the Assyrians; and from behind these, which rested on the ground, the New Persian bowmen shot their arrows with deadly effect. When forced to retreat they shot backwards as they fled. The ordinary infantry were armed with swords and spears, and had little defensive armor.

The great national standard of the New Persians was the famous "leathern apron of the blacksmith," originally unadorned, but ultimately covered with jewels. The cavalry generally carried a more ordinary standard, consisting primarily of a pole and a cross-bar, ornamented with rings, bars and tassels.

The infantry was the largest body of the army. In sieges the New Persians opened trenches near the walls, and advanced along them under cover of hurdles to the ditch, which they filled up with earth and fascines; after which they attempted escalade, or brought movable towers, armed with rams or balistæ, close to the walls, and battered the defenses until a breach was effected. Sometimes they raised mounds against the walls, to attack the upper part. A prolonged siege was then turned into a blockade, the town was invested, water was cut off, and provisions were kept out, so that the besieged were eventually forced by hunger and thirst to surrender.

The leading classes were the great nobles, the court officials, and the *dikhans*, or landed proprietors, who generally lived on their estates, superintending the cultivation of the soil, on which they employed the free labor of the peasants. The standing army was chiefly recruited from the dikhans and the peasants, whose habits were simple. Polygamy was rare, though lawful. Zoroaster's maxims commanding industry, purity and piety were fairly observed. Women were not kept in seclusion.

All classes, except the very highest, among the New Persians were free from oppression, though they had no voice in the government. Most of the Sassanidæ desired to govern with mildness and justice. The system introduced by Khosrou Nushirvan, and maintained by his successors, secured the masses in their rights, as the provincial rulers were well watched and well checked. Tax-gatherers were not allowed to exact more than their share, for fear that their conduct would be reported and punished. Great care was taken that justice should be honestly administered; and a person who felt aggrieved could appeal to the king, whereupon the case was again tried in open court at the gate, or in the open square, in the presence of the king, the Magi, the great nobles and the people. But the highest class—the king's near relatives, the great court officers, the generals—were at the mercy and caprice of the king, who disposed of their lives and liberties at his pleasure; this class being arrested, imprisoned, tortured, blinded, or put to death, without trial when the king chose to pronounce sentence.

KINGS OF PERSIA.

THE ACHÆMENIDÆ.

B. C.		B. C.	
	ACHÆMENES.	425	XERXES II.
	Six other kings.	425	SOGDIANUS.
	CAMBYSES I.	424	DARIUS NOTHUS.
558	CYRUS THE GREAT.	405	ARTAXERXES MNEMON.
529	CAMBYSES II.	359	ARTAXERXES OCHUS.
522	SMERDIS.	338	ARSES.
521	DARIUS HYSTASPES.	336	DARIUS CODOMANNUS.
486	XERXES THE GREAT.	331	End of the Medo-Persian Empire.
465	ARTAXERXES LONGIMANUS.		

THE SASSANIDÆ.

A. D.		A. D.	
226	ARTAXERXES I.	483	BALAS, or PALASH.
240	SAPOR I.	487	KOBAD I. (deposed in 498).
271	HORMISDAS I.	498	ZAMASP.
272	VARAHRAN I.	501	KOBAD I. restored.
275	VARAHRAN II.	531	KHOSROU NUSHIRVAN.
292	VARAHRAN III.	579	HORMISDAS IV.
292	NARSES.	591	KHOSROU PARVIZ (deposed in 591).
301	HORMISDAS II.	591	BAHRAM.
309	SAPOR II.	591	KHOSROU PARVIZ restored.
379	ARTAXERXES II.	628	SIROES, or KOBAD II.
383	SAPOR III.	629	ARTAXERXES III.
388	VARAHRAN IV.	630	SHAHR-BARZ.
399	ISDIGERD I.	630	PURANDOCHT.
420	VARAHRAN V.	631	Six insignificant sovereigns.
440	ISDIGERD II.	632	ISDIGERD III.
457	HORMISDAS III.	651	End of the New Persian Empire.
459	PEROZES.		

SECTION X.—ISLAM'S RISE AND THE SARACEN EMPIRE.

THE peninsula of Arabia has the form of a large and irregular triangle, and is situated between Persia, Syria, Egypt and Ethiopia. Its extreme length is about fifteen hundred miles, and its mean breadth is about seven hundred miles. It contains several lofty mountain chains, but the greater portion of the country consists of level, sandy and arid plains, which support very few inhabitants. Water can only be obtained with great difficulty. There is very little wood to shelter from the direct and intense rays of a tropical sun. The winds are not refreshing breezes, but frequently come loaded with pestilential vapors, or raise eddying billows of sand that have overwhelmed caravans and entire armies.

The high lands of Arabia bordering on the Arabian Sea are distinguished by a superior abundance of wood and water, and for this reason this portion of the peninsula has been called *Arabia Felix*, or "Arabia the Happy." But the groves, even of this favored district, are thinly scattered. The streams, though pure, are small; and the country could be considered delightful by persons who have been unaccustomed to

WANDERING ARABS

seeing vegetation, and who have often felt the want of a cooling shade or a refreshing drink. Arabia Felix is now called *Yemen*. The northern part of Arabia is occupied by ranges of naked, rocky mountains, whence it obtained the name of *Arabia Petræa*, or "Arabia the Stony." But in spite of its rugged and desert aspect, this region was in ancient times the center of a flourishing commerce, being the great high road of trade between Egypt and South-eastern Asia. The modern name of Arabia Petræa is *Hedjaz*. The division of Arabia anciently known as *Arabia Deserta*, or "the Desert Arabia," is now comprehended under the names of *Oman, Lasha* and *Nedshed*.

Arabia is to-day, as it has always been in the past, governed by a multitude of petty chiefs, or *sheikhs*, usually independent of each other. The government is mainly patriarchal in character, the various sheikhs exercising the supreme authority of a father over his family. Some of the sheikhs live intrenched in castles, while some preside over cities, and some are leaders of the wandering Bedouins of the desert.

The Arabs are a Semitic people, thus belonging to the same great ethnological stock with the ancient Assyrians, Babylonians, Syrians, Hebrews, Phœnicians and Carthaginians. Of the seven great Semitic nations the Arabs only remained unknown and undistinguished until the time of Mohammed. The Arabs claim their descent from Abraham through Ishmael, his son with his concubine, Hagar, whom he had driven into the desert wilderness. This claim is confirmed by the unerring evidence of language. Nine-tenths of the Arabic roots are identical with the Hebrew, and a plain glossological relation is shown by a similarity of grammatical forms.

Thus the Arabs, as well as the Jews, are descended from Abraham; but while the Jews have a history from the time of Abraham, the Arabs have none until the time of Mohammed, twenty-five centuries after Abraham. During that long interval the nomad wanderers of the desert roamed to and fro, engaged in mutual wars, thus verifying the prediction in Genesis concerning Ishmael: "He will be a wild man; his hand will be against every man, and every man's hand against him."

Wherever such wandering races exist—whether in Arabia, Turkestan or Equatorial Africa—"darkness covers the earth, and gross darkness the people." There the earth has no geography, and the people have no history. During the whole period of twenty-five centuries from Abraham to Mohammed, the Arabs were not a nation, but only a multitude of tribes, either stationary or wandering. The nomad or Bedouin is the true type of the race as it exists in Northern Arabia. The Arab of the South is in many respects different—in language, in manners and in character— thus confirming the old opinion of a double origin of the Arabic race. But they remain an unmixed people.

The Northern Arab in his tent has remained unchanged since the time of Abraham. As he is proud of his blood, of his freedom, of his tribe, and of his ancient customs, he desires no change. He is in the Old World what the North American Indian is in the New. The chief virtues of the Northern Arab are the same as those of the North American Indian—courage in war, cunning, wild justice, hospitality and fortitude. But the Arab is of a better race than the Indian—more reflective, more religious, and with a thirst for knowledge. The pure air and the simple food of the Arabian plains keep the Arab in perfect health; while the necessity of constant vigilance against his enemies, from whom he is unprotected by rock, forest or fortification, quickens his perceptive faculties.

In all his pleasures, dangers and fatigues, the Arab makes the horse and the camel of the desert his associates rather than his servants; and these animals seem to have obtained an actual superiority in Arabia, from being raised into the condition of companions of their masters. The horse of Arabia is remarkable alike for speed, temper, and power of endurance; and it is notable that the best breeds of this animal in Europe, Asia and Africa have been derived from an Arabian stock. The Arab regards the camel and the dromedary of the desert as scarcely inferior to his horse. This patient and powerful animal supplies him with milk for his sustenance, transports his property and family from one part of the desert to another, and enables him to pursue or flee from his enemy with almost incredible speed when occasion demands it.

The Arabs boast that their country has never been subdued, but the greater portion of it has very little to tempt the cupidity of a conqueror. We have seen that Esar-haddon, King of Assyria, penetrated into the country in the seventh century before Christ. In the reign of Trajan the Romans made Arabia Petræa a Roman province. Yemen, or Arabia Felix, was sometimes subject to the New Persian Empire of the Sassanidæ. About the time of Mohammed's appearance —toward the end of the sixth century of the Christian era—the southern portion of the peninsula was ruled by the Negus of Abyssinia.

The chief ancient Arabian cities were in Yemen, or Arabia Felix; but their fame was destined to be eclipsed by the glories of Mecca and Medina, both in the Hedjaz, the ancient Arabia Patræa. These two cities have been the great sanctuaries of the national religion. Mecca was a place of considerable trade from the most ancient period, being situated at the intersection of two important routes—that between Syria and Arabia Felix, and that between Ethiopia and South-eastern Asia.

Commerce flourished under the sanctuary of religion. The Kaaba, or temple of Mecca, was considered the national metropolis of the Arabic faith, before Judaism and Christianity appeared in the peninsula. The custody of the Kaaba raised the tribe of Koreish, descendants of the most illustrious of Ishmael's twelve sons, to the condition of a priesthood, thus elevating them to a rank above the other Arab tribes. The failure of the Abyssinians in their attempt to storm the Kaaba, in the very year of Mohammed's birth, may be regarded as the great check that impeded, or rather prevented, the further spread of Christianity in Arabia.

Mecca is located in a winding valley at

THE KAABA IN MECCA.

the foot of three barren mountains. The soil is a rock, and the waters are brackish. The pastures are distant from the city, and good fruits can not be obtained at any nearer place than the gardens of Tayef, about seventy miles away.

The Arabs believe that Mecca was founded by Adam, and that its temple, the Kaaba, was built by Abraham. They ascribe the early prosperity of the city to Ishmael, who established his residence there, because, as the Arabian traditions assert, the brackish well of Zemzem was the one to which the angel directed Hagar. Mecca must have been a very ancient city, if, as the commentators believe, it was the Mesha mentioned by Moses as inhabited by Joktan's posterity.

Medina—called *Yatreb* before the appearance of Mohammed—possesses more natural advantages than Mecca; but it is not situated so conveniently for traffic. The people of Medina seem always to have been jealous of the supremacy claimed by the Meccans, and this was probably the reason why they espoused the cause of Mohammed when he was banished by their rivals.

The ancient Arabs zealously cultivated literature. They were enthusiastically devoted to poetry and eloquence, for both of which their rich harmonious language affords peculiar facilities. A meeting of the Arab tribes was held annually, and at these assemblies the Arab poets recited their productions, and those which were judged the best were preserved in the public treasury. The most celebrated of these compositions were the seven poems known as *Moallakat*, written on Egyptian silk in golden letters, and suspended in the Kaaba, or temple of Mecca.

The Arabs did not place a similar importance upon science. Their history consisted only of genealogical tables. Their astronomy was only a rude knowledge of the stars sufficient to mark the variation of the seasons, and they almost entirely neglected the mechanical arts. They were in the habit of saying that God had given them four peculiarities—turbans instead of diadems; tents instead of houses; swords instead of fortresses; and poems instead of written laws.

The Arabs have also a sense of spiritual things, and this sense seems to have a root in their organization. The ancient religion of Arabia was the Sabean idolatry, consisting in the worship of the sun, the moon and the stars; but long before Mohammed's time the Arabs were distracted by a great variety of beliefs. Some of the tribes adhered to their ancestral creeds. Others embraced the Persian Magism; others Judaism; while several tribes became Christian. When Christianity was introduced into Arabia it was unfortunately deeply tinged with men's devices. The various Christian Arab tribes were animated by a fierce sectarian spirit, and hated each other more bitterly than Jews or pagans. The vivid imaginations of the Arabs caused them to investigate subjects beyond the powers of human comprehension; and the result was such a multitude of new doctrines that one of the early Christian Fathers described Arabia as the country most prolific in heresies.

Thus when Mohammed appeared, the Arabian religion was a jumble of monotheism and polytheism—Judaism, Christianity, Magism and idolatry. There had been at one time a powerful and intolerant Jewish kingdom in Arabia Petræa. At another period the Negus of Abyssinia had established Christianity in Yemen, or Arabia Felix, as already noticed. But neither Judaism nor Christianity had ever been able to conquer the whole Arabian nation; and at the end of the sixth century—when Mohammed made his appearance—Sabeism, or the worship of the heavenly bodies, was the prevailing religion of Arabia.

The Arabs say: "The children of Shem are prophets, the children of Japhet are kings, and the children of Ham are slaves." As the Arabs have no temples, no priesthood, no religious forms, their religion is not so formal and more instinctive, like that of children. The Koran, the sacred book of the Mohammedans, says: "Every child is born into the religion of nature; its parents make it a Jew, a Christian or a Magian."

Mohammed appeared about the end of the sixth century of the Christian era; and in a few years he united all the warring Arab tribes in one religious faith and consolidated them into one nation. His successors wielded their mighty and enthusiastic forces against the neighboring countries—Syria, Persia, Egypt and North Africa—and triumphed wherever they moved. Mohammed certainly had the rare gift of natural empire. To him, more than to any other of the great characters of history, was given

"The monarch mind, the mystery of commanding,
The birth-hour gift, the art Napoleon,
Of wielding, moulding, gathering, welding, banding,
The hearts of thousands till they moved as one."

Mohammed, or Mahomet—the great lawgiver of the Arabs, and the founder of a religion which has prevailed over large portions of Asia and Africa for the last twelve centuries—was born at Mecca in A. D. 569.

He belonged to one of the most illustrious families of Arabia. This family was of the priestly tribe of the Koreish, and of the particular branch of Hussein, to which belonged the guardianship of the Kaaba, or temple of Mecca, which contained the Black Stone, believed by the Arabs to have covered Abraham's tomb. The branch of Hussein also held the office of chief magistrate of Mecca.

Mohammed's grandfather, Abd al Motalleb, had held three high dignities; but he, as well as his son Abdallah, Mohammed's father, died before Mohammed grew to manhood. The chief magistracy of Mecca passed to Mohammed's uncle, Abu Tâleb, and the only patrimony inherited by the lawgiver of Arabia and founder of Islam was reduced to five camels and a slave. Mohammed's father, Abdallah, was an idolator; but his mother, Emina, was a Jewess, who had been converted to Christianity, and from whose early instructions the great Arabian Prophet probably derived the religious impressions for which he was distinguished even in boyhood. As both his parents died while he was still a child, he was cared for by Abd al Motalleb and Abu Tâleb, the latter of whom became a tender guardian of the orphan boy.

Mohammed's youth had been unstained by vice, and his honorable character early obtained for him the title of *Al Amîn*, "the Faithful," a title given him by common consent. At one time he tended sheep and goats on the hills in the vicinity of Mecca. At Medina, after he acquired celebrity, he referred to this, saying: "Pick me the blackest of those berries; they are such as I used to gather when I fed the flocks at Mecca. Verily, no prophet has been raised up who has not performed the work of a shepherd."

MOHAMMED.

The believers in the divinity of Mohammed's mission have thrown a halo of wonders around his infancy. Though their Apostle was destitute of worldly wealth, their accounts represent his birth as rich in prodigies. Like that of other great men who have astonished the world, it was accompanied by signs in the heavens and miracles on earth. It was believed that the "prophetic light" which surrounded him was so intense that it served his mother for a lamp and shone with a brilliancy that illuminated the country as far as Syria. It was also believed that the sacred fire of the Persians, which had burned without interruption for a thousand years, was forever extinguished, and that the palace of Khosrou Parviz was rent by an earthquake, which leveled fourteen of its towers to the ground.

These omens were designed to prefigure the failure of the royal line of the Sassanidæ and the conquest of the New Persian Empire by the Arabs after the reign of fourteen kings. Mohammed's biographers mentioned a vast number of other supernatural prognostications, equally marvelous. Mohammed's devout followers would have been ready to attest on oath to the reality of these wonders.

At the age of thirteen he accompanied Abu Tâleb in a caravan journey to Syria. Tradition has made this mercantile journey remarkable by several wonderful indications of his subsequent greatness. At the fair of Bosrah he is said to have met the famous Nestorian monk, Felix, or Sergius, surnamed Bahira, whom Christian writers accused of having afterwards assisted the founder of Islam in preparing the Koran. Thenceforth Mohammed seems to have actively engaged in trade.

At the age of twenty-five he engaged in the service of a rich and noble widow named Khadijah, for whose commercial interests he made another caravan journey to Syria, to sell her merchandise at Damascus. When the caravan returned to Mecca, and his adventure had proven successful, Khadijah, then forty years old, became interested in the young camel-driver. She was wise, virtuous and attractive, and was so pleased with the young man's industry, zeal and intelligence that she soon gave him her hand in marriage, and made him master of her splendid fortune. Mohammed, who had the reputation of being the handsomest man of the tribe of Koreish, and who had a passion for women which the Arab morality does not condemn, and which legalized polygamy has sanctioned, was a kind, affectionate and faithful husband to Khadijah during their union of twenty-five years. As long as she lived, he did not take to himself another wife.

After his marriage with Khadijah, Mohammed ranked with the chief citizens of Mecca, but he was not corrupted by prosperity. The first use which he made of his good fortune was to relieve his kind uncle and guardian, Abu Tâleb, who had fallen into distress. He placed Abu Tâleb above want, and undertook the education of a part of his family.

Little is known of Mohammed's history for the next fifteen years. Khadijah sympathized with her husband in his religious tendencies, and was his first convert. His character was marked by thoughtfulness and austerity. He had an ardent imagination; and his extreme sobriety in most things surpassed that of an Anchorite, and inclined him to religious meditation and lofty reveries. Externally he displayed that serious demeanor which distinguishes the better portion of an Oriental people—a dignified manner, and a pleasing and commanding expression of countenance.

Mohammed seems to have begun his extraordinary religious reformation by endeavoring to fix his own belief and to free it from the gross superstitions of his countrymen. Being the grandson and the nephew of the high-priest of an idol, and powerful and revered for his connection with the temple of the Kaaba, Mohammed had too strong an understanding to discover a divinity in this rude emblem, or in the idols surrounding it. His love of solitude and retirement aided him in his speculations upon the great mystery of the nature of the Deity.

Every year, for a month at a time, Mohammed retired to a cave in Mount Hira, three miles from Mecca, where he devoted himself to prayer, fasting and meditation. In the solemn obscurity of this retirement he laid the foundation of his future greatness. There he meditated the scheme of his religion. Sadness came over him in view of the evils of this world. He beheld with sorrow the calamities of Arabia, the abandonment of its ancient manners and the introduction of foreign customs. His Christianized Jewish mother had taught him that the Jews were still looking for the champion of Israel, and that Jesus had promised to those who loved him the Comforter, who should lead them all to the truth.

By communing with his own soul, Mohammed recognized the existence of the divinity as an eternal Spirit, omnipresent, omnipotent and omniscient—a beneficent Being, incapable of being represented by any corporeal image. For fifteen years he brooded in silence over this sublime idea, developed it by meditation, and exalted his imagination by reveries. One of the Suras of the Koran, believed to belong to this period, is as follows:

"By the declining day I swear!
Verily, man is in the way of ruin;
Excepting such as possess faith,
And do the things which be right,
And stir up one another to truth and steadfastness."

About this time Mohammed began to have visions of angels, especially of Gabriel. He saw a light and heard a voice, and had sentences like the Sura just quoted put into his mind. These communications were accompanied by strong convulsions, during which Mohammed would fall to the ground, foaming at the mouth. Weil considers these convulsions epilepsy, while Sprenger regards them to have been a form of hysteria accompanied with catalepsy. Mohammed himself declared: "Inspiration descends on me in two ways. Sometimes Gabriel cometh and communicateth the revelation, as one man to another. This is easy. But sometimes it is as the ringing of a bell, which rends me in pieces, and grievously afflicts me."

One day, when Abu Bekr and Omar sat in the Mosque at Medina, Mohammed came suddenly upon them, lifting up his beard and looking at it; whereupon Abu Bekr said: "Ah thou, for whom I would sacrifice father and mother; white hairs are hastening upon thee!" Mohammed responded: "Yes, Hûd and its sisters have hastened my white hairs." Abu Bekr asked: "And who are its sisters?" Mohammed replied: "The *Inevitable* and the *Striking*." The three Suras containing this account are called the "Terrific Suras." But these last Suras appeared at a later period than the one now referred to.

At this time Mohammed's visions and revelations possessed *him*. He did not possess nor control *them*. In after years the Prophet's spirit was more subject to the Prophet. But the Koran is an unintelligible book if unconnected with its author's biography. All the incidents of his life assumed shape in some revelation. A separate revelation was given to encourage or to reprove him. In his later years the too subservient revelation came to appease the jealousy of his wives whenever he took to himself a new one. Nevertheless, in the beginning he was as much surprised at his visions as were others. A systematic arrangement of the Suras would make the Koran the best biography of the founder of Islam. As may be said of David and his Psalms, so it may be said of Mohammed, that his life hangs suspended in his hymns, the Suras, as in votive pictures, each being an account of some grave experience.

It is impossible to read the detailed accounts of this part of Mohammed's life and have any doubts of his sincerity. His first converts were his bosom-friends and the people of his household, who were intimately acquainted with his private life. A man does not easily commence an ambitious course of deception at the age of forty. As Mohammed had lived until that time as a quiet, peaceful and unobtrusive citizen, he would have gained nothing by such a career. Long years passed before he was able to make but a few converts. During these weary years he was the object of contumely and hatred to the Koreish, then the ruling tribe of Mecca. His life was in constant danger from that tribe, and nothing could be more hopeless than his position during the first twelve years of his public preaching. Nothing but a strong conviction of the reality of his mission could have sustained him through this long period of failure, loneliness and contempt. During all these long years the wildest imagination could not have pictured the wonderful success which the future was to bring forth.

The following is a Sura in which Mohammed found comfort in God and His promises:

"By the rising sunshine!
By the night when it darkeneth!
Thy Lord had not removed from thee,
Neither hath he been displeased.
And verily the future shall be better than the past.
What! did he not find thee an orphan,
And give thee a home?
And found thee astray, and directed thee?"

In this Sura Mohammed referred to the death of his mother, Emina, in his seventh year; his father having died but a few months previously. Many years afterward he visited her tomb, and raised his voice and shed bitter tears. Replying to the questions of his companions, he said: "This is the grave of my mother; the Lord hath permitted me to visit it, and I asked leave to pray for her, and it was not granted. So I called my mother to remembrance, and the tender memory of her overcame me, and I wept."

Mohammed's grandfather, Abd al Motalleb, who was eighty years of age when he took his orphan grandson, treated the child with the greatest indulgence. Mohammed's uncle, Abu Tâleb, who adopted the boy after Abd al Motalleb's death, brought him up as his own son, making him sleep by his bed and go with him wherever he went. And though Abu Tâleb himself, who was then of a venerable age and universally respected, never accepted his nephew's teaching, he protected Mohammed from his enemies after he had declared himself a prophet and assumed an inspired position. Therefore Mohammed had very good reason to bless the Providence which had provided such kind and efficient protectors for his orphaned childhood.

Mohammed did not pretend to found a new religion, as that would have alarmed the jealousies of all parties among his countrymen and united their discordant views into a general opposition. His professed object was simply to restore the only true and primitive faith, such as had existed in the days of the patriarchs and the prophets, from Adam to Jesus. The fundamental doctrine of this ancient worship, which Mohammed sought to purify from the corruption which had infected it among a frail and degenerate race of men, was the UNITY OF GOD. A principle so simple and obvious, which had never been denied by any sect, and which presented nothing difficult to comprehend, was a broad foundation for a popular and universal religion, and this was an advantage fully appreciated by Mohammed.

With the Jews, who adhered to their ancient ceremonial, he maintained the authority of the Pentateuch and the inspiration of the Hebrew prophets. With the Christians, he admitted the divinity of Christ's mission and the truth of the Gospel, making the revelations of the Old and New Testaments the basis of his own preaching. But he took especial care to conciliate the Arabs, who were the more immediate objects of his endeavors. He manifested an extreme indulgence to their prejudices, while lamenting the madness and folly of their idolatrous worship. He spared their popular traditions and ceremonies, at least such of them as suited his views, and he even made them more attractive by giving the Divine sanction to customs already hallowed by immemorial usage.

In A. D. 609, when Mohammed was forty years of age, and after he had matured his plans and acquired a reputation for sanctity corresponding in some degree with the exalted and venerable office which he was about to assume, he announced his mission, proclaiming the cardinal principle of his creed: "*There is no god but Allah, and Mohammed is His Apostle.*" His faithful wife, Khadîjah, was the first person to whom he made this revelation, and she became his first convert, as already noticed. His next two proselytes were his two adopted children, Ali and Zeid.

Ali was the son of Mohammed's uncle and guardian, Abu Tâleb, who had become so poor that he found it difficult to support his family. "Prompted by his usual kindness and consideration," in the language of Mr. Muir, Mohammed went to his wealthy uncle, Abbas, and proposed that each of them should adopt one of Abu Tâleb's children, and that was accordingly done. Mohammed's other adopted son, Zeid, belonged to a Syrian tribe, and had been taken captive by marauders, sold into slavery, and fallen into the possession of Khadijah, by whom he was presented to her husband.

At length Zeid's father heard where his son was, and went to Mecca and offered a large sum to ransom him. Mohammed had become very fond of Zeid, but called him and offered him his choice of going or staying. Zeid said: "I will not leave thee; thou art in the place to me of father and mother." Mohammed then took him to the Kaaba and touched the Black Stone, saying: "Bear witness, all here! Zeid is my son. I shall be his heir, and he mine." The father then returned home satisfied, and thenceforth Zeid was known as *Zeid ibn Mohammed*, "Zeid the son of Mohammed."

It is said that when Ali was about thirteen years of age Mohammed was on one occasion praying with him in a retired glen near Mecca, whither they had gone to avoid the ridicule of their opponents. Abu Tâleb passed by, saying: "My nephew! what is this new faith I see thee following?" Thereupon Mohammed replied: "O my uncle, it is the religion of God, His angels and prophets, the religion of Abraham. The Lord hath sent me as His Apostle; and thou, uncle, art most worthy to be invited to believe." Abu Tâleb responded: "I am not able, my nephew, to separate from the customs of my forefathers, but I swear that while I live no one shall trouble thee." Mohammed then said to Ali: "My son, he will not invite thee to anything which is not good; wherefore thou art free to cleave to him."

Another early and important proselyte was Abu Bekr, an opulent citizen of Mecca, the father of Mohammed's favorite wife, Ayesha, and afterwards the Prophet's successor. Ayesha said: "I cannot remember the time when both my parents were not true believers." Mohammed said of Abu Bekr: "I never invited any to the faith who did not show hesitation, except Abu Bekr. When I proposed Islam to him, he at once accepted it." Abu Bekr was thoughtful, calm, tender and firm. He is still known as *Al Sadîch*, "The True One." Another of his titles is "The Second of the Two," so called because he was Mohammed's only companion in the latter's flight from Mecca. Hassan, the poet of Medina, thus says of Abu Bekr:

"And the second of the two in the glorious cave,
While the foes were searching around,
And they two were in the mountain—
And the Prophet of the Lord, they well knew
Loved him more than all the world;
He held no one equal unto him."

Mohammed once asked Hassan if he had composed any poetry about Abu Bekr, and the poet repeated the preceding lines; whereupon Mohammed laughed so heartily that he showed his back teeth, and said: "Thou hast spoken truly, O Hassan! It is just as thou hast said."

Abu Bekr was at that time a successful merchant, and was in possession of about forty thousand *dirhems*. But he expended most of this sum in purchasing the freedom of Moslem slaves who were persecuted by their masters for their religion. Abu Bekr was a man of influence among the Koreish. This powerful tribe, the rulers of Mecca, who from the first treated Mohammed with contempt, gradually became violent persecutors of the Prophet and his followers. Their chief wrath was directed against the unprotected slaves, whom they exposed to the scorching sun, and who, in their intolerable thirst, sometimes recanted and acknowledged the idols. Some of the slaves remained firm, and afterwards triumphantly exhibited their scars.

Mohammed, Abu Bekr, Ali, and all who were connected with powerful families, were safe for a long time. The chief protection in such a disorganized society was the principle that each tribe must defend every one of its members at all hazards. Mohammed very naturally desired to win over members of the great families, but he felt bound to take equal pains with the poor and helpless, as is shown by the following incident, related by Muir: "The Prophet was engaged in deep converse with the chief Walid, for he greatly desired his conversion. Then a blind man passed that way, and asked to hear the Koran. But Mohammed was displeased with the interruption, and turned from him roughly." The Prophet was, however, afterwards grieved to think that he had slighted one whom God had perhaps chosen, and had paid court to a reprobate. So his remorse assumed the form of a divine message, embodying itself thus:

"The Prophet frowned and turned aside
Because the blind man came to him.
Who shall tell thee if he may not be purified?
Or whether thy admonition might not profit him?
The rich man thou receivest graciously,
Although he be not inwardly pure.
But him who cometh earnestly inquiring,
And trembling with anxiety,
Him thou dost neglect."

During the first three years after announcing his mission Mohammed had gained but fourteen disciples. Being then forty-three years old, and feeling sufficiently assured of success to make a more open avowal of his mission, he directed Ali to prepare an entertainment of a lamb and a bowl of milk, to which forty guests were invited. When these guests were assembled, Mohammed addressed them thus:

"Friends, I this day offer you what no other person in Arabia can offer—the most valuable of all gifts, the treasures of this world and of that which is to come. God has commanded me to call you to his service. Who among you will be my Vizier, to share with me the burden and the toils of this important mission, to become my brother, my Vicar and my ambassador?"

The guests heard this address with silent surprise. The impatient Ali at length answered: "I will be your Vizier, O Apostle! and obey your commands. Whoever dares to oppose you, I will tear out his eyes, dash out his teeth, break his legs, and rip open his body." But the guests in general received the Prophet's announcement with contempt and ridicule.

Mohammed was not discouraged by the small success of his first effort, but labored with indefatigable zeal for the accomplishment of his design. His ardor was not daunted by any ridicule, any reproaches or any affront. He preached to the people of Mecca in the market-place, and waited at the Kaaba for the pilgrims who visited that consecrated spot from all portions of Arabia. He represented to them the grossness of the religious rites which they came to practice. He appealed to their reason, and implored them to acknowledge the One True God (Allah)—the Creator, and the omnipotent, omnipresent and omniscient Ruler, of the entire universe.

But Mohammed's progress was slow at first. He had to encounter the deep-rooted prejudices of his countrymen, who were offended by his audacity and presumption. He was assailed by envy and malice, and was accused of endeavoring to subvert the old and venerated religion of his country. The citizens of Mecca, especially, were incensed at Mohammed's attack on the sanctity of their temple. They were alarmed for their gods, which already appeared to be toppling from their pedestals. They saw that the worship which was their principal means of support was menaced with extinction, and they determined to nip in the bud this attempt to sap the foundation of their wealth and consequence.

A deputation of the leading men of Mecca appeared before Abu Tâleb with this remonstrance: "Unless thou impose silence on thy nephew and check his audacity, we shall take up arms in defense of our gods. The ties of blood shall not restrain us from drawing the sword." Abu Tâleb was so alarmed at this threat that he exhorted Mohammed to relinquish his apparently hopeless task. But the zealous Prophet replied: "Spare thy remonstrances; though the idolators should arm against me the sun and the moon, planting the one on my right hand

and the other on my left, they would not turn me aside from my resolution."

Mohammed did not encourage his followers to martyrdom, but permitted them to dissemble to save themselves. One day he found one of his disciples weeping bitterly because ill treatment had forced him to abuse his master and worship the idols. The Prophet asked the sorrowing disciple: "But how dost thou find thy heart?" To this the disciple answered: "Steadfast in the faith." Mohammed replied: "Then if they repeat their cruelty, thou mayest repeat thy words."

Mohammed also had an hour of vacillation. Weary of the apparently hopeless struggle with the Koreish, and seeing no way of overcoming their bitter hostility, he entertained the plan of compromise. After preaching Islam five years he had only about fifty converts. Such of his followers as had no protectors he advised to flee to the Christian kingdom of Abyssinia. Pointing to the west, he said: "Yonder lies a land wherein no one is wronged. Go there and remain until the Lord shall open a way for you." About twenty who went to that land were kindly received. This exodus showed the strength of faith of these Moslem exiles, who gave up their native land rather than renounce Islam. But it was not long until they heard that the Koreish had been converted by Mohammed, whereupon they returned to Mecca.

The following were the facts connected with the conversion of the Koreish. One day, when the leading citizens of Mecca were sitting near the Kaaba, Mohammed made his appearance among them, and commenced reciting in their hearing one of the Suras of the Koran. In this Sura three of the goddesses worshiped by the Koreish were named. When he came to their names he added two lines in which he conceded that their intercession might avail with Allah. The Koreish were so delighed at this acknowledgment of their deities that, when Mohammed added another line calling on them to worship Allah, they all prostrated themselves on the ground and adored the One True God. Then they arose and expressed their satisfaction, and agreed to be his followers and accept Islam, on condition that their goddesses and favorite idols were to be respected.

As soon as Mohammed had gone home his mind was troubled. The compromise appears to have lasted long enough for the Moslem exiles in Abyssinia to hear of it and to return to their homes in Arabia. But finally the Prophet recovered himself and took back his concession. The verse of the Sura concerning it was canceled, and another was inserted, declaring that the three goddesses were simply names invented by the idolators. Ever afterward the intercession of the idols was condemned with scorn. But Mohammed thus records this relapse, in the seventeenth Sura of the Koran:

"And truly, they were near tempting thee
From what we taught thee,
That thou shouldst invent a different revelation;
And then they would have inclined unto thee.
And if we had not strengthened thee,
Verily thou hadst inclined to them a little.
Then thou shouldst not have found against us any helper."

Very naturally the persecution of Mohammed's followers became hotter than ever. A second band of Moslem exiles went to Abyssinia. Mohammed's life was only spared through the protecting care of the venerable Abu Tâleb. The persecutors threatened the old man with deadly enmity unless he gave up Mohammed. But though Abu Tâleb agreed with them in their religion and worshiped their gods, he refused to surrender his nephew to them.

Once, when Mohammed had disappeared, and his uncle suspected that the Koreish had seized him, Abu Tâleb armed a band of Hâshimite youths with dirks and went to the Kaaba to release him from the Koreish. But on the way Abu Tâleb was informed that Mohammed was found. In the presence of the Koreish, Abu Tâleb then told his young men to draw their dirks, and said: "By the Lord! had ye killed him, not one of you had remained alive."

Abu Tâleb's boldness cowed the violence

of the Koreish for a time; but as Mohammed's unpopularity increased, the Prophet and all his party were obliged to seek refuge with the Hâshimites in a secluded quarter of Mecca belonging to Abu Tâleb. Omar's conversion about this time only increased the rage of the Koreish, who formed an alliance against the Hâshimites, agreeing that they would neither buy from them nor sell to them, and that they would not intermarry with them, nor have any dealings whatever with them. This oath was committed to writing, sealed, and hung up in the Kaaba.

For several years the Hâshimites remained shut up in their fortress, frequently deprived of the necessaries of life. Their friends sometimes secretly supplied them with provisions, but the cries of the hungry children were frequently heard on the outside. They were blockaded in their intrenchments. But many of the leading people of Mecca began to take pity upon the besieged, and finally it was suggested to Abu Tâleb that the bond hung up in the Kaaba had been eaten by the ants, so as to be valid no longer. This was found to be the case, whereupon it was decided that the league was ended, and the Hâshimites returned to their homes.

But other misfortunes were in store for the founder of Islam. His good uncle, Abu Tâleb, soon died; and his faithful wife, Khadijab, also went to her grave not long afterward. Having thus lost his guardian and protector, Mohammed retired from Mecca, taking Zeid with him as his only companion on a mission to Tâyif, sixty or seventy miles east of Mecca, in hopes of converting the inhabitants of that place.

We can sarcely think of the Prophet in this lonely journey without sympathy. He was on a mission to preach the doctrine of One True God to idolators. But he failed to make any impression upon them, and as he left the town he was followed by a howling mob, who hooted him and pelted him with stones. Finally they left him, and in the shadow of some trees he betook himself to prayer. The Moslems have preserved his words, which they believe to have been as follows:

"O Lord! I make my complaint unto Thee of the feebleness of my strength and the weakness of my plans. I am insignificant in the sight of men. O Thou most merciful! Lord of the weak! Thou art my Lord! Do not abandon me. Leave me not a prey to these strangers, nor to my foes. If Thou art not offended, I am safe. I seek refuge in the light of Thy countenance, by which all darkness is dispersed and peace comes. There is no power, no help, but in Thee."

Mohammed's faith, in that hour of prayer, was the same as that of Luther praying for protection against the Pope. It formed a part of the universal religion of nature. Certainly a man of such zeal and earnestness was not an impostor. A man going alone to summon an idolatrous city to repentance must at least have been sincere, must have believed in his own doctrine.

But the hour of triumph was now at hand. No amount of error, no bitterness of prejudice, no vested interest in falsehood, can permanently resist the determined conviction of a single soul. If a zealous leader believe a truth strongly enough to maintain it through good and ill report, the vast multitude of half-believers will finally come round to him. And generally the success finally comes very suddenly, after long and weary years of trial and disappointment. Momammed's triumph came almost as suddenly. His religion had made some progress in other parts of Arabia.

At one of the great annual fairs at Mecca, Mohammed preached his mission to the merchants assembled from all portions of Arabia. Some citizens of Yatreb, the city afterwards called *Medina*, were among his hearers. At Yatreb and in its vicinity there had for a long time been many powerful tribes of Jewish proselytes. In their conflicts with the idolators, they had frequently predicted the speedy advent of a great prophet and lawgiver like Moses. The Jewish influence at Yatreb was great, and the idolators there were distracted by bitter quarrels among themselves.

We must remember that at this time Mohammed taught a kind of modified Judaism. He came to restore the monotheistic religion of the honored patriarchs, Abraham, Isaac and Jacob. He constantly quoted the Jewish sacred books—the Old Testament and the Talmud—for his authority. He professed to be an inspired prophet, but not a teacher of any new doctrine. His declared mission was to revive the universal monotheism which God had taught to man in the very beginning—the religion of all true patriarchs and prophets.

The essential doctrine of Mohammed's religion at this time was the Unity of God and His supremacy and providence. The duty of this new religion was *Islam*, or submission to the Divine will. Its worship consisted of prayer and alms-giving. At this time the Prophet did not make belief in himself the main point of his religion. That religion consisted in professing the Unity of God, and in submitting wholly to God. The Mohammedans, or followers of Mohammed, were called *Moslems*, or *Mussulmans*, "true believers."

The semi-Judaized pilgrims from Yatreb to Mecca were quite prepared to accept Mohammed's teachings. At the time of the pilgrimage the Prophet met many of them, and they promised to become his disciples. They took the following pledge: "We will not worship any but the One God; we will not steal, nor commit adultery, nor kill our children (female); we will not slander at all, nor disobey the Prophet in anything that is right." This was subsequently known as the "*Pledge of Women*," because it did not require them to fight for Islam. This faith made rapid progress among the idolators at Yatreb—much more than the Jewish system. The Jews required too much of their proselytes. They insisted on these proselytes becoming Jews, and demanded a change of all their previous customs; but Mohammed simply asked for submission.

About this time Mohammed had the celebrated dream or vision, in which he was carried by the angel Gabriel on a winged steed to Jerusalem, where he met all the prophets of God and was welcomed by them, after which he was carried on the same steed and in company with the same angel to the seventh heaven into the presence of God. This vision was so vivid that Mohammed deemed it a reality, and maintained that he had been to Jerusalem and to heaven. This and the Koran itself were the only miracles that he ever claimed.

As the Moslems at Yatreb had entered into a second pledge—a pledge to receive Mohammed and his friends, and to protect them—the Prophet ordered his followers at Mecca to repair secretly in small parties to Yatreb. Mohammed and Abu Bekr, and their families, remained quietly at Mecca until all the rest of the Mussulmans had fled.

The Koreish were so utterly amazed at these events that they did not know what to do. They could not understand why the Prophet himself remained, and why his disciples had fled. They could not comprehend why he remained unprotected in their midst. They contemplated assassinating him, but feared that his tribe would take a bloody vengeance on his murderers. Finally they proposed to seize him, and also that a number of men, one from each tribe and family, should at the same moment plunge their dirks into him. Some thought it would be better to send an assassin to waylay him on his way to Yatreb.

While the Koreish were discussing these alternatives, they received information that Mohammed and Abu Bekr had also fled. The enemies of the Prophet instantly repaired to the houses of the illustrious fugitives. They found the young Ali in Mohammed's house, and asked him where his father was. Ali replied: "I do not know. I am not his keeper. Did you not order him to go from the city? I suppose he is gone."

As the Koreish did not obtain any more information at Abu Bekr's house, they sent out parties of armed men, mounted on swift horses and camels, to search the entire route to Yatreb and to bring the refugees back to Mecca. The pursuers returned in a few days, saying that there were no indications of any persons having fled in that direction, and that if the fugitives had gone that way they would certainly have overtaken them.

Instead of going north to Yatreb, Mohammed and Abu Bekr had concealed themselves in the cave of Thor, on a hill about five or six miles south of Mecca. In this cave the fugitives remained hidden three days and nights, in imminent peril from their pursuers, who, it is said, once came to the mouth of the cave, but, seeing spiders' webs spun across the opening and a pigeon's nest with two eggs near it, reached the conclusion that no human being could have entered the cave recently, and hurried away. The fugitives heard the voices of their pursuers at the mouth of the cavern. The morning light penetrated through a crevice in the roof of the cave. The trembling Abu Bekr, who had shed many bitter tears at his master's desperate fortunes, said: "We are only two. If one of them were to look down, he would see us." Mohammed replied: "Think not so, Abu Bekr. We are two, but Allah is in our midst, a third."

Being satisfied the next day that the heat of the pursuit had abated, the illustrious refugees came out of the cave and mounted the camels which Abu Bekr's son had privately brought to them from Mecca, thus starting for Yatreb, leaving Mecca on the right. They were once overtaken by a band of pursuers, but escaped by means of supplications and promises. As a certain writer has truly said, "What a moment for history! One thrust of a lance might have changed the destiny of half the world."

Mohammed's flight from Mecca to Yatreb —which occurred in the summer of A. D. 622—is called the *Hegira*, and is the point from which the Mohammedans reckon time, as the Christian nations do from the birth of Christ; though this computation was not introduced until some years after the Prophet's death.

The Mohammedan era truly begins with the Hegira. Mohammed entered Yatreb in triumph, being enthusiastically welcomed by his followers, who now regarded him as a sovereign, as well as an apostle and prophet. He changed the name of Yatreb to *Medinet al Nabi*, "The City of the Prophet," or *Medina*, "The City," as it is still called.

Mohammed's fortunes now arose, but his character degenerated. He had borne adversity and opposition with sublime faith and patience, but was not able to bear prosperity so well. Previous to that time he had been a prophet and apostle, teaching God's truth to those who would accept it, and commending himself to every man's conscience by the manifestation of that truth. He now became a politician—the head of a party, contriving expedients for its success. Hitherto, truth was his only weapon; thenceforth, force constituted his chief means. He no longer sought to convince his antagonists, but endeavored to force their submission by the terror of his power. The tone of his revelations changed, adapting themselves to his necessities; and he claimed inspiration for every action, even for taking an additional wife.

Thus Mohammed yielded to the temptation which Christ resisted. Up to the Hegira the Prophet of Mecca might also truthfully have said: "My kingdom is not of this world." But after that date the sword was to serve him as his most faithful servant in building up Islam. His ends were the same as before. His object was still to establish the worship of the one true and living God. But his means thereafter were of the earth, earthy. He no longer contented himself with the arts of persuasion, but assumed a tone of command. He declared that the period of long suffering and patience was past, and that his mission and that of every Moslem was to propagate the dominion of Islam by the sword. The duty of all Mussulmans was to destroy the temples of the infidels, to overthrow the idols, and to pursue the unbelievers to the remotest quarters of the world.

Said Mohammed: "The sword is the key of heaven and of hell. A drop of blood shed in the cause of Allah, a night spent in arms, is of more avail than two months of fasting and prayer. Whoever dies in battle, his sins are forgiven." This promise, with the assurance that every man's death is decreed by Fate, made the Moslems boldly face death in battle. They were assured that no man could die until the appointed moment. Until that moment arrived, he was safe from the enemy's darts; but when it did arrive, he would drop dead in his own house or expire in his bed, if not on the battle-field. It is no wonder that under such teaching the soldiers of Islam have ever been distinguished for their reckless bravery.

Mohammed did not only promise the glories of Paradise as the reward of the valor of his followers, but the riches of this world were also to be divided among them. Thus the new religion attracted the wandering Bedouins of the Arabian desert, not so much from the sublime dogma which it inculcated of the unity and spirituality of God, as from the sanction which it gave to pillage, and the rights it conferred on the conquerors over the wealth, women and slaves of the conquered.

Nevertheless, at the very time when Mohammed shared the treasures won by the united forces of his followers, he did not depart from the simplicity of his early life. His house and his mosque at Medina were entirely destitute of ornament. His dress was coarse, and his food consisted of only a few dates and a little barley bread. While preaching every Friday, the Mohammedan Sabbath-day, he leaned against a palm tree. He did not indulge in the luxury of a wooden chair until after the lapse of many years. Mohammed was also distinguished for his benevolence and his concern for the poor. One of his teachings was that the poor would get to heaven seventy years before the rich. He was grave and dignified in his manner.

Islam promised to be a noble religion when Mohammed started out in his career. He accepted all the essential truths of Judaism. He recognized Moses and Jesus as true teachers. He taught that there was one universal religion, the substance of which was faith in one universal Supreme Being, submission to His will, trust in His providence, and good-will to His creatures. The only worship which God required were prayer and alms. Says Mr. Muir, a marvelous and mighty work had been wrought by these few precepts.

From time immemorial Mecca and all Arabia had been buried in spiritual lethargy. The influences of Judaism, Christianity and philosophy had been feeble and transient. Dark superstitions prevailed, the mother of dark vices. And now, in thirteen years of preaching, a body of men and women had risen who rejected idolatry, worshiped the One True God, lived lives of prayer, practiced chastity, benevolence and justice, and were ready to do and suffer anything for the truth. All this was the result of the deep conviction in the soul of this one man.

Mohammed, who had exhibited such great qualities as a prophet and a religious teacher, now also displayed the characteristics of the warrior and the statesman. He had finally obtained a position at Medina whence he was able to act on the Arabs with other forces than those of eloquence and sentiment. And now the man who for forty years had been a simple citizen and led a quiet family life—who for thirteen years afterward had been a despised and persecuted but patient teacher of the Unity of God —passed the last ten years of his wonderful career in raising and organizing a fanatical army of warriors, destined to conquer half the civilized world. The simple, earnest zeal of the original believers in Islam raised up a power which then took the sword and conquered with it.

Influence is the reward of patient, long enduring faith, and ambition serves itself with this influence for its own purpose. This is more or less the history of every religion and of every political party. Sects are not founded by politicians, but by men of faith, by men to whom ideas are realities, by men who are willing to die for those ideas. Such faith always triumphs in the end, makes many converts, becomes a great power. Ambitious men make use of these deep and strong convictions for their own purposes.

Mohammedanism was a powerful religious movement founded on the sincerest conviction, but gradually turned aside, and used for ambitious objects and temporal triumphs. Mohammed himself led the way in thus diverting his religion from divine objects to purely human ones. He is perhaps the greatest illustration of the vast multitude of noble souls who have sought high ends by low means.

Mohammed, who had hitherto always been so kind-hearted and affectionate, was now capable of the greatest cruelty toward those who resisted his purpose. This tendency manifested itself in his treatment of the Jews. He hoped to form an alliance with them against the idolators. He had acknowledged the divine authority of the Jewish religion, and appealed to the Hebrew Scriptures to prove the truth of his own mission. He conformed to the Jewish ritual and customs, and made Jerusalem his Kibla, toward which he turned in prayer five times a day. He therefore expected that the Jews would receive him as a prophet, but they refused to do so. He then gradually departed from their customs, changed his Kibla to Mecca, and finally denounced the Jews as obstinate unbelievers.

About a year after his settlement at Medina, the despised and persecuted outcast of Mecca proclaimed a holy war against the Koreish. Ambuscades were stationed to annoy their commerce, by seeking to seize the caravans in the narrow defiles of the mountains. The ill success of the first efforts were atoned for by Mohammed in person on the plain of Bedr, one of the usual watering stations, about forty miles from Mecca, in January, A. D. 624.

Mohammed's spies had brought him news that a caravan of the idolators, consisting of a thousand camels richly laden, was on its home journey from Syria. He advanced with a small body of his followers to intercept this caravan. He was so poorly provided with cavalry that his troops could muster only two horses and seventy camels, mounting these by turns. Mohammed had caused to be erected a temporary wooden structure, overshadowed with green boughs, for his own personal safety. He had likewise provided a fleet camel, ready harnessed, in order that he might escape captivity in case of defeat.

When Mohammed had drawn up his army, he prayed earnestly for victory. Burning with zeal and mutual hatred, the troops on both sides rushed furiously to the charge. The troops of the Koreish outnumbered those of Mohammed three to one, but the superiority of numbers was overbalanced by the reckless intrepidity of religious fanaticism. While the Moslems bravely resisted the assaults of their enemies, their leader fervently addressed the Lord of Heaven and Earth in their behalf.

Seated with Abu Bekr in his wooden sanctuary, with his eye fixed on the battlefield, Mohammed exclaimed: "Courage, my children, and fight like men! Close your ranks, discharge your arrows, and the day is your own!" He continued exhorting them until the mantle fell from his shoulders; after which he started as if from a trance, and exclaimed: "Triumph! Abu Bekr! triumph! Behold the squadrons of heaven flying to our aid!" After thus rekindling the enthusiasm of his followers, Mohammed mounted his horse, placed himself at their head, and led them on to victory.

The Koran ascribes the glory of this triumph to the Divine aid; and the Mohammedan historians relate that the angelic chivalry, headed by the archangel Gabriel, did frightful execution with their invisible swords on the terrified idolators. Mohammed claimed the fifth part of the booty, by a special revelation. He spoke bitterly of his enemies, as their bodies were cast into a pit. He looked fiercely at one of the prisoners who were brought before him. The unhappy man exclaimed: "There is death in that glance!" Mohammed presently ordered him to be beheaded. Two days later another was ordered to execution. This second victim asked piteously: "Who will take care of my little girl?" "Hell-fire," replied Mohammed, who instantly ordered the unfortunate man to be cut down.

Mohammed did not make the faith of his followers dependent upon success. The same year of his victory at Bedr, he suffered a severe defeat at Ohud, six miles from Medina, where he himself was wounded. This disaster imperiled his reputation, and his followers began expressing doubts of his pretensions to Divine favor. But with his usual address, he ascribed the defeat to their sins, and assured them that the seventy martyrs who had fallen in the field were already participating in the joys of Paradise.

Mohammed's defeat at Ohud tended to increase his pride and fanaticism. The Jews became special objects of his enmity. A Jewess who had written verses against Mohammed was assassinated by a Moslem, and the Prophet praised the murderer for the deed in the public mosque. Another aged Jew was murdered by order of Mohammed for the same offense. A quarrel between some Jews and Moslems induced Mohammed to attack the Jewish tribe. This tribe surrendered after a siege of fifteen days; whereupon Mohammed ordered all the prisoners to be killed; but, at the urgent request of a powerful chief in Medina, the Prophet permitted them to retire into exile, cursing them and their intercessor.

Mr. Muir mentions other cases of the murder of Jews by Mohammed's command. All these facts are derived from contemporaneous Mussulman historians, who glorify their Prophet for these acts. The worst of this class of actions on the part of Mohammed was the deliberate execution of seven or eight hundred Jewish prisoners, who had surrendered at discretion, and the sale of their wives and children into slavery. Mohammed selected the most beautiful one of these women for his concubine.

About this time Mohammed began multiplying wives and receiving revelations permitting him to do so beyond the usual limit of his law. He added one after another to his harem, until he had ten wives, besides his slaves. He made presents of three beautiful female slaves taken in war, one to his father-in-law, and one to each of his two sons-in-law.

Thus the stormy and triumphant years of the Arabian pontiff-sovereign were passed in battles with the Syrians, the Koreish and the Jewish tribes. But the great object of his most ardent desires was the conquest of Mecca. He viewed that city as the future seat of his religion and his true country. He wished to restore there the glory of his illustrious ancestors, and to surpass it by that which he had achieved for himself.

The Meccans had suffered more severely in the war than their enemies. They depended for their prosperity, and almost for their existence, on commerce; and now they beheld their trade nearly annihilated, their caravans plundered and their flock's swept away. They made one great effort, and besieged Mohammed in Medina, but were repulsed after suffering a severe loss. The Prophet exclaimed: "Hitherto they have sought us; it is now our turn to go in search of them." After this defeat the Meccans appear to have lost all courage. Mohammed rapidly became the most powerful prince in Arabia. His followers accepted his words as the inspired oracles of God. They had such veneration for him that a hair which fell from his head, and the water in which he had washed, were preserved in the belief that they contained some divine virtue. The faith of his followers was confirmed by the revelations which he professed to receive from Allah, through the medium of the archangel Gabriel, and which he communicated orally to those around him.

In A. D. 628 Mohammed marched against Mecca. He found the city too strongly fortified for his means of attack, and consequently concluded a truce very much against the will of his followers, thus securing a peaceful entrance into the city the next year (A. D. 629). He now regarded his power as established, and therefore sent ambassadors inviting the most powerful monarchs of the world, especially Khosrou Parviz, King of Persia, and Heraclius, the Eastern Roman Emperor, to embrace Islam. The Persian sovereign treated the demand with contempt, while the Emperor Heraclius rejected it with mildness and civility.

On the banks of the river Karasu, Khosrou Parviz received a letter from "Mohammed, the camel-driver of Mecca," ordering him to abjure the errors of that faith in which his fathers had lived, and to embrace the religion of the One True God, whose Apostle Mohammed declared himself to be. The Great King was so indignant at this insulting message that he tore the letter into fragments, which he cast into the passing stream. Upon hearing of this, the Arabian Prophet exclaimed: "It is thus that Allah will tear the kingdom and reject the supplications of Khosrou!"

The zealous Mohammedan historian who records this circumstance is sure that all the miseries which imbittered the last years of Khosrou Parviz were attributable to this sacrilegious deed. He also says that the waters of the river, which until then had supplied the means of irrigation to a large extent of country, shrank in horror into their present deep and scanty channel, where, he says, they have ever since remained useless and accursed.

In the meantime Mohammed continued his hostilities against the Jews and the neighboring Arab tribes. At the capture of the fortress of Khaibar, a Jewess placed a poisoned shoulder of mutton upon his table to test his claims as God's Apostle. Mohammed ate only a mouthful, but this was sufficient to plant the seeds of a fatal disease in his constitution.

Every moment added to the numbers of the Moslem sect. Ten thousand Bedouin Arabs joined Mohammed's army, and the opening of the gates of Mecca to the Prophet and his followers was the final consummation of the triumph of Islam. In A. D. 629 Abu Sofian surrendered the keys of the holy city of Arabia to Mohammed, who made his triumphal entrance with unparalleled magnificence. He did homage to the national faith by worshiping in the Kaaba; and his presence produced such an effect that many of his former enemies, the chief guardian of the idolatrous sanctuary among them, declared themselves his disciples.

Soon afterward Mohammed commenced his first foreign war. The ambassador whom he had sent to the Byzantine governor of Bosrah had been murdered at the little town of Muta, south of the Dead Sea; and Mohammed despatched an army under his adopted son Zeid to avenge the insult. Zeid and two of his sucessors lost their lives in battle; but Khaled, the son of Walid, won a decisive victory, and returned to Medina laden with a vast amount of booty.

This success encouraged Mohammed to break his truce with the Meccans. Notwithstanding their remonstrances and offers of submission, he marched against their city. The fiery Khaled forced an entrance, and Mohammed had great difficulty in preventing his followers from massacring his fellow-citizens. Thus Mecca was conquered and the Koreish submitted. Eleven men and six women, who had been conspicuous among his old enemies, were proscribed; but the rest of the population of the city were spared. The Kaaba was purified by Mohammed's orders; all traces of idolatry being removed from this national sanctuary, except the celebrated Black Stone, an aërolite venerated by the Arabs from an unknown age, the reverence for which was so deeply fixed in their hearts that it was not easily eradicated. The Meccans embraced Islam, and a perpetual law prohibited any unbeliever from entering the holy city.

Ambassadors now flocked from all sides to congratulate the new temporal and spiritual ruler. For the few remaining years of his life Mohammed may be considered the ruling sovereign of Arabia, and three years after the submission of Mecca he effected the complete subjugation of the entire desert peninsula. The Prophet's generals marched from the shores of the Red Sea to those of the Persian Gulf and the Indian Ocean. The Arab tribes throughout the peninsula acquiesced, one by one, in the Prophet's authority. All paid tribute or accepted Islam. His enemies were all under his feet; his doctrines were accepted; and the rival prophets, Aswad and Museilama, were overcome. At the period of his last pilgrimage to the Kaaba, in A. D. 632, one hundred and fourteen thousand Mussulman soldiers marched under the Prophet's banner.

The Arab chieftain who governed that portion of Irak west of the Euphrates under the suzerainty of the Persian king, and the Arabian viceroy of Yemen, the province in South-western Arabia ruled by the Negus of Abyssinia, embraced Islam; so that Arabia was now entirely liberated from the yoke of foreign powers, and the Arabs considered themselves an independent united nation.

During the six years of his reign, Mohammed fought personally in nine battles or sieges, and his generals led his followers in fifteen military expeditions. Nearly all of these proceedings were confined to Arabia; but the Prophet's ambition was not satisfied with success in his own country, and he directed his attention to Palestine and Syria. The wealth and fertility of Syria attracted his cupidity; and for the purpose of anticipating the military preparations of the Emperor Heraclius, he determined to invade that part of the Eastern Roman Empire.

Accordingly an army of thirty thousand Moslems was assembled, and a holy war was solemnly proclaimed against the Romans. The Arabs reluctantly entered upon this struggle; as it was the harvest season and a time of scarcity, when their labor was imperiously required in the field. But they vainly begged for a dispensation, and urged their different excuses—lack of money, horses and provisions, their ripening crops, and the burning summer heats. The indignant Apostle exclaimed: "Hell is much hotter!"

The Arabs then took the field, and entered upon a painful and weary march. Ten men rode by turns on the same camel, and the suffering from thirst was intense. After a ten days' journey in a burning desert, the Moslems reposed by the waters and palm-trees of Tabuc, a town midway between Medina and Damascus. There they were informed that the Roman army had decamped, and thus ended the war. The distressed condition of his followers probably induced Mohammed to decline hazarding his fame and fortunes against the military forces of the Eastern Roman Empire.

The Mussulmans call the ninth year of the Hegira the *Year of Embassies*, because of the extraordinary concourse of ambassadors and visitors who had been attracted to Mecca that year by the Prophet's fame, and who came to acknowledge his power or to implore his protection. These devotees were said to "outnumber the dates that fall from the palm-tree in the season of ripeness." Various arrangements were made to consolidate the strength of the infant monarchy. Officers were appointed to collect the ecclesiastical revenues, and the opprobrious name of tribute was exchanged for that of *alms*, or *oblation*, for the service of religion.

Mohammed assumed great state in his household. His camp included all his wives, who rode on camels and were inclosed within pavilions of embroidered silk. He was followed by a vast number of victims for sacrifice, crowned with garlands of flowers. Every spot where he halted and said his prayers became consecrated; and the manner in which he conducted the various religious rites, from cutting his hair and nails to the solemn act of casting stones at the devil, is still faithfully followed by the Moslems.

Mohammed was now in the sixty-third year of his age. His physical vigor had perceptibly declined during four years; but he still performed the duties of a king, a general and an apostle. Finally he was seized with a fever, attended by occasional delirium. Finding his condition critical, he caused himself to be conveyed to the mansion of his favorite wife, Ayesha. He expressed to her his belief that his disease had its origin in the poisoned mutton set before him by the Jewess at Khaibar.

As he felt his danger increasing and his end approaching, he recommended himself to the prayers of his faithful followers, and asked forgiveness of all whom he might have offended. Said he: "If there be any man among you whom I have struck unjustly, I submit myself to be scourged in return. If I have injured any man's reputation, let him proclaim my faults. If I have taken any one's property, or owe money to any one, let him demand justice. that I may satisfy him."

A voice in the multitude responded: "Yes, you owe me three drachms of silver." The dying Apostle paid the debt, and thanked his creditor for demanding it in this world, rather than accusing him at the Judgment Day. He then freed his slaves, ordered the affairs of his burial, calmed the lamentations of his friends, and pronounced a benediction upon them. Until his final hour he continued acting the character of God's Apostle, evincing the same remarkable fortitude and presence of mind that he had exhibited on the battle-field. He continued performing his devotions in the mosque until within three days. When, finally, he was too feeble, he assigned that duty to Abu Bekr; and it was supposed that he thus intended to appoint his old friend as his successor; but he expressed no opinion or desire on this subject, and appeared to leave the matter wholly to the judgment of his followers.

Mohammed contemplated the approach of death with perfect calmness, and recited the words which he declared that he had heard from the archangel Gabriel. He repeated what he had before affirmed, that the archangel Azriel would not take away his soul until he had obtained permission from him. This permission the Prophet finally pronounced aloud. The moment of his soul's departure arrived. His head reclined in the lap of his favorite wife, Ayesha, and he fainted from excess of pain. Upon regaining consciousness, he fixed his eyes upon the ceiling, and uttered his last words: "O God! pardon my sins! I come to rejoin my brethren in heaven!" With this exclamation, the founder of Islam ended his mortal life on the 8th of June, A. D. 632—in the tenth year of the Hegira.

The Arabs could scarcely realize that they had lost their Apostle. The frantic populace of Mecca rushed in crowds to the house of Mohammed, where they received the unexpected tidings of his death. Wild with grief, Omar declared that Mohammed was not dead, but in a trance. Drawing his cimeter, he threatened to strike off the head of any one who should say that the leader of the faithful was no more. The grave Abu Bekr calmed the excited multitude. Mohammed was buried the day after his death, amid the grief of his followers. Abu Bekr and Omar offered the following prayer: "Peace be unto thee, O Prophet of God; and the mercy of the Lord, and His blessing! We bear testimony that the Prophet of God hath delivered the message revealed to him; hath fought in the ways of the Lord until God crowned his religion with victory; hath fulfilled his words commanding that God alone is to be worshiped in Unity; hath drawn us to himself, and been kind and tender-hearted to believers; hath sought no recompense for delivering to us the faith, neither hath sold it for a price at any time."

To this fervent prayer all the assembled multitude exclaimed: "Amen! Amen!"

Such is the story of the founder of the last of the great monotheistic religions. Mohammed was a great man—one of the greatest that any age or country produced. He was a man of the deepest convictions and of the purest purposes, but in the hour of triumph he employed low means for a good end. He fully believed in his visions and revelations, and in his own inspiration.

After ages have speculated upon the problem of his true character—whether he was a mere fanatic, sincerely believing all that he preached, and carried away by his enthusiasm; or whether he was only an ingenious and successful hypocrite. But that is not the proper issue of the question; as no impostor, civil or religious, could ever succeed in establishing a permanent influence over the minds of millions of the human race.

Mohammed has not until recently received justice from Christian writers, who until a quarter of a century ago have been disposed to see everything bad and nothing good in the founder of Islam. Nothing but a feeling of bigotry and narrow-mindedness can induce the belief that Mohammed was an impostor, a fraud, a hypocrite. He was in his own age and country a great religious reformer. He urged a whole nation onward in the most essential of all steps in the investigation of truth. He led his countrymen from an absurd and degrading idolatry, from a priestly slavery which corrupted morals and encouraged all vices by a system of expiations, to a belief in an omnipotent, omniscient and omnipresent God, the same Deity worshiped by Jews and Christians.

Mohammed acknowledged himself to be nothing more than a mere man. He made no pretensions to miraculous power, but he felt himself commissioned to perform a great work of religious reformation. He was no impostor for declaring this to be a call from Heaven, but he allowed his zeal and fanaticism to lead him into intolerance and cruelty, and to accomplish a good end by low means.

Mohammed was the reformer of the Arabs. He taught his countrymen to acknowledge and reverence the One True God, the Lord of Heaven and Earth. But from the time that he adopted force as the means for the propagation of his religion, his life lost its purity, and his temper its mildness, and policy entered into his religion.

Though invested with the ensigns of royalty, Mohammed despised its pomp, and was indifferent to its luxuries. His familiarity, which endeared him to his companions, was extended to the humblest of his countrymen, whose wishes and complaints he always listened to patiently. He even entertained them occasionally at his table, or shared with them their homely meal, while they occupied benches around the mosque. When he was not engaged in matters of greater importance, he ignored the forms and restraints of official etiquette, and condescended to participate in the amusements or jocular conversation of his friends. While at the head of his army, he maintained the stateliness and grave taciturnity of a Roman Emperor. But while with his soldiers, he was able to unbend himself without sacrificing his authority. He participated in their pastimes and pleasantries with the most remarkable degree of freedom.

Mohammed courted no distinction beyond others in food or apparel. His usual fare were dates and water, or a small quantity of barley bread, the abstemious diet of his countrymen. He sat cross-legged on the ground while he ate. When he traveled, he shared his scanty morsel with his servant, who usually rode behind him on the same camel. It is said that he also was in the habit of performing the most humble and menial duties of the family. He did not disdain to mend his own shoes or patch his coarse woolen coat. He milked the sheep, kindled the fire, swept the floor, and served the guests at his own table. His liberality in bestowing alms amounted to extravagance, and frequently left him without money or provisions for his own household.

The Arabs had been accustomed to unrestricted freedom in love and marriage. Mohammed forbade incestuous marriages, restricted the right of divorce, and punished dissoluteness, but allowed every Mussulman to have four wives. He raised himself above the laws which he imposed on others, by successively marrying fifteen women after the death of his wife, Khadijah. Female society and perfumes were the two things on earth which most highly delighted him. He declared that the fervor of his piety was heightened by these enjoyments, and his religion made adequate provision for them. Yet all the inmates of his harem were childless, and not a son survived to support his old age, or to uphold the royal and pontifical dignities after his death. His daughter Fatima was the only one of his eight children by Khadijah that lived to enjoy his paternal tenderness. She married Ali in the first year of the Hegira, and became the mother of an illustrious posterity.

Mohammed claimed to have received from the archangel Gabriel a volume bound in silk and gems, written with a finger of light, and containing the Divine decrees. He disclosed the contents of this precious book only in fragments, said to have been committed to writing by an amanuensis, as the founder of Islam is said to have been unable to read or write. The writing was dictated by Mohammed himself, and was executed on palm-leaves, scraps of leather and the shoulder-bones of sheep, to be distributed among the faithful. Moslems regard this holy book as the word of God. Allah, and not Mohammed, is considered its author.

Allah handed it to Mohammed through the medium of the archangel Gabriel. Two years after Mohammed's death these fragmentary writings were collected and published by Abu Bekr as the holy book of the the information necessary for the guidance and spiritual welfare of mankind. Like the Jews, the Mohammedans hold their sacred book in the most extraordinary veneration. They will not allow it to be read, or even touched, by any person of a different religion. They handle it with the greatest respect, never holding it below the girdle, and always first performing their legal ablutions. They swear by it, consult it on all momentous occasions, take it with them to battle, and inscribe verses from it upon their banners and clothing, as they formerly did upon their coins.

PREACHING THE KORAN.

The Moslems speak in terms of the highest rapture concerning the literary merits of the Koran. The most learned Mussulman doctors have pronounced the style of this sacred volume to be inimitable. It is universally conceded to be written with great elegance and purity of language. It is in prose, but is measured into chapters and verses, like David's Psalms. The sentences have the sweet cadence of poetry, and usually end in a long continued chime, which in many cases interrupts the sense and occasions unnecessary repetition; but this metrical charm is highly appreciated by the Arabs, whose ears are delighted with musical cadence.

Koran, meaning "that which ought to be read."

The Koran, as containing the revelations said to have been made to Mohammed, is accepted by the Moslems as containing all

The Koran teaches the fundamental Jewish and Christian doctrines, along with many old Arabian and Persian maxims. As before noticed, its essential doctrine is the absolute Unity and supremacy of God, in opposition to the old Arabian polytheism on the one hand and the Christian Trinity on the other. The doctrine was proclaimed in Mohammed's words, which long constituted the war cry of the Mussulmans: "*There is no God but Allah, and Mohammed is His Apostle.*" Christian writers have usually used the word *Prophet*, instead of Apostle, in this connection; but this is incorrect, as Mohammed himself never made any pretension to the gift of prophecy, and as the Arabic word *resoul*, used in the Mussulman creed, means "one who is sent"—a missionary or apostle.

This sacred volume declares that Adam, Noah, Abraham, Moses and Jesus were Allah's prophets, but that Mohammed was greater than any of them. It accepts the Pentateuch, the Psalms, the Gospels and the Koran as sacred books. It teaches the doctrines of Eternal Decrees, or absolute Predestination; of future rewards and punishments; of an intermediate state after death; of the Resurrection and Judgment; and of angels and demons. All who reject the Koran—Jews, Christians, Magians, etc.—are consigned to an eternal "hell-fire." There are separate hells for Christians, Jews, Sabeans, Magians, idolators, the hypocrites of all religions, and wicked Moslems. All Moslems, whatever their sins, shall finally be admitted to a paradise of sensual enjoyments—wicked Mohammedans only after a temporary future punishment; but the righteous, and those who die in battle for the propagation of Islam, instantly after the Judgment.

The Koran requires all Mussulmans to pray five times a day, to cleanse themselves from all impurities by frequent washings or ablutions, to give alms, to fast during the whole month of Ramadân, to abstain from wine and gaming, to refrain from all vice and crime, to make pilgrimages to Mecca, and to propogate Islam by the sword. The prohibition of wine and swine's flesh, the practice of circumcision, and the observance of the Sabbath on Friday, are also a part of the Mohammedan creed; though circumcision is not mentioned in the Koran. Like the old Jewish system, and like other Oriental religions, Mohammedanism sanctions polygamy.

The Koran describes the angels and demons as having pure and subtile bodies, created of fire, and being free from all carnal appetites and desires. The four archangels are Gabriel, the angel of revelation; Michael, the friend and protector of the Jews; Azriel, the angel of death; and Israfil, the angel of the Resurrection, whose duty it will be to sound the trumpet at the Judgment Day. According to the Mohammedan belief, every human being has two guardian angels, who attend him and record all his good and evil deeds. The Mohammedan doctrine concerning angels was adopted from the Jews, who acknowledged that they derived it from the Magians of Persia.

The Mohammedan creed relating to demons and genii was likewise obtained from the Jews, some of whom assert that the genii were begotten before the Deluge. This is assumed on the authority of the Mosaic account, that "the sons of God saw the daughters of men, that they were fair, and they took them wives of all which they chose," etc. The Jewish genii, or *shedim*, have wings with which they fly from one end of the world to the other, as do the ministering angels; but they eat, drink, have offspring, and die.

The demons described in the Koran are fallen angels. Eblis, or Satan, was at first one of the angels nearest to Allah's presence, and was then called *Azazel*. The Koran tells us that he was cast out of heaven because he refused to pay homage to Adam at the time of the Creation. The genii are intermediate creatures, neither entirely spiritual nor wholly earthly. They were created of fire, like the angels, but of grosser kind, requiring food and drink for their sustenance, and being subject to passions and death like ordinary mortals.

Some of the genii were good, believing in the Koran and in Mohammed's divine mission, and were accordingly capable of salvation. Others were infidels, and were therefore doomed to eternal damnation. The genii existed long before the creation of Adam. At first they were possessed of virtue and goodness, but in the course of time they fell into almost universal corruption and wickedness, whereupon Eblis was sent to drive them to a remote and desolate part of the earth, where they were then confined. As some of this generation still remained, an ancient Persian king made war upon them and forced them to retire to the mountains of Kaf.

There are several ranks and degrees of genii, such as the *peris*, or fairies—beautiful female spirits, who believe in Allah and His Apostle, and endeavor to do good in this world; and the *deev*, or giants, who often make war upon the peris, take them captive, and confine them in cages, which they hang upon the trees, where they are soon found by other peris, who come daily to feed them with the most fragrant odors, which are their ordinary food. Both good and bad genii are able to make themselves invisible at pleasure. Their chief resort is the mountain of Kaf; but they also dwell in ruined cities, unoccupied houses, at the bottom of wells, in woods, in pools of water, and among the rocks and sand-hills of the desert.

The Orientals still consider shooting stars to be arrows shot by the angels against the genii who transgress their limits and approach too near the forbidden regions of bliss. The genii are said to carry off beautiful women, whom they detain as their wives and companions. Many of the evil genii delight in mischief for its own sake. They injure and mislead travelers, raise whirlwinds, and dry up springs in the desert. The *ghoul* is a kind of subordinate evil genius which feeds on the flesh of men and women whom he decoys to his haunts in wild and barren places for the purpose of killing and devouring them. When it is difficult to obtain food in this way, this lesser evil genius approaches nearer to the dwelling-places of man, and enters the graveyards for the purpose of feeding upon the carcasses of the dead. The *afrite* is a powerful evil genius.

A respect for magic and the power of enchantments naturally prevailed among a people who devoutly believed these traditions regarding genii and demons. It was believed that Solomon's throne and army were conveyed through the air at a word, by virtue of the possession of a ring. Among other Arab traditions are those of the wonderful lamp, or the magical palace of Aladdin, the city of the statues visited by Zobeide, Ali Baba's cavern, and the transformation of the subjects of the King of the Black Isles into fishes.

Magicians were believed to possess powers superior, if not equal, to those of the genii. They had the power of transporting themselves and others through the air, and of transforming men and animals into any shape they chose, if no contrary influence was used in opposition to them. Like the genii, magicians were good and bad; and the good magician of to-day might be an evil one to-morrow. The history of the Arabs contains numerous instances of enchantment, which the best informed among their sheikhs and philosophers believe, the same as do the most ignorant of the common people. Mohammed himself believed in the agency of magicians, and inserted numerous passages in the Koran to enable the faithful to counteract their spells.

Concerning the intermediate state after death, the Koran declares that when a corpse is laid in the grave, it is received by an angel, who notifies it of the coming of two examiners, who are two black livid angels, of a frightful appearance, named Monkir and Nakir, who order the corpse to sit upright, and examine him concerning his faith as to the Unity of God and the mission of Mohammed. If the dead person answers in the affirmative, these terrible angels permit the body to rest in peace; but if he replies in the negative, they beat him on the temple with iron maces, till he roars out with anguish so loud that he is heard by all in the universe except men and genii. Then they press the earth on the corpse, which is gnawed and stung until the Resurrection by ninety-nine dragons with seven heads each; or their sins will become venomous beasts, the grievous ones stinging like dragons, the smaller like scorpions, and the others like serpents. The orthodox Mohammedans have their graves made hollow, so that they may sit up more easily while they are examined by the angels. The sect of the Mótazalites reject the doctrine of the examination of the sepulcher.

The Koran declares that the archangel Azriel, who separates the soul from the body, performs his office with ease and gentleness towards the good, and with violence towards the wicked. The soul then enters into that state which the Moslems call *Al Rerzakh*, the interval between death and the Resurrection. If the departed person was a believer, he is met by two angels, who convey his soul to heaven.

Concerning the Resurrection, the orthodox Mohammedan doctrine is that both body and soul will be raised; while Ebu Sina and the Arabian philosophers maintained that the Resurrection was only spiritual, and others asserted that it was only corporeal. Mohammed taught that a man's body was entirely consumed by the earth, except the *os coccygis*, or rump-bone, which he said was the first formed in the human body and would remain uncorrupted until the Judgment Day, as a seed from which the entire human frame was to be renewed. Mohammed said that this renewal was to be effected by a forty days' rain which Allah would send, and which would cover the earth to the height of twelve cubits and cause the bodies to sprout forth like plants.

The Mohammedans declare that the exact time of the Resurrection is a profound secret to all except Allah Himself, and that the archangel Gabriel himself was unable to enlighten Mohammed on this point. But the Moslems say that the approach of that great day may be known from certain signs which are to precede it.

The lesser signs are: 1. The decay of faith among men. 2. The advancing of the meanest persons to eminent dignity. 3. That a maid-servant shall become the mother of her mistress, or master; by which is meant that towards the end of the world men shall be abandoned to sensuality, or that the Mohammedans shall then take many captives. 4. Tumults and seditions. 5. A war with the Turks. 6. Great distress in the world, so that a man in passing another's grave shall say: "Would to God I were in his place." 7. That the provinces of Irak and Syria shall refuse to pay their tribute. 8. That the buildings of Medina shall reach to Ahâb, or Yahâb.

Besides these lesser signs, there are a number of greater signs preceding the Judgment Day. The first sign is the sun's rising in the west. Next is the appearance of a gigantic beast, said by some to reach to the clouds and to heaven when her head is only out, and to appear for three days, but only to show a third part of her body. This monster is described as having the head of a bull, the eyes of a hog, the ears of an elephant, the horns of a stag, the neck of an ostrich, the breast of a lion, the color of a tiger, the back of a cat, the tail of a ram, the legs of a camel, and the voice of an ass. Some say that this monster will appear three times in several places, bringing the rod of Moses and the seal of Solomon with her; that she is so swift that none can overtake or escape her; and that she will strike all the believers on the face with the rod of Moses, thus marking them with the word *Mûmen* (believer), and mark the unbelievers on the face with the word *Câfer* (infidel), so that every person may be known for what he really is. This beast is also to demonstrate the vanity of all religions except Islam, and is to speak Arabic. This is the Mohammedan Beast of Revelations.

The third sign is a war with the Greeks and the capture of Constantinople by seventy thousand Jews, when the walls of that city shall fall down while they exclaim: "There is no god but Allah; Allah is most great!" While they are dividing the spoil they will hear of the appearance of Antichrist, whereupon they shall leave all and return back.

The fourth sign is the coming of Antichrist, called *Al Masîh al Dajjâl*, "the false or lying Christ," and simply *Al Dajjál.* This being is to have only one eye, and to be marked on the forehead with the letters C. F. R., meaning *Cáfer,* or infidel. The Moslems say that the Jews call this beast Messiah Ben David and pretend that he is to come in the last days and to be lord of both land and sea, and that he will restore the kingdom to them. This beast is to ride an ass, to be followed by seventy thousand Jews of Ispahan, and to remain on earth forty days, one of which will be a year in length, another a month, another a week, and the rest ordinary days. This monster will devastate every place but Mecca and Medina, which he will not enter, as those two cities will be guarded by angels; but he will be finally killed by Jesus, who will encounter him at the gate of Lud. Mohammed is said to have foretold of about thirty Antichrists, one of which was of greater note than the others.

The fifth sign will be the descent of Jesus on earth, who is to appear near the white tower of Damascus, when the people have returned from the capture of Constantinople. He is to embrace the Mohammedan religion, marry a wife, beget children, kill Antichrist, and finally die after a residence of twenty-four or forty years upon earth. The Moslems say that under Jesus there will be great security and plenty in the world; that all hatred and malice will cease; when lions and camels, bears and sheep, shall live in peace, and a child shall play with serpents unhurt.

The sixth sign shall be a war with the Jews, of whom the Mohammedans shall make a religious slaughter, so that the very trees and stones shall discover those who hide themselves, except the tree called *Gharkad,* the tree of the Jews.

The seventh sign is the eruption of Gog and Magog, or Yájúj and Májúj. After passing the Lake of Tiberias, which the vanguard of their vast army will drink dry, these barbarians will come to Jerusalem and there greatly distress Jesus and his companions; until at his request Allah will destroy them and fill the earth with their carcasses, which some time afterward Allah will send birds to carry away, at the prayers of Jesus and his followers. Their bows, arrows and quivers the Moslems will burn for seven years together; and finally Allah will send a rain to cleanse the earth and make it fertile.

The eighth sign is a smoke which shall fill the entire earth. The ninth sign is an eclipse of the moon. Mohammed is reported as having said that there would be three eclipses before the last hour—one in the east, another in the west, and the third in Arabia. The tenth sign is the apostasy of the Arabs from Islam and their return to idolatry; after the death of all in whose heart there was faith equal to a grain of mustard-seed, none but the very worst of men being left alive. They say that Allah will send a cold odoriferous wind, blowing from Syria Damascena, which shall sweep away the souls of all the faithful and the Koran itself, so that men will remain in the grossest ignorance for a hundred years.

The eleventh sign will be the discovery of a vast heap of gold and silver by the retreating of the Euphrates, which will cause many to be destroyed. The twelfth sign will be the demolition of the Kaaba, or temple of Mecca, by the Ethiopians. The thirteenth sign will be speaking of beasts and inanimate things. The fourteenth sign will be the breaking out of fire in the province of Hedjaz, or in Yemen. The fifteenth sign will be the appearance of a man of the descendants of Kahtân, who shall drive men before him with his staff.

The sixteenth sign will be the coming of the Mahdi, or director; concerning whom Mohammed prophesied that the world should not have an end until one of his own family should govern the Arabs, whose name should be the same as his own, and whose father's name should likewise be the same as his father's name, and who should fill the world with righteousness. The sect of the Shyites believe this person to be now alive, and concealed in some secret place, until the time of his manifestation; as they suppose that he is the last of the twelve Imâms, named Mohammed Abu 'Ikasem, as their prophet was, and the son of Hassan al Askeri, the eleventh of that succession. He was born at Sermanrai in the 255th year of the Hegira. The seventeenth sign will be a wind which shall sweep away the souls of all who have but a grain of faith in their hearts.

After the presiding signs before the Resurrection, the immediate sign of the presence of that great event will be the first blast of the trumpet, which they believe will be sounded three times. The first is called the *blast of consternation*, at the hearing of which all creatures in heaven and earth shall be struck with terror, except those whom Allah shall please to exempt therefrom. This first blast shall shake the earth and level all buildings and even the very mountains, melt the heavens and darken the sun; while the stars shall fall, on the death of the angels, who hold them suspended between heaven and earth. The sea shall be dried up, or turned into flames; and the sun, moon and stars shall be thrown into it. Women who give suck shall forsake their infants, and even the she-camels which have gone ten months with young shall be utterly neglected. All kinds of animals will run together into one place, in terror at the sound of the trumpet and the sudden shock of nature.

The second blast will be the *blast of examination*, when all creatures, both in heaven and earth, shall die or be annihilated, except those which Allah shall please to exempt from the common fate; and this shall occur in the twinkling of an eye, or in an instant; only Allah surviving, with heaven and hell, and the inhabitants of those two places, and the throne of glory. Azriel, the angel of death, will be the last to die.

Forty years later will occur the *blast of the Resurrection*, which shall be sounded the third time by the archangel Israfil, who, along with Gabriel and Michael, will be previously restored to life. At Allah's command, Israfil shall call together all the dry and rotten bones, and other dispersed parts of the bodies, and the very hairs, to judgment. After setting the trumpet to his mouth by the Divine order, and calling together all the souls from all quarters, he will throw them into his trumpet, from which, on his giving the last sound at the command of Allah, they will fly forth like bees and fill the entire space between heaven and earth; after which they will repair to their respective bodies, which the opening earth will permit to rise. Mohammed himself will be the first to rise. The earth will be prepared for this birth by the rain which is to fall constantly for forty years, and which will resemble the seed of a man and be supplied from the water under the throne of Allah, called *living water*, by the efficacy and virtue of which the dead bodies shall spring forth from their graves, as corn sprouts forth by common rain, until they become perfect; after which breath will be breathed into them, and they will sleep in their sepulchers until they are raised to life at the last trump.

In one place the Koran says that the Judgment Day will last one thousand years, and in another place fifty thousand years. Mohammedan commentators use several devices to reconcile this apparent contradiction. Those who are destined to partake of eternal happiness will arise from the dead in honor and security; and those who are doomed to misery, in disgrace and under dismal apprehensions. Mankind will be raised perfect in all their parts and members, and in the same state in which they were born, barefooted, naked and uncircumcised. When Mohammed was telling this circumstance to his wife Ayesha, she, fearing that the rules of modesty might thereby be violated, objected that it would be indecent for men and women to look upon one another in that condition. But he answered her that the serious and weighty character of the business of that day would not allow them to make use of that liberty.

Others assert that Mohammed declared that the dead should arise dressed in the same clothes in which they died.

Mohammed also declared that the believers whose good works are few shall go on foot at the last day. Those who are in great honor with Allah and more acceptable to

Him shall ride on white-winged camels with saddles of gold. The infidels, whom Allah will cause to make their appearance, shall crawl with their faces on the earth, blind, deaf and dumb.

Mohammed also said that Allah shall fix certain distinguishing marks on ten classes of wicked men. The professors of Zendicism will appear in the form of apes. Those who have been greedy of filthy lucre, and who have enriched themselves by public oppression, will appear in the form of swine. The usurers will be brought with their heads reversed and their feet distorted. The unjust judges will wander about blind. Those who glory in their own works will be blind, deaf and dumb, understanding nothing. The learned men and doctors, whose actions contradict their sayings, will gnaw their tongues, which will hang down upon their breasts, while corrupted blood flows from their mouths like spittle, so that everybody shall detest them. Those who have injured their neighbors will have their hands and feet cut off. The false accusers and informers will be fixed to the trunks of palm-trees or stakes of wood. Those who have indulged their passions and voluptuous appetites, but refused Allah such part of their wealth as was due to him, will smell worse than a corrupted corpse. The proud, the vainglorious and the arrogant will be clothed in garments daubed with pitch.

The Mohammedans believe that the genii and irrational animals, as well as mankind, shall be judged on the last day; when the unhorned cattle shall take vengeance on the horned, until entire satisfaction shall be given to the injured. When mankind are assembled together to be judged, the angels will keep them in their ranks and order while they attend for that purpose. This attendance some say shall last forty years, others seventy, others three hundred, and others as high as fifty thousand years; each vouching Mohammed's authority.

During this space they will stand looking up to heaven and suffer grievous torments, both the just and the unjust, though with great difference. The limbs of the just shall shine gloriously, and their sufferings shall be comparatively light and last only long enough to say the appointed prayers; but the unjust will have their faces obscured with blackness and disfigured with all the marks of sorrow and deformity. Their pain will be heightened by a sweat which will stop their mouths, and in which they will be immersed in different degrees according to their demerits, some to the ankles only, some to the knees, some to the middle, some to the mouth, and others to the ears.

This sweat will be caused by the vast multitude crowding together and trampling on one another's feet, and also by the near and unusual approach of the sun, which will be as near as a mile. Their skulls will boil like a pot, and they will all be bathed in sweat. The good will be protected by the shade of Allah's throne; but the wicked will be so miserably tormented with this sweat, and also with hunger and thirst, and a stifling air, that they will cry out: "Lord, deliver us from this anguish, though thou send us into hell-fire."

When those who have risen shall have waited the limited time, Allah will appear to judge mankind; Mohammed undertaking the office of intercessor, after it shall have been declined by Adam, Noah, Abraham and Jesus, who shall beg deliverance only for their own souls. On this solemn occasion Allah will come in the clouds, surrounded by angels, and will produce the books wherein the actions of every human being are recorded by their guardian angels, and will command the prophets to bear witness against those to whom they have been respectively sent.

Then every person will be examined concerning all his words and actions, uttered and done by him in this life, in order to oblige every person to make public confession and acknowledgment of Allah's justice. They shall give an account of how they spent their time, how they acquired and employed their wealth, wherein they exercised their bodies, and what use they made of their learning. But Mohammed affirmed that at least seventy thousand Moslems should be permitted to enter Paradise without any previous examination.

Each person shall answer the foregoing questions, and defend himself as best he can, seeking to excuse himself by throwing the blame of his evil deeds on others, so that a dispute shall arise even between the soul and the body, as to which of them their guilt ought to be ascribed. The soul will say: "O Lord, my body I received from thee; for thou createdst me without a hand to lay hold with, a foot to walk with, an eye to see with, or an understanding to apprehend with, till I came and entered into this body; therefore, punish it eternally, but deliver me." The body will make this apology: "O Lord, thou createdst me like a stock of wood, having neither hand that I could lay hold with, nor foot that I could walk with, till this soul, like a ray of light, entered into me, and my tongue began to speak, my eye to see, and my foot to walk; therefore, punish it eternally, but deliver me."

Allah will then propound to both soul and body the following parable of the blind man and the lame man. A certain king, having a pleasant garden, in which were ripe fruits, sent two persons to keep it, one of whom was blind and the other lame, the blind being unable to see the fruit, and the lame to gather it. The lame man, however, seeing the fruit, persuaded the blind man to take him upon his shoulders; and by that means he easily gathered the fruit, which they divided between them. The lord of the garden, coming some time after, and inquiring after his fruit, each began to excuse himself. The blind man said he had no eyes to see with, and the lame man that he had no feet to approach the trees. But the king, ordering the lame man to be set on the blind, passed sentence on and punished them both. And in the same manner will Allah deal with the body and the soul. As these apologies will not avail on that day, so will it also be in vain for any one to deny his evil actions, since men and angels and his own members, nay, the very earth itself, will be ready to bear witness against him.

The trial and judgment will only last as long as the milking of an ewe, or the space of time between the two milkings of a she-camel. Some explain those words so frequently used in the Koran, "Allah will be swift in taking an account," to mean that He will judge all creatures in the space of half a day; and others say that it will be done in the twinkling of an eye. Each person will have the book wherein all the actions of his life are written delivered to him; which books the righteous will receive in their right hand and read with entire satisfaction; but the wicked will be obliged to take them against their wills in their left hand, which will be bound behind their backs, their right hand being tied up to their necks.

The Moslem will be judged by his actions. The archangel Gabriel holds a balance, whose scales are large enough to hold both heaven and earth; one of the scales being suspended over heaven, and the other over hell. The books wherein one's good deeds are written will be thrown into one of the scales, and the books in which are recorded his evil actions will be cast into the other scale. According as the scales incline, sentence will be given; and those whose good works shall weigh the heavier will be sent to heaven, while those whose evil works preponderate will go to hell.

After this examination, every creature will take vengeance one of another, or have satisfaction rendered them for the injuries which they have suffered. The angels will then take a part of the good works of him who offered the injury and give them to him who suffered it. The angels will then say; "Lord, we have given to every one his due; and there remaineth of this person's good works so much as equaleth the weight of an ant." Allah will of his mercy cause it to be doubled unto him that he may be admitted into Paradise; but if his good works be exhausted and there remain only his evil deeds, and there be any who have not yet received satisfaction from him, Allah will order that an equal weight of their sins be added to his, that he be punished instead.

After the brutes shall have also taken vengeance of one another, Allah will order them to be changed into dust; whereupon the wicked men, who will be reserved for a more grievous punishment, shall exclaim: "Would to God that we were dust also." Some Moslems believe that those of the genii who are true believers will undergo the same fate as the irrational animals, and will be rewarded only by being converted into dust; but others assign the genii a place near the confines of Paradise, where they will enjoy sufficient felicity, though they be excluded from that delightful abode. All Moslems agree that the unbelieving genii will be doomed to eternal punishment, and be cast into hell with the infidels of the human race. The devil and his companions are classed with unbelieving genii.

After the trials and judgment, those who go to heaven, or Paradise, will take the right-hand way, and those who are destined to hell-fire will take the left; but both must pass the bridge of *Al Sirât*, which is laid over the midst of hell, and is finer than a hair and sharper than the edge of a sword, while being also beset with briers and hooked thorns. The righteous shall pass over this bridge with wonderful ease and swiftness, like lightning or the wind, Mohammed leading the way; but, on account of the extinction of the light, the wicked soon become entangled among the thorns of this extremely narrow bridge, and thus soon miss their way and tumble down headlong into hell, which is gaping beneath them. The bridge of Al Sirât in Islam seems to be the same as the bridge of Chinevat in the Zoroastrian religion, and the bridge of hell mentioned by the Jews.

The seven apartments of hell are seven stories, one below another, designed for as many different classes of the damned. The first or highest story, called *Jehennam*, is for the wicked Moslems, who will be released after suffering a temporary punishment, and admitted into Paradise. The second story, called *Ladhâ*, is for the Jews; the third, called *Al Hotama*, for the Christians; the fourth, called *Al Sâîr*, for the Sabeans; the fifth, called *Sakar*, for the Magians; the sixth, called *Al Jahîm*, for the idolators. The seventh or lowest story, and the worst of all, is called *Al Hâwiyat*, and is for the hypocrites of all religions. A guard of nineteen angels will be set over each of these seven stories or apartments; and to these angels the damned will confess the just judgment of Allah, and beg them to intercede with Him for some alleviation of their pain, or that they may be delivered by being annihilated.

The Koran gives an appalling description of hell and the torments of the damned. This place is represented as a receptacle full of smoke and darkness, dragged forward with roaring noise and fury by seventy thousand angels, through the opposite extremes of heat and cold; while the wretched victims of the Divine wrath are also tormented by the hissing of numerous reptiles and the scourges of hideous demons, whose recreation consists in the cruelty and pain which they inflict upon the unhappy wretches who have been consigned to that miserable abode. Concerning the fate of the unbelievers—as the Moslems designate all who reject Islam—the Koran repeatedly declares, "they must remain therein forever." The punishments vary according to the degrees of guilt; those who are punished most lightly of all being shod with shoes of fire, the heat of which will cause their skulls to boil like a cauldron.

Only the unbelievers, or those who reject the Koran, shall thus be consigned to eternal damnation. Wicked Moslems, or those who accept Islam, but whose evil actions overbalance their good deeds, shall expiate their sins during different periods of torment. Some say that these wicked Mussulmans shall be released after they shall have been scorched and their skins burned black, and shall afterwards be admitted into Paradise; and when the inhabitants of that delightful place shall contemptuously call them infernals, Allah will answer their prayers by taking from them that opprobrious title.

Others believe that while these wicked Moslems remain in hell they shall be de-

ISLAM'S RISE AND THE SARACEN EMPIRE.

prived of life, or be cast into a profound sleep, so that they shall be less sensible of their torments; and that they shall afterwards be received into Paradise, and there revive on their being washed with the water of life; though some suppose they will be restored to life before they come forth from their place of punishment, so that they may have little taste of their pains when they bid adieu to them.

These wicked Mohammedans shall be kept in punishment not less than nine hundred years, nor more than seven thousand. They shall be distinguished by the marks of prostration on those parts of their bodies with which they used to touch the ground in prayer, and over which the fire will therefore be powerless. They will be relieved by the mercy of Allah, at the intercession of Mohammed and the blessed. Thereupon those who have been dead will be restored to life, as has been related; and those whose bodies shall have contracted any sootiness or filth from the flames and smoke of hell will be immersed in one of the rivers of Paradise, called the *river of life*, which will wash them whiter than pearls.

The wall or partition separating Paradise from hell is called *Al Orf*, or *Al Aráf*. Some Mohammedan writers say that Al Aráf is a sort of limbo for the patriarchs and prophets, or for the martyrs and those who have had the greatest reputation for sanctity; among whom will also be angels in the form of men. Other Moslem writers say that such will be placed on Al Aráf whose good and evil works exactly counterpoise each other, and therefore deserve neither reward nor punishment; and these will be admitted into Paradise on the last day, after they shall have performed an act of adoration, which will be attributed to them as a merit, and will make their good works overbalance their bad acts. Other Mussulman writers suppose that Al Aráf will be a place for those who have gone to war without their parents' permission, and therein suffered martyrdom; being excluded from Paradise for their disobedience, and escaping hell because they were martyrs to Islam. This partition wall is so narrow that those who stand thereon shall converse with the inhabitants of both Paradise and hell, while the blessed and the damned themselves will likewise be able to talk to one another.

All Moslems, whatever their sins, are eventually to become dwellers of Paradise. That delightful abode is all that the Moslem imagination can portray of sensual felicity. Mohammed promised to the faithful an unlimited indulgence of the corporeal propensities, and addressed his allurements to these carnal ideas, painted in the gayest colors that the Oriental fancy could invent; as the untutored Arab could not have comprehended the nature of abstract enjoyment; or understand the elements of happiness in pure and spiritual pleasures.

After the righteous have passed the sharp bridge of Al Sirât, and before they enter Paradise, they will be refreshed by drinking at Mohammed's pond. This is described to be an exact square, of a month's journey in compass. Its water is supplied by two pipes from *Al Cawthar*, one of the rivers of Paradise, and is whiter than milk or silver and more odoriferous than musk, with as many cups set around it as there are stars in the firmament. Whoever drinks of this water thirsts no more forever. This is the first taste which the blessed will have of their future and now near-approaching felicity.

The Môtazalites and some other Mohammedan sects assert that Paradise is to be created hereafter, but the orthodox maintain that it was created before the world. These latter describe it as situated above the seven heavens, or in the seventh heaven, and next under Allah's throne. The earth of this delightful abode is of the finest wheat flour, or of the purest musk, or of saffron. Its stones are pearls and jacinths. The walls of its buildings are enriched with gold and silver. The trunks of its trees are of gold; and the most remarkable is the tree called *Tûba*, or the *tree of happiness*. This tree stands in Mohammed's palace, but a branch of it will reach to every true believer's house, and it will be laden with pomegranates, grapes, dates and other fruits of wonderful size and of tastes unknown to mortals. If a man desire to eat of any particular kind of fruit, it will be immediately presented to him; or if he choose flesh, birds ready dressed will be set before him in accordance with his desire. The boughs of the tree Tûba will bend down spontaneously to the hand of the person who would gather of its fruits; and will supply the blessed with silken garments, as well as food, and also with beasts to ride on, ready saddled and bridled, and adorned with rich trappings, which will burst forth from its fruits. This tree is so large that a person mounted on the fleetest horse could not gallop from one end of its shade to the other in a century.

The Koran mentions the rivers of Paradise as the chief ornament of that delightful abode. Some of these rivers are described as flowing with water, some with milk, some with wine, and others with honey; all taking their rise from the root of the tree Tûba. Two of these rivers are named *Al Cawthar* and the *River of Life*. This delightful abode is also watered by a vast number of lesser springs and fountains, the pebbles of which are rubies and emeralds, the earth of which is of camphor, the beds of which are of musk, and the sides of which are of saffron. The most remarkable of these springs and fountains are Salsabîl and Tasnîm.

But all these glories just mentioned will be eclipsed by the resplendent and ravishing girls of Paradise, called *Hûr al oyûn*, because of their large black eyes. These blooming damsels are created of pure musk, and are free from all the natural impurities, defects and inconveniences incident to the female sex. They are of the strictest modesty, and are secluded from public view in pavilions of hollow pearls, so large that one of them will be no less than four parasangs, or, as some say, sixty miles long, and as many broad.

The Mohammedans call this happy mansion *Al Jannat*, "The Garden." Sometimes they call it *Jannat al Ferdaws*, "the Garden of Paradise;" *Jannat Aden*, "the Garden of Eden;" *Jannat al Mâwa*, "the Garden of Abode;" *Jannat al Naim*, "the Garden of Pleasure;" etc. By these several appellations some understand so many different gardens, or at least so many places of different degrees of felicity. There are at least a hundred such gardens, the very meanest of which will afford its inhabitants so many pleasures and delights that one would suppose they must be overwhelmed by them, had not Mohammed taught that Allah will give to every one the abilities of a hundred men, in order to qualify the blessed for a full enjoyment thereof.

Besides Mohammed's pond, there are two fountains springing from a certain tree near the gate of Paradise. The blessed will also drink of one of these, in order to cleanse their bodies and carry off all excrementitious dregs, and they will wash themselves in the other. At the gate each person will be met and welcomed by the beautiful youth appointed to serve and wait upon him, one of them running ahead, to bring the tidings of his arrival to the wives destined for him. Each person is also met at the gate by two angels, carrying the presents which Allah sent him. One of these angels will invest the new comer with a garment of Paradise, and the other will put a ring on each of his fingers, bearing inscriptions alluding to his happy condition.

There are eight gates of Paradise. Mohammed declared that no person's good works will gain him admittance to Paradise, and that even he himself shall be saved only by the mercy of Allah, and not by his merits. But the Koran constantly teaches that the felicity of each person will be proportioned to his deserts, and that there will be different degrees of happiness. The most eminent degree is reserved for the prophets, the second for the doctors and teachers of Allah's worship, the third for the martyrs, and the lowest for the remainder of the righteous, according to their several merits. Mohammed asserted that the poor will enter Paradise five centuries before the rich. He also declared that when he took a view of Paradise he saw that most of its inhabitants were the poor, and that when he looked down in-

ISLAM'S RISE AND THE SARACEN EMPIRE.   1381

In hell most of its wretched inmates were women.

When the blessed have entered Paradise the whole earth will then be as one loaf of bread, which Allah will reach to them with his hand, holding it like a cake. For meat they will have the ox Balâm and the fish Nûn, the lobes of whose livers will suffice for the seventy thousand Moslems who shall be admitted to Paradise without any examination.

From this feast every one will be dismissed to the mansion designed for him, where he will enjoy a degree of felicity proportioned to his merits, but vastly exceeding comprehension or expectation. The very humblest Moslem in Paradise will have eighty thousand servants; seventy-two blooming damsels of immortal youth and dazzling beauty, breathing musk, for wives, in addition to the wives he had in this world; and a vast tent of pearls, jacinths and emeralds. He will also be waited upon by three hundred attendants while he eats, will be served in golden dishes, three hundred of which shall be set before him at once, each containing a different kind of food, the last morsel of which will be as grateful as the first. He will also be supplied with three hundred kinds of liquor in golden vessels, and with all the wine he desires. Though forbidden in this life, wine will be freely allowed to be drunk in the next, as the wine of Paradise will not intoxicate. The flavor of this wine is delicious beyond description, as the water of Tasnîm and the other fountains used to dilute it is wonderfully sweet and fragrant.

When an impudent Jew, on one occasion, remarked to Mohammed that so much eating and drinking would necessarily require proper evacuations, the Prophet replied that the inhabitants of Paradise will not need to ease themselves, as all superfluities will be discharged and carried off by perspiration, or a sweat as odoriferous as musk, after which their appetite shall return afresh.

The Koran also promises the righteous in the next life garments and furniture of the most indescribable magnificence. They are to be attired in the richest silks and brocades, mainly of green, which will burst forth from the fruits of Paradise, and will also be supplied by the leaves of the tree Tûba. They will be adorned with bracelets of gold and silver, and with crowns set with pearls of unparalleled brilliancy. They will have silken carpets, enormous litters, couches, pillows, and other elegant furniture embroidered with gold and precious stones.

The happy dwellers of Paradise will enjoy a perpetual youth. No matter at what age a Moslem may die, he will be in his prime and vigor in the next world, or about thirty years of age, which age he will never exceed. The same will be the case of the damned, in order that they may the more severely feel their torments. Upon entering Paradise the Moslems will be of the same stature with Adam, who is represented as being sixty cubits high. If they desire children their wives will conceive, otherwise not; and these children shall immediately attain to thirty years of age and to the stature of sixty cubits. Mohammed declared: "If any of the faithful in Paradise be desirous of issue, it shall be conceived, born, and grown up within the space of an hour." In like manner if any one shall have a taste for agricultural pursuits, whatever he shall sow will spring up and come to maturity in a moment.

The blessed inhabitants of Paradise will likewise be entertained with the delightful songs of the archangel Israfil, who has the most melodious voice of all Allah's creatures. They will also be charmed with the musical voices of the lovely daughters of Paradise. Even the trees themselves will celebrate the Divine praises with a harmony surpassing all that mortals have ever heard. To this will be joined the sound of the bells hanging on the trees, which will be put in motion by the wind proceeding from Allah's throne, so often as the blessed desire music. The very clashing of the golden-bodied trees, whose fruits are pearls and emeralds, will exceed human imagination; thus adding to the enjoyments of the pleasures of the sense of hearing.

Such are the delights of all the happy

dwellers of Paradise, even those of the humblest. Those who shall obtain a higher degree of felicity will enjoy "such things as eye hath not seen, nor hath ear heard, nor hath it entered into the heart of man to conceive." Mohammed said that the humblest of the inhabitants of Paradise will see his gardens, wives, servants, furniture, and other possessions occupy the space of a thousand years' journey; but that he who will behold the face of Allah morning and evening will be in the highest favor with him. Al Ghazâli believes that this favor is that additional or superabundant reward which the Koran says will give such exquisite delight that all other pleasures of Paradise will be forgotten and lightly esteemed in comparison therewith. The same Mohammedan author says that every other enjoyment is equally tasted by the very brute beast who is turned loose into luxuriant pasture. This fully refutes the assertions of those who say that the Mohammedans admit of no spiritual pleasure in the next life, but make the happiness of the blessed to consist only in corporeal enjoyments.

From the whole tenor of the Koran it is evident that what Mohammed told his followers of Paradise is to be taken literally, and not metaphorically; and the general and orthodox doctrine is that the whole is to be strictly believed in the obvious and literal acceptation. When the Mohammedans wish to bind the Christians in the strongest and most sacred manner, they make them swear that if they violate their engagement they will affirm that there will be corporeal pleasures and black-eyed girls in the next world.

The Koran also affirms that Allah will make no distinction of sexes in the reward or punishment, in the future life, of good or evil conduct in this world. Women who are wicked and who reject Islam will in the next life suffer the torments of the damned in hell; while those who are righteous and believe the Koran will enjoy the felicities of heaven, but nothing is said about husbands or paramours being provided for them. The general notion is that good women will not be admitted into the same abode in Paradise as the men, but will be assigned a separate place of happiness where they will enjoy all sorts of delights. It is, however, believed that a man in Paradise will enjoy the company of those women who were his wives in this world, or such of them as he shall desire. It is said that an old woman, on one occasion, desired Mohammed to intercede with Allah that she might be admitted into Paradise; but he told her that no old women would enter that happy abode. This answer set the poor old woman crying, whereupon Mohammed explained himself by saying that Allah would then make her young again.

The Koran lays great stress on Allah's absolute decree and predestination of good and evil. The orthodox Mohammedan doctrine is, that whatever occurs in this world, whether good or bad, proceeds wholly from the Divine will, and is irrevocably fixed and recorded from all eternity in the preserved table; Allah having secretly predetermined, in the most minute particulars, the adverse and prosperous fortune of every human creature in the world, and also his faith or infidelity, his obedience or disobedience, and therefore his eternal happiness or misery after death; which fate or predestinaton it is impossible to avoid by any foresight or wisdom.

Mohammed makes great use of this doctrine in the Koran for the advancement of his designs; encouraging his followers to fight with courage and desperation for the propagation of Islam, by representing to them that all their caution could not avert their inevitable fate or prolong their lives for a moment; and deterring them from rejecting him as an impostor, by picturing to them the danger they would thereby incur, by the just judgment of Allah, of being abandoned to seduction, hardness of heart, and a reprobate mind, as a punishment for their obstinacy.

Many Mohammedan divines have regarded this doctrine of absolute election and reprobation as derogatory to the goodness and justice of Allah, and to make Him the author of evil. These divines have therefore invented several subtle distinctions and raised several disputes to explicate or soften this doctrine; and different Mohammedan sects have arisen, according to their several methods of explaining this controverted point, some of these sects going to the extreme of holding the direct contrary opinion of absolute free agency in man.

The Koran lays particular stress upon Mohammed's declaration already alluded to: "The sword is the key of heaven and of hell. A drop of blood shed in the cause of Allah, a night spent in arms, is of more avail than two months of fasting and prayer. Whoever dies in battle his sins are forgiven." This promise, with the assurance that the appointed time of every man's death is decreed by Fate, made the Moslems boldy face death in battle, and accounts largely for that religious fanaticism which carried the dominion of Islam over so large a portion of Asia and Africa in so short a time.

A scene of tumult and confusion followed Mohammed's death. His neglect to name his immediate successor was a political error that proved fatal to the unity and stability of his empire. His death was the signal for immediate rivalry for power between the two leading parties among his followers. On the day of his burial they were assembled to deliberate on the choice of a new sovereign. A schism seemed inevitable. Swords were drawn, and the hasty structure of Mohammedan greatness appeared tottering to its fall, when the tumult was stilled by the timely magnanimity of Omar, who renounced his own pretensions in favor of Mohammed's father-in-law, the companion of his flight; and ABU BEKR was accordingly proclaimed *Khalif*, or "Commander of the Faithful"—a title subsequently assumed by his successors.

Abu Bekr was unable to lead the armies of the faithful, because of his advanced age. He appointed Khaled, surnamed the *Sword of God*, his general, and devoted himself to prayer, penitence, and the administration of justice. Abu Bekr was energetic, brave, chaste and temperate, and proved himself quite equal to the difficulties of the situation. Within a few months after his accession, his troops struck such a series of blows against the rebellion which showed itself against his authority, that very soon the entire Arab nation, except the tribe of Gassan, made their submission to his sway.

Moseilama, the most important of the rivals who contended against Abu Bekr, had a large following, and fought a pitched battle with Abu Bekr's army of forty thousand men. Moseilama repulsed Abu Bekr's army at the first encounter, the latter losing twelve hundred warriors; but Moseilama was defeated and slain in the second engagement, and Khaled, "the Sword of God," the commander of Abu Bekr's army, conveyed to Medina the tidings of his own victory and the spoils of the defeated foe. Soon afterward the other rebellious Arab tribes acknowledged Abu Bekr's authority, and the first Khalif was at liberty to extend the dominion of Islam into foreign lands.

The Mussulmans were still inspired by the same religious enthusiasm. They believed that their swords, their wealth and their power were destined to no other object than that of extending the worship of the One True God, the All-knowing, All-seeing and All-powerful. It mattered not what part each man took, provided he labored with all his efforts to this end.

Thus far the victories, the doctrine and the revolution wrought by Mohammed had not extended beyond the frontiers of Arabia. Changes of opinion in an illiterate nation, of which the language had never been studied by its neighbors, did not appear of adequate importance to enlist the attention of mankind. The revolutions of the little republics of Western Arabia had never produced any effects in other lands; and the Arab union under one dominion, thus suddenly accomplished by a new religious doctrine, appeared likely to be of brief duration.

The rise of Islam attracted no attention at Constantinople, at Antioch or at Alexandria. Yet the first twelve years following Mohammed's death were occupied with Mussulman conquests which astound the imagination.

These fanatical conquerors were entirely ignorant of geography, and of the interests, strength, policy and languages of the nations which they attacked. They had no regular plans of campaign, no projects to strengthen themselves by alliances, or to establish secret correspondence in the countries which they were about to invade. The instructions given by the Khalifs to the commanders of their armies were simple and general. Neither Mohammed nor his successors made any change in the rude armor and irregular manner of fighting to which the Bedouins of the Arabian desert were accustomed.

The Mussulman soldiers were half naked. Their infantry were armed only with bows and arrows. Their cavalry carried lances and cimeters. Their horses were indefatigable, and were unequaled for their docility and spirit. But they did not maneuver in large or regular masses. They were ignorant of those charges of modern cavalry which bear down battalions by their irresistible weight. Moslem warriors advanced single-handed in front of the army to signalize themselves by acts of personal prowess, and, after several strokes of their flashing cimeters, escaped from their foes by the swiftness of their steeds. Battles were protracted skirmishes, in which the hostile troops did not engage rank to rank. The conflict frequently continued several days; and only after their enemies, exhausted by unusual fatigue, were routed, did the Arabs become terrible in pursuit.

The Asiatic provinces of the Eastern Roman Empire and the dominions of the New Persian Empire of the Sassanidæ, alternately devastated by war, had undergone a great change in the seventh century, both in their political condition and in the character of the people. The fortresses were dismantled. Confidence in the defenses of the frontiers was at an end. The administration was disorganized, and obedience to the civil power was imperfect and irregular. The provincials had commenced an active participation in the affairs of their country, and had become soldiers, though not very efficient ones.

At this time we first find mention of military bodies proportioned to the extent of the Eastern Roman Empire—armies of a hundred thousand men, though their valor and discipline were such as to lead us to believe that they consisted entirely of militia. The names of the officers incidentally mentioned in history are Syrian, not Greek. The Syrian cities seem to have had an independent existence, and their own magistrates directed their affairs, while the interests of the Empire were forgotten in the interests of the provinces. The Moslems did not attack the Syrians or the Persians by surprise; but before their invasion they gave their enemies a threefold choice—to embrace Islam, and thus share all the honors, rights and privileges of true believers; or to submit on condition of paying tribute; or to try the fortune of war.

In A. D. 633 the Khalif Abu Bekr sent expeditions into the Roman province of Syria, and into Irak, where Iyas, the Persian feudatory, the successor of Noman, son of Al Mondar, held his court at Hira, on the western branch of the Euphrates. The irresistible Khaled led two thousand Arabs across the Arabian desert to the branch stream, where he was aided by Al Mothanna, chief of the Beni Sheiban, who had been a subject of Iyas, but had revolted and placed himself under Abu Bekr's protection.

Khaled quickly conquered the kingdom of Hira, took in succession Banikiya, Barasuma and El Lis, descended the river to Hira, the capital, and there defeated the Persian cavalry under Asadsubeh and their Arab allies. As the city of Hira then was ungarrisoned, Iyas submitted to the victorious Khaled, and agreed to pay a tribute of two hundred and ninety thousand dirhems.

After his army had been increased by reinforcements to eighteen thousand men, Khaled marched southwards to reduce the entire region between the Arabian desert and the Eastern or real Euphrates. Obolla, the most important city of the southern region at that time, was situated on a canal or backwater derived from the Euphrates, near the modern Bassora. It was a great emporium for the Indian trade, and was known as the *limes Indorum*, or "frontier city towards India."

The Persian governor of Obolla was a certain Hormuz, or Hormisdas, who garrisoned the city with twenty thousand men. Khaled completely defeated Hormuz and killed him with his own hand. Obolla surrendered, and a vast booty fell into the possession of the victorious Saracens. After liberally rewarding his soldiers, Khaled sent a fifth of the spoils, with a captured elephant, to the Khalif Abu Bekr at Medina. The strange animal astonished the simple natives of Medina, who, in wonderment, inquired of one another: "Is this indeed one of Allah's works, or did human art make it?"

Khaled's conquests of Hira and Obolla were soon followed by other victories, which added the whole region between the Arabian desert and the Euphrates, from Hit to the Persian Gulf, to the Saracen dominion; and the conquered territory was placed under the authority of Mohammedan governors. Thus Persia was deprived of the protection hitherto afforded her by a vassal Arab kingdom on the west side of the Euphrates, and was brought into direct contact with the great Mohammedan empire along her entire western frontier. Thenceforth the New Persian Empire was exposed to open attack on that side for a distance of more than four hundred miles, with several rivers as the only barrier between her enemy and her capital. Soon after his conquest of Hira and Obolla, the renowned Khaled was suddenly recalled from the banks of the Euphrates to take the command of the Saracen forces in Syria.

In the meantime the Khalif Abu Bekr had resolved on an invasion of Syria, and a Saracen army under Abu Obeidah had already marched to invade that country. The spirit which animated the early Mussulmans is illustrated in the instructions given by the Khalif to Abu Obeidah. Said the Khalif: "Remember that you are always in the presence of Allah, always at the point of death, always in expectation of judgment, always in hope of Paradise. Avoid, then, injustice and oppression. Study to preserve the love and confidence of your troops. When you fight the battles of Allah, bear yourselves like men, and turn not your backs upon the enemy. Let your victories never be sullied by the blood of women or children. Destroy not the fruit-trees, neither burn the standing corn. Do no damage to the flocks and herds, nor kill any beasts but such as are necessary to your sustenance. Whatever treaty you make, be faithful to it, and let your deeds be according to your words. As you advance into the enemy's country, you will find some religious persons who live retired in monasteries, designing to serve God in that way. Let them alone, and neither hurt them nor destroy their houses. But you will find, also, another sort of men, who belong to the synagogue of Satan, and who have shaven crowns. Cleave their skulls. Give them no quarter till they either embrace our faith or pay tribute."

The two classes of Christian religionists here indicated were the monks and the secular clergy. The monks had obtained Mohammed's favor by some act of kindness which they had extended to him in his youth. So says an Arab tradition.

The Moslems regarded Jerusalem with as much veneration as did the Jews and Christians, and Abu Bekr felt that the capture of so holy a city would give immense prestige to the cause of Islam. In his celebrated directions to his generals he exhibits much knowledge of the country as well as great political wisdom. But these directions are yet more remarkable for their almost verbal coincidence with a passage in the Book of Revelations, which most commentators have considered a prophetic description of the Saracens.

The Syrians at first regarded the invasion as simply one of the usual incursions of the wandering Bedouin tribes of the Arabian desert, and they bestowed upon the Arabs the name of *Saraken*, or "marauders," which had been applied to a plundering horde on the Syro-Arabian frontier for many centuries. This is the origin of the word *Saracen*, a name which soon became a terror to the civilized world.

The Emperor Heraclíus was seriously alarmed at this formidable Arabian invasion of his dominions, and sent a large detachment to meet the enemy on the frontiers. This Byzantine army was defeated with great slaughter, but the imperialists gained a victory over a Moslem division under Abu Obeidah at Gaza. The Khalif Abu Bekr

SARACEN ARMOR.

invested Amru with the chief command of the invading expedition, but assigned Abu Obeidah's division to Khaled, who attacked Bosrah, one of the frontier towns of Syria on the Arabian border.

Romanus, the governor of Bosrah, counseled the inhabitants to surrender; and when they indignantly deprived him of his command, he treacherously admitted the Arabs into the fortress at night. The next day, in the presence of his astonished fellow-citizens, he publicly professed his belief in Mohammed's religion. This was the commencement of a series of desertions which dealt a fatal blow to the rapidly declining Eastern Roman Empire. All the discontented, all whose ambition or cupidity outran their advancement or their fortune, all who had any secret injury to avenge, were sure to be received with open arms by the Saracen conquerors and to share their fortunes. In provinces where the Roman commanders had never been able to levy a cohort, the Saracen army was received by fugitives with a readiness which clearly demonstrates that it is the government which destroys courage, and not the climate.

The capture of Bosrah by the Saracens was speedily followed by an attack on Damascus, which was still one of the most flourishing of Syrian cities. This aroused the attention of the Emperor Heraclíus, who led an army of seventy thousand men for the relief of the beleagured city. The Christians were defeated in the great battle of Aiznadin, in the South of Palestine, July 30, A. D. 634; in which they lost fifty thousand men. A few weeks later the Christian arms sustained another crushing defeat from the Saracens under Khaled, on the banks of the Yermûk, near the Lake of Tiberias, in the North of Palestine, August 22, A. D. 634—a battle in which seventy thousand Christians laid down their lives.

These two decisive battles sealed the fate of Syria, which was thus lost to the dominion of the Eastern Roman Emperor; and the death-blow was struck to the Roman power in Asia. It was said that Mohammed, after viewing the lovely and fertile plains in which Damascus is located, from one of the neighboring heights, proclaimed it to be the earthly paradise designed for the inheritance of true believers. The fiery Khaled related this tradition to his enthusiastic soldiers as he led them to attack the walls of this renowned ancient city, thus exciting their ardor for the siege to an insane fury.

The defeat of the Roman forces in the

ISLAM'S RISE AND THE SARACEN EMPIRE.

great battles of Aiznadin and Yermouk led to the fall of Damascus, one side of which was stormed by Khaled just as the other side capitulated to Abu Obeidah. A warm dispute arose between the two victorious Saracen generals as to the claim of the citizens to the benefit of the capitulation; but mercy finally prevailed, and the lives of the Damascenes were spared.

The Khalif Abu Bekr died on the very day of the capture of Damascus, August 3, A. D. 634. His memory was justly venerated, not only because he showed the Saracens the road to conquest beyond the confines of Arabia, but because he gave the Mohammedan religion its permanent form, by collecting the scattered passages of the Koran, and arranging them in the order in which they are found at the present day. Thus Abu Bekr published the first edition of the Koran.

Abu Bekr's character was remarkable for generosity and moderation. He did not reserve for himself any portion of the vast wealth acquired by his conquering armies, but distributed his share to his soldiers and to the poor. He was always easy of access, and no petitioner for mercy or claimant for justice went unheard from his presence. Both by precept and example, he labored to preserve the republican simplicity so remarkable in the early history of the Saracens. Though the partisans of Ali consider Abu Bekr a usurper, they still reverence his memory because of his moderation and virtue.

Abu Bekr had reigned only two years. Just before his death, he named Omar as his successor in the Khalifate. Omar said: "I do not want the place." Abu Bekr replied: "But the place wants you." After being saluted by the acclamations of the army, OMAR was made Khalif (A. D. 634). During the reigns of the two peaceful religious devotees—Abu Bekr and Omar—the Moslems achieved their most wonderful conquests.

Omar had given brilliant proofs of his valor during Mohammed's wars, but he regarded the dignity of Khalif as putting an end to his military career and demanding from him an exclusive attention to religious affairs. During a reign of ten years he was entirely absorbed in directing the affairs of the faithful, giving an example of moderation and justice, of abstinence and contempt for external ostentation. His food consisted of barley bread or dates; his drink was water; and the garment in which he preached to the people was patched in twelve places. A Persian satrap who came to do homage to Omar found the Khalif sleeping on the steps of the mosque at Medina.

Omar was informed of the capture of Damascus, soon after his accession to the Khalifate; but, instead of manifesting any gratitude, he gave way to the promptings of petty jealousy by transferring the command of the army under Khaled to Abu Obeidah. The fall of Damascus was followed by the capture of Emesa and also by that of Baalbec, or Heliopolis; after which the Saracens laid siege to Jerusalem.

The siege of the holy city of the Jews and Christians brought the rival religions of Islam and Christianity into especial hostility, as all Christendom had its attention directed to Jerusalem, regarding that sacred spot as the outward pledge of the truth and triumph of the religion of Jesus. During a siege of four months the religious enthusiasm of the besieged kept apace with the fanatical zeal of the assailants. The walls of the holy city of David and Christ were thickly planted with crosses, banners blessed by the priests, and miraculous images. But all this Christian zeal was unavailing. Sophronius, the Patriarch of Jerusalem, who directed the efforts of the besieged, was forced to capitulate. But he refused to open the gates of the Holy City until the Khalif Omar should come in person to receive so important a surrender and to guarantee the capitulation by his word.

Jerusalem was as sacred in the eyes of the Mohammedans as in those of the Jews and Christians. Omar started on his pious pilgrimage; the camel which he rode being also laden with his baggage, which consisted only of a sack of wheat, a wooden bowl, and a water bag, all of which were suspended from the saddle to supply his necessities during the journey. Besides this equipage, as another characteristic of the simplicity still prevalent among the Saracens, the Khalif's dress consisted of camel's hair, coarse and torn; while his only attendant and escort was a slave.

In this guise Omar reached the Moslem camp, in sight of Jerusalem, where he recited the public prayers and preached a sermon to his soldiers. He exclaimed: "Good and victorious Lord! grant us a victory unstained with blood." The Khalif's attendants pitched his tent of camel's hair cloth; after which he sat down upon the ground and signed the capitulation, by which he promised to leave the Christians of Jerusalem liberty of conscience in religious worship, the undisputed possession of the Church of the Holy Sepulcher, and absolute protection in person and property, on the payment of a moderate tribute, and entered the Holy City in triumph (A. D. 637.)

In his triumphal entry, the Khalif marched at the head of his victorious troops, in familar conversation by the way with the Christian Patriarch, Sophronius, whom he hoped to protect from the fanaticism of his followers by this exhibition of confidence. This was not the only evidence of good faith displayed by Omar. He refused to pray in any of the Christian churches, lest the Mussulmans should take advantage of the circumstance to convert them into Mohammedan mosques. The Khalif and the Christian Patriarch visited the Church of the Resurrection together; and at the hour of prayer Omar declined offering his adorations in the inside of this Christian sanctuary, preferring the steps of the porch, where he spread his mat and performed his devotions.

Omar caused the spot which was covered with the ruins of Solomon's Temple to be cleared of its rubbish and prepared for the erection of a magnificent Mohammedan mosque, which still bears this renowned Khalif's name; Omar himself setting the example of clearing it to his soldiers, by removing some of the rubbish in his robe.

At the end of ten days, the Khalif returned to Medina in the same simple and unostentatious manner, and there passed the remainder of his life in offering up his devotions at the Prophet's tomb.

In the year following the capture of Jerusalem (A. D. 638) the Saracens completed the conquest of Syria by making themselves masters of the great cities of Aleppo and Antioch. Aleppo, the ancient Berhœa, was valiantly defended for four months, but was finally carried by storm; and its governor, Gukinna, and several of his officials embraced the Moslem faith. Antioch and Cæsarea were taken more easily; and the Emperor Heraclius fled from Syria, his son following him to Constantinople after several unsuccessful efforts. The Byzantine army dispersed or deserted to the Moslems. Tyre and Tripoli were treacherously surrendered to the invaders. The remaining Syrian cities soon afterward opened their gates to the triumphant Saracens by capitulation, and Syria was forever lost to the Eastern Roman Empire. Thus in six years from their first invasion of Syria and Palestine, the Saracens had effected the subjugation of those Roman provinces, and secured their conquests by occupying the mountain-fortresses on the Cilician frontier.

The Saracens followed up the conquest of Syria by the subjugation of the New Persian Empire. The recall of Khaled from his victories in the Lower Euphrates region allowed Persia a breathing-spell. The Persians embraced the opportunity to arouse disaffection in the newly-acquired Saracen province of the Sawâd, west of the Euphrates. Rustam, the Persian commander, sent emissaries to the towns of the Sawâd, urging them to revolt and offering to aid such a rising with a Persian army. The Moslem situation was critical, but Rustam's troops were beaten in detail. Al Mothanna and Abu Obeidah defeated the Persian generals, Jaban, Narses and Jalenus, in three battles and drove their shattered armies back upon the Tigris; thus restoring the Saracen authority in the Sawâd.

The victorious Arabs even extended their

ENTRY OF THE KHALIF OMAR INTO JERUSALEM.

conquests across the Euphrates into Mesopotamia, into the very heart of the New Persian Empire. But here the Saracens suffered a severe reverse. When Rustam was informed of the defeat of his generals, he sent an army under Bahman-Dsul-hadjib, or "Bahman the beetle-browed," to watch the victorious Saracens. This Persian army encamped upon the Western Euphrates at Koss-en-natek, near the site of Kufa. To raise the courage of his soldiers, Rustam intrusted Bahman with the Persian sacred standard, the celebrated *durufsh-kawani*, or leather apron of the blacksmith Kavah, which was elegantly adorned with silk and gems, and is said to have measured eighteen feet long by twelve feet wide. The Persian tradition states that Bahman had thirty thousand men and thirty elephants. The Arabs under Abu Obeidah had only nine or ten thousand men.

Bahman is said to have given Abu Obeidah the alternative of crossing the Euphrates or allowing the Persians to cross it. The Saracen general preferring the bolder course, threw a bridge across the river and thus conveyed his army to the east side, in spite of the dissuasions of his officers. Then begun the "Battle of the Bridge." The Persian horse-archers, covered with their scale armor, were drawn up in a solid line behind their elephants. The Saracen cavalry were galled severely by showers of Persian arrows, and sought to engage at close quarters; but the Arab horses were terrified at seeing the huge elephants, and were further alarmed by the tinkling of the bells hung around their necks, so that they refused to advance. The Saracens then dismounted and assailed the Persians on foot.

The encounter was then furious, but Abu Obeidah was defeated and killed by his reckless courage. He observed a white elephant in the center of the Persian army; and, regarding this huge animal as the object of Persian superstition, he fought his way with irresistible valor towards the elephant and cut off his trunk. Maddened with pain, the infuriated beast rushed upon his assailant and trampled him to death. Dispirited by the loss of their commander, the Saracens fled in confusion, falling back upon their newly-made bridge, which was found to have been broken, either by the victorious enemy or by a rash Arab who sought to give his side the courage of despair. The pursuing Persians slew many of the Arabs and drove others into the stream, where they were drowned. Only five thousand Arabs escaped, and two thousand of these dispersed to their homes. The veteran Arab leader Salit was also slain, and Al Mothanna was severely wounded. The last remnant of the defeated Saracen army was only saved by dissensions among the victorious Persians, which induced Bahman to return to Ctesiphon.

The defeated Arabs under Al Mothanna retired to El Lis, and that commander sent to the Khalif Omar for reinforcements, which soon arrived under the command of Jarir, Abdallah's son. While Al Mothanna was preparing to resume the offensive, the Persian general Mihran anticipated him by leading a body of picked men across the Euphrates and making a dash at Hira; but Al Mothanna hastily collected his widely scattered troops, and defeated the Persians in a desperate battle on the canal El Boweib, near the menaced city, Mihran himself being slain. The defeated Persians recrossed the Euphrates and returned unmolested to Ctesiphon, but all Mesopotamia was at the mercy of the triumphant invaders, who soon extended their ravages to the Tigris and the near vicinity of the great Persian capital.

The youthful Isdigerd III., the New Persian king—the last of the illustrious dynasty of the Sassanidæ—proposed to negotiate with the Saracen general, and the following conversation took place between the New Persian king and the Saracen ambassador.

Said Isdigerd III.: "We have always held you in the lowest estimation. You Arabs have hitherto been known in Persia either as merchants or as beggars. Your food is green lizards, your drink salt water, your clothes hair-cloth. But lately you have come in large numbers to Persia, you have tasted good food, you have drunk sweet water, you have worn good clothes. You have told your countrymen of these things, and they are flocking hither to partake of them. But, not satisfied with all that you have thus obtained, you wish to force a new religion upon us. You appear to me like the fox of our fable, who went into a garden where he found plenty of grapes. The generous gardener would not disturb a poor, hungry fox; but the animal, not content with eating his fill, went and brought all the other foxes into the garden; and the indulgent owner was forced to kill them to save himself from ruin. However, as I am satisfied that you have been impelled by want, I will not only pardon you, but load your camels with wheat and dates, that when you return you may feast your countrymen. But, if you are insensible to my generosity, and continue to remain here, you shall not escape my just vengeance."

The chief ambassador of the Saracens replied thus: "What you have said of the former condition of the Arabs is true. Their food was green lizards; they buried their infant daughters alive; nay, some of them feasted on dead carcasses and drank blood; they robbed and murdered, and knew not good from evil. Such was our state. But Allah in His mercy has sent us, by a holy Prophet, a sacred volume which teaches us the true faith. By this we are commanded to war against infidels. We now solemnly require you to receive our religion. If you consent, not an Arab shall enter Persia without your permission, and our leaders will only demand the established taxes which all believers must pay. If you do not accept our religion, you are required to pay the tribute fixed for infidels. If you reject both these propositions, you must prepare for war."

The Persian king rejected these degrading conditions, and the war was renewed with all the vigor of which the tottering New Persian Empire was capable. King Isdigerd III. sent an army of one hundred and twenty thousand men under Rustam to recover Irak. Al Mothanna, the Saracen commander, had died of his wound, and was succeeded by Sa'ad Ibn Abi Wakas, who with thirty thousand men occupied the Sawâd, acting wholly on the defensive, but relying for success on the reckless valor of his fanatical followers. The Saracen forces had concentrated at Cadesia, or Kadisiyeh, where they rested upon a fortified town.

The Persians challenged the Saracens to combat, and thus brought about the great battle of Cadesia, in the year A. D. 636. Sa'ad Ibn Abi Wakas had pitched his camp outside the walls of Cadesia; his position being protected on each side by a canal, or branch stream, derived from the Euphrates, and flowing south-east into the Sea of Nedjef. Sa'ad himself occupied the Cadesian citadel, from which he directed the operations of his troops, who were led in the fight by Khaled. The Persians filled up El Atik, the more eastern of the branch streams, with reeds and earth, and in this way crossed the channel.

The Arabs rushed to the attack at midday, when Sa'ad gave the signal by shouting from his watch-tower: "Allah akbar" (God is great.) On the advance of the Persian elephant corps the Saracen cavalry fled, but the Saracen archers and other infantry finally repulsed the Persians in the evening. Thus ended the first day of the battle of Cadesia—the "day of concussion."

As the Saracens received reinforcements from Syria during the second day of the battle, that day was called the "day of succors." The morning was passed in skirmishes and single combats between the champions of each side. By these single duels the Persians lost two of their best generals, Bendsuwân and Bahman-Dsulhadjib. When the Arabs were fully reinforced, they attacked the Persians with cavalry and with camels dressed up to resemble elephants, thus driving the Persian cavalry from the field with heavy loss; but the Persian infantry held their ground and their cavalry finally rallied, so that when night arrived the result was indecisive, though the Persians had lost ten thousand in killed and wounded, and the Arabs only two thousand.

On the third day of the battle—the "day

of embittered war"—some Persian deserters informed the Arabs that the elephants could be disabled by wounding them in the proboscis or in the eye. The Arabs therefore directed their main attack upon the elephants, and wounded the two which led the others, whereupon the entire body of elephants fled in full speed across the canal El Atik to Ctesiphon. The cavalry and infantry of the two armies then contended with swords and spears, and when night arrived the Persians fled across the canal El Atik.

The third day of the battle was followed by the "night of snarling"—a time of horrid noise and tumult, when the cries of the soldiers on both sides were thought to resemble the yells and barks of dogs and jackals. Two of the bravest of the Arabs, Toleicha and Amru, crossed El Atik with a few followers, and entered the Persian camp under cover of the darkness, slaughtered many, and caused a panic in the enemy's lines. A general engagement followed, which lasted into the next day; and thus the "night of snarling" can scarcely be separated from the "day of cormorants"—the last of the four days of the great battle of Cadesia.

On the fourth and last day of the battle the Persians again occupied their old ground in the tract between the two canals, having recrossed El Atik. But a wind arose at noon and blew great clouds of sand into the faces and eyes of the Persians, while the Arabs suffered but little, their backs being turned to the storm. A part of the Persian army finally lost ground; as Hormuzan, satrap of Susiana, and Firuzan fell back.

Just then a sudden violent gust tore away the awning that shaded the Persian general's seat, blowing it into the canal El Atik. Rustam sought among his baggage mules a refuge from the violence of the storm; but then Hillal, son of Alkama, began cutting the cords of the baggage and strewed it upon the ground. Rustam was severely injured by a bag which fell, and he endeavored to save himself by swimming across El Atik; but Hillal rushed after him, drew him to the shore and killed him, and then, mounting the vacant throne, shouted with all his might: "By the Lord of the Kaaba, I have killed Rustam."

These words created a general panic among the Persians, who mostly fled hastily to El Atik, some swimming across the stream, others crossing where it had been filled up, but thirty thousand perishing in the waves, while the few who stood their ground were cut to pieces. Ten thousand Persians lost their lives on the battle-field during the preceding night and the day, while the Saracen slain numbered six thousand. The capture of the Persian national standard, the *durufsh-kawani*, or blacksmith's apron, was considered the most serious loss.

Jalenus conducted the retreat of the defeated Persian army. Sa'ad Ibn Abi Wakas sent three detachments to pursue the fleeing foe. One of these Arab detachments, under Sohra, overtook and massacred the Persian rear-guard under Jalenus at Harrar, the Persian leader himself being among the slain. The greater part of the fleeing Persian hosts found shelter behind the walls of Ctesiphon.

By the great defeat of her army at Cadesia, Persia lost all hope of recovering the territory on the west side of the Euphrates, but she did not yet despair of preserving her independence. The Arabs, after their great victory, consolidated their dominion in the Sawâd, and laid the foundations of the cities of Bassora and Kufa.

The next year (A. D. 637) the triumphant Mohammedans resumed the offensive, and Sa'ad Ibn Abi Wakas led an army of twenty thousand men from Kufa to Perisabor, or Anbar, and there crossed the Euphrates into Mesopotamia. When King Isdigerd III. was informed of this invasion and of the threatened Arab attack upon Ctesiphon, he called a council of war to consider the best course to pursue. This council decided that the great Persian capital must be evacuated; but Isdigerd III. was so reluctant to leave Ctesiphon that he waited until the Saracen general with sixty thousand men had reached Sâbât, only a day's march from the Persian capital, before he could be induced to retreat. He then fled hastily from Ctesiphon, with a small part of the treasures which the Sassanidæ had accumulated there during four centuries, and retired to Holwan, a strong city in the Zagros mountain-range.

When Sa'ad Ibn Abi Wakas heard of the Persian king's flight from his famous capital, he sent a detachment in pursuit. This Saracen detachment overtook the Persian rear-guard and cut it to pieces; but King Isdigerd III. made good his retreat to Holwan, where he soon concentrated an army of more than a hundred thousand men.

The Saracen army under Sa'ad Ibn Abi Wakas entered Ctesiphon without opposition. This renowned Persian capital was a rich prize to the conquering Arabs. The Arabian writers never tire of describing its palaces and gardens, its opulent houses and pleasant fields, its fountains and flowers, the beauty of its site, the elegance of its edifices, the magnificence and luxury of their furniture, or the amount of the treasures contained therein. The royal palace of Khosrou Parviz—the Takht-i-Khosrou—particularly excited their admiration.

This splendid palace was built of polished stone, and had in front of it a portico of twelve marble pillars, each one hundred and fifty feet high. The palace was four hundred and fifty feet long, one hundred and eighty feet wide, and one hundred and fifty feet high. The hall of audience, in the center, was one hundred and fifteen feet long and eighty-five feet high, with a magnificent vaulted roof, bedecked with golden stars, so arranged as to represent the motions of the planets among the twelve signs of the Zodiac. In this noble hall the Persian king was accustomed to sit on a golden throne, to hear causes and dispense justice to his subjects.

The treasury and the different apartments of the noble palace were full of gold and silver, of costly rubies and precious stones, of jeweled arms and dainty carpets. The glass vases of the spice magazines contained an abundance of musk, camphor, amber, gums, drugs and delicious perfumes. In one apartment was found a carpet of white brocade, four hundred and fifty feet long and ninety feet wide, with a border worked in precious stones of different colors, to represent a garden of all kinds of lovely flowers. The leaves were formed of emeralds; the blossoms and buds of pearls, rubies, sapphires, and other precious gems.

One of the objects found in the treasury was a horse made entirely of gold, bearing a silver saddle set with a countless number of jewels. Another object discovered in the treasury was a silver camel with a golden colt.

A coffer belonging to King Isdigerd III. was captured at the bridge over the Nahrwân canal, as its guardians were about to carry it off. Among the contents of this coffer were a robe of state embroidered with rubies and pearls, several garments made of gold tissue, the crown and seal of Khosrou Nushirvan, and ten pieces of silk brocade. The victorious Saracens also obtained possession of the armory of Khosrou Nushirvan. This armory contained that great Persian king's helmet, breastplate, greaves and armpieces, all of which were of solid gold adorned with pearls, six "cuirasses of Solomon," and ten costly cimeters. The works of art and one-fifth of the entire booty were sent by trusty messengers to the Khalif Omar at Medina. The remainder of the spoils was of such enormous value that when Sa'ad Ibn Abi Wakas distributed it among his sixty thousand soldiers, each one's share amounted to twelve thousand dirhems (about sixteen hundred dollars of our money.)

Thus the "sons of the desert" were enriched by the possession of wealth far beyond their comprehension. They had learned to appreciate silver, but were entirely ignorant of the value of gold; and an Arabian soldier, who desired to exchange gold, which he had never seen, for silver, which he had learned to prize, went around, saying: "I will give any quantity of this yellow metal for a little white."

Tabari says that after Sa'ad Ibn Abi Wakas had captured Ctesiphon, he was anxious to go in pursuit of the Persian king, but was restrained by despatches from the Khalif Omar, commanding him to remain at the Persian capital, and to employ his brother Hashem and the experienced Arab general, El Kakâa, in the further prosecution of the war against the Persians.

Hashem was sent with twelve thousand men against the fugitive Persian sovereign, whose forces, said to have numbered more than a hundred thousand men, under the command of Mihran, were drawn up at Jalula, near Holwan. After maneuvering about six months, Hashem ventured upon an engagement and was victorious, the Persians leaving a hundred thousand dead upon the field, their commander being among the slain. Jalula at once surrendered, and the conquering Arabs obtained fresh treasures. Among the precious articles found in one of the Persian tents was the figure of a camel with its rider, in solid gold. The value of the booty is estimated at twenty million dollars of United States money, each Arab soldier engaged in the battle obtaining about ten thousand dirhems, equal to about thirteen hundred dollars.

On hearing of the defeat of his army in the battle of Jalula, King Isdigerd III. fled from Holwan to Rei, a large Persian town near the Caspian Sea, near the site of Teheran, the modern Persian capital. The fugitive Persian monarch left a large detachment under Khosrou-sum to defend Holwan to the last extremity. Khosrou-sum rashly led his force against the Arabs under El Kakâa, but was defeated at Kasr-i-Shirin and his army entirely dispersed. Holwan immediately surrendered; the Saracen conquest of Shirvan, Mah-sabadan and Tekrit followed; and by the end of A. D. 637 the banner of Islam waved over the entire region west of the Tigris, from the site of Nineveh to that of Susa.

There was a lull in hostilities during the year A. D. 638, but the Saracens renewed their aggressions upon Persia in the following year (A. D. 639). Otba, the Saracen governor of Bassora, sent an expedition across the Shat-el-Arab into Susiana, the population of which deserted to the invaders, who were thus enabled to defeat Hormuzan, the Persian satrap of the province, in two battles, and to force him to cede a part of Susiana, including the important city of Ahwaz, to the Saracen dominion.

Shortly afterwards, Ala, the Saracen governor of Bahrein, led an expedition into Persia proper, crossing the Persian Gulf in vessels; but Shehrek, the Persian satrap, collected a large army and drove Ala to the coast. As the Arab fleet had been engulfed by the waves, Ala escaped by land with great difficulty, through the aid of troops sent to his assistance from Bassora by Otba, who defeated Shehrek, thus rescuing Ala.

In the following year (A. D. 640) King Isdigerd III. incited Hormuzan, the satrap of Susiana, to make a desperate effort to recover the territory which he had been forced to cede to the conquering Arabs. Aided by Shehrek, the satrap of Persia proper, Hormuzan attacked the Saracens unawares; but was speedily driven from Ram-Hormuz to Shuster, where he was besieged for about six months, during which eighty indecisive battles are said to have been fought before the walls.

At length Al Berâ, son of Mâlik, one of Mohammed's companions, and who was believed by many to be endowed with the prophetic spirit, announced that victory was about to incline to the Moslem side, but that he himself would be slain. After a chance arrow had killed Al Berâ, thus fulfilling one-half of his prediction, the Arabs felt certain that the other half would be verified by victory for their side, and fought with such fanatic ardor that their expectations were soon realized. They won the town of Shuster; but Hormuzan retired into the citadel, where he maintained himself successfully until Abu Sabra, the Saracen general, agreed to spare his life and send him to Medina, where his fate should be decided upon by the Khalif.

After arriving at Medina, Hormuzan obtained an audience with the Khalif Omar. Being handed a cup of water, which he had requested, pretending thirst, Hormuzan looked around suspiciously, as if he expected to be stabbed while drinking. Omar instantly said: "Fear nothing; your life is safe till you have drunk the water." The crafty Persian captive flung the cup to the ground, and Omar saw that he was outwitted, but that he must keep his word. Hormuzan then became an Arab pensionary, and soon afterwards embraced Islam. His province, Susiana, was occupied by the Saracens and annexed to their dominions.

Sa'ad Ibn Abi Wakas—the victor of Cadesia and the great Saracen commander—had built a magnificent palace for himself at Kufa, which city he made his headquarters and his capital; but the Khalif Omar caused this palace to be destroyed. Sa'ad's subordinates grew envious of his power and position, and made frequent complaints to the Khalif Omar concerning the great commander's pride, luxury and injustice. Omar finally heeded these complaints by recalling Sa'ad from Kufa to Medina and appointing Ammâr Ibn Yâser in his place.

In A. D. 641 King Isdigerd III., who was still at Rei, felt encouraged by the news of the change of Moslem commanders, and thus hoped to recover his lost provinces. From the citadel of Rei the Persian king sounded the call to battle. His envoys spread themselves through Media, Azerbijan, Khorassan, Gurgan, Taberistan, Merv, Bactria, Seistan, Kerman, and Farsistan, or Persia proper; collecting contingents of troops in all these provinces, and concentrating their forces at the little town of Nehavend, about fifty miles south of Hamadan, the ancient Ecbátana. With such zeal was the Persian king's call to arms responded to by his subjects that the Persian army so suddenly collected at Nehavend numbered one hundred and fifty thousand men. This large army was placed under the command of Firuzan, one of the Persian nobles who had commanded at Cadesia.

The Persians contemplated making a descent on Holwan, retaking Ctesiphon, crossing the Euphrates into the Sawâd, and destroying the new cities of Kufa and Bassora. But the Saracens were on the alert, and anticipated the threatened invasion of Irak. The Khalif Omar hastily commissioned Noman, son of Mokarrin, the Arab commander at Ahwaz, to concentrate the Saracen troops stationed in Irak, Khusistan and the Sawâd, to assume command of the whole, and to prevent the threatened Persian invasion by marching immediately upon Nehavend, and, by striking a decisive blow against the disciples of Zoroaster, to destroy forever the Magian fire-worship.

Noman accordingly led thirty thousand Saracen troops against the Persian army under Firuzan, which was strongly intrenched in front of Nehavend. After the two armies had faced each other for two months and the stores of the Arabs began to fail, Noman spread a report that the Khalif Omar was dead, broke up his camp and commenced a hasty retreat. This stratagem completely succeeded. Firuzan quitted his intrenchments and pursued the fleeing Saracens, overtaking them on the third day, when the great and decisive battle of Nehavend began (A. D. 641).

After drawing up his army in line of battle and making some arrangements concerning the command in case of his own death, Noman addressed his soldiers thus: "My friends, prepare yourselves to conquer or to drink the sweet sherbet of martyrdom. I shall now cry 'God is great' three times. At the first cry, you will gird up your loins; at the second, mount your steeds; at the third, point your lances and rush to victory or to Paradise. As for me, I shall be a martyr."

Without a pause, the fanatical Arab leader then mounted a milk-white steed and gave the signal for battle by thrice shouting the famous tekbir, or war-cry, "*Allah akbar*" (God is great). At the second call, every Arab soldier was upon his horse; and at the third, which the entire Moslem army repeated, the Saracens charged with irresistible fury, and only the clash of steel was for some time heard amid the clouds of dust which arose beneath their feet. The Persians at length gave way, and Noman advanced his standard and went in pursuit, but a volley of arrows from the retreating foe checked his advance and ended his mortal career, so that he fell in the moment of victory.

Maddened by the death of their leader, the fanatical Saracens pressed on more furiously than before, driving the Persians in headlong flight. Thirty thousand Persians were pierced by the Arab lances, and eighty thousand were drowned in the deep trench by which they had surrounded their camp. Firuzan, with four thousand men, fled northward toward Hamadan, but was overtaken by El Kakâa in a narrow pass and put to the sword. The victorious Arabs triumphantly entered both Nehavend and Hamadan.

The great battle of Nehavend was the death-blow to the New Persian Empire of the Sassanidæ; though King Isdigerd III., fleeing continually from place to place, prolonged an inglorious existence ten years longer (A. D. 641-651). But he was a monarch without a kingdom; as his empire rapidly fell under the Saracen dominion after the *Fattah-hul-Futtûh*, or "Victory of Victories," as the triumphant Arabs called the battle of Nehavend. One Persian province after another was occupied by the "sons of the desert;" and finally, in A. D. 651, their conquering hosts reached Merv, where the last scion of the house of Sassan had for some years found a refuge. In the same year (A. D. 651) the unfortunate monarch was murdered by a miller for the sake of his elegant clothes, and his body was cast into the mill-stream. Such was the sad fate of Isdigerd III., the last of the Sassanidæ.

The Mohammedan conquest of Persia was followed by a cruel persecution of the Magi. The followers of Zoroaster were massacred without mercy, and but a handful of daring souls ventured to adhere to the religion of their fathers. Persia was simply a province of the great Saracen Empire for two centuries, during which period the Persian people embraced the Mohammedan religion.

Before the final conquest of Persia by the Moslems, Egypt had been wrested from the Eastern Roman Empire and brought under the Saracen dominion. The Arabs easily effected the conquest of Egypt; as the Copts, the descendants of the ancient Egyptians, though Christians, were severed from the established Christian Church by a theological dispute, and preferred the Mohammedan yoke to the persecutions which they had endured from the orthodox Christians. Even during Mohammed's lifetime, the Copts of Egypt had proposed negotiations to the Moslem Arabs; and after the Saracen conquest of Syria, the Khalif Omar consented to the invasion of Egypt by the valiant Amru, who had earnestly urged the Khalif thereto.

After a month's siege, in A. D. 639, the frontier fortress of Pelusium surrendered to the Arabs, thus opening the way to the Saracen invasion of the Nile land. As Alexandria had during a thousand years, the period of the Macedonian and Roman dominion in Egypt, been the capital of that renowned ancient land, Memphis, the ancient capital, had sunk to the rank of a secondary city. Nevertheless, Memphis still had a large population, which was almost exclusively Coptic, or native Egyptian; while Alexandria was largely inhabited by Greeks. Memphis surrendered to the Saracen invaders after a siege of seven months.

Amru's march from Memphis was a series of skirmishes and victories; and, after twenty-two days of battle, the triumphant Saracens pitched their tents before the gates of Alexandria. After the lapse of a thousand years, this magnificent Greek city in Egypt had risen to the rank of the second city of the Eastern Roman Empire, while it had from its very origin been the great emporium of the world's commerce and the great seat of intellectual culture and civilization.

The Greek inhabitants of Alexandria made a determined resistance to the Saracen attacks, and were abundantly supplied with the means of defense. The siege was conducted for four months with a fury almost unparalleled in the annals of war. Amru's sword glittered in the van, in every sally and assault. On one occasion the Arabs were repulsed, and Amru and his slave were taken prisoners and brought into the presence of the Byzantine governor of the city. Amru was not recognized as the Saracen leader, but his haughty demeanor began to excite suspicion, when his slave, with remarkable presence of mind, struck him in the face and commanded him to keep quiet in the presence of his superiors. The crafty slave then proposed to send Amru to the Mussulman camp under the pretext of obtaining money for his own ransom. The unsuspecting Christians were thoroughly deceived, as they allowed Amru to depart to the Moslem camp; but they soon found cause to repent of their credulity, as no pacific embassy came from the camp of the Arabs, who hailed their commander's return with the most tumultuous acclamations of joy. Alexandria finally surrendered to the besieging Saracens on the 22 of December, A. D. 640, after a siege in which they had lost twenty-three thousand men.

Amru wrote the following account of his victory to the Khalif Omar: "I have taken the great city of the West. It would be impossible for me to describe all its grandeur, all its beauty. Let it suffice to you to know that it contains four thousand palaces, four thousand baths, four hundred theaters, or places of public amusement, twelve thousand shops for the sale of vegetables fit for the food of man, and forty thousand tributary Jews. The city has been taken by force of arms, without treaty or capitulation, and the Mussulmans are impatient to seize the fruits of their victory."

Omar rejected the proposal to pillage the captured city, and ordered his officers to restrain the rapacity of their soldiers and to preserve the wealth of the city for the public service. The Arab conquerors took a census of the population of the city, imposed a tribute upon it, and assessed a land-tax according to the annual rental of estates. Many of the inhabitants embraced Islam; but the bulk of the population held fast to the Christian faith, and the Coptic Church in Upper Egypt and the Greek Church of Alexandria are not entirely extinct at the present day.

One circumstance connected with the Saracen conquest of Egypt was an irreparable loss to the literary world—the destruction of the great Alexandrian library. It is said that seven hundred thousand volumes were at that time collected in the temple of Serápis and the royal palace. John the Grammarian ventured to solicit of the victorious Amru the gift of the royal manuscripts, which, he said, the Arabs had ignored as of no value in sealing up the magazines and repositories of wealth. Amru was disposed to comply with this request; but, as he did not have the power to separate any of the spoil, the Khalif's consent was necessary. Amru wrote to Omar, asking how he should dispose of the great library. The Khalif replied thus: "If these writings of the Greeks agree with the Koran, they are useless, and need not be preserved; if they disagree, they are pernicious, and should be destroyed." Accordingly that great store of ancient learning was sacrificed to the bigotry and fanaticism of an ignorant barbarian monarch. The books are said to have been used in heating the four thousand baths of the city, and six months are said to have been scarcely sufficient for their destruction.

The conquest of Egypt was most opportune to the Arabs, as the possession of this fertile country could not have been more useful to them at any other time. Arabia was then suffering from a famine, and the Khalif Omar earnestly solicited a supply of corn for his starving subjects His request was instantly granted. A train of camels was despatched in a continuous chain from Memphis to Medina, a distance of three hundred miles, bearing on their backs the produce of the gardens and granaries of Egypt, for the relief of the starving Arabs.

The tediousness of this mode of conveyance suggested to the Saracen Khalif the project of opening a maritime communication between the Nile and the Red Sea—an experiment which had been vainly undertaken by the Ptolemies and by the Roman Emperor Trajan. The resources of the Arabs were equal to the accomplishment of this design, and a canal eighty miles long was opened by Amru's soldiers. Their inland navigation continued until the Saracen Khalifs removed their capital to Damascus.

Amru's description of Egypt in his letter to the Khalif Omar was as follows: "O commander of the faithful! Egypt is a compound of black earth and green plants, between a pulverized mountain and a red sand. The distance from Syene to the sea is a month's journey for a horseman. Along the valley descends a river, on which the blessing of the Most High reposes both in the evening and morning, and which rises and falls with the revolutions of the sun and moon. When the annual dispensation of Providence unlocks the springs and fountains that nourish the earth, the Nile rolls his swelling and sounding waters through the land. The fields are overspread by the salutary flood, and the villagers communicate with each other in their painted barks. The retreat of the inundation deposits a fertilizing mud for the reception of the various seeds. The crowds of husbandmen that blacken the fields may be compared to a swarm of industrious ants, and their native indolence is quickened by the lash of the taskmaster and the promise of the flowers and fruits of a plentiful increase. According to the vicissitudes of the seasons, the face of the country is adorned with a silver wave, a verdant emerald, or the deep yellow of a golden harvest."

This letter satisfied the Khalif's anxiety to learn something of Egypt. The phenomenon of a country alternately a garden and a sea was new to the "sons of the desert." But Amru's ambition was not satisfied with a single conquest. He therefore carried his arms westward, and soon made himself master of the entire region between the Nile and the desert of Barca.

In the midst of his career of conquests, the Khalif Omar's life was ended by the dagger of an assassin (A. D. 644). A Persian slave, in revenge for a private injury, watched his opportunity, and, while the Khalif was engaged in morning prayers in the mosque at Medina, plunged a dagger into his heart. During Omar's reign of ten years (A. D. 634-644), the Saracens wrested Syria and Egypt from the Eastern Roman Empire, and absorbed in their dominion the whole of the New Persian Empire of the Sassanidæ; taking thirty-six thousand cities, towns and castles, destroying four thousand Christian churches and Magian temples, and erecting fourteen hundred Mohammedan mosques.

Omar is celebrated for his piety, justice, abstinence and simple manners, which caused him to be more highly reverenced than his successors, notwithstanding all their grandeur. Says an Arabian historian: "His walking-stick struck more terror into those who were present than another man's sword." His severity and simplicity, bordering on barbarism, form a striking contrast to the luxury and magnificence of his successors. He had no state or pomp. He lived in an humble dwelling. He passed his mornings in preaching or praying in the mosque at Medina; and during the remainder of the day he was to be seen clothed in a tattered robe in the public market-place, where he administered justice to all comers, directed the affairs of his constantly-growing empire, and received ambassadors from the most powerful Oriental princes.

Omar's memory is regarded with the highest veneration by the sect of the *Sunnites*, or Sunnees, and is most bitterly execrated by the *Shyites*, or Sheahs. The Arabs are indebted to him for the era of the Hegira. Before his reign they counted their years from such events as wars, famines, plagues, remarkable tempests, or harvests of unusual plenty. He was the first who established a police in Medina and in the other great cities of his empire. Before his reign the Arabs, so accustomed to lawless independence, would not tolerate any restraint; and the great conquests of the Saracens had brought such a multitude of strangers in the Moslem capitals that cities became almost as insecure as places of residence as the open country. Omar also established a regular system of pay for troops in the field, and instituted pensions for the wounded and disabled soldiers. Had it not been for the provision made for their support in their declining years, Mohammed's old companions, those who had borne the dangers and difficulties that beset the founder of Islam in the earlier part of his career, having been rendered incapable of acquiring fresh plunder by wounds and age, would have perished miserably.

During the reigns of Abu Bekr and Omar the Mussulmans had lost none of the religious enthusiasm with which Mohammed had inspired them. As yet, no private ambition, no jealousy, no personal interest or passion, had alloyed that zeal for extending the dominion of Islam which directed all their efforts to war and conquest and caused them to meet death with as much exultation as victory. The Saracen commanders, born in free Arabia and accustomed to complete independence of mind and will, rendered implicit obedience to the Khalif; but they felt that they were not subject to a master, because his will was so precisely in conformity with their own. But a new question arose after Omar's assassination, both in the civil government and in the army. The Saracen armies had been recruited from foreign lands, and, though they partook of the religious enthusiasm of the Arabs, they introduced a new character and a new kind of ambition into the Saracen army.

The two Khalifs who succeeded Omar resided constantly at Medina, and maintained the genuine Moslem faith pure and uncorrupted, along with the simplicity of manners which characterized their predecessors. But these two Khalifs were surrounded by persons who no longer held fast to the former Arab purity of character, and who brought confusion and civil war into a government hitherto remarkable for its simplicity.

Omar, by his will, appointed six commissioners to elect a new Khalif, and these now chose OTHMAN, who had been Mohammed's secretary. Othman was already an old man, and incapable of supporting the burden of government. His principal recommendation to the office was his pliant disposition. The rage for conquest among the Saracens was not abated by the change of sovereigns. The Saracen armies in Syria penetrated into Asia Minor and Armenia, wresting more territory from the Eastern Roman Empire, while the Khalif's forces in Egypt extended their conquests into Nubia. The Arabs did not limit their exertions to land; but Moawiyah, the Saracen governor of Syria, fitted out a fleet which wrested the islands of Cyprus and Rhodes from the Eastern Roman Empire. The conquerors broke into pieces the celebrated Colossus of Rhodes, and the fragments were sold to a Jew, who loaded nine hundred camels with the metal of which the gigantic statue was composed.

In the midst of the Saracen victories, the Khalif's Egyptian army revolted, and marched into Arabia to besiege Othman in Medina, so that the Saracen capital became a scene of civil war. Othman's weakness had rendered him odious to his warlike subjects. Ali's exertions appeased the discontents of the rebels for a time; but as they had cause to suspect that the Khalif meditated vengeance, they retraced their steps and assassinated Othman in his palace by poniarding him, while he covered his heart with the Koran (A. D. 655). This copy of the Koran, stained with Othman's blood, is still preserved at Damascus. Othman had published a new edition of the Koran. He had also given away vast sums in charity, but when murdered he still had an amount of money equal to fifty million dollars.

Immediately after the assassination of Othman, ALI, Mohammed's cousin and son-in-law, the husband of the Prophet's daughter Fatima, was chosen and proclaimed Khalif. Ali's accession was the signal for new civil and political disorders, which threatened the speedy ruin of the Saracen Empire, and which was the cause of that religious schism which rent the creed of Islam in twain. The discontented faction was called *Môtazalites*, or separatists. The spirit of discord was aggravated by the charge that Ali was an accomplice in the assassination of Othman. Ali's old and bitter enemy, Ayesha, Mohammed's widow, excited a revolt in Arabia against the new Khalif, under the pretext of avenging the murder of Othman, notwithstanding that she helped to instigate that crime. Moawiyah headed a revolt in Syria against the Khalif's authority, while the Khalif's turbulent army in Egypt also set his rule at defiance.

A great battle was fought at Bassora between the partisans of the Khalif Ali and the adherents of Ayesha. Ayesha herself took part in the conflict, riding upon a camel in a kind of wooden tower or cage. With her shrill voice she animated her troops to the combat, and her tower was pierced by numberless darts and javelins. Her army was defeated and she was taken prisoner. This engagement was called the *Battle of K'horaiba*, or the *Day of the Camel*. Ali spared the life of Ayesha and even assigned her a large pension.

Moawiyah, who had in the meantime been chosen Khalif in Syria, was a far more dangerous enemy and rival to the Khalif Ali. Moawiyah was the son of Abu Sofian, Mohammed's old rival. Upon hearing of the assassination of Othman, Moawiyah had declared himself the avenger of the commander of the faithful. He displayed Othman's blood-stained garments in the mosque at Damascus, whereupon sixty thousand Moslems swore to support his standard. By his pretended zeal for Islam, Moawiyah had won the friendship of many of Mohammed's companions, while his descent from the Koreish procured for him the support of many who had yielded with reluctance to Mohammed's sway.

Ali marched against Moawiyah, and the rival armies met in the plains of Saffien, on the west bank of the Euphrates, where they remained facing each other for almost a year, while ninety days were spent in indecisive skirmishing. At length when Moawiyah found his forces diminishing, he adopted a singular expedient, on Amru's recommendation. He ordered a copy of the Koran to be fixed on the top of a pike, and directed a herald to proclaim in the presence of both armies that he was willing to decide all disputes in conformity to a precept of this sacred volume. Ali was forced by his own soldiers to consent to a truce with his rival, and two commissioners were chosen to regulate the terms of peace. The rival Khalifs submitted, and Ali retired to Kufa, while Moawiyah returned to Damascus.

The two commissioners chosen to decide which of the two Khalifs was to retain the Mussulman scepter were Abu Musa, on the part of Ali, and Amru, on the part of Moawiyah. The two umpires agreed to depose both the rival Khalifs and to elect a new man to succeed them, and this seemed to be the most practicable course. In accordance with this agreement, the two umpires first announced to the people that Ali had ceased to be Khalif, whereupon the crafty and treacherous Amru instantly declared that Moawiyah consequently remained in undisputed possession of the Khalifate. From this treacherous act is dated the schism which still exists in the Mohammedan world between the Sunnites and the Shyites.

The Ottoman Turks are Sunnites, while the modern Persians are Shyites. The difference between these two Mohammedan sects or parties was originally more political than religious. The Sunnites consider themselves the orthodox Mohammedans, and are traditionists, acknowledging the authority of the first three Khalifs, from whom most of the traditions were derived. The Shyites asserted Ali's divine and indefeasible right to succeed Mohammed, and therefore they regard the first three Khalifs and all the Ommíyades and Abbássides as usurpers.

The Persians were the first Mohammedan nation that joined the Shyite sect, and that faith has prevailed among them for almost four centuries. The spirit of hostility between these two sects of Islam is rancorous and irreconcilable, even surpassing the antipathy which each of them entertain toward the Christians, Jews or others. The wars which have arisen from the political and religious controversies between these two Mohammedan sectaries have been stamped more deeply with the character of implacable animosity, and have caused more misery and bloodshed, than any struggles that ever desolated Christendom. The *Wahawbees*, a third of the leading Mussulman sects, arose but little more than a century ago, and their history will be given in its proper place.

Amru's treachery was immediately followed by a renewal of the civil war, but no decisive battle was fought. The Saracen Empire, founded on a long course of victories, seemed on the point of crumbling to pieces. At length some enthusiasts met accidentally at Mecca and commenced discussing the calamities that threatened the ruin of Islam. One of them remarked that none of the claimants of the throne deserved to reign, because they had jointly and separately inflicted great sufferings on the faithful and brought the Moslem religion into jeopardy. Three of them then agreed to devote themselves to the public good, and to assassinate Amru, Moawiyah and Ali on the same day. Amru and Moawiyah escaped, but Ali was assassinated (A. D. 660).

Ali's memory is justly reverenced by the Moslems. He was inferior to his predecessors in statesmanship, but he was unquestionably the most amiable of the Khalifs. His mildness, placidity, and yielding disposition caused him to be beloved in private life, but these qualities were fatal to him in a time of internal dissension and civil war. His family continued to be revered long after his death.

The Shyites recognized Hassan, Ali's son and Mohammed's grandson, as the lawful Khalif; but Hassan, desirous of putting an end to civil bloodshed, renounced all claims to the Khalifate in a treaty with MOAWIYAH, who was thus left sole Khalif without opposition, and was the founder of the dynasty of the *Ommíyades*, which occupied the Saracen Khalifate for almost a century (A. D. 660-752).

Moawiyah made the beautiful city of Damascus the capital of the Saracen Empire, as he preferred the abject submission and servile habits of the Syrians to the haughty independence of the Bedouins of the Arabian desert. Oriental despotism then succeeded to the liberty of the desert. Fanaticism was still kept alive in the Saracen army, but a new principle of government guided the prudence of the Khalifs and concealed their

3—18.-U. H.

vices. Moawiyah caused his son Yezid to be acknowledged as his colleague, thus securing the Khalifate to his family by anticipation. When this principle was once admitted, the Khalifate became hereditary in the family of Abu Sofian, Mohammed's earliest and most inveterate enemy.

Communication was maintained through all portions of the Saracen dominions by means of posts, introduced by the Khalif Moawiyah about seven centuries before they were established in France. The same Khalif laid the foundations of a maritime force, which served to connect the Saracen provinces.

Moawiyah reigned twenty years, during which he restored tranquillity to the Saracen Empire, and renewed the career of Moslem conquest which had been suspended during the period of civil war. Besides seeking to extend Islam, the Mussulman conquests now served to establish the supremacy of a new reigning family, which united the despotic habits of the ancient Oriental monarchs with the fanaticism of the Moslem votaries. The Khalif's armies traversed Northern Africa and founded the famous city of Kairwan, or Cairouan, south of Tunis.

For seven years—from A. D. 668 to 675—the Saracens besieged Constantinople, renewing the attack with vigor every summer during this period; but the Byzantine capital was saved by means of the newly discovered *Greek Fire*. This was a new and fortunate discovery which chemistry accidentally revealed to the Byzantine Greeks, at a time when there was neither courage, patriotism nor talent among those people sufficient to repel so formidable an enemy. Callinícus of Heliopolis discovered a compound of naphtha, pitch and sulphur. Naphtha, or liquid bitumen, is a bright, tenacious and highly inflammable oil, which springs from the earth and catches fire as soon as it comes into contact with the air.

Callinícus of Heliopolis, the discoverer of Greek Fire, was one of the Khalif's subjects, but a Christian; and, instead of disclosing his secret to the Saracens, he went to Constantinople and made it known to the Byzantine Greeks, who thus used it in the defense of Christendom. The secret of this destructive composition was said to have been revealed to Constantine the Great by an angel from heaven, and was carefully kept by the Greeks for more than four centuries.

This inflammable compound, when once set on fire, could not be extinguished by water, which only increased its fury. Only sand and vinegar had any effect upon it. It adhered to wood with destructive tenacity, and, when thrown upon combatants in battle, insinuated itself between the joints of their armor and destroyed them by a torturing death. It was poured over the walls of towns upon the heads of storming parties, launched in red-hot balls of stone and iron, or shot in arrows or javelins twisted round with flax and tow which had been steeped in the inflammable oil. At sea it was used in fireships, or blown through long copper tubes from the prows of vessels, which thus assumed the appearance of fire-breathing monsters. When it struck anything it instantly exploded with terrific noise, dense smoke, and a fierce, almost inextinguishable flame.

Ignorance increased the terror of its victims, who saw it approaching in the form of a fiery serpent, until it fell in a burning shower upon ships and men. The sea would be covered with this flaming oil after an hour's fight, and would thus have the appearance of a sheet of fire. The Saracen fleets were repeatedly destroyed by this inflammable composition; and the most valiant Saracen warriors, who were never daunted by the near aspect of death, recoiled from the terrors and tortures of this liquid fire, which crept beneath their armor and clung to every limb.

Upon Moawiyeh's death, in A. D. 680, his son YEZID became Khalif. The Fatimites, or adherents of Ali and his wife Fatima, Mohammed's daughter, were disgusted with Yezid's vices. Ali's second son, Hossein, had served at the siege of Constantinople. The injustice which his family had suffered revived a feeling of loyalty toward him and suggested the thought of making him Khalif. The inhabitants of Kufa invited him to come to that city, and a list was sent to Mecca of one hundred and forty thousand Moslems in Irak who announced themselves in favor of his cause and were ready to take up arms as soon as he should make his appearance on the banks of the Euphrates.

Hossein accordingly left Mecca, with an escort of forty cavalry and a hundred infantry, at the head of a large multitude of women and children, and traversed the Arabian deserts, hoping to reach his partisans in Irak before Yezid's officers could obtain information of his designs; but his expectations were disappointed, as Obeidollah, governor of Kufa, had detected and put to death Hossein's faithful agent. As Hossein aproached the frontier of Irak, the hostile appearance of the country told the melancholy news, and his fears were confirmed by the tidings that four thousand of Yezid's troops were marching to intercept him. He pitched his tent by the brook of Kerbela, as he found it impossible to retreat when he was encumbered with so large a family.

Obeidollah had issued the following peremptory order to his officers: "Bring me Hossein or his head." The governor's troops soon surrounded Hossein's camp at Kerbela. Hossein vainly endeavored to negotiate a peace and return to his home. His little band, true to his fortunes and determined to share his fate, drew up to meet the governor's troops. The women and children, terrified by the certain prospect of death, manifested their sorrow in loud and bitter lamentations.

Obeidollah's archers showered their arrows upon this defenseless host. Twenty lost their lives in a charge, but those who survived maintained the struggle against a largely superior force with unshaken constancy until their thirst was rendered unendurable by the intense heat of the day. As they were cut off from all communication with the river, they were unable to obtain any relief. Their cavalry dismounted and fought on foot, generously throwing themselves between their leader and the enemy's swords, and each one saluting him, as they successively passed to the deadly encounter, with these words: "Peace be with thee, thou son of the Apostle of Allah! Fare thee well."

The only respite of these brave men was the hour of prayer, and Hossein wept as he saw the last of this gallant little band of martyrs expire with Spartan heroism by his side. His brothers then rushed to the deadly conflict and perished with their slain comrades. His eldest son sought revenge in the thickest of the combat, and perished after sustaining ten different assaults with unflinching valor.

Hossein was overcome with feelings of anguish, which he was unable any longer to suppress. He seated himself at the door of his tent, alone, weary and wounded, and prayed to Allah. His infant child was brought to his arms, and while pressing it to his bosom he saw an arrow pierce it to its heart. His little nephew ran to embrace him, but his head was cut off with a blow from a saber.

Hossein was wounded in the mouth while quenching his thirst with a drop of water. His foes gathered thickly about him. His sister Zeinab rushed from her tent in a transport of horror, and implored the governor's general not to allow Mohammed's grandson to be murdered in his presence. Hossein threw himself into the midst of his enemies, frantic with despair, and the bravest of them retreated before his desperate charge. They were held at bay by a feeling of awe until their cowardice was reproached by the remorseless Shamer, whose memory is still execrated by the faithful. Finally Hossein fell covered with thirty-three wounds.

Thus, on the 10th of October, A. D. 680, Mohammed's family was extirminated in the very empire which he had founded. Hossein's memory is still dear to the Shyites of Persia and India, and multitudes of pilgrims pay their devotions at his shrine. The anniversary of his martyrdom—called the *Day of Hossein*—is an occasion of weeping and lamentation; and on these occasions the affecting incidents of these events are so vividly represented that travelers would think that the outbursts of grief which they witness were caused by some recent overwhelming calamity. The hatred of the Shyites towards the Sunnites is prolonged by this solemnity.

Under the Ommiades the empire of the Saracens and the religion of the Koran were carried eastward to the Indus and northward beyond the Oxus into Central Asia, as well as westward across Northern Africa to the Atlantic. The westward progress of the Moslems was attended with extraordinary success. The Saracen conquest of Northern Africa was accomplished between the years A. D. 655 and 689, during the reigns of Moawiyah and Yezid.

After leading his victorious army through the modern Morocco, Akbab spurred his horse into the waters of the Atlantic opposite the Canary Isles, and, brandishing his cimeter, exclaimed: "Great God! why is my progress checked by these waves? Fain would I publish to the unexplored kingdoms of the West that Thou art the sole God, and that Mohammed is Thine Apostle! Fain would I cut down with this sword those rebels who worship other gods than Thee!"

But the final conquest of Northern Africa by the Saracens was only effected after a stubborn resistance from the Moorish and Berber races; and when Hassan, the Saracen governor of Egypt, took and destroyed Carthage, the metropolis of Africa, in A. D. 698, after a siege of nine years, his resentment was so provoked by the resistance of the Christians that he gave up that beautiful city to the flames as soon as it surrendered, and Rome's former rival was finally and utterly destroyed. Many of the inhabitants were massacred; many escaped to Constantinople; while others were scattered along the shores of Italy, Sicily and Spain. Those who preferred their country to their religion by embracing Islam were transported to Kairwan, the new African capital founded by the Arab conquerors; and the "ancient queen of Africa" has never since risen from her ruins.

Thirty thousand Moors in the North-west of Africa embraced Islam in one day, and were enrolled in the Saracen army. All the Moorish tribes, resembling the roving Arabs in there customs and manners, and born under a similar climate, soon adopted the name, language and religion of their Saracen conquerors. The final conquest of the Moors and Berbers was achieved in A. D. 709; thus establishing the religion of the Koran and the dominion of the Saracens from the Indus on the east to the Atlantic on the west.

No sooner had the Saracens completed the conquest of Northern Africa than they were invited into Spain by Count Julian, a Visigothic noble, in revenge for an injury which he had received from his sovereign, Roderic, or Rodrigo, the ruling Visigothic King of Spain. Count Julian, then in command of the important Spanish fortress of Ceuta, on the African shore of the Strait of Gibraltar, betrayed that post to the Saracens.

In A. D. 711 Muza, the Saracen governor of Northern Africa, sent a large Arabian and Moorish army under Tarik across the narrow strait between Africa and Spain; and that strait has ever since been called *Gibraltar*, meaning Gibel al Tarik, or Hill of Tarik. King Roderic sent an army with orders to drive the Moslem invaders into the sea, but this army was routed. Roderic then assembled all his forces, which are said to have numbered almost a hundred thousand men. The hostile armies encountered each other at Xeres de la Frontera, on the Guadalete, not far from Cadiz, in A. D. 711. This great and decisive battle forever ended the Visigothic kingdom in Spain.

Roderic attended his army, with a crown of pearls on his head, clothed in a flowing robe of silk and gold, and reclining in an ivory chariot drawn by two white mules. The effeminate and luxurious Goths, though numerically superior to the Saracen invaders, were unable to resist the fierce onset of the fanatical Mohammedan warriors; and the last three days of this memorable and decisive conflict were little more than a disastrous rout, fatal to the Gothic dominion in Spain. Roderic escaped from the battle-field, but was drowned in the Guadalete.

After a gallant defense, Merida, the Visigothic capital of Spain, surrendered to the Saracens. Almost all the Spanish cities quietly submitted to the invaders ; and before the end of A. D. 713 the Saracen dominion was established over the whole of Spain except the mountainous region of Asturias, in the North, to which a small body of Visigoths under their prince, Pelayo, retired, and which stronghold they held successfully against the Mohammedan conquerors, thus laying the foundations of the Christian states which eventually grew into the modern Kingdom of Spain.

The conquering Saracens made Cordova the capital of their dominion in Spain; and this country was at first governed by Saracen Emirs, or viceroys, but eventually became an independent Moslem kingdom, the Moslem dominion lasting eight centuries. Multitudes of Arabs, or Saracens, migrated to Spain from Syria and Arabia, and settled in the conquered country, so that Spain soon became as thoroughly Arab as the southern shores of the Mediterranean.

No sooner had Spain been added to the Mussulman dominion than Muza, its conqueror, experienced the ingratitude of despotic courts. He was arrested at the head of his army by a messenger from the reigning Khalif, who ordered him to hasten to Damascus, there to render an account for the abuse of power with which he was charged.

After the Saracens had thus succeeded in entering Europe by way of the Strait of Gibraltar, they made another desperate effort to push their way into the same continent by way of the Bosphorus, when in A. D. 717 they renewed their attack on Constantinople; but, after a vigorous siege of thirteen months and another gallant defense by the Byzantine Greeks, under the Emperor Leo III., the Moslems were again repulsed by means of Greek Fire, whereupon they relinquished their attacks in despair and retired.

After their conquest of Spain, the Saracens resolved to push their arms across the Pyrenees, and to extend their dominion and religion over France, and, if possible, over all Europe. Zama, the Khalif's general, crossed the Pyrenees and seized Narbonne and the neighboring provinces of Septimania. The Saracen frontier now bordered on the dominion of the Merovingian kings of the Franks, who claimed Southern Gaul as a part of their territories, though they had never thoroughly subdued that region. The Arabs established their headquarters at Narbonne, and their cavalry ravaged the country as far north as Lyons and Besançon.

The Khalif now resolved upon a serious effort to extend his dominion over all Southern Europe—to conquer France, Germany and Italy; after which his victorious hosts were to descend the Danube to its mouth, overwhelm the Eastern Roman, or Byzantine Empire, and thus surround the Mediterranean with a mighty Mohammedan empire. For this enterprise the Khalif assembled a powerful army in Spain, collected from that country, from Northern Africa, Egypt, Syria and Arabia, and placed it under the command of Abderrahman, the Saracen governor of Spain, who was an able and experienced general. Abderrahman entered France and marched triumphantly northward, desolating the country along his route with fire and sword, to the very center of France, and established his camp between Tours and Poitiers.

Christendom was now in extreme peril. No idea of the general interest of honor, or of the general defense, appeared to form a bond of union among the Christian nations of the West. The dukes ruling over the Gallic tribes of Southern France began to negotiate with the Mussulman invaders and to submit. It seemed impossible for the whole of the Frankish dominions to escape Moslem conquest; and if France had yielded to the warriors of Islam, all Europe must have yielded to the religion of the Koran, as there was no nation in the rear of the Franks that was in a condition to resist the triumphant course of the Mohammedan invaders—no other Christian nation that had made any progress toward civilization; none

which, by its valor, its policy, its means of defense, or the number of its soldiers, could entertain any hope of victory in case the Franks were conquered.

The imminent peril to Europe and Christianity was plainly realized by the valiant Frankish leader Charles Martel, the most illustrious Christian warrior of his time. This renowned Mayor of the Palace—as the prime minister of the Frankish king was called—rallied to his standard his brave Franks and also all the Germanic tribes as far north as the North Sea, and advanced southward to stay the further progress of the Saracens.

The two armies which encountered each other on the plain between Tours and Poitiers, in the very heart of France, in October, A. D. 732, one hundred years after Mohammed's death, to decide whether Europe was to be thenceforth Christian or Mohammedan, were the most gigantic military hosts seen in Gaul since the time of the memorable defeat of the Huns under Attila at Châlons, in A. D. 451.

For seven days the mighty armies of Christendom and Islam confronted each other and engaged merely in skirmishing; but on the eighth day the Saracens fiercely assailed the Frankish hosts, and the battle lasted all day. The desperate struggle was renewed with terrific fury the next morning, and finally the Arab hosts were put to flight. Their valiant leader, Abderrahman, was slain, and the remnants of the shattered Moslem host fled in utter dismay. Three hundred thousand Moslems are said to have fallen on this sanguinary field. Although the Saracen army effected its retreat into Spain without further check, this great battle was decisive, as it put an end forever to the Saracen efforts to conquer Europe. The Frankish leader, Charles, was surnamed *Martel*, or "the Hammer," from the power with which he dealt the heavy blows which shattered the Saracen forces.

Isidore, Bishop of Beja, in Portugal—who flourished a little later—gave the following account of this famous conflict· "The Franks were planted like an immov-

SARACENS ATTACKING CONSTANTINOPLE.

able buttress, like a wall of ice, against which the light-armed Arabs dashed themselves to pieces without making any impression. The Mussulmans advanced and retired with great rapidity, but they were mowed down by the swords of the Germans. Abderrahman himself fell under their blows. Meanwhile, night began to fall, and the Franks lifted up their arms as if to petition their leader for rest. They wished to reserve themselves for the next day's fight, for they saw the distant country covered with Saracen tents. But when, on the following morning, they formed for battle, they perceived that the tents were empty, and that the Saracens, terrified by the dreadful loss they had sustained, had retreated in the middle of the night, and were already far on their way."

Thus the tide of Mussulman conquest was rolled back, and Europe was saved to the Christian religion. Had the Saracens triumphed in this memorable battle, the Christian religion would have been wiped out of existence, and all Europe would have become Mohammedan. The battle of Tours—as this celebrated engagement is called—was therefore one of the most decisive battles in the world's history—a battle as decisive as those of Marathon and Châlons. Had any of these three great battles resulted differently, the whole fate of Europe would have been changed.

The Saracens held on to their province of Septimania twenty three-years longer; but in A. D. 755 they were driven from Southern France across the Pyrenees into Spain by Pepin the Little, the son and successor of Charles Martel and the founder of the Carlovingian dynasty of the Franks. The Moslems never regained a footing in France, but their kingdom in Spain continued to flourish.

The Saracens destroyed many old and flourishing cities in Spain, and founded many new ones. They left the institutions of the country unchanged in other respects, except that they substituted the authority of the Saracen Khalif for that of the native Spanish king. The national assemblies, the nobility, the courts of justice, and the laws remained. The Christian Spaniards obtained toleration for their worship, and were only forbidden to speak against the religion of their Moslem conquerors. Cordova remained the capital of the Saracen dominion in Spain, even after this part of the Mussulman empire became an independent Mohammedan kingdom.

The Saracen Empire and the religion of Islam now extended from Western India and the Turkish lands in Central Asia beyond the Oxus westward to the Alantic, including the Spanish peninsula in Europe; and throughout this vast domain the will of the Khalif ruling at Damascus was law.

There was justice in the charge made by the Mohammedans and by the Jews that at this time Christianity was tinctured with idolatry. It is also true that at this time Islam was purer in the practical morality of its devotees than was Christianity, whose monks and nuns were guilty of the most disgraceful and degrading licentiousness, such vices as drunkenness and prostitution being the rule, and not the exception, among them.

The Khalif made it an invariable rule to appear at the great mosque for prayer, and to preach there on Friday, the Mohammedan Sabbath, or day which the Moslems devote to public worship. But this was the only occasion on which he presented himself to the people, and he was then accompanied with all the pomp of royalty. The rest of his life was passed in the Paradise of Damascus—the name which the Orientals assign to the gardens of the palace. There the sovereign of the mighty Saracen Empire reposed under fresh and blooming bowers, amid gushing fountains, and breathing an air fragrant with the most delightful perfumes. Thus the court of the Ommiyades at Damascus was as luxurious as that of the generality of Oriental monarchs, and quite in contrast to the simplicity of the first Khalifs at Medina.

But while the character of the Khalifs had undergone an entire change, the Saracen people retained that spirit of activity and energy which seemed to promise them the dominion of the world, and which would soon have enabled them to complete their conquests had they not been abandoned by their leaders. The complete transformation of the Oriental nations which was effected in so short a time is one of the wonders of history.

The Arabs never had any affection for the dynasty of the Ommíyades, whose armies were therefore composed of soldiers from the newly-conquered and newly-converted nations—the Syrians, the Persians and the Egyptians—nations noted for their pusillanimity and effeminacy. Mohammed taught these people to think and to act, and the enjoyment of thought and action was as lively and as deep as it was new to them. The rapid metamorphosis of the timid and indolent Orientals into valiant Mussulmans may be regarded as the most brilliant example of the advantages which a lawgiver may derive from that desire for knowledge and improvement and that love of action which are inherent in man and which become their own reward when once aroused by a sufficient object.

The Khalifs issued their commands in Mohammed's name, calling themselves his lieutenants, and were obeyed without hesitation; but their authority was not really despotic, as they were merely organs of the public will. Every Mussulman was absorbed in one single thought, one sole passion; and every effort was directed to the great purpose of establishing the triumph of Islam. The first four Khalifs attempted nothing in their own name. They reaped no personal enjoyment from the enormous power which they wielded, and the exercise of their authority excited no jealousy.

During the most brilliant period of the Mohammedan conquests, the Saracen army acted continually with a republican spirit, urging forward its generals without the check of any responsibility. This universal passion, this devotion of all to the cause of all, developed the activity of the Oriental nations in so brilliant and unexpected a manner, inspired the sons of the pusillanimous Syrians with courage and endurance, suggested to them ingenious maneuvers in the art of war, and maintained their constancy unshaken through danger and privation.

This complete self-education, this all-pervading sentiment, put in action all the talents and virtues of the Saracens, rendered them happy under all the vicissitudes of war and fortune, and constituted a reward for the valor of the believers far more certain than the black-eyed maidens promised them in Paradise. Patriotism, glory and personal happiness flourished on the frontiers of the Saracen Empire and in the Saracen army long after a mortal corruption had fastened itself upon the center.

The obscure and inglorious Khalifs of the Saracen Empire continued conquering countries which they never saw, and of which they did not even know the names, long after their government had become corrupted with all the vices of a despotic court, long after the most illustrious men had fallen a sacrifice to the caprices of tyranny; and the election or deposition of the commanders of a heroic soldiery was constantly brought about by the vilest intrigues.

The cause of this was that these conquering troops fought for the Moslem religion, and not for the Khalif. They obeyed the dictates of their own consciences, and not the orders from the palace. They regarded themselves free, and ministers of God. They only discovered that they were no longer free citizens, and therefore ceased to be men, long after they had been accustomed to the scenes of civil war and to the treachery and baseness of their leaders.

Fourteen Khalifs of the dynasty of the Ommíyades, founded by Moawiyah, reigned at Damascus for almost a century with great success and glory (A. D. 660–752); but were all this time regarded by a large party in the East as usurpers, and were reproached with being descended from the most inveterate enemy of Mohammed. In A. D. 752 MERVAN II., the last of the Ommíyades, was deposed and put to death by Abul Abbas al Saffah, a descendant of Abbas, an uncle of Mohammed.

ABUL ABBAS AL SAFFAH then became

ISLAM'S RISE AND THE SARACEN EMPIRE.

Khalif, thus founding the dynasty of the *Abbássides*, so illustrious in the later Saracen history. This important revolution caused the dismemberment of the vast Saracen Empire. Three different parties arose, and these were distinguished by three different colors. The badge of the Abbássides was black, that of the Ommíyades was white, and that of the Fatimites was green.

The throne of Abul Abbas, surnamed *Al Saffah*, or "The Sanguinary," was raised in blood. He massacred all the Ommíyad princes whom he could seize, broke open the tombs of all the Ommíyad Khalifs, burned their mouldering remains, and scattered the ashes to the winds. This cruelty was accompanied with treachery. The defeated Ommíyades accepted a peace which was offered to them, and relied with confidence on the oaths of their victorious rival.

Some authors say that twenty-four, others say ninety, members of the Ommíyad family were invited to a feast of reconciliation, where the new treaty of friendship was to be sealed. They met without suspicion. According to a preconcerted arrangement, a poet presented himself before Abdallah Abu Ali, the uncle of the Khalif, who had given the feast. This poet recited some verses enumerating the crimes of the Ommíyades, calling for vengeance on their heads, and pointing out the danger of their existence to the dynasty of the Abbássides. He exclaimed: "Allah has cast them down; why dost thou not trample upon them?"

TOMBS OF THE KHALIFS AT DAMASCUS.

The poet's merciless exhortation was at once acted upon. Abdallah gave the signal to the executioners whom he had already prepared, and ordered all the guests to be beaten to death with clubs in his presence. When the last victim had fallen under the hands of the executioner, he ordered the bodies to be thrown on a pile and carpets to be spread over the ghastly heap. The festive board was then placed upon their palpitating bodies while they still breathed, and the orgies of the Abássides were prolonged amidst the groans of their dying rivals.

The only one of the Ommíyades who escaped this horrid massacre was Abderrahman, the youngest son of the last Khalif of the fallen dynasty. This prince fled from Syria and wandered over Africa as a fugitive, but while in the valleys of Mount Atlas he ascertained that the white banners of the Ommíyades still waved in triumph over Spain. He instantly proceeded to that country, and in A. D. 755 he presented himself to his partisans on the coast of Andalusia. They saluted him as the true Khalif, and all Spain soon acknowledged his authority. He assumed the title of *Emir al Mumenim,* or "Commander of the Faithful," which the people of the West corrupted into the barbarous name of *Miramolin.* This was the beginning of the *Western Khalifate* of Cordova, which lasted two hundred and seventy-six years (A. D. 755-1031). Thus the Mohammedan world was now divided into two independent Khalifates.

ABDERRAHMAN, the first Khalif of Cordova, died after a glorous reign of thirty-two years (A. D. 755-787). His son HIXEM I. (A. D. 787-796) and his grandson ALHAKEM I. were contemporaries of Charlemagne, the great Frankish Emperor of Western Christendom, and fought successfully against his generals several times. Near the middle of the eighth century an independent Moslem kingdom arose in North-western Africa, the modern Morocco, under the dynasty of the *Edrisides* of Fez, who declared themselves descendants of the Fatimite branch of Mohammed's family, and who recognized neither the Western nor the Eastern Khalif.

Abul Abbas al Saffah, the first of the Abbásside Khalifs of the East, died in A. D. 752, after a reign of but two years, and was succeeded by ABU JAAFAR, surnamed AL MANSUR, or "the Victorious," who rendered his name illustrious by founding Bagdad, on the Tigris, about fifteen miles from the ruins of Ctesiphon, and making this new city the capital of the Eastern Khaliphate. After the court of the Abbássides had been fixed at Bagdad, the new city grew so rapidly that during the reign of its founder the funeral of a popular Mohammedan saint was attended by eight hundred thousand men and sixty thousand women of Bagdad and the neighboring villages.

The court of the Abbássides at Bagdad was maintained in the utmost grandeur and magnificence. Nothing in the Eastern Khalif's palace was calculated to remind the observer of the simple and austere manners of the primitive Mohammedans. Watch was kept at the gate by a numerous guard, shining in gold and bristling with steel. The apartments of the palace were decorated with every ornament that could be procured by means of wealth and luxurious art. Every delicacy of the most sumptuous table was sought for to gratfy the Khalif's palate; and when he traveled, four hundred camels were scarcely sufficient to carry his kitchen furniture. Seven thousand eunuchs were employed in attendance on his person or as a guard to his women. The court of the Abbássides was celebrated for its patronage of literature and men of learning; and Bagdad became the great center of Arabian civilization, learning, wealth and refinement.

Abu Jaafar al Mansur—the second Abbásside Khalif and the founder of Bagdad—was involved in many bloody civil wars; but in spite of these troubles, and the expense of a magnificent pilgrimage to Mecca, he amassed treasure valued at about one hundred and fifty million dollars of our money during the twenty-five years of his reign, and left all of this vast sum behind him when he died. This renowned Khalif was a covetous, perfidious and cruel sovereign; but he was also amiable in private life, as well as brave, prudent and learned. It is believed that he gave the first impulse to literature among the Saracens.

AL MOHDI, or MAHADI, who became Khalif of Bagdad upon the death of his father, Abu Jaafar al Mansur, in A. D. 779, was an able and successful sovereign, though his reign was disturbed by wars and sectarian controversies. One of the remarkable incidents of his reign was a rebellion headed by the one-eyed impostor Mokanna, who was so hideously ugly that he covered his face with a veil. This impostor's adventures have been rendered familar to English readers by Moore's poem of *Lalla Rookh*.

The Khalif Al Mohdi, or Mahadi, squandered the treasures left to him by his father in various ways. He made a magnificent pilgrimage to Mecca, a distance of a thousand miles, with such a retinue as to enable him to carry snow sufficient through the desert to preserve his accustomed luxuries. His fruits and liquors were served daily in the scorching sands of the Arabian desert with the same coolness and freshness which they possessed when he partook of them in his palace at Bagdad.

Al Mohdi's brilliant reign was ended by a murder designed for another, but of which he was the victim. The tragic end of this illustrious Khalif illustrates a trait in the moral character of the Oriental nations. He had numerous wives, his favorite one being named Hasfana. One of the neglected and jealous of his females inserted a deadly poison in a beautiful pear and then gave it to Hasfana, who handed it to the Khalif, utterly ignorant of its contents. Al Mohdi ate it and died (A. D. 784).

MUSA, Al Mohdi's son and successor, died after a reign of but two years, and was succeeded by his uncle HAROUN AL RASCHID, or *Aaron the Just*, the celebrated Khalif whose name is so well known to the readers of the *Arabian Nights*. He is specially famous as a patron of literature. He was always surrounded by learned men, both at home and on his travels. He made it a rule to attach a school to every mosque which he erected.

Haroun al Raschid was the friend of Charlemagne, the great Frankish Emperor of Western Christendom, to whom he sent two embassies, one in A. D. 801 and the other in A. D. 807. The first embassy carried the keys of the Holy Sepulcher at Jerusalem, which this renowned Khalif presented to the great Christian Emperor. The second embassy presented to Charlemagne a clock ornamented with automaton figures which moved and played on various musical instruments. This is one of the evidences of the superiority of the Saracens of that age over the Christian nations in the mechanical arts.

The court of Haroun al Raschid abounded with men of learning and genius. The illustrious Khalif selected a philosopher to counsel him and take care of his conscience. The rules which he prescribed to this philosopher illustrate his character, and are as follows: "Never instruct me in public; never be in haste to give me your advice in private. Wait till I question you; answer in a direct and precise manner. If you see me quitting the path of rectitude, gently lead me back to it, without any harsh expressions; but never address me in equivocal terms."

The Eastern Roman Empire had become so weak that the Emperors did not hesitate to purchase peace from the Saracens by the payment of tribute. The Emperor Nicephorus I. determined to release himself from this badge of servitude, and accordingly sent a letter of defiance to the Khalif Haroun al Raschid, alluding to his own predecessor, the Empress Irene, in the following terms: "The Empress considered you as a *rook*, and herself as a *pawn*. That pusillanimous female consented to pay a tribute, when she should have demanded twice as much from the barbarians. Restore, therefore, the fruits of your injustice, or abide by the decision of the sword."

The Byzantine ambassador who carried the letter to the Khalif cast a bundle of swords at the foot of that potentate's throne. Haroun al Raschid ordered these swords to be stuck in the ground, and then severed them all at one blow, without turning the edge of his cimeter. The Khalif answered the Eastern Roman Emperor's letter thus: "In the name of the most merciful God! Haroun al Raschid, Commander of the Faithful, to Nicephorus, the Roman dog! I have read thy letter, O thou son of an unbelieving mother! Thou shalt not hear, thou shalt behold my reply."

Immediately a Saracen army of one hundred and thirty thousand men appeared in the Eastern Roman Emperor's provinces of Asia Minor, under the black standard of the

Khalif; and the entire territory was made to feel the terrible vengeance of Haroun al Raschid. The presumptuous Nicephorus was glad to retract his defiance and to return to submission.

In his internal administration Haroun al Raschid was guided principally by his two ministers, Yahia ben Khaled and Giafar, who belonged to the old family of the Barmecides, and whose ancestors had belonged to the Magian priesthood and had charge of the fire-temple of Balkh, the ancient Bactria, through many generations before the rise of Islam. This family is said to have been of royal Persian blood, and when they came to the court of the Abbásside Khalifs at Bagdad they were exceedingly wealthy.

Yahia had been the instructor of Haroun al Raschid in the latter's boyhood, and when Haroun became Khalif he appointed his tutor to the office of Grand Vizier. When Yahia was obliged to relinquish his post on account of old age, the Khalif at once conferred the office upon the retired minister's son Giafar, whose abilities equaled those of his illustrious father.

Giafar was the most admired writer and the most eloquent orator of his time, and in the administration of his office he displayed the accuracy of a man of business and the comprehensive ideas of a statesman. His acquirements made him the Khalif's companion as well as his minister, and Haroun finally grew so attached to Giafar that he appointed the minister's elder brother Fadhel to the office of Grand Vizier, so that the affairs of state might not deprive him of the pleasure of Giafar's society.

The brothers Giafar and Fadhel were all powerful for seventeen years, but finally their entire family was suddenly involved in disgrace, and the treatment which Haroun al Raschid then accorded them is an ineffaceable blemish on the character of that illustrious Khalif. The circumstances which led to this result are said to have been as follows.

Haroun was passionately fond of his sister Abassa, and preferred her society to all else except Giafar's conversation. The Khalif would have enjoyed these two pleasures together by taking Giafar with him in his visits to Abassa, but the laws of the harem prevented that by forbidding all except near relations from being introduced there. At length Haroun conceived the scheme of removing this obstacle by uniting Giafar and Abassa in marriage. They were accordingly married, but with the express condition that they were never to meet except in the Khalif's presence. Both groom and bride promised this, but their mutual affection proved so strong that the promise was violated, and two children were born of this unequal marriage. Haroun remained ignorant of this event for some time, but when it could be concealed from him no longer the Khalif became furious with rage and resolved on the most cruel revenge. He ordered Giafar to be put to death, and all the property of the entire race of the Barmecides to be confiscated and the whole family to be imprisoned. Thereupon Giafar was beheaded in the antechamber of the royal apartment, which he had sought to request an interview with the implacable Haroun, and his father and brothers were put to death in prison. Abassa and her two children were thrown into a well, which was closed over them.

The massacre of the Barmecides was regarded as a public calamity. An Oriental writer says that all of them enjoyed the singular happiness of being loved as much when in the zenith of their greatness as they had been in a private station, and of being praised as much after their disgrace and ruin as when they had been in the height of their glory. The following stanzas were written on their fall:

"No, Barmec! time hath never shown
  So sad a change of wayward fate,
Nor sorrowing mortals ever known
  A grief so true, a loss so great.

Spouse of the world! thy soothing breast
  Did balm to every woe afford;
And now, no more by thee caressed,
  The widowed world bewails her lord."

This horrible massacre is an exception to the mildness and equity which generally characterized the reign of Haroun al Raschid, and illustrates the state of society at that period and the tendency of despotism itself. The supreme pontificate of Islam and the secular authority of the Khalifate of Bagdad were united in the hands of the Khalif, who, being invested with the mantle, signet and staff of the Prophet, and bearing the title of Commander of the Faithful, exercised supreme temporal and spiritual power, without any other restriction than the vague ordinances of religion.

The brilliant reign of Haroun al Raschid has always been referred to as the most glorious period of the Arabian dominion. The wealth and adopted luxury of conquered nations had given a refinement to social life and a splendor to the court of Bagdad previously unknown to the Mohammedans. Flourishing towns sprung up in every portion of the Saracen dominions. Commerce by land and sea increased with the luxury of wealth; and Bagdad, the capital of the Eastern Khalifate of Islam, rivaled Constantinople, the capital of the Eastern Empire of Christendom, in magnificence.

Haroun al Raschid died of despondency produced by ill-omened dreams, in the year A. D. 807, after dividing his dominions between his sons AL MAMOUN and AL AMIN. A civil war soon broke out between the brothers, and the feeble and timid Al Amin was easily overthrown by his more powerful brother, who thus became sole master of the Eastern Saracen Empire (A. D. 813).

Al Mamoun was one of the most illustrious of the Khalifs of Bagdad, and was especially distinguished for the magnificent style of his court and his patronage of letters. At his marriage a thousand of the largest pearls were showered on the head of his bride, and lands and houses were distributed by lot among the guests. The Khalif bestowed a sum equal to four million dollars in a single gift.

Al Mamoun ordered his ambassadors and agents in other countries to collect books for his use. The volumes of Grecian science and literature were collected at Bagdad from Constantinople, Armenia, Syria and Egypt. These works were translated into Arabic, and Al Mamoun exhorted his subjects to diligently study them. He attended the assemblies of the learned, whom he had invited to his court from all countries. The Khalif's example was imitated in Egypt and all his other provinces, and even in Spain by the Khalifs of Cordova.

In the plains of Sinaar, and again in those of Kufa, the Khalif Al Mamoun's mathematicians accurately measured a degree of the great circle of the earth, and reckoned the entire circumference of the globe to be twenty-four thousand miles; thus exhibiting a degree of mathematical knowledge hitherto unattained.

During Al Mamoun's reign the Saracens conquered the island of Crete (A. D. 823), which they held for more than a century, during which period it was their chief market for the sale of the captives which they took from the various countries bordering on the Mediterranean. The principal Saracen fortress in the island was called Chandak, whence its modern name, *Candia.*

In A. D. 827 the Saracens of Africa attacked the island of Sicily, and gradually overran the largest and western portion of that island, making Palermo the chief naval station for their piratical squadrons. Syracuse maintained its independence for half a century, but was finally captured by the Moslem freebooters in A. D. 878, whereupon the whole island of Sicily passed under Mussulman sway, and the Greek language and the Christian religion gave way to the Arabic tongue and the worship of Islam.

The Arabian squadrons, issuing from the Sicilian ports, ravaged the Italian coast, and captured and pillaged one hundred and fifty towns in Calabria and Campania. The daring pirates even attacked Rome and plundered its shrines beyond the walls; but the city made a determined resistance, through the vigilance and energy of Pope Leo IV., who brought about an alliance of the maritime states of Gaëta, Naples and Amalfi against the Saracen freebooters. In A. D. 849 the allied fleet defeated the Saracen fleet off the port of Ostia, and immediately after the battle the Arabian galleys were dashed ashore and destroyed by a violent tempest. But the Saracens obtained a firm footing in Southern Italy, and would have extended their dominion over all Italy had the Eastern and Western Khalifates been united.

Thus during the ninth century, under such enlightened Khalifs as Haroun al Raschid, Al Mamoun, and several of their successors, the Arabs, or Saracens, carried science and literature to the highest degree of perfection. Bagdad, Cairo and Cordova became famous as the seats of learning and civilization, while the greater part of Christian Europe was slumbering in the darkness of barbarism. The Arabs taught the arts, sciences, literature and poetry wherever they established their dominion and religion. Architecture and music flourished in all the Arabian cities of Asia, Africa and Spain. Agriculture, manufactures and commerce were encouraged.

To the Saracens we are indebted for several sciences, such as chemistry and algebra, and our mode of notation, called the *Arabic* figures, as well as our system of notes in music. They cultivated grammar, philosophy and medicine, and translated into Arabic the works of Plato and Aristotle, of Euclid and Apollonius, of Ptolemy, Hippocrates and Galen, and those of other eminent ancient writers, both Latin and Greek. The Saracen civilization exerted a great influence upon Christian Europe throughout the Dark and Middle Ages. Thus during the Dark Ages it was Islam, and not Christendom, that led in civilization and enlightenment.

A Vizier founded a college at Bagdad by the gift of a sum equal to three and a half millions of dollars. This college was attended by six thousand students, from every class in life, from the noble to the mechanic. All the Mohammedan cities from Samarcand, in Turkestan, to Cordova, in Spain, had their colleges and libraries. A private doctor refused the invitation of the Khan of Bokhara to visit his capital, because the transportation of his books would have required four hundred camels. In Egypt the public library contained one hundred thousand volumes, and these were free for the gratuitous use of every student. The public libraries of Spain contained six hundred thousand volumes.

The Arabians excelled in mathematical studies, and cultivated the science of astronomy with brilliant success. The Khalif Al Mamoun supplied the costly instruments of observation, and the same unclouded horizon and the same spacious level was still afforded by the land of the primitive Chaldæans. From the reigns of the Abbássides to the times of Tamerlane's grandchildren the stars were diligently observed without the aid of the glasses; and the astronomical tables of Bagdad, Samarcand and Cordova correct some minute errors, without renouncing Ptolemy's theory, and without making any progress in the direction of discovering the solar system. In the Oriental courts the truths of science could be recommended by ignorance and folly only; and the Arabs, like the ancient Chaldees and Later Babylonians, were encouraged in the study of astronomy by the vain predictions of astrology, believing that they read human destiny in the stars.

The Arabs have been deservedly applauded in the science of medicine. The names of Mesna and Geber, of Razis and Avicenna, are classed with the Grecian masters. In the city of Bagdad eight hundred and sixty physicians were licensed to exercise their lucrative profession. In Spain the lives of the Christian princes were intrusted to the skill of Saracen physicians; and in Italy the school of Salerno, the legitimate offspring of the Saracens, revived the precepts of the healing art in Europe.

The origin and improvement of the science of chemistry is to be ascribed to the industry of the Saracens. They first invented and named the alembic for the purpose of distillation, analyzed the substances of the three kingdoms of nature, tried the distinction and affinities of alkalis and acids, and converted the poisonous minerals into soft and salutary medicines. But the chemistry of the Arabs, like their astronomy, was mingled with superstition; and they wasted long lives and ample fortunes in the researches of alchemy, hoping thus to find the elixir of immortal youth, or the philosopher's stone, which could transmute all substances into gold.

The Saracens obtained the first elements of the liberal sciences from the Greeks. John of Damascus translated the writings of the Greek physicians into Arabic, thus giving the first impulse to scientific study among the Khalif's subjects. Translations were subsequently made of the works of the Greek astronomers and philosophers. The court of Bagdad bestowed the most munificent patronage upon men of learning, while the literature of Constantinople was buried in unfrequented libraries.

In philosophy the Arabs greatly admired Aristotle, but they learned to distinguish only in words where he distinguishes in things. They translated Ptolemy's description of the earth, and combined it with a better knowledge of the globe and of the starry heavens, their acquaintance with the latter being an ancient acquisition. The sum of their important observations in the science of geography transmitted to us are contained in Abulfeda's Arabic work, to which we are indebted for much of our knowledge of the countries with which the Arabs held intercourse.

But the Arabs often perverted the use of Greek learning, which they did not always fully comprehend. Astrology, the interpretation of dreams, fortune telling, and many other superstitions which have descended to our own times, were developed among the Saracens.

The *Arabian Nights* is a work strongly national in its character, and is well known in Christendom. Neither the author of these tales nor the date of their composition can be ascertained with certainty. Some ascribe this work to a Syrian, others to an Egyptian, and others think that it was written by various authors of various ages; but all who are familiar with the subject agree that these tales represent correctly Oriental habits, feelings and superstitions. They are universally read and admired throughout Asia by the old and young men of all ranks. The Bedouin Arabs of the desert will sit around their fires in the evening, and listen to these stories with such attention and delight that they will entirely forget the fatigue and hardship of their day's journey. The supernatural portion of the *Arabian Nights* is founded on matters firmly fixed in the Mohammedan belief.

The Saracens made many improvements in arts and manufactures. They instructed the Franks in the art of weaving before Charlemagne's time, and introduced many Eastern vegetables into Europe. The fair of Bagdad was the principal market for silk. The Saracens learned the art of clock-making from the Greeks of Constantinople, and carried it to a high degree of perfection. The Arabs are said to have invented tournaments, which were introduced from them into Italy and France.

The Saracens also originated a new style of architecture, which is characterized by an expression of boldness and extravagance peculiar to the Orientals. They had fountains and jets of water even in their sleeping apartments, because the Koran commands frequent ablutions, and because the Bedouins of the desert considered water and shady places as the greatest luxuries. The court of the Abbásside Khalifs at Bagdad surpassed the splendor of that of the Eastern Roman Emperors at Constantinople in the abundance of gold, of pearls, and of precious stones. The Saracen cities bore hardly the least resemblance to those of Europe. Their walls enclosed large spaces of ground, beautifully cultivated. Many of these cities were built in the midst of deserts, and were the markets and places of deposit for the neighboring tribes.

Notwithstanding the splendor of the court of Bagdad, the empire of the Abbásside Khalifs was distracted by rebellions, civil wars and the contentions of religious sects. Although the Abbássides relinquished all efforts at foreign conquest, they continued to surround themselves with all the pomp and magnificence of the most powerful martial princes.

The Khalif AL MOTASSEM, Al Mamoun's successor (A. D. 833-841), is said to have had one hundred and thirty thousand horses in his stables; which is twice the number of cavalry possessed by Napoleon Bonaparte in the zenith of his power and glory. Al Motassem is said to have loaded each of his horses with a pack of earth, which was carried fifty miles to raise a mountain in Irak-Arabi, on which a palace called *Samara* was erected. It is likewise said that this Khalif had eight sons and eight daughters; that he reigned eight years, eight months and eight days; that he was born in the eighth month of the year, was the eighth Khalif belonging to the dynasty of the Abbássides, fought eight battles, had eight thousand slaves, and left eight million pieces of gold in his treasury.

AL MOKTADOR (A. D. 907-932) was the last of the Abbásside Khalifs celebrated in history, and the splendor of the court of Bagdad seems to have been at its height during his reign. A body of troops numbering one hundred and sixty thousand infantry and cavalry were assembled under arms on the occasion of receiving an ambassador from the Eastern Roman Emperor. The state officers and the favorite slaves of the Khalif stood around him, glittering with gold and gems; and near these were seven thousand eunuchs, black and white. Gorgeous boats and barges covered the Tigris. Thirty-eight thousand pieces of tapestry were hung in the palace; a hundred lions were exhibited in show; and the eyes of the spectators were delighted with the spectacle of a tree of gold and silver spreading out into eighteen branches, on which sat a variety of golden birds among the golden leaves. By the ingenious mechanism of this remarkable artificial tree, the birds warbled in harmony, and the leaves waved in the wind. This proficiency of the Arabs in mechanical science is confirmed by abundant evidence.

The extensive Saracen Empire had now reached its highest pinnacle of glory and greatness; and the mighty fabric of Moslem dominion, torn by religious and political dissensions, soon declined in power and importance, and before the close of the ninth century it fell to pieces, dissolving into many petty Mohammedan kingdoms.

The Khalifs of Bagdad and Cordova each claimed to be Mohammed's true successor, and each denounced his rival's pretensions. In the meantime the Turkish tribes were pressing into the Saracen Empire in the East in the same manner that the Teutonic tribes had pressed into the Western Roman Empire. The governors of the various Saracen provinces gradually made themselves independent; and many dynasties, mainly Turkish, sprung up, acknowledging but a nominal allegiance to the Khalif of Bagdad.

A number of sects likewise arose among the Mohammedans, the same as they arose among the Christians, and each sect regarded the others as heretics. Those who announced themselves as Mohammed's orthodox followers always recognized the Khalif of Bagdad as the spiritual head of Islam, so that the Abbásside Khalifs retained something of the power of a Pope long after they had lost that of an Emperor.

At the beginning of the ninth century there were two rival Khalifates in the Mohammedan world, just as there were two rival Empires in Christendom. Each Christian Empire was an enemy of the Moslem Khalifate next to it, and on terms of friendship with the distant Mussulman Khalifate. The Khalifs of Cordova were the natural foes of the Western Christian Empire, while the Khalifs of Bagdad were the natural enemies of the Eastern Empire of Christendom; but there was usually peace and friendship between the Western Empire and the Eastern Khalifate, and between the Eastern Empire and the Western Khalifate.

And in the same manner as the two Christian Empires decayed and split up into many kingdoms, so the two great Saracen Khalifates, torn by religious and political dissensions, soon declined in power and importance, and gradually fell to pieces. Before the close of the ninth century numerous petty Mohammedan kingdoms arose from the fragments of the once-vast empire of the Khalifs.

These new Mussulman states acknowleged but a nominal allegiance to the Abbásside Khalif at Bagdad or the Ommíyad Khalif at Cordova, and some of these small Moslem powers went on conquering at the expense of the Christians. During the ninth century independent Saracen powers sprung up in the great Mediterranean islands of Sicily and Crete, which had been conquered from the Eastern Roman Empire. Although the civil power of the Khalifs was thus subverted, the religion of Mohammed remained in all the countries in which it had been established.

The frequent revolutions in the Khalifate of Bagdad ceased to have any influence on the rest of the world. Each successive Khalif lost some province by revolt. The Khalifs perceived the decline of enthusiasm and courage, and even of physical vigor, among their subjects, from the time that all noble objects had ceased to be presented to their ambition or their activity. The Khalif Al Motassem—whom we have already mentioned—endeavored to supply this want of native courage and vigor by procuring young slaves, bred in the mountain region of the Caucasus, whom he trained in military duties and formed into a guard, to which he intrusted the protection of his palace. These troops were of the Turkish race.

As the Saracens became more and more enervated by a long course of wealth and luxury, the Khalifs of Bagdad were obliged to recruit their armies from the more vigorous Turkish and Tartar tribes which roamed over the vast steppes of Central Asia. These barbarian mercenaries soon became numerous and formidable, and, becoming stronger than their masters, soon established their power over the Abbásside Khalifs, as the Prætorian Guards of Rome had done over their Emperor.

The rivalry between the mercenary troops and the Syrians effectually disgusted the latter with military pursuits, so that the Turks were soon the only soldiers of the Khalifs of Bagdad. The slavery in which they had been reared rendered them less faithful, but not more obedient. They were the authors of most of the revolutions in the palace of Bagdad. They dethroned or assassinated those Khalifs who refused to be the obsequious instruments of their insolence and rapacity.

Finally, in A. D. 936, the Turkish mercenaries elected a chief of their body, calling him *Emir al Omara*, or "Chief of Chiefs." This official became the real ruler of the Khalifate of Bagdad. He kept the Abbásside Khalif a prisoner in his own palace, reducing him to that life of poverty, penitence and prayer which Mohammed's early successors had imposed upon themselves by choice. The Turks would have assumed the nominal authority if their conversion to Islam had not made it indispensable to maintain a phantom of a Khalif as the spiritual head of the Mohammedan religion. The Khalifs of Bagdad were treated with great ceremony while in office, but were hurled from the throne whenever it suited the Turks, and substitutes were appointed in their stead. Several of the dethroned Abbásside Khalifs became beggars.

Thus we see that the history of the Saracen Empire is marked by one period of brilliant conquest, a second of stationary but rather precarious greatness, and a third of rapid decline. The Arabian dominion is likewise distinguished by the strong contrast which it presents to the European nations of that time. The splendid palaces of the Khalifs, their numerous guards, their treasures of gold and silver, the populousness and wealth of their cities, constitute a striking spectacle in comparison with the rudeness and poverty of the contemporary European nations.

As a rule the history of Oriental despots is stained by atrocious crimes. The history of the Khalifs of Bagdad is the history of a series of tyrants, whose dark and bloody deeds, perpetrated by unbridled passion or jealous policy, rank with those of the bloodstained court of the Byzantine Emperors. The crimes are ill redeemed by ceremonious devotion and acts of trifling or ostentatious humility, or even by a rigorous justice in chastising the offenses of others, the best trait of Mohammedan sovereigns.

Mohammedanism was first established by religious zeal and fanaticism, and its earliest form was that of paternal authority. Mohammed did not give liberty to the Arabs, nor did he impose a despotism upon them. His countrymen had been accustomed to liberty before his time, and he was careful not to alarm the spirit of Arabian freedom by acts or ordinances hostile to it. He neither destroyed nor preserved the republican institutions of Mecca, but he exalted above them the power of inspiration—the divine voice which must silence all the counsels of human prudence. He founded no political despotism. That was the work of religious faith only.

The character of the Arabian government and people has been strikingly portrayed by the events of their history during the brilliant period of their ascendency. This character made the Saracen Empire prosperous. A characteristic circumstance in the Arabian conquests was, that whoever embraced the Moslem faith was thereafter reckoned among the victorious people, and became as free as the conquerors themselves. The Saracen nation did not stand as much in awe of the unlimited power of the Khalifs as of Allah and His Apostle, whom the Khalifs themselves feared, or professed to fear.

The loftiness of character imparted to the whole Arab nation became the source of splendid undertakings. The Arabian laws were mainly founded on the common principles of the understanding, and maintained their influence for this reason. In general, the Arabian government was so intimately connected with the doctrines of the Mohammedan religion that the description of the one necessarily involves that of the other.

Under the Mohammedan rule Spain enjoyed a greater degree of prosperity and a higher state of civilization than at any previous period. The tenth century was the culminating period of the power and glory of the Khalifate of Cordova, which increased in strength and greatness as the Western Empire of Christendom became weaker. But the Saracen power in Spain soon began to decline; and in the year A. D. 1031 the Khalifate of Cordova was dissolved into a number of small Moslem states, which were gradually conquered by the Christians from their fastnesses in the mountain region of Asturias in the North of Spain.

In the course of time arose the Christian kingdoms of Aragon, Castile, Leon, Navarre and Portugal, which waged continual wars against the Mussulman kingdom of Granada in the South of Spain. The kingdom of Granada was founded in A. D. 1238, and was conquered in A. D. 1492 by the united power of Aragon and Castile under the rule of Ferdinand V. and Isabella I. With the conquest of Granada ended the Mohammedan power in Spain, after it had existed in that country almost eight centuries (A. D. 712-1492), under the dominion of the Ommíyad Khalifs of Cordova, and under the Moorish kings of Granada.

Egypt, as a province of the Saracen Empire, was governed by Arab Emirs, or viceroys, for more than two centuries. Multitudes of Arabs settled in the country, and great numbers of Egyptians accepted Islam. The Coptic Church gave way to the religion of the Koran, so that Egypt gradually changed from a Christian to a Mohammedan country. This period was likewise marked by great disturbances. Riots and tumults were of frequent occurrence, and several general revolts also took place, but these were all suppressed. In A. D. 868 AHMED, the Saracen Emir, renounced his allegiance to the Khalif of Bagdad, and established an independent Moslem kingdom in Egypt, which lasted thirty-seven years, when it was subdued by the Khalif of Bagdad, and a long period of anarchy followed.

In the meantime a new Arab kingdom arose in Northern Africa. In A. D. 908 MOHAMMED, surnamed AL MEHDI, or the Leader, the chief of the Shyite sect of the Moslems, renounced the authority of the Khalif of Bagdad and founded an independent Mussulman Khalifate in North Africa.

He made himself Khalif, or both civil and religious ruler of the new Moslem monarchy, which he and his successors extended over all Northern Africa. This dynasty of Khalifs was the Edrisides, or Fatimites, already alluded to as descendants of Mohammed's daughter Fatima, Ali's wife. The Fatimite Khalifs were formidable rivals of the Abbásside Khalifs of Bagdad.

In A. D. 970 AL MUEZZEDDIN, or MOEZ, the fourth of the Fatimite Khalifs of Northern Africa, conquered Egypt, at a time when the country was in a state of anarchy and when the people were suffering from a severe famine. The Fatimite army carried large supplies of corn with them, and, by distributing these to the starving people, obtained their submission to the spiritual and temporal claims of the African Khalif. Al Muezzeddin made Egypt the seat of his dominion, founded a new city in the vicinity of the ruins of Memphis and named it *Cairo*, or *Kahíra*, "City of Victory," at the same time making it the capital of his vast dominions. Thus Egypt became again an independent and powerful state.

Thus there were now three leading Khalifates in the Mohammedan world—those of Bagdad, Cordova and Cairo. The Fatimite Khalif of Cairo denounced the Abbásside Khalif of Bagdad as an impostor, and declared himself the only legitimate successor of Mohammed, as the descendant of the Prophet's daughter. His claims were diligently preached throughout the Oriental world, and a serious schism thus arose in the ranks of Islam. · The Fatimite Khalifs soon extended their dominion over Syria and Arabia, and Palestine again became the battle-field of the rival armies of Egypt and the East. The Fatimite dynasty ruled Egypt for two centuries (A. D. 970—1171).

The division of the Eastern or Abbásside Khalifate in the tenth century by the rise of a third Khalifate, that of the Fatimites in North Africa and Egypt, struck a fatal blow at the political power of the Khalifs of Bagdad. In the meantime the Seljuk Turks under their mighty Sultan, Togrul Beg, conquered Persia and drove the original Moslem masters of that country eastward into India, about the middle of the eleventh century, when Mahmoud of Ghaznee made extensive conquests in Northern India, bringing that immense region under the Mohammedan faith.

The dominion of the sovereign of the once vast Saracen Empire was now reduced to the city of Bagdad, and all his provinces had set up independent Mohammedan governments. Thus by the middle of the eleventh century the Khalif of Bagdad had become a mere petty prince. Although he was still highly reverenced as Mohammed's successor, his sacred character did not save him from the aggressions of the neighboring tribes, or from the tyranny of his own mercenary troops.

In A. D. 1055 the Khalif solicited the aid of Togrul Beg, the conquering Sultan of the Seljuk Turks, against his enemies. The powerful Sultan instantly came to the weak Khalif's relief, and was rewarded with the temporal power of the Khalif, who retained only the possession of Bagdad and the exercise of his spiritual functions as Mohammed's successor. By this proceeding and by his own victories, the Seljuk Turkish Sultan became master of all Western Asia and the acknowledged leader of the Mohammedan world.

The Khalif of Bagdad remained the spiritual head of Islam two centuries longer, until A. D. 1258, when the conquering Mongolian hordes under Zingis Khan's successors stormed and sacked Bagdad. The fifty-sixth successor of Mohammed was trodden under foot by the Tartar cavalry amid the plunder of the city; and two hundred thousand of the inhabitants of the former seat of Arabian learning and splendor were massacred, the work of destruction and ruin continuing for forty days. Such was the melancholy end of the once-mighty Saracen dominion.

The Saracens who were renowned among their own countrymen for their attainments in literature and science must now be mentioned. TABARI and MAÇOUDI were eminent Arabian historians who flourished in the ninth century. AVERRHOES became celebrated by his commentary on Aristotle. ACHMET was a renowned astronomer.

GEBER, the chemist, flourished in the eighth century; but little is known of his history, though his writings contain so many facts that he is regarded as the founder and father of chemistry. He was familiar with almost all of the chemical processes in use as late as the eighteenth century. But, as a philosopher, he did not rise above the level of his time; as he explained phenomena by "occult causes," and firmly believed in and sought the "philosopher's stone." Geber's work is the oldest chemical treatise known. It was translated from Arabic into Latin by Golius, of Leyden, who called it *Lapis Philosophorum*. An English translation by Richard Russell appeared in 1678.

AVICENNA, the celebrated Arabian physician and philosopher, was born near the city of Bokhara in A. D. 980, and died in A. D. 1037. He devoted his time to the study of mathematical science, logic, medicine and theology. He was the author of numerous writings on philosophy and medicine, the most important being his commentary on the *Metaphysics* of Aristotle, and his famous *Canon*, the sovereign authority in medical science for centuries.

ABULFEDA, the distinguished Mohammedan historian and geographer, wrote a compendious History of Mankind, particularly valuable because of the information it gives concerning the early Khalifs. His principal work is *The True Disposition of Countries*, in which the description of Syria, his native country, is the most authentic and interesting part. Abulfeda was born in A. D. 1273, and died in A. D. 1331.

SARACEN KHALIFS.

THE FIRST FOUR KHALIFS.

A. D. 632	ABU BEKR.	A. D. 644	OTHMAN.
634	OMAR.	655	ALI.

THE OMMIYADES.

A. D. 660	MOAWIYAH.	A. D. 717	OMAR II.
680	YEZID I.	719	YEZID II.
683	ABDULLAH.	723	HESHMAN.
684	MERVAN I.	743	WALID II.
689	AB AL MALIB.	744	YEZID III.
704	WALID I.	744	MERVAN II.
714	SOLYMAN.		

THE ABBASSIDES.

A. D. 752	ABUL ABBAS.	A. D. 933	AL RADI.
754	AL MANSUR.	939	AL MOKTAKI.
779	AL MOHDI.	943	AL MOSKTASSI.
784	MUSA 'L HADI.	944	AL MOTI.
786	HAROUN AL RASCHID.	973	AL TAY.
807	AL AMIN.	991	AL KADER.
813	AL MAMOUN.	1031	AL KAYMEN.
833	AL MOTASSEM.	1079	AL MOKTADI.
841	AL WATHEK.	1099	AL MOSTAZHER.
846	AL MOTAWAKKEL.	1124	AL MOSTARSHID.
861	AL MONTASSER.	1141	AL RASCHID.
862	AL MOSTAIM.	1142	AL MOKTASI.
865	AL MOTAZ.	1167	AL MOSTANJID.
868	AL MOHTADI.	1178	AL MOSTADI.
869	AL MOTAMED.	1187	AL NASER.
892	AL MOTADED.	1234	AL ZAHER.
901	AL MOKTASSI.	1235	AL MOSTANSER.
907	AL MOKTADOR.	1252	AL MOSTASEM.
932	AL KAHER.	1258	End of the Khalifate of Bagdad.

SECTION XI.—THE SARACEN KINGDOM OF CORDOVA.

IT is needless here to repeat the account of the Saracen invasion and conquest of Spain by Tarik, and the overthrow and death of Roderic, the last Visigothic King of Spain, at Xeres de la Frontera in A. D. 712. The Arabian conquest of Spain was accompanied by great cruelty on the part of the conquerors. The country was at first held as a province of the undivided Saracen Empire, and the government was administered by Emirs, or viceroys, appointed by the Ommíyad Khalifs reigning at Damascus.

After the rapid conquest of Spain by the Saracens, the unoccupied lands and the lands which had been deserted by their former inhabitants were distributed among the Arab chiefs, and the towns were soon filled with merchants and persons of consequence, who migrated to Spain from Africa and Arabia in great numbers, bringing with them to their new homes their wives, families and property, with many of the luxuries of the Eastern nations, hitherto unknown in Europe. Arabian customs and manners were then introduced into Spain, and during the next three centuries that European country was as throughly Arab as the African shores on the oppsite side of the Mediterranean.

The twenty different Emirs, or viceroys, who had been sent by the Ommíyad Khalifs ruling at Damascus to govern Spain during a period of more than forty years after the Saracen conquest of the country, were generally so cruel and oppressive that rebellions and civil wars were frequent; and this newly-acquired Arabian province was distracted by the jealousies and hatreds, the mutual distrusts, the open revolts, the thirst for revenge, which characterized the administration of the Emirs who followed one after another in such quick succession, in consequence of the frequent revolutions which so deplorably disorganized Mohammedan society in Spain, when no sheikh or wali would recognize a superior, and when the Christian Spaniards of Asturias were consolidating their infant power and were naturally on the alert to every advantage that they might gain over the hated Moslems.

The danger with which the Mussulman dominion in Spain was menaced by the existing condition of affairs was fully recognized by all the principal Arab sheikhs, and about eighty of them assembled at Cordova to consult upon the means of establishing a more efficient and settled government for their new country. These sheikhs were resolved that so fine a country—abounding in all the treasures of the earth, and capable of being the seat of a great and powerful kingdom—should no longer be ruined by misgovernment. They accordingly came to the conclusion that it would be better to declare themselves wholly independent of the Khalif, who then ruled all the Saracen dominions from Damascus, and to elect a sovereign of their own, who would live among them and protect their rights.

The accomplishment of this design was rendered easy by the revolution at Damascus by which the dynasty of the Ommíyades was overthrown and succeeded by that of the Abbássides, who thus usurped the Khalifate of Islam. All the Arabian dominions except Spain submitted to the usurper Abul Abbas, the first of the Abbásside Khalifs. The Moors of Spain refused to acknowledge the sovereignty of the new Khalif, and turned their eyes toward Abderrahman, the last surviving son of the last Ommíyad Khalif of Damascus, who had escaped the massacre of his kindred by the Khalif Abul Abbas, by being absent on a hunting excursion.

As soon as the melancholy tidings of the fate of his kindred had reached Abderrahman, he took refuge among the Bedouins of the Arabian desert, and afterwards among those of Africa. His misfortunes, his learning, his gentle manners and handsome person, soon won the affection of the desert nomads, who frequently saved him from the toes of his family, who pursued him relentlessly.

Hadib, the Saracen governor of Barca, though a beneficiary of the Ommíyades, was now the most enterprising and persistent in hunting down the fugitive heir of the fallen dynasty. One night a troop of Hadib's cavalry surrounded the tents of the Bedouins, and demanded to know if they did not have a young Syrian among them, describing accurately the person of the prince, which description had been anxiously forwarded by the Khalif Abul Abbas to all the Emirs of the vast Saracen Empire. The Bedouins, recognizing their guest in the person sought, and shrewdly suspecting that the visit of Hadib's cavalry meant no good for the refugee prince, replied that the youth had been hunting with some companions, but that he might be found in a valley which they pointed out to him at some distance.

As soon as Hadib's troops had departed, the faithful Bedouins awoke their guest and acquainted him with what had transpired. With tears in his eyes, Abderrahman thanked them for this evidence of their affection, and fled farther into the desert, attended by some of the more resolute youths of the tribe. After various adventures the fugitive prince arrived safely among the Moors in the North-west of Africa, where he was welcomed with joy by a noble sheikh to whom he was related.

This amiable and talented young prince appeared to be the only person capable of uniting the distracted interests of the Arabs and Moors of Spain. One of the assembled sheikhs informed his fellows of the career and adventures of the youthful refugee. The Sheikhs unanimously exclaimed: "Let Abderrahman be our sovereign!" They instantly sent deputies to the prince, assuring him of their own fidelity, and of the submission of the Arab, Moorish, Syrian and Egyptian tribes in Spain, but neither disguising nor belittling the difficulties with which he would be obliged to contend.

Abderrahman replied: "Noble deputies, I will unite my destiny with yours; I will go and fight with you. I fear neither adversity nor the dangers of war. If I am young, misfortune, I hope, has proved me, and never yet found me wanting." The young prince also said that he was bound to mention the subject to the friends who had protected him, and to ask their advice. Thereupon an aged sheikh, a kinsman of the prince, replied: "Go, my son, the finger of Heaven beckons thee! Rely on us ah; the cimeter alone can restore the honor of thy line." The youth of the entire tribe were eager to accompany the prince, but he selected only seven hundred and fifty well-armed cavalry for his adventurous expedition.

Abderrahman landed on the coast of Andalusia early in A. D. 755, and was enthusiastically welcomed by the sheikhs and people of the province, who made the air ring with their joyful acclamations. His appearance, his station, his majestic mien, his open countenance, won the support of the multitude; and his march to Seville was one continued triumph, twenty thousand voices cheering his progress, while twenty thousand cimeters, wielded by vigorous hands, were at his disposal. The surrounding towns instantly sent deputies offering their submission and their services to the young prince. Yussuf, the Emir, or viceroy, of the Abbásside Khalif at Damascus, fled in consternation from province to province of Spain, to muster a force sufficient to oppose Abderrahman's triumphal march; but Yussuf was overthrown in several bloody and desperate battles and soon forced to surrender; and in the brief space of a year ABDERRAHMAN I. had triumphed over all his enemies, in spite of their valor and numbers, and found himself securely established on the throne of Cordova as the first Arabian King of Mohammedan Spain (A. D. 755).

Thus began the independent Saracen kingdom in Spain, at a time when England was still divided into the seven kingdoms of the Saxon Heptarchy, and when the

THE GARDENS OF THE ALCAZAR AT SEGOVIA.

PURSUIT OF THE OSTROGOTHS BY BELISARIUS.

great Carlovingian dynasty of Frankish monarchs had just assumed the emblem of royalty and laid the foundation of Charlemagne's great Empire in Western Christendom. For the next three centuries this Mohammedan kingdom in Spain was the most wealthy, the most magnificent and the most highly civilized state in Europe.

hammedan laws are such as Mohammed delivered to the Arabs in the Koran, and are therefore immutable. But he was careful to appoint good and just magistrates in all the cities of Spain, and released his Christian subjects from the payment of much of the tribute money hitherto exacted from them, thus materially improving their condition.

He likewise encouraged commerce, and provided employment for labor, by having dock-yards established all along the Spanish coast—a great advantage to a country whose cities were filled with merchants who were trading to every quarter of the world then known.

Abderrahman I. improved his capital by a countless number of works of art. He narrowed the channel of the Guadalquivir by means of gigantic embankments, and transformed the space thus rescued from the waters into immense gardens, in the center of which arose a tower, commanding an extensive view. There were many expert architects, masons and workmen among the Arabs, and there was some remnant of skill among the Latin Spaniards, whose ancestors had been familiar with Roman art in the days of the ancient Cæsars.

Abderrahman I. utilized all the architectural talent of the age in erecting at Cordova a celebrated edifice, one of the most superb mosques in the world. This grand structure still remains—a splendid monument of the interesting and enlightened nation over which Abderrahman I. reigned. This magnificent edifice was supported by three

ALCAZAR.

Abderrahman I. began his reign as sovereign of Cordova by making such regulations as were likely to secure good order and prosperity to his new kingdom. He was unable to originate any new laws; as the Mo-

hundred and sixty-five marble columns, had nineteen curiously constructed gates of bronze, and was lighted by four thousand seven hundred lamps, which were kept constantly burning.

To Abderrahman I. has been ascribed the first transplanting of the palm-tree into the congenial climate of Spain. The Orientals manifest an ardent fondness for trees, and are in the habit of connecting the planting of them with interesting personal and family-occurrences. The Arabic poets complimented the taste of the amiable Abderrahman I. by representing him as appreciating such refined feelings as he contemplated the graceful tree and apostrophized it in the following words:

"Beautiful palm! thou art, like me, a stranger in these places; but the western breezes kiss thy branches, thy roots strike into a fertile soil, and thy head rises into a pure sky. Before the cruelty of Abul Abbas banished me from my native land, my tears often bedewed thy kindred plants of the Euphrates; but neither they nor the river remember my grief. Beautiful palm! thou canst not regret thy country!"

The authority of Abderrahman I. was acknowledged by all of Spain except by the Christians of Asturias, in the North. The great mass of the Moslems in Spain were ardently attached to Abderrahman; but the new dynasty of the Abbássides at Damascus had many partisans in the country, and these greatly disturbed Abderrahman's reign by their frequent insurrections, which were only crushed after many active and bloody campaigns. Charlemagne, the great Frankish sovereign of Western Christendom, led an expedition into Spain to assist the rebels in one of these struggles; and this invasion resulted in the annexation of that part of Spain north of the Ebro to the Frankish dominion, but soon after Charlemagne had returned to his own dominions Abderrahman recovered the territory which the Frankish monarch had conquered. Abderrahman I. also conducted several wars against the Christian kingdom of Asturias, but failed in his effort to conquer that kingdom.

Abderrahman I. was a just and generous sovereign, scrupulously honorable in all his dealings, loving justice and promoting religion. He founded schools and encouraged literature in his kingdom. Mohammedan Spain found in its own first monarch a hero and a lawgiver to lay the foundation of her prosperity. Abderrahman I. died in A. D. 787, after a glorious reign of thirty-two years (A. D. 755-787).

Abderrahman I. was succeeded as King of Cordova by his youngest son, HIXEM THE GOOD, who was defeated in an effort to conquer the Christian kingdom of Asturias. Upon Hixem's death, in A. D. 796, he was succeeded by his son, ALHAKEM THE CRUEL, a whimsical tyrant, during whose reign Charlemagne's son Louis invaded Spain and took a number of fortified towns. Charlemagne erected the territory thus acquired into the *Spanish March*, over which a Frankish governor was appointed, his residence being fixed at Barcelona.

Alhakem the Cruel had a troubled reign. His character, when developed by circumstances, was found to combine two traits frequently united—love of luxury and love of blood. To gratify his thirst for blood, and under pretexts more or less just, he caused three hundred heads to be cut off at one time, four hundred at another time. In the indulgence of his love of luxury he neglected the interests of his kingdom and the happiness of his subjects. He passed all of his time in his palace with his female slaves, listening to vocal and instrumental music, or witnessing the lascivious dance. In A. D. 815 he relinquished the cares of royalty to his son, so that he might unreservedly enjoy its sensual pleasures; and he surrounded himself with a well-paid guard of five thousand men, for the better protection of his person against his outraged subjects.

This guard necessitated a new expense, and new taxes were accordingly levied. The cruelty with which those who resisted the levy were punished provoked a riotous rebellion. In a few minutes the streets of Cordova were strewed with the dead bodies of the rioters, three hundred having undergone

THE SARACEN KINGDOM OF CORDOVA.

the horrible torture of impalement. The suburbs were leveled and their inhabitants were exiled; eight thousand refugees fleeing to Fez, in Africa, and fifteen thousand to Alexandria, in Egypt. These refugees held Alexandria until they were bribed to retire to Crete, in which island they founded the city of Chandak, or Candia.

The cruel Alhakem now fell a victim to remorse, so that solitude was intolerable to him, and sleep almost impossible. He would be in the habit of calling up his singers and dancers in the dead of night, and send for his ministers and judges. When the ministers and judges had listened and looked on, waiting anxiously and vainly for information concerning the public business which demanded their presence, he would coolly order them to go home.

Alhakem the Cruel died in A. D. 821, and was succeeded by his son ABDERRAHMAN II., a magnanimous and beloved sovereign, during whose reign the piratical Northmen, or Normans, from Scandinavia, barbarously ravaged the coasts of Spain and Portugal, even destroying half of the city of Seville. These marauding *Sea-Kings* were so terrible that they were usually permitted to retire unmolested to their ships. For two years drought and locusts afflicted Spain, and were followed by a famine, which was alleviated by Abderrahman II. importing corn from Africa. In the early part of this reign a law of succession was enacted preventing many of the miseries which had hitherto proceeded from the uncertainty of the law as to the inheritance of the throne of Cordova. Abderrahman II. beautified and adorned his capital, and introduced a sufficient quantity of pure water by means of leaden pipes. By his boundless liberality he attracted natives and foreigners of genius, talent and learning to his court.

Upon the death of Abderrahman II,, in A. D. 852, the throne of Cordova descended to his son, MOHAMMED I., a man of letters and a friend to genius, but also a persecutor of his Christian subjects. Mohammed I. died in A. D. 886; and his son and successor, ALMONDHIR, reigned but two years, being killed in battle with Calib, son of the rebel Omar ben Hafs, in A. D. 888. ABDALLA was the next sovereign of Cordova; but the formidable adventurer, Calib, who marshaled an army of sixty thousand men, reigned at Toledo, as sovereign of half of Mohammedan Spain. Calib's father, Omar, had been a laborer of Ronda; but, after annoying the country as a petty robber in Andalusia, he proceeded to the Pyrenees, where he became a king. Both Omar and his son Calib after him defied the whole power of the kingdom of Cordova.

ABDERRAHMAN III., Abdalla's grandson, ascended the throne of Cordova in A. D. 912. His reign is regarded as the golden age of the Mohammedan dominion in Spain. Before he became king he was the universal favorite of the nation, because of his mild manners, his generosity and his wonderful progress in learning. By the universal acclamation of his Moslem subjects, he was hailed as "prince of believers," and "defender of the faith of God." He was therefore the first of the sovereigns of Cordova to assume the spiritual honors of Khalif.

Abderrahman III. regarded it as his first duty to exterminate the audacious rebels who had so long distracted his kingdom, and he accordingly sent his renowned uncle Almudafar with a select army of forty thousand men against Calib, who was defeated on the banks of the Jucar, losing seven thousand men, while three thousand of the royal troops were likewise slain. The entire kingdom was then speedily brought back to its allegiance to the crown of Cordova, and Abderrahman III. soon afterward subdued the Mohammedan kingdom of Fez, in Northwestern Africa. In the early part of his reign he was also engaged in wars against the Christians of Asturias.

But the great Khalif Abderrahman III. did not acquire his glory by military achievements alone, as he delighted much more in cultivating the arts of peace. He was rewarded for his virtues by the affections of his subjects and the prosperity of his kingdom. In his internal administration he was distinguished for his great capacity of mind, for his boundless liberality, for his unparalleled magnificence and his inflexible justice. Still he did not feel perfectly happy, as he remarked that he had known but fourteen days of real enjoyment during his reign of fifty years.

Abderrahman III. displayed his taste and luxury in the founding of a palace and a city, about six miles from Cordova, which he named after his wife, *Zehra*, or *Azhara*. The mosque in this new city rivaled that of Abderrahman I. at Cordova. The roof of the palace was upheld by over four thousand pillars of variegated marble, and the floors and walls were of the same costly material. The principal apartments were adorned with exquisite fountains and baths, and the whole were surrounded with the most magnificent gardens, in the midst of which arose a pavilion, which was supported on pillars of white marble ornamented with gold. A fountain of quicksilver was constantly playing in the center of the pavilion, thus reflecting the sun's rays in a new and wondrous manner.

Abderrahman III. showed himself capable of a sublimity of justice by an example similar to that of the Elder Brutus of Rome. He had intended his second son, Alhakem, for his successor; and for this reason his elder son, Abdalla, entered into a conspiracy to assassinate the heir-apparent or to consign him to life-long imprisonment. The plot was detected, and the would-be fratricide confessed his guilt. Alhakem pleaded for his brother, saying that Abdalla had been misguided by evil counselors.

The royal father's answer to this plea was worthy of "the proudest Roman of them all." Said the king: "Thy humane request becomes thee well, and if I were a private individual it should be granted, but *as a king* I owe both to my people and my successors an example of justice. I deeply lament the fate of my son; I shall lament it through life; but neither thy tears nor my grief shall prevent the punishment of his crime." The unfortunate prince was strangled to death, and the stern father was never afterwards happy, though he had acted from a sense of public duty. He once addressed the following pathetic verses to a friend: "The days of sunshine are past—dark night approaches, the shadows of which no morn will ever dissipate!"

The reign of Abderrahman III. has been regarded as the most brilliant period in the history of Saracen Spain. Commerce flourished, and wealth was accumulated in an unparalleled degree. A powerful navy was organized and maintained in full activity. The arts and sciences were cultivated with ardor, as their professors were rewarded with princely liberality. Many splendid public works were undertaken in the chief cities of Mohammedan Spain. The sovereign was the friend of industry, of merit and of poverty; and the fame of Abderrahman III. was so widespread that rich embassies came to visit him even from the Eastern Emperor at Constantinople.

Thus, two centuries after its origin, the Arabian kingdom of Cordova had attained the highest pinnacle of its prosperity. Its merchants were extremely wealthy. It had many manufactories of silk, woolen, cotton and linen, which employed tens of thousands of the people. Plate and jewelry of its own manufacture were everywhere seen. The land was fertilized by diligent and skillful irrigation; and rice, sugar and cotton were extensively cultivated. The landholders or farmers of Spain were much more prosperous under the Arab dominion than they had been in the feudal times of the Visigothic kings, who exacted one-third of the produce of the land as a tribute, whereas the Arabian rulers only demanded a tenth.

The commerce of the Moslems in the Mediterranean was more extensive than that of the Christian nations, and their naval power was superior. Abderrahman III. built a larger vessel than had ever been seen before, and loaded it with valuable merchandise, to be sold in the East. This vessel returned laden with goods for the Western Khalif's use, and also brought a number of beautiful female slaves, skilled in music and dancing, to enliven the royal banquets.

So great was the opulence of this flourishing Moslem kingdom in Spain that the governors of the provinces and the judges vied with the sovereign himself in the magnificence of their palaces and gardens; and, like him, they were surrounded by artists, poets, philosophers and others, who were distinguished by their superior talents, and who were entertained by their patrons in the most sumptuous manner. Numerous public libraries and academies were established in all the large cities of Spain, for the advancement of science and literature. At this period the science of medicine was little known outside of the Mohammedan world, but the physicians of Cordova were held in such high estimation that Christian princes came to the court of the Western Khalif to be cured of disease.

Abderrahman III. died in A. D. 961, and was succeeded by ALHAKEM II., who emulated his predecessor's virtues—a rare circumstance in the history of flourishing kingdoms. He disliked war, loved peace, and manifested an intense fondness for literature. His agents were constantly employed throughout the East in purchasing scarce and curious books. He himself wrote to every distinguished author for a copy of his works, for which he paid handsomely; and wherever he was unable to purchase a book he caused it to be transcribed. The catalogue of his library, though unfinished, numbered forty-four volumes. When he ascended the throne he intrusted the care of his library to one of his brothers, and assigned the duty of protecting literary institutions and of rewarding the learned to another brother, in order that he might devote his chief time to the affairs of state, and yet not neglect the interests of learning and literature. Thus the reign of Alhakem II. was the Augustan Age of Arabic literature in Spain.

This good monarch committed an act of tyranny, but the sequel is much to his credit. He sought to purchase an adjoining field in order to enlarge a garden. The owner refused to sell the field, whereupon the Khalif forcibly took possession of it. The owner complained to the cadi, or local magistrate, who took a sack and slung it across the back of a mule, and proceeded to the lot, where he found the Khalif busy pointing out a site for a pavilion. He requested permission to fill his sack with earth. After doing so, he respectfully asked the Khalif to assist him to lift the sack to the mule's back. Thinking some jest was intended, the Khalif good-naturedly attempted to lift one end of the sack, but found it too heavy. Thereupon the cadi exclaimed: "O prince, if thou canst not now lift so small a portion of the field thou hast usurped as is contained in this sack, how wilt thou bear the weight of the whole of it upon thy head in the Judgment Day!" The Khalif thanked his fearless monitor and restored the field to its owner.

The reign of Alhakem II. ended with his death, in A. D. 976, when his son, HIXEM II., ascended the throne of Cordova at the age of eleven years; the queen mother appointing a regent in the person of her secretary, a man of remarkable genius, valor and activity, who is best known by his surname, Al Mansur, "the Conqueror"—a title given him on account of his victories over the Christian Spaniards. He is said to have won fifty-four battles, and to have finally died of chagrin because he had been defeated in one battle. Al Mansur, who acted as a sovereign, was an enlightened statesman and active ruler, as well as a most able general and valiant soldier. He encouraged science and art, and munificently rewarded merit. His death, in A. D. 1002, at an advanced age, was a misfortune to the Khalifate of Cordova, which then rapidly decayed and soon fell to pieces.

The imbecile Hixem II. had been cast into prison by a usurper, and was supposed to have been dead; but one of the Arab chiefs showed him to the populace, used him as a puppet, and, in consideration of certain successes, was intrusted by the weak king with the privilege of converting revocable into hereditary fiefs. Some of the most powerful of the governors were thus drawn into the king's interest for a time, but thenceforth each of them aimed at a separate and independent sovereignty.

Suleiman, the rival of Hixem II., used the same ruinous means against his opponent, and gave the governors of Calatrava, Saragossa, Medina Cœli and Guadalaxara the hereditary and irrevocable possession of their governments, thus securing their powerful aid. This was the signal for the formation of many independent and rival Mohammedan kingdoms out of the territory of the Khalifate of Cordova, thus causing the ruin of Mohammedan Spain.

The last Khalif of Cordova was HIXEM III., who was called to the throne by the Spanish Arabs in A. D. 1026, against his own wishes. He sought to deserve the affections of his subjects, to redress wrongs, to encourage industry, to administer justice impartially, to relieve the poor, and to repress the exactions of the local magistrates. The governors resisted; whereupon he took the field against them; but they were too formidable for him, so that he was obliged to treat with open rebels. His failure where success was impossible was treated as a crime by the fickle multitude, and a mob paraded the streets of his capital and demanded his deposition, whereupon he gladly retired to private life (A. D. 1031). His virtues were remembered for ages, and the Arabic writers all represent him as too good for his times.

With the dethronement of Hixem III., in A. D. 1031, ended the illustrious dynasty of the Ommíyades; and the kingdom of Cordova, the Western Khalifate of Islam, fell to pieces. This powerful Saracen monarchy in Spain appeared to sink suddenly and to fall at once. Less than thirty years had passed since the great Al Mansur had wielded the resources of Africa and Spain, threatening the wholesale destruction of the Christians, whom he had driven into an obscure corner of the Spanish peninsula. But by A. D. 1031 Africa was lost; the Christian Spaniards occupied two-thirds of Spain; the petty independent Arabian governors—the boldest of whom had trembled at Al Mansur's name—openly insulted the ruler of Cordova, whose authority was confined to the capital and its immediate vicinity. Says a historian: "Assuredly, so astounding a catastrophe has no parallel in all history!"

The most prominent cause of the ruin of the Khalifate of Cordova was the division of the kingdom into the petty governments which were made hereditary in the families of the successful partisans who first obtained the fiefs. Thus the Arab nation in Spain retrograded from a powerful central government—a government sufficiently strong to protect the rights of all, with its subordinate powers properly distributed—back to the barbarian Feudal System, which, since the fall of the Western Roman Empire, had brought such terrible evils upon Europe, through the degradation of the many and the conflicting selfishness of the few.

During the next two centuries after the dissolution of the Khalifate of Cordova, which had so suddenly fallen from the zenith of its splendor and glory, its fine capital fell into the possession of the Christian Spaniards. The annals of these two centuries—from A. D. 1031 to 1238—are mainly a record of bloody battles, sieges, treasons, rebellions, persecutions, and petty successes of rival Arabian and Moorish chieftains; thus indicating a decay of the national spirit and the lack of a central, controlling energy—the convulsions of a body whose "whole head is sick and whose heart is faint."

From the dissolution of the Khalifate of Cordova, in A. D. 1031, to the founding of the Moorish kingdom of Granada, in A. D. 1492, Mohammedan Spain was without a supreme chief, excepting the *Almoravides* and the *Almohades*, the fleeting conquerors who invaded the Spanish peninsula from Africa and whose empire had but a transient and ephemeral existence. The portion of Spain that had escaped the progressive advances of the rising Christian kingdoms of Aragon, Castile, Leon, Navarre and Portugal fell under the dominion of petty Mohammedan kings, whose obscure feuds are not of sufficient importance to demand consideration in this work.

The Kingdom of Cordova embraced Valencia, Murcia, Granada, Andalusia, Portugal, and nearly all of Castile. These limits were extended under some of the more powerful sovereigns. Under Abderrahman I. the kingdom included Catalonia, Aragon and Leon; and even Asturias paid him tribute. Thus the entire Spanish peninsula was for a short time under the Saracen dominion, though Charlemagne for a portion of this time exercised a precarious authority in Catalonia and Aragon. But the Arabs had great trouble in maintaining those portions of their acknowledged possessions which bordered on the plains at the foot of Asturias, as the Christians were increasing in numbers every year, and were gradually extending their territories by prosecuting an almost incessant warfare against their conquerors. The wars between the Christian Spaniards and the Saracens continued, with few intervals of peace, during the entire period of the Mohammedan dominion in Spain.

In spite of their national animosity, a Christian Spaniard would sometimes marry a Moorish maiden, and many a young Moslem warrior would hazard countless difficulties and perils for the sake of obtaining his Christian bride. These intermarriages between the hostile nations were usually preceded by many romantic adventures, as they were invariably opposed by the relatives of both parties, and as the lover's ingenuity was put to the test to devise expedients for seeing and conversing with the maiden of his choice. Their correspondence was sometimes held by means of flowers, which the Orientals are in the habit of arranging in such order as to convey the same meaning as a written billet, each flower having an idea or word universally understood assigned to it.

The Arabs and Moors were an industrious people, and the agriculture of Spain was in a most flourishing condition during their occupation of the country. They introduced plantations of sugar, rice and cotton, and these products were cultivated by means of the labor of negro slaves. The Moors of Spain made the first paper manufactured in Europe; and their carpets and silks, their gold and silver embroidery, their manufactures in steel and leather, were long unrivaled.

We are indebted to the Saracens of Spain for the elements of many of the useful sciences, especially chemistry. They introduced the simple Arabic figures which we use in arithmetic. They taught mathematics, astronomy, philosophy and medicine; and were so superior in knowledge to the Christian nations of Europe that many Christians of all nations went to be educated in the Arabian schools of Cordova.

Abderrahman I. exhibited an excellent taste in selecting Cordova for the capital of his kingdom; as that city was surrounded by a most delightful country, adorned with groves of orange and citron, which were reflected in the clear waters of the Guadalquivir, on the picturesque banks of which were immense gardens, with their gay kiosks, and palaces ornamented with all the agreeable and striking characteristics of Saracen architecture. The Arabs connected the Oriental taste for gardens with the study of botany—a favorite pursuit, by which they ascertained the medicinal qualities of herbs. Thus the Saracen physicians, like the Jewish, became celebrated.

The Arabs and Moors of Spain differed very much from the Christian nations of Europe in their domestic manners, as well as from the simplicity of the primitive Arabs, because they had adopted much from the Persians, the Syrians and the Turks. The costume of the men was a long, loose robe, over large trousers, fastened around the waist with a girdle of embroidered leather, in which they carried a dagger. The robe was sometimes of cloth, sometimes of silk. The turban worn on the head was sometimes of silk, sometimes of muslin, and was frequently embroidered with gold.

The Moorish women lived in seclusion, having separate apartments of their own, where their husbands were the only male visitors admitted. They were taught to work embroidery and to play on the lute, but their mental culture was totally neglected, and most of their time was devoted to adorning their persons. They wore the large Turkish trousers, short open robes and long veils; and their dresses were often elegantly embroidered with gold and beads, in imitation of pearls. For seats they used low cushions, and mats or carpets spread over the floor. Their meats were served by slaves, on tables elevated but a few inches from the ground. They abstained from drinking wine, because the Koran forbids it; but they made a kind of sherry from the grape, were very fond of coffee, and drank sherbets, or the juice of fruits prepared with water and sugar. They ate very little meat, but were skilled in the art of making all kinds of pastry and confectionery, which generally formed the principal portion of every repast.

The government of the Khalifs was of that patriarchal kind which regards the sovereign as the father of a large family, whose children are permitted to come before him and address their complaints to him. The Arab sovereigns were empowered to appoint their own successors; and some of them bequeathed the crown to a younger son, in preference to an elder one, if they thought the younger would make the better monarch.

The Arabs and Moors deprived the Christians who remained among them of their civil rights, but protected them in the free exercise of their religion. Under the Mohammedan dominion in Spain the Jews in that country passed their happiest period in Europe, and the Jewish mediæval literature then attained its most thorough development.

SECTION XII.—EGYPT UNDER THE FATIMITES.

E have alluded to the rise of the new Arab kingdom of the Fatimites in Northern Africa, founded in A. D. 908 by the revolt of MOHAMMED AL MEHDI, the leader of the Shyite sect of the Mohammedan world, who then renounced his allegiance to the Khalif of Bagdad, and made himself Khalif, or both civil and religious ruler of the new state, which he and his successors enlarged by conquests over all Northern Africa. This dynasty became the formidable rivals of the Abbásside Khalifs of Bagdad, and assumed the title of Fatimites, in honor of their famous ancestress Fatima, Mohammed's daughter.

As we have also seen, MOEZ, or MUEZZEDDIN, the fourth of the Fatimite Khalifs of North Africa, conquered Egypt in A. D. 970, when that country was in a condition of anarchy and its inhabitants were suffering from a severe famine. The Fatimite army obtained the submission of the starving people of Egypt to the temporal and spiritual pretensions of the African Khalif, by distributing among them the large stores of corn which they carried into the country.

After conquering Egypt, Al Muezzeddin made that country the seat of his dominion, and founded the new city of Cairo, or Kahíra, "City of Victory," which he made the capital of his dominions. Thus Egypt again assumed the rank of an independent and powerful kingdom. The Fatimite Khalif of Egypt and North Africa denounced the Abbásside Khalif of Bagdad as an impostor, and declared himself the only legitimate successor of Mohammed. The claims of the Fatimite Khalif were diligently preached throughout the East, thus giving rise to a serious schism in the ranks of Islam. The Fatimite Khalifs soon enlarged their dominions by the conquest of Syria and Arabia, and Palestine again became the battleground of the rival armies of Egypt and the East. Egypt was governed by the Fatimite dynasty for two centuries, from A. D. 970 to 1171.

The most noted of the Fatimite Khalifs was AL HAKEM, who reigned from A. D.

996 to 1021. He was either a madman or a cruel monster. At the beginning of his reign he was a zealous Mohammedan, and began a rigorous persecution of the Jews and the Christians within his dominions. He compelled the Christians to bear heavy wooden crosses through the streets, and to every Jew he bound a calf's head to remind them of their idolatry at Sinai. He afterwards substituted a heavy wooden bell for the calf's head.

In A. D. 1020 Hakem, who had fallen under the influence of Hamza, a wandering fanatic, proclaimed himself the incarnation of the Deity, and commanded his subjects to worship him. Says Gibbon: "At the name of Hakem, the lord of the living and the dead, every knee was bent in religious adoration; his mysteries were performed on a mountain near Cairo; sixteen thousand converts signed his profession of faith." Hakem now severely persecuted the Mohammedans, as well as the Jews and the Christians. He destroyed the Christian Church of the Resurrection at Jerusalem, and a thousand other Christian churches in Syria and Egypt. But he soon ceased his persecution of the Christians, and permitted them to rebuild their churches.

In his civil administration Hakem ruled cruelly and tyrannically. He constantly interfered in the private affairs of his subjects, especially the women, and punished all infractions of his arbitrary decrees in the most barbarous manner. He condemned the Egyptian women to the utmost seclusion, forbidding them to show themselves in the streets. On one occasion he observed what appeared to him to be a woman standing in the streets of Cairo, in defiance of his edict; but when he approached the object, he discovered that it was only a lay figure made of pasteboard, holding in its hand a card on which was a writing accusing the Khalif's sister of immorality. Hakem was so enraged that he set his soldiers upon the people of Cairo, many of whom were brutally massacred. He ordered an inquiry into his sister's morals; but she, in alarm for her life, caused him to be assassinated, A. D. 1022.

After the assassination of Hakem, the fanatical Hamza fled to Syria, and in the fastnesses of Mount Lebanon established the sect of the *Druses*, who still consider Hakem their Messiah.

The later Fatimite Khalifs were feeble sovereigns, monarchs only in name; the real power being exercised by their Grand Viziers, or chief ministers. The Khalif was confined either in the mosque or in the seraglio, as his disposition inclined him, and the Grand Vizier conducted the affairs of state in his name. This produced repeated contests for power, thus reducing the country to great weakness.

In the reign of the Khalif ADHED one of the rival claimants for supremacy appealed to the Christian King of Jerusalem for aid, and the other to the Turkish Sultan of Damascus. Both these rulers were indifferent to the Khalifate of Cairo, and each responded to the appeals made to him, hoping thereby to subvert that power and annex it to his own dominions. Almeric, the Christian King of Jerusalem, led his own army; but the forces of Noureddin, Sultan of Damascus, were led by the Emir Shiracouh, a Kurd by birth, and his nephew Saladin.

Three successive expeditions resulted in making Shiracouh master of Egypt, and he was then invested by the Khalif Adhed with the office of Grand Vizier of Egypt. Shiracouh lived but two months after this; and while accepting the office of Grand Vizier, he always styled himself the subject of Noureddin, the Sultan of Damascus, and his Emir in Egypt. When Shiracouh died, his nephew Saladin became his successor. Saladin was generally regarded as deficient in talent, and too much given to pleasure to have much authority in the army. Adhed hoped that Saladin's weakness would enable him to recover his lost power, and for some time it appeared that he would be successful. But Saladin's true nature now awoke, and he soon made himself master of the Fatimite Khalif.

Noureddin, King of Damascus, now ordered Saladin to put an end to the Fatimite Khalifate. Saladin, fearing that so daring a proceeding would provoke a popular outbreak, hesitated. But one of his council mounted the oratory before the Khatib, or general reader, and offered the public prayer in the name of the Khalif of Bagdad. The solemn tranquillity of devotion was not disturbed by any cry of astonishment, any outburst of rage and indignation, at this insult to national principles. The will of the court spread through Egypt in a few days, and the Egyptians silently submitted to the overthrow of their altars. During this revolution, Adhed, the last Fatimite Khalif, was confined to his bed with his last illness, and he died in utter ignorance of what had transpired (A. D. 1171). Thus ended the dynasty of the Fatimite Khalifs after ruling for more than two and a half centuries (A. D. 908–1171).

Saladin immediately seized the dead Khalif's treasures, and confined the unfortunate sovereign's children in the seraglio. The Sultan of Damascus confirmed Saladin in his office. The green silk of the Fatimites in Egypt gave way to the black ensigns of the Abbássides, thus ending the schism of two centuries in the Mohammedan world.

Saladin acknowledged the authority of Noureddin as long as that Sultan of Damascus lived; but when Noureddin passed to his grave, the valiant Kurd proclaimed himself Sultan of Egypt and Syria—a usurpation which was ratified by the Khalif of Bagdad, the spiritual head of Islam, through gratitude to the destroyer of the rival Khalifate.

Saladin—whose chief fame rests on his wars in Palestine with the Christian Crusaders from Europe—died in A. D. 1193; whereupon his dominions were divided among his three sons, who became Sultans of Aleppo, Damascus and Egypt. Egypt fell to the share of Aziz, and was thus again separated from Syria. Saladin's descendants repulsed the attacks of the European Crusaders upon Egypt, as we shall see in another section of this volume.

Malek Sala, one of Saladin's successors, bought a multitude of captives from the great Mongol conqueror, Zingis Khan, and organized them as his body-guard under the name of *Mamelukes*. Other captives from the region around the Caspian Sea were brought to Egypt. The Mamelukes were the flower of the Egyptian army, and appreciated their power from the beginning. They dethroned Malek Sala, and made their leader, Ibeg, Sultan of Egypt (A. D. 1254). The Mamelukes ruled Egypt for one hundred and thirty years, raising up and pulling down Sultans at their pleasure. Towards the end of the fourteenth century the Circassian Mamelukes outnumbered the Turkish Mamelukes, when the former overpowered the latter, making their own leader Sultan of Egypt; and for the next century Egypt was a prey to anarchy until the conquest of the country by the Ottoman Turks in A. D. 1517.

SECTION XIII.—THE WESTERN EMPIRE RESTORED.

LLUSION has been made to the deposition of Chilperic III., the last Merovingian King of the Franks, by PEPIN THE LITTLE, the son of Charles Martel and the founder of the Carlovingian dynasty of Frankish kings, A. D. 752. Pepin's elevation to the Frankish throne was the result of a compact between himself and Pope Zachary, based on considerations of mutual interest. Pepin needed the Pope's sanction to legitimatize his crown; while the Pope needed the aid of the Frankish arms, by which he was elevated ultimately to the position of a temporal and territorial sovereign. This alliance between the Carlovingians and the Papacy became a principle of regeneration and progress for France and all Western

Europe. A strong monarchical government was now established, clothed with the power to make itself universally respected; and at the same time the Papacy became a fixed predominant authority for the management of the affairs of the Church.

Thus when the last of the feeble descendants of Clovis was dethroned by Pepin the Little, the Frankish kingdom, by being brought into close political connection with the Holy See, became the leading state in Europe; and the foundation was laid for the system of policy which has since prevailed in Europe, by the combination of the highest ecclesiastical authority with the most extensive civil power.

Many circumstances had previously tended to give the Pope, as the Bishop of Rome was called from an unknown period, great and commanding authority over the Christian nations of the West. Among the most influential of these circumstances was the extravagant claim to the ancient dominion of the Cæsars, seriously put forth by the Eastern Roman Emperors, when they lacked the means and the ability to uphold their pretensions. Weary of the pride and cruelty of the Byzantine Greeks, the Italians supported the papal power as a counterpoise to the imperial authority, and were eager to have the Bishop of Rome recognized as the Head of the Christian Church, for the purpose of guarding against the usurpation of the title by the Patriarch of Constantinople.

The recognition of Pepin's elevation to the Frankish throne was thus something more than a mere form, being a ratification of his claims by the only authority that was respected by the nations of Western Christendom. In return Pepin furnished military assistance to the Popes in their wars with the Lombards, and openly proclaimed himself the champion of the Church. Astolph, King of the Lombards, seized Ravenna, the capital of the Exarchate, and menaced Rome. In A. D. 753 Pope Stephen II. visited Paris, the Frankish capital, as already related, to implore Pepin's assistance. Pepin swore to cross the Alps to the Pope's aid the next year, and was crowned at St. Denis by Pope Stephen II., with great pomp, being at the same time invested with the title of *Patrician of the Romans.*

The following year, A. D. 754, Pepin led a large army into Italy, defeated the Lombards, and compelled King Astolph to agree to cede to the Pope all the territory which he had conquered. Pepin then returned to his dominions, and Astolph at once broke his promise, ravaged the Romagna, besieged Rome and demanded the Pope's surrender. Pepin immediately crossed the Alps a second time and chastised the Lombard king so severely that he was obliged to surrender the Exarchate of Ravenna and the Pentapolis for the sake of peace. Pepin conferred these territories upon the Pope, thus elevating him to the dignity of a temporal as well as a spiritual ruler. The Frankish king retained the sovereignty of these provinces, but the Pope obtained their rich revenues. This was the beginning of the Pope's temporal power, which lasted until 1870.

Under the protection of Pepin the Little, some active English missionaries proclaimed the religion of a crucified Jesus to the savage inhabitants of Germany. The most celebrated of these Anglo-Saxon missionaries was Boniface, or Winfried, who preached the Gospel in Hesse, where he built the abbey of Fulda, and who founded bishoprics and colleges for education among the Thuringians, the Franks and the Bavarians, and manifested such zeal that he acquired the title of "the Apostle of the Germans." After being appointed Archbishop of Mayence, Boniface in his old age undertook another mission to the heathen Finlanders, who murdered the noble missionary. Through the influence of the Carlovingian kings, the bishoprics and colleges which Boniface had established became closely united with the Roman See, and the abbey of Fulda was especially free from all jurisdiction except that of the Pope.

The whole of the reign of Pepin the Little was marked by warlike enterprises. In A. D. 752 he undertook to expel the Saracens from the province of Septimania. He drove them successively from all the Septimanian cities, and finally besieged Narbonne, the capital of the province, which some Gothic citizens betrayed to him in A. D. 759. By this success the war was decided in favor of the Frankish monarch, and Septimania became ultimately a Frankish province.

The great duchy of Aquitaine, embracing a fourth part of the territory of modern France, cast off its allegiance to the Frankish sovereign, but Pepin reduced it to submission. The war commenced in A. D. 760 and continued eight years. The Duke of Aquitaine made an obstinate resistance, but was put to death by his own people in A. D. 768, and the Frankish king's authority over the duchy was restored. This triumph ended the career of Pepin the Little. On his return from Aquitaine, Pepin was seized with a violent fever at Saintes. He was removed with great difficulty to St. Denis, where he died September 24, A. D. 768, at the age of fifty-four, after a reign of almost twenty-seven years—eleven as Mayor of the Palace, and almost sixteen as King of the Franks.

In accordance with Pepin's will, the Frankish dominions were divided between his sons, CHARLES and CARLOMAN—a repetition of the pernicious policy which had proved so destructive to the Merovingian dynasty. The mutual jealousy of Charles and Carloman would have exploded in civil war, but for the judicious interference of their mother, Bertha. Three years after their accession, A. D. 771, Carloman died suddenly, and his widow and children fled to the Lombards. His brother Charles, who is better known by his French name, CHARLEMAGNE, or Charles the Great, was declared sole King of the Franks by the voice of the estates of the kingdom.

The accession of Pepin the Little to the Frankish throne was the triumph of the Teutonic element over the Latin-Celtic race in Gaul. The predominance of this Germanic element was still more marked in the reign of Charlemagne, who proved himself one of the greatest sovereigns in the world's history. This prince had acted a conspicuous part in his father's wars in Italy, and displayed more than ordinary abilities, both as a general and a statesman. He distinguished himself in the suppression of the revolt in Aquitaine, and deservedly acquired the fame of recovering that fine province to the Frankish dominions.

The protection granted to Carloman's family threatened to produce a rupture with the Lombard king Desiderius. There was another ground of hostility between Charlemagne and Desiderius. Charlemagne had married the Lombard king's daughter, and afterwards divorced her. Desiderius menaced war, but lacked the means to execute his threats. Charlemagne would have crossed the Alps to chastise the Lombard monarch, had not a more formidable foe appeared on the eastern frontier of the Frankish dominions.

This new enemy was the Saxons, who were the only German people who had never submitted to the dominion of the Franks, and whose country extended from the mouths of the Elbe southward to Thuringia, and westward nearly to the Rhine. The Saxons had not yet become Christians, and were still worshipers of Odin and Thor. They frequently devastated the frontier provinces of the Christian Franks, and displayed particular animosity toward the Christian churches and clergy. A Christian missionary, St. Libuinus, had vainly endeavored to convert the Saxons by denouncing God's vengeance against their paganism; but they were so exasperated by his reproaches that they expelled him from their country, burned the church erected at Daventer, and massacred the Christians.

The general convocation of the Franks, called from the time of meeting the *Champ de Mai*, or "Field of May," was then assembled at Worms under the presidency of Charlemagne. This assembly considered the massacre at Daventer a *casus belli*, and accordingly declared war against the Saxons. As the Assembly of the Champ de Mai was both a convention of the estates of the Frankish kingdom and a review of the military power of the Franks, a Frankish army was in immediate readiness. Charlemagne

CHARLEMAGNE.

ROLAND AT THE BATTLE OF RONCESVALLES.

THE WESTERN EMPIRE RESTORED.

crossed the Rhine, captured the important Saxon fortress of Eresburg, destroyed the Saxon idols, and in A. D. 772 compelled the Saxons to accept a treaty of peace and to give hostages for their good behavior. No sooner had Charlemagne returned home from his first Saxon campaign, than he was summoned to Italy to rescue Pope Adrian I. from the wrath of the Lombard king Desiderius, who was so enraged at the Pope's refusal to recognize Carloman's sons as Kings of the Franks that he actually invaded the Pope's dominions and besieged Rome itself. Charlemagne forced a passage over the Alps, and was actually descending from the mountains before the Lombards were aware that he had begun his march.

After vainly endeavoring to check the Franks in the defiles, Desiderius abandoned the field and shut himself up in his capital, Pavia, which withstood a year's siege, during which Charlemagne visited Rome and was very enthusiastically received by the Pope and the citizens. The whole body of the clergy appeared with banners in their hands, and Pope Adrian I. received the great monarch in the church of St. Peter, the people singing: "Blessed is he that cometh in the name of the Lord." Soon after he had returned to camp, in A. D. 774, Pavia surrendered. Desiderius and his queen were made prisoners, and spent the remainder of their days in separate cloisters. Charlemagne, placing the iron crown of the Lombard kings upon his own head, assumed the title of King of Italy; thus putting an end to the Lombard monarchy, which had existed in Northern Italy for two centuries (A. D. 571-774).

Thenceforth Charlemagne's full title was *King of the Franks and Lombards and Patrician of the Romans.* The Lombard nobles were permitted to retain their estates and titles as his vassals. In A. D. 776 they plotted against Charlemagne, and were aided by the Eastern Roman Emperor, Leo IV. The great Frankish monarch crossed the Alps in midwinter, crushed the revolt, and filled all the important offices in Lombardy with Franks.

While Charlemagne was engaged in Italy the Saxons expelled the Frankish garrisons from their territory. But after the conquest of the Lombards, Charlemagne again led a large army into the Saxon country, subdued the barbarians a second time, and compelled the Saxon chiefs to agree to the Peace of Paderborn in A. D. 777. The warlike Saxon duke, Witikind, refusing to accept the treaty, fled to the Danes.

In the same year that Charlemagne ended his second war with the Saxons (A. D. 777), the Saracen Emir of Saragossa sought refuge at the Frankish court and solicited Charlemagne's aid in his struggle with the King of Cordova, offering to become tributary to the Frankish king in return for such assistance. Charlemagne promised to help the Emir, and in A. D. 778 he led an expedition over the Pyrenees into Spain. The Frankish monarch dismantled Pampeluna and Saragossa, and annexed all that portion of Spain between the Pyrenees and the Ebro to the Frankish dominions, in consequence of the disputes that distracted the Mohammedans in Spain. After his great victory at Saragossa, Charlemagne was recalled home by a new and more dangerous revolt of the Saxons.

As the Frankish monarch was recrossing the Pyrenees into France, his rear-guard, under the command of his nephew Roland, was treacherously attacked and cut to pieces by the Basques in the pass of Roncesvalles, Roland himself being among the slain. The battle of Roncesvalles gave rise to many romances, and was celebrated in the poetry of the Middle Ages.

A more minute account of this famous encounter will be interesting. The celebrated valley of Roncesvalles is the line of communication between France and Navarre, and the road through it is rugged and tortuous, with narrow gorges between steep mountains. While the Franks were toiling through these defiles, the Basques and Saraceus formed ambuscades on the summits of the mountains, hidden by the dense forests which there abound.

After the greater portion of the Frankish

CHARLEMAGNE CROSSING THE ALPS.

army had passed, the Basque mountaineers suddenly rushed down the declivities and assailed the Frankish rear-guard and the divisions intrusted with the charge of the baggage. The Franks were surprised, but not disheartened. They made a desperate resistance, and vainly endeavored to cut their way to the main body of their army. The assailants had the advantage of a light equipment and a favorable position, and the entire rear-guard of the Franks was cut off. The baggage was plundered before Charlemagne was aware of their peril, and the Basque mountaineers disappeared so rapidly with their booty as to elude all pursuit.

Though the legendary account of the battle of Roncesvalles contains very little truth, it is of great historical importance, as no history ever possessed a wider influence than this romantic tale. By singing the song of Roland the Normans were encouraged at the battle of Hastings, and by it the French were inspired to their most glorious deeds.

According to this legend Charlemagne had almost conquered Spain in a war which lasted more than seven years. The Saracen king, whom the romances call Marsiles, in dread of total ruin held a council of his most prominent Emirs and nobles, who unanimously recommended him to conciliate Charlemagne by immediate submission. With the usual inconsistency of romance, a Saracen ambassador is said to have taken a stand near the Spanish marches, and he addressed the Frankish sovereign thus: "God protect you! Behold here are presents which my master sends; and he engages, if you withdraw from Spain, to come and do you homage at Aix la Chapelle."

Charlemagne is said to have summoned his twelve Paladins to council to deliberate upon the offer made by the Saracen ruler of Spain. Roland was strenuously opposed to negotiating with a non-Christian, declaring that it was the duty of Christians to rescue Spain from the dominion of the crescent, and to place it again under the banner of the cross. But two of the Paladins. Ganelon and the Duke Naimes, maintained that it was contrary to the rules of chivalry to refuse grace to a vanquished foe.

Charlemagne, whom the romances represent as a perfect model of chivalry, yielded to the arguments of the advocates of peace, and inquired which of his peers would undertake to return with the Saracen ambassador and convey a suitable answer to Marsiles, the Saracen sovereign of Spain. Ganelon offered his services, but Roland contemptuously declared that he was unfit for such a duty, and offered himself instead.

A spirited debate arose in the council. Ganelon was so exasperated by the scorn with which his pretensions were treated by Roland, and by the imputations upon his loyalty and courage, that he said indignantly to his rival: "Take care that some mischief does not overtake you." Roland, who did not possess the quality of moderation among some other virtues, replied: "Go, you speak like a fool! We want men of sense to carry our messages; if the king pleases, I will go in your place." Ganelon angrily answered: "Charles is commander here; I submit myself to his will." Thereupon Roland loudly laughed—an act of discourtesy which so offended the other Paladins that they unanimously recommended Ganelon as the most suitable ambassador to the court of Marsiles.

The Saracen ambassador had obtained private information of the angry discussion which had occurred in the king's council. Upon returning to the Saracen court he took every opportunity to remind Ganelon of the insult which he had suffered, and, though he did not succeed immediately, he certainly weakened the Paladin's loyalty and led him secretly to consider the possibility of revenging himself by treasonable means.

At his first interview with Marsiles, Ganelon maintained the pride and dignity of a French chevalier. Said the Saracen King of Cordova: "Charles is now old; he must be close upon a hundred years of age; does he not think of taking some repose?" Ganelon firmly replied: "No! no! Charles is ever powerful; so long as he has around him the twelve peers of France, but particularly Oliver and Roland, Charles need not fear a living man."

But subsequent conversations enabled the Saracen sovereign to work upon Ganelon's cupidity and his jealousy of Roland so effectually that he consented to give him such information as would enable him to cut off the rear of the Frankish army when it returned to Roncesvalles in accordance with the terms of the treaty.

Ganelon returned to Charlemagne's camp and informed the Frankish king that Marsiles had agreed to become his vassal and to pay tribute. Charlemagne at once ordered his army to return to France, the king personally assuming command of the van, while the rear-guard under Roland followed at a little distance through the pass of Roncesvalles with the baggage and plunder.

Meanwhile Marsiles had collected a vast army from his subjects in Spain, and from the numerous auxiliaries of Northern and Central Africa. According to Ganelon's instructions, the Saracen ruler of Spain sent large detachments of his troops to occupy the woods and mountains overhanging "the gloomy Roncesvalles' strait."

When the Franks were involved in the pass they were suddenly assailed simultaneously in front, flank and rear. Oliver climbed a tree for the purpose of obtaining some idea of the number of the enemy. Seeing that the Saracen hosts were vastly superior to the Franks, he called out to Roland: "Brother in arms! the infidels are very numerous, and the Christians are few; if you sounded your horn King Charles would bring succor."

Roland replied: "God forbid that my lineage should be dishonored by such a deed! I will strike with my good sword Durandel; and the infidels falling beneath my blows will discover that they have been led hither by their evil fate."

Oliver repeated: "Sound your horn, companion in arms! the enemies hem us in on every side" Roland reiterated: "No! our Franks are gallant warriors; they will strike heavy blows and cut through the host of the foul paynim." Roland then prepared his troops for action. Archbishop Turpin, who perceived that the conflict would be desperate and bloody, ordered the Frankish soldiers to kneel and to join in a general confession of faith, after which he conferred upon them absolution and his episcopal benediction.

The Christian Franks made a heroic defense, but numerical superiority eventually prevailed over valor. "Down went many a noble crest; cloven was many a plumed helmet. The lances were shivered in the grasp of Christendom's knights, and the swords dropped from their wearied arms." Turpin, Oliver and Roland still survived, and feebly resisted. At length Roland turned to Oliver, exclaiming: "I will sound my horn, Charles will hear us, and we may yet hope again to see our beloved France." Oliver replied: "Oh! shame and disgrace, why did you not sound when first I asked you? The best warriors of France have been sacrificed to your temerity; we must die with them!" But Turpin insisted that the horn should be blown as a signal to the king, whereupon Roland blew such a blast that the blood spurted from his mouth, thus opening his wounds afresh and pouring forth in torrents.

Charlemagne, who was then almost a hundred miles distant, heard the sound, and said: "Our men are engaged at disadvantage; we must haste to their assistance." The traitor Ganelon replied: "I do not believe it." The Frankish monarch was thus dissuaded from going to Roland's aid. With his dying breath, Roland again blew a wailing blast from his horn. Charlemagne understood the character of the sound, and exclaimed: "Evil has come upon us; those are the dying notes of my nephew Roland!" The Frankish king accordingly returned to Roncesvalles; but Roland and all his comrades lay dead in the pass, and Charlemagne was only able to honor their corpses with Christian burial.

Such are the salient points in the old romance on which the song of Roland is founded. The narrative was accepted as a historical fact until the very close of the Middle Ages; and when King John the Good, of France, shortly previous to the disastrous battle of Poitiers, reproached his nobles that there were no Rolands in his army, an aged knight replied: "Sire, Rolands would not be wanting if we could find a Charlemagne."

As the Saracen Emir of Saragossa had violated his promise to do homage to Charlemagne, the Frankish king organized the conquered territory into a Frankish province called *Marca Hispanica*, or the "Spanish March." The governor of this province had jurisdiction over Rousillon, Catalonia, and the infant kingdoms of Aragon and Navarre; and his capital was Barcelona.

While Charlemagne was fighting against the Mohammedans in Spain, the Saxons again took up arms against the Franks; but after his return from Spain, Charlemagne again invaded and ravaged the territories of the Saxons, and again subjugated those fierce people after a series of desperate encounters. The victorious Frankish king compelled many of the conquered Saxons to join his armies in a war against the Slavonians in the East of Europe.

On the march against the Slavonians, the Saxons in Charlemagne's army fell suddenly upon the Frankish soldiers and massacred many of them. This treachery was terribly avenged by the Frankish monarch, who devastated the Saxon territory and caused four thousand five hundred Saxons whom he had made prisoners to be put to death. The Saxons now renewed the war, but after sustaining a severe defeat on the Hase they were obliged to submit, and Saxony became a portion of the Frankish Empire. Witikind, the Saxon chief, swore fealty to the Frankish monarch, received Christian baptism, and he and his people embraced Christianity. Bishoprics, monasteries and churches rapidly sprung up in the Saxon country. The eight bishoprics were those of Osnabruck, Minden, Verden, Bremen, Paderborn, Munster, Halberstadt, and Hildersheim.

In the year A. D. 786, not long after Charlemagne had established the Margraviate of Brandenburg as a check against the destructive inroads of the Slavonians, his nephew, Thassilo, Duke of Bavaria, endeavored to cast off the yoke of Frankish supremacy, with the aid of the wild Avars, who had established themselves in the East of Europe. Thassilo was subdued, but revolted again the next year (A. D. 787). The treacherous Bavarian duke was defeated, made prisoner, and punished for his faithlessness by perpetual imprisonment in the cloister at Fulda, in Hesse. Charlemagne then incorporated the dukedom of Bavaria with the great Frankish Empire, and established the Eastern Margraviate to check the incursions of the Avars.

The Avars, the descendants of the savage Huns, who, under the leadership of Attila, had desolated Europe more than three centuries before, still occupied the forests and morasses of Pannonia, and were in such close proximity to Bavaria that Charlemagne determined to attempt to reduce them under his dominion. Accordingly he invaded their country in A. D. 791 with an overwhelming force and subdued them, thus becoming master of Western Pannonia.

Five years later (A. D. 796), Charlemagne's son, Pepin, King of Italy, stormed the remaining defenses of the Avars and inflicted dreadful slaughter upon them, thus compelling them to submit to the Frankish power. Almost the whole of the treasures which Attila had carried away from Western Europe was recovered by Pepin; and the Avar chieftain, Thudan, and his leading warriors embraced Christianity, and were baptized at Aix la Chappelle. The entire kingdom of the Avars was thus annexed to Charlemagne's dominions.

On the death of queen Hildegard in A. D. 783, Charlemagne married Fastrade, a woman of low birth, but of vindictive and haughty disposition. This marriage was unfortunate for the king; as Fastrade filled his mind with jealousies and suspicions, instigated him to cruel deeds, and induced him to oppress the nobles and the people. This conduct created disaffection, and in A. D. 789 led to the formation of a plot for the deposition of Charlemagne and the placing of his son Pepin upon the Frankish throne. The detection of the conspiracy was followed by the punishment of those engaged in it, but Charlemagne never again recovered the complete confidence of his subjects.

Pope Leo III., the successor of Adrian I., upon his accession in A. D. 796, sent the Roman standard to Charlemagne, entreating the great Frankish monarch to send a deputy to Rome to receive the allegiance of the Roman people; thus showing that the Popes then acknowledged the sovereignty of the most powerful ruler of Western Christendom. In A. D. 799 the relatives of the preceding Pope brought an accusation against

CHARLEMAGNE ORDERING THE CUTTING DOWN OF THE SACRED OAK.

THE WESTERN EMPIRE RESTORED.

Leo III., attacked him in the open street, overwhelmed him with a shower of blows, and confined him half dead in the prison of the monastery. But the Pope made his escape and fled to Charlemagne, who received him with the utmost respect and sent him back to Rome loaded with honors, promising soon to follow him to Italy.

In A. D. 800, according to his promise to the Pope, Charlemagne, who had now become master of all France, Germany and Italy, and of North-eastern Spain, went to Italy for the twofold purpose of quelling the rebellion of the Lombard Duke of Benevento and rescuing Pope Leo III. from his insurgent subjects. Charlemagne's visit to Rome to investigate the charges against the Pope resulted in Leo's acquittal and in the punishment of his enemies.

The grateful Pontiff rewarded the great Frankish king for his friendly assistance, and promptly executed a design which he had doubtless planned with the visiting sovereign. On Christmas day, in the year 800 A. D., as the great Frankish monarch was attending divine service in the Church of St. Peter, Pope Leo III. placed the golden crown of the Roman Empire upon his head and saluted him with the title of "*Emperor of the Romans;*" while the people in the church shouted: "Long life to Charles Augustus, crowned by the hand of God great and pacific Emperor of the Romans." The crowning of Charlemagne at Rome was regarded as a revival of the Roman Empire of the West, and Charlemagne was considered a successor of the Cæsars. The capital of Charlemagne's Empire was Aix-la-Chapelle. There were now two great Empires in Christendom—that of the East with Constantinople for its capital, and that of the West with Aix-la-Chapelle for its seat of government. The division which had for a long time existed in the Christian Church now ended in a complete separation; and thus arose the Eastern, or Greek Catholic, and the Western, or Roman Catholic Churches.

It was held that the Western Roman Empire had not ceased to exist when Romulus Augustulus was dethroned by Odoacer in A. D. 476, but that it had been simply merged in the Eastern Roman Empire. The imperial authority had been represented in the West by the Exarch of Ravenna, and the Eastern Emperor's right to rule had not been disputed in theory, but the most powerful of the barbarian kings had been proud to govern with titles conferred upon them by the Eastern Cæsars.

The Iconoclastic War had created bitter animosity in the West toward the court of Constantinople, and thus produced a state of feeling which rendered it impossible to effect any actual reunion between the Eastern and Western Empires and Churches of Christendom. Events tending to widen the breach followed in rapid succession.

The Romans regarded the Empress Irene, who then reigned at Constantinople, as a usurper. They maintained that she could not be Cæsar and Augustus, and that they had as good a right as the East to elect the Cæsar. They insisted that Rome was rightfully the capital of the Empire; and thus, in choosing Charlemagne, they declared that they were exercising an inalienable right, and merely resuming the privileges which had so long been held in abeyance without being lost.

Thus Charlemagne was declared the successor of Constantine VI. as temporal head of Christendom, and he was numbered as sixty-eighth in order through the Eastern line of Emperors from Augustus, the founder of the Roman Empire. This claim was denied at Constantinople, as it was in direct conflict with the pretensions of the Eastern Roman Emperors. Thus the two Emperors in Christendom—the one reigning in the East and the other in the West—each claimed to be the only true Cæsar.

The death of Fastrade having again left Charlemagne a widower, he intended marrying the Eastern Empress Irene, but the contemplated match was prevented by the dethronement of Irene. Her successor, Nicephorus I., dreaded Charlemagne's power and sought his alliance. A treaty was negotiated between the two Emperors in A. D. 803, fixing the boundaries of their dominions in Italy. The Eastern Emperor renounced his claim to Rome and the Exarchate of Ravenna, but retained Venice, Istria, the coast of Dalmatia and the cities of Calabria. It was hoped that Western Christendom might now be united under the Pope as the spiritual head, while the new Western Emperor was to be secular ruler. The Western Empire, thus revived in Charlemagne, lasted one thousand and six years, from A. D. 800 until 1806, when it was subverted by Napoleon Bonaparte.

Maddened by the oppressive system of military service and by the payment of tithes to the Church, the Saxons rose in rebellion against the Frankish power; but they were finally reduced to submission in the year A. D. 804, and ten thousand Saxon families were forced to settle among the Franks, while colonies of Franks were settled in the Saxon countries. Thus ended the war which for thirty-two years Charlemagne had waged against the Saxons, for the purpose of punishing them for their repeated aggressions and extending his empire and the Christian religion.

In the midst of his victorious career, Charlemagne was alarmed by the appearance of a new enemy on the coasts of France, in A. D. 807; and, though the Frankish monarch repelled their incursions, his mind was distracted with sad bodings for the future of his subjects. This new foe of the Franks—the Northmen, Norsemen, or Normans, from the bleak shores of Scandinavia—were actuated by thirst for plunder, further stimulated by the desire of revenging the wrongs suffered by their pagan brethren, the Saxons. They had little time to perpetrate any devastation at their first landing in France, as they fled when they received tidings of the great Frankish monarch's approach. Charlemagne beheld their departing ships without exultation, and, bursting into tears, predicted that those *Sea-kings* would shortly prove a terrible scourge to Southern and Western Europe.

The monk of St. Gall stated that when Charlemagne was asked the cause of these tears, he replied: "My faithful friends, do you inquire why I weep thus bitterly? Assuredly it is not that I dread any annoyance to myself from the piracy of those wretches; but I am deeply affected to find that they have dared to visit these coasts even in my life-time; and violent grief overwhelms me when I look forward to the evils they will inflict on my subjects."

Charlemagne's Empire extended from the Baltic and North Seas on the north to the Ebro in Spain and Central Italy on the south, and from the Atlantic Ocean on the west to the Save, the Theiss, the Oder and the Lower Vistula on the east. The Rhineland —the home of the Eastern Franks—was the center of his vast realm.

His favorite capital, Aix la Chapelle, was embellished with a palace, a chapel, and works of art, such as marbles and mosaics from Italy and sculptures from Greece. The city was also adorned with an excellent library, a richly endowed college, and a school of sacred music. The superb chapel from which this famous city derived its present name was a most magnificent structure. The dome was embellished with a globe of solid gold. The gates and balustrades were of bronze, the vases and chandeliers of gold and silver, while the ornaments displayed an elegance unparalleled in that region.

Charlemagne was now the most powerful monarch in the world, and his greatness was recognized by all Christendom and Islam. The Anglo-Saxon kingdoms in Britain and the little Christian kingdom in Spain sought his protection; while the great Khalif of Bagdad, Haroun al Raschid, sent two embassies to seek his friendship, bringing valuable gifts to the great Emperor; the first embassy, in A. D. 801, presenting the keys of Jerusalem and the Holy Sepulcher, and the second embassy, in A. D. 807, presenting a curious clock.

Charlemagne passed the remainder of his life and reign in perfecting the internal organization of his dominions. This was a task of almost superhuman difficulty, because of the many dissimilar nations under his dominion. The success which crowned his efforts did more to perpetuate his fame than all his great military achievements, and his greatest glory was the extension of Christianity and the revival of civilization in Europe. Germany had been little more than a heathen wilderness at the time of his accession, its only towns being those on the Rhine and the Danube founded by Roman colonies.

Charlemagne's government of his dominions was strictly personal. It was an absolute monarchy disguised under aristocratic and popular forms and institutions. The Emperor originated and proposed all laws, and these were discussed in the national assemblies, one of which convened in May and the other in the fall, and which were attended by the dukes, counts, bishops and other leading men of the Empire. These national assemblies were simply authorized to deliberate and advise, the Emperor alone having the right to decide what should become law.

The *capitularies* or laws of Charlemagne still remaining show the wide range over which the Emperor's care and wisdom extended. His laws embrace almost every conceivable subject of legislation, from matters of the highest moral, ecclesiastical and political importance, down to the most minute details of domestic economy.

One of Charlemagne's great objects was to diminish the power of the dukes and counts, who were almost independent sovereigns, and who were the principal obstacles in the way of the Emperor's efforts to administer justice among his subjects. He wholly abolished the title of duke in Germany. For the defense of the long and exposed frontier of his great Empire, he organized the border districts of Germany into *Marks*, or *Marches*, also known as *Margraviates*, or *Margravates;* and over these he placed margraves or marquises, whose chief duty was to drive back or conquer the neighboring tribes.

The principal of these marks were Brandenburg in the North-east, formed to check the inroads of the Slavonians; Austria, or the Eastern mark, designed to check the incursions of the Avars, or Huns, into Bavaria; and Carinthia, which extended from the Adriatic to the Danube.

Charlemagne established order and improved the administration of justice throughout his vast dominions. The counts were mainly intrusted with the administration of justice, and these were aided by various grades of deputies. The Emperor also appointed a peculiar class of officials called *missi dominici*, who were charged with the duty of visiting every portion of the Empire four times a year, to hear appeals from the lower tribunals, and to report to the Emperor concerning the general state of the country. An appeal might be made from the judgments of these lower tribunals to the royal tribunal, over which the Palsgrave presided.

Charlemagne was a liberal friend of the Church, but was not its slave by any means. He fully and readily recognized the benefits which Christianity conferred upon his dominions; and he employed the means which the Church furnished him, in his earnest desire to protect the poor and humble class of his subjects against the rich and powerful.

He also sought to improve the morals of the clergy, who, since the fifth century, had been guilty of crimes not fit to be mentioned. He issued an edict as follows: "We are informed that many monks are addicted to debauchery, even to unnatural sins." * * * * "We command our monks to cease swarming about the country, and we forbid our nuns to practice fornication and intoxication. We shall not allow them any longer to be prostitutes, thieves and murderers." * * * * "And priests are forbidden to haunt the taverns and market-places for the purpose of seducing mothers and daughters." Says a certain writer: "The degradation of the clergy became so complete that organized concubinage was welcomed as a safeguard against promiscuous licentiousness, as preferable to the mischief which the unbridled passions of the pastor might inflict upon his flock."

Charlemagne was fond of learning and of learned men, and therefore sought the society of ecclesiastics, the only class that in this age of darkness and ignorance possessed any education; but he was always their master, kind and generous, and never their instrument. He founded many bishoprics and monasteries and bestowed rich estates upon them, and compelled the payment of tithes throughout the Empire for the support of the clergy. In every part of the Empire, but more especially in Germany, he elevated the bishops, abbots and higher clergy to a more important position in the state than they had ever before held, with the view of making them a counterpoise to the secular nobility.

Charlemagne encouraged the arts, agriculture, commerce and literature. He made the greatest exertions for the advancement of civilization among his subjects, and founded schools and cathedrals for the diffusion of intellectual enlightenment and Christianity.

This great Emperor, who did so much to dispel the intellectual darkness which universally prevailed in Europe, and who gave such enlightened protection and encouragement to learning and the diffusion of knowledge, was himself an ardent student, and set a bright example to the world by his patient and arduous efforts to store his mind with knowledge. He encouraged learned men to settle in his dominions, and delighted to have their society and to converse with them upon subjects in which he felt an interest. He spent his moments of relaxation, even in the midst of his most important campaigns, in the society of these learned men.

Charlemagne's most trusted friend and counselor was Alcuin, the famous Anglo-Saxon monk, one of the greatest scholars of his time. Alcuin took up his residence at Charlemagne's court in A. D. 781, and died in A. D. 804. He was the Emperor's tutor during this period, and instigated many of the great sovereign's most useful acts. History furnishes few more striking spectacles than that of the great Western Emperor, surrounded by the princes and princesses of his family and the learned personages of his brilliant court, all sitting as pupils at the feet of their Anglo-Saxon preceptor Alcuin, in the "school of the palace" at Aix la Chapelle. The course of study which these august academicians pursued embraced the *trivium* and *quadrivium*, or "the seven liberal arts," with a special attention to grammar, psalmody and the theory of music; and as Alcuin excelled in the exposition of the Scriptures, the mysteries of theology were not forgotten in his lectures.

Charlemagne's best gift to his people was the system of education which he established throughout his dominions. As early as A. D. 789, acting on Alcuin's advice, the Emperor addressed a circular letter to the bishops, ordering them to establish elementary schools in their cathedral cities, for the free instruction of the children of freemen and the laboring classes. Each monastery was required to maintain a school for the study of the higher branches of learning. Many of the seminaries then established in different parts of Germany and France are still in existence. Charlemagne encouraged learned men from all parts of Europe to settle in these monastic schools as professors. These schools became so many places of refuge for the professors, and the wise plan of their founder made them the sources of permanent and great blessings to mankind, and particularly to the districts in which they were located.

Charlemagne was tall and broad-chested—of heroic stature and majestic presence. He was gracious and graceful in his manner, and spoke with great clearness and precision. He was able to converse fluently in Latin, and thoroughly understood Greek. He was plain and simple in his habits. He dined off four dishes, his favorite dish being newly-killed venison roasted on the spit. He was temperate in drinking and abhorred drunkenness. His favorite works of history and Augustine's *City of God* were frequently read aloud to him during his meals. Born a German, he was a German in everything as long as he lived. He prided himself on his Teutonic blood, and strove to maintain the ancient German customs, especially the old heroic ballads of his ancestors. He was always attired in the national Frankish costume, only appearing in the Roman dress

THE WESTERN EMPIRE RESTORED.

upon rare state occasions. In private life he was of very estimable character, being a kind master, a tender husband and an affectionate father.

Following the fatal custom of the Merovingian kings and of his father, Charlemagne, in A.D. 813, made a will, which he caused to be signed by the bishops and the other great lords, dividing his Empire between his three sons, Charles, Pepin and Louis, also appointing them his lieutenants during his life-time. But soon after this arrangement, the two eldest sons died, and the great Emperor associated his surviving son, Louis, with him in the government.

The death of his eldest son weighed heavily upon Charlemagne's mind, and he at once passed from a state of vigorous health to the infirmity and decrepitude of old age, so that he was unable to walk without assistance. He repaired to his chapel, arrayed in his imperial robes, with a golden crown upon his head, and supported by his son Louis. Taking the crown from his head and placing it on the altar, he exhorted his son to be a good sovereign and a good man, and commanded him to take the crown and place it on his own head.

Charlemagne now relinquished all the cares of government and occupied himself in acts of devotion, passing his few remaining days in reading the Scriptures, in prayer and in deeds of charity. His strength gradually failed, and in January, A.D. 814, he became so weak that he was unable to swallow anything but a little water. When, on the 28th of that month, he felt the moment of dissolution approaching, he gathered sufficient strength to make a sign of the cross with his right hand; and then quietly composing himself in his bed, he murmured in a low and faltering voice: "Into Thy hands, O Lord, I commend my spirit."

Charlemagne died in the seventy-second year of his age and the forty-fourth of his reign. His body was deposited in a vault in his chapel, and was placed upon a magnificent throne of gold, dressed in the imperial robes, with a crown on his head, his sword by his side, and the Bible between his knees; but the hair shirt of the penitent was under the imperial robes, and he still bore the pilgrim's purse which he carried in all his pilgrimages to Rome. The tomb was filled with gold and silver, and was scented with the choicest perfumes; while a triumphal arch was erected, bearing a long inscription. In the year A.D. 1001 the Emperor Otho III. robbed the tomb of its riches; and all that now marks the spot where the great Emperor's remains are deposited is the inscription "Carlo Magno" in the pavement.

The glory of the Carlovingian dynasty expired with Charlemagne, and the Empire which had been established by his wisdom and policy soon crumbled to pieces during the reigns of his feeble and inglorious successors, who, by their folly and vices, destroyed the vast dominion which their great ancestor had built up. The entire history of the period is confused and entangled by the divisions which the sovereigns made of their territories between their children, by the rapid changes of territory and the succession of sovereigns distinguished only by their names.

Louis was in Aquitaine when his illustrious father died. In his journey thence to Aix la Chapelle he was everywhere welcomed with acclamations of joy by the populace, because he had won the affections of the people of Aquitaine by his gentleness and his mild disposition, which acquired for him the surname of *Le Debonnaire*, "the Goodnatured"—a name expressive of qualities valuable in private life, but not the best adapted to the government of a great Empire in so stormy a period.

In A.D. 816, two years after his accession, he received the imperial crown from Pope Stephen V.; and soon afterward he committed the usual error of Frankish sovereigns by dividing the monarchy among his three sons, thus still more enfeebling an authority already greatly weakened by the folly of the government. By this arrangement LOUIS LE DEBONNAIRE made his eldest son, Lothaire, his partner in the imperial government, while conferring Aquitaine on Pepin and Bavaria on Louis.

Bernard, the nephew of Louis le Debonnaire, was invested with the crown of Italy as a fief of the Empire. He was so indignant at Lothaire's elevation that he raised the standard of revolt, but was deserted by his troops, whereupon he was taken prisoner, tried, and condemned to death. Louis commuted the punishment and caused the young prince's eyes to be put out, three days after which Bernard died. For the purpose of guarding against new troubles, the Emperor confined three of Charlemagne's natural sons in a monastery, compelling them to take the monastic vows.

After these rigorous acts Louis le Debonnaire became distracted with remorse, and he reproached himself with being the murderer of his nephew and the oppressor of his brothers. These feelings were aggravated by the artifices of the clergy, who finally induced the Emperor to accuse himself in a general assembly and to solicit the prelates to admit him to public penance. The clergy pretended to be greatly edified by the monarch's actions, but they perceived how easily a man of such feeble mind could be made a mere instrument to their power, and readily profited by the mistaken devotion which degraded the imperial majesty.

After the death of his first wife, Louis le Debonnaire had married Judith, daughter of the Count of Bavaria, and had by her a son who was afterwards Charles the Bald, King of France. This child seemed to be excluded from the succession by the partition made in favor of the three sons of the first marriage; but Louis was persuaded to make a new division and to obtain the consent of Lothaire, who was chiefly interested in opposing this new arrangement, and who soon had cause to regret his complaisance.

In A. D. 829 the three princes united in a project to restore the original arrangement, and were effectively assisted by Vala, Abbot of Corbie, who, though considered a saint, did not scruple to place himself at the head of a faction. Prodigies were invented to inflame the credulous masses; and the most odious charges were brought against the government, the Empress being particularly accused of being criminally intimate with Count Bernard, a minister who had made himself obnoxious by his stern inflexibility. The imbecile Emperor humbled himself to the rebels, and his Empress was confined in a cloister. Louis himself narrowly escaped a similar fate, and was forced to proclaim a general amnesty, the only apparent effect of which was to increase the insolence of the seditious.

No sooner had this rebellion been suppressed, in A. D. 832, than a multitude of errors produced another. Louis le Debonnaire again proceeded to exercise his sovereign powers; recalled Judith to court when her ambition was inflamed by a desire for revenge; banished Vala, who had acquired great popularity by his pretensions to sanctity; and finally disinherited his two sons, Lothaire and Pepin, thus giving them a pretext for their unnatural hostility. He even rendered himself obnoxious to his able minister, Count Bernard, by yielding to the influence of a monk who had unfortunately gained his confidence.

The Emperor's three sons—Lothaire, Pepin and Louis—assembled their forces in Alsace in A. D. 832, and prepared to march against their father and sovereign. Pope Gregory IV. joined them under the pretense of mediating between them and the Emperor, but displayed all the zeal of an ardent partisan, and threatened the feeble sovereign with the terrors of excommunication. Thereupon several of the loyal prelates of France sent a spirited remonstrance to the Pope, whom they accused of treason to the Emperor, and whom they also threatened with excommunication for excommunication, and even with deposition, in case he persisted in his rebellion.

Agobard, Bishop of Lyons, the most renowned of the Frankish prelates, dissented from his brethren, and joined Vala and the monk Ratbert in asserting that the Pope possessed the jurisdiction of universal judge, not being amenable to any human tribunal. Relying on the principles of his supporters, Gregory IV. replied to the remonstrance of the loyal prelates in haughty terms, hitherto unparalleled, and asserted an authority not previously claimed by any Pope.

The crafty Lothaire sent the Pope to propose terms of peace to the Emperor. By the intrigues of Gregory IV., Louis le Debonnaire suddenly lost all support, and was obliged to surrender at discretion; after which he was dethroned by a tumultuous assembly, and the imperial crown was conferred on his son. The Pope then returned to Rome.

For the purpose of giving permanency to this revolution, Ebbo, whom Louis le Debonnaire had elevated from a servile condition to the bishopric of Rheims, proposed the following extraordinary and iniquitous method. Said he: "A penitent ought to be excluded from holding any civil office! Therefore a king who is a penitent must be incapable of governing. Consequently, to subject Louis to penance will forever bar his way to the throne."

Ebbo's advice was followed by the Emperor's enemies, who forced Louis le Debonnaire to perform public penance in the monastery of St. Medard de Soissons and to sign a written confession; after which they stripped him of his royal robes, clothed him in the habit of a penitent, and immured him in a cell. They employed Agobard to write a vindication of all these horrors.

But the prelates had ventured too far. The demands of outraged nature and the voice of justice made a strong impression upon the people's mind. Lothaire became universally detested, and a new revolution, in A. D. 834, restored Louis le Debonnaire to the Frankish throne. But his superstitious weakness now became more conspicuous than ever. He refused to resume the imperial title until he had received absolution, professed the most profound submission to the Pope, and, after a brief suspension, restored Agobard to his former authority.

A repetition of the same errors naturally led to the same unfortunate consequences. On the death of his son Pepin, in A. D. 840, Louis le Debonnaire divided his dominions between Lothaire and Charles, thus excluding Louis, who immediately appealed to arms. While the Emperor was marching against this rebellious son, tortured with grief, and terrified by an eclipse of the sun which he considered an evil omen, he was attacked with illness in the vicinity of Mayence, where he died in the twenty-eighth year of his reign (A. D. 840), after bequeathing to his favorite son Charles the provinces of Burgundy and Neustria; the latter of which was subsequently called *Normandy*.

It was during the reign of Louis le Debonnaire that the Saracens, who had subdued Sicily, infested the Mediterranean and threatened to make themselves masters of Italy; while the Normans continued their ravages on the coast of Germany and France. Thus, with enemies on the north and south, and with discord, crime and civil war raging within, Western Europe at this time presented a most deplorable spectacle.

No sooner had LOTHAIRE ascended the imperial throne than he prepared to deprive his brothers LOUIS and CHARLES of their dominions; but they took the field against their ambitious eldest brother, and defeated him in a sanguinary battle of three days at Fontenay, in Burgundy, in the year A. D. 841, on which occasion so many of the Frankish nobles and soldiers were slain that no successful resistance could be made to the ravages of the Norman freebooters.

For the purpose of obtaining the aid of the Saxons, Lothaire had promised to suspend Charlemagne's laws, which compelled them to observe the ordinances of Christianity. This gave his brothers a pretext to attempt to procure his dethronement. A large assembly of bishops was convened at Aix la Chapelle, and the two victorious princes preferred their complaint before this body. The bishops examined the charge, and then declared that Lothaire had forfeited his right to the imperial dignity, which they conferred on his triumphant brothers.

But Lothaire was still sufficiently formidable to defy the decree of the bishops, and forced his brothers to consent to a new partition. Thus was concluded the Partition Treaty of Verdun, in A. D. 843, by which the sons of Louis le Debonnaire divided among themselves the great Frankish Empire which their illustrious grandfather, Charlemagne, had built up. Lothaire took Italy, Burgundy and Lorraine; the name of the last-named province being a corruption of *Lotharingia*, or land of Lothaire. Louis obtained Germany, and is therefore called *the German*. Charles, surnamed *the Bald*, received France. The *Treaty of Verdun* (A. D. 843) is one of the most important events in the history of Europe, as it marks the beginning of France and Germany as separate nations.

SECTION XIV.—THE NEW CARLOVINGIAN KINGDOMS.

AFTER the dissolution of Charlemagne's Empire by the Partition Treaty of Verdun, in A. D. 843, the new kingdoms which arose from the fragments of that Empire remained under that great Emperor's descendants for different periods of time. Thus Italy was governed by one branch of the Carlovingian dynasty until A. D. 887; Germany was ruled by another branch of the same dynasty until A. D. 911; France remained under a third branch until A. D. 987; while the minor kingdoms of Lorraine, Burgundy and Provence also remained under Carlovingian princes for some time.

The Carlovingian Kings of France, Germany and Italy were monarchs only in name; the great dukes and counts virtually exercising all the powers of sovereignty, leaving to the sovereigns only the empty title of royalty. During the reigns of these weak Carlovingian princes, the Northmen ravaged the coasts of France and Germany, the Slavonians and Avars desolated the eastern frontiers of Germany, while the Saracens devastated the southern coasts of Italy.

Lothaire's kingdom extended from the duchy of Beneventum on the south to the North Sea on the north, lying between Germany and France; the Rhine dividing it from the former, and the Rhone separating it from the latter. Lothaire, who, as we have seen, took the imperial title, associated his son Louis in the government, making him ruler over Lombardy. Lothaire's capital was Aix la Chapelle.

The dominions of Louis the German, who was called *King of the East Franks*, embraced all the German territories east of the Rhine. The principal state of Germany was East Francia, or Franconia, which comprised the valleys of the Main, the Neckar and the Lahn; Saxony and Thuringia lying to the north of it, and Suabia and Bavaria, embracing the territory of the ancient Alemannia, to the south and south-east.

The dominions of Charles the Bald, who was styled *King of the West Franks*, embraced all the territory of modern France except the eastern part comprised in Lorraine, Burgundy and the provinces east of the Rhone. Paris was the capital of this kingdom.

The division of the great Carlovingian Empire by the Treaty of Verdun was made according to the languages spoken by the different populations. Pure German was spoken east of the Rhine; while the modern French began to be formed in Western Francia, or France, by the mingling of the Frankish with the Latin-Celtic elements; and Lothaire's kingdom acted as a wall or partition between the two kingdoms in which the French and German tongues were respectively spoken.

In the meantime the Saracens, who had conquered Crete, commenced their efforts to obtain possession of Sicily in A. D. 827. The struggle lasted half a century, until finally, in A. D. 878, the Saracens took Syracuse and overran the whole of Sicily; but the Arabs had long before this begun to direct their efforts to the mainland of Italy. From the Sicilian ports the Moslem squadrons ravaged the Italian coast at their pleasure. Encouraged by the dissensions of the cities of Southern Italy, the Saracens firmly established themselves in the southern end of the Italian peninsula, and extended their ravages to the vicinity of Rome, finally laying siege to the Eternal City itself. Had the Saracens been united they might have acquired possession of the entire Italian peninsula.

Rome was saved by the courageous action of Pope Leo IV., who successfully resisted the Saracen attacks upon the city, and who induced the cities of Gaëta, Naples and Amalfi to enter into a league against the Arab invaders. The combined fleets of these confederated cities severely defeated the Arabian fleet off Ostia, and the remnant of the vanquished squadron was destroyed by a tempest. The Pope was unable to prevent the Saracens from plundering the churches and shrines within the walls of Rome. After the Mussulman invaders had retired, he inclosed this portion of the city—the Vatican quarter—with a strong wall, and called it, in honor of himself, the *Leonine City*, A. D. 852.

The Emperor Lothaire died in A. D. 855, after ordering himself to be clothed in a monkish dress—a convenient act of devotion by which bad sovereigns imagined that their crimes might be expiated at the moment of death. His dominions were divided among his sons—LOUIS II. taking Italy with the imperial title; LOTHAIRE II. obtaining Lorraine, and CHARLES receiving Provence. Thus Charlemagne's vast Empire was divided into a number of petty states, the mutual jealousies of which produced constant bloodshed.

Rome was saved from further Mohammedan attacks by the advance of the Emperor Louis II. into Southern Italy. The Saracens were successful in capturing Bari, by which they were enabled to command the Adriatic and to make their power severely felt in Southern Italy. This led to a league of the Eastern Emperor Basil I. and the Western Emperor Louis II., who thus united their forces to drive the Moslem invaders from Italy. The army of Louis II. besieged Bari by land, while the Byzantine fleet assailed the city by sea, and in A. D. 871 the beleagured city was forced to yield to this combined attack of the forces of the two Empires of Christendom.

The most important result of the expulsion of the Saracens from Bari was the revival of the Byzantine or Greek power in Southern Italy. The weakness of the Carlovingian dynasty in Italy had enabled the Eastern Emperor to capture many of the Saracen castles. The province called the Theme of Lombardy extended northward to Salerno. The Greek cities of Naples and Amalfi and the Lombard rulers of Benevento and Capua likewise acknowledged the Eastern Emperor as their suzerain, but they were not always to be depended upon. The feuds of the rulers of Northern Italy protected the Byzantine Greeks of the southern portion of the peninsula from interference during this period.

Louis the German was unable to defend his dominions against the ravages of the Northmen, who assailed the exposed points of the German coast with impunity, sailed up the navigable rivers, ravaged the country along their shores, and attacked and almost destroyed Hamburg about A. D. 847, the archbishop fleeing to Bremen, which town became the seat of the northern archbishopric of Germany. Louis the German also carried on war against the Slavonians to compel them to acknowledge his supremacy, and was frequently involved in hostilities with his brother, Charles the Bald, King of France, who was constantly seeking to enlarge his own dominions.

The most unfortunate of the Frankish states was France, under the dominion of Charles the Bald, a monarch inheriting his father's weakness and his mother's turbulent spirit. During this imbecile prince's reign the new Kingdom of France was in a condition of anarchy. Brittany, Aquitaine, and Septimania or Languedoc were practically independent, and were only reduced to a state of semi-allegiance to the King of France after a long and severe struggle.

As France was distracted by dissensions between the clergy and the nobility, who were so intent on their own petty jealousies that they abandoned their country to its foes, Charles the Bald was unable to defend his kingdom against the ravages of the Northmen, who, starting from the islands and mainlands of Scandinavia, soon made France one of the main objects of attack, ascending the navigable rivers in their light but swift and strong galleys, no storm being sufficiently fierce to keep them to the open sea. Being pagans and cherishing a bitter animosity toward Christianity, they never spared a monk or a monastery.

In the very year of the battle of Fontenay, A. D. 841—two years before the Treaty of Verdun—these piratical Northmen ascended the Seine as far as Rouen, and pillaged and burned that city. They renewed their incursions every year, and in A. D. 845 a band of Northmen under the famous chieftain, Ragnar Lodbrog, reached Paris. Charles the Bald abandoned his capital without striking a blow, and the Northmen plundered the city and its rich churches and abbeys, after which they consented to a treaty with Charles the Bald, who bribed the daring freebooters to retire by the payment of seven thousand pounds of silver—a proceeding which only made the insolent corsairs the more eager to return.

In A. D. 857 the Northmen again took Paris, and massacred many of its inhabitants. A third time they attacked the city in A. D. 862, but were vigorously resisted by Robert the Strong, whom Charles the Bald had made Count of Paris and governor of the region between the Seine and the Loire. But the weakness of Charles the Bald enabled the Northmen to inflict serious damage upon France during the next five years, and in 866 Count Robert the Strong lost his life in battle with the famous Norman chief, Hastings.

The weakness of Charlemagne's successors had stimulated the ambition of the Popes to establish their authority over all the monarchs of Europe, and a circumstance which transpired about this time contributed in a considerable degree to their success. In A. D. 862 Lothaire II., King of Lorraine, divorced his wife, Teutberga, on a false charge of incest. She had first justified herself by the ordeal of boiling water; but was afterwards convicted on her own confession, or, more properly, on a declaration extorted by threats and brutal violence. Lothaire II. then married his concubine Valdrada, and persuaded a council of bishops assembled at Aix la Chapelle to sanction his actions.

The flagrant iniquity of this proceeding somewhat justified the Pope's interference, and it was perhaps his duty to have reproved Lothaire II., but Pope Nicholas the Great determined to bring the King of Lorraine to trial for his outrageous proceedings. The Pope accordingly assembled a council of the Church at Mayence; and this body examined into the affair, and, contrary to the universal expectation, decided in Lothaire's favor. Nicholas the Great deposed the bishops who had been mostly instrumental in procuring this decision, and sent a legate to threaten the King of Lorraine with prompt excommunication if he did not at once recall Teutberga.

The intimidated sovereign submitted, even giving up Valdrada to be conveyed a prisoner to Rome; but she escaped on the way and returned to Lorraine, where she was restored to her former honors; while Teutberga, wearied out by the contest, consented to nullify her own marriage, and acknowledged Valdrada as legitimate queen. Pope Nicholas the Great was dissatisfied with this turn of affairs,but he died in A. D. 867; and his successor, Adrian II., was a man of more moderation and contented himself with summoning Lothaire II. to Rome. That monarch swore on the Holy Sacrament that he was innocent of the crimes charged against him; and his death, which occurred soon afterward (A. D. 869), was universally regarded as a punishment for his perjury.

Upon the death of Lothaire II., without issue, his Kingdom of Lorraine was seized by his uncles, Charles the Bald, King of France, and Louis the German, King of Germany, to the exclusion of his eldest broth-

CORONATION OF CHARLEMAGNE, ST. PETER'S, ROME.

er, the Emperor Louis II. Thus Cisjurane Burgundy—including the district between the Meuse and the Scheldt—and the counties of Lyons and Vienne were annexed to the territories of the King of France, while the remainder of the Kingdom of Lorraine fell under the dominion of Louis the German.

Vainly did Pope Adrian II. threaten King Charles the Bald of France with the punishment of a usurper. Supported by the renowned Hincmar of Rheims, the King of France issued a manifesto asserting the supremacy of the state over the church, and declaring that *free* men would not submit to enslavement by the Bishop of Rome. The Pope soon found means to annoy the disobedient monarch. Charles the Bald had confined his two youngest sons, Lothaire and Carloman, in a monastery. Lothaire, who was lame and sickly, became resigned to his fate; but Carloman resisted his father's determination, and was encouraged in his rebellion by the Pope. Carloman was eventually defeated, and was obliged to seek refuge at the court of his uncle, Louis the German.

The death of the Emperor Louis II. without male issue, in A. D. 875, induced the King of France and the Pope to lay aside their jealousies. Pope Adrian II. even wrote a flattering letter to Charles the Bald. His successor, John VIII., went so far as to crown the King of France Emperor at Pavia on Christmas day, A. D. 875—an act which brought on a war between Charles the Bald and his brother, Louis the German. Louis invaded France in A. D. 876, but died in August of the same year (A. D. 876), dividing his dominions among his three sons, CHARLES THE FAT, CARLOMAN and LOUIS, in accordance with Frankish custom. Charles the Bald made an ineffectual effort to deprive these princes of their territories, but was defeated with loss and disgrace, while his own dominions were frightfully devastated by the Northmen.

After the death of the Emperor Louis II., the Saracens renewed their destructive ravages in Southern Italy, and were aided by the Duke of Naples, who, though nominally a vassal of the Eastern Roman Emperor, was virtually an independent sovereign. Terrified at the progress of the Saracen marauders, Pope John VIII. urgently summoned the Emperor Charles the Bald to his aid, in A. D. 877, threatening to deprive him of the imperial crown in case he refused.

Charles the Bald obeyed the Pope's mandate; but no sooner had he arrived in Italy than he received intelligence that his nephew Carloman, the son of Louis the German, was on the march to wrest from him the imperial crown. Charles the Bald hastened to return to France, but was deserted by his nobles on the way and attacked with a sudden illness, of which he died miserably in a wretched hut by the way-side (A. D. 877). Thus deprived of aid, the Pope was obliged to purchase the safety of Rome by paying tribute to the Moslems.

During the period embraced in the reigns of Louis the German in Germany, and Charles the Bald in France, the *Feudal System*, which we will describe hereafter, was finally established in all the Carlovingian dominions. The government of the provinces and districts, which had been formerly held during pleasure or for life, was made hereditary by a capitulary enacted in the last year of the reign of Charles the Bald; and thus the power of the Frankish nobles was established on the ruins of the royal authority.

About this time also the Gauls and the Franks began to be amalgamated into one nation; and the language of France, which had been previously a mixture of Latin and German, began to settle down into the two dialects known as the *langue d' oc* and the *langue d' oui;* the former, which was spoken in the South of France, being the parent of the Provençal, or the language of the Troubadours; and the latter, which was the language of the North of France, being that from which the modern French is derived.

The division of Germany between the sons of Louis the German, upon that king's death, in A. D. 876, did not last long; as Carloman and Louis soon died, leaving Charles the Fat sole King of Germany. Carloman, during his brief reign, had seized the crown of Italy, after the death of Charles the Bald, King of France.

Upon the death of Charles the Bald, in A. D. 877, his only surviving son, LOUIS THE STAMMERER, became King of France; but died in A. D. 879, after a reign of less than two years, leaving the crown of France to his two sons, LOUIS III. and CARLOMAN, who reigned jointly—Louis III. in the North of France, and Carloman in Aquitaine and Burgundy. Some months after the death of Charles the Bald a posthumous son was born, named Charles, afterwards surnamed *the Simple*.

Louis III. and Carloman reigned together in harmony; but during their reign Duke Boso, Carloman's father-in-law, the brother-in-law of Charles the Bald, rebelled, and dismembered the Kingdom of France by founding a new kingdom east of the Rhone. A council held at Mante, in Dauphiny, declared that they had been divinely inspired to confer the Kingdom of Arles, or, as it is more generally styled, the Kingdom of Burgundy and Provence, upon Duke Boso. Pope John VIII. sanctioned this council's action and personally crowned the new king. Boso was a wise and politic monarch, and preserved his little kingdom safe from all the calamities which afflicted the rest of France. The new Kingdom of Burgundy and Provence, the capital of which was Arles, remained independent for more than a century and a half, during which Provence was the center of elegance and refinement.

Pope John VIII. endeavored to make Boso King of Italy after the death of the last king, Carloman, the son of Louis the German; but Charles the Fat, King of Germany, made himself King of Italy and compelled the Pope to crown him Emperor. Charles the Fat was unable to quell the disturbances among the Italian nobles, or to check the aggressions of the Saracens.

The sons of Charles the Bald did not reign over France any length of time. After being disastrously defeated by the Northmen under Hastings at Sancourt, near Abbeville, Louis III. died in August, A. D. 882; and Carloman died in A. D. 884. The right of inheritance descended to Charles the Simple, then only in his fifth year; but the nobles of France, perceiving that an infant sovereign would precipitate the ruin of the kingdom in the existing condition of the country, conferred the French crown on the Emperor Charles the Fat, King of Germany and Italy.

Thus Charles the Fat, the son of Louis the German, was King of Germany, Italy and France, and Emperor of the West; uniting under his scepter all the dominions of Charlemagne exept the new Kingdom of Burgundy and Provence founded by Boso. Charles the Fat lacked genius and courage, and was destitute of the capacity requisite for the management of so large an Empire. He was proud and cowardly. He rendered himself contemptible by his gluttony, and infamous by his disregard of treaties.

Soon after becoming King of France, Charles the Fat purchased a peace from the Northmen by disgracefully yielding to them the province of Friesland, in the Netherlands, and stipulating to pay them tribute; but he again provoked their hostility by repeated acts of treachery, and they again attacked France more furiously than ever before. Advancing through the country, under their famous chieftain, Rollo, they burned Pontoise and besieged Paris in overwhelming force, in A. D. 885.

This siege is celebrated in history and romance for the valiant resistance of the besieged. Eudes, Count of Paris, the son and successor of Count Robert the Strong, had put the capital into a good state of defense, and strengthened the garrison by the addition of several brave nobles, among whom the most conspicuous were two bishops, Goslin and Ansheric. The garrison under Eudes bravely defended the city for a year and a half, anxiously expecting the approach of King Charles the Fat to raise the siege. After a long delay, he led an army from Germany to the relief of Paris; but although almost certain of victory, he lacked the spirit to risk an engagement, and bribed the Northmen to withdraw by the payment of a ransom of eight hundred pounds of silver (A. D. 886).

THE NEW CARLOVINGIAN KINGDOMS.

The three kingdoms composing the Empire of Charles the Fat were disgusted with the imbecility and incapacity of the Emperor, as displayed in this disgraceful and cowardly peace with the Northern pirates; and a spirit of revolt manifested itself throughout his dominions, which culminated in the dethronement of Charles the Fat in all his kingdoms in A. D. 887. The Germans, who were the first to revolt, elected a new king in the person of ARNULF, an illegitimate son of Carloman, King of Bavaria, brother of the dethroned Charles the Fat. Italy became distracted between the Dukes of Friuli and Spoleto, who contested for the Italian crown. The nobles of France offered the crown of their kingdom to Count EUDES, the heroic defender of Paris, who had already been made Duke of France by Charles the Fat.

Thus, with the deposition of Charles the Fat, in A. D. 887, the reunited Carlovingian Empire finally fell to pieces, never to be restored; and the Carlovingian dynasty ceased to rule in Italy. The unhappy Charles the Fat became hopelessly insane after his dethronement. He was deserted by his servants and driven from his palace, and would have suffered from want of the common necessaries of life but for the compassion of Luitbart, Bishop of Mayence, under whose generous protection the unfortunate ex-monarch ended his miserable existence, dying in A. D. 888, the year after his deposition.

Arnulf, who became King of Germany after the deposition of Charles the Fat, in A. D. 887, was a brave and active sovereign, and defeated the Northmen so severely at Louvain, or Löwen, in A. D. 891, that they gave Germany but little trouble afterwards. To check the incursions of the Slavonians and the Avars, he called in the aid of the Magyars, or Hungarians, a wild Tartar tribe from the Ural, who were skillful horsemen and archers. After subduing the Avars, or Huns, or driving them from the valleys of the Theiss and the Danube, the Magyars, under their valiant chieftain, Arpad, settled in that region, since called *Hungary*.

In the struggle which ensued between Beranger, Duke of Friuli, and Guido, Duke of Spoleto, for the possession of the Italian crown, after the dethronement of Charles the Fat, Guido was victorious, and was crowned Emperor. Beranger solicited the aid of Arnulf, King of Germany, who willingly responded to the summons and invaded Italy in A. D. 894. After taking Rome, Arnulf set aside both Beranger and Guido's son, Lambert—Guido having died during the struggle—and was himself crowned Emperor by Pope Formosus. Arnulf's power in Italy was but nominal, and he soon returned to Germany. After Lambert's death, in A. D. 899, BERANGER made himself King of Italy. The leading rulers in the North of Italy then were the Duke of Friuli, the Count of Tuscany and the Archbishop of Milan; the latter two bearing but a nominal allegiance to the King of Italy.

Arnulf died in A. D. 899 and was succeeded by his son, LOUIS THE CHILD, whose short reign of twelve years (A. D. 899–911) was most unfortunate for Germany. The Magyars, or Hungarians, who had just established themselves in the valleys of the Theiss and the Danube, in the country previously occupied by the Avars, now became a far more terrible scourge than either the Slavonians or the Avars, and made the most destructive inroads into Germany and Italy for more than a century. These fierce barbarians ravaged Germany annually during the reign of Louis the Child, from whom they exacted a yearly tribute.

The Hungarian army consisted of huge masses of cavalry, and was victorious in almost every battle with the Germans, whose army consisted mainly of infantry. As Germany was an open country without fortresses or towns in which the people could find refuge, many of them were massacred, and many more were carried into captivity by the Hungarians. Louis the Child was unable to resist these barbarians, who ravaged Germany so terribly that they reduced the country almost to a desert. The Carlovingian dynasty in Germany ended with the death of Louis the Child in A. D. 911.

The Magyars, or Hungarians, also swept over the Alps and ravaged Northern Italy with fire and sword; while the Northmen under Hastings captured, plundered and destroyed the city of Luna, which they mistook for Rome; and the Saracens kept Southern Italy in a state of terror until A. D. 916, when the warlike Pope John XII. took the field against them, aided by many of the princes of Southern Italy and by a fleet sent by the Eastern Emperor, and severely defeated the Moslems, thus putting a stop to their outrages.

Besides the misery caused by the ravages of the Saracens, the Northmen and the Hungarians, all Italy suffered from the misfortunes produced by the frequent revolutions which kept the unhappy country in a condition of constant strife and inflicted much suffering upon the inhabitants. Adalbert, the great Count of Tuscany, was chiefly instrumental in raising Beranger to the throne of Italy. But Adalbert soon became dissatisfied with Beranger's rule, and called in LOUIS of Provence, Boso's son, to overthrow him and seize the Italian throne for himself. Louis did not long remain King of Italy, as the Tuscan king-maker found him a less pliant instrument than he had expected, and therefore soon dethroned him. RODOLPH of Burgundy next appeared to contest with Beranger for the throne of Italy, and Beranger was finally assassinated.

Rome was at this time virtually ruled by Marozia, an infamous woman who had won notoriety as the mistress of one Pope, the mother of a second, and the grandmother of a third, and the account of whose career constitutes the most disgraceful page in the history of the Papacy. Upon Beranger's death Marozia sought to strengthen herself by marrying HUGH of Provence, who had assumed the Italian crown and had been acknowledged King of Italy by Pope John XI., Marozia's son. Marozia introduced Hugh into the Castle of St. Angelo; but the Romans, under the leadership of Alberic, Marozia's legitimate son, refused to permit Hugh to enter the Eternal City, and confined him to the castle, from which he was soon driven by Alberic. Marozia was cast into prison; the Pope was restricted to the exercise of his spiritual functions; and Alberic ruled Rome for twenty years, restoring the old republican institutions to a limited degree. His son Octavian succeeded him, and ruled Rome for some time as Consul. Upon the death of his uncle, Pope John XI., Octavian made himself Pope with the title of John XII.; but his infamous life soon disgusted all Europe.

Though driven from Rome, Hugh of Provence remained master of the rest of Italy, but he was such an infamous tyrant and plundered his subjects so shamefully that they soon conspired against his authority. The most formidable of these plots, which was supported by most of the Italian nobles, aimed at the elevation of Beranger, Marquis of Iorea, to the throne of Italy. Hugh detected this conspiracy, and Beranger was obliged to flee; but finally Hugh was driven from Italy into his native Provence, leaving his son LOTHAIRE as King of Italy (A. D. 945). Lothaire died in A. D. 950, after a reign of five years, and his death was ascribed to Beranger of Iorea, who at once ascended the Italian throne with the title of BERANGER II. Beranger's cruel persecution of Lothaire's young and beautiful widow Adelaide, because she refused to marry his son Adalbert, brought in the interference of Otho the Great, King of Germany, who assumed the Lombard crown at Milan in A. D. 951, and the imperial crown at Rome in A. D. 962, thus annexing Italy to the Germano-Roman Empire.

Count Eudes had been elected King of France upon the deposition of Charles the Fat, in A. D. 887, in grateful recognition of his services in defending Paris against the Northmen. His authority, which was limited to the provinces between the Meuse and the Loire, was firmest in Anjou, but was not recognized in Aquitaine, and was merely nominal south of the Loire. Even in the territories which acknowledged his scepter there were several princes whose submission to the sovereign was only nominal, such as the Counts of Flanders and Anjou.

The people of France soon became dissatisfied with the vigorous administration of Eudes; and the Count of Vermandois joined with the Archbishop of Rheims to restore the rightful heir, Charles the Simple, to the throne of France. After a short struggle, Eudes generously ceded to his young rival the sovereignty of the region between the Seine and the Meuse, and the court of Charles the Simple was established on the banks of the Moselle. Eudes died in A. D. 898, after enjoining the nobles of France to acknowledge Charles the Simple as their sole sovereign. Robert, the brother of Eudes, became Duke of France; while the old Carlovingian dynasty was restored in the person of CHARLES THE SIMPLE, who now became undisputed monarch of the country.

The most remarkable event of the reign of Charles the Simple was the permanent settlement of the Northmen, or Normans, in France, A. D. 912. Under their most celebrated chieftain, Rollo, or Rolf, the Northmen everywhere defeated the French forces, took Rouen, which they converted into a military post, and so terrified King Charles the Simple that he resolved to purchase peace on any conditions, as he was too weak to resist them, and too poor to bribe them. Accordingly, he sent a bishop as an ambassador to Rollo, offering to give him his daughter in marriage, and to grant the province of Neustria, embracing a large region in the North-west of France, to the Norman chieftain, on condition that Rollo and his followers should cease their depredations, acknowledge the King of France as their suzerain, and embrace Christianity. Rollo, to whom religion was a matter of total indifference, accepted all these conditions, stipulating that the feudal sovereignty of the duchy of Brittany, or Bretagne, should be ceded to him, and this was granted.

The region thus granted to Rollo and his followers was named *Normandy*, from its new settlers, who were thereafter known as *Normans*. Rollo made Rouen his capital, and as he and his followers had an interest in the land, they kept back their rude countrymen from further aggressions, thus constituting a most effectual barrier to France from this previously exposed quarter.

When Rollo went to take the oath of fealty to his new feudal sovereign, he was told that it was necessary for him to kneel and kiss the king's foot. He indignantly refused to perform so humiliating a ceremony. But the courtiers of Charles the Simple insisted upon this point of etiquette, and the Norman chief finally consented to do the act by proxy, ordering one of his followers to kiss the royal foot for him. The rude Norman soldier, instead of kneeling down to salute the king's foot, caught it up and performed the ceremony by lifting it to his mouth, thus causing the monarch to fall backward violently from his seat. The Northmen showed their want of respect by bursting into a loud shout of laughter; and as the French were in no condition to resent the insult, they were obliged to allow it to pass without remark.

Rollo received in marriage the princess Gisèle, the daughter of King Charles the Simple, and became one of the most loyal of the French monarch's subjects. He faithfully observed his promise not to molest the French, relinquished his predatory habits, established schools and framed a code of wise laws. He proved himself a wise, able and prudent ruler; and Normandy rapidly reached a high state of prosperity under his beneficent rule. He caused the ruined churches to be rebuilt, the towns to be walled and fortified, the land to be carefully cultivated, and justice to be impartially administered. The barbarian Normans adopted the French language, manners and customs with marvelous facility, so that in a few generations they became assimilated to the people among whom they had settled; and Normandy soon became celebrated for its progress in the industrial arts and in commerce and civilization.

The weakness and incapacity of Charles the Simple became constantly more apparent. The government was entirely in the hands of his minister, Haganon, a man of low birth, hated by the nobility and despised by the masses. Haganon's insolent use of his power provoked a rebellion of the nobles, headed by Robert, a brother of King Eudes. Instead of levying an army, King Charles the Simple convened a council of the Church, in which he procured the excommunication of his enemies. ROBERT was crowned King of France at Rheims, in A. D. 922.

Charles the Simple endeavored to recover his lost crown; but was defeated in a bloody battle at Soissons, in June, A. D. 923, in which Robert was slain in the moment of victory. Robert's son, Hugh the Great, or the Abbot, might have made himself King of France; but preferred conferring the crown on RAOUL, or RODOLPH, Duke of Burgundy. Rodolph won the support of the nobles by lavish grants of the land still belonging to the crown.

In A. D. 929 Charles the Simple again attempted to regain his lost crown, but was taken prisoner; and his queen, Elgiva, and her nine-year-old son found refuge at the court of her brother Athelstan, King of England. Herbert, Count of Vermandois, had obtained possession of the person of the unhappy Charles the Simple, under the pretense of undertaking his defense; but he detained him in captivity, for the purpose of procuring good terms from Rodolph by threatening to liberate his rival. In this way Herbert obtained some territory from the new king; and the captive Charles the Simple died soon afterward (October, A. D. 929), said to have been poisoned by the Count of Vermandois.

Though Rodolph was nominally King of France, all the real power of the state was exercised by Hugh the Great, Count of Paris, who had elevated him to the throne. Besides his hereditary property, Rodolph enjoyed the revenues of so many abbeys that he is frequently called *the Abbot*. The possessions of the Church had already grown to such dimensions that they had attracted the cupidity of the laity, and this glaring abuse continued to prevail during this and the following age, though the Pope frequently attempted to check it.

King Rodolph died in A. D. 936, after a reign of less than seven years, without any children. Rollo, the first Duke of Normandy, had died about three years before, transmitting Normandy and the feudal supremacy of Brittany to his son William, surnamed *Longue epée*, "Long-sword," who also inherited his father's virtues. Upon King Rodolph's death, Hugh the Great, Count of Paris and Duke of France and Burgundy, still retained possession of the supreme power. Hugh refused the crown of France a second time, either because he disliked the royal title or because he dreaded the jealousy of the French nobles.

Supported by Dukes William Long-sword of Normandy and Herbert of Vermandois, Hugh invited Louis, the son of Charles the Simple, to return from his place of refuge in England and assume the crown of France. The young prince's uncle, Athelstan, King of England, feared that some act of treachery was intended, and sought to dissuade his nephew from complying with the request of the Count of Paris; but Louis was eager to return to his native land, and Hugh's character removed all grounds for apprehension. Louis accordingly returned to France, and was received with the greatest respect; and Count Hugh the Great conducted him to Rheims, where he was crowned King of France.

Thus began the reign of LOUIS D' OUTREMER, the surname signifying *the Stranger*, because of his early exile in England. He had been carefully educated by his uncle, King Athelstan, and displayed more courage, vigor and ability than most of the Carlovingian sovereigns; but he was destitute of honor and integrity, and these defects rendered all his other qualities ineffectual. Although Count Hugh the Great had invited Louis to return to his native France, he did not have the slightest intention to relinquish the administration of the kingdom. The young king sought to exercise the power of government; but his independent spirit alarmed Hugh, who then became the enemy of the monarch whom he had elevated to the throne of France, placed him under restraint.

and refused to restore his liberty until he had ceded the county of Laon, which was almost the only portion of the royal domains that remained unappropriated.

Hugh the Great had been excommunicated by several Church councils, and even by the Pope. The clergy, particularly the bishops of Lorraine, accordingly espoused the cause of Louis d' Outremer, and thus began a civil war which lasted several years. Hugh's chief ally in this struggle was William Long-sword, Duke of Normandy, who was one of the bravest nobles of France. The king was supported by the Count of Flanders, who had a private quarrel with the Duke of Normandy, whom he caused to be assassinated under circumstances of the greatest treachery. The murdered duke left a young son named Richard, whom King Louis d' Outremer brought to court under pretense of undertaking the care of his education. The Count of Flanders instigated the king to murder this orphan Duke of Normandy; but, by a stratagem of Osmond, his governor, the young duke was rescued from the king's power and placed under the protection of his uncle, the Count de Senlis.

Hugh the Great had renounced his allegiance to Louis d' Outremer, and declared himself a vassal of Otho the Great, King of Germany, who now invaded France and reduced Louis d' Outremer to great distress. In A. D. 945 Louis was made a prisoner by the Count de Senlis, and only recovered his freedom when he consented to restore several places which he had unjustly seized in Normandy. Young Richard of Normandy was at length established in his hereditary dukedom. He was a good and pious ruler, distinguished for his personal graces and moral qualifications; and the Norman historians called him Richard *Sans Peur*, "the Fearless," and relate numerous anecdotes of his piety, charity and intrepidity.

In the midst of his troubles, Louis d' Outremer died, in A. D. 954, in the thirty-third year of his age, from the effects of a fall from his horse, leaving behind him two sons, Lothaire and Charles. LOTHAIRE was only fourteen years old, but was elevated to the throne of France by Count Hugh the Great, who was still the real ruler of the kingdom. Lothaire's mother and her brother, St. Bruno, conducted the government so well in the young king's name that France enjoyed profound tranquillity for three years. Hugh the Great died in A. D. 956, two years after the death of Louis d' Outremer, and was succeeded as Count of Paris and Duke of France by his eldest son, Hugh Capet.

Otho the Great, King of Germany, had seized Lorraine, an ancient fief of the French crown, and bestowed it on Charles, Lothaire's brother, in order to secure its possession to the German crown. This arrangement was distasteful to the French king and people, Lothaire being indignant at the loss of the province, and the French people considering their honor degraded by one of their princes becoming tributary to a foreign monarch.

Upon the death of Otho the Great, Lothaire attempted to recover the duchy of Lorraine, and, without waiting to publish a declaration of war, invaded the dominions of Otho II., the new King of Germany, whom he almost made a prisoner at Aix la Chapelle. So thoroughly was Otho II. taken by surprise that he was obliged to rise from the table where he was dining and trust to the fleetness of his horse for escape. Lothaire plundered the palace of Aix la Chapelle of everything valuable, and carried the booty with him back to Paris.

Otho II. retaliated upon Lothaire by invading France with an army of sixty thousand men, in A. D. 978, and advanced to the very gates of Paris; but Hugh Capet had put the capital in such a good state of defense that Otho II., on hearing of his preparations, sent him word that he would make him hear so loud a litany as would make his ears tingle. Accordingly, one morning he posted his army on the heights of Montmartre, which overlook Paris, and there he made his troops sing a Latin psalm as loud as they could brawl. The German soldiers made a prodigious noise, and so many voices brawling at once made themselves heard from one end of the city to the other. After venting his rage in this empty menace, Otho II. marched back to Germany. On his return to his own dominions, the German monarch had to cross the river Aisne; but, as his army arrived on the banks of the stream late in the day, Otho II. and a part of his army only could pass over. The stream rose to such a height during the night that the second division was unable to ford the stream. In this dilemma it was attacked by the French king, and Otho II. had the mortification to see his army defeated, without being able to render it any aid. At length he sent the Count of Ardennes over in a small skiff, to challenge Lothaire to single combat. The French nobles would not allow their sovereign to accept this challenge, declaring that they did not wish to lose their own king, and that they would not recognize the German monarch as a sovereign under any circumstances. Peace was finally concluded between the Kings of France and Germany in A. D. 980, Lothaire renouncing his pretensions to Lorraine, contrary to the advice of Hugh Capet and the wishes of the French people. Lothaire died in A. D. 986. His son and successor, LOUIS LE FAINÉANT, "the sluggard," reigned but little over a year, dying in May, A. D. 987. The only Carlovingian prince now surviving was Lothaire's brother Charles, Duke of Lorraine; but his character was odious to the French people, and his acceptance of Lorraine as a fief of the German Empire was regarded as an act of treason against his country. The French nobles therefore rejected Charles, and elected HUGH CAPET to the dignity of King of France. Hugh Capet was immediately afterward solemnly crowned at Rheims, July 1, A. D. 987, and his accession was the real beginning of the French monarchy. Thus ended the Carlovingian dynasty, which had reigned over France, Germany and Italy for several centuries.

CARLOVINGIAN SOVEREIGNS.

CARLOVINGIAN KINGS OF THE FRANKS.

A. D. 752	PEPIN THE LITTLE.
768	CHARLEMAGNE, or CHARLES THE GREAT (and CARLOMAN until 771).
800	Charlemagne crowned Emperor of the West.
814	LOUIS LE DEBONNAIRE.
840	CHARLES THE BALD.
841	Frankish Empire divided by the Partition Treaty of Verdun.

CARLOVINGIAN KINGS OF ITALY, BURGUNDY AND LORRAINE.

A. D. 843	LOTHAIRE I., Emperor, and King of Italy, Burgundy and Lorraine.
855	LOUIS II., King of Italy, and Emperor (until 875).
855	LOTHAIRE II., King of Lorraine (until 869).
855	CHARLES, King of Provence (until 879).

CARLOVINGIAN KINGS OF GERMANY.

| A. D. 841 | LOUIS THE GERMAN. |
| 876 | CHARLES THE FAT (and CARLOMAN and LOUIS until 877). |

CARLOVINGIAN KINGS OF FRANCE.

A. D. 841	CHARLES THE BALD.
877	LOUIS THE STAMMERER.
879	LOUIS III. (until 882) and CARLOMAN (until 884).

CARLOVINGIAN KING OF GERMANY, ITALY AND FRANCE.

| A. D. 884 | CHARLES THE FAT (deposed in 887 and Empire again divided). |
| 887 | End of the Carlovingian dynasty in Italy. |

CARLOVINGIAN KINGS OF GERMANY.	
A. D. 887	ARNULF.
899	LOUIS THE CHILD.
911	End of the Carlovingian dynasty in Germany.

CARLOVINGIAN KINGS OF FRANCE.	
A. D. 887	EUDES.
898	CHARLES THE SIMPLE.
922	ROBERT.
923	RODOLPH.
936	LOUIS D' OUTREMER.
954	LOTHAIRE.
986	LOUIS LE FAINÉANT.
987	End of the Carlovingian dynasty in France.

SECTION XV.—THE NORTHMEN AND THEIR RELIGION.

CANDINAVIA comprises the two peninsulas in the North of Europe occupied by the three modern kingdoms of Denmark, Sweden and Norway. The geographical peculiarity of this country is its proximity everywhere to the sea, and the vast extent of its coast line. The larger peninsula, Sweden and Norway, with the Arctic Ocean on the north, the Atlantic on the west, the channels of Skagerrack and Cattegat on the south, and the Baltic Sea and Gulf of Bothnia on the east, penetrated on all sides by creeks, friths, and arms of the sea, surrounded with innumerable islands, studded with lakes, and cleft with rivers, is only equaled by Switzerland in the sublime and picturesque beauty of its mountains.

The smaller peninsula, Denmark, surrounded and penetrated likewise by the sea on all sides, is almost level; its most elevated portion being only about a thousand feet above the ocean. It comprises an area of but twenty-two thousand square miles, but is so penetrated with bays and creeks that it has four thousand miles of coast. Like the larger and more northern peninsula, it is surrounded with many islands, which are so closely grouped together, particularly on its eastern coast, as to constitute an archipelago.

The Scandinavians, or Northmen—also known as Norsemen or Normans, and in English history as Danes—destined to play so important a part in the world's history, were a portion of the great Teutonic, or Germanic, division of the Aryan branch of the Caucasian race.

We have observed that modern ethnology teaches that all the races which inhabit Europe, with some insignificant exceptions, are descended from the prehistoric Aryans, whose home was in Central Asia. This is clearly demonstrated by the new science of comparative philology. The closest resemblance exists between the seven linguistic divisions of the Aryan branch of the Caucasian race—those of the Hindoos, the Medo-Persians, the Greeks, the Romans, the Germans or Teutons, the Celts, and the Slavonians; and it is a most remarkable circumstance that, from the earliest period of history to our own times, a powerful people, speaking a language belonging to one or the other of these Aryans families, should have largely swayed the destinies of mankind.

Before the birth of Christ the Romans called the peninsula of Denmark the *Chersonesus Cimbrica*, "the Cimbric peninsula" —a name derived from the Cimbri, who made the Roman Republic tremble for its existence a little more than a century before

Christ, striking more terror into the hearts of the Romans than any event since the time of Hannibal.

As we have seen, more than three hundred thousand barbarians, issuing from the peninsula of Denmark and the neighboring regions of Germany—Cimbri and Teutons—rolled like an avalanche over Gaul and Southern Germany. They encountered and vanquished four Roman armies in succession, until they were eventually overthrown by the military skill and genius of Marius. After this irruption was checked, the great northern bee-hive did not molest civilized Europe for several centuries—not until the Goths, Vandals and other Scandinavian nations began the migrations which finally overwhelmed the dominion of imperial Rome.

In the fifth century of the Christian era the Scandinavian tribe of Jutes, from the peninsula of Jutland, united with the kindred Germanic tribes of Angles and Saxons from the North of Germany in their invasion, conquest and settlement of England. In the ninth and tenth centuries the Scandinavians, under the name of Northmen, Norsemen, or Normans, ravaged all the coasts of continental Europe; while at the same time, under the name of Danes, they raided and terrorized the British Isles for two centuries.

If we look at the map of Europe we perceive the close natural resemblances between the geography of the northern part of the continent and that of the southern portion. The Baltic sea is to the North what the Mediterranean is to the South. The peninsula of Denmark, with its many bays and islands, corresponds to Greece and its archipelago. Modern geography teaches that an essential condition of civilization is the extent of coast line, in comparison with the superficial area of a country. Races and nations seem to be adapted to the countries which they inhabit.

The great Aryan migration westward from Central Asia was divided into two streams, by the Caspian and the Black Sea, and by the Caucasus, the Carpathian and the Alps mountains. The Teutonic, or Germanic nations—Saxons, Franks and Northmen—were thus turned to the North, and spread themselves along the coast and peninsulas of the Baltic. The Græco-Latin nations were distributed through Syria, Asia Minor, Greece, Italy, Spain and Southern France.

Each of these vast European divisions of the Aryan branch of the Caucasian race, stimulated to mental and moral activity by its proximity to water, developed its own peculiar forms of national character, which were afterwards combined in modern European society. The North of Europe developed individual freedom, while social organization was a product of the South. The North gave force, the South culture. From the North were derived that respect for individual rights, that sense of personal dignity, that energy of the single soul, which constitute the essential equipoise of that high social culture, that literature, philosophy, arts, laws, etc., which proceeded from the South. The romantic admiration of woman came from the South, but a better respect for her rights and the sense of her equality came from the North.

These two elements of freedom and civilization, always antagonistic, have been hostile in most ages of the world's history. The individual freedom of the North has been equivalent to barbarism, as displayed in the destroying avalanche which rolled down from time to time over the South, nearly sweeping its civilization out of existence, and overwhelming its arts, literature and laws in one common ruin. The civilization of the South had passed into luxury, had produced effeminacy, until individual freedom had been swallowed up in a grinding despotism.

A third element—Christianity—has united these two powers of Northern freedom and Southern culture together into equipoise and harmony in modern civilization. Christianity develops the sense of personal responsibility by teaching the mutual dependence and common brotherhood of all human society. The Christian element saves modern civilization from the double danger of a relapse into barbarism

THE NORTHMEN AND THEIR RELIGION.

and an over-refined luxury. The modern European nations which are the most advanced in civilization, literature and art are likewise the most thoroughly pervaded with the love of freedom; and the most civilized nations of the world are likewise the most powerful, not the most effeminate.

The Danes and Normans, along with their Germanic kinsmen, the Angles, Saxons and Jutes, furnished almost the entire population of England by means of the successive conquests by the Anglo-Saxons, Danes and Normans. These rude Northmen colonized themselves in every portion of Northern Europe, and even as far south as Italy and Greece, everywhere leaving the familiar stamp of their ideas and habits in all of modern civilization.

Many of the old Northern ideas are still mingled with our methods of thought. We retain the names of the Teutonic and Scandinavian gods in the designation of five of our week-days—Tuesday, Wednesday, Thursday, Friday and Saturday. The popular assemblies, or Things, of the Northern nations were the origin of our modern Parliaments, Diets, Congresses, National Assemblies, Legislatures, etc. Our trial by jury was of Scandinavian origin; and Montesquieu tells us that we are indebted to the Northern nations for that desire for freedom which is one of the main elements in Christian civilization—the most glorious inheritance of all. The modern nations which have led the world in civilization and liberty are the English speaking nations, the direct descendants of Anglo-Saxons, Danes and Normans.

The Teutonic, or Germanic, race developed its special civilization and religion in Scandinavia. As the Scandinavians were cut off from the rest of the world by stormy seas, they could there unfold their ideas and become themselves. We must therefore turn to Scandinavia to study the Germanic religion and to discover the influence exercised on modern civilization and the present character of Europe—an influence freely recognized by great historians.

Montesquieu says: "The great prerogative of Scandinavia is, that it afforded the great resource to the liberty of Europe, that is, to almost all of liberty there is, among men. The Goth Jornandes calls the North of Europe the forge of mankind. I would rather call it the forge of those instruments which broke the fetters manufactured in the South."

Geijer, in his Swedish History, says: "The recollections which Scandinavia has to add to those of the Germanic race are yet the most antique in character and comparatively the most original. They offer the completest remaining example of a social state existing previously to the reception of influences from Rome, and in duration stretching onward so as to come within the sphere of historical light."

Scandinavian society was divided into two classes—the landholders, or bondsmen, and the thralls, or slaves. The thralls consisted of prisoners taken in war and their children, and their duties were to perform domestic service and to till the soil. War was the chief pursuit of the landholder, and courage was his chief virtue.

Scandinavian institutions were patriarchal. The head of the family was the chief and priest of the tribe; but all the freemen in a neighborhood met in the Thing, and there decided disputes, laid down social regulations and determined on public measures. Therefore the Thing was the legislature, the court of justice and the executive council, all in one. The Land-Thing, or All-Thing, was an annual meeting of the freemen of the whole country in some central place to settle national affairs. At this meeting the king was chosen for the entire community, who sometimes appointed subordinate officers called *Yarls*, or earls, to preside over large districts.

A marked trait among the Scandinavians was respect for women, as Tacitus had noticed among their kinsmen, the Germans. Women were admired for their modesty, sense, and force of character, rather than for the fascinations preferred in the South of Europe. When Thor described his battle with the sorceress he was answered:

"Shame, Thor! to strike a woman!" The wife was expected to be industrious and domestic, and she carried the keys of the house. The Sagas frequently mention wives who divorced their husbands for some offense and took back their dowry.

The *Skalds*, or bards, were a highly honored and distinguished class among the Scandinavians; and their songs constituted the literature and history of this remarkable people. The people listened to the pulsation of its own past life, but not as to the inspiration of an individual mind. The greatest Scandinavian kings and heroes desired the praises of the Skalds, and feared their satire. The style of these Skalds was figurative, sometimes bombastic, frequently obscure.

The old Norse, or Scandinavian, language was distinguished from the Alemannic, or High German, and from the Saxon, or Low German. The languages of Norway, Sweden and Denmark, of the Faroe Isles and of Iceland, have all been derived from the Norse; just as the German, Dutch and English have been derived from the ancient Germanic, or Teutonic.

From the earliest times the Scandinavians, as well as the Saxons, were distinguished for their maritime hardihood, their ardent passion for adventure and their contempt for death. They navigated the Northern seas with more courage and freedom than the Greeks and Romans manifested in the Mediterranean. They did not come to anchor when the stars were obscured by clouds. They did not despair when they lost sight of land. On board every Norman vessel was a cast of hawks or ravens; and when the adventurers were uncertain in what direction lay the land, they let one of the birds fly, knowing that he would instinctively make for the nearest coast, and by his flight they steered their course.

The great peculiarity of the raids of the Northmen was their maritime character; and these daring and skillful navigators encountered the tempests of the dreary Northern Ocean and the heavy roll of the stormy Atlantic in vessels so small and light that they floated on the surface of the waves like eggshells, and ascended the rivers of Germany, France and England for hundreds of miles, without check from the shallows or rocks. In these fragile barks the intrepid Northern *Sea-kings* made the most extraordinary maritime discoveries.

Though the Norman leaders assumed the proud title of *Vikings*, or Sea-kings, their respective dominions were confined to the deck of the vessel which each commanded, and when the expedition had ceased all superiority was at an end. As soon as a Sea-king announced his intention of undertaking some buccaneering enterprise he was certain to have multitudes of adventurous youth ready to volunteer their services as his associates. It was a matter of absolute indifference whither an adventurous Sea-king would steer, provided that there was a reasonable opportunity for plunder.

These piratical crews effected a landing when they were least expected. They showed no mercy to age or sex, and the fate of those who submitted was the same as those who resisted; but the Christian churches and clergy were the special objects of vengeance, because the Northmen considered their mission to be to avenge the insults offered to Odin and the persecutions which the worshipers of that deity had suffered from Christian sovereigns.

Almost the entire information which we possess concerning these Northern pirates is obtained from the *Sagas*, or songs of the *Skalds*, or bards. These strange compositions are unlike any other form of literature, being records of adventure in verse or measured prose, in which historical events and chronology are utterly ignored. The Scandinavians honored their Skalds, or bards, more than their priests.

The character of a Viking, or Sea-king, was not in the least disgraceful, being eagerly sought by men of the highest rank, and was only accorded to such as had given distinguished evidence of their heroism in battle and their skill in navigation. According to an old Scandinavian maxim, in order to obtain glory for bravery, a man should attack a single enemy, defend him self against two, and not yield to three, but he might flee from four without disgrace.

The Scandinavian warrior's highest ambition was to die in battle. He believed that he should then pass to the happy halls of Odin. Ragnar Lodbrog died singing the pleasure of receiving death in battle, saying: "The hours of my life have passed away; I shall die laughing." In describing a duel, Saxo said that one of the champions fell, laughed and died. Some, when sick, would leap from a rock into the sea, rather than die in their beds. Others, when dying, would be carried into a field of battle. Others induced their friends to kill them. The Icelandic Sagas abound with stories of single combat, or *holm-gangs*.

When not fighting, the Norman warriors were engaged in feasting, of which they were very fond; and the man who was able to drink the most beer was considered the best. The custom of drinking toasts came from these Northmen. As the English give their sovereign, and the Americans their President, the first health on public occasions, so the Northmen began with a cup, first to Odin, and afterward to other deities, and then to the memory of the dead, in what they called grave-beer.

Sir Walter Scott has described the character of a Northern Sea-king with such poetic force and historic accuracy that the following extract will dispense with the necessity of further description:

"Count Witikind came of a regal strain,
And roved with his Norsemen the land and the main;
Wo to the realms which he coasted! for there
Was shedding of blood and rending of hair,
Rape of maiden and slaughter of priest,
Gathering of ravens and wolves to the feast!
When he hoisted his standard black,
Before him was battle, behind him wrack;
And he burned the churches, that heathen Dane,
To light his band to their barks again.

On Erin's shores was his outrage known,
The winds of France had his banners blown;
Little was there to plunder, yet still
His pirates had forayed on Scottish hill;
But upon merry England's coast,
More frequent he sailed, for he won the most.

So far and wide his ravage they knew,
If a sail but gleamed white 'gainst the welkin blue
Trumpet and bugles to arms did call,
Burghers hastened to man the wall;
Peasants fled inland his fury to scape,
Beacons were lighted on headland and cape;
Bells were tolled out, and aye as they rung
Fearful and faintly the gray brothers sung,
'Save us, St. Mary, from flood and from fire,
From famine and pest, and Count Witikind's ire.'"

The French historian Thierry has collected the main characteristics of a Sea-king from the Icelandic Sagas, as follows: "He could govern a vessel as a good rider manages his horse, running over the oars while they were in motion. He would throw three javelins to the mast-head and catch them alternately in his hand without once missing. Equal under such a chief, supporting lightly their voluntary submission, and the weight of their coat-of-mail, which they promised themselves would soon be exchanged for an equal weight of gold, the pirates held their course gayly, as their old songs express it, along the track of the swans. Often were their fragile barks wrecked and dispersed by the North seastorm, often did the rallying sign remain unanswered, but this neither increased the cares nor diminished the confidence of the survivors, who laughed at the wind and waves from which they had escaped unhurt. Their song in the midst of the tempest was:

'The force of the storm helps the arms of our rowers,
The hurricane is carrying us the way which we should go.'"

Every Norman king, whether on sea or land, had a select band of companions, called *Kempe*, who were warriors pledged to the personal service of their leader, and whose sole hope of promotion sprung from the performance of some achievement, the fame of which might be spread over the North by the songs of the Skalds. Each Viking laid down rules for the government of his own champions, and he whose regulations were the most rigid and rigorous was rewarded with fame.

Thus it is said that Hiorolf and Half, the

sons of a King of Norway, both devoted themselves to maritime adventure, or, more properly speaking, to piracy. Hiorolf collected many ships and manned them with every kind of volunteers from both serfs and freemen, but he was defeated in all his expeditions. Half had a single ship; but his crew were all picked men, at first only twenty-three in number and all of royal descent, afterwards increased to sixty. Half's band carried terror to all the shores of Western Europe for eighteen years.

In order to be admitted into the company a champion was required to lift a large stone which lay in front of Half's residence and which the united strength of twelve ordinary men could not move. These champions were forbidden to take women and children, to seek a refuge during a tempest, or to dress their wounds before the end of the battle.

Finally, when Half was returning to enjoy the wealth which he had gained by his piracies and maraudings, his vessel, overladen with plunder, appeared about sinking within sight of the coast of Norway. The gallant crew instantly drew lots to decide who should cast themselves into the sea for the purpose of saving their chieftain and the cargo. Those on whom the lot fell immediately jumped overboard, laughing, and swam to the shore; and the vessel, thus relieved of some of the heavy weight, safely reached the harbor.

A Viking seldom condescended to the blandishments of courtship. If he heard of any noble or royal damsel famed for beauty, he instantly demanded her from her father, and, in case of refusal, equipped a vessel to take her away forcibly. If he succeeded in this enterprise, he usually brought along her dowry at the same time, and was thus able to boast of a double victory.

A Swedish pirate named Gunnar, having heard the Skalds celebrate the charms of Moalda, a Norwegian princess, sent to her father Regnald a peremptory demand for his fair daughter's hand in marriage. Regnald scornfully rejected the suitor, but, aware of the consequences of such a refusal, made instant preparations for defense. Before marching against the Swedish pirates, the Norwegian king caused a cavern to be hollowed out in the mountains, and concealed the princess and his choicest treasures within, leaving the princess an adequate supply of provisions.

No sooner were Regnald's arrangements completed than the fierce Gunnar appeared off the Norwegian coast. Regnald met the Swedish pirates on the shore, and a desperate battle ensued, in which the Norwegian king was defeated and slain. After his victory Gunnar sought the place where the fair Moalda was concealed, and carried away the princess and her treasures to Sweden.

A conquest of this kind was frequently followed by several others, as polygamy was sufficiently common among these Northern adventurers. The fair ones themselves could not view with indifference those heroes who risked their lives to obtain their hands, and whose exploits were immortalized by the Skalds and sung in all Scandinavian families.

Sometimes these Scandinavian warriors, like the Malays of Java, were seized with a kind of frenzy, produced by an excited imagination or by the use of stimulating liquors. In this condition they were called *berserker*, a word which often occurs in the Sagas. While under the influence of this madness the champions committed the wildest extravagances. They danced about, foamed at the mouth, struck indiscriminately at friends and foes, destroyed their own property, and, like the mad Orlando, warred against inanimate nature, tearing up rocks and trees.

Siwald, King of Sweden, had five sons, and all of them became *berserker*, swallowing burning coals and throwing themselves into the fire when the fit was on them. They and their father were slain by Halfdan, who had been previously dethroned by Siwald, the nation having become impatient of the extravagances of the frantic princes. Halfdan had a contest with another berserker, named Hartben, who came to attack him, accompanied by twelve champions.

Hartben was a formidable pirate, but when he was under the influence of the fit his twelve champions had as much as they could do to prevent him destroying right and left. Halfdan challenged Hartben and his entire crew—an insult which so inflamed Hartben that he was instantly seized with a fit of frenzy, during which he killed six of his champions, and rushed against Halfdan with the remaining six, but these were all slain by the irresistible blows of Halfdan's mace.

The sons of Arngrim, King of Heligoland, were the most famous pirates of their time, and are said to have suffered severely from the berserk madness. When under its influence they massacred their crews and destroyed their shipping. Sometimes they landed on desert places and vented their fury on the stocks and stones. After the fit had left them they lay quite senseless from sheer exhaustion.

It was about the opening of the ninth century, during the brilliant reign of Charlemagne, that the freebooting Northmen began their destructive inroads. For several centuries they were the terror of Western and Southern Europe. Their depredations brought tears to Charlemagne's eyes, and after his death they pillaged and burned the chief cities of France and Germany, even his own splendid palace at Aix la Chapelle. The daring pirates especially infested the coasts of France, England and Ireland.

Ragnar Lodbrog, King of the Danish Isles, was expelled from his dominions with the aid of the Franks. He retaliated by invading France, sailing up the Seine to Paris, and plundering all the churches, A. D. 845. He finally fell into the power of King Ella of Deira, one of the petty Anglo-Saxon monarchs in Britain, who threw him into a dungeon, where he suffered a torturing death by the venom of innumerable serpents.

The Northmen almost destroyed Hamburg in A. D. 847. In A. D. 857 they took Paris a second time and massacred its inhabitants. In A. D. 862 they besieged Paris a third time ; and, though the Parisians made a vigorous resistance, the Northmen, under

3—20.-U. H.

their renowned leader, Hastings, ravaged France frightfully for the next five years. Under Rollo, the Northmen again besieged Paris in A. D. 885, but were bribed to withdraw. Rollo renewed his inroads ; and the ravages of the Northmen in France only ceased when King Charles the Simple allowed Rollo and his followers to settle in that portion of North-western France to which they gave the name of *Normandy*, A. D. 912.

About the same time when the Norman ravages began in France and Germany, the same intrepid marauders, under the name of Danes, commenced their destructive inroads into England, which country suffered fearfully from their depredations for two centuries; these raids only ceasing when Canute the Great, King of Denmark, conquered England and became monarch of that kingdom also, as he afterwards did of Norway and Sweden. Finally in A. D. 1066, William, Duke of Normandy, invaded England, and, by his great victory at Hastings over the Saxon King Harold, became King of England, the whole fate of which was thus entirely changed. During the same period the Danes also ravaged Ireland, until they were defeated in battle with Brian Boru at Clontarf in A. D. 1014.

The Northmen also carried their inroads into Spain, Italy and Greece. In A. D. 844 a band of these sea-rovers sailed up the Guadalquivir and attacked the city of Seville, then in possession of the Arabs, took the city, and afterwards fought a battle with the army of King Abderrahman II. The followers of Mohammed and the worshipers of Odin—the turbaned Arabs and Moors, and the fair-haired Norwegians—here encountered each other, each far from his mother country, each having pursued a line of conquest, and these two coming in contact at their farthest extremes.

In A. D. 866 the Sea-kings of Norway appeared before Constantinople, and afterwards a band of these Northern, pirates, or Varangians, composed a body-guard of the Eastern Emperors.

The Northmen in Italy entered the ser-

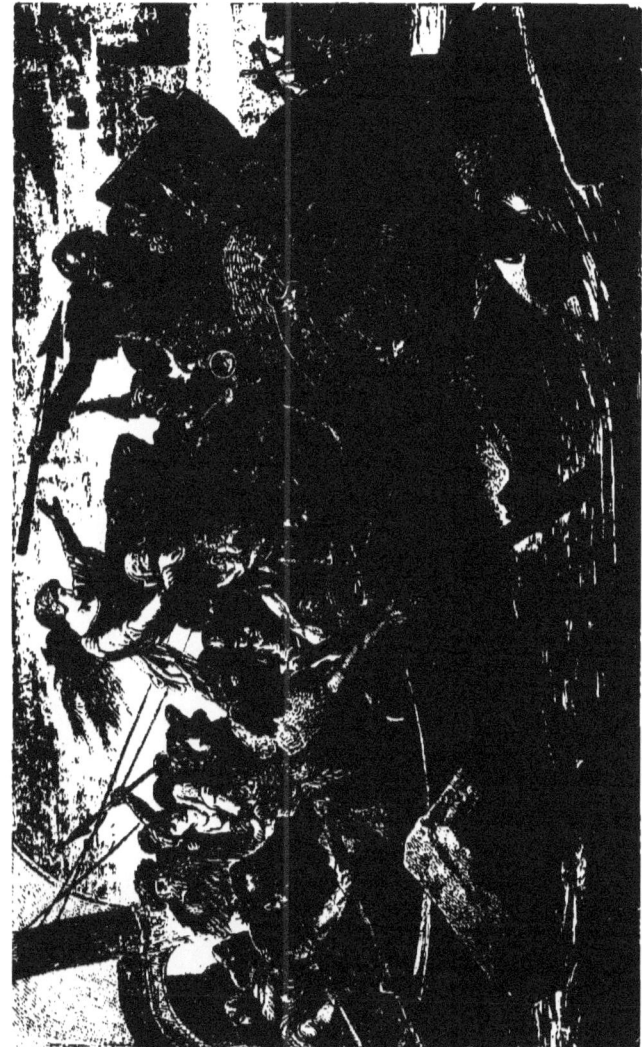

MARAUDING EXPEDITION OF THE NORTHMEN.

LEIF ERIC DISCOVERING THE SHORES OF VINLAND.

vices of different princes, and under Count Rainalf they built the city of Aversa in A. D. 1029. The Norman knights defeated the Saracens in Sicily, thus enabling the Eastern Emperor to reconquer that island. They afterwards established themselves in Southern Italy and took possession of Apulia. The Pope and the Germano-Roman Eastern and Roman Emperors then formed a league against them, but the Papal and German army was utterly defeated by three thousand Normans, and Apulia was afterwards received and held by the Normans as a papal fief.

In A. D. 1060 Robert Guiscard, a valiant Norman chieftain, became Duke of Apulia and Calabria, and laid the foundation of the Kingdom of Naples and Sicily. Count Roger, Robert Guiscard's brother, with but a few followers, conquered Sicily, routing vast numbers of the Saracens and completely subduing the island after thirty years of war. In the meantime Roger's brother Robert crossed the Adriatic sea and besieged and took Durazzo, after a fierce battle, in which the Norman soldiers of the Eastern Emperor fought with their Norman kinsmen.

About A. D. 875 Harald Harfager, "the Fair-haired," founded the Kingdom of Norway, and Gorm the Old laid the foundations of the Kingdom of Denmark; while the Ynglingar founded the Kingdom of Sweden a little later, or about A. D. 900. When Harald Fairhair endeavored to clear Norway of the pirates they swarmed over Europe.

About A. D. 875 Rurik, a Norman Varangian chieftain, was called upon by the people of Novgorod to be their ruler; and he thus laid the foundations of the Russian Empire, the name *Russian* being given to those Slavonian people because Rurik belonged to the Scandinavian tribe of Russ.

The Sea-kings of Norway discovered Iceland in A. D. 860 and settled it in A. D. 874. Greenland was discovered by Icelandic Northmen in A. D. 982 and settled in A. D. 986. They colonized the western shores of Greenland, where they built churches and established diocesan bishoprics, which lasted from four to five centuries. Finally in A. D. 1000 these Northern sea-rovers, sailing from Greenland, discovered the coast of Labrador, Nova Scotia and New England, and built houses on the south side of Cape Cod five centuries before the discovery of America by Christopher Columbus. They left no vestige of their presence in New England, unless it be the mysterious old tower at Newport, Rhode Island, which many believe to have been built by these Northern explorers. These facts, long regarded as mythical, have been established to the satisfaction of European scholars by the publication of Icelandic contemporaneous annals.

The central idea of the Scandinavian religion was the free struggle of soul against material obstacles, the freedom of the Divine will in its conflict with the antagonistic powers of nature. The Scandinavian gods were perpetually at war. This system was a dualism, in which sunshine, summer and development were waging constant battle with storm, snow, winter, ocean and terrestrial fire. The characteristics of the people were the same as those of the gods. Their occupation was war, their duty was courage, their virtue was fortitude. Their history and their destiny were made up in the conflict of life with death, of freedom with fate, of choice with necessity, of good with evil.

This conflict in the natural world was particularly apparent in the annual renewal of the struggle between summer and winter. Accordingly the gods of light and heat were the friends of the Scandinavians, and the gods of darkness and cold were their foes. As Typhon, the burning heat of summer, was the Satan of Egypt; so the Jötuns, or ice-giants of the North, were the Scandinavian devils.

Some virtues are naturally associated together, such as the love of truth, the sense of justice, courage and personal independence. The opposite class of virtues naturally grouped together are sympathy, mutual helpfulness and a tendency to social organization. In the moral world is the serious antagonism of truth and love. Most cases of conscience presenting a real difficulty resolve themselves into a conflict of truth and love. It is no easy matter to be true without hurting the feelings of others, nor is it easy to sympathize with others without yielding a little of our inward truth. The same antagonism is seen in the religions of the world. The religions in which truth, justice and freedom are developed tend to isolation, coldness and hardness; while the religions which develop brotherhood and human sympathy tend to luxury, effeminacy and slavery.

The Germanic and Scandinavian religion, which was the natural development of the Teutonic organization and moral character, was one of the first of these two classes of religions—a religion in which the essential elements were truth, justice, self-respect, courage and freedom. Like the gods of Greece, those of Scandinavia were human, with moral attributes. They were finite beings, with limited powers. They carried on a warfare with hostile and destructive elements, in which they were finally to be vanquished and destroyed, but that destruction was to be followed by a restoration of the world and the gods.

Such was the idea in the Germanic and Scandinavian religion. Courage was man's chief virtue; cowardice was his unpardonable sin. The sure way to Valhalla, the Scandinavian Paradise, was "to fight a good fight" and to die in battle. Odin sent his Choosers to every battle-field to select the heroic dead for his companions in the joys of heaven, where they sat with him drinking beer from the skulls of their slaughtered foes. Those who escaped with their lives on the battle-field, or who died a natural death, were excluded from this happy abode, as being too cowardly for Odin's society.

The resemblance between the Scandinavian and Zoroastrian mythologies has frequently been remarked. Each is a dualism, with its good and evil gods, its worlds of light and darkness, in opposition to each other. Each has behind this dualism a dim presence, a vague monotheism, a supreme Deity, an infinite and eternal Being, an omnipotent, omnipresent and omniscient God. In each system the evil powers are conquered for the present and bound in some subterranean prisons, but are to break out hereafter, to battle with the gods and subdue them, being themselves destroyed at the same time. Each system speaks of a great conflagration, in which every thing will be destroyed; after which there will be a new earth, more beautiful than the first, to be the abode of peace and joy. In each system man's duty is war, though the Zend Avesta regards this war as rather a moral conflict, while in the Edda it is represented more grossly as a physical struggle.

The tone of Zoroaster's theology is higher throughout and more moral than that of the Scandinavians, but there is a singular correspondence between these two systems in their details. Odin, in the Scandinavian system, corresponds to Ahura-Mazda in the Zoroastrian system; and in the same way Loki corresponds to Angra-Mainyus, the Æsir to the Amshaspands, the giants of Jötunheim to the Daêvas, the giant Ymir to the ox Adudab, Baldur to the Redeemer Sosiosh.

The creation of the man and woman, Ask and Embla, in the Scandinavian theology, is correlated to Meshia and Meshiane, in the Zend-Avesta. The Scandinavian bridge Bifröst, which reaches to heaven, resembles the Zoroastrian bridge Chinevat, which ascends from the top of the mountain of Albordj to heaven. The Scandinavian Surtur, the watchman of the luminous world at the South, seems to correspond to the dog Sirius (Sura), the watchman who keeps guard over the abyss Duzahk, as described in the Zend-Avesta.

The ancient Germans and Scandinavians called the earth *Hertha*, which is the name assigned to this goddess by Tacitus, while the Zend-Avesta called it *Hethra*. Himmel, the German name for heaven, is derived from the Sanskrit word *Himmala*, signifying the name of the Himalaya mountains, on the northern boundary of India, believed by the primitive Aryans to be the abode of their gods.

As already noticed, Iceland was settled from Norway in the ninth century; and in

A. D. 874 a republic was founded in that dreary island, which was very flourishing for several centuries. A remarkable social life developed there, which preserved the Scandinavian ideas, manners and religion in their purity for many centuries, and whose *Eddas* and *Sagas* are the main source of our knowledge of the Scandinavian race. In that remote and barren region of the earth, where icy seas spread desolation over thousands of square miles and make such vast areas impenetrable, where ice mountains abound, and where volcanoes with terrible eruptions destroy whole regions of inhabited territory in a few days with lava, volcanic sand and boiling water, the purest form of Scandinavian life was developed to its highest degree.

The Scandinavian religion is described in the two Eddas. The elder, or poetic Edda, consists of thirty-seven poems, first collected and published at the close of the eleventh century. The younger, or prose Edda, is ascribed to the renowned Snorro Sturleson, who was born of an illustrious Icelandic family in the year A. D. 1178, led a turbulent and ambitious life, was twice chosen supreme magistrate, and was finally killed A. D. 1241. The chief part of the prose Edda is a full synopsis of Scandinavian mythology.

The elder Edda is the fountain of this mythology, and consists of old songs and ballads, transmitted from an immemorial past by popular tradition, but first collected and committed to writing by Sæmund, an Icelandic Christian priest in the eleventh century. Sæmund was a Skald, or bard, no less than a priest; and one of his own poems, *The Sun-Song*, is in the elder Edda. The word *Edda* signifies *great-grandmother*.

The poetic, or elder Edda, is in two parts —the first comprising mythical poems respecting the gods and the creation; the second embracing the legends of the Scandinavian heroes. The latter of these two parts contains the original and ancient fragments from which the German *Nibelungenlied* was subsequently derived. These songs of the elder Edda are to the famous mediæval German poem what the pre-Homeric ballad literature of Greece about Troy and Ulysses was to the Iliad and Odyssey as reduced to unity by Homer.

The first poem in the first portion of the poetic Edda is the *Völuspa*, or *Wisdom of Vala*. The Vala was a prophetess endowed with great supernatural knowledge. Some antiquarians regard the Vala as the same as the Nornor, or Fates. They were dark beings, whose wisdom was terrible even to the gods, resembling the Greek Prometheus in this particular. The Völuspa describes the universe before the creation, in the morning of time, before the great Ymir lived, when sea and shore had no existence. The Völuspa commences as follows, Vala speaking:

"I command the devout attention of all noble souls,
Of all the high and the low of the race of Heimdall;
I tell the doings of the All-Father,
In the most ancient Sagas which come to my mind.

"There was an age in which Ymir lived,
When was no sea, nor shore, nor salt waves;
No earth below, nor heaven above,
No yawning abyss and no grassy land.

"Till the sons of Börs lifted the dome of heaven,
And created the vast Midgard (earth) below;
Then the sun of the south rose above the mountains,
And green grasses made the ground verdant.

"The sun of the south, companion of the moon,
Held the horses of heaven with his right hand;
The sun knew not what its course should be,
The moon knew not what her power should be,
The stars knew not where their places were.

"Then the counselors went into the hall of judgment,
And the all-holy gods held a council.
They gave names to the night and new moon;
They called to the morning and to midday,
To the afternoon and evening, arranging the times."

The Völuspa proceeds to an account of how the gods assembled on the field of Ida, and how they went on to create metals and vegetables, and afterwards the race of dwarfs who preside over the powers of nature and the mineral world. Vala then relates how the three gods, Odin, Hönir and

Lodur, "the mighty and mild Aser," found Ask and Embla, the Adam and Eve of the Scandinavian legends, lying without soul, sense, motion or color. Odin gave them their souls, Hönir their intellects, Lodur their blood and colored flesh. Next follows the discription of the ash-tree Yggdrasil; of the three Norns, or sisters of destiny, who tell the Aser of their doom, and of the end and renewal of the world, and how one being mightier than all shall finally arrive, in the following lines:

"Then comes the mighty one to the council of the gods,
He with strength from on high who guides all things,
He decides the strife, he puts an end to the struggle,
He ordains eternal laws."

The *Song of Hyndla*, another of the poems of the Edda, contains a prediction of one who shall come, mightier than all the gods, and put an end to the strife between Aser and the giants. The Song of Hyndla begins thus:

"Wake, maid of maidens! Awake, my friend!
Hyndla, sister, dwelling in the glens!
It is night, it is cloudy; let us ride together
To the sacred place, to Valhalla."

After describing the heroes and princes born of the gods, Hyndla sings as follows:

"One shall be born higher than all,
Who grows strong with the strength of the earth;
He is famed as the greatest of rulers,
United with all nations as brethren.

"But one day there shall come another mightier than he;
But I dare not name his name.
Few are able to see beyond
The great battle of Odin and the Wolf."

Among the poems of the elder Edda is a Book of Proverbs, like those of Solomon in their wise observations on human life and manners. This poem is styled the *Havamal*, and contains one hundred and ten stanzas in its proverbial section, mainly quatrains. Some specimens are the following:

"Carefully consider the end
Before you go to do anything,

For all is uncertain, when the enemy
Lies in wait in the house.

"The guest who enters
Needs water, a towel, and hospitality.
A kind reception secures a return
In word and in deed.

"The wise man, on coming in,
Is silent and observes,
Hears with his ears, looks with his eyes,
And carefully reflects on every event.

"No worse a companion can a man take on his journey
Than drunkenness.
Not as good as many believe
Is beer to the sons of men.
The more one drinks, the less he knows,
And less power has he over himself.

"A foolish man, in company, had better be silent.
Until he speaks no one observes his folly.
But he who knows little does not know this,
When he had better be silent.

"Do not mock at the stranger
Who comes trusting in your kindness;
For when he has warmed himself at your fire,
He may easily prove a wise man.

"It is better to depart betimes,
And not to go too often to the same house.
Love tires and turns to sadness
When one sits too often at another man's table.

"One's own house, though small, is better,
For there thou art the master.
It makes a man's heart bleed to ask
For a midday meal at the house of another.

"One's own house, though small, is better;
At home thou art the master.
Two goats and a thatched roof
Are better than begging.

"It is hard to find a man so rich
As to refuse a gift.
It is hard to find a man so generous
As to be always glad to lend.

"Is there a man whom you distrust,
And who yet can help you?
Be smooth in words and false in thought,
And pay back his deceit with cunning.

"I hung my garments on two scarecrows,
And, when dressed, they seemed
Ready for the battle.
Unclothed they were jeered at by all.

"Small as a grain of sand
Is the small sense of a fool;

THE NORTHMEN AND THEIR RELIGION.

Very unequal is human wisdom.
The world is made of two unequal halves.

"It is well to be wise; it is not well
To be too wise.
He has the happiest life
Who knows well what he knows.

"It is well to be wise; not well
To be too wise.
The wise man's heart is not glad
When he knows too much.

"Two burning sticks placed together
Will burn entirely away.
Man grows bright by the side of man;
Alone, he remains stupid."

The sort of proverbial wisdom thus found in the Havamal may have had its origin in the prehistoric past, when the ancestors of the Scandinavians migrated from Central Asia. These proverbs resemble the fables and maxims of the Hitopadesá, or Salutary Counsels of Vishnu Sárman, as found in the Sanskrit literature.

Odin's Song of Runes is another of the poems of the elder Edda. The Runes were the Scandinavian alphabet, used for lapidary inscriptions, of which a thousand have been discovered in Sweden, and from three to four hundred in Denmark and Norway, mainly upon tombstones. The Runic alphabet has sixteen letters, with the powers of F, U, TH, O, R, K, H, N, I, A, S, T, B, L, M, Y. The letters R, I, T and B almost resemble the Roman letters of the same significations. These Runes were believed to possess a magical power, and they were carved on sticks and then scraped off and used as charms. Eighteen different kinds of these Rune-charms are mentioned in this song.

A song of Brynhilda mentions different Runes which she will teach Sigurd. "*Runes of Victory* must thou know, to conquer thine enemies. They must be carved on the blade of thy sword. *Drink-Runes* must thou know to make maidens love thee. Thou must carve them on thy drinking-horn. *Runes of freedom* must thou know, how to deliver the captives. *Storm-Runes* must thou know, to make thy vessel go safely over the waves. Carve them on the mast and the rudder.

Herb-Runes thou must know to cure disease. Carve them on the bark of the tree. *Speech-Runes* must thou know to defeat thine enemy in council of words, in the Thing. *Mind-Runes* must thou know to have good and wise thoughts. These are the Book-Runes, and Help-Runes, and Drink-Runes, and Power-Runes, precious for whoever can use them."

The second portion of the poetic Edda contains the legends of the old heroes, particularly of Sigurd, the Achilles of Northern romance. This part of the elder Edda likewise contains the Song of Volund, the Northern Smith, the German Vulcan, capable of making swords of powerful temper. These songs and ballads are all grave and serious, sometimes tender, characterized somewhat by the solemn tone of the old Greek tragedy.

Snorro Sturleson may have transcribed most of the prose Edda from the manuscripts to which he had access, and from the oral traditions which had been preserved in the memory of the Skalds. His other principal work was the *Heimskringla*, or collection of Saga concerning Scandinavian history. In his preface to this last book he says that he "wrote it down from old stories told by intelligent people;" or from "ancient family registers containing the pedigrees of kings," or from "old songs and ballads which our fathers had for their amusement."

The prose Edda commences with "The deluding of Gylfi," an ancient king of Sweden, who was celebrated for his wisdom and his love of knowledge, and who resolved to visit Asgard, the home of the Æsir, to learn something of the wisdom of the gods. But the gods foresaw his coming, and prepared various illusions to deceive him. Among the things that he saw were three thrones raised one above another.

"He afterwards beheld three thrones raised one above another, with a man sitting on each of them. Upon his asking what the names of these lords might be, his guide answered: 'He who sits on the lowest throne is a king; his name is Har (the High or Lofty One); the second is Jafnhar (i. e.

equal to the High); but he who sitteth on the highest throne is called Thridi (the Third).' Har, perceiving the stranger, asked him what his errand was, adding that he should be welcome to eat and drink without cost, as were all those who remained in Háva Hall. Gangler said he desired first to ascertain whether there was any person present renowned for his wisdom.

"'If thou art not the most knowing,' replied Har, 'I fear thou wilt hardly return safe. But go, stand there below, and propose thy questions; here sits one who will be able to answer them.'

"Gangler thus began his discourse: 'Who is the first or eldest of the gods?'

"'In our language,' replied Har, 'he is called Alfadir (All-Father, or the Father of All); but in the old Asgard he had twelve names.'

"'Where is this God?' said Gangler; 'what is his power? and what hath he done to display his glory?'

"'He liveth,' replied Har, 'from all ages, he governeth all realms, and swayeth all things great and small.'

"'He hath formed,' added Jafnhar, 'heaven and earth, and the air, and all things thereunto belonging.'

"'And what is more,' continued Thridi, 'he hath made man, and given him a soul which shall live and never perish, though the body shall have mouldered away, or have been burnt to ashes. And all that are righteous shall dwell with him in the place called Gimli, or Vingólf; but the wicked shall go to Hel, and thence to Niflhel, which is below, in the ninth world.'"

The Eddas teach the following cosmogony: In the beginning there was neither sea nor shore, nor any refreshing breeze. There was no heaven or earth—nothing but one vast abyss, without herb and without seas. There was no sun, moon or stars. After this a bright shining world of flame appeared to the South, and a dark and cloudy one toward the North. Torrents of venom flowed from the dark world into the abyss, freezing it and filling it with ice. But the air oozed up through it in icy vapors, and these were melted into living drops by a warm breath from the South. These drops produced the giant Ymir, from whom proceeded a race of wicked giants. These same drops of fluid seeds, children of heat and cold, afterwards produced the mundane cow, the milk of which fed the giants. Then followed the mysterious appearance of Börs, who had three sons, Odin, Vili and Ve. These killed the giant Ymir and created Heaven and Earth out of his body, after which they created the first man and woman, Ask and Embla. After this disappearance of Chaos, Odin became the All-Father, the creator of gods and men, with Earth for his wife, and the powerful Thor for his eldest son.

This cosmogony is development, or evolution, and creation combined. The Brahmanic, Gnostic and Platonic theories suppose the visible world to have emanated from God by a succession of fallings from the most abstract spirit to the most concrete matter. The Greeks and Romans believed that everything came by a process of evolution, or development from an original formless and chaotic matter. There is a remarkable similarity between the Greek account of the origin of the gods and men and the Scandinavian account of the same beings. Both systems commence in materialism, and are in complete antagonism to the spiritualism of the other theory; and the cosmogony of the Eddas reminds us of the modern scientific theories of the origin of all things from nebulous vapors and heat.

After giving the preceding account of the creation of the world, of the gods and the first pair of mortals, the Edda speaks of day and night, of the sun and the moon, of the rainbow bridge from earth to heaven, and of the Ash-tree where the gods sit in council. Night was the daughter of a giant, and was of a dark complexion, like all the rest of her race. She married one of the Æsir, or children of Odin; and their son was Day, a child who was light and beautiful, like his father. The Sun and the Moon were two children; the Sun being the girl, and the Moon the boy—a peculiarity of gender which still prevails in the German language. The Edda tells us that the Sun and the Moon each drive round the heavens daily with horses and chariot, and says that their speed is caused by fear upon being pursued by two gigantic wolves from Jötunheim, or the world of darkness.

The bridge Bifröst is the rainbow, woven of three hues, and by which the gods ride up to heaven daily from the holy fountain under the earth. Three maidens—Norns, or Fates—dwell near this fountain, below the great Ash-tree, and decide the fate of every human creature. These Norns, or Fates, are named Urd, Verdandi and Skuld—three words signifying "past," "present" and "future." Our word *wierd* is derived from Urd. The red in the rainbow is burning fire, which prevents the front-giants of Jötunheim from ascending to heaven, or Asgard, which contains Valhalla, the Scandinavian paradise, where the gods feast daily with all the heroes who have died in battle, drinking mead and eating the flesh of a boar.

Odin and the other Scandinavian gods did not live quietly in Valhalla, and the Edda narrates numerous interesting accounts of adventures performed by them. One of these legends describes the death of Baldur the Good, who was loved by all beings. Having been tormented with bad dreams, indicating that his life was endangered, he related them to the assembled gods, who made all creatures and things, living and dead, swear not to do him any harm. This oath was taken by fire and water, by iron and all other metals, by stones, earths, diseases, poisons, beasts, birds and creeping things.

After taking this oath, all animate and inanimate things amused themselves at their meeting in setting up Baldur as a target; some hurling darts or shooting arrows at him, and some cutting at him with axes and swords; and as nothing hurt Baldur, it was regarded as a great honor done to him. But wicked Loki, or Loke, who was envious of this honor to Baldur, assumed the form of a woman, and asked the goddess who had administered the oath, whether all things had taken it. The goddess replied that everything had taken it, except one little shrub called mistletoe, which she considered too young and feeble to do any harm. Accordingly Loki got the mistletoe, brought it to one of the gods, and persuaded him to throw it at Baldur, who fell dead, pierced to the heart.

The grief at Baldur's death was intense. A special messenger was despatched to Hela, Queen of Hell, to ascertain if Baldur might be ransomed on any terms. This messenger rode for nine days through dark chasms until he crossed the River of Death and entered Hela's kingdom, where he made known his request. Hela replied that it should now be definitely ascertained if Baldur was so universally beloved as was represented, and that she would permit him to return to Asgard if all creatures and all things would weep for him. The gods then despatched messengers through the world to humbly implore all things to weep for Baldur, which they did at once. The crocodiles and the most ferocious beasts melted in tears. Fishes wept in the water, and birds in the air. Stones and trees were covered with pellucid dew-drops.

Thinking their mission accomplished, the messengers then returned to the gods, but found an old woman sitting in a cavern, and entreated her to weep Baldur out of Hell. But the woman declared that she could gain nothing by such a course, and that Baldur might stay where he was, like other people as good as he; thus acting on the selfish principle of non-intervention. Thus Baldur remained in the halls of Hela, but the old woman did not go unpunished. She was shrewdly suspected of being Loki himself in disguise, and upon inquiry such was found to be the case. Thereupon Loki was hotly pursued, and, after changing himself into many forms, was caught and chained under sharp-pointed rocks below the earth.

The adventures of Thor, the god of storms and thunder, are very numerous. The most interesting account of his adventures is that concerning his journey to Jö tunheim, where he visited his enemies, the giants of Cold and Darkness. As he was obliged to pass the night in the forest, on his way to Jötunheim, he came to a spacious hall, with an open door, which extended from one side to the other. In this vast hall Thor went to sleep, but was aroused by a terrible earthquake, whereupon he and his companions crept into a chamber which communicated with the hall. At daybreak they found an immence giant sleeping near them, so large that they had passed the night in the thumb of his glove. They traveled with this giant all day, and the next night Thor regarded himself as justified in killing him, as he was one of their enemies. Thor launched his mallet at the giant's head three times with terrific force, and the giant awoke three times to ask whether it was a leaf or an acorn that had fallen on his face.

After taking leave of their gigantic and invulnerable enemy, Thor and his companions arrived at Jötunheim and the city of Utgard, entering the city of the king, Utgard Loki. This king inquired what great exploit Thor and his companions were able to perform. One claimed to be a great eater, whereupon the king of giants summoned one of his servants named Logi, and placed a trough filled with meat between them. Thor's companion ate his share; but Logi ate both meat and bone, and the trough into the bargain, and was regarded as having triumphed over his rival. Thor's other companion was a great runner, and was set to run with a young man named Hugi, who so surpassed him that he reached the goal before his competitor had gotten half-way.

The king then asked Thor what he was able to do. Thor answered that he would engage in a drinking-match, and was presented with a large horn filled with liquor, which he was requested to drink at a single draught, and which he expected to be able to do with ease, but when he looked into the horn the liquor appeared to be scarcely diminished. He tried the second time, and diminished it very little. A third draught only reduced the quantity of liquor a half inch.

Thereupon Thor was laughed at, and called for some new feat. The king answered: "We have a trifling game here, in which we exercise none but children. It is merely to lift my cat from the ground." Thor exerted himself with all his might, but was able only to raise one foot, and was again laughed at. Thereupon he became angry, and called for some one to wrestle with him. King Utgard then said: "My men would think it beneath them to wrestle with thee, but let some one call my old nurse Eld, and let Thor wrestle with her."

Thereupon a toothless old woman entered the hall, and wrestled with Thor, who began to lose his footing after a desperate struggle, and he went home extremely mortified. But it afterward appeared that all this was illusion. Three blows from Thor's mallet, which had been directed against the giant's head, had fallen on a mountain, which the giant had dexterously put between, and made three ravines in it, which still remain.

The triumphant eater was Fire, disguised as a man. The successful runner was Thought. The horn out of which Thor attempted to drink was connected with the ocean, which was diminished but a very few inches by his tremendous draughts. The cat was the great Midgard Serpent, which goes around the world, and Thor had actually pulled the earth slightly out of its place. The old woman was Old Age. It is apparent from this old Scandinavian legend that the gods are idealizations of human will arrayed in antagonism to the powers of nature. The battle of the gods and the giants represents the struggles of the soul against the inexorable laws of nature, of freedom against fate, of the spirit with the flesh, of mind with matter, of human hope with change, disappointment and loss; "the emergency of the case with the despotism of the rule."

According to this mythology of the Edda, a time will come when the world will be destroyed by fire and afterward renewed. Several terrible disasters will precede this destruction—dreadful winters, wars and desolations on earth, cruelty and deceit; while the sun and the moon will be devoured, the stars will be hurled from the sky, and the earth will be violently shaken. The Wolf Fenrir, the awful Midgard Serpent, Loki and Hela will come to battle with the gods. The great Ash-tree will shake with fear. The Wolf, Fenrir, will break loose and open his immense mouth. The lower jaw will extend to the earth, and the upper one to heaven. The Midgard Serpent, beside the Wolf, will vomit forth floods of poison. Heaven will be rent in twain, and Surtur and the sons of Muspell will ride through the breach. These are the children of Light and Fire, whose abode is in the South, and who appear to belong neither to the race of gods nor to that of giants, but to a third party, who only interfere at the end of the struggle.

While the battle between the gods and the giants is in progress, the two parties will keep their respective bands apart on the battle-field. In the meantime Heimdall, the door-keeper of the gods, will sound his mighty trumpet, which will be heard through the entire universe, to summon the gods to battle. The gods, or Æsir, and all the heroes of Valhalla will arm themselves and go to the scene of conflict. Thor will fight with the Midgard Serpent, whose life he will destroy, but will himself die by being suffocated with the floods of venom. Odin will combat the Wolf, which will swallow him; but at that instant Vidar will set his foot on the Wolf's lower jaw, and take hold of the upper jaw, which he will tear apart. This feat he will accomplish because he will have on his foot the famous shoe, the materials of which have been collecting for ages, it being made of the shreds of shoe-leather which are cut off in making shoes, and which the religious Scandinavians were careful to throw away for this very reason. Loki and Heimdall will fight and kill each other. Surtur will then dart fire over the entire earth, and the whole universe will be consumed in the general conflagration.

The restitution of all things will follow, and a new heaven and a new earth will rise out of the sea. Two gods, Vidar and Vali, and two human beings, a man and a woman, will survive the general conflagration, and will inhabit heaven and earth with their posterity. Thor's sons will come with their father's mallet and put an end to the war. Baldur and the blind god Hodur will come up from Hell; and the Sun's daughter, more beautiful than its mother, will take its place in the sky.

Physical circumstances caused changes in the mythologies, whose origin was similar.

VICTORY—VALHALLA.

Thus Loki, the god of fire, belongs to the Æsir, because fire is antagonistic to frost, but represents the treacherous and evil subterranean fires, which in Iceland destroyed with lava, sand and boiling water more than was injured by cold.

The following passages extracted from the prose Edda give the reader the best possible account of the old Norse pantheon.

"OF ODIN.

"'I must now ask thee,' said Gangler, 'who are the gods that men are bound to believe in?'

"'There are twelve gods,' replied Har, 'to whom divine honors ought to be rendered.'

"'Nor are the goddesses,' added Jafnhar, 'less divine and mighty.'

"'The first and eldest of the Æsir,' continued Thridi, 'is Odin. He governs all things, and although the other deities are powerful, they all serve and obey him as children do their father. Frigga is his wife. She foresees the destinies of men, but never reveals what is to come. For thus it is said that Odin himself told Loki, "Senseless Loki, why wilt thou pry into futurity? Frigga alone knoweth the destinies of all, though she telleth them never."

"'Odin is named Alfadir (All-father), because he is the father of all the gods, and also Valfadir (Choosing Father), because he chooses for his sons all those who fall in combat. For their abode he has prepared Valhalla and Vingólf, where they are called Einherjar (Heroes or Champions). Odin is also called Hangagud, Haptagud, and Farmagud, and, besides these, was named in many ways when he went to King Geirraudr.' * * *

"OF THOR.

"'I now ask thee,' said Gangler, 'what are the names of the other gods? What are their functions, and what have they brought to pass?'

"'The mightiest of them,' replied Har, 'is Thor. He is called Asa-Thor and Auku-Thor, and is the strongest of gods and men. His realm is named Thrúdváng, and his mansion Bilskirnir, in which are five hundred and forty halls. It is the largest house ever built. Thus it is called in the Grímnismál:

"Five hundred halls
And forty more,
Methinketh, hath
Bowed Bilskirnir.
Of houses roofed
There's none I know
My son's surpassing."

"'Thor has a car drawn by two goats called Tanngnióst and Tanngrisnir. From his driving about in this car he is called Auku-Thor (Charioteer-Thor). He likewise possesses three very precious things. The first is a mallet called Mjölnir, which both the Frost and Mountain Giants know to their cost when they see it hurled against them in the air; and no wonder, for it has split many a skull of their fathers and kindred. The second rare thing he possesses is called the belt of strength or prowess (Megingjardir). When he girds it about him his divine might is doubly augmented; the third, also very precious, being his iron gauntlets, which he is obliged to put on whenever he would lay hold of the handle of his mallet. There is no one so wise as to be able to relate all Thor's marvelous exploits, yet I could tell thee so many myself that hours would be whiled away ere all that I know had been recounted.'

"OF BALDUR.

"'I would rather,' said Gangler, 'hear something about the other Æsir.'

"'The second son of Odin,' replied Har, 'is Baldur, and it may be truly said of him that he is the best, and that all mankind are loud in his praise. So fair and dazzling is he in form and features, that rays of light seem to issue from him; and thou mayst have some idea of the beauty of his hair when I tell thee that the whitest of all plants is called Baldur's brow. Baldur is the mildest, the wisest, and the most eloquent of all the Æsir, yet such is his nature that the judgment he has pronounced can never be altered. He dwells in the heavenly mansion called Breidablik, in which nothing unclean can enter. As it is said,

"'Tis Breidablik called,
Where Baldur the Fair
Hath built him a bower,
In that land where I know
The least lothliness lieth."'

"OF NJÖRD.

"'The third god,' continued Har, 'is Njörd, who dwells in the heavenly region called Noátún. He rules over the winds, and checks the fury of the sea and of fire, and is therefore invoked by sea-farers and fishermen. He is so wealthy that he can give possessions and treasures to those who call on him for them. Yet Njörd is not of the lineage of the Æsir, for he was born and bred in Vanaheim. But the Vanir gave him as hostage to the Æsir, receiving from them in his stead Hœnir. By this means was peace reëstablished between the Æsir and Vanir. Njörd took to wife Skadi, the daughter of the giant Thjassi. She preferred dwelling in the abode formerly belonging to her father, which is situated among rocky mountains, in the region called Thrymheim, but Njörd loved to reside near the sea. They at last agreed that they should pass together nine nights in Thrymheim, and then three in Noátún. One day, when Njörd came back from the mountains to Noátún, he thus sang :

"Of mountains I'm weary,
Not long was I there,
Not more than nine nights;
But the howl of the wolf
Methought sounded ill
To the song of the swan-bird."

" 'To which Skadi sang in reply:

"Ne'er can I sleep
In my couch on the strand,
For the screams of the sea-fowl.
The mew as he comes
Every morn from the main
Is sure to awake me."

" 'Skadi then returned to the rocky mountains, and abode in Thrymheim. There, fastening on her snow-skates and taking her bow, she passes her time in the chase of savage beasts, and is called the Ondur goddess, or Ondurdís. * * * *'

"OF THE GOD FREY, AND THE GODDESS FREYJA.

" 'Njörd had afterwards, at his residence at Noátún, two children, a son named Frey, and a daughter called Freyja, both of them beauteous and mighty. Frey is one of the most celebrated of the gods. He presides over rain and sunshine, and all the fruits of the earth, and should be invoked in order to obtain good harvests, and also for peace. He, moreover, dispenses wealth among men. Freyja is the most propitious of the goddesses; her abode in heaven is called Fólkváng. To whatever field of battle she rides, she asserts her right to one half of the slain, the other half belonging to Odin. * * * *'

"OF TYR.

" 'There is Tyr, who is the most daring and intrepid of all the gods. 'T is he who dispenses valor in war, hence warriors do well to invoke him. It has become proverbial to say of a man who surpasses all others in valor that he is *Tyr-strong*, or valiant as Tyr. A man noted for his wisdom is also said to be "wise as Tyr." Let

THE GOD TYR.

me give thee a proof of his intrepidity. When the Æsir were trying to persuade the wolf, Fenrir, to let himself be bound up with the chain, Gleipnir, he, fearing that they would never afterwards unloose him, only consented on the condition that while they were chaining him he should keep Tyr's right hand between his jaws. Tyr did not hesitate to put his hand in the monster's mouth, but when Fenrir perceived that the

Æsir had no intention to unchain him, he bit the hand off at that point, which has ever since been called the wolf's joint (úlflidr). From that time Tyr has had but one hand. He is not regarded as a peacemaker among men.'

"OF THE OTHER GODS.

" 'There is another god,' continued Har, 'named Bragi, who is celebrated for his wisdom, and more especially for his eloquence and correct forms of speech. He is not only eminently skilled in poetry, but the art itself is called from his name *Bragr*, which epithet is also applied to denote a distinguished poet or poetess. His wife is named Iduna. She keeps in a box the apples which the gods, when they feel old age approaching, have only to taste of to become young again. It is in this manner that they will be kept in renovated youth until Ragnarök. * * * *

" 'One of the gods is Heimdall, called also the White God. He is the son of nine virgins, who were sisters, and is a very sacred and powerful deity. He also bears the appellation of the Gold-toothed, on account of his teeth being of pure gold, and also that of Hallinskithi. His horse is called Gulltopp, and he dwells in Himinbjörg at the end of Bifröst. He is the warder of the gods, and is therefore placed on the borders of heaven, to prevent the giants from forcing their way over the bridge. He requires less sleep than a bird, and sees by night, as well as by day, a hundred miles around him. So acute is his ear that no sound escapes him, for he can even hear the grass growing on the earth, and the wool on a sheep's back. He has a horn called the Gjallar-horn, which is heard throughout the universe. * * * *

" 'Among the Æsir,' continued Har, 'we also reckon Hödur, who is blind, but extremely strong. Both gods and men would be very glad if they never had occasion to pronounce his name, for they will long have cause to remember the deed perpetrated by his hand.

" 'Another god is Vidar, surnamed the Silent, who wears very thick shoes. He is almost as strong as Thor himself, and the gods place great reliance on him in all critical conjunctures.

" 'Vali, another god, is the son of Odin and Rinda; he is bold in war, and an excellent archer.

" 'Another is called Ullur, who is the son of Sif, and step-son of Thor. He is so well skilled in the use of the bow, and can go so fast on his snow-skates, that in these arts no one can contend with him. He is also very handsome in his person, and possesses every quality of a warrior, wherefore it is befitting to invoke him in single combats.

" 'The name of another god is Forseti, who is the son of Baldur and Nanna, the daughter of Nef. He possesses the heavenly mansion called Glitnir, and all disputants at law who bring their cases before him go away perfectly reconciled * * * *'

"OF LOKI AND HIS PROGENY.

" 'There is another deity,' continued Har, 'reckoned in the number of the Æsir, whom some call the calumniator of the gods, the contriver of all fraud and mischief, and the disgrace of gods and men. His name is Loki or Loptur. He is the son of the giant Farbauti. * * * * Loki is handsome and well made, but of a very fickle mood, and most evil disposition. He surpasses all beings in those arts called Cunning and Perfidy. Many a time has he exposed the gods to very great perils, and often extricated them again by his artifices. * * . * *

" 'Loki,' continued Har, 'has likewise had three children by Angurbodi, a giantess of Jötunheim. The first is the wolf Fenrir; the second Jörmungand, the Midgard Serpent; the third Hela (Death). The gods were not long ignorant that these monsters continued to be bred up in Jötunheim, and, having had recourse to divination, became aware of all the evils they would have to suffer from them; their being sprung from such a mother was a bad presage, and from such a sire, one still worse. All-father therefore deemed it advisable to send one of the gods to bring them to him. When they came he threw the serpent into that deep ocean by which the earth is engirdled. But the monster has grown to such an enormous size that, holding his tail in his mouth, he encircles the whole earth. Hela he cast into Niflheim, and gave her power over nine worlds (regions), into which she distributes those who are sent to her, that is to say, all who die through sickness or old age. Here she possesses a habitation protected by exceedingly high walls and strongly barred gates. Her hall is called Elvidnir; Hunger is her table; Starvation, her knife; Delay, her man; Slowness, her maid; Precipice, her threshold; Care, her bed; and Burning Anguish forms the hangings of her apartments. The one half of her body is livid, the other half the color of human flesh. She may therefore easily be recognized; the more so, as she has a dreadfully stern and grim countenance.

"'The wolf Fenrir was bred up among the gods; but Tyr alone had the daring to go and feed him. Nevertheless, when the gods perceived that he every day increased prodigiously in size, and that the oracles warned them that he would one day become fatal to them, they determined to make a very strong iron fetter for him, which they called Læding. Taking this fetter to the wolf, they bade him try his strength on it. Fenrir, perceiving that the enterprise would not be very difficult for him, let them do what they pleased, and then, by great muscular exertion, burst the chain, and set himself at liberty. The gods, having seen this, made another fetter, half as strong again as the former, which they called Drómi, and prevailed on the wolf to put it on, assuring him that, by breaking this, he would give an undeniable proof of his vigor.

"'The wolf saw well enough that it would not be so easy to break this fetter, but finding at the same time that his strength had increased since he broke Læding, and thinking that he could never become famous without running some risk, voluntarily submitted to be chained. When the gods told him that they had finished their task, Fenrir shook himself violently, stretched his limbs, rolled on the ground, and at last burst his chains, which flew in pieces all around him. He thus freed himself from Drómi, which gave rise to the proverb "*at leysa or lædingi eda at drepa or dróma*" (to get loose out of Læding, or to dash out of Drómi), when anything is to be accomplished by strong efforts.

"'After this, the gods despaired of ever being able to bind the wolf; wherefore Allfather sent Skirnir, the messenger of Frey, into the country of the Dark Elves (Svartálfaheim) to engage certain dwarfs to make the fetter called Gleipnir. It was fashioned out of six things; to wit, the noise made by the footfall of a cat; the beards of women; the roots of stones; the sinews of bears; the breath of fish; and the spittle of birds. Though thou mayest not have heard of these things before, thou mayest easily convince thyself that we have not been telling thee lies. Thou must have seen that women have no beards, that cats make no noise when they run, and that there are no roots under stones. Now I know what has been told thee to be equally true, although there may be some things thou art not able to furnish a proof of.'

"'I believe what thou hast told me to be true,' replied Gangler, 'for what thou hast adduced in corroboration of thy statement is conceivable. But how was the fetter smithied?'

"'This I can tell thee,' replied Har, 'that the fetter was as smooth and soft as a silken string, and yet, as thou wilt presently hear, of very great strength. When it was brought to the gods they were profuse in their thanks to the messenger for the trouble he had given himself; and taking the wolf with them to the island called Lyngvi, in the Lake Amsvartnir, they showed him the cord, and expressed their wish that he would try to break it, assuring him at the same time that it was somewhat stronger than its thinness would warrant a person in supposing it to be. They took it themselves, one after another, in their hands, and after attempting in vain to break it, said, "Thou alone, Fenrir, art able to accomplish such a feat."

"'"Methinks," replied the wolf, "that I shall acquire no fame in breaking such a slender cord; but if any artifice has been employed in making it, slender though it seems, it shall never come on my feet."

"'The gods assured him that he would easily break a limber silken cord, since he had already burst asunder iron fetters of the most solid construction. "But if thou shouldst not succeed in breaking it," they added, "thou wilt show that thou art too weak to cause the gods any fear, and we will not hesitate to set thee at liberty without delay."

"'"I fear me much," replied the wolf, "that if ye once bind me so fast that I shall be unable to free myself by my own efforts, ye will be in no haste to unloose me. Loath am I, therefore, to have this cord wound round me; but in order that ye may not doubt my courage, I will consent, provided one of you put his hand into my mouth as a pledge that ye intend me no deceit."

"'The gods wistfully looked at each other, and found that they had only the choice of two evils, until Tyr stepped forward and intrepidly put his right hand between the monster's jaws. Hereupon the gods, having tied up the wolf, he forcibly stretched himself, as he had formerly done, and used all his might to disengage himself, but the more efforts he made, the tighter became the cord, until all the gods, except Tyr, who lost his hand, burst into laughter at the sight.

"'When the gods saw that the wolf was effectually bound, they took the chain called Gelgja, which was fixed to the fetter, and drew it through the middle of a large rock named Gjöll, which they sank very deep into the earth; afterwards, to make it still more secure, they fastened the end of the cord to a massive stone called Thviti, which they sank still deeper. The wolf made in vain the most violent efforts to break loose, and, opening his tremendous jaws, endeavored to bite them. The gods, seeing this, thrust a sword into his mouth, which pierced his under jaw up to the hilt, so that the point touched the palate. He then began to howl horribly, and since that time the foam flows continually from his mouth in such abundance that it forms the river called Von. There will he remain until Ragnarök."

There are also goddesses in the Valhalla, of whom the Edda mentions Frigga, Saga, and many others.

The Scandinavians had very simple religious ceremonies. Their worship was at first held in the open air, like that of the followers of Zoroaster; but in later times they built temples, some of which were very splendid. The Scandinavians had three great festivals during the year. The first was held at the winter solstice, on the longest night of the year, called the Mother Night, believed to be the one which produced the rest. This great feast was called *Yul*, from which is derived the English *Yule*, the old name for Christmas, which festival took its place when the Scandinavians became Christians. The festival of Yul was in honor of the sun, and was held with sacrifices, feasting and great mirth. The second Scandinavian festival took place in the spring, in honor of the earth, to supplicate fruitful crops. The third festival was likewise held in the spring, and was in honor of Odin. The sacrifices were of fruits, afterwards of animals, and in later times occasionally of human beings.

The Scandinavians believed in divine interposition and in a fixed destiny, but especially in themselves and in their own force and courage. Some of them laughed at the gods; some challenged them to fight with them, believing only in their own might and main. One warrior calls for Odin, as a foeman worthy of his steel, and it was regarded as lawful to fight the gods. The quicken-tree, or mountain-ash, was believed to have great virtues, because it afforded aid to Thor on one occasion.

The Northern nations had their soothsayers, as well as their priests. They likewise believed that the dead could be made to speak by the power of Runes. These Runes were called *Galder*; and another kind of magic, principally practised by women, was called *Seid*. These wise women were believed to be able to raise and allay storms.

and to harden the body so that it could not be cut by the sword. Some charms could give preternatural strength; others the power to cross the sea without a ship, to create and destroy love, to assume different forms, to become invisible, to give the evil eye. Garments could be charmed to protect or destroy the person wearing them. A horse's head, set on a stake, with certain imprecations, was the cause of terrible mischief to an enemy.

Very few remains of temples have been found in Scandinavia; but the most important remains of the religion of Odin and Thor are found in the usages and languages of the descendants of the worshipers of those famous gods. These descendants of the Northmen—in Norway, Sweden and Denmark, in England and Normandy—as well as their Teutonic kinsmen in Germany and Holland, all retain recollections of the principal deities of the Scandinavian mythology, in the names of Tuesday, Wednesday, Thursday, Friday and Saturday. The sleep of the English-speaking people is still tormented by Mara, the night-mare; and Old Nick is said to be descended from Nokke, the Evil One.

The ancient Scandinavians held solemn sacrifices at the great temple of Upsala, in Sweden, every ninth year. The king and all the leading citizens were required to be present and bring offerings. Multitudes assembled on these occasions, and no one was excluded, except for some base or cowardly action. Nine human beings, usually slaves or captives, were sacrificed; but even a king was made a victim in times of great calamity. Earl Hakon, of Norway, offered his son in sacrifice to obtain a victory over some pirates. The bodies were buried in groves, which were thereafter considered sacred. Odin's Grove, near the temple of Upsala, was regarded as sacred in every twig and leaf.

Though such Scandinavian tribes as the Goths had been converted to Christianity through the exertions of their celebrated bishop, Ulfilas, who was born A. D. 318 and consecrated a bishop A. D. 348, the great bulk of the Scandinavian nation in its own home in the North still held fast to the worship of Odin and Thor and the other deities of the Scandinavian pantheon, until about the year A. D. 1000, when the Northmen began to accept Christianity.

The process of conversion was in progress for several centuries, during which there were several relapses into paganism; so that no exact time can be fixed for the conversion of any Scandinavian nation, much less for that of the various branches of the Scandinavian stock separately inhabiting Denmark, Norway and Sweden, and colonized in Iceland and Greenland, in Normandy and England.

A Christian mission was established in Denmark in A. D. 822, and the Danish king was baptized; but the overthrow of this Christian monarch restricted the missionary labors. In A. D. 829 an effort at conversion was made in Sweden, by St. Ansgar, "the Apostle of the North," who remained in that country a year and a-half; but the mission there was soon overthrown. St. Ansgar then established schools at Hamburg, in Northern Germany, where he educated Danish and Swedish boys to preach the religion of Christ to their countrymen in their own language. But the Normans laid waste this city in A. D. 847, as already noticed, and destroyed the Christian schools and churches.

About the year A. D. 850 a new effort at conversion was made in Sweden, and the Swedish king submitted the subject to his council, or Diet, composed of two assemblies; and this Diet decided to permit Christianity to be preached and practiced in Sweden, seemingly on the ground that this new god, Christ, might aid the Swedes in their dangers at sea when Odin, Thor and the other Scandinavian gods were unable to afford them the required assistance. Thus, according to the independent character of these Northmen, Christianity was neither allowed to be imposed upon the Swedes by their own king against their will, nor to be excluded from the use of those who chose to adopt it. The new religion took its chances with the old Scandinavian system, and many of the Danes and Normans believed in worshiping both Odin and Jesus at the same time.

Harald Bluetooth, King of Denmark, in the last half of the tenth century, favored the diffusion of Christianity, and was himself baptized with his wife and son; at first believing that the Christian God was more powerful than the old heathen Scandinavian gods; but finally reaching the conclusion that Odin, Thor and the Northern deities were evil spirits. Some of the Danes believed that Christ was a god to be worshiped, but that he was less powerful than Odin or Thor. King Harald Bluetooth's son and successor, Sweyn, the conqueror of England, apostatized to paganism in A. D. 990 and expelled the Christian priests from Denmark. But Sweyn's son and successor, Canute the Great, who began to reign in A. D. 1014, was converted to Christianity in England, and became a zealous friend of that religion. These fierce warriors, however, became rather poor Christians. Adam of Bremen says: "They so abominate tears and lamentations, and all other signs of penitence which we think salubrious, that they will neither weep for their own sins nor at the death of their best friends."

Thus, in these Northern kingdoms, the Christian religion grew through several centuries, like the leaven gradually infusing itself into the national life. Adam of Bremen, who was an eye-witness, tells us that the Swedes were very susceptible to religious impressions. Says he: "They receive the preachers of the truth with great kindness, if they are modest, wise and able; and our bishops are even allowed to preach in their great public assemblies."

In the middle of the tenth century an effort was made in Norway by King Hakon the Good to establish Christianity, which he had learned in England. Hakon proposed to the All-Thing, the great national assembly of Norway, that the entire nation should renounce the religion of Odin and Thor, worship God and Christ, observe Sundays as festivals and Fridays as fasts. He was confronted with great opposition, which threatened to break out in a general insurrection; so that the good king had to yield, and even himself to drink a toast to Odin and to indulge in the heathen practice of eating horse-flesh.

Succeeding Kings of Norway again introduced Christianity; but their subjects adhered to the worship of Odin and Thor, though they were willing to accept Christian baptism, and only by degrees did they renounce their old worship and their habits of piracy. King Olaf the Saint, who ascended the throne of Norway in A. D. 1015, effected the final triumph of Christianity in Norway, but in so cruel a manner that his subjects turned aginst him; so that he was easily deprived of his kingdom by Canute the Great of Denmark.

In the year A. D. 1000 the All-thing, or popular assembly of Iceland, adopted Christianity, but with the condition that the Icelanders might likewise retain their old worship and be permitted to eat horse-flesh and to expose their infants. When the All-thing broke up, the assembled multitudes went to the hot baths to be baptized, preferring hot water to cold for this rite.

During this period the Scandinavians appear to have lost their faith in their old religion and to have been in a transition state. One Norman warrior declared that he relied more on his own arms and strength than upon Thor. Another asserted: "I would have thee know that I believe neither in idols nor spirits, but only in my own force and courage." Another warrior told King Olaf the Saint of Norway: "I am neither Christian nor Pagan. My companions and I have no other religion than confidence in our own strength and good success."

There is no doubt that for a long time Christianity was very lightly esteemed by these Northern nations. They were willing to be baptized and to accept some of the outward ceremonies and festivals of the Roman Catholic Church, which were considerately made to resemble those of their own religion. Christianity, however, met many of the wants of this noble branch of the human race, and their race instincts were well adapted to promote an equal development of all sides of Christian life.

The Latin races of Southern Europe received Christianity as a religion of order; the Northern races accepted it as a religion of freedom. These two phases of Christian development in Europe have been clearly defined since the great Reformation in the sixteenth century. In the South of Europe the Roman Catholic Church, by its ingenious organization and its complex arrangement, had introduced culture and discipline into life. In the North of Europe the Protestant Reformation, by appealing to the individual soul, awakened conscience and stimulated to individual and national progress. The Latin nations of Southern Europe accepted Christianity chiefly as a religion of feeling and sentiment; while the Teutonic nations in Northern and Central Europe accepted the same system as a religion of truth and principle.

Thus when the Saxon monk, Luther, struck against the ecclesiastical despotism of the Papacy and the Romish hierarchy, he was supported by all the Teutonic nations of Northern and Central Europe—by Northern Germany, by England and Holland, by the three Scandinavian kingdoms of Denmark, Sweden and Norway, and by the republic of Iceland. Without the Teutonic nations in Germany, England and Scandinavia, there could have been no Protestantism in Europe. England produced the "Morning Star of the Reformation" in the immortal Wickliffe. Germany, the cradle of the Reformation, gave the world the founder of Protestantism in the intrepid Luther. Scandinavia furnished the valiant "Lion of the North," the great Swedish monarch Gustavus Adolphus, who at the head of his Protestant hosts gave the final triumph to the Reformation by dying the death of a hero in the moment of victory, fighting for religious liberty, for freedom of spirit.

The Scandinavian races at this very day, in Denmark, Sweden and Norway, and their Teutonic kinsmen, the Germanic races in North Germany and Holland, in England and her dependencies, and in the United States of America, are almost the only Protestant nations of the world; thus showing that the old instincts still run in the blood and cause these races to seek light, freedom and progress, and not to give way to the luxury of emotion or to the satisfaction of repose, in having every opinion settled for them and every action formally prescribed.

SECTION XVI.—DUCHY OF NORMANDY.

HE nations that successively invaded Southern Europe from the ninth to the eleventh century were originally descended from the same stock ; but when they had obtained a settlement in any country by conquest they gradually adopted the arts of the vanquished, thus relinquishing their predatory habits for the more useful pursuits of agriculture. The next horde of invaders would not recognize these degenerate warriors as their countrymen, and inflicted the same calamities upon them that they caused the original inhabitants to suffer. The Saxons in Britain, the Goths and Franks in Gaul, found in the Danes and Normans the avengers of the cruelties which they had previously perpetrated upon the Britons and Gauls. The severe persecution of the Saxons by Charlemagne caused many of their bravest warriors to flee to Scandinavia, where their accounts of the cruelties to which the worshipers of Odin and Thor were subjected aroused their Northern brethren to preparations for vengeance, and in Charlemagne's reign the coasts of France were first visited by Norman pirates.

Rollo's invasion during the reign of

Charles the Simple was the last of their freebooting raids into France; and we have seen that that weak French monarch entered into a treaty with Rollo, ceding to the Norman leader the province of Neustria, and giving him his daughter in marriage, on condition that Rollo would cease his devastations and acknowledge the suzerainty of the French sovereign. After obtaining possession of his new duchy, thenceforth called *Normandy*, Rollo, or Rolf, assumed the title of ROBERT I., Duke of Normandy, making Rouen his capital, A. D. 912.

The remains of the Celtic Gauls, who had endured cruel oppression from the Franks, readily submitted to the equitable administration of Duke Robert I.; the number of whose subjects was constantly increased by parties of the aboriginal natives, who sought, under a new master, relief from the oppression of their former conquerors.

But the Normans did not succeed so well in gaining the affections of the people of Brittany, or Bretagne, whom Charles the Simple, unable to conquer himself, had transferred to the Norman duke. This province, embracing the North-western part of Gaul, was called *Armorica* by the Romans, and was inhabited by the bravest of the Celtic Gauls, who had successfully resisted most of the invaders who had seized on the rest of Gaul.

When the Anglo-Saxons had established themselves in Britain, many of the ancient Britons fled to Armorica, with the consent of the ancient inhabitants of that province, who acknowledged them as brethren of the same origin. The new comers settled along the entire northern coast, as far as the territory of the Veneti, now called *Vannes*; and this province thereafter was named *Brittany*, or *Bretagne*. The increase of the population of this extreme western province of France, and the great number of people of the Celtic race and language thus assembled within a small area of territory, preserved them from the irruption of the Roman tongue which had by degrees become prevalent in all other portions of Gaul, under a form more or less corrupt.

Remembering the evils that had driven them into exile, the Bretons entertained a bitter antipathy to all foreign domination; and, under all vicissitudes of fortune, they were eager to embrace every opportunity to assert their independence. Under the leadership of their counts, or *Tierns*, as they were called by the Normans, Alan and Berenger, the Bretons made a determined resistance to Duke Robert I. of Normandy, who had great difficulty in subduing them. The conquering duke seems to have used his victory with moderation, and to have been satisfied with receiving homage from the leaders of the revolted Bretons as their feudal lord.

The conduct of Duke Robert I. and his successors forms an honorable contrast to that of their contemporaries. Robert I. gave his subjects a charter, provided for the due administration of justice and encouraged emigration into his dominions. The Norman historians describe the tranquillity and security of Normandy during his reign by assuring us that ornaments of gold and silver were exposed unguarded on the public highways without danger of being carried away by thieves or robbers. In A. D. 927 Robert I. resigned his sovereignty to his son WILLIAM, surnamed LONGUE-EPÉE, "Long-sword," and passed the remaining three years of his life in retirement.

During the first years of the reign of William Long-sword an insurrection of the Bretons and a more formidable rebellion of the Normans broke out, but he suppressed both these risings by his valor and prudence; and, following in his father's footsteps, he applied himself with diligence to the improvement of his dominions. The Danes maintained a friendly intercourse with their kinsmen in Normandy; and when Harald Bluetooth, King of Denmark, was dethroned by his rebellious son Sweyn, he sought refuge at the court of Duke William Long-sword, whose friendship and valor were instrumental in effecting his restoration to the Danish throne.

William Long-sword seems to have been fated to afford aid to princes in misfortune.

When Hugh the Great, Count of Paris, sought to deprive Louis d' Outremer of the throne of France, William exerted his utmost endeavors in behalf of the legitimate sovereign of France, and was mainly instrumental in securing him on the throne. With like generosity, William espoused the cause of Herbin, Count of Montreuil, who had been expelled from his dominions by his treacherous neighbor, Arnold, Count of Flanders. The Duke of Normandy defeated the usurper in a decisive battle, and refused every reward offered him by the restored nobleman. But this expedition caused William Long-sword's death. Arnold, exasperated at his defeat, determined upon the employment of treachery, as open force had failed. He solicited an interview with William in an island of the Somme, craftily separated the duke from his attendants, and then caused him to be assassinated, A. D. 943.

The murdered William Long-sword was succeeded as Duke of Normandy by his son RICHARD, a mere boy, surnamed SANS PEUR, "the Fearless;" but the administration of public affairs was undertaken by four Norman nobles, the chief of whom was Bernard, Count of Harcourt, usually called Bernard the Dane. Louis d' Outremer, King of France, who owed his crown to William Long-sword, with base ingratitude, plotted with Hugh the Great, Count of Paris, to deprive William's youthful son and successor of his dominions. For this purpose Louis led a large army into Normandy, under the pretext of avenging the murder of William Long-sword; but after being received at Rouen as a friend, he seized on the person of the youthful Duke Richard the Fearless, and sent him off to Paris under the pretense of having him properly educated.

Instigated by the Count of Flanders, Louis d' Outremer designed the assassination of Richard, but the young duke was rescued from the danger by the fidelity of his tutor Osmond. This faithful attendant went to the castle of Laon, where Richard was confined, and, under the pretense of going to feed his horse, conveyed him out of the castle enveloped in a truss of hay. They proceeded to the residence of the Count de Senlis, Richard's maternal uncle, safely reaching their place of refuge.

In the meantime the gratitude of a prince who had been benefited by William Long-sword was about to be displayed by the restoration of William's son to his dominions. Bernard, Count of Harcourt, had successfully exerted himself to arouse discord between the King of France and the Count of Paris, and had also sent a secret message to Harald Bluetooth, King of Denmark, informing him of the condition of affairs, and entreating him to assist in delivering Normandy from the dominion of the King of France.

King Harald Bluetooth came at the first summons; and the Normans, under the leadership of Bernard of Harcourt, hastened to join him. The King of France was unable to withstand the combined forces in the field, and solicited an interview to arrange terms of peace. While Kings Harald Bluetooth and Louis d' Outremer were discussing the conditions, a Norman who recognized Herbin, Count of Montreuil, in the French king's army, bitterly reproached him for his ingratitude; and when Herbin made a haughty reply, a Dane who was present struck him dead. This was the signal for a general engagement, which began before the Kings of France and Denmark were aware of the occurrence. The battle ended in the total defeat of the French, and King Louis d' Outremer was taken prisoner. The captive monarch was treated with great respect, but was obliged to restore Normandy to young Richard the Fearless, and to pay a heavy ransom for his freedom.

Richard the Fearless inherited all the noble qualities of the Norman race, and preserved the security and tranquillity of his dominions, though surrounded by formidable foes. His marriage with the daughter of Hugh the Great, Count of Paris, alarmed King Louis d' Outremer, who accordingly entered into an alliance with King Otho II. of Germany, King Conrad of Burgundy and Count Arnold of Flanders, to overwhelm both the Duke of Normandy and the Count of Paris. But the allies were everywhere unsuccessful. After failing to make any impression on Paris they marched into Normandy, but Richard cut off some of their best troops in an ambuscade, and repulsed them from the walls of Rouen with heavy loss.

On the death of Hugh the Great, Count of Paris, Duke Richard the Fearless was appointed guardian to his minor children, and by his fidelity in the execution of that office he again aroused the hostility of the King of France. The Normans were everywhere successful, after a long struggle, and Richard finally triumphed over the treachery and the forces of his foes, compelling them to beg for peace. In A. D. 987 Hugh Capet, the son of Count Hugh the Great, with the aid of his former guardian, made himself King of France; so that the Norman duke had a friend on the French throne. Duke Richard the Fearless spent the rest of his reign in profound peace; and at his death, in A. D. 996, the duchy of Normandy was one of the most flourishing states in Europe.

The next Duke of Normandy was RICHARD THE GOOD, the son of Richard the Fearless. The early portion of his reign was disturbed by a peasant insurrection and by a rebellion of his illegitimate brother, the Count de Hiemes. After subduing the rebels, Richard the Good confined his brother in prison for five years. The brother finally made his escape, when he suddenly appeared in a squalid dress before Richard while hunting, and earnestly besought forgiveness. The duke granted him his pardon and restored all his former possessions.

At this period Ethelred the Unready was King of England, and maintained himself against the Danes with great difficulty. In order to obtain a powerful ally, he married Emma, sister to Duke Richard the Good of Normandy; but all the assistance that he could procure failed to repel the invasion of Sweyn, King of Denmark. King Ethelred the Unready was obliged to flee from England and to live for some time in exile at the court of his Norman brother-in-law.

Robert the Pious, King of France, having united with some of the princes bordering on Normandy, Duke Richard the Good found himself unable to resist the allies without aid, and he accordingly solicited the aid of the Danes. The Danes sent a large army to Richard's aid, but the Norman duke soon discovered that his allies were more injurious to his cause than were his enemies. The King of France having agreed on terms of peace, the Danes were so enraged at losing the prospect of plunder that they turned their arms against Brittany and perpetrated the most dreadful outrages in that province; so that Duke Richard the Good was obliged to bribe them to retire by the payment of a large sum of money. The intercourse between Denmark and Normandy seems to have declined thenceforth.

The character of Duke Richard the Good for honor was so great that Geoffrey, Count of Brittany, with whom the duke had been frequently at war, nominated Richard for regent of that province while he was absent on a pilgrimage. Geoffrey was killed by accident, but Richard acted as a faithful guardian to his children, and when they attained their majority he gave them immediate possession of their father's territories.

On the death of King Ethelred the Unready, in A. D. 1016, Canute the Great, King of Denmark, Sweyn's son, became King of England; whereupon Ethelred's widow, Emma, and her two children were obliged to take refuge at her brother's court in Normandy. The Norman duke prepared to invade England in his sister's behalf, but his fleet was shattered by a storm, whereupon he concluded peace with Canute the Great, and gave him Emma as his wife.

The sons of Ethelred the Unready seemed thus to have lost all chance of inheriting the throne of England; but the sons and successors of Canute the Great died several years later without heirs, and Edward the Confessor, one of Ethelred's sons, returned from exile and became King of England.

Richard the Good died in A. D. 1027, after a long and peaceful reign, leaving behind him two sons, Richard and Robert. RICHARD III. died the next year after his father (A. D. 1028), after a reign of eighteen months, suspected of having been poisoned by his brother Robert, who became his successor on the ducal throne of Normandy, and who is called ROBERT THE DEVIL. The early portion of Robert's reign was disturbed by insurrections, but he subdued the malcontents so completely that he considered it safe for him to go on a pilgrimage to Palestine. His health was thoroughly undermined by the climate of Asia, so that he was obliged to complete his journey in a litter. Another Norman pilgrim, returning from Jerusalem, met Robert, who was carried by four Saracens, and asked the duke what account he should give of him on his return. Robert replied: "Tell my friends that you saw me borne into Paradise by four devils." The invalid duke died on his return at Nice, in Bithynia, without any legitimate heir.

Before starting for the Holy Land, Duke Robert the Devil had nominated his illegitimate son William as his successor on the ducal throne of Normandy, and this choice was ratified by the Norman states; but when Robert's death became known in Europe, several of the ducal family sought to have William set aside. The states of Normandy, however, resolutely adhered to their former decision; and WILLIAM II. triumphed over all his competitors, after a series of struggles.

These wars proved the source of William's future prosperity, as they supplied him with an army inured to battles and inspirited by repeated success, and with this army he was enabled to profit by the opportunities which fortune presented to him. Edward the Confessor, King of England, became disgusted with his Anglo-Saxon subjects and abandoned himself to his Norman favorites. He was especially disgusted with the family of the famous Earl Godwin, who would have succeeded to the English throne, as Edward had no direct heirs; but Edward bequeathed the English crown to Duke William II. of Normandy. Upon Edward's death, in A.

D. 1066, Earl Godwin's son, Harold, made himself King of England; but the Norman duke invaded England with the flower of his chivalry, defeated and killed Harold in the decisive battle of Hastings, and thus conquered England and became its king, with the title of William the Conqueror. Thenceforth the history of Normandy is so intimately connected with that of England and France that it is no longer necessary to treat of it separately.

In A. D. 1016—fifty years before the Norman conquest of England—some adventurers from Normandy laid the foundation of a new kingdom in Italy. Forty Norman gentlemen, while returning from a pilgrimage to Jerusalem, saved the city of Salerno, which was about to be seized by the Saracens, and would not accept any of the rewards which were offered to them by the gratitude of the inhabitants. The fame of this exploit spread through Italy, and induced several Italian princes to take into their pay troops of Norman adventurers, who were always willing to sell their services. They had been so useful to the Duke of Naples in his struggle with the Prince of Capua that he conferred upon them considerable territory located between the two cities, where they founded the city of Aversa in A. D. 1029.

This establishment attracted other Norman adventurers to Southern Italy. Three sons of Tancred of Hauteville, a gentleman from Normandy—one of whom was William Fier-a-bras, or Bras-de-fer, "Iron-arm"—laid the foundation of a new principality for their family, A. D. 1046. They wrested Apulia from the Catapan, a magistrate acting under the authority of the Eastern Emperor, after which they shared the conquest with the other officers. William Iron-arm was chosen Count of Apulia by his soldiers; and was succeeded by his brothers, Drogon and Humphrey, who, being subsequently joined by their younger brother, Robert Guiscard, soon became formidable to the Italians.

Pope Leo IX., fearing that these Norman adventurers would not respect the property of the Church any more than they did that of the laity, formed an alliance against them, having previously excommunicated them. These Normans, scarcely numbering three thousand, sent the Pope a most respectful message, promising to do homage to him for their fiefs; but Leo IX. refused their offer, whereupon they cut his army to pieces and took him prisoner. They did not, however, do the Pope any injury, but prostrated themselves before him, and after he had given them absolution they gave him his liberty.

What these Normans had offered to Pope Leo IX. was accepted by the next Pope, Nicholas II. In A. D. 1060 Robert Guiscard took the oath of fealty to this Pope, after receiving from him the investiture of all the conquests which he had acquired in Apulia and Calabria, and all that he might afterwards gain in those provinces or in Sicily. These Norman adventurers attacked the forces of the Eastern Empire in Southern Italy and the Saracens in Sicily with equal vigor and success. Victory followed victory in such rapid succession that they at length obtained actual possession of the territories to which the Pope had given them empty titles. Thus powerful vassals were attached to the Head of the Church, valuable feudal rights were acquired, and new means of aggrandizement were obtained.

Sicily was conquered by Count Roger, Robert Guiscard's brother, who, with a small Norman force, routed vast numbers of Saracens, thus completing the subjugation of the island after thirty years of war. Robert Guiscard, who was the greatest soldier of his time, by extending his conquest throughout Southern Italy, put an end to the dominion of the Eastern, or Byzantine, Emperors in Italy. He afterwards led a large army, officered by Norman knights, into the other territories of the Eastern Empire; crossing the Adriatic and capturing Durazzo, after a seven months' siege, and after a desperate battle, in which his Normans fought with the Norman soldiers in the army of the Eastern Emperor; after which he marched eastward and threatened Constantinople, but was recalled by Pope Gregory VII. (Hildebrand) to defend the Head of the Church against his inveterate enemy, Henry IV., King of Germany and Emperor of the West.

Roger II., the son of Roger I., Robert Guiscard's brother, ruled over the Norman territories in Italy and Sicily, and founded the Kingdom of Naples and Sicily; but the Norman dynasty in Southern Italy became extinct in A. D. 1194, with the death of William III.

DUKES OF NORMANDY.

A. D. 912	ROLLO, ROLF, or ROBERT I.	A. D. 1106	HENRY I. } Kings of England.
927	WILLIAM LONG-SWORD.	1135	STEPHEN.
943	RICHARD THE FEARLESS.	1144	MATILDA and GEOFFREY PLANTAGENET.
996	RICHARD THE GOOD.		
1027	RICHARD III.	1151	HENRY II.
1028	ROBERT THE DEVIL.	1189	RICHARD THE LION-HEARTED. } Kings of England.
1035	WILLIAM II. (the conqueror of England).		
		1199	ARTHUR, and JOHN of England.
1087	ROBERT II.	1204	Normandy annexed to the crown of France.

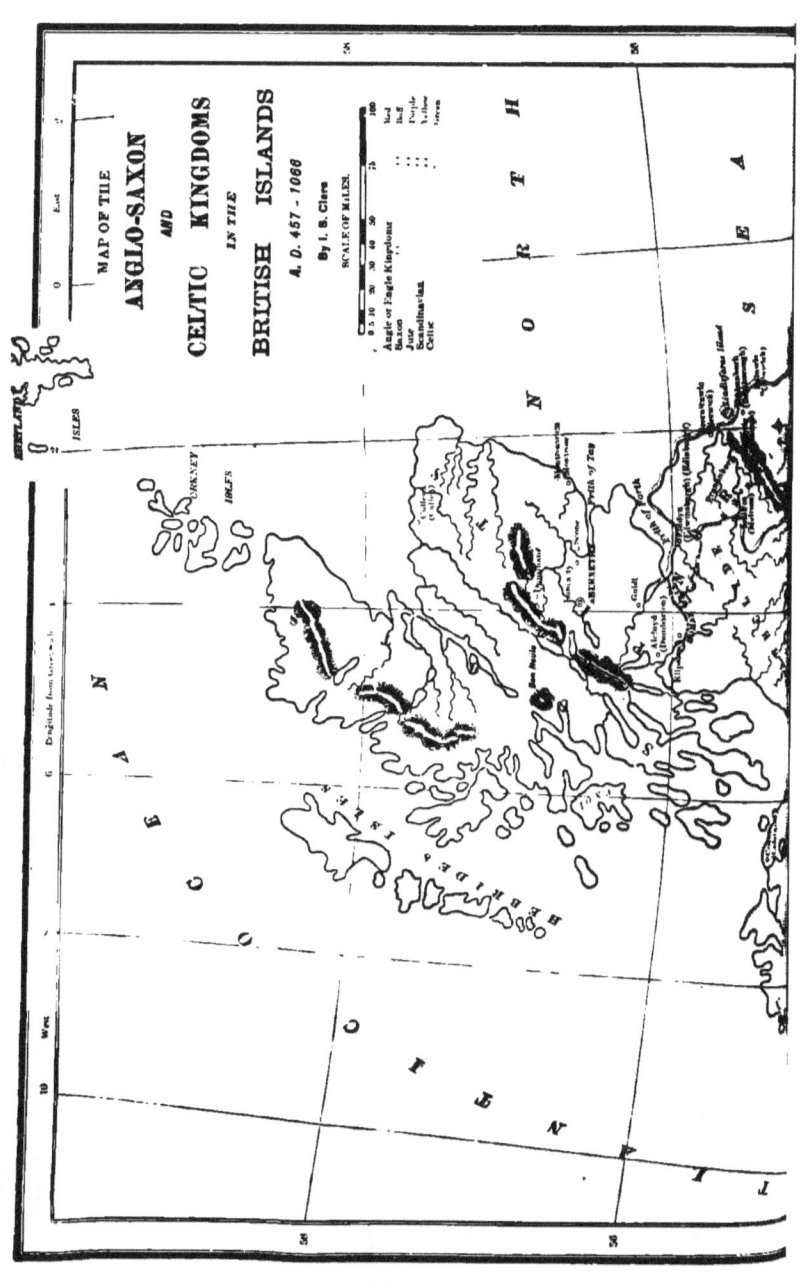

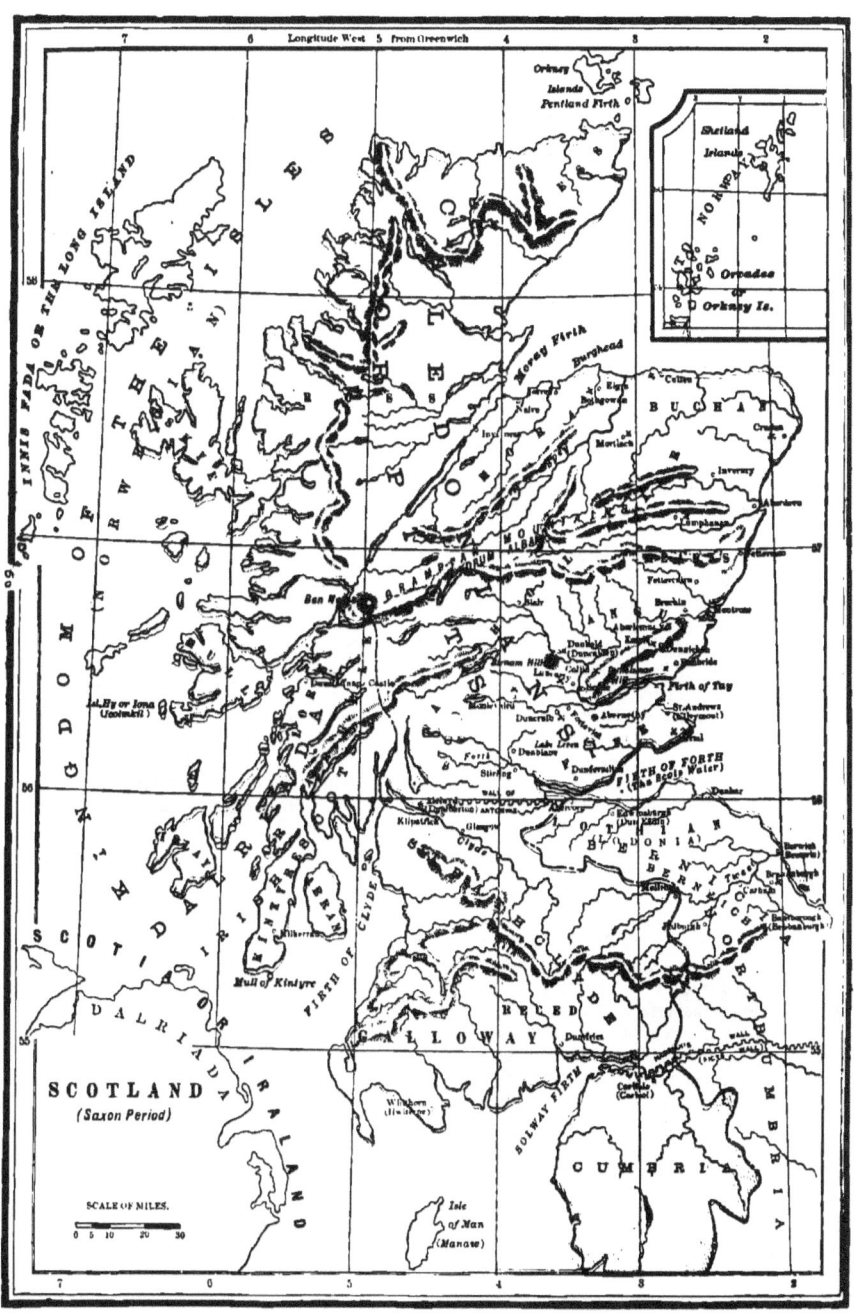

SECTION XVII.—DANES AND NORMANS IN ENGLAND.

E HAVE seen that in the year A. D. 827, the seven kingdoms of the Anglo-Saxon Heptarchy in Britain—Wessex, Essex, Sussex, Kent, East Anglia, Mercia and Northumberland —were united into one great kingdom under EGBERT, King of Wessex, who thus became the founder of the Kingdom of Angleland, or England. Egbert was a sovereign of great natural abilities, and had been educated at Charlemagne's court. He was the ancestor of all the sovereigns who have since swayed the scepter of the English realm.

It was now almost four centuries since the Anglo-Saxons first settled in Britain. They had begun to value the arts of peace, and hoped that under the government of one sovereign they might enjoy tranquillity and peace, but this fond hope was soon doomed to disappointment. As their savage ancestors in the middle of the fifth century had robbed the more civilized Britons of their homes and their country, so in the ninth century the Anglo-Saxons in Britain were themselves subjected to the ravages of the freebooting Danes, as the Northmen from the peninsula and islands of Denmark were called. The barren peninsulas of Scandinavia were too poor to support so numerous and adventurous a race, to whom the stormy sea was more attractive than the land, while beyond that sea lay fertile countries and cities stored with wealth. These Danes, or Northmen—like the Saxon pirates four centuries before—found the broad estuaries of Britain especially attractive.

In all the maritime regions of Western Europe the churches resounded daily with the following doleful addition to the litany: "From the fury of the Northmen, good Lord, deliver us!" In England, as in Continental Europe, the progress of these Scandinavian marauders was marked by the smoke of burning villages; and the helpless Saxons fled in dismay wherever the standard of the black raven appeared. Neither rich nor poor were spared; but the churches were the special objects of violence, because their vaults contained gold, silver and other treasures.

It was in A. D. 832—five years after Egbert had become over-lord of all England —that the heathen Danes began their raids upon that country. During his reign the savage freebooters contented themselves with raids upon the English coast during the summer of each year, retiring to their light vessels with their booty for the winter, and sailing back to their strongholds on the shores of the Baltic and North Seas. King Egbert, the founder of the English monarchy, died in A. D. 838, after a reign of eleven years, and at a time when his strong hand was most needed to defend his kingdom against the devastations of the Danish corsairs.

Egbert's son and successor, ETHELWOLF, was a weak and inefficient monarch, who began his reign by bestowing the three south-eastern provinces—Essex, Kent and Sussex—upon his eldest son, Athelstan, and soon afterward departed with his youngest and favorite son, Alfred, on a pilgrimage to Rome. In utter disregard of the miseries of his subjects, the imbecile king passed a year in prayers and offerings at the various holy places, while the Danes became more formidable than during his father's reign.

Landing from their little vessels and scattering themselves over the country in small bands, the intrepid pirates made spoil of everything that came in their way—goods, cattle and people. If opposed by a superior force, the daring freebooters fled to their boats, sailed away and invaded some distant quarter, where they were not expected. Thus all England was kept in constant alarm, and the people of one part of the realm did not dare to go to the aid of another portion, for fear that their own families and possessions would be exposed to the fury of the daring marauders.

In the meantime Athelstan died, and his brother Ethelbald joined a party of nobles who desired to dethrone his father. Had not King Ethelwolf consented to a division of the kingdom by relinquishing the western and more peaceful portion to his son, civil war might have been added to the horrors from which the unhappy country was suffering.

While returning through France, King Ethelwolf married the princess Judith, daughter of King Charles the Bald of France. Her only importance in English history is her influence over her little step-son Alfred, whose bright youthful mind she stimulated by the reading of a book of Saxon poetry which she numbered among her treasures. Like the young Saxons in general, Alfred had been brought up in such ignorance that he had not been taught to read, and he was twelve years old when his step-mother showed him and his brothers the book of Saxon poetry. This book was beautifully written and ornamented, and his step-mother told Alfred and his brothers that she would give it to the one who would soonest learn to read it.

Alfred applied himself with so much diligence and zeal that in a short time he was able to read the book to his step mother, who gave it to him as his reward. Thenceforth he took the greatest delight in study, but he had two great difficulties to encounter. There were very few books to be had, and there were very few people who were able to teach him anything. But, in spite of all these obstacles, he soon became one of the most learned men of his time; and his perseverance procured incalculable benefits to himself and to his countrymen.

On the death of King Ethelwolf, in A. D. 857, after a reign of nineteen years, his third son, ETHELBERT, succeeded to his father's throne; and he and his brother ETHELBALD reigned jointly until Ethelwolf's death, in A. D. 860, when Ethelbert became sole King of England. Upon Ethelbert's death, six years later (A. D. 866), a still

ALFRED'S STEP-MOTHER TEACHING HIM THE SAXON POEMS.

younger brother, ETHELRED I., became his successor. The Danes continued their piratical incursions with ever-increasing assurance. In one of their raids they captured Edmund, the tributary King of East Anglia, offering to him the alternative of death or apostasy. If he became a pagan and turned to the worship of Odin and Thor, he might continue to hold his kingdom, as their vassal. But he scorned this insulting proposition, and was bound to a tree and made a target for their arrows, until they became weary of their brutal sport, when they finally beheaded him. He was honored as a saint and a martyr, and his martyrdom is commemorated in the name of the place of its occurrence—Bury St. Edmunds.

King Ethelred I. lost his life in battle with the Danes, at Nottingham, A. D. 871, and was succeeded by his youngest brother, Alfred, who was thus called from his favorite studies to the toils and heavy responsibilities of royalty. Thus began the reign of ALFRED THE GREAT, the best sovereign that ever wore the English crown, the real founder of the English monarchy.

Alfred was twenty-two years of age when he ascended the throne of England. For eight years he warred bravely, and often successfully, against the heathen Danes, who had seized Wilton and were in possession of the entire country north of the Thames, having subdued Mercia, Northumberland and East Anglia, after their victory at Nottingham, where King Ethelred I. was killed. The Mercians were hostile to Alfred, and no dependence could be placed upon the provinces of the kingdom. The cultivation of the lands was neglected, through fear of constant Danish incursions; and all the churches and monasteries were burned to the ground.

Soon after his accession to the throne, Alfred marched against the daring invaders of his kingdom with but a few troops, but was defeated in a desperate battle. This misfortune did not abate Alfred's diligence, and he was in a short time enabled to hazard another engagement; but the Danes so dreaded his courage and activity that they proposed terms of peace, which he considered advisable to accept. By this treaty the invaders agreed to retire from the kingdom, but they violated their engagement by simply removing from place to place, burning and destroying wherever they went.

As the Danes were thus disregardful of treaties, and as their numbers were constantly increased by fresh arrivals of their countrymen from Denmark, Alfred's situation became extremely precarious, and some of his subjects sought safety by fleeing to Wales or to Continental Europe. Alfred vainly endeavored to remind the refugees of their duty to their country and their king, but his remonstrances were so ineffectual that he was obliged to provide for his own safety. He therefore relinquished the ensigns of royalty, dismissed his servants, dressed himself as a peasant, and lived for some time in the house of a herdsman, who had been intrusted with the care of his cattle.

In this manner did the great and good Alfred become a fugitive among his Anglo-Saxon subjects; but he still resolved to remain in his kingdom, watching for the slightest opportunity to strike an effective blow for its deliverance from the devastations of its heathen invaders. In his solitary retreat in Somersetshire, at the confluence of the rivers Parret and Thone, he amused himself with music and supported his humble lot with the hopes of better fortune. The wife of the herdsman by whom he was sheltered was ignorant of the true rank of her guest. Being called away one day the good woman set him to watch some cakes that were left baking over the fire; but Alfred was so intent on mending his bow that he let the cakes burn, and received a violent scolding from the angry woman when she returned. Concerning this story there are two old Latin verses that quaintly express the good woman's sharp reproof:

"*Urere quos cernis panes gyrare moraris,*
Quum nimium gaudes hos manducare calentes."

Translated into English these verses are as follows:

"There don't you see the cakes on fire?
Then wherefore turn them not?
You are glad enough to eat them
When they are piping hot."

The Danes grew careless as they met with no opposition, and Alfred was enabled to collect a small force from a chosen band of followers who had remained faithful to their king. With this band he took shelter in the forests and marshes of Somersetshire, and fortified himself on an island of firm ground in the midst of a bog. There hidden from the invaders, he was often enabled to surprise them by a night attack. Thus the drooping spirits of his Anglo-Saxon subjects were revived, and the little island court was well provided with the means of subsistence by forage.

The life of Alfred the Great was full of the most interesting incidents. Among the many anecdotes related about him is one told by the old English historians, affording a striking illustration of his benevolence, and being evidence of the privations which he, along with his trusty adherents, suffered during their seclusion in Somersetshire. One day during the winter, which happened to be unusually rigorous, he had sent all his attendants out to endeavor to procure fish or some kind of provisions. This enterprise was considered so difficult that the king and queen only were excused from the employment. When they had gone, the king, according to his custom, whenever he had an opportunity, took a book and commenced reading, while his queen, Elswitha, was employed in her domestic affairs.

Before the king and queen had been thus engaged for any length of time, a poor pilgrim who was accidentally passing that way knocked at the door and begged for something to eat. The kind-hearted king called Elswitha and requested her to give the poor man part of what provision there was in the fort. The queen, finding only one loaf of bread, brought it to Alfred, to show how scant was their store, also representing the distress under which the family would labor should they return unsuccessful from their foraging.

The humane king was not to be thus deterred from his charitable purpose, but rather rejoiced inwardly at this test of his benevolence, and cheerfully gave the poor Christian one-half of the loaf; consoling the queen with the religious reflection that "He who could feed five thousand with five loaves and two fishes, could make, if it so pleased him, that half of the loaf suffice for more than their necessities." When the pilgrim had departed, Alfred returned to his reading, and felt that inward satisfaction which most certainly follows a benevolent action. Nor was his charitable deed long unrewarded, as his companions returned with a quantity of provisions so great that they were not subjected to any similar inconveniences during their seclusion.

In the meantime Ubba, the chief of the Danish leaders, spread consternation and dismay over the entire kingdom, and now carried terror through Wales unopposed. The only time when he encountered resistance was while returning from the castle of Kenworth, into which the Earl of Devonshire had retired with a small military force. This brave soldier discovered that it was impossible for him to endure a siege, and was aware of the danger of surrendering to a perfidious foe; so he determined, by one desperate effort, to sally out and force his way through the besieging Danes, sword in hand. This proposal was embraced by all his followers; and the Danes, secure in their numbers and in their contempt for their enemies, were routed with terrific slaughter, and Ubba, their general, was slain.

This great victory again restored courage to the dispirited Saxons, and Alfred took advantage of their favorable disposition and prepared to animate them to a vigorous exertion of their superiority. He accordingly soon apprized them of the place of his seclusion, and instructed them to be prepared to move against the foe at a moment's warning. But none were found who would endeavor to give information concerning the number and position of the enemy. Not knowing, therefore, in whom he could confide, he undertook the perilous task himself.

Availing himself of a talent which he had cultivated in times of peace, Alfred disguised himself as a harper and boldly entered the Danish camp near Ethandune, where he tried all his musical arts to please. His songs and jokes so delighted the Danish soldiers that they introduced him to the tent of Guthrum, their leader, who entertained him royally for several days. Alfred had every opportunity there to learn the character and intentions of the Danes. He found them lazy and negligent, despising the English and fearing no attack. Having obtained the information he desired, he returned to his retreat, detached proper emissaries among his subjects, and ordered them to meet him in the forest of Selwood, which summons they gladly obeyed.

The moment was favorable, and Alfred swiftly and secretly collected his forces. He directed his most violent attack against the most unguarded quarter of the enemy. So suddenly did he fall upon the Danish encampment that the Danes were taken completely by surprise. So little did they expect to behold an army of English, whom they had thought utterly conquered, that they offered but a faint resistance, and were totally routed, with dreadful slaughter, notwithstanding their superiority of numbers. Their chief, Guthrum, fled, and with his surviving warriors took refuge in a fortified camp in the vicinity; but as they were unprepared for a siege, hunger compelled them to surrender in less than a fortnight on Alfred's own terms, which were dictated by a policy nobler than revenge.

The north-eastern coasts of England were already depopulated by the ravages of the Danes. Alfred resolved to make friends out of his late enemies by granting them large tracts of land in permanent possession, on condition that they should cease their ravages and exchange the fierce worship of Odin for the mild and gentler faith of Christ. Softened by terms so much more generous than he had a right to expect, Guthrum accepted Alfred's proposal and received Christian baptism, with the Christian name of Athelstan. Thirty of his nobles followed his example. Such of the vanquished Danes as did not choose to embrace Christianity were permitted to embark for Flanders, under the command of their valiant leader, Hastings.

Thus Alfred's struggle with the Danes ended in his complete triumph in the year A. D. 878. He had now attained the meridian of his glory, and possessed a greater extent of territory than any of his predecessors had ever ruled. The Kings of Wales did him homage for their possessions, and the Northumbrians accepted the king he had selected for them. Danish and Saxon England were separated by the Roman military road, known as *Watling Street*, which extended from London to Chester. As the Anglo-Danes were absorbed in their new possessions, they did not often molest Alfred's dominions; though the new hordes of Danes which were constantly arriving from beyond the sea threatened to crowd out the earlier occupants of the island.

Alfred the Great employed the twelve years of comparative peace and tranquillity, which followed, in civilizing his subjects and cultivating the arts of peace, and in protecting his kingdom and repairing the damages which it had sustained by war. London and several other cities which the Danes had burned were now rebuilt. The English coast was guarded by a powerful fleet, designed to repel any future incursions of the Danes; while a regular militia was established throughout the kingdom and trained to defend the land.

The good Alfred did not neglect the education of his subjects. He found them sunk in the grossest ignorance and barbarism, in consequence of the continual disorders of the government and the ravages of the Danes. He asserted that when he became king he did not know of one person south of the Thames, and but few south of the Humber, who understood the prayers in the churches; and this is not surprising in an age when many a king "made his mark" at the foot of charters and treaties, because he was unable to write his name. So little was learning prized by the great in Alfred's time that Asser, the biographer of Alfred, states with astonishment that the king taught his youngest son, Ethelward, to read, before he instructed him in hunting.

Almost all the monasteries, with their libraries, had been destroyed by the Danes; and all the customs of peaceful and orderly life had been broken up by the terror of the ravages of the fierce freebooters. The good monarch first restored peace and security, after which he founded schools and required every owner of two hides of land to send his children to these schools for instruction. He founded the university of Oxford and endowed it with many privileges. He invited learned men and artisans from Continental Europe. He employed these learned men in translating Greek and Latin books into the Saxon, or English, of his time; while he had the artisans occupied in enriching his kingdom with useful arts and manufactures.

Alfred himself was the most learned man in his kingdom. He made considerable progress in such studies as grammar, rhetoric, philosophy, geometry and architecture, and was an excellent historian. He understood music, and was acknowledged to be the best Saxon poet of the age. He left many literary works behind him, and some of these are still in existence. He was the founder of English prose-writing. The *Anglo-Saxon Chronicle*, first reduced to regular form in his time, was kept for centuries by the monks of Abingdon and Peterborough, and is our main authority for early English history.

Among the works which Alfred wrote or translated were a History of the World by Orosius and the *Consolations of Philosophy* by Boëthius, as well as some inestimable versions of the Psalms, the Gospels, and other portions of the Scriptures. Alfred's piety was as conspicuous as his prowess, and in those days of ignorance he enlightened by his pen, as much as by his example, the people over whom he ruled. The following version of the Lord's Prayer in the Saxon tongue, as found in Alfred's translation, is a sample of the English language in his time:

"Fæder ure thu the earth on heafenum, si thin mama gehalgod, to be cume thin rice, Gewurthe hin willa on earthen swa swa on heafenum, urne ge dægwanlican hlaf syle us to daeg; and forgyf us ure gyltas, swa swa we forgivath urum gyltendum, and ne geladde thu us or consenung ac alyse us of yfle."

Alfred always carried a book in the bosom of his robe, so that he might be able to profit by it whenever he had a spare moment, and in this way he acquired a very extensive knowledge without neglecting any of his duties. He divided his time into three equal parts; devoting one-third to religion and to study, another third to sleep and refreshment, and the remaining third to the affairs of state. As there were no clocks or watches in use in England at that time, he contrived to measure time by the burning of candles. These candles were painted in rings of different breadths and colors—so many colors as he had things to attend to—and thus he knew by the burning of these candles when he had been employed a sufficient time at any one thing. But he discovered that when the wind blew upon his candles they burned faster; and to remedy this inconvenience, he invented lanterns to put them in.

Alfred made a new collection of the laws of Ethelbert, Offa and Ina, and to these he added some enactments of his own. He established a regular police, and revived the old Saxon division of the kingdom into shires, or counties, and subdivided the counties into hundreds, and the hundreds into *tithings*, or tens, for the better administration of justice. The tithings consisted of ten families each; the hundreds, of a hundred families each. All the members were held responsible for a crime committed within their number, and were bound to produce the offender before the proper court. An innocent man could always clear himself by bringing ten of his neighbors, members of the same hundred, who would testify under oath to his integrity of character, or to his absence from the place where the crime was alleged to have been committed. This is supposed to have been the origin of our later and now universal custom of trial by jury.

So well regulated was the police which Alfred established that violence and disorder entirely disappeared from the land, and it is said that he had golden bracelets hung near the public highways, which no robber dared to touch. But the good king never deviated from the nicest regard for the liberty of his people; and the following remarkable sentiment is preserved in his will: "*It is just the English should forever remain as free as their own thoughts.*"

Alfred's last years were disturbed by fresh incursions of the Danes, under their famous leader, Hastings. After these barbarians had been driven from France by a famine.

they landed on the Kentish coast and spread their ravages over that part of England. Alfred encountered them with his usual energy, and finally restored peace to his kingdom after a severe struggle of several years.

The skillful foreign artisans whom Alfred invited from Continental Europe to instruct his countrymen were of such great service that the English goldsmiths soon became very expert. Their skill was proven by the discovery of a golden ornament at Athelney, Alfred's place of concealment in Somersetshire during his distress. This ornament, which is supposed to have been worn by Alfred himself, is of very beautiful workmanship and elegantly engraved with various figures, and bears the following inscription in Saxon characters: "Alfred commanded me to be made."

But the workmen who were the most highly esteemed were the blacksmiths, because they could make swords and other implements of war. Every soldier of rank was constantly attended by his smith to keep his arms in order. The chief smith was an officer of great dignity at court. At table he sat next to the priest, and was entitled to a draught of every kind of liquor brought into the hall.

Thus, we see that a thousand years ago King Alfred the Great laid the foundations of those institutions which have placed England at the head of European civilization, enlightenment, progress and liberty— those institutions which have been the priceless inheritance of the Anglo-Saxon race, and which have made the English-speaking nations the leaders of modern civilization.

King Alfred the Great died in A. D. 901, after a reign of thirty years, in the fifty-second year of his age, and was buried at Winchester, his capital. His entire reign had been devoted, with the most intense zeal and diligence, to the advancement of the best interests of his subjects. He had fought fifty-six battles with the Danes by land and sea, and had excelled most sovereigns in his labors as lawgiver and judge; yet he found time to acquire more learning and write more books than most men of uninterrupted leisure. He proved his moral greatness in conquering himself and in tempering justice with kindness; and we can vainly search all history for any human character more near perfection than that of Alfred the Great, who has never been surpassed by any English sovereign as a scholar, a soldier or a statesman.

Concerning this estimable king, a certain writer says: "To give a character to this prince, would be to sum up those qualities which constitute perfection. Even virtues seemingly opposite were happily blended in his disposition; persevering, yet flexible; moderate, yet enterprising; just, yet merciful; stern in command, yet gentle in conversation. Nature also, as if desirous that such admirable qualities of mind should be set off to the greatest advantage, had bestowed on him all bodily accomplishments, vigor, dignity, and an engaging open countenance."

Under Alfred and his successors the *Witenagemote*, or "Meeting of the Wise Men," was convened alternately at different places —generally at Winchester, the capital of Wessex, for the southern shires; at Gloucester, for the western shires; at London, for the eastern shires; and at York, for the northern shires, after the *Danelagh*, the region ceded to the Danes by Alfred, ceased to be distinguished from the rest of England. At Winchester, Gloucester and London the king "wore his crown" in turn on the three great festivals of the Christian year; and all persons who had petitions to make, or wrongs to be righted, might bring their suit thither. No important proceedings were transacted without the advice of the "wise men." With their concurrence Alfred and his successors required each maritime town to provide and maintain a ship for the defense of the English coast; and it was early settled that the English people could not be taxed without their consent.

These old Saxon names have a meaning. Thus *Egbert* signifies "bright eye;" *Ethelred*, "noble in council;" *Athelstan*, "the noble stone;" *Edward*, "the prosperous guardian;" *Edwin*, "prosperous in battle," etc.

Alfred's eldest son, Edmund, had died before his father, and his second son, Ethelward, preferred a private and studious life to the cares and responsibilities of royalty; and therefore the Witenagemote, or "Assembly of the Wise Men," chose Alfred's third son, Edward, who accordingly became his illustrious father's successor on the throne of England, and is known as EDWARD THE ELDER, so surnamed because he was the first King of England bearing the name of Edward. He was equal to his renowned father as a warrior, but was greatly inferior to him in science and literature. His sister, Ethelfleda, "the Lady of Mercia," was as fond of war as himself, and aided him in many of his military enterprises. Edward the Elder founded the university of Cambridge in A. D. 915.

Edward's cousin, Ethelwolf, attempted to seize the English crown, but was defeated; whereupon he joined the Danes, and invited fresh hordes of them from their homes beyond the sea to attack his native land. Edward was assisted in his defense by his warlike sister Ethelfleda; and the fame of his success gained for him the voluntary homage of the sovereigns of Wales, Northumbria, Strathclyde and Scotland, A. D. 924. These kingdoms had suffered as much as Saxon England from the ravages of the freebooting Danes, and their rulers were glad to place themselves under the protection of the victorious Edward the Elder. Edward's own dominions extended as far north as the Humber, while he was over-lord of the entire island of Britain and of the Western Isles.

Edward the Elder died in A. D. 925, and was succeeded on the English throne by his eldest son, ATHELSTAN, one of the greatest of the Saxon Kings of England. During Athelstan's reign England was renowned in Europe for her wealth and splendor. Five of his sisters were the wives of sovereigns or great lords in Continental Europe. One of these sisters was married to Charles the Simple, King of France · another to Hugh the Great, Count of Paris, the "kingmaker" of France; and Editha, the highest of all in rank, to Otho the Great, King of Germany, afterwards Emperor. These royal intermarriages and the constant intercourse between England and the Continent developed much commerce. Athelstan enacted various laws for the encouragement of commerce, one of which was that any merchant who had made three long voyages on his own responsibility should be admitted to the rank of thane.

Several foreign princes were intrusted to Athelstan's care and instruction. The nearest to him was his royal nephew, afterward Louis d' Outremer, King of France, who learned from his uncle to act with spirit and efficiency amid the troubles attending the decline of the Carlovingian dynasty.

Athelstan is regarded as one of the ablest of the Saxon Kings of England. He was most courteous in his manners and was much beloved by his subjects. It is said that his hair was bright yellow and that he wore it beautifully plaited.

By adding Northumberland to his own immediate dominion, Athelstan became sole king of all the Saxons and Danes in Britain, as well as over-lord of all the Celtic principalities in the island; but his government was not sufficiently strong and vigilant to keep his vassals in subjection. The Welsh and the Scots aided each other in a revolt against the Saxon king's supremacy; and this rising had not been very long suppressed before a grand conspiracy of Scots, Welsh and Irish with Danes beyond the sea threatened Athelstan's dominion.

Aulaff, one of the Danish leaders, tried the stratagem which Alfred the Great had practiced so successfully—disguising himself as a minstrel and entering Athelstan's camp. The English king was highly delighted with Aulaff's music, and, thinking that he was a poor boy, gave him a piece of money. Aulaff was too proud to keep the coin, and when he got out of Athelstan's tent he buried it in the ground. An English soldier happened to see him in this act, and thinking this very strange, examined the pretended minstrel's face, and discovered that he was Prince Aulaff, but allowed him to depart.

When the Danish prince had reached a safe distance, the English soldier informed King Athelstan of the discovery which he had made. The king reproved the soldier for letting so dangerous an enemy escape, whereupon the soldier replied: "I once served Aulaff and gave him the same faith that I have now given to you; and if I had betrayed him, what trust would you have reposed in my truth? Let him die, if such be his fate, but not through my treachery. Secure yourself from danger, and remove your tent, lest he should assail you unawares."

Athelstan was very much pleased with the honest soldier's answer, and acted on his advice. It was very well that he did, as Aulaff with a select band of Danish warriors broke into Athelstan's camp that very night and killed a bishop who had pitched his tent upon the spot where the English king's had stood. The noise of the attack awakened the Saxons, and a general battle ensued, which lasted all night and the following day, and is known in English history as the battle of Brunanburgh, or the *Long Battle*. In this great battle Athelstan completely defeated and routed the Danes, and his triumph was sung by English minstrels as the most glorious of victories.

Upon Athelstan's death, in A. D. 941, his brother, EDMUND I., became King of England, at the age of eighteen years. He subdued the Celtic kingdom of Strathclyde, which he bestowed upon Malcolm I., King of Scotland, on condition that that monarch should do him homage and defend the northern coast against the Danes.

The Danes whom Alfred the Great had permitted to settle in Northumberland had caused great trouble in England. They were constantly rising in rebellion and endeavoring to make themselves independent of Saxon rule. Prince Aulaff, who had escaped from the Long Battle and taken refuge in Ireland, was now their leader. King Edmund's youth and inexperience gave him hope of better success in a new effort. Aulaff accordingly collected a large army, but this army was utterly defeated by the English under King Edmund, and the whole of the Danelagh in Northumberland was reduced to submission.

Edmund had displayed so much wisdom and courage that there was every hope that his reign would be a happy one, when it was suddenly brought to a tragic end. He had banished a notorious robber named Leolf from the kingdom, but Leolf had the audacity to return and to come into the hall and take a seat at the royal table. The young king ordered the robber to leave the room, but Leolf refused to obey, which so enraged the king that he sprang from his seat, seized the robber by the hair and threw him down. Leolf thereupon drew his dagger and stabbed the young monarch to the heart. Thus died King Edmund I. by the assassin's hand, at the age of twenty-four years, after reigning seven years, A. D. 948.

Edmund's two little sons, Edwy and Edgar, were too young to succeed their father; and so the Witenagemote elected EDRED, Edmund's brother, King of England in their stead. At the beginning of Edred's reign the Danes of Northumberland again rebelled, but Edred speedily subdued them. With the aid of his great minister, St. Dunstan, he adopted effectual means to prevent them from disturbing the peace of the kingdom, and held them in submission with a firm hand. He no longer permitted them to be governed by their own prince, but put them under the jurisdiction of an English governor, and garrisoned all their chief towns with English troops.

St. Dunstan, Edred's famous minister, was the most remarkable man of his time. He was an Englishman, born of noble parents, and endowed with extraordinary talents. He was educated for the Church, and when quite young was famous for his learning and accomplishments. He was able to paint and engrave. He copied and adorned books with the most elegant designs. He wrought curious patterns in gold and silver. Above all, he won the king's esteem by the songs which he composed and sang to the music of his harp.

In those days and long afterward it was dangerous to have too much knowledge. St. Dunstan's rivals at court accused the distinguished churchman of magical arts, and caused his disgrace and banishment. This change of fortune did not crush St. Dunstan's ambition, but only directed it in a new channel. He dug a cell so small that he could neither stand erect in it nor stretch out his limbs when he laid down. In this cell he occupied himself constantly, either in religious devotion or in making ingenious and useful things of iron and brass. Many foolish stories are related about the temptations to which the devil subjected him, and how he resisted these temptations.

He imagined that the devil, in human form, paid him frequent visits. One day, while he was busily engaged at work, the devil popped his head into the window and asked him to make something for his Satanic majesty. St. Dunstan thereupon seized the devil by the nose with a pair of red-hot tongs and held him there, while he roared out in anguish.

These, and a thousand other stories equally ridiculous, were seriously told, and implicitly believed by the English people, thus gaining for St. Dunstan the reputation which he desired. He now again appeared before the public, and soon acquired so much influence over King Edred that the king not only consulted him about religious matters, but also intrusted him with the direction of the affairs of state.

St. Dunstan now determined to make an innovation in the Church in England, by introducing the order of monks which had already existed in other European countries for several centuries. These monks lived in absolute seclusion from the rest of mankind, having taken the three vows of celibacy, personal poverty, and obedience to the head of the monastery, called the *Abbot*, or the *Superior*. St. Dunstan himself became Abbot of Glastonbury.

The old clergy were called *Seculars*; and a bitter contest at once commenced between the two orders, which agitated the entire kingdom and finally caused a civil war. The secular clergy were very numerous and wealthy, and were in possession of all the offices in the Church; but St. Dunstan wielded all the power of the king, who had become indolent and helpless from ill health, and who thus allowed his minister to do as he pleased.

King Edred died in A. D. 955, and was succeeded on the English throne by his nephew EDWY, the eldest son of the murdered King Edmund. Edwy was then only sixteen years old. He was possessed of virtues and abilities which would have made him a great popular favorite had he not unhappily engaged in the religious disputes and taken part with the secular priests against the monks. His brief reign of three years was the beginning of that bitter struggle between the Church and the royal power which raged throughout Europe for centuries.

Edwy had a beautiful female cousin named Elgiva, whom he loved dearly, and whom he married before his coronation, against the advice of his best counselors. St. Dunstan, and Odo, Archbishop of Canterbury, both declared it to be sinful for a man to marry his cousin, and did all in their power to mar the happiness of the young couple. On the day of Edwy's coronation, when the nobles were feasting in the great hall of the palace, the young king retired from the scene of drunken riot to the more agreeable society of his wife and her mother. St. Dunstan rudely followed the king into his wife's apartment, upbraiding him with all the bitterness of ecclesiastical rancor, and pushed him back by main force into the company he had quitted.

St. Dunstan's enemies now advised the young king to punish this insult, and accordingly Edwy called upon the great churchman to give an account of the money which he had received as treasurer of the kingdom during the preceding reign. This account the haughty abbot refused to give in; whereupon he was deprived of all his civil and ecclesiastical emoluments and banished from the kingdom. St. Dunstan's exile only tended to increase his reputation for sanctity. The people regarded the abbot as a true saint, and their superstitious reverence was kept up by pretended messages from heaven. Crucifixes, altars, and even horses, were said to have been gifted with the power of speech, in order to harangue in the exiled churchman's favor.

In the meantime Odo, Archbishop of Canterbury, took up the cause of St. Dunstan with great zeal, and incited the Danes of Northumberland to revolt against King Edwy and to proclaim Edgar, the King's younger brother, as their sovereign. Odo also pronounced a divorce between Edwy and Elgiva. The church party gained the ascendency; and Archbishop Odo, with a party of soldiers, broke into the palace and cruelly branded the young queen's beautiful face with a red-hot iron, in order to destroy her beauty; after which they carried her away as a prisoner to Ireland, where they commanded her to remain in exile for the rest of her life.

Edwy, unable to withstand the power of the Church, consented to a divorce. Elgiva, after being cured of her wound and after obliterating the marks which had been made to deface her beauty, returned from her banishment, and got as far as Gloucester, on her way to join Edwy, whom she still considered her husband; but she fell into the power of Archbishop Odo's adherents, who put her to death in the most cruel manner, the sinews of her limbs being cut and her body being mangled, so that she died in the most cruel agony. Her unhapyy husband died of a broken heart soon afterward, A. D. 959; and his brother, EDGAR THE PEACEABLE, ascended the English throne without any further opposition; while St. Dunstan, who had raised an army to support his pretensions, returned to his former power as virtual ruler of the state.

Edgar the Peaceable was but sixteen years old when he became undisputed King of England, his rebellious arms having made him master of a large portion of the kingdom before his unfortunate brother's death. Edgar was completely under the influence of St. Dunstan and the monks; and these monks, who were the only historians of the time, wrote the history of his life and praised him as the greatest, wisest and best king that ever lived ; representing him as a great statesman, a man of great ability and virtue, and likewise a saint. Notwithstanding this praise from the monks, Edgar was a consummate hypocrite, because he was guilty of the most enormous crimes, while falsely accusing the secular clergy of all kinds of wickedness.

Edgar was, however, an active and efficient sovereign, and governed his kingdom wisely and well. He enacted good laws, and administered justice so well that travelers no longer had any fear of robbers. Whilst Edgar was regardless of his own morals, he was very careful about those of his subjects. Instead of setting them a good example, he sought to promote religion by laws. Amongst other laws, he ordained that every Sunday should be rigidly observed, and that the Sabbath should commence at three o'clock on Saturday afternoon and end at sunrise on Monday.

One of Edgar's first acts was to make St. Dunstan Archbishop of Canterbury. The new Primate found exercise for his great talents and indomitable will in reforming the English convents after the strict rule of the Benedictine order of monks, which had arisen in Italy almost four centuries before, and which had already done good service to the world by copying and preserving the greatest treasures of ancient literature. The quiet retreat within convent walls afforded to many weak souls the only opportunity for a holy life, amid the corruptions and tumults of the Dark Ages.

The monks are only to be blamed when they presumed to judge the duties of others by their own, and to cast contempt and insult on relations which had been regarded as sacred. Hitherto the parish priests in England were permitted to marry, though certainly not encouraged to do so. For this reason the monks, or regular clergy, held the parish priests, or secular clergy, in disdain, and induced Edgar to enact several laws which placed them at an unjust disadvantage. The English people and country thanes sided with their pastors, but St. Dunstan was successful in driving out many of the married priests and filling their places with his monks.

At this time Wales and a great part of England were infested by wolves. In order to get rid of them, Edgar ordered that the Welsh kings should bring him three hundred wolves' heads yearly, instead of paying him an annual tribute in money and cattle. This plan was so successful that the wolves in that country were almost exterminated.

Edgar maintained a large fleet, which checked all hostile movements of the Danes, either within his own dominions or beyond the seas. He kept his ships sailing constantly around the island of Britain, in order to make his sailors expert.

It was during Edgar's reign in England that the Normans settled in France, and this for a time afforded room for all the fresh Scandinavian hordes that left their native homes in the cold and barren North. The duchy of Normandy, which these Normans founded in the North-west of France, was to have an important part in the history of England.

Edgar gained many victories over the tributary, but not always submissive, princes of Wales, Scotland, Ireland, the Orkneys, and the Isle of Man. On one occasion, while he was making his annual inspection of all the English coasts, his barge was rowed up the river Dee by eight vassal kings.

By St. Dunstan's advice, Edgar divided Northumbria into three great earldoms. Deira, south of the river Tees, became the modern Yorkshire; the central portion, between the Tees and the Tweed, retained the old name of Northumbria or Northumberland; and the portion north of the Tweed, now called Lothian, was bestowed upon the King of Scots as an English fief. Lothian became the favorite residence of the Scottish kings, who established their capital at *Edwin's borough*, or Edinburgh, named after Edwin, the first Christian King of Northumbria.

King Edgar the Peaceable died in A D. 975, after a reign of sixteen years; leaving two sons, Edward, by his first wife, and Ethelred, whose mother, Elfrida, was still living. Elfrida was ambitious to have her son placed on the English throne; but the overpowering influence of St. Dunstan placed the crown on the head of Edward, who was then a boy of thirteen years. This harmless youth treated everybody kindly and gently, and was very liberal to his ambitious step-mother; but this had no effect upon Elfrida, who relentlessly pursued her innocent young step-son, and finally brought him to a tragic death, after a troubled reign of three years, for which reason he was called EDWARD THE MARTYR.

In the fourth year of his reign (A. D. 878), while Edward the Martyr was hunting near Corfe Castle, in Dorsetshire, where his ambitious and ungrateful step-mother lived, he rode up to the castle, entirely alone and unsuspicious of any danger, to make her a passing visit. Elfrida received her kingly step-son with much pretended kindness. As he declined to dismount, she gave him a cup of wine; and while he was drinking, one of Elfrida's domestics, who had been instructed for that purpose, stabbed him in the back. Finding himself wounded, Edward put spurs to his horse, and galloped off; but, fainting from the loss of blood, he fell from his horse; and, his foot sticking in the stirrup, he was dragged along by the horse until he was dead.

As Elfrida was the head of the party opposed to the monks, these latter considered Edward as having fallen in the cause of religion, and for that reason they styled him *Edward the Martyr*. The monks affirmed, and the superstitious people very readily believed, that many miracles were performed at his tomb.

ETHELRED II., surnamed THE UNREADY, the son of Edgar and Elfrida, was then made King of England, at the age of ten years. He was of an amiable disposition, and was much affected by his step-brother's cruel death, shedding many bitter tears. His wicked mother regarded this as a reproach to herself, and she became so angry that she seized a large wax candle and beat the poor boy almost to death. Ethelred never forgot this beating, and to the day of his death he could not bear the sight of a wax candle.

Though Elfrida had now obtained the object of her ambition, she was anything but happy, being stung by the remorse of conscience. To atone for her crime, she founded monasteries, performed penances, and did all that the priests required; but none of these things could calm the upbraidings of her own conscience or restore her peace of mind. She finally retired to a nunnery, where she passed the remainder of her life in fasting and prayer.

The reign of Ethelred II. lasted thirty-eight years (A. D. 978-1016), and was full of trouble for himself and his subjects; as the Danes, who had not molested England for a long time, recommenced their inroads with terrible fury. In A. D. 980 a small band of Danish adventurers landed upon the English coast, ravaged the kingdom to some extent, and then escaped with their booty. These piratical incursions were continued for several years.

Emboldened by their success, and encouraged by the distracted condition of England, the Danes invaded the kingdom in A. D. 991 with a great force. King Ethelred II. had sufficient warning of their coming, and ample time for preparation to resist them; but he neglected to make any provision for defense, and thus acquired the surname of *the Unready*, which expressed only too well his weak and inefficient policy toward them.

The Danes advanced into the heart of England, and Ethelred II. bribed them to retreat by paying them sixteen thousand pounds of silver, which only insured their return in greater force, with a demand for twenty-four thousand pounds; and Ethelred II., to comply with this demand, levied upon his subjects an odious tax called *Danegelt*.

In A. D. 993 Sweyn, King of Denmark, and Hakon Jarl, King of Norway, invaded England, sailing up the Humber and ravaging the country far and wide. The next year (A. D. 994) they entered the Thames with ninety-four vessels and besieged London, but the merchants and mechanics were braver than the king or the nobles, and the besiegers were finally driven off. Fully a third part of the islands of Britain and Ireland, with all the smaller islands belonging to them, were now in the grasp of the "Raven;" and the most trusted favorites of King Ethelred II. sold his kingdom to his enemies by bribing the Danes to withdraw—a proceeding which always insured their speedy return. The kingdom only gained one year's respite, as the Danes returned again the next year, and were again bribed to retire.

King Ethelred II. was only ready for action at the wrong time. He wasted the force of his kingdom in ravaging Cumberland, because King Malcolm II. of Scotland refused to help him to buy off the Danes; and he rashly invaded Normandy, to punish its people for having harbored and encouraged the Danes. It was known that the plunder of England was regularly exchanged, on the warves of Rouen, the capital of Normandy, for the wines of France; but Ethelred's expedition failed, as the peasantry on the Norman coast armed themselves " with hook and with crook, with fork and with pike, with club and with flail," and made so valiant a resistance that the English gladly sought refuge in their own ships.

Sweyn, King of Denmark, had a sister named Gunilda, a women of great virtue and abilities, who married an English nobleman and became a Christian. This woman had for a long time beheld with grief and horror the devastations perpetrated in England by her barbarous countrymen. By her intercession, a treaty of peace was concluded between the English and the Danes. She offered herself, her husband and her son as securities for the fidelity of the Danes, whose repeated breaches of faith had made the English thoroughly distrustful of them.

After this conclusion of peace between the English and the Danes, King Ethelred II. sought to conciliate both classes of Danes by marrying Emma, sister of Duke Richard the Good of Normandy and at that time the most beautiful princess in Europe.

One of the Danish officers made the following report to King Sweyn concerning the condition of England under Ethelred the Unready: "A country naturally powerful; a king asleep, solicitous only about his pleasures, and trembling at the name of war; hated by his people, and laughed at by strangers. Generals, envious of each other; and governors ready to fly at the first shout of battle."

But still measures which had been adopted might have secured peace to England, but for an act as unwise as it was wicked and barbarous. In A. D. 1002 King Ethelred II. was persuaded by his counselors to issue secret orders to his officers to massacre all the Danes in England on the 13th of November, the day of the Feast of St. Brice. This cruel order was executed with shocking barbarity; and men, women and children were massacred indiscriminately.

Among the victims was Gunilda. The wretch who had the custody of her and her family first caused her husband and son to be murdered before her eyes, though they were English. When the assassins approached her, she calmly warned them of the consequences of their action. In the agony of despair, she declared that her sufferings would be avenged by her royal brother, who was a great and powerful sovereign, to whom she was very dear, and who would punish her murder by the total ruin of the English king and people.

Her prophecy was fulfilled to the letter. A few Danes who were so fortunate as to escape boarded a vessel and sailed to their native country, where they informed King Sweyn of the cruel fate of their countrymen in England. Sweyn was roused to fury by the news of his sister's cruel death, and he at once collected a large army, with which he invaded England. In a few years he obtained entire possession of the country, and was acknowledged King of England; King Ethelred the Unready and his wife and two sons fleeing to Normandy.

After Sweyn had been master of England for ten years, he died A. D. 1014; whereupon Ethelred II. returned to England and acted with such unexpected energy and courage that the Danes were forced to return to their own country. If Ethelred II. had been wise and prudent he might have reëstablished himself on the throne of England, but his conduct was such as to alienate the affections of his supporters.

Canute the Great, King of Denmark, Sweyn's son and successor, now returned to England; and after the death of Ethelred II., in A. D. 1016, he disputed the possession of the English crown with Ethelred's son and successor, EDMUND IRONSIDE, so surnamed on account of his personal courage and hardihood, whom he compelled to divide the kingdom with him. But one month after this division Edmund Ironside was murdered at the instigation of Edric, Duke of Mercia, one of Ethelred's most treacherous favorites; whereupon CANUTE THE GREAT, King of Denmark, became sole King of England, A. D. 1017.

There were now five English princes who might have been aspirants for the crown, but not one of these was of age or character sufficient to dispute it with the victorious Danish king. Edmund's own brother died the next year; his half-brothers, the sons of Ethelred II. and Emma, were in Normandy with their uncle, Duke Richard the Good; and his two little children were sent by Canute the Great to King Olaf Skotkonung of Sweden, with a hint that they should be put out of the way, but the Swedish king chose the more generous construction of this request by sending the infant princes to be educated at the court of King Stephen the Pious of Hungary.

Canute the Great had already summoned a council of the whole kingdom at London, which chose him by an almost unanimous vote to be King of England. Like a wise monarch, he then sought to conciliate his English subjects, and to show his confidence in them he sent almost all his Danish troops back to Denmark, after paying them liberally by a tax imposed on the English. He also restored the laws and customs of Athelstan and Edgar the Peaceable, and provided for the security of life and property by a strict administration of justice. To silence the claims of the young sons of Ethelred the Unready to the English crown, he proposed to marry their widowed mother, Emma, who gave her consent.

Canute the Great, though brought up in the worship of Odin and Thor, embraced Christianity. He was a very pious king, according to the standard of that age. He bestowed much wealth upon churches and monasteries, and went on a pilgrimage to Rome, whence he wrote a kind and fatherly letter to his subjects, telling them of the events of his journey and describing the gifts and honors bestowed upon him by the Pope and by Conrad II., King of Germany, in whose coronation as Emperor he bore a distinguished part; also referring to the privileges which he had been able to obtain for his subjects. He acknowledged that the early years of his reign were oppressive, and promised redress, assuring them that he needed no money which must be obtained by injustice. The following is a sample of this "King's English:" "First above all things, are men one God ever to love and worship, and one Christendom with one consent to hold, and Canute King to love with right truthfulness."

Canute the Great was tall in stature, and very strong physically; of fair complexion, and celebrated for his beauty. His hair was thick and long, and his eyes were bright and sparkling.

England enjoyed many years of tranquillity during his reign. Canute employed himself in making new laws and in promoting the prosperity of the kingdom. Poetry was the favorite art of the time, and the king did not disdain the character of a poet. The first stanza of a poem which he wrote on hearing the monks of Ely singing, as he was passing by on the water, is still on record, and is as follows:

"Cheerful sang the monks of Ely,
As Canute the king was passing by;
Row to the shore, knights, said the king,
And let us hear these churchmen sing."

This poem was afterwards sung in the churches, which gives us a strange idea of the sacred poetry of the times of the Saxon and Danish kings of England.

Canute's courtiers, desiring to flatter him by exalting his power, once told him that he was lord alike of sea and land, and that he had only to command and both would obey him. In order to rebuke their flattery, and to show them how impious and foolish such praises were, he ordered his throne to be carried to the sea-shore at Southampton, and sat down upon it while the tide was rising. As the waters approached, Canute said: "O sea, I am thy lord and master; thou art under my dominion; the land upon which I tread is mine; I charge thee, therefore, to come no nearer, nor dare to wet the feet of thy sovereign. Roll back thy waves! How darest thou thunder and foam in my presence?" He sat some time pretending to expect that the waves would obey; but they continued rising higher and higher, until they touched the king's feet, whereupon he turned to his courtiers and rebuked them, bidding them to remember that there is only One who can say to the billowy deep: "So far shalt thou go and no farther." He afterwards hung up his crown over the altar in Winchester Cathedral, and never again wore it.

Before his death Canute the Great wore the crowns of four kingdoms—having been King of Denmark since the death of his father Sweyn in A. D. 1014; and having conquered England in A. D. 1017, Sweden in A. D. 1025, and Norway in A. D. 1027. He was thus the sovereign of a great Scandinavian empire, and one of the most powerful monarchs of his time. He was often obliged to quit his island-kingdom to resist the inroads of his neighbors on the Continent of Europe. In one of these campaigns the Saxon Earl Godwin won Canute's gratitude by his wonderful energy and valor; and was rewarded by marriage with the king's daughter, as well as by his sovereign's confidence and esteem.

Canute the Great died in A. D. 1036, leaving three sons—Sweyn and Harold by a first marriage, and Hardicanute, the son of Emma. Hardicanute should have succeeded to the English throne by his parents' marriage contract; but as he was absent in Denmark at the time of his father's death, and as he was hated by the Anglo-Danes, HAROLD HAREFOOT, so surnamed from his swiftness in running, usurped the English crown and seized his renowned father's treasures. Earl Godwin upheld the rights of Hardicanute, and the dispute was settled by a division of the kingdom, Hardicanute having all the shires south of the Thames, and Harold the rest of the realm. It was agreed that the territory assigned to Hardicanute should be governed by Emma until her son's return from Denmark. Harold soon won Earl Godwin to his interest by promising to marry his daughter and to declare her children heirs to the English crown.

The two sons of Ethelred II. and Emma were still living in Normandy under the protection of their uncle, Duke Richard the Good. In order to get them into his power, Harold forged a letter in Emma's name, earnestly inviting them to come to England, where, they were told, they would be joyfully welcomed by the people, and one of them would be acknowledged as king. Still further to deceive the princes, the letter was filled with abuse of Harold himself. The letter was written so much like their mother's style that the innocent and confiding princes were utterly deceived. Alfred, the most active of the two princes, trusting himself wholly to a few Normans on board some ships, sailed for England. Soon after he had landed he was met by Earl Godwin, who professed the greatest friendship for him and loaded him with caresses. But the treacherous earl took advantage of the prince's confidence, seized him at night and sent him to Ely, where he was actually murdered, or died in consequence of cruel treatment.

As soon as Emma heard of her son's fate she fled into Flanders; and Harold seized the whole kingdom, but did not long enjoy the fruits of his cruelty and ambition, as he died in A. D. 1039. HARDICANUTE had joined his mother in Flanders, and as soon as he heard of the death of Harold Harefoot he came to England and was joyfully welcomed by the people; but he soon lost their affections by tyranny and dissipation, and died a drunken wretch, in A. D. 1041, after a short and uneventful reign of two years.

The ill conduct of Harold Harefoot and Hardicanute had disgusted the English people with the Danish kings, and they therefore determined to restore the Saxon dynasty.

Accordingly EDWARD THE CONFESSOR, the only surviving son of Ethelred the Unready and Emma, was proclaimed King of England. Being of a timid and unambitious disposition, Edward the Confessor did not desire to be king, but finally yielded to the solicitations of Earl Godwin, then the most powerful subject in the English kingdom.

The restoration of the Saxon dynasty was hailed with enthusiastic joy throughout England, and was for a long time celebrated by an annual festival called *Hokeday*. Says the old Saxon chronicle: "Before Harold, King, buried were, all folk chose Edward to king at London." Edward the Confessor married Edgitha, daughter of Earl Godwin. He abolished the tax called *Dane-gelt*, first imposed by King Ethelred the Unready to raise money to bribe the Danes to withdraw from England.

The joy of the English people at the restoration of their Saxon kings was soon clouded by disappointment. Edward the Confessor had been brought up in Normandy, and had many favorites among the Normans. He loved the land of his education and early years better than that which he was called upon to govern. He conferred most of the high offices in the Church and about his court on his Norman favorites, who despised the civil freedom and sneered at the barbarous language and manners of the English. These Normans were unable to understand a government in which every

KNIGHT OF ST. JOHN.

LADIES OF THE ORDER OF ST. JOHN.

KNIGHTS TEMPLAR.

SUPERIOR OF THE ORDER OF GERMAN KNIGHTS.
BROTHER-OF-THE-SWORD (SCHWERTBRUDER).

THE RELIGIOUS ORDER OF KNIGHTHOOD.

churl might have his place in the great council of the nation, and under which the poorest man's hut was as inviolable as the earl's castle.

Edward the Confessor also introduced the Norman fashion of wearing loose trowsers, and substituted the Norman title of *baron* for the old Anglo-Saxon word *thane*. The English nobles, particularly Earl Godwin, were highly offended at the king's partiality for the Normans.

The hostile feeling between the king's Norman favorites and the English came to a violent outbreak when Eustace, Count of Boulogne, a great Norman lord from over the Channel, came to visit his brother-in-law, King Edward the Confessor, with a large retinue. Returning through Dover, the count's followers endeavored to force themselves into free quarters in the houses of the citizens. The master of one house lost his life in defending his home, and the entire city rose in tumult to avenge his death. In the conflict that ensued, almost forty persons were killed on both sides.

The angry count, hastening back to King Edward the Confessor, complained bitterly of the insult to his dignity and demanded the punishment of the offenders. The king at once ordered a military execution, with all the horrors of fire and sword; but Earl Godwin, who was Governor of Dover, refused to execute the sentence, telling Count Eustace that law, not violence, was supreme in England, and that if he brought his complaint into a court of justice all who were guilty would certainly be punished.

For thus defending his countrymen, Earl Godwin and his four sons were banished from England; and their governments, embracing one-third of all the kingdom, were conferred on others. Their private estates were confiscated; and even Edward's queen, who was a daughter of Godwin, was imprisoned in a convent. Nothing remained to oppose the Norman party at court; and within a few months, William II., Duke of Normandy, came with a great retinue to visit the English king. The Norman duke was received with great honors, and conducted himself in such a manner as to win Edward's confidence and good will. It was believed that at this meeting King Edward the Confessor, who was childless, promised to recommend his Norman cousin to the Witenagemote, or "Meeting of the Wise Men," as a candidate for the crown of England.

But Earl Godwin was still remembered by the English people as their champion, and he also had powerful friends abroad. His son Harold raised a squadron in Ireland, while Godwin collected a still larger fleet in the ports of Flanders. Both united their forces at the Isle of Wight, and sailed to London, followed along the coast by a constantly increasing multitude of supporters, who expressed their resolution to live or die with the great earl. The king's levies stood on the north bank of the Thames; but Godwin's army, summoned only by his own will, crowded the southern bank. The earl held back his forces; as he said that he would rather die than do or permit any irreverent act toward his lord the king.

The Witenagemote, now summoned to decide whether England should be governed by native or foreign rulers, assembled in arms outside the walls of London. Godwin took his place in the assembly with his four brave sons. He knelt and laid his battle-ax at the king's feet; then rose and requested permission to defend himself against the unjust charges which had been brought against himself and his house. His short but eloquent speech was received with shouts of approval. The voice of his countrymen pronounced him innocent, and decreed that all the honors and estates of which he, his sons and followers, had been deprived be restored to them. The queen was brought back from her convent, and resumed her true place in the court.

All the Norman-French in England were declared outlaws, because they had given the king bad advice and had brought unrighteous judgments into the kingdom. A third decree restored the "good laws" of Edward the Confessor's earlier days. When it was first decided to submit Godwin's cause to the votes of a free people, and not to the sword, the Norman bishops, priests and knights, who had been preying upon the English nation, took horse and fled from the kingdom. Even the Primate relinquished his holy office and sought refuge beyond the Channel. A better day dawned upon England when her own best men acquired the direction of her destinies, but Earl Godwin did not live long to enjoy his honors. His son Harold succeeded him in all his dignities, and became more popular than his renowned father, his noble qualities having already won the confidence of the king and the people.

Under Harold's ministry the Witenagemote ordered an English invasion of Scotland; and this invasion was executed by Siward, Earl of Northumberland, a chief of extraordinary strength and courage, one of whose ancestors was reputed to have been a Norwegian bear. Macbeth, Thane of Moray, had murdered his kinsman, Duncan, and usurped the Scottish throne. But Duncan's son, Malcolm III., surnamed Canmore, now asserted his rights, and Earl Siward's victory elevated him to the throne of his ancestors. Macbeth lost his life in battle four years afterward.

Malcolm Canmore had passed fifteen years in exile at the court of Edward the Confessor, where he relinquished his Gaelic, or Celtic, speech and costume, and acquired that foreign culture which ever afterward prevailed in the Scottish government, however odious it may have been to the Scottish people for a time. The history of Malcolm Canmore was much like that of his patron and over-lord. Both passed their youth in exile—Edward the Confessor in Normandy, and Malcolm Canmore in England; and each exchanged his native language, tastes and habits for those of more cultivated nations.

Edward the Confessor, advancing in years and having no son, sent to Hungary for his nephew, the only surviving son of Edmund Ironside; but the prince died a few days after his arrival in England, leaving his son Edgar, with two sisters, as the only remaining descendants of Cerdic, the founder of Wessex and the ancestor of Egbert.

Edgar the Atheling was a feeble child, and it was then thought necessary that a King of England should be born and bred in his kingdom. The Witenagemote was therefore obliged to seek another successor to the English throne, and they are believed to have chosen Harold, who, though claiming no descent from Odin, was the greatest living Englishman in all the mental and physical qualities befitting a king, as his illustrious father had been before him.

Since his father's death, Harold had been intrusted with the chief administration of the English government. He had conquered the Welsh and established the suzerainty of the English king over Scotland. His strong hand had maintained the honor and safety of England everywhere.

On one occasion, while cruising for pleasure in the English Channel, he had been shipwrecked upon the coast of Normandy; and, according to the barbarous custom of that time, he was seized and held for ransom ; but when Duke William of Normandy heard of Harold's capture he instantly ordered him to be released, and welcomed him at the Norman court with splendid hospitality.

Before being permitted to depart from Rouen, the capital of Normandy, Harold was obliged to enter into engagements with Duke William II., the nature of which is not exactly known. Some writers say that he promised to sustain Duke William's claims to the throne of England, and to give him possession of the castle and well of Dover, and of several other fortresses which Harold held under his oath of allegiance to King Edward the Confessor, even during the life of that monarch. But these statements are made by Harold's bitter enemies, who, after his death, sought in every possible way to blacken his memory, thus trying to make it appear that the life-long champion of English independence swore to betray his country to the Normans.

After returning to England, Harold, by his bravery and prudence, vastly increased his influence. His brother Tostig had been appointed Earl of Northumberland; but his merciless enforcement of justice in that distracted part of England enraged the people, who rose in rebellion, being assisted by Edwin and Morcar, grandsons of the former earl. Harold was sent to crush the revolt; but when he discovered that some of the charges against his brother were well founded, he persuaded King Edward the Confessor to confirm Morcar in the possession of the earldom of Northumberland. Harold likewise obtained the government of Mercia for Edwin, Morcar's brother; and he married their sister, widow of the Welsh prince, Griffith, whom he had conquered.

King Edward the Confessor died January 5, 1066. On his death-bed he extended his hand to Harold, saying: "To thee, Harold, my brother, I commit my kingdom." Notwithstanding his weakness and errors, Edward was dearly loved by his subjects; and the later sovereigns of England were well aware that the surest way to gain the popular favor was to promise the enforcement of the laws.

Edward the Confessor was the first English monarch who was believed to be able to cure scrofula by the touch of his hand, and for that reason that dreadful disease was called *King's Evil*. About a century after his death he was canonized as a saint, and for that reason he is called *the Confessor*. He was buried in the West Minster, a magnificent church which had been dedicated to St. Peter a few days before; the building of which had mainly occupied his later years. This splendid church is the historic Westminster Abbey, the burial-place of England's renowned heroes and statesmen.

The English princes are buried at Windsor. The tomb of Edward the Confessor is among the most imposing objects of Westminster Abbey, and near it is the stone chair in which every English sovereign sits at his coronation.

On the very day of the burial of Edward the Confessor, HAROLD II. was crowned King of England. A memorable year thus opened with these ceremonies. Before this year (A. D. 1066) had ended, England had suffered two great invasions, one from the north and the other from the south, had raised and maintained greater fleets and armies than she had seen before, and finally submitted to the yoke of a foreign conqueror.

Tostig, Harold's brother, was a traitor to his kinsman and his country. He instigated Harald Hardrada, King of Norway, to invade England and make that country the seat of a great Scandinavian empire like that of Canute the Great. With a fleet larger than any that had ever before issued from any Northern port, joined by ships from Iceland, the Orkney's, Scotland, Flanders, and the Danish settlements in Ireland, the Norwegian king sailed southward along the eastern shores of England, burned Scarborough and Holderness, landed on the coast and defeated the English under Edwin and Morcar in a desperate battle near York. That city opened its gates to the Norwegian invader before King Harold of England could come to its rescue. He had left the defense of the northern counties of England to their own earls, while he himself watched the southern coast, where the Norman invasion was expected. But when he was informed of the defeat of Edwin and Morcar, he marched northward with the utmost haste.

King Harold of England encountered King Harald Hardrada of Norway at Stamford Bridge, in Yorkshire, September 25, A. D. 1066. When the hostile armies were drawn up in battle array, the English king offered his brother Tostig wealth and a part of his kingdom if he retired from the struggle. Tostig asked: "If I accept these terms, what will you give my ally, the King of Norway?" Harold replied: "Seven feet of English soil, or, as he is very tall, perhaps a little more." This ended the conference; and the battle which followed lasted all day, Tostig and Harald Hardrada being defeated and both slain. In the midst of a banquet held at York in honor of this victory, King Harold of England received tidings that Duke William II. of Normandy had landed in Sussex with a formidable army.

Duke William heard of the death of Edward the Confessor and the accession of Harold while hunting in the park near Rouen, and he was instantly seized with ungovernable rage. He immediately sent an embassy summoning Harold to relinquish the crown of England. Harold indignantly refused to do so, and even banished from England all the Normans who had been growing wealthy in English offices and estates through the favor of Edward the Confessor. Duke William II. was neither displeased nor disappointed, as Harold's defiant response opened the way for the movement which the Norman duke had long in contemplation.

William collected an army of sixty thousand knights from the chivalry of Normandy, and soon had a fleet of almost a thousand vessels prepared to transport this army across the Channel into England. Pope Alexander II. blessed and encouraged the enterprise, on condition that England, when conquered, should be held as a fief of St. Peter. The great battle which was to decide the fate of England was fought at Senlac, nine miles from the seaport of Hastings, in Sussex, October 14, A. D. 1066. King Harold fought on foot at the head of his infantry; but his best soldiers had perished in the campaign against King Harald Hardrada of Norway, and the rest were wearied with forced marches, while the Normans were fresh and confident.

The Pope's intervention on the side of the Norman duke disheartened the English, who had endeavored to drown their terrors during the night before the battle by revelry which did not have the effect of making their hands more steady or their hearts stronger. Both sides, however, fought with a bravery worthy of the prize for which they were contending, and the battle raged furiously from morn till eve. At one time a cry arose that the Duke of Normandy was slain, and his troops gave away in almost every part of the field; but William, galloping bare-headed over the sanguinary field, finally succeeded in rallying his panic-stricken followers.

Finally Harold was struck in one eye with an arrow and fell dead from his horse, while his two brothers were likewise slain, and the English ranks were broken. The scattered hosts were pursued with terrific slaughter, and the Duke of Normandy held possession of the bloody field. The Pope's consecrated banner took the place of Harold's standard; and on the same spot the Norman Conqueror erected the altar of a magnificent abbey, that perpetual prayers might be offered for the repose of the souls that had passed away in that terrible conflict.

After the battle of Hastings the important towns of Dover, Canterbury and Winchester readily surrendered to William the Conqueror. Earls Morcar and Edwin, along with Stigand, Archbishop of Canterbury, endeavored to crown Edgar the Atheling at London; but the Northern earls had plans of their own more important to them than the defense of their native land against the triumphant arms of a foreign conqueror. They withdrew their forces; and Edgar the Atheling, the young king-elect, with most of his adherents, hastened to the Conqueror's camp and tendered their submission. The leading men in the South of England —churchmen and statesmen—seeing no further hope of successful resistance, solicited the triumphant Duke of Normandy to accept the English crown; hoping that the holy office of anointing and coronation would effect as great a change in the Norman Conqueror as it had in Canute the Great half a century before, and thus convert the stern invader into a wise and beneficent monarch.

The crowning of WILLIAM THE CONQUEROR at Westminster Abbey, on Christmas Day, A. D. 1066, completed the *Norman Conquest* of England. The native Anglo-Saxon monarchy was forever ended, and the whole destiny of England was changed, in consequence of the result of the battle of Hastings, which was thus one of the most important battles in all history.

The Norman Conquest of England was more than the mere substitution of a foreign dynasty for the native Saxon kings, as the Conqueror stamped the impress of his race up-

EDITH FINDING THE DEAD BODY OF HAROLD.

on the English nation and gave it a new direction by ingrafting the Norman character and institutions upon the old Anglo-Saxon civilization.

Having sketched the political history of Anglo-Saxon England up to the time of the Norman Conquest, we will now take a brief view of the social life of the English people before they were reduced under the dominion of a foreign king and became subject to foreign laws and customs. By this time the Saxon and Danish sea-rovers had settled into orderly people, tilling the soil, working the mines and conducting an active commerce with the European Continent. English women were celebrated for their embroidery in gold thread, which was highly valued in the cities of France and Flanders.

The houses of the English were low wooden structures, with a hole in the roof instead of a chimney, and with wooden benches for chairs. A few very wealthy men had glass in their windows; but none had carpets, though the walls were frequently covered with elegantly embroidered tapestry.

The tunic which the men wore was bound in round the waist with a belt, and generally extended no lower than the knees, only kings and nobles wearing them down to the feet. People of rank wore over this tunic a short tunic, or *surcoat*, made of silk and elegantly embroidered and ornamented. The rich wore a linen shirt, shaped much like a modern shirt. The poor wore no shirt, and had only a tunic made of coarse cloth. The slaves wore an iron collar around the neck, and were clad in tunics open at the sides.

The pictures of the Anglo-Saxons generally represent them as having gone bare-headed; though they occasionally wore fur caps. The hair was parted in the middle, and hung down over the shoulders in waving ringlets. No mustache was worn; and the beard was shaven on the top of the chin, the rest of it growing long and being kept very smooth, and usually being divided in the middle and hanging down in two points.

The ladies wore a linen under-dress with long tight sleeves, and over this dress a wide robe or gown, fastened round the waist by a belt, and long enough to conceal the feet. The head-dress was a square piece of linen or silk, so put on as to conceal the hair and neck, and showing only the face.

The old historians write about their curls and crisping-pins, but their pictures show us nothing but the face peeping through the folds of their *cover-chief*. While the men among the Anglo-Saxons were constantly adopting new fashions, the women made little or no change in their styles of dress for three centuries.

Both sexes wore mantles, more or less splendid, according to their rank; also a profusion of gold ornaments, fringes and bracelets. The stockings of the Anglo-Saxon beaux were of gay colors, often red and blue. At one time they cross-gartered their legs, as the Scotch Highlanders still do.

The Anglo-Saxon nobles spent most of their revenues in giving great feasts to their friends and followers. These feasts were more remarkable for their abundance than for their elegance. The meat was usually dressed by boiling. The Anglo-Saxons do not seem to have had grate or fire-places, but made a fire on the ground, and placed a kettle over it.

At these feasts they sat on long benches, at large square tables, and every person took his place according to his rank. But if any one took a higher place than that to which he was entitled, he was degraded to the bottom of the table, and all the company were at liberty to pelt him with bones.

These tables were set out with exceeding nicety, and were covered with clean table-linen. Every person had a separate drinking-horn, there being no glasses. They had knives and wooden spoons, but no forks.

As before remarked, the Anglo-Saxons were very ignorant, being able neither to read nor to write. Besides feasting, hunting and fighting, they passed their time in other ways. In rainy weather and winter evenings they played with their dogs, sharpened their arrows and brightened their spears.

Anybody who was able to sing a song, to play on a harp or to relate an amusing story was much courted and valued; and this caused some people to make it their business to learn all these accomplishments. These persons were called *gleemen*, now generally styled minstrels, and were in the habit of roving about the country, from house to house and from castle to castle, singing their songs and telling their stories, which were usually in verse. Everybody made these gleemen welcome, and was glad to see them.

Even in war times, when it was dangerous for other people to travel, the gleeman went everywhere without being molested; as no one would hurt a poor gleeman, who was always so pleasant and so entertaining a guest. Alfred the Great visited the Danish camp in the character of a gleeman.

Sometimes the Anglo-Saxons amused themselves by playing back-gammon, which was invented by the Welsh, who so named it from two words in their language, *back cammon*, or little battle.

The relations between the nobles and the common people underwent some important changes under the later Saxon kings. Many free land-holders, unable to maintain their independence, attached themselves to powerful lords, engaging to follow them in war, and sealing the agreement by the ceremony of *homage*. The vassal knelt before his new master, thus promising to be "*his man* for life and limb." The same ceremony was repeated, with greater magnificence, when the King of Scots did homage to Edgar the Peaceable or Edward the Confessor for his earldoms of Cumbria and Lothian, or when the great Duke of Normandy rendered princely fealty to the King of France.

SECTION XVIII.—RISE OF THE GERMANO-ROMAN EMPIRE.

 N THE death of Louis the Child, the last Carlovingian sovereign of Germany, in A. D. 911, the Dukes of Franconia, Saxony, Suabia, Bavaria and Lorraine elected Duke Conrad of Franconia to the dignity of King of Germany, a prince well adapted to the government of a great people. Germany thus became an elective monarchy, and so remained until 1806.

CONRAD I. spent his reign of seven years in the field, repressing the incursions of the barbarous Hungarians into Germany. His authority was disputed by some of the more powerful nobles or princes of Germany, particularly by Henry, Duke of Saxony. In A. D. 918 Conrad I. received a mortal wound in a war with the Bavarians, and on his death-bed he advised the nobles to confer the German crown on his old antagonist, Henry of Saxony, whom he regarded as most worthy of it.

In accordance with the avowed wish of Conrad I., the Dukes of Franconia, Saxony, Suabia, Bavaria and Lorraine, elected HENRY I. to the office of King of Germany. He is usually called HENRY THE FOWLER, from a tradition that the messengers who brought him the tidings of his election found him hunting among the Hartz mountains with his falcons. His election was at first opposed by the Dukes of Bavaria and Suabia, but they were at length obliged to submit.

Henry the Fowler was the first of five successive Saxon Kings of Germany, who occupied the German throne for a little over a century (A. D. 918–1024). He was the wisest and most vigorous sovereign that had reigned over Germany since the time of Charlemagne. Soon after his accession the Hungarians renewed their invasions of Germany. In A. D. 924 Henry captured one of their leaders; and, in order to obtain his release, the Hungarians agreed to cease their incursions for nine years, on condition that the German monarch should pay them tribute.

After this truce Henry the Fowler seized Lotharingia, or Lorraine, which had consti-

MAP OF EUROPE A.D. 1000 By I. S. Clare

tuted a part of France, and gave it to a duke who held it as a fief of the German crown. As such it formed a part of the German kingdom many centuries. Henry likewise conducted several wars against the Slavonians. He forced the Duke of Bohemia to become his vassal, and subdued the Wends, who occupied the region to the north-east of Germany.

When the nine years' truce with the Hungarians had expired they renewed their inroads; but Henry the Fowler had occupied the interval in making preparations to resist them, and he defeated them so severely in a great battle at Merseburg, in A. D. 933, that they did not molest Germany again during his reign. Henry's grateful subjects bestowed upon their able sovereign the honored title of "*Father of the Fatherland.*"

After his great victory over the Hungarians at Merseburg, Henry the Fowler took the field against the Danes, who had invaded Saxony and Friesland, compelled them to retreat into their own country, and wrested from them the territory between the Eider and the Schlei, which in modern times constituted the duchy of Holstein.

Henry's internal administration was as successful as were his wars with the neighboring nations. He reorganized the German armies; and by training the nobles and their vassals to fight as cavalry he placed his army in a condition to fight the wild Hungarians on equal terms and to defeat them. Appreciating the importance of towns as places of defense and refuge for his subjects against such a barbarous foe as the Hungarians, he fortified the towns already existing with strong walls, and founded new towns which he likewise fortified. He also caused numerous fortresses to be erected at important points, and towns gradually grew up around these citadels.

Henry compelled every ninth freeman to reside in the nearest fortress or town as a builder or defender. The remaining eight freemen provided for his support and furnished the fortress with stores, by contributing one-third of their produce. All public meetings and festivities were required to be held in the towns, which were made the seats of the courts of justice. King Henry the Fowler endeavored to encourage the growth of the German towns in many ways, and the effect of his efforts continued for a long time after his death.

Thus Henry the Fowler became the founder of the *burghers*, a new class among the German people. The towns were naturally the centers of commerce, and the burghers became the trading class and the natural antagonists of the lawless nobles. Therefore, in the struggles which subsequently occurred between the nobles and the king, the burghers were the firm and useful supporters of the sovereign, thus rewarding the fostering care of Henry the Fowler. After making Germany the leading power of Europe, Henry sought to make himself Emperor, but this was prevented by his death, A. D. 936.

OTHO I., THE GREAT, the son of Henry the Fowler, was chosen by the German nobles to succeed his father on the throne of Germany. The new sovereign was twenty-four years of age at his accession, and had been married for several years to the princess Edith, the daughter of Edward the Elder, King of England, and therefore the granddaughter of Alfred the Great. The part which the great dukes took in the coronation ceremonies of Otho the Great showed the firmness of the royal power in Germany. The Duke of Lotharingia, or Lorraine, acted as chamberlain; the Duke of Franconia as carver; the Duke of Suabia as cupbearer; and the Duke of Bavaria as master of the horse.

Soon afterwards Thankmar, the king's half-brother, aided by the Dukes of Franconia and Lorraine, rebelled against Otho; but was slain in the early part of the struggle. Thereupon Henry, the king's full brother, who aspired to the German crown, headed the rebellion. Otho the Great fought valiantly for his throne, and finally crushed the revolt. Both of the rebel dukes—those of Franconia and Lorraine—were slain, and Prince Henry submitted and received his kingly brother's pardon.

3—23.-U. H.

In A. D. 945 the duchy of Bavaria became vacant, and King Otho the Great bestowed it upon his brother Henry, who atoned for his past rebellious behavior by his gallant attacks upon the Hungarians. Otho bestowed the duchy of Lorraine upon Count Conrad, who afterward married Luitgard, the king's only daughter. The German king retained the duchy of Franconia in his own possession. Upon the death of Hermann, Duke of Suabia, in A. D. 949, Otho conferred that duchy upon his own son Ludolf, who had married Hermann's daughter.

In this way all the great duchies came into the possession of the king and those who were immediately dependent upon him. Thus Otho the Great became more powerful than his ancestors had been, but he was not content to be king only in name. He was the real ruler of his dominions, and governed as well as reigned, having the power and ability to force his vassals to discharge their duties towards their suzerain.

Otho the Great was a great warrior as well as a vigorous ruler. He aided his brother-in-law, Louis d' Outremer, King of France, against Hugh the Great, Count of Paris, and William Long-sword, Duke of Normandy. The Danes had recovered the territory which Henry the Fowler had wrested from them; but Otho the Great drove them northward again and reoccupied the lands between the Eider and the Schlei, erecting the Mark of Schleswig for the defense of that part of the German frontier.

Otho the Great also compelled the Duke of Poland and King Harald Bluetooth of Denmark to become his vassals, and these two countries were considered fiefs of the German crown for the next two centuries. The German frontier was extended along the Baltic coast and between the middle Elbe and the Oder by the territory wrested from the Slavonians by the German generals. Otho the Great settled the territories which he and his generals conquered with German colonies, and made exertions to extend Christianity among the pagan tribes which were reduced under the German dominion. For this purpose he founded many bishoprics, among which was the archbishopric of Magdeburg, founded A. D. 968.

In A. D. 951 the attention of Otho the Great was called to Italy. The Italian king Beranger II. sought to force Adelaide, his predecessor Lothaire's young and beautiful widow, to marry his son Adalbert, and when she refused he cast her into prison and treated her with great cruelty. She made her escape, and appealed to Otho the Great, who was a chivalrous knight, for protection. Otho crossed the Alps, defeated Beranger, married Adelaide, and assumed the title of *King of the Lombards*, but allowed Beranger II. to retain the Italian crown as his vassal (A. D. 951).

Otho's son, Ludolf of Suabia, headed a new rebellion in Germany against his father, and was aided by Conrad of Lorraine, the Archbishop of Mayence, and others ; and Otho the Great suppressed the revolt only after a sharp struggle. He then made his brother Bruno, Archbishop of Cologne, Duke of Lorraine, and Burchard, the son-in-law of Henry of Bavaria, Duke of Suabia. Otho made his eldest son, William, who was already a priest, Archbishop of Mayence.

These troubles encouraged the Hungarians to undertake another invasion of Germany. They entered Bavaria in strong force in A. D. 955. Otho the Great marched against them and defeated them so disastrously at Lechfeld, near Augsburg, as to finally break their power and put an end to their invasions of Germany. But Otho's victory was very dearly purchased; as his son-in-law Conrad, who had sought by his gallant deeds to wipe out the disgrace of his former treason, and many others of the bravest of the German leaders, were among the slain. Thenceforth until the thirteenth century the Hungarian kings were nominally subject to the German sovereigns.

After years of violence and discontent in Italy, during which the Lombard nobles won the inveterate hostility of Pope John XII., whose infamous life had disgusted all Europe, the Pope urged Otho the Great to put an end to all disorders by assuming the

RISE OF THE GERMANO-ROMAN EMPIRE.

imperial crown. Otho went to Italy in the latter part of A. D. 961, after first securing the succession of his young son Otho by causing him to be crowned King of Germany at Aix la Chapelle. Otho the Great caused himself to be crowned King of Lombardy at Pavia with the Iron Crown of the Lombard kings, and was crowned Emperor by the Pope at Rome with the golden crown of the Roman Empire, February 2, A. D. 962.

The three German kings who had reigned just before Otho the Great had been neither Kings of Lombardy nor Emperors, but thenceforth the German sovereigns claimed both the Lombard and imperial crowns as their right. The Emperor was regarded as occupying a much higher and more important position than a mere feudal sovereign, and was therefore considered to be entitled to more perfect allegiance. Accordingly the Kings of Germany attached a much greater importance to their imperial than to their royal dignity.

Thus was founded the *Holy Roman Empire of the German Nation*, the name of which signifies the hold which it had upon the imaginations and affections of the people of Germany and Italy at that period. The Holy Roman Empire was at that time the leading power in Christendom. The Emperor, as King of Germany, was elected by the Diet of German princes, but he could receive the imperial crown from the Pope only.

The connection of the German kingdom with the Roman Empire was productive of many results in Germany. There had been very little truly national feeling among the Germans before the reign of Otho the Great. They only thought of themselves as Franks, Saxons, Suabians, Bavarians, Lotharingians, etc.; with scarcely any union as one people or nation. But when the German kings acquired the right to be crowned Roman Emperors, the German people themselves became the imperial nation. They accordingly began to take pride in the German name. A national sentiment was thus aroused, which the Germans never afterwards abandoned.

Nevertheless, taking all in all, Germany was no better off for its connection with the Empire. By being Emperors, the Kings of Germany became involved in struggles in which their native kingdom had no interest. They thus wasted much German blood and treasure, and lost almost all real power. While the German kings were absent from Germany, sometimes for years at a time, carrying on distant wars, their great vassals at home ruled as sovereign princes within their own respective dominions. When the kings returned and endeavored to assert their rights as feudal monarchs, they frequently discovered that they had spent almost their entire strength, and were able to do very little against a united and formidable aristocracy. Thus the development of Germany into a powerful centralized monarchy like England or France was prevented, and the German kingdom was ultimately divided into many practically independent small states.

Although Pope John XII. had urged Otho the Great to assume the imperial crown, he soon became his enemy. The Pope discovered that the Emperor was not content with an empty title. Enraged at the progress of the imperial authority, and by the Emperor's remonstrances against his vices, he took advantage of Otho's absence in pursuit of Beranger II. to enter into a secret alliance with Adalbert, the son of his old enemy, for the expulsion of the Germans from Italy; at the same time inviting the Hungarians to invade Germany.

Otho the Great received the news of the Pope's treachery with great indignation, and promptly returned to Rome, where he compelled the nobles and the people to renew their oath of allegiance. He then summoned a council, in which Pope John XII. was accused of the most scandalous immoralities, and when the Pope refused to appear before the council he was condemned as contumacious, after having been twice summoned in vain, and was then solemnly deposed, Leo VIII. being elected Pope in his place. Pope Leo VIII. was fully devoted to the German interests, and took an oath of obedience and fidelity to the Emperor. He even issued a bull ordaining that Otho the Great and his successors should be clothed with the right of appointing the Popes and investing bishops and archbishops, and that none should dare to consecrate a bishop without the Emperor's permission.

This fatal blow was unpopular with the bishops, who complained that Leo VIII. had subverted at one blow the structure which his predecessors had toiled for two centuries to raise. When the deposed Pope John XII. returned to Rome, after the Emperor's departure, he easily procured the deposition of Leo VIII. and the acknowledgment of his own claims. The restored Pope commenced to practice great crulties against his enemies, but in the midst of his career he was assassinated by a young noblemen whom he had rivaled in the affections of his mistress. This Pope's crimes had inspired such horror that many of the Romans believed that Satan in proper person had struck the fatal blow which sent John XII. to his final account, "with all his imperfections on his head."

The adherents of Pope John XII. still refused to acknowledge Leo VIII., and chose Benedict VI. as the successor of the murdered Pope, without consulting the Emperor. But the return of Otho the Great threw them into confusion. Benedict VI. hastily tendered his submission to Leo VIII., who banished him; and the Roman nobility and clergy promised the Emperor that they would never confer the papal dignity on any but a German.

On the death of Leo VIII. the papal electors, according to their promise, chose John XIII. to the Papacy, by the Emperor's permission. Pope John XIII. was too grateful to the German sovereign to resist the encroachments of the imperial power on the city of Rome and on the Church. The turbulent Romans revolted, and cast Pope John XIII. into prison; but Otho the Great soon came and suppressed these disturbances, restored John XIII. and severely punished the authors of the revolt. Thus the political system of the Papacy seemed utterly ruined. The Pope ruled the Roman states simply as the Emperor's viceroy, not as an independent sovereign; and, instead of being considered the supreme umpire of monarchs, he was reduced to the condition of a subject.

Otho the Great made an unsuccessful effort to annex Southern Italy to the Germano-Roman Empire, even going so far as to engage in war with the Eastern Roman Emperor Nicephorus Phocas for that purpose. Otho the Great spent his last years almost wholly in Italy. In A. D. 967 he caused his son, Otho II., to be crowned Emperor, and associated him in the government. In A. D. 972 Otho II. was married to Theophania, the daughter of the Eastern Roman Emperor Nicephorus Phocas. Otho the Great then returned to Germany, where he died A. D. 973.

OTHO II. was thus left sole Emperor, and King of Germany. He was nineteen years old at his father's death. As he had many of his father's best traits, it was expected that he would be a sovereign of more than ordinary merit, but this promise was blasted by his early death.

In the beginning of the reign of Otho II., Henry the Wrangler, Duke of Bavaria, and son of the Henry who had caused so much trouble to Otho the Great, rebelled against the new Emperor; but the revolt was easily suppressed, and Henry the Wrangler was deprived of his duchy and imprisoned. Harald Bluetooth, King of Denmark, then attempted to throw off his allegiance, as did also the Duke of Poland afterwards, but both were reduced to submission.

In A. D. 978 Lothaire, King of France, attempted to seize Lotharingia, or Lorraine, when Otho II. was at Aix la Chappelle. The French captured that city and almost took the Emperor prisoner. Otho II. then invaded France at the head of a large German army and encamped on the heights of Montmartre, before Paris; but that capital was too strongly defended to be taken, and the approach of winter obliged the German monarch to retreat back to Germany. A treaty of peace was finally made, by which the King of France relinquished all claim to Lorraine.

The death of the Emperor Otho the Great was the signal for new convulsions in Italy. The feudal lords aspired to independence; the cities endeavored to establish freedom; and Pope John XIII. sought to uphold the imperial cause, but was arrested by Cincius, the head of the popular party, and was strangled in prison.

Cincius and his faction chose Boniface VII. to the Papacy; while the aristocratic party, headed by the counts of Tuscany, elected Benedict VII. Boniface VII. was soon driven from Rome, and sought refuge at Constantinople, where he strenuously urged the Eastern Emperor to invade Italy. The Eastern Emperor accordingly espoused his cause, uniting with the Saracens in Southern Italy, and subduing Apulia and Calabria.

When Otho II. returned to Germany, Pope Boniface VII. came back to Italy, made himself master of Rome, and cast his rival, Benedict VII., into prison, where he was starved to death. Four months later Boniface VII. died suddenly, and was succeeded by John XV.

Otho II. was always more of an Italian than a German in his sympathies, and in A. D. 980 he went to Rome, never to return to Germany. He endeavored to carry out his father's policy toward Southern Italy, the conquest of which he attempted with the aid of the Lombard Duke of Benevento. But the Southern Italians formed an alliance with the Saracens, and severely defeated the forces of the Emperor Otho II. in the sanguinary battle of Crotona, A. D. 982 ; thus saving the Lombard Theme for the Eastern Emperor, whose power in Italy was vastly strengthened by this victory. Otho II. only escaped capture by his skill in swimming.

Upon the death of Otho's ally, Pandulf Ironhead, Duke of Benevento, that duchy fell into decay and finally broke up into many small states, most of which fell under the dominion of the Eastern Emperor. The Romans endeavored to recover their independent municipal government during the latter portion of the reign of Otho II., and set up a Consul named Crescentius, who forced Pope John XV. to acknowledge his authority.

The Emperor Otho II. died A. D. 982, and was succeeded as King of Germany by his infant son OTHO III., who had been solemnly proclaimed his father's successor by a Diet at Verona, in Northern Italy, before his father's death ; and the Empress Theophania was left regent for her infant son. Duke Henry of Bavaria attempted a revolution, but all the other great German nobles remained faithful to the infant Otho III., and the Bavarian duke gladly submitted upon condition of being left in possession of his duchy.

Theophania's regency was able and popular. The frontiers of the Empire were firmly maintained, and its internal affairs were wisely administered. The Empress-regent conferred the Mark of Austria upon Leopold I. of Babenberg, who extended his territories by subduing a part of the Hungarian dominions and colonizing it with German settlers. The Babenberg family continued to rule Austria until its extinction in the thirteenth century, when it was succeeded by the House of Hapsburg, which has ever since held sway there.

Otho III. was carefully educated by tutors selected for that purpose by his mother. The most celebrated of these instructors was the renowned Gerbert, Archbishop of Rheims, the most learned man of his time, under whom the young German king made such remarkable progress that his courtiers called him "The Wonder of the World." In A. D. 996, when he was scarcely sixteen, Otho III. proceeded to Rome at the head of a large German army, put an end to the Consular government, and was crowned Emperor by Gregory V., a German Pope, whom he had caused to be placed in the chair of St. Peter.

As soon as Otho III. had left Rome, Crescentius excited the city to revolt against the Emperor, set up a Greek as Antipope, and appealed to the Eastern Emperor for aid.

Otho III. promptly returned to Rome, deposed the Antipope and cruelly tortured him, and besieged the Castle of St. Angelo, in which Crescentius had taken refuge. The Emperor drew Crescentius from the castle by promising to accept his surrender, and then treacherously put him to death. Self government in Rome was now ended, and the imperial power was supreme.

Though the Emperor Otho III. was a German by race, he was an Italian in feelings and tastes. He even dreamed of reviving the ancient glories of the Roman Empire and of reigning as master of the world with Rome for his capital, but his ambitious schemes were ended by his early death. One of his last acts was the elevation of his preceptor Gerbert to the Papacy with the title of Sylvester II. Being the most profound scholar and the most daring thinker of his time, Pope Sylvester II. used his power in the interest of science and learning.

Concerning this renowned Pope, Mosheim says: "The genius of the famous pontiff was extensive and sublime, embracing all the branches of literature; but its more peculiar bent was turned toward mathematical studies. Mechanics, geometry, astronomy, arithmetic, and every other branch of knowledge that had the least affinity to these important sciences, were cultivated by this restorer of learning with the most ardent zeal, and not without success, as his writings abundantly testify; nor did he stop here, but employed every method that was proper to encourage and animate others to the culture of the liberal arts and sciences. The effects of this noble zeal were visible in Germany, France and Italy, both in this and in the following century; as by the writings, example and exhortations of Gerbert, many were incited to the study of physic, mathematics and philosophy, and in general to the pursuit of science in all its branches. If, indeed, we compare this learned pontiff to the mathematicians of modern times, his merit, in this point of view, will almost totally disappear under such a disadvantageous comparison; for his geometry, though it be easy and perspicuous, is merely elementary and superficial. Yet, such as it was, it was marvelous in an age of barbarism and darkness, and surpassed the apprehension of the pygmy philosophers, whose eyes, under the auspicious direction of Gerbert, were just beginning to open upon the light. Hence it was that the geometrical figures, described by this mathematical pontiff, were regarded by the monks as magical operations, and the pontiff himself was treated as a magician and a disciple of Satan."

The Emperor Otho III. was poisoned in A. D. 1002 by Stephania, the widow of Crescentius, who had suffered shameful treatment from the Germans. In accordance with his request, he was buried in the same tomb with Charlemagne at Aix la Chapelle; and when the tomb was opened the body of the great Frankish Emperor was seen sitting on its marble throne, clad in the imperial robes.

Otho III. was succeeded as King of Germany by Henry, Duke of Bavaria, who is known as HENRY II., THE SAINT; so surnamed on account of his love for the Church and the clergy, as particularly displayed in founding the cathedral and archbishopric of Bamberg. He was elected king in A. D. 1003; and, as a relative of his four immediate predecessors, he was the last of the five successive Saxon Kings of Germany. The great nobles had acquired a state of semi-independence, and Henry II. had great difficulty in making them acknowledge his accession, but he finally succeeded in doing so.

The Duke of Poland had renounced his allegiance to the German king, and had conquered Silesia and Bohemia, but was reduced to submission and compelled to do homage to Henry II. after a struggle of fourteen years, being also obliged to surrender Bohemia and Meissen. Nevertheless, Poland was but nominally dependent upon Germany; and after the death of Henry II., the Polish duke, Boleslas I., made himself King of Poland.

In A. D. 1004 King Henry II. became King of Italy, as well as of Germany; and in A. D. 1014 he was crowned Emperor at Rome by Pope Benedict VIII. He was a generous friend of the Church, and was afterwards canonized as a saint by the Pope, wherefore his title.

During the reign of Henry II. the title of the Kings of Germany, which had been that of *King of the East Franks and Saxons*, was changed to that of *King of the Romans*. The German king only became *Emperor of the Romans* when crowned by the Pope; but Henry II. chose the new title for the purpose of establishing the principle that the German king only had the right to the imperial crown. The condition of Germany had likewise undergone vast changes by this time, in consequence of the rapid growth of the towns which had arisen, mainly around cathedrals, monasteries, fortresses, and the castles of the great nobles.

Upon the death of Henry II. in A. D. 1024, Duke Conrad of Franconia was chosen King of Germany with the title of CONRAD II. He was the first of the four Frankish Kings of Germany, who in succession occupied the German throne for a century and a year (A. D. 1024-1125). Conrad II. was descended from the Conrad who had married a daughter of Otho the Great, being thus related to the Saxon dynasty. He was forty years of age at his accession, and his reign was marked by firmness and wisdom. He sought to strengthen the royal power by lessening that of the dukes, in which he succeeded very well. He made his son Henry, who gave promise of great ability, Duke of Bavaria, Suabia and Carinthia; thus drawing those duchies into an active support of the crown. Conrad II. was likewise a friend of the burgher class, and by favoring the cities he won the support of the citizens, who regarded him as their natural protector against the nobles.

In A. D. 1026 Conrad II. was crowned King of Italy, and the following year he was crowned Emperor at Rome by Pope John XIX., who bought the Papacy. In A. D. 1032 Conrad II. became King of Burgundy, the crown of that kingdom having been bequeathed to him by Rodolph III., whose niece, Gisela, was Conrad's wife. The crown of Burgundy thus became a legitimate possession of the German kings, but they were unable to assert their claims on account of their weakness, and the greater portion of the Burgundian kingdom passed into the possession of the Kings of France. Conrad's title to Burgundy was disputed by Duke Ernst of Suabia, who, considering himself the rightful heir to the Burgundian kingdom, because he was the son of Gisela by a former marriage, disputed Conrad's title to that kingdom; but the nobles refused to follow him, and he was imprisoned by Conrad II., who, however, afterwards liberated him.

Conrad's reign was marked by many wars. He crushed several rebellions of the Duke of Bohemia, repulsed an invasion by the Poles, and compelled the Polish king Micislas II. to do homage for his crown and to surrender Lusatia, which Henry II. had granted to Boleslas I. Conrad II. also conquered the Slavonic tribes on the Oder and the lower Elbe. King Stephen the Pious of Hungary attempted an invasion of Germany, but was defeated by Conrad's son Henry in A. D. 1031, and was forced to make peace.

In A. D. 1037 Conrad II. issued an edict decreeing that no holder of a fief should be deprived of his lands except by the judgment of his peers, thus making all fiefs in his dominions hereditary. At first this law was enforced only in Lombardy, but at length it was likewise extended to Germany. It was a great gain for the minor vassals, because it freed them from the power of their immediate lords to a great extent, and made them dependent upon the king for protection. Conrad II. founded the cathedral of Spire, where he and his successor were buried.

Conrad II. died in A. D. 1039, and was succeeded by his son, HENRY III., who had been crowned King of Germany and King of Burgundy during his father's life-time. Henry III. inherited many of his father's best qualities; and, by pursuing his father's policy of depressing the great German princes and nobles and protecting the lower vassals in their rights, he made himself the most powerful sovereign that Germany had since the reign of Charlemagne. He raised the Germano-Roman Empire to its height, and extended his suzerainty over Bohemia, Poland and Hungary.

Henry III. bestowed the duchies of Bavaria, Suabia and Carinthia upon men who were willing to hold them as his dependent vassals; having received these duchies from his father. He pursued a similar course with the duchy of Upper Lorraine, and defeated Gottfried, Duke of Lower Lorraine, who opposed him, and whom he compelled to retire into Italy.

Henry III. exerted himself earnestly to maintain peace and the reign of law in his dominions, and in A. D. 1043 he proclaimed a general peace throughout Germany. He enforced this decree and was successful in abolishing private wars among the nobles. He was a liberal patron of learning, and endeavored to reform the abuses of the Church for the purpose of fitting it for its great mission.

At this time the Church was steeped in corruption, from which there appeared to be no escape, and this corruption necessarily weakened the Church. The great cause of this weakness was simony, or the crime of buying and selling ecclesiastical preferment, which robbed the Church of its sanctity as a profession, and enabled the temporal power to interfere with its preferments. There was a secondary cause of weakness from an ecclesiastical standpoint—the marriage of the clergy—which prevented the priests from devoting themselves exclusively to the task of rendering the Church independent of the State and the most powerful body on earth, and which deprived the clergy of the semi-miraculous character which the most ascetic arrogated to themselves, and displayed them to the laity as only men. Simony was a real cause of corruption; the marriage of the clergy was an obstacle in the way of papal ambition.

When Pope Benedict VIII. crowned Henry II. Emperor he made him swear to remain faithful to him and his successors.

Henry III. sought to bring the Church up to its true position by treating the Popes as his dependents and by appointing German Popes, who would be free from the petty local jealousies of the Italians, and who would therefore devote their energies to the whole of Christendom.

The factions of the Roman nobles and citizens prevented the consolidation of the papal power; and three rival Popes, each remarkable for his scandalous life, at once shared the revenues of the Church between them (A. D. 1045); but these were finally induced to abdicate by John Gratian, a very pious and learned priest, who was then elected Pope with the title of Gregory VI. The Emperor Henry III. caused Gregory VI. to be deposed, and Clement II., a German, to be chosen to the Papacy.

The most remarkable of the deposed Popes was Benedict IX., who was the son of a Tuscan count, and who was raised to the Chair of St. Peter at the early age of ten years. His vices caused the Romans to raise rivals against him; but, as he was supported by the aristocratic faction, he would doubtless have held his place had he not been bribed to resign in favor of Gregory VI. The chief agent in these transactions was Hildebrand, a Tuscan monk, who had raised himself by the force of his own talents and by his reputation for piety to a high position in the Church, that of Archdeacon of Rome, and to a commanding influence in the Roman state.

Gregory VI. was undoubtedly a better ruler than his immediate predecessors. He expelled the robbers and freebooters who infested the roads around Rome; he opened a secure passage for the pilgrims who desired to visit the shrine of St. Peter; and he vigorously exerted himself to reform the administration of justice. Henry III. did an imprudent act in deposing such a Pope at the instigation of the enemies of order. The next Pope, Clement II., felt great aversion to the proceeding, and consented to his own elevation with the greatest reluctance. In A. D. 1046 Pope Clement II. crowned Henry III. Emperor.

HENRY III. OF GERMANY DEPOSES POPE SYLVESTER III.

RISE OF THE GERMANO-ROMAN EMPIRE.

To the great regret of the Italian people, and particularly the citizens of Rome, Gregory VI. and Hildebrand were driven into exile. They retired to the monastery of Clugni, where Gregory died of vexation, leaving Hildebrand the heir of his wealth and his resentment. Clement II. was poisoned by an emissary of Benedict IX., nine months after his consecration; and his successor, Damasus II., who was also elected Pope by the instrumentality of the Emperor Henry III., shared the same fate.

When Hildebrand was informed of these events he instantly started for the imperial court, hoping to have some influence in the nomination of the next Pope; but on the way he ascertained that the German Diet at Worms, under the Emperor's direction, had elected Bruno, Bishop of Toul, to the Chair of St. Peter, with the title of Leo IX.

Leo IX., who was a kinsman of the Emperor Henry III., commenced with vigor a reformation which was destined to accomplish more than Henry III. either desired or believed possible. In the end the Papacy became the powerful and relentless rival of the Empire, with both the will and the ability to inflict many humiliations and losses upon it. Leo IX. made an uncompromising war upon the practice of simony, for which no effort at defense was made, but it had become too universal a practice to be destroyed in a single reign.

The Emperor Henry III. engaged in several wars with the Hungarians, whose king he forced to do homage for his crown.

Henry III. died in A. D. 1056, in the fortieth year of his age; and his son, HENRY IV., then a child of six years, succeeded him as King of Germany. The young king's mother, Agnes, acted as regent, and her weak government enabled the great German nobles to recover almost all the power of which they had been deprived by Conrad II. and Henry III. In A. D. 1061 Hanno, Archbishop of Cologne, compelled Agnes to resign the regency, and obtained possession of the young king's person, with the design of making himself his guardian and the real ruler of Germany.

Adalbert, Archbishop of Bremen, a powerful prelate, who was jealous of Hanno, endeavored to take the young monarch from him, and ultimately was successful, as Henry IV. had a thorough dislike for the stern Hanno and a decided preference for the gay and lively Adalbert. But Adalbert was a bad preceptor, as the young king's education was neglected under him, so that he became imbued with low tastes, and grew up to be wayward and passionate. Adalbert taught Henry IV. to consider the German dukes his natural enemies, and implanted in him an inveterate animosity toward the Saxons.

In A. D. 1065 Henry IV. was declared of age, having reached the age of fifteen. He established his capital at Goslar, in Saxony, and retained Adalbert as his most trusted counselor. He commenced his reign by treating the Saxons with unnecessary harshness, and acted as if he designed annexing the duchy of Saxony to the royal lands. The next year the German princes forced Adalbert to leave the court, but Henry IV. persisted in the mistaken policy which he had inaugurated.

Queen Agnes had raised Otho of Nordheim, a powerful Saxon Count, to the position of Duke of Bavaria. Without just cause, Henry IV. deprived Otho of his duchy, bestowing it upon Guelf, son of the Margrave Azzo of Este, who had married a descendant of the ancient Bavarian dynasty of Guelf. Thereupon Otho commenced plotting with Magnus, the son and heir of the Duke of Saxony. The conspiracy failed, and both were imprisoned. Otho was soon released, but Henry IV. retained Magnus in captivity.

Upon the death of the Saxon duke, the Saxon nobles proceeded to Goslar and demanded that King Henry IV. should liberate their young duke. The king's refusal to comply with this demand produced a revolt of the Saxons, and in the civil war which ensued Henry IV. was at first defeated and driven from the Saxon territory. He took refuge in Worms, that city having remained faithful to him. Elated by their success, the Saxons indulged in a series of outrages which shocked the whole German nation and caused such a reaction that Henry IV. was soon enabled to take the field against them with a large army and to gain a decisive victory over them in a bloody battle on the Unstruth, near Langensalza, A. D. 1075.

Promises made to the Saxon rebels in the king's name induced them to submit; but Henry IV. soon violated these promises, displaced many of the Saxon nobles, and gave their lands to his own vassals. In strange contrast with this conduct, he restored to Otho of Nordheim his Saxon lands, and made him administrator of the duchy of Saxony, although Otho was his most relentless enemy.

King Henry IV. was very much mistaken in supposing that he had quieted the disturbances in his kingdom by this proceeding. The whole of Germany was pervaded by a feeling of profound discontent. Rudolf of Suabia, Otho of Nordheim, and a multitude of other enemies of the king were simply waiting for an opportunity to cast off the royal authority; and Henry's tyranny had left him few friends among any class of the German people.

We have now reached an important crisis in the struggle between the papal and the imperial power. The power of the Emperor had reached the zenith of its greatness, and was destined to fall by the dauntless energies of Hildebrand, the humble Tuscan monk, whose talent and whose position as minister of the Popes, and afterwards as Pope himself, made him the controller of the destinies of nations.

From the time of Leo IX. the Popes employed every means suggested by ambition to render their dominion complete and universal. They did not simply aspire to the character of supreme lawgivers in the Church, but asserted themselves to be the lords of the world, the arbiters of the fate of empires, supreme rulers over all Emperors, kings and princes; ruling as Christ's Vicegerents on earth.

The controlling spirit of the papal court was Hildebrand. He was a man of unyielding will and intense ambition, and conceived at an early day a plan that aimed not simply at reforming the Church of the abuses and corruptions which pervaded it, but of rendering the ecclesiastical power independent of and superior to the civil. With this object in view he laid down two principal rules, one that the clergy should not marry, and the other that no temporal prince should confer any ecclesiastical benefice, as was then generally the case in Germany, England and most other European countries.

There is no doubt that Hildebrand sincerely desired to bring the Church back to its primitive purity, and in this work he deserves the gratitude of all good men. But he blundered in not being satisfied with this reformation, and in aiming to render the civil power in all Europe subject to the will of the Bishop of Rome, and exalting the clergy, headed by the Pope, into a superior and independent body, placing them above and free from all obedience to the civil law, exempting them from taxation, and rendering them dependent only upon the Pope for their guidance and control.

During the reigns of Popes Leo IX., Victor II., Stephen IX., Benedict X., Nicholas II., and Alexander II.—embracing a period of a quarter of a century—Hildebrand was the controlling spirit of the Roman court. His haughty and aggressive policy pervaded the acts of these Popes and foreshadowed the bold career which he had marked out for himself when he became Pope, as he intended to be. While only Archdeacon of Rome he began his reforms, wisely seeking to constitute the clergy a compact and harmonious body dependent upon the Pope.

Leo IX., on whom the Emperor Henry III. had conferred the Papacy, was a Pope of virtuous principles and strict integrity, but he was a man of infirm purpose and weak in understanding. Hildebrand perceived the advantages that might be derived from the Pope's character, and in his first interview with Leo IX. he gained such an ascendency over the Pope's mind that thenceforth Leo IX. was simply a passive instrument in the power of his adviser.

Leo IX. naturally feared that the circumstance that he owed his nomination to the Emperor and his election to the German Diet would render him unpopular in Italy; but Hildebrand smoothed the way, and by his personal influence secured to Leo IX. a favorable reception at Rome. This service was rewarded by a multitude of dignities. Hildebrand soon united in his person the titles and offices of cardinal, sub-deacon, abbot of St. Paul, and keeper of the altar and treasury of St. Peter. The clergy and people of Rome applauded these proceedings, because Hildebrand had induced Leo IX. to gratify the national vanity by submitting to the form of a new election immediately after his arrival in the Eternal City.

Pope Leo IX. made unremitting exertions to reform the clergy and the monastic orders; but in the fifth year of his pontificate he marched against the Normans, who were ravaging Southern Italy, and was taken prisoner. Though the triumphant Normans showed every respect to the captive pontiff, the misfortune weighed heavily upon Leo's proud spirit, and his grief was aggravated by the reproaches of some of his clergy, who condemned him for desecrating his holy office by appearing in arms. The unfortunate Pope died of a broken heart soon after his release, and the deposed Benedict IX. seized the opportunity to recover the papal throne.

Hildebrand was opposed to the imperial influence, but he hated the nearer and more dangerous power of the Italian nobles more intensely, and therefore he became an active and energetic opponent of their creature, Benedict IX. The monks supported one whom they rightly considered the pride and ornament of their body, and by their means Hildebrand acquired such a commanding influence over the Roman people that he could rightly represent himself to the Emperor as their delegate in electing a new Pope.

The Emperor Henry III. nominated a German bishop to the papal dignity, who assumed the name of Victor II., and the cardinal-monk hoped to exercise the same authority under the new Pope that he had possessed under Leo IX. But Pope Victor II. soon became weary of having "a viceroy over him;" and he sent his ambitious minister into France with the title of legate, under the honorable pretext of correcting the abuses that had crept into the Church in that kingdom.

Hildebrand executed his task more rigorously than would have been prudent in a less popular minister. He excommunicated several immoral priests and bishops, and even sentenced some monks to death for a breach of their monastic vows. After a year's absence in France, Hildebrand returned to Rome more powerful than ever, and Pope Victor II. was willing to receive him as his chief counselor and minister.

Through the reigns of Victor II. and several of his successors, Hildebrand managed with consummate skill to make himself the trusted counselor, and practically the guide and master of each, pursuing with unflinching resolution the carefully matured design by which he intended to augment and strengthen the papal power. Nor was he entirely disinterested in this work, as his eye seems to have been fixed on the Chair of St. Peter from the beginning, and each step taken by him brought him nearer thereto. He aspired to be not merely Bishop of Rome, but he meant to be absolute Head of Christendom and to dictate to the world.

The death of the Emperor Henry III. and the accession of his infant son Henry IV. was a circumstance which Hildebrand was sagacious enough to perceive might prove advantageous to the papal power in its struggle with the imperial, and he made secret preparations for the contest. The death of Pope Victor II., speedily followed by that of his successor, Stephen IX., delayed Hildebrand's intentions, but did not alter them, as circumstances forced him to appear as an advocate of the imperial authority.

In the name of Pope Stephen IX., Hildebrand gave orders that the married priests should be displaced and separated from their wives, and exerted himself to incite the populace against the offending clergy. He succeeded so well in this task that in some instances the priests fe'' .ictims to the fanatical fury of the mo⊦ The virtues of celibacy were held ⋂ to popular admiration, and Hildebrand's invectives against marriage and the sanctity of a single life were listened to with delight.

The secular clergy were compelled to adopt the unsocial and demoralizing principles of the monks; and when all family affections were pronounced sinful, and the pastor's feelings concentrated on the interests of his profession, the Popes had secured, in the entire body of the Church, the implicit obedience and the absolute support which had hitherto been characteristic of the monks only.

On the death of Pope Stephen IX., the aristocratic faction, presuming upon the minority of Henry IV., rushed into the Vatican church with a body of armed men at night, and there proclaimed John, Bishop of Velitri, one of their own body, Pope, with the title of Benedict X. Hildebrand was informed of this when he was returning from Germany, the news being brought to him by the terrified cardinals and bishops who had fled from Rome. He assembled the fugitives at Sienna, and induced them to elect the Bishop of Florence to the Papacy with the title of Nicholas II. The sanction of the Emperor Henry IV. was easily obtained for the last-named Pope's election, and the imperial court was persuaded that in placing Nicholas II. on the papal throne it was supporting its own interests.

Circumstances soon occured which proved that the Germans had been deceived. Pope Nicholas II. convened a Church council at Rome, in which it was decreed that the cardinals only should in future have a voice in the election of the Pope; but to avoid any open breach with the Emoeror, a clause was added, reserving to him all due honor and respect. A proceeding less equivocal soon followed. The Normans who had settled in Southern Italy had become more amenable to the Church than they had been in the days of Pope Leo IX. The thirst for conquest had abated, and the Normans were now desirous of obtaining some security for their territories. They therefore tendered their alliance and their feudal allegiance to the Pope, on condition that he confirmed their titles. By Hildebrand's advice, Pope Nicholas II. conferred the principality of Capua on Richard Guiscard, and bestowed the title of duke on Robert Guiscard, with the investiture of all the lands that he had conquered, or might conquer, in Sicily, Apulia and Calabria.

The Pope willingly granted that to which he had no right—a proceeding which might have cost him dear if the Emperor Henry III. had been yet living. In return, the Normans gave the Pope their aid to punish his enemies in the Roman territory. The lands of the turbulent Roman aristocracy were cruelly ravaged; and the depopulation of the country around Rome even at the present day must be ascribed to the desolation wrought by the Normans on this occasion.

While Hildebrand was maturing his plans to reëstablish the Papacy, many circumstances occurred which proved the expediency of establishing a central controlling power in the Church. For almost two centuries the ecclesiastics of Milan had been independent of the Pope, and their Church had become the scandal of Italy. They openly sold benefices and flagrantly practiced immoralities, until at length a respectable part of the laity requested the Pope's interference. Peter Damian was sent to Milan as a papal legate; but the Milanese priests incited the populace to a formidable insurrection, and the infuriated mob threatened to murder the legate for menacing their independence. Undismayed by the threats made against him, Peter Damian ascended a pulpit in one of their principal churches and delivered such an effective discourse that the rioters submitted and encouraged him to pursue his investigation.

The legate's inquiry developed the fact that almost every priest in Milan had bought his preferment and lived with a concubine. After an obstinate resistance, the archbishop was induced to confess that he had transgressed the Church canons; but he was pardoned by the legate, on condition of swearing with his clergy to observe the ecclesiastical rules in the future. But no sooner had the legate departed from Milan than the clergy assailed the archbishop for betraying the rights of their Church, and forced him to retract the conditions to which he had so recently sworn. The troubles in Milan were renewed, and the profligacy of the clergy appeared to have been increased by the temporary interruption.

Before Pope Nicholas II. was able to make any effort to put an end to these disorders, he fell a victim to a fatal disease; and his death produced a great change in the political condition of Italy, as Hildebrand instigated the Church party to set both the Emperor and the aristocracy at defiance. Without waiting for the Emperor's sanction, the cardinals and bishops conferred the Papacy on Anselm, Bishop of Lucca, who assumed the title of Alexander II.; but the counts of Tuscany, hoping to recover the lands that had been wrested from them by the Normans, declared that they would sustain the Emperor's right of nomination. The Roman nobles had hitherto been indebted for their partial success to their support of a national prelate. They soon discovered that their strength had departed when they gave their assistance to a foreign competitor.

With the support of a German and Lombard army, Cadislaus, who had been chosen Pope by the German king, appeared before the gates of Rome; but the citizens refused to admit him. At first the imperialists obtained some advantages; but when Duke Godfrey arrived, with an auxiliary force of Normans, the fortunes of the war changed, and Cadislaus was forced to make a hasty retreat. He sought refuge in the Castle of St. Angelo, where he was closely besieged. Soon afterwards Henry IV., instigated by the Archbishops of Bremen and Cologne, recognized Alexander II. as the legitimate Pope; and Cadislaus, thus finding himself abandoned by his imperial protector, fled in disguise from the Castle of St. Angelo to his native diocese, where he died in obscurity.

During the brief pontificate of Alexander II., Hildebrand was the real ruler of the Church. As soon as the war with Cadislaus was ended, he directed his attention to the affairs of Milan, excommunicating the perjured archbishop, and ordering that all the priests who were married or who lived in concubinage should be ejected from their cures. With the support of the populace and a large body of the nobles, the papal legate enforced the decree against the marriage or concubinage of the priests, and made the clergy solemnly swear that in the future they would regard no election of bishop as valid unless it was confirmed by the Pope.

The excommunicated archbishop resigned his see, and sent the insignia of his office, the pastoral rod and ring, to the German king. Godfrey, a deacon of Milan, was appointed by the imperial council to fill the vacancy; but the citizens of Milan refused to receive him, and chose Atto, a nominee of the Pope, for their archbishop. A fierce war raged between the rival prelates; and Pope Alexander II., exasperated by the aid that the German sovereign gave to Godfrey, summoned that monarch to appear before his tribunal on a charge of simony and granting investitures without the Pope's approval.

But neither the cares nor the ambition of Pope Alexander II., or, more properly, of his instigator, Hildebrand, were restricted to Italy. By means of the popularity which the monkish orders had secured throughout Europe by their pretensions, Hildebrand established an interest for himself in every country of Christendom. His faithful agents kept a strict watch over the proceedings of King Henry IV.; papal legates were sent to Denmark and Norway; the allegiance of the King of Bohemia was secured by permission to wear the miter; and by the Norman Conquest of England, encouraged and sustained by Pope Alexander II. and Hildebrand, the virtual independence of the Anglo-Saxon Church was destroyed.

Although Hildebrand supported the Duke

of Normandy in conquering England and usurping its crown, he did not show the same favor to the Normans in Italy. With the aid of the forces of the Countess Matilda, a devoted adherent of the Church and an heiress to considerable territory, he compelled them to relinquish the territory which they had wrested from the Pope. Desirous of retaining this sovereignty, Hildebrand violently opposed a marriage between the countess and Godfrey Gobbo, a son whom her step-father had by a former wife, before his marriage with her mother. For this marriage Godfrey Gobbo was excommunicated, but Hildebrand secretly intimated that he might be reconciled to the Church by making proper submissions.

During the reign of Pope Alexander II. more had been done to extend the papal authority than during any previous pontificate; but this was wholly owing to Hildebrand, in whose hands Alexander II. was a mere instrument. To raise Hildebrand's fame, the monks published tales of the many miracles which he performed, and these stories were readily believed by the superstitious populace and tended greatly to extend Hildebrand's influence.

Upon the death of Pope Alexander II., in A. D. 1073, Hildebrand was elected Pope. Most of the statesmen in Christendom dreaded his accession to the Papacy, but none were willing to provoke his resentment by interfering to prevent his election. The irregular and precipitate manner in which he was chosen apparently shows that some opposition was dreaded by his partisans, and Hildebrand himself found it necessary to silence opposition by affecting submission to the Emperor. He wrote to Henry IV. that he had been chosen against his will, that he had no desire for the papal office, and that he would not be consecrated without the imperial sanction. Deceived by this hypocrisy, the German king ratified the irregular election, and Hildebrand ascended the papal throne with the title of Gregory VII. Thus began the reign of the greatest of all the Popes.

Pope Gregory VII. soon struck a decisive blow at simony, the abuse which he had been unable to reach in his subordinate position. In France and Germany the bishops were either nominated or confirmed by the sovereign, and in England by the Parliament. The parish priests and other clergy received their positions from the nobles. The ceremony by which these offices were conferred was styled *Investiture*. The practice frequently led to the purchase of the offices with money, so that they were often bestowed on incompetent persons.

Pope Gregory VII. was determined to put an end to this practice, denouncing it as simony; but as more than half of the lands in Germany had been granted to churchmen as feudal fiefs, it was very apparent that any effort to render these independent of the German king would strike a terrible blow at that sovereign. But the resolute Pope did not shrink from the task, as it was the first step in the undertaking by which he intended to bring the Emperor to his feet.

As soon as Gregory VII. was secure on the papal throne he began to put in execution his favorite plan for securing the independence of the Church by preventing lay interference in the collation of benefices. In less than a month after his election he sent a legate into Spain to reform the ecclesiastical abuses in that country, but chiefly to claim for the Church all the conquests that had been recently made from the Moors, under the pretense that before the Saracen conquest of Spain that country had been tributary to the successors of St. Peter.

King Henry IV. was so much daunted by this and other displays of the new Pope's vigor that he sent a submissive letter to Gregory VII., acknowledging his former errors in his dispute with the preceding Pope, ascribing these errors to his youth and to the influence of evil counselors, desiring the Pope to arrange the troubles in the Church of Milan at his pleasure, and promising to aid him in everything with the imperial authority.

The two great objects of Gregory VII. were the enforcement of the celibacy of the clergy and the papal right to the investiture of bishops. The enforcement of the celibacy of the clergy was a matter of discipline, defended on plausible grounds of expediency. The advocates of celibacy pleaded that a clergyman unencumbered with the cares of a family could devote his entire attention to the flock intrusted to his charge, and that a bishop without children would be free to exercise his patronage without being perverted by domestic affection.

The opponents of celibacy contended that men were thus forced to sacrifice the noblest and best of human feelings, that they were thus denaturalized and cut off from the influences of social life, that the Church became the country and the home of every person who embraced the ecclesiastical profession. After ordination the priest and the bishop were no longer Germans, Englishmen, Frenchmen, or Italians; they were Romans—ministers and peers of a mighty empire that claimed the dominion of the entire world.

Like the envoy or ambassador of any foreign government, a member of the Romish hierarchy obeys the laws of the state in which his master may have placed him, and for a time respects the local magistrate's authority; but his priestly order is his country, the Pope is his natural sovereign, and their welfare and their honor are the proper objects of his public care. The constant sight of such a sacrifice of the natural feelings of mankind was obviously calculated to gain the respect of the laity and to acquire credence for the superior sanctity that was believed to invest a priest's character.

The determination of Pope Gregory VII. to destroy the practice of lay investitures was defended on more plausible grounds. The administration of ecclesiastical patronage by the Emperor and other temporal sovereigns was liable to great abuses, and had actually led to many. These monarchs supplied vacancies with the ignorant, the depraved and the violent. When they had to appoint a bishop they sought for the qualifications of a soldier or a politician. In the Dark Ages, when monarchs and nobles were scarcely able to write their own names, when the knowledge of the alphabet even in aristocratic families was so rare as to be considered a spell against witchcraft, and when the fierce qualities of a warrior were esteemed more highly than the Christian virtues, it appeared almost necessary to render appointments in the Church independent of the state.

But to this obvious expediency Pope Gregory VII. added a claim of right as Christ's Vicar on earth and heir of his visible throne. However preposterous such claims may appear, Hildebrand deserves the credit of higher and purer motives than those of personal aggrandizement, mingling in his schemes for extending his own power and that of his successors. It cannot be denied that the corporate authority which he procured for the Church became a source of much benefit in many European countries during the Middle Ages, overawing the violent, protecting the forlorn, mitigating the prevailing ferocity of manners, and supplying the defects of civil institutions in various ways.

Gregory VII. assembled a general council of the Church at Rome, where he ordained, with the consent of the bishops present, that if any one should accept investiture from a layman, both the giver and the receiver should be excommunicated; that the prelates and nobles who advised the Emperor to claim the collation of benefices should be excommunicated; and that all married priests should dismiss their wives or be deposed. The Pope himself communicated these decrees to the sovereigns of Europe, in letters that fully attest his consummate abilities. His claims for the universal supremacy of the Church and of the Papacy were presented in a tone of humility and candor, well calculated to gain the support of the unthinking and the unwary. His dictations assume the form of affectionate suggestions, and his remonstrances resemble those of a tender and affectionate father.

But Gregory VII. did not confine his exertions simply to words. He forced the

Normans to relinquish their conquests in Campania; proposed a crusade against the Saracens, who were threatening Constantinople; and offered a province in Italy to Sweyn II., King of Denmark, under the pretense that the inhabitants were heretics.

King Henry IV. was not deceived by Hildebrand's professions. He hated the Pope in his very heart, and had good reason to believe that the animosity was reciprocal. He therefore beheld with mingled jealousy and indignation a new power established which surpassed his own, and he entered into a secret alliance with the Normans in Southern Italy against their common foe.

In the meantime a conspiracy was organized against the Pope in Rome itself by some of the aristocracy, whose privileges he had infringed upon. Cincius, the Prefect of the city, arrested Gregory VII. while he was celebrating mass on Christmas day, and cast him into prison; but the Roman populace soon forced the liberation of the great pontiff, and Cincius would have been torn to pieces by the indignant mob had it not been prevented by the Pope's own interference, all who participated in this act of violence being banished from the city.

Now came the great crisis in the struggle between the papal and the imperial power. Gregory VII. had waited for two years before breaking with King Henry IV. The wily Pope chose his opportunity sagaciously when the German king was engaged in a life and death struggle with the revolted Saxons. Thus, in A. D. 1075, while this fierce Saxon rebellion was in progress, Hildebrand addressed a haughty and imperious letter to Henry IV., commanding him to abstain from simony, and to discontinue the practice of investiture by the ring and cross, which he claimed were emblems of spiritual dignity, whose bestowal was inherent in the Pope only.

In this emergency the German king promised compliance with the Pope's demand, but upon the suppression of the Saxon rebellion he refused to be bound by his promise. This refusal brought matters to a crisis, and the resolute Pope determined to strike an effective blow. As the promise of King Henry IV. had been wrung from him while he was engaged in a life and death struggle with the Saxon rebels for the preservation of his crown, it was only natural that he should disregard it, not simply for this reason, but because most of the lands in Germany were held by churchmen, and had Gregory's wishes been carried out these spiritual princes would have owed allegiance to the Pope only.

Gregory VII. had an equally great interest at stake. If he humbled King Henry IV. he would not merely settle the question of investitures, but would establish the principle upon which he intended that the future policy of the Roman court should rest—that the Pope, as Christ's Vicar on earth, was above all earthly sovereigns and was entitled to give them laws.

In A. D. 1075, when Henry IV. refused to comply with the Pope's demands concerning investitures, Gregory VII. summoned the German king to appear before him at Rome to answer the charges which the Saxons and others had brought against him. Henry IV. was enraged at what he considered an act of priestly interference, and refused to comply with the Pope's order. He therefore convened a synod of the German bishops at Worms, in A. D. 1076, and caused sentence of deposition to be pronounced against Pope Gergory VII. on a charge of simony, murder and atheism.

Instead of being disheartened by the German king's violence, Pope Gregory VII. convened a council of the Church at Rome; solemnly excommunicated Henry IV.; declared him no longer King of Germany; absolved his subjects in Germany and Italy from their allegiance to him; deposed several prelates in Germany, France and Lombardy; and published a series of papal constitutions, in which the claims of the Popes to supremacy over all sovereigns were boldly avowed.

The most important of these claims, which constitute the basis of the political system of the Papacy, were:

That the Pope alone can be called universal.

That he alone has a right to depose bishops.

That his legates have a right to preside over all bishops assembled in a general council.

That the Pope can depose absent prelates.

That he alone has a right to use imperial ornaments.

That princes are bound to kiss his feet, and his only.

That he has a right to depose Emperors.

That no synod or council summoned without his commission can be called general.

That no book can be called canonical without his authority.

That his sentence can be annulled by none, but that he may annul the decrees of all.

That the Romish Church has been, is, and will continue, infallible.

That whoever dissents from the Romish Church ceases to be a catholic Christian.

And, that subjects may be absolved from their allegiance to wicked princes.

Some cautious prelates advised Gregory VII. not to be too hasty in excommunicating his sovereign; but the Pope made the following memorable reply to their remonstrances: "When Christ trusted his flock to St. Peter, saying, 'Find my sheep,' did he except kings? Or when he gave him the power to bind and loose, did he withdraw any one from his visitation? He, therefore, who says that he cannot be bound by the bonds of the Church, must confess that he cannot be absolved by it; and he who denies that doctrine, separates himself from Christ and his Church."

Henry IV. did not expect so bold a move on the part of the Pope. Both sides prepared for war, but all the advantages were on the side of Hildebrand. At the very beginning of the struggle, Gobbo, the most vigorous supporter of the Emperor, died; and his widow, the countess Matilda, placed all her resources at the Pope's disposal. So ardently did this princess espouse the interests of Gregory VII. that their mutual attachment was suspected of having transgressed the bounds of innocence. The Duke of Dalmatia, gratified by the title of king, and the Norman king of Sicily, proffered aid to the Pope; and even the Mohammedan sovereign of Morocco courted his favor by liberating the Christian slaves in his dominions.

Henry IV. did not know where to look for support. He had alienated all classes of his subjects by his tyranny, and their discontent was widespread and deep. The Pope very well knew that the German nobles would eagerly seize upon any pretext to rebel against their unpopular king. The result fully justified the Pope's expectations. In every quarter of the dominions of Henry IV.—in Germany and Italy—the monks preached against their sovereign and the prelates who sustained him. A few remained faithful to Henry IV., but the great majority sided with his foes, who openly accepted the papal sentence; and Germany was divided into two hostile factions. The Saxon nobles eagerly embraced a religious pretext to renew their rebellion, and the king's enemies throughout his dominions were glad to cloak their hatred of their sovereign under the guise of zeal for religion, while the Pope energetically fomented the rebellion.

Thus commenced the *War of Investitures*, which had a deep significance, being really a struggle between the Papacy and the Empire for supremacy. The Dukes of Suabia and Carinthia demanded a change of dynasty. Even the prelates who had been most zealous in instigating Henry IV. to defy the Pope, terrified by threats of excommunication, deserted his cause. The German princes and nobles who opposed their king met in a Diet at Tribur, attended by two papal legates, to depose Henry IV. and elect a new King of Germany. Realizing the extent of his danger, Henry IV. sought to influence the Diet, and was so far successful that it was agreed that he should be given a year in which to make his peace with the Pope, but if at the end of that time the papal sentence of excommunication was not removed a new king should be chosen.

The prelates and nobles of Lombardy alone maintained their courage, and boldly retorted the Pope's excommunications. Hoping to gain their efficient aid, Henry

IV. determined to cross the Alps, instead of waiting for the arrival of Gregory VII. in Germany. The hardships which the unfortunate monarch underwent during this journey, in the depth of a rigorous winter; the perils to which he was exposed from the malice of his enemies; the sight of the sufferings of his queen and child, who could only travel by being inclosed in the hides of oxen, and thus dragged through the Alpine passes—all this would have broken a sterner spirit than this king's.

Henry IV. entered Lombardy utterly disheartened, and he thought only of conciliating his powerful foe by submission. After obtaining a conference with the Countess Matilda, he persuaded her to intercede for him with the Pope; and her intercession, supported by the leading nobles of Italy, induced Gregory VII. to grant an interview to his sovereign.

Thus throwing himself upon Hildebrand's generosity, King Henry IV., on January 21, A. D. 1077, started for the castle of Canossa, where the Pope was then sojourning, with his devoted friend, the Countess Matilda. The German king was forced to submit to the greatest indignities ever heaped upon imperial majesty. He was forced to dismiss his attendants at the first barrier, and when he reached the second he was obliged to lay aside his imperial robes and assume the dress of a penitent. For three whole days he was compelled to stand barefooted and bareheaded, without tasting a mouthful of food, in the outer court of the castle, in the midst of one of the severest winters that had ever been known in Northern Italy, imploring God and the Pope for the pardon of his transgressions.

After undergoing this humiliation, Henry IV. was admitted into the haughty pontiff's presence, and only obtained the suspension of the excommunication, not its removal, notwithstanding all his submission; the Pope only promising that Henry IV. should be tried with justice for his "crimes," and if found innocent he should be restored to his throne, but if proven guilty he should be punished with the full rigor of Church law.

This harsh treatment sank deep into the German king's mind, and his hostility to the Pope was aggravated by Gregory's acceptance of a grant of the Countess Matilda's possessions for the use of the Church, which would legally revert to the Empire after her death. The reproaches of the Lombards also induced him to repent of his degradation, and he renewed the war with the Pope by a dishonorable attempt to arrest Gregory VII. and the Countess Matilda.

In the meantime the discontented nobles of Germany had convened a Diet at Fercheim, which deposed their humbled sovereign, and elected Duke Rudolf of Suabia to the dignity of King of Germany. This transaction greatly perplexed the Pope, who dared not declare against Henry IV., because he was powerful in Italy; and if he abandoned Rudolf he would ruin his own party in Germany. He therefore determined to remain neutral in the struggle, and in the meantime he directed his attention to the internal condition of the Church, which had been distracted for some time by the controversy concerning the eucharist.

No article of faith was better calculated to exalt the power of the priesthood than the doctrine of transubstantiation, as it represented them as daily working a miracle equally stupendous and mysterious. Though its nature was incomprehensible, this circumstance only increased the reverence with which it was regarded. It is not therefore surprising that the Romish priesthood has ever manifested intense zeal in defending an opinion which has so materially strengthened its influence. A celebrated French priest, Berenger of Tours, assailed this doctrine with ridicule and with argument; but in his eightieth year Berenger was induced by Gregory VII. to renounce his former opinions; and transubstantiation was generally accepted as an article of faith of the Romish Church.

In the meantime the war had been going on in Germany and Italy between the partisans of Henry IV. and those of his rival. Rudolf of Suabia. The pride of the Germans revolted at the indignity to which their

EMPEROR HENRY IV. A SUPPLIANT TO POPE GREGORY VII.

RISE OF THE GERMANO-ROMAN EMPIRE.

sovereign had been subjected, and they rallied to his support, enabling him to gain a victory over Rudolf. Lombardy, particularly Milan and Ravenna, remained faithful to Henry IV.; but the monks and the clergy everywhere sustained the Pope as the champion of their order against the secular power; and the common people also gave him their sympathy, as they regarded him as sprung from themselves, believing that he was seeking to free them from oppression.

The imperial party simply considered the Pope the greatest subject of the Emperor, invested by him with his bishopric and its possessions, in support of which view they cited the examples of Otho the Great and Henry III., who had judged, deposed and appointed Popes. The papal party claimed that the Pope was above all earthly sovereigns, as things spiritual are above things temporal, and reminded their antagonists that the coronation by the Pope alone could make a King of Germany an Emperor. The true cause of Henry's weakness was the discontent caused in Germany by his tyranny.

After the discontented German nobles had chosen Rudolf of Suabia to the German throne, in March, A. D. 1077, Henry IV. returned to Germany, where he was joined by a large party who had been exasperated by the shameful treatment to which the Pope had subjected him. The cities were particularly loyal to him. A victory gained by Rudolf over Henry at Mülhausen induced the Pope to depart from his cautious attitude of neutrality. Gregory VII. accordingly excommunicated Henry IV., and sent a golden crown to Rudolf.

The indignant Henry IV. thereupon summoned a council in the mountains of the Tyrol, pronounced the deposition of Gregory VII., and proclaimed Guibert, Archbishop of Ravenna, Pope. Thereupon Gregory VII. made peace with the Normans, and with their aid and that of the Countess Matilda he bade defiance to his enemies. But in the meantime Rudolf was defeated and slain in the battle of the Ulster, A. D. 1180; and Henry IV. forced the discontented party in Germany to submit to his authority, after which he led his victorious army across the Alps into Italy and turned his arms against the Pope.

Upon entering Lombardy the German king was received with great joy. The Countess Matilda vainly endeavored to check his advance, and her army was defeated near Mantua, while her capital, Florence, was threatened by Henry IV. The German king advanced to Rome and laid siege to the city, continuing the siege for three years, retiring every summer to avoid the heat, and returning again every winter.

The Pope's ally, Robert Guiscard, the Norman duke of Southern Italy, having invaded the dominion of the Eastern Emperor, the latter entered into an alliance with Henry IV. and supplied him with money. Robert Guiscard's absence in the East deprived Hildebrand of his ablest champion and allowed the German king to have his way in Italy. The imperial troops overran Tuscany, and many of the Countess Matilda's adherents deserted the papal cause.

Henry IV. carried the Leonine City, or the Vatican quarter of Rome, and forced the Pope to take refuge in the Castle of St. Angelo. Finally the city proper opened its gates to the German king, who thereupon took possession of Rome; and Guibert, Henry's Pope, was consecrated on Palm Sunday, A. D. 1084, with the title of Clement III. After his consecration, the new Pope crowned Henry IV. Emperor of the Romans.

Gregory VII., secure in the impregnable Castle of St. Angelo, still held out against Henry IV., but finally received help from Robert Guiscard, who returned from the East and led a large army towards Rome, consisting partly of Saracens from Sicily, who were the subjects of Roger, Robert Guiscard's brother. The Emperor Henry IV. retired from Rome upon the approach of the Norman leader, who entered the city without opposition, A. D. 1084.

A tumult which broke out among the citizens of Rome so enraged the Normans that they gave up the city to pillage, remorselessly sacking it and destroying the Cœlian quarter by fire. The triumphant Normans conducted Gregory VII. to the citadel of Salerno, where he fell a victim to a fatal disease, A. D. 1085; dying unconquered, and repeating with his last breath the excommunications which he had hurled against the Emperor Henry IV., the Antipope Clement III., and their adherents. He viewed his own conduct in the struggle with complacency, frequently boasting of the justice of his cause, and exclaiming: "I have loved righteousness and hated iniquity, and it is therefore I die an exile."

Thus died the great Hildebrand, the founder of the political system of the Papacy. The character of this remarkable man was formed by his age and developed by the circumstances surrounding him. He was the representative both of popery and democracy, principles seemingly inconsistent, but which have been frequently found in alliance in ancient, mediæval and modern times. He shielded the people with the sanctity of the Church. He gave stability to the Church with the strength of the people. He displayed abilities of the highest order, in the course of his long career as the secret and as the acknowledged ruler of the Papacy. He won the enthusiastic admiration of the multitude by his pretensions to ascetic piety. The soldiers considered him a brave warrior and a successful general. The higher ranks of the clergy yielded in the council to his fervid eloquence and political skill.

His very faults proved to be among the elements of his success. He was severe, vindictive and inexorable. He did not know forgiveness. None of his enemies could elude the patient search and the constant vigilance with which he pursued those against whom his wrath was directed. He was in the habit of witnessing the execution of those whom he condemned to death. The serenity of his countenance and the placidity of his manners while he presided over tortures and massacres was awful to contemplate. It is therefore not surprising that the power of this remarkable churchman should have swept over Christendom like a torrent, hurrying everything into the vortex of his new and wonderful politico-religious system.

The death of Gregory VII. did not end the struggle which he commenced, but only gave the Emperor Henry IV. a brief respite. The cardinals elected Victor III. as the great pontiff's successor in the Chair of St. Peter. The new Pope gained several advantages over the imperial party during his brief reign. The next Pope, Urban II., the friend and pupil of Hildebrand, began his pontificate by sending an encyclical letter to the Christian churches, declaring his intention to adhere to the political system of the great pontiff. With the support of the Normans, Urban II. entered Rome, and assembled a council of one hundred and fifteen bishops, in which the Emperor, the Antipope and their adherents were solemnly excommunicated. Urban II. also negotiated a marriage between Guelf, son of the Duke of Bavaria, a prominent leader of the imperial cause in Germany, and the Countess Matilda. From this union are descended the modern Dukes of Brunswick and Luneburg, and the present royal family of England.

The Emperor Henry IV. marched into Italy, and gained several important advantages, though vigorously opposed by Guelf; but the papal intrigues raised enemies against him in his own family. His eldest son, Conrad, rebelled and was crowned King of Italy by Urban II. This revolt obliged the Emperor Henry IV. to relinquish his recent acquisitions and to retire toward the Alps.

A Church council was convened at Placentia, where so many bishops assembled that no church was large enough to contain them, and they were obliged to deliberate in the open air. This council reënacted most of the decrees of Gregory VII., and organized the First Crusade, of which we shall speak hereafter. Paschal II., the successor of Urban II., also pursued Hildebrand's policy, and easily triumphed over the

RISE OF THE GERMANO-ROMAN EMPIRE.

Antipope, who died of a broken heart. Pope Paschal II. convened a Church council at Rome to consolidate the papal power, and procured the enactment of a new oath to be taken by all ranks of the clergy, by which they abjured all heresy, and promised implicit obedience to the Pope, to affirm what the holy and universal Church affirms, and to condemn what the Church condemns (A. D. 1104).

The Emperor Henry IV. had returned to Germany in A. D. 1085, and gave his personal attention to the war with the Saxons, who had set up two kings after the death of Rudolf of Suabia; but they now became weary of the war, and submitted to the Emperor in A. D. 1087. Henry IV. had learned wisdom in the bitter school of experience, and he now treated the Saxons with leniency, thus restoring peace to Germany for awhile.

In A. D. 1099 the Emperor Henry IV. caused his second son, Henry, to be crowned King of Germany, and the younger monarch took a solemn oath not to attempt to seize the government during his father's life-time. But in A. D. 1104 the younger Henry, instigated by Pope Paschal II., violated his solemn oath by rebelling against his father. The younger Henry gained the advantage of his father, treated him with great cruelty, and compelled him to sign his abdication from the German throne at Engelheim, in A. D. 1105.

The Duke of Lorraine endeavored to restore the aged Emperor, but Henry IV. died of a broken heart in A. D. 1106. Even after his death he was relentlessly pursued by the hostility of the Pope. The dead Emperor's body was denied Christian burial, and lay in a stone coffin in an unconsecrated chapel at Spire for five years. It was only in A. D. 1111, when the papal sentence of excommunication was removed, that the remains of Henry IV. were properly buried.

Though HENRY V., the new King of Germany, had profited by the Pope's aid during his rebellion against his father, he no sooner became king than he became as resolute a champion of the right of investiture as his father had been. The Pope still forbade ecclesiastics to receive investiture from the German king and even to take an oath of allegiance to him, but Henry proved to be a more formidable enemy to the Papacy than his unfortunate father had been. In A. D. 1111 he led an army to Rome, made Pope Paschall II. prisoner, and compelled the pontiff to crown him Emperor and to issue a bull securing to the Emperor the right of investiture.

Upon the Emperor's return to Germany, Pope Pachall II., influenced by the remonstrances of the cardinals, annulled his treaty with Henry V., renewed all his former demands, and permitted several provincial Church councils to excommunicate the Emperor. But the Pope did not ratify the sentence of excommunication until after the death of the Countess Matilda, when the disputes about her inheritance caused new animosities between the Empire and the Papacy.

Matilda bequeathed her extensive territories to the Pope; but the Emperor claimed them, and seized Tuscany, which he held until his death. The Popes did not relinquish their claims to Matilda's dominions, though they were unable to maintain them. Under Gelasius II. and Calixtus II., the successors of Paschal II., who pursued the same policy as their immediate predecessors, the war of investitures was renewed.

Finally, in A. D. 1122, the question of investitures was settled. A concordat, or treaty, was concluded at Worms—therefore called the *Concordat of Worms*—between the Emperor Henry V. and Pope Calixtus II.; the Emperor relinquishing the right of investiture by ring and staff, and granting to the clergy the right of free election; and the Pope consenting that the temporal possessions of the Church of Germany should be received from the Emperor—a concession which made the Church in Germany a National Church. The ring and crozier, the emblems of spiritual authority, were to be conferred by the Pope alone. The loss of Henry V. as Emperor of the Romans was his gain as King of Germany; but the greatest of all gains was that of the Pope, who became independent of the Emperor in everything, while the Emperor still received his crown from the Pope. The independence thus gained by the Papacy was the certain way to papal supremacy.

This settlement established peace between the Emperor and the Pope, but during the remainder of his reign Henry V. was engaged constantly in contests with his rebellious nobles, particularly in the North of Germany. Henry V. died in A. D. 1125, leaving no children, and thus ending the Frankish, or Franconian dynasty, which had occupied the German throne for a century and a year (A. D. 1024-1125).

LOTHAIRE, Duke of Saxony, was chosen by the German princes to succeed Henry V. on the throne of Germany; but his accession was resisted by the Hohenstaufens, Conrad and Frederick of Suabia; and in order to oppose them with success Lothaire made such concessions to the Church that Pope Innocent II., who crowned him Emperor, ventured to declare the new sovereign his vassal. Lothaire was supported by Duke Henry the Proud of Bavaria, who married the Emperor's daughter, and who received the duchy of Saxony and the Italian lands of the Countess Matilda, thus becoming the most powerful noble in Germany. In A. D. 1134 the Hohenstaufen princes, Conrad and Frederick of Suabia, submitted to the Emperor Lothaire, who died in A. D. 1138. Thus ended the period of the supremacy of the Germano-Roman Empire; while the ascendency of the Romish, or Latin Church, which continued during the Crusades, commenced.

SECTION XIX.—EMPIRE OF THE SELJUK TURKS.

N the eleventh century a new power arose in Western Asia, which swayed the destinies of that quarter of the world for about a century. This new power was the Seljuk Turks, who derived their name from SELJUK, a famous chief, who was obliged to leave the court of Bighoo Khan, the sovereign of the Turks of Kipzak, who inhabited the plains of Khozar. Seljuk and his followers emigrated from the steppes of Tartary to the plains of Bokhara, early in the eleventh century.

Seljuk died at a very advanced age; and his son Michael was known to Mahmoud of Ghizni, the celebrated Afghan conqueror of Persia and India, by whom he was greatly honored, and who is said to have persuaded him to cross the Oxus and settle in Khorassan. The first lands which this Turkish tribe received from the Ghiznivide dynasty were granted by Massoud, Mahmoud's successor, A. D. 1037. Massoud was obliged to enter into a treaty with the Seljuk Turks on account of his inability to oppose their progress. TOGRUL, the Turkish leader, assumed the title and state of a sovereign at Nishapur, in Khorassan.

From that point Togrul extended his conquests westward, encouraged thereto by the distracted condition of the dominions of the Khalif of Bagdad. Leaving his brother Daood in Khorassan, he advanced into the Persian province of Irak, which he subdued. He then marched against Bagdad, captured that city, and took the Khalif Al Kaymen prisoner. After this he led an expedition against Mosul and its vicinity, which he soon conquered; after which he returned to Bagdad in triumph, and was there received by Al Kaymen with great pomp.

We are told that the Turkish monarch approached the Commander of the Faithful on foot, accompanied by his nobles, who laid aside their arms and joined in the procession. The Khalif appeared with all the equipage of state that belonged to his high office, seated on a throne, which was concealed by a dark veil. The celebrated *bourda*, or black mantle, of the Abbássides, was thrown over his shoulder, while his right hand held Mohammed's staff.

Togrul kissed the ground, stood in a respectful posture for a short time, and was then led to the Khalif, near whom he was seated on a throne. His commission was then read, appointing him the lieutenant, or Vicegerent, of the Vicar of the Holy Prophet, and the lord of all the Mohammedans. He was invested with seven dresses, and seven slaves were bestowed upon him; this ceremony implying that he was appointed to rule the seven regions subject to the Khalif of Bagdad. A veil of gold stuff, scented with musk, was thrown over his head, on which were placed two crowns, one for Arabia and the other for Persia. Two swords were girt on his loins, to signify that he was ruler of the East and the West. This display satisfied the Khalif's pride, and the Turkish chieftain was pleased to receive a sanction for his conquests from the spiritual head of Islam, who was still considered by orthodox Moslems the only source of legitimate authority.

Togrul quickly subdued all Persia, and adopted measures to organize a permanent dominion in that country. He appears to have possessed all the good and bad qualities of a Tartar chieftain. He was violent in temper and insatiable of conquest, but was likewise distinguished for his courage, frankness and generosity. His family and tribe were converted to Islam when Seljuk first settled near Bokhara. The Khalif of Bagdad greeted Togrul on his first victories in Persia with the title of *Rukun u Deen*, "the Pillar of the Faith," and he seems to have promoted with zeal the religion which he professed. He erected many mosques, and patronized pious and learned men.

Togrul died A. D. 1063, and was succeeded by his nephew ALP ARSLAN, "the Conquering Lion," who was noted for his valor, generosity, and love of learning. The Mohammedan writers represent him as one of the best among Asiatic sovereigns, as he was certainly one of the most renowned. But he was a cruel persecutor of the Christians of Armenia, Georgia and Iberia, and such are the actions which the Mussulman historians describe as the most commendable. It was his custom to put a large iron collar—or, according to some writers, a horseshoe—as a mark of ignominy, on the back of every Christian who refused to renounce his religion and accept Islam. His invasion of Georgia, and the severities with which he treated the inhabitants of that country who manifested reluctance to embrace the Moslem faith, aroused the court of the Eastern Roman Emperor to a sense of its imminent peril from the Turkish armies, which had by this time advanced into Asia Minor as far west as Phrygia.

The Eastern Emperor Romanus Diogenes led his armies against the invaders, and by his skill and courage forced them back upon their frontier. Romanus Diogenes desired to improve his success, and marched into Armenia and Azerbijan. He encountered Alp Arslan near the village of Konongo, in Azerbijan. The Turkish monarch was confident in his own courage and that of his own army, but trembled at the thought of shedding Moslem blood, and offered liberal terms to the Eastern Roman Emperor.

The Mohammedan historians tell us that Romanus Diogenes ascribed Alp Arslan's moderation to a wrong cause, and insolently replied that he would listen to no terms unless the Turkish sovereign abandoned his camp to the Roman army and surrendered his capital, Rei, as a pledge of his sincere desire for peace.

When Alp Arslan heard this reply he prepared for action. Romanus Diogenes was confident of victory, and Alp Arslan resolved not to survive defeat. The Turkish monarch made a display of pious resignation by tying up his horse's tail and clothing himself in a white robe or shroud, perfumed with musk. He exchanged his bow and arrows for a cimeter and mace; while his conduct, his dress and his speeches proclaimed to every soldier that if he was unable to preserve his earthly dominion by a victory over the unbelievers he was determined to obtain a crown of martyrdom.

The troops of Romanus Diogenes began the engagement and were at first victorious; but the Emperor had led them too far, and when he desired to retreat to his camp his ranks were thrown into a panic by the cowardice and treachery of his followers. Alp Arslan took advantage of the crisis, and a general charge of his entire army completed the defeat of the Christian host. The Emperor Romanus Diogenes was wounded and taken prisoner by an obscure officer whom Alp Arslan at a general review on the morning of that day had threatened to disgrace on account of his mean and deformed appearance.

The illustrious prisoner was taken before the Turkish Sultan, who treated him with the greatest kindness and consideration. At their first conference, Alp Arslan asked his captive what he would have done if he had conquered. The haughty Romanus Diogenes answered: "I would have given thee many a stripe." This reply excited no anger in the conqueror, who simply smiled and asked the captive Emperor what he expected would be done to him. The Emperor replied: "If thou art cruel, put me to death; if vainglorious, load me with chains and drag me to thy capital; if generous, grant me my liberty."

Alp Arslan, being neither cruel nor vainglorious, released his distinguished prisoner, gave all his captives dresses of honor, and bestowed upon them every mark of respect and friendship. To requite these favors, Romanus Diogenes agreed to pay a large ransom and a fixed tribute annually; but he could never recover his throne, which had been usurped during his absence. Alp Arslan was preparing to restore the deposed Emperor to the Byzantine throne by force of arms, when he was informed that the unfortunate Romanus Diogenes had been imprisoned and put to death by his subjects.

After his triumph over the armies of the Eastern Empire, Alp Arslan determined on a still more arduous enterprise. He desired to establish the dominion of Seljuk's posterity over their native country, and he summoned his warriors to invade those immense regions whence their fathers had issued. His power now extended from Arabia to the Oxus, and his army consisted of two hundred thousand soldiers. He marched into Khorasm and subdued most of that country, after which he built a bridge over the Oxus and crossed that stream without opposition, but his proud career was now approaching its end.

Alp Arslan's operations in Khorasm had been prolonged by the resistance of a small fortress called *Berzem*, defended by a chief named Yusuf. Incensed that his grand designs should have been delayed by so contemptible a fortress, the Turkish Sultan, after taking it, ordered its gallant defender to appear before him, and reproached him for his insolence and obstinacy in resisting the Turkish army. Yusuf was provoked to a violent reply, and Alp Arslan so far forgot himself as to order his captive to be put to a cruel death. Thereupon Yusuf drew his dagger and attacked the Turkish Sultan. The guards rushed in; but Alp Arslan, who considered himself unrivaled for his skill in archery, seized his bow and ordered his guards to stand aloof, and they obeyed him. The Sultan missed his aim; and before he could draw another arrow he fell under Yusuf's dagger, but the assailant instantly received death from a thousand of the Sultan's followers, while the wounded Sultan was conveyed to another tent.

Said the dying Alp Arslan to those around him: "I now call to mind two lessons which I received from a reverend sage. The one bade me despise no man; the other, not to estimate myself too highly, or to confide in my personal prowess. I have neglected what his wisdom taught. The vast numbers of my army, which I viewed yesterday from an eminence, made me believe that all obstacles would yield to my power. I have perished from my errors, and my end will show how weak is the power of kings and the force of man when opposed to the decrees of destiny."

Alp Arslan lived long enough to transmit his dominion to his worthy son, MALEK

SHAH, A. D. 1073. The dying Sultan entreated his son and successor to intrust the chief direction of public affairs to the wise and pious Nizam ul Mulk, a deservedly famous minister, to whose virtue and ability he ascribed the success and prosperity of his own reign. Alp Arslan's remains were interred at Merv, in Khorassan; and the following impressive sentence was inscribed on his tomb: "All who have seen the glory of Alp Arslan exalted to the heavens, come to Merv, and you will behold it buried in the dust."

Under Nizam ul Mulk's wise administration the empire of the Seljuk Turks attained the highest prosperity, and Persia enjoyed a degree of tranquillity which it had not seen for a long time. But this worthy minister had no military talents. In the few army operations in which he was engaged he appears to have trusted more to his piety than to his valor. When foiled in his effort to obtain possession of a castle in the province of Fars, or Persia proper, he consoled himself by the philosophical reflection that "a man should not become impatient from disappointment, as it could not cure, but it doubled the pain." When the same fortress capitulated, because the fountains which supplied it became dry, he attributed his success entirely to his prayers.

The Sultan Malek Shah's generals conquered almost all of Syria and Egypt; and this renowned sovereign was more fortunate than his valiant father, as he subdued Bokhara, Samarcand and Khorasm, and even received homage from the Tartar and Turkish tribes beyond the Jaxartes, compelling the sovereign of the remote country of Kashgar to coin money in his name and to pay him a yearly tribute.

It is said that when Malek Shah was crossing the Oxus the ferrymen on that river complained that they were paid by an order on the revenues of Antioch. The renowned Sultan spoke to his minister; and Nizam ul Mulk replied: "It is not to defer payment of their wages, but to display your glory and the wide extent of your dominions." Malek Shah was pleased with this flattery, and the boatmen's complaints ceased when they discovered that they could negotiate the bill without loss. This circumstance is curious, as showing something of the monetary system of that time.

Malek Shah is said to have traveled over his vast empire twelve times. During his reign the Seljuk dominions extended from the Mediterranean in the west almost as far east as the Great Wall of China; and prayers were every day offered for his health in the mosques of Jerusalem, Mecca, Medina, Bagdad, Ispahan, Rei, Bokhara, Samarcand and Kashgar.

Oriental historians relate numerous incidents to show the goodness and greatness of Malek Shah. It is said that, on coming out of a mosque, before he fought a battle with his brother, who disputed his title to the Turkish crown, he asked Nizam ul Mulk what he had prayed for. The illustrious minister replied: "I have prayed that the Almighty may give you victory over your brother." The Sultan responded: "And I prayed that God may take my life and crown if my brother is worthier than I to reign over the faithful." This noble sentiment was crowned with the success it sought as the reward of superior piety and virtue.

But Malek Shah's character is marked with a blemish which all his glories cannot eradicate. He listened to Nizam ul Mulk's enemies and disgraced the old and virtuous minister, who soon afterward perished by an assassin's dagger. Malek Shah's fortunes seemed to decline from the hour of his worthy minister's fall; and the Turkish nation, which for half a century had revered the sage whom the Sultan destroyed, saw without regret the changed fortune of its ungrateful sovereign.

Malek Shah survived his illustrious minister but a few months. He was greatly attached to the city of Bagdad, and desired to make that seat of the Eastern Khalifs the capital of his vast empire, endeavoring to persuade the Khalif Al Moktadi to remove to another place. The Khalif requested a delay of ten days, which was granted; but during that brief period the renowned Sultan was seized with a sudden illness, which put an end to his life, A. D. 1092.

Few sovereigns have attained to the glory and power of Malek Shah. Under his sway Persia enjoyed a longer period of tranquillity than during any other period of her history; and this tranquillity was attributable to the wise administration of Nizam ul Mulk, in whom the great Sultan implicitly confided until within a few months of his death. Persia was greatly improved during this period, many colleges and mosques being erected, and agriculture being promoted by the construction of canals and watercourses.

Learning was also encouraged, and an assembly of astronomers from every portion of Malek Shah's dominions was employed for several years in reforming the calendar. Their labors established the *Jellalean*, "the Glorious Era," which began March 15, A. D. 1079. Its name *Jellalean* was in honor of the Sultan, one of whose titles was *Jellaledeen*, "the Glory of the Faith." This great work is a remarkable evidence of the attention given in the empire of the Seljuk Turks to one of the noblest of all sciences.

For a period of forty-eight years after Malek Shah's death, from A. D. 1092 to 1140, the Turkish Empire was distracted by civil wars. Malek Shah's four sons all occupied the Turkish throne in succession. SANJAR, one of these, held the government of Khorassan at the time of his father's death, and had little share in the troubles that followed; but from the time of the death of his brother MAHMOUD, in A. D. 1140, he may be considered the reigning Sultan.

Sanjar always resided in Khorassan, whence he extended his dominion eastward beyond the Indus, and northward beyond the Jaxartes. He compelled Byram Shah, a Ghiznivide sovereign, whose capital was Lahore, in the Punjab, to pay him tribute. To render his magnificence more complete, the kingdom of Khorassan was bestowed on Sanjar's cupbearer—a circumstance which has caused Sultan Sanjar's flatterers to say that he was served by kings.

But Sanjar, after a long reign, marked by remarkable success and splendor, experienced the most cruel reverses. He undertook a distant expedition into Tartary, to attack Ghour Khan, the sovereign of Kara Khatay, in which he suffered a signal defeat, his army being almost wholly cut to pieces, his family being made prisoners, and all his baggage being plundered. He escaped to Khorassan with a few followers, and was there reminded by a flattering poet that "the condition of God alone was not liable to change."

Sanjar afterwards suffered greater misfortunes. The Turkoman tribe of Ghuz had withheld their usual tribute of forty thousand sheep. Sanjar marched against them to force them to make payment, but was defeated and taken prisoner. At first he was treated with respect, but he was soon exposed to every hardship and insult that barbarity could inflict. The savage Turkomans placed him upon a throne during the day, and confined him in an iron cage at night.

During Sanjar's captivity of four years among the Turkomans, his dominions were ruled by his favorite Sultana, at whose death he made his escape, but died soon after gaining his liberty. The desolate and deplorable condition of his dominions, most of which had been ravaged by the barbarians of Ghuz, preyed on his spirits and plunged him into a melancholy from which he never recovered. The Oriental writers passed high eulogiums upon Sanjar, representing him as no less celebrated for his humanity and equity than for his valor and magnificence.

After Sanjar's death, in A. D. 1157, Iran, or Persia, remained distracted for forty years by the wars between the different branches of the Seljuk dynasty. The last to exercise power was TOGRUL III., who overcame most of his rivals and defeated a conspiracy of his nobles, after which he abandoned himself to every kind of excess. After the death of Sanjar, the ruler of Khorassan became an independent sovereign, and the discontented nobles of Persia invited him to invade their country. He defeated Togrul III., who was slain in the battle, being then intoxicated.

Thus ended the Seljuk dynasty in Persia, which had reigned from the time of Togrul I. for a period of one hundred and fifty-eight years. A branch of the dynasty, which ruled over the province of Kerman, the ancient Carmania, had assumed the title of Sultan; but they exercised little more than the power of viceroys, and paid or withheld homage according to the strength or weakness of the Sultans of Persia. The Emirs, or governors of cities and provinces, had renounced their allegiance, and exercised sovereign authority under the modest title of Atta-begs, "fathers or guardians of the peace."

Jakush, the sovereign of Khorasm who conquered Togrul III., was a descendant of the monarch of that country who had been the cupbearer to Sultan Sanjar. At his death he bequeathed his kingdom to his son Mohammed, whose reign was splendid and successful at its beginning. But Mohammed fell before the great Mongol chieftain, Zingis Khan, who defeated his armies, pillaged his dominions and took most of his family captive. These misfortunes broke Mohammed's heart, and he died on a small island in the Caspian Sea.

His son Jellal u Deen, the last of this dynasty of kings, bore up with exemplary fortitude against the conquering avalanche that had overwhelmed his father, but he finally sunk under the vicissitudes of fortune. He fled before the Mongols, took refuge among the hills of Kurdistan, and was slain by a barbarian whose brother he had put to death (A. D. 1250).

The families of the Turkish generals who had subdued Asia Minor, Syria and Egypt cast off their allegiance to the Seljuk Sultans during the civil wars between the sons of Malek Shah. The most important of the new kingdoms which sprung from the wrecks of the Turkish dominions in Western Asia was that of the Sultans of Iconium, or Roum, in Asia Minor, noted for its connection with the Crusades. The Seljuks of Roum were first brought into notice by Sultan Solyman. Their first capital was Nice, but after the Crusaders took that city Iconium became their seat of government.

The dynasties of Iconium and Aleppo, which had been brought into contact with the Crusaders, finally both fell before the victorious arms of Sultan Saladin of Egypt. The Khalifs of Bagdad enjoyed a qualified independence, having cast off the Seljuk yoke, and made themselves masters of Irak Arabi, or the province of Bagdad.

SECTION XX.—PERSIA AND THE GHIZNIVIDE EMPIRE.

FTER the Arabian conquest of Persia in A. D. 641, Arabian governors were appointed in the conquered country, and colonies from the burning sands of Arabia spread over the cold regions of Khorassan and Balkh. These colonies flourished in the soil to which they were transplanted. As before remarked, Persia remained under the dominion of the Khalifs for more than two centuries, during which the Persian people became Mohammedans. Persian history during this period is to be found in the history of the Moslem conquerors of the country, and even there it occupies a small and unimportant space. The only events of consequence are petty revolts of insubordinate governors, who attempted to erect their provinces into hereditary principalities when the power of the Khalifs declined.

Many of the Persians who refused to accept Islam fled to other lands to escape death or oppression; but the fury of religious enthusiasm soon spent itself, and when the Khalif's person was no longer regarded as sacred the Persian scepter was ready to fall from the grasp of Omar's and Ali's feeble successors. So dazzling a prize soon tempted the ambitious native chieftains of

Persia; and it was soon obtained by a man of humble origin, but ennobled by his valor, generosity and wisdom.

This man was YAKOOB (Jacob) BEN LEIS, the son of a pewterer of Seistan. When young he worked at his father's trade, but all his gains were squandered among boys, with whom his boldness and prodigality made him a favorite. As he grew up, tempted by the distracted condition of his country, he became a robber, and was followed by those whom his liberality from childhood had attached to his fortunes. The number of his attendants and the success of his enterprises soon gave him wealth. The change from the successful robber to the renowned chieftain was easy in such a condition of society. His assistance was sought by the usurping governor of Seistan, and he profited by the confidence thus reposed in him by at once seizing the person of his ally and the authority which he had assumed.

The Khalif of Bagdad gladly received the alliance of Yakoob ben Leis, and gave him a commission to make war against his rebellious tributaries; but the bold and unscrupulous adventurer again betrayed his trust, making himself master of most of Eastern Persia. The Khalif sent an army commanded by his brother, who defeated Yakoob near Bagdad; but Yakoob was undismayed by this casual reverse, and soon recruited his forces, after which he marched against Bagdad. The Khalif sent another mission to Yakoob, who was dangerously ill when it reached his camp.

Yakoob ordered that the Khalif's envoy should be brought into his presence, and that his sword, some coarse bread and dried onions should be laid before him. Yakoob said to the envoy: "Tell your master that if I live, this sword shall decide between us. If I conquer, I will do as I please; if I am conquered, this coarse fare will suffice for me." This speech, indicating his stern resolution, is the last act recorded of Yakoob ben Leis, who died two days later, A. D. 877, transmitting almost all of Persia to his brother Amer.

The Oriental writers describe Yakoob ben Leis as a person whose manners were most pleasant and conciliatory, while also characterized by great simplicity. The attachment of his followers to his person and fortunes was extreme, and the playmates of his boyhood attained the most exalted positions in the government.

AMER, Yakoob's brother and successor, showed a very different disposition by his conduct towards the Khalif of Bagdad, addressing him a respectful letter, and consenting to hold Persia as the nominal vassal of the Khalif. He prospered for some years, during which he sent yearly presents to the Commander of the Faithful. But this loyalty did not last, as disagreements and wars arose. Unable to enforce his authority, the Khalif instigated a chief of Transoxiana to attack his rebellious vassal.

Amer sent one of his generals against the Transoxianian chief, but this general was defeated; and Amer resolved to advance across the Oxus, in opposition to the advice of his counselors. He led an army of seventy thousand men in this expedition. The Tartar chieftain did not have more than twenty thousand men; but valor overcame numbers, and the Persians were utterly routed. Amer fled, but was taken prisoner after his horse had fallen.

The fortunes of Amer's family fell with him. His grandson TAKER struggled for power in his native province; but after a reign of six years his authority was subverted by one of his own officers, who seized him and sent him a prisoner to Bagdad. The only prince of the family who attained any eminence was a chief named Kuliph, who established himself in Seistan and maintained his power over that province until Mahmoud of Ghizni defeated him and made him prisoner.

From the fall of the dynasty of Yakoob ben Leis to the rise of Mahmoud of Ghizni is a period of almost a century; during which Persia was divided between the two families of Samanee and Dilamee—the first reigning over Eastern Persia and Afghanistan, and the other over Western Persia. These

PERSIA AND THE GHIZNIVIDE DYNASTY.

two dynasties distracted Persia by their wars.

ISMAIL SAMANEE traced his descent from Bahram Choubeen, the warrior who contended with Khosrou Parviz for the Persian crown. Oriental writers represent him as brave, generous, pious and just. He took Amer prisoner, and when that prince offered to ransom himself by revealing immense treasures Ismail spurned the offer, saying: "Your family were pewterers. Fortune favored you for a day, and you abused her favors by plundering the faithful. That wicked act has rendered your fall as rapid as your rise. Seek not to make my fate like yours, as it would be if I soiled my hands with such sacrilegious wealth!"

But Ismail's virtue underwent a severer test. After he had taken the city of Herat, his army was greatly in need of money. Ismail had given his word not to levy a contribution on that city, but his soldiers clamored that he should consider their merits and necessities before a pledge which he had given too hastily. Ismail was firm; and as his army became more distressed every hour, he ordered them to march away, lest the temptation to violate his word should be too great. He pitched his camp not far from Herat, where his wants were relieved by a singular accident. In a dry well were found several boxes of treasures, which proved to be part of Amer's wealth which had been stolen by one of his servants from the palace of Seistan. Ismail rejoiced at this good fortune. He paid his soldiers, and bade them learn from what had occurred that God would never desert the man who withstood temptation and preserved his faith inviolate.

The Dilamee family received their name from their native village, and traced their descent to the ancient Persian kings, but the first of the dynasty mentioned in history was the fisherman Dilam. His son, ALI BUYAH, who held a command in the Persian army, defeated the governor of Ispahan, who held his authority under the Khalif of Bagdad. By the immense plunder obtained by this victory Ali Buyah at once acquired renown. He drove the Khalif from his capital, but the Khalif made a treaty with him, appointing him viceroy of Fars and Irak. Accidental discoveries of treasures gave him immense wealth and promoted his advance in power by enabling him to enlarge his territory, so that he became master of all the provinces from Khorassan to Bagdad. After a few generations this dominion was transferred to Mahmoud of Ghizni, with whom commenced the Ghiznivide empire.

The Ghiznivide empire derives its name from Ghizni, or Ghazni, a city of Afghanistan, about sixty miles south of Cabul. The history of the Ghiznivide sovereigns has usually been included in that of Persia, though their dominions were not always comprised within the limits of Persia proper. The founder of the Ghiznivide empire was ABUSTAKEEN, a noble of Bokhara, who, about the year A. D. 976, renounced his allegiance to Munsoor, a prince of the Samanee dynasty, and retired to Ghizni at the head of seven or eight hundred followers. By successful wars with the Persians, Abustakeen was enabled to establish a petty principality, with Ghizni for its capital.

SUBUCTAGEEN, one of Abustakeen's successors, turned his arms against Hindoostan, for the purpose of acquiring fame and plunder, and extending Islam. Subuctageen defeated Jypaul, the sovereign of Northern India, captured Cabul, and overran the fine province of the Punjab, in his first campaign; and in his second he was still more successful. After being severly defeated, Jypaul submitted, agreeing to pay tribute.

The zeal of young Mahmoud, Subuctageen's son, spurned these offers. He vehemently urged his father to make no compact with idolators. When the Hindoo prince heard of Mahmoud's intolerance he bade him beware how he drove brave men to despair. Said he: "My followers, who appear so mild and submissive, will, if they are irritated, soon change their character. They will murder their wives and children, burn their houses, loosen their hair, and rush upon your ranks with the energy of men whose only desire is revenge and death."

Subuctageen knew that there was truth in this threat, and disregarded his son's advice. But within a year the armies of Ghizni overran Jypaul's territory with frightful slaughter. Subuctageen died soon afterwards, and was succeeded by his son MAHMOUD, A. D. 977. Mahmoud ascended the throne of Ghizni at a ripe age, when his powers were matured by experience in war and government. His ruling passions were devotion to the Mohammedan religion and the love of military glory. Both these passions had become ardent from restraint, and blazed forth on his accession to power with a lustre which, according to a Mohammedan author, filled the whole world with terror and admiration.

After securing the friendship of the Khalif of Bagdad, and marrying a Tartar princess, Mahmoud of Ghizni began a religious war against the idolators of Hindoostan, and this war occupied most of his reign. He was completely successful in his first two campaigns. Unable to defend his dominions, Jypaul resolved to heroically sacrifice his own life to propitiate the gods whom he adored, hoping to see the divine interposition manifested for the defense of the national religion. He transferred the government of his dominions to his son, after which he mounted a funeral pile and prayed that his death amid the flames might expiate those sins which he imagined had subjected his unhappy kingdom to the Divine vengeance.

Anundpal, Jypaul's son and successor, was as unfortunate as his father. His army, encamped near the Indus, is said to have exceeded three hundred thousand men. Mahmoud seems to have regarded it with some apprehension. He remained in sight of it for forty days without coming to an action, defending his camp by a deep intrenchment. His enemies at length determined to attack him. The trench was carried by the fury of the first assailants, and many of Mahmoud's army were slain; but in the midst of this success Anundpal's elephant took flight, thus carrying dismay and confusion among the Hindoo ranks, so that Anundpal's troops instantly fled, and were pursued for two days, during which more than twenty thousand were slain.

Mahmoud followed up his victory by advancing into Hindoostan, destroying temples and idols, and seizing the wealth of those whom he had vanquished. On his return to Ghizni he celebrated a festival, at which he displayed to the admiring and astonished people golden thrones, magnificently ornamented, constructed from the plunder of twenty-six thousand pounds of gold and silver plate, with fourteen hundred and eighty pounds of pure gold, seventy-four thousand pounds of silver, and seven hundred and forty pounds of set jewels.

Mahmoud led his next expedition against Jannaser, a famous site of Hindoo worship, seventy miles north of Delhi. The temple at that place was destroyed by the fanatic zeal of Mahmoud, who broke its famous idol, Jugsoom, and sent its fragments to Ghizni to be converted into steps for the principal mosque, so that the faithful might tread on the mutilated image of superstition as they entered the temple of the One True God. Mahmoud passed the next two years in the conquest of Cashmere and the hilly provinces in its vicinity. Many of the people in all the territories conquered by Mahmoud and annexed to his empire were forced to accept Islam.

While Mahmoud was establishing his authority in Khorassan, Hindoostan obtained a brief respite of a year. When he had accomplished this task he prepared to attack the celebrated Hindoo city of Kinoge. Though the distance was great and the obstacles numerous, Mahmoud began his march with a hundred thousand cavalry and thirty thousand infantry—the flower of his army. His movements were so rapid that the city was utterly surprised and fell an easy prey to the invader. He then conquered Meerut, a great and opulent principality. He took the holy city of Muttra, and broke all the idols in the place, but did not destroy its great and solid temples. In the letters which he wrote to Ghizni he gave the most glowing description of the architecture of these elegant structures. When he returned to his capital his own share of the plunder was estimated at two million two hundred and fifty thousand dollars in money, fifty-three thousand captives, three hundred and fifty elephants, and a vast quantity of jewels. The private spoil of the army was much greater.

After this triumph Mahmoud seemed disposed to indulge himself with a period of rest. He employed some of the wealth which he had amassed in adorning his capital. The nobles of Ghizni imitated their king's example, and Ghizni soon rivaled the most celebrated Oriental cities in the elegance and magnitude of its public and private edifices. The grand mosque erected by Mahmoud surpassed every other structure. The beauty of the marble of which it was constructed, and the superior style of its architecture, were admirable, as were also the elegance of the carpets and the golden branch-lights with which it was ornamented. Mahmoud's vanity was flattered by hearing this favorite edifice styled the "Celestial Bride."

Mahmoud sent an account of his victories written in verse to the Khalif of Bagdad, with a variety of valuable presents. This poetic eulogy was read publicly at the Khalif's capital, and every means was employed to stimulate Mahmoud's pride and bigotry to further exertions in the Mohammedan cause.

Mahmoud's zeal and avarice required no stimulant. He had heard of a rich Hindoo temple in Gujerat, the priests of which boasted of the power of their famous idol Somnauth, and ascribed all the misfortunes of Northern India to the impiety of the inhabitants. Mahmoud resolved to destroy this idol. He marched to Somnauth, which the Persian authors describe as a lofty castle situated on a narrow peninsula, bounded by the ocean on three sides.

No sooner had Mahmoud encamped near the temple than a herald from the castle informed him that the god Somnauth had brought the Mohammedans before the walls of this temple that he might blast them with his wrath. Mahmoud smiled at the idol's threatened vengeance, and gave orders for the attack the following morning.

The Hindoos were driven from the walls at the first assault, and assembled about their idol, vainly imploring its aid. As they found no supernatural assistance at hand, they rushed upon their Moslem enemies with the fury of despair, and drove them back from their walls. Night put an end to the frightful carnage, and the assault was renewed on the following morning with increased vigor. Mahmoud's warriors mounted the walls everywhere, but were everywhere cast down headlong by the Hindoos, whose eyes are said to have been streaming with tears, while their bosoms were burning with rage. They believed that the god whom they adored had abandoned them, and their only desire for life was to take vengeance on their enemies. Their desperate valor forced Mahmoud to raise the siege.

The Hindoos were unexpectedly reinforced, and the battle was renewed. Mahmoud saw his soldiers were exhausted and giving way before the foe. He sprang from his horse, prostrated himself on the ground, and implored God to favor the one whose desire was to advance the glory of His holy name. He remounted his steed in an instant, seized one of his bravest generals by the hand, invited him to charge the enemy, and win either a glorious victory or a crown of martyrdom. When Mahmoud's soldiers saw that their sovereign was resolved not to survive defeat, they determined to share his fate and again rushed into battle with irresistible fury. The Hindoos fled in all directions, and Mahmoud's valor was crowned with a brilliant victory.

The inhabitants of Somnauth had watched the battle with extreme solicitude, and when they saw that all was lost they abandoned the walls which they had so gallantly defended. Many of them put to sea with their families and property, but were pursued and captured. The spoil found in the temple was immense. But the destruction of the famous idol—a gigantic image fifteen feet high—was the glory claimed by Mahmoud.

After giving the image a blow with his mace, Mahmoud ordered it to be broken and that two fragments of it should be sent to Ghizni, one to be placed at the doorway of the great mosque, and the other in the court of his palace. Two pieces were to be sent to Mecca and Medina. Some Brahmans came forward at this moment and offered several millions of money if Mahmoud would spare the idol. Mahmoud's officers advised him to accept the ransom; but he exclaimed that he desired the title of a breaker, not a seller, of idols, and ordered that the idol should be instantly demolished. It was accordingly burst open, and a vast quantity of rich jewels was discovered within, the value of which far exceeded the ransom which had been offered by the Brahmans.

Mahmoud extended his dominions by conquest until his empire equalled in power the New Persian Empire of the Sassanidæ under the Sapors and the Khosrous, extending to Bokhara and Kashgar on the north, to Bengal and the Deccan on the east and south, and to Bagdad and Georgia on the west. Mahmoud died in a magnificent palace which he had vainly styled "The Palace of Felicity." Just before he expired he took a last and mournful view of his army, his court, and the vast treasures which he had amassed by his wonderful successes. He is said to have burst into tears at the sight.

Mahmoud's court was splendid beyond example. The edifices which he erected were noble monuments of architecture, and he was a most liberal patron of learned men and poets. We are indebted to his love of literature for all that remains of the history of ancient Persia contained in the noble epic poem entitled the *Shah Nameh*, "Book of Kings," written by Firdusi, the celebrated Persian poet of the eleventh century.

The dark shades of Mahmoud's character were his love of war and his religious persecution. In every country which he subdued the horrors of war were increased by religious fanaticism. The desolation wrought by his conquering hosts is illustrated by a popular tale. Mahmoud's Vizier pretended to know the language of birds. One day, as Mahmoud and his Vizier were walking in a forest, they observed a couple of owls perched together on a tree. Mahmoud desired to know the subject of their conversation. The Vizier, after pretending to listen to the birds, replied: "The old owl is making a match with the other for her daughter. She offers a hundred ruined villages as her dowry, and says, 'God grant a long life to Sultan Mahmoud, and we shall never want for ruined villages.'"

Mahmoud died A. D. 1028, and the decline and fall of the Ghiznivide dynasty was as rapid as its rise. MASOUD, Mahmoud's son and successor, made several incursions into Hindoostan to maintain the tranquillity of the territories acquired by his father in that country; but the Seljuk Turks made inroads into his own dominions and completely defeated him.

Masoud was succeeded by his brother MADOOD, and the Ghiznivide empire declined very rapidly during the latter's reign. For more than a century the history of this empire presents nothing but an uninteresting and disgusting detail of petty wars, rebellions and massacres. During BYRAM's reign Ghizni was captured by Souri, an Afghan prince of Ghour; but Byram, favored by the attachment of the inhabitants, recovered his capital and took his enemy captive.

Byram disgraced his victory by the cruelties which he inflicted on his captive, in retaliation for the disgrace which he had suffered. He caused Souri to be stripped, painted black, then mounted upon a lean bullock, with his face turned in an opposite direction from the animal's head, and to be carried through the streets of Ghizni in that condition. After being exposed to all the insults of the mob, Souri was put to death by the most cruel torture, and his head was sent to Sanjar, the Seljuk Turkish Sultan, in token of triumph.

Allah, Souri's brother, upon hearing of his fate, summoned his mountaineers to arms, and led them to Ghizni, breathing vengeance against his brother's murderers. The fury of the Afghans was irresistible. Byram was thrown from his elephant, saved his life with difficulty, and fled into Hindoostan. His army was totally routed, and the victorious Allah entered Ghizni, which suffered for a full week from the fury of his soldiers, who perpetrated the most shocking horrors, sparing neither age nor sex. The humble shed, the stately palace, the sacred temple, all were involved in one common ruin. Many of the nobles and priests who had been made captive were conveyed to Ghour, and there publicly put to death, their blood being used to wet the mortar for repairing the walls of that city.

Byram's cruelty was visited on his posterity. His grandson, KHOSROU II., was taken captive by Allah and put to death, thus ending the dynasty whose fame in history may be solely assigned to Mahmoud. They were overthrown by a family which had for a long time submitted to them, but whose doubtful allegiance was a source of constant uneasiness; as the princes of Ghour, who were descended from Tobak, and who boasted that their ancestors had successfully opposed Feridoon, reluctantly submitted to the sovereigns of Ghizni. The situation of their country, amid rugged and barren mountains, was favorable to insurrection; and their power increased as that of Mahmoud's successors declined, until they finally rose on the ruin of the Ghiznivide dynasty, ascending not only the throne of Ghizni, but also that of Hindoostan. The Ghiznivide empire ended A. D. 1160, when Persia had been under the dominion of the Seljuk Turks for a century and a half, as already related.

BRESCIA, ITALY.

CHAPTER II.

MEDIÆVAL CIVILIZATION.

SECTION I.—THE FEUDAL SYSTEM AND CHIVALRY.

I WILL now proceed to give an account of the *Feudal System*, or form of government which prevailed throughout Europe during the Middle Ages. The barbarians who overthrew the Western Roman Empire divided the conquered lands among themselves. The chief of each of these tribes of barbarians was called a *king*. Under him were other chiefs or leaders called *barons*. Under each of these barons were still other chiefs, and under each of these last was a large body of people. The military organization was kept up in the conquered countries. The barbarian conquerors devoted themselves entirely to war, leaving the tilling of the soil to the conquered inhabitants, who became slaves or *serfs*. The serfs were bought and sold with the lands on which they lived.

The kings and barons owned large stone castles, to which they retired when attacked by an enemy. All the personal property of the conquered people was divided by lot among the conquerors; but the lands were regarded as the property of the king, not to retain, however, but to grant to his followers. The king kept a portion of the lands for his own use. These were called *crown-lands*; and the king's power depended upon the extent of his private estates. The remainder of the lands was bestowed on his subordinate chiefs, the barons, to be held by them for life. At the death of a chief or baron, his portion of land, called a *feud*, or *fief*, was again taken by the king, who then bestowed it on some other baron. From the term *feud*, the word *feudal* is derived; and by the Feudal System is meant the system based on the feuds or fiefs.

Those to whom the king granted fiefs were called *vassals of the crown*, or *liegemen*. The giver of the lands was called a *liege-lord*, or *lord-paramount*, or *suzerain*. The king bestowed the lands on his vassals on condition that they should join him with a certain number of soldiers whenever he should call them to arms. To do this they bound themselves every year by a solemn oath, which was called *swearing fealty*. The king, who was lord-paramount or liege-lord, in return, swore to protect his vassal, and not to continue in arms more than forty days at a time, nor to war against the Church. On the same condition, the vassals of the crown distributed their lands among their followers or vassals. Thus each vassal bestowed fiefs and sub-fiefs on his vassals, each of whom did homage for his lands to his liege-lord. So there were many grades of fiefs and sub-fiefs.

These fiefs, which were at first granted only for life, at length became hereditary in the families of the great vassals of the crown, each of whose estates at his death passed into the possession of his eldest son. In the same manner, great offices and their titles, such as *duke, marquis, count* or *baron*, finally became hereditary also. In this way originated the exclusive privileges yet enjoyed by the nobility of Europe.

STORMING OF WARWICK CASTLE, ENGLAND.

The great oppression and abuses to which the Feudal System gave rise led to the establishment of a remarkable institution throughout Europe about the beginning of the eleventh century. This peculiar institution called *Chivalry*, originated in the piety of some nobles who wished to give to the profession of arms a religious tendency. These nobles devoted their swords to God, and bound themselves by a solemn oath to use them only in the cause of the weak and the oppressed. Those who took upon themselves

TOURNAMENT AT NUREMBERG

THE EMPEROR FREDERICK BARBAROSSA KNIGHTING YOUNG NOBLEMEN.

these vows were called *knights*. Very soon every noble aspired to the honor of being a knight; and the result was that much attention was given to the education of the young, for more than physical power was needed for admission to knighthood.

The aspirant to knighthood was required to be brave, courteous, generous, truthful, obedient, and respectful to his superiors in age or rank, and also to the ladies. The result of the development of these virtuous and noble qualities was that the candidate for knighthood became kind and affable to all who were below him in rank or fortune. The young noble who aspired to knighthood was placed at a very early age under the care of some noble distinguished for his chivalrous qualities, who, in his castle, instructed the young aspirant to knighthood in all the duties of Chivalry.

The ceremonies of admission to the order of knighthood were somewhat singular. The candidate was first placed in a bath, to denote that in presenting himself for knighthood he must present himself washed from his sins. When he left the bath he was clothed; first, in a white tunic, to signify the purity of the life he was vowing to lead; then, in a crimson vest, to denote that he was called upon to shed blood; and lastly, in a complete suit of black armor, which was an emblem of death, for which he must always be prepared. He took an oath to speak the truth, to maintain the right, to protect the distressed, to practice courtesy, to defend the Christian religion, to despise the allurements of ease, and to vindicate the honor of his name.

The knight was dressed in a suit of armor which protected his whole person. This armor was sometimes made of mail, that is, links of iron forming a kind of net-work dress, which a sword or a lance could not easily penetrate. Often this armor consisted of plates of iron, which protected the whole body of the knight. The aggressive weapons of a knight were a lance twelve or fifteen feet in length, a large sword, a dagger, and sometimes a battle-ax, or a steel club called a *mace-at-arms*. The knight's war horse, like himself, was protected by a covering of mail or iron plate.

Those knights who traveled about from place to place, independent of each other, were called *knights-errant*. Sometimes a great entertainment, called a *tournament*, was given by some king or rich prince, at which a mock combat was held for the knights to display their skill in the use of arms. A vast number of ladies and gentlemen assembled to witness these friendly trials of skill. At the conclusion of the exercises, the judges, who were usually old knights, declared the victors; and the prizes were presented to the successful knights by the noblest or most beautiful lady present.

The good effects of the institution of Chivalry were many. While it protected the defenseless and down-trodden in that warlike and barbarous period, the Middle Ages, it contributed much to the final overthrow of feudalism and the revival of European civilization, which had disappeared with the fall of the Western Roman Empire. Commerce increased, talent and invention received encouragement, the arts and the sciences began to flourish, and many new towns were built and peopled.

SECTION II.—THE PAPACY, HIERARCHY AND MONACHISM.

HE Pope, or Head of the Church, assumed command or authority over all the princes and kingdoms of Christendom. He regarded the Empire of Germany and all other Christian kingdoms as papal fiefs. From the eleventh to the sixteenth century the papal power was at its height. During that period the power of the Pope was so great that the most powerful monarch of Europe could be subjected to the greatest humiliation by His Holiness,

CATHEDRAL OF COLOGNE.

The most powerful, the most illustrious, and the ablest of the Popes, and the one who raised the papacy above every other power in Christendom, was Gregory VII. (Hildebrand), who compelled Henry IV., King of Germany, to come to Italy and stand three days and three nights barefooted and bareheaded, without tasting a mouthful of food.

The two punishments by the influence of which the Pope endeavored to maintain his authority were the *interdict* and the *excommunication*. The papal punishment by the interdict was forbidding or interdicting divine service to be publicly performed. When a nation was under an interdict, the churches were all closed, the bells were not rung, the dead were thrown into ditches and holes without any funeral ceremonies, diversions of all sorts were forbidden, and everything presented an appearance of gloom and mourning. An interdict was leveled at a village, a city, a state, or a nation; but an excommunication was directed against individuals.

A person excommunicated by the Pope was regarded as unholy and polluted; and every person was forbidden to come near him or render him any friendly assistance. If the sentence of excommunication could be enforced, as in most cases it could, the proudest and most powerful monarch could become, by a single decree of the Holy See, a miserable outcast.

The power and influence of the clergy during the Middle Ages was almost as great and important as was that of the nobles and the princes. Besides their ecclesiastical dignities, the superior clergy often held the most important offices of state; and by degrees great numbers of the archbishops, bishops and abbots acquired extensive possessions, so that they finally became as powerful and influential as most of the princes. The magnificent cathedrals and abbeys, adorned with all the productions of art, fully attested the greatness of the ecclesiastical residences.

CASTLE AND MONASTERY OF ILLOCK, HUNGARY.

Monachism, or *Monasticism*, had its birthplace in the East, where a life of solitude and devotion to the contemplation of divine subjects was by degrees adopted by so many that about the close of the third century of the Christian era the Egyptian Antonius, who had divested himself of all his vast possessions and selected the desert for his residence, collected the hitherto scattered *monks*, or *monachi*, as they were called, into enclosed places styled *monasteries*, *abbeys*, *cloisters* or *convents*. In these monasteries the monks lived together in fellowship; and Pachomius, the disciple of Antonius, gave the fraternity a rule.

Monasticism soon extended into Western Europe. In the sixth century, Benedict of Nursia established a monastery on Mount Casino, in Southern Italy, and thus became the founder of the famous order of *Benedictine* monks, which rapidly spread into all European countries and built many cloisters. Numerous orders of monks arose in the course of time, among which were the *Augustinians*, so called from the famous St. Augustine. Other noted monastic orders were the *Cistercians*, the *Premonstrants*, and the *Carthusians*.

Two celebrated monkish orders arose in the thirteeth century—the *Franciscans* and the *Dominicans*. The order of Franciscans was founded by the pious Francis of Assisi, a wealthy merchant's son, who, in 1226, renounced all his possessions, clothed himself in rags, and went from place to place, begging and preaching the gospel. His wonderful zeal for the salvation of souls made for him many disciples, who, following his example, renounced their worldly possessions, fasted, prayed, and supported themselves by alms and donations. The order of Franciscans became wide-spread throughout Europe. About the same time arose the order of Dominicans, founded by the learned Spaniard, Dominicus. The chief aim of the Dominican monks was the extinction of all heretical doctrines and the preservation of the predominant faith in its original purity. The Dominicans took a vow of absolute poverty, and sought to gain heaven by austerity of manner and by a strict religious devotion. The court of the *Inquisition*, with all its horrible examinations, dungeons and tortures, was assigned to the Dominicans for the extermination of heretics, as all who differed with the established Church were called. The Franciscan monks, who mingled with the people, were chiefly engaged in the salvation of souls; while the Dominicans, who gave their attention to the sciences, filled, by degrees, the chairs of the European universities.

All monks were obliged to take the three vows of celibacy, personal poverty, and obedience. Females who took upon themselves the obligations of Monachism were called *nuns*, and their cloisters or convents were styled *nunneries*. The monastic orders were the strongest support of the power of the Pope, who endowed them with privileges and removed them from the authority of the bishops.

Monachism proved a blessing to humanity during the dark and barbarous period of the Middle Ages. It preserved the remains of ancient civilization, afforded an asylum or place of refuge for the down-trodden and the oppressed, and diffused morality and intellectual enlightenment and softened the rude manners of those benighted times by the preaching of the gospel and by the establishment of schools for education.

SECTION III.—MEDIÆVAL LEARNING AND LITERATURE.

URING the whole mediæval period of a thousand years—known also as the Middle Ages —Europe, under feudalism, was slumbering in the darkness of barbarism, ignorance and superstition. All the learning was in the possession of the clergy, and most of them were only able to read their prayer-books and write their names. During the Dark Ages, kings and nobles were unable to write their own names.

The first half of the mediæval period is known as the *Dark Ages*. The Saracens or Arabians were then leaders in learning and the arts. The great names among the Arabians of this period were ACHMET, the astronomer; GEBER, the chemist; and AVICENNA (980-1037), the eminent physician and philosopher. FIRDUSI, a renowned Persian poet, flourished early in the eleventh century. Two illustrious names appear among the Anglo-Saxons of Britain in the eighth century—"THE VENERABLE" BEDE (672-735), the church historian, and ALCUIN (725-804), a famous scholar, the tutor of Charlemagne.

The great seats of learning in Europe, during the Middle Ages, were the famous universities of Oxford, in England; Paris, in France; Bologna, in Italy; and the Moorish university of Cordova in Spain. These were attended by thousands of students from different parts of Europe. The students and professors mostly begged their way, as poverty was considered no disgrace when it was endured for the sake of learning. Latin was the universal language of the learned, all over Christian Europe. Other famous schools arose at Cambridge, in England; Prague, in Bohemia; Toulouse and Montpelier, in the South of France; Padua, in Italy; and Salamanca, in Spain.

The great French philosopher, ABELARD (1079-1142)—who flourished in the first part of the twelfth century—is regarded as the founder of the Scholastic philosophy.

The *Schoolmen* were those philosophical writers who devoted themselves to subtle points of theology and metaphysics. The most eminent of the Schoolmen were the Italian Dominican monk, THOMAS AQUINAS (1224-1274), "the Angelic Doctor," and the Scottish Franciscan monk, DUNS SCOTUS (1265-1308), "the Subtle Doctor"— both of whom flourished in the thirteenth century, and who were the founders respectively of the *Thomists* and the *Scotists*. Other famous schoolmen were ANSELM (1033-1108), Archbishop of Canterbury, and PETER LOMBARD (1100-1160), an Italian monk. The English monk, ROGER BACON (1214-1294), "the Admirable Doctor," and the Italian monk, ALBERTUS MAGNUS, (1193-1280)—both of whom flourished in the thirteenth century—were Schoolmen celebrated for their investigations in physical science, and both were punished as magicians. The *Mystics* sought to build up a religion of feeling, of poetry and of imagination, in opposition to the system of the Schoolmen, who sought to blend science with revelation. The most renowned of the Mystics was THOMAS À KEMPIS (1380-1471), who was born in Germany, but flourished in France during the fifteenth century—the closing period of the Middle Ages —and whose great work, *Imitatione Christi* "Imitation of Christ," has been translated into all languages.

The Northern and Eastern nations of Europe kept their own languages. The mingling of the Northern barbarian conquerors with the Celtic and Latin races of Southern and Western Europe gave rise to the modern French, Italian, Spanish and Portuguese. The blending of Norman-French with the Anglo-Saxon, or Old English, gave us the modern English.

In Italian literature we find three illustrious names, all of whom flourished at Florence—"the Athens of the Middle Ages"—in the fourteenth century. The first and greatest of these was the renowned dramatic poet, DANTE (1265-1321), who, in his *Divine Comedy*, describes his visions of Hell, Purgatory and Paradise The next was PETRARCH (1304-1374), also a great dramatic poet, famous for his *Odes to Laura*. The third was Petrarch's cotemporary, BOCCACCIO (1313-1375), the great novelist, who, by his novels and tales, became the creator of Italian prose, his great work being *Decameron*. Petrarch and Boccaccio were mainly instrumental in restoring ancient civilization and literature.

English literature arose in the time of King Edward III., in the fourteenth century. The *Travels* of SIR JOHN MANDEVILLE (1300-1372) were the earliest English prose. GEOFFREY CHAUCER (1328-1400) —" the Father of English poetry "—wrote *Canterbury Tales*. JOHN GOWER (1320-1402)—called "Moral Gower"—was another great English poet; as was also WILLIAM LANGLAND (1332-1400), the author of *Piers Plowman*. JOHN WYCLIFFE (1324-1384)— the great Oxford professor, divine and reformer—made the first English translation of the Bible.

Two great French historians flourished during the fourteenth and fifteenth centuries—FROISSART (1337-1410) and COMINES (1445-1509). Lyric poetry was cultivated by the *Minnesingers* and *Meistersingers* in Germany, and by the *Troubadours* in the South of France. The great German epic poem of the *Nibelungen Lied*; the Spanish poem of the *Cid*, who fell in the war against the Moors in 1099; and the British poem of *King Arthur and the Knights of the Round Table*, were the most famous productions of mediæval heroic poetry. The mediæval architecture displayed itself mostly in magnificent cathedrals in the Gothic style which still remain as monuments of the Middle Ages.

SECTION IV.—TOWNS, COMMERCE AND SOCIAL LIFE.

TOWARD the close of the eleventh century all the European nations gradually grew more wealthy and powerful. The towns emerged into importance. Cities are always the centres of civilization. As civilization advanced new towns arose, especially in Germany and Italy, and the old towns recovered their ancient greatness. The real importance of the German towns began with the *Hanseatic League*, which was of the greatest importance to commerce and freedom. The Hanseatic League, comprising seventy cities and towns, maintained powerful fleets and defended themselves in the Northern seas against piracy. In Italy the Lombard cities arose to greatness, and finally threw off the nominal yoke of the German Emperor. The great Italian republics of Venice, Genoa, Pisa and Florence engrossed the commerce of the Mediterranean and the East.

The growth of towns gave rise to various industries, and trade and commerce began to flourish. The woolen manufacture of Flanders was among the earliest industries. This had become important in the twelfth century, and "Flemish stuffs" were sold in distant lands. Ghent and Bruges were the chief seats of this industry. The weavers of these cities were noted for their democratic spirit. In England, for two centuries after the Norman Conquest, the export of wool, the great staple of that country, was the only commerce. But in the fourteenth century, King Edward III., the father of English commerce, brought Flemish artisans to England, and thus introduced the finer manufacture of woolen cloths. From that period England increased in wealth, and a merchant's occupation became honorable.

The commerce of the South of Europe was conducted by the republics of Venice, Genoa and Pisa. The Crusades increased

GREAT ITALIAN WRITERS.

the wealth and extended the commerce of these Italian city-republics. The towns of Marseilles, Nismes and Montpelier, in Southern France, and Barcelona, in Spain, had a flourishing commerce. The introduction of the silk-manufacture at Palermo, in Sicily, in 1148, was the beginning of manufacturing industry in Italy. Silk soon became a staple manufacture of the towns of Lombardy and Tuscany, and their laws enforced the cultivation of mulberries. The silk-manufacture soon spread into Southern Europe and into Catalonia, in Spain.

The growth of commerce, in the course of time, led to the establishment of moneyed institutions. Most nations in the Middle Ages treated the lending of money for profit as a crime. This trade was at first entirely conducted by the Jews, who were long subjected to cruel persecution, being maltreated and swindled to a shameful extent. In the thirteenth century the merchants of Lombardy and Southern France took up the trade in money by beginning the business of remitting money on bills of exchange and of making profits on loans. The "Lombard usurers," in spite of much prejudice, established themselves in all the leading commercial centers of Europe. As the practical utility of this business was soon recognized, this ancient prejudice gradually died away. The earliest bank of deposit is said to have been that of Barcelona, in Spain, founded in 1401. The bank of Genoa was established in 1407, and soon became a great power.

The growing wealth of Europe led to the diffusion of comforts and luxuries among the people. Dwelling-houses were improved. Chimneys and window-glasses first came into use in the fourteenth century. Fantastic fashions prevailed. Long-toed shoes came into general use. The toes of these were so long that they had to be fastened to the knees with gold chains. Ignorance and superstition was the rule. Books were few and high-priced. Implicit faith was placed in stories of giants and magicians, dragons and enchanted palaces. In the short intervals of peace in the Middle Ages, hunting and hawking were favorite amusements. Even the clergy were very fond of field-sports.

MIGHT MAKES RIGHT.

CHAPTER III.

THE CRUSADES.

SECTION I.—THE FIRST CRUSADE.

FROM the time of the triumph of Christianity over the paganism of the Roman world in the fourth century, it had been a custom among the people of Christian Europe to make pilgrimages to Jerusalem for the purpose of expiating a sinful life, praying at the Holy Sepulcher, and exhibiting gratitude for heavenly mercies. As long as Syria and Palestine formed a part of the Byzantine, Greek, or Eastern Roman Empire, access to the Holy City was secured to these pilgrims. While the Holy Land remained under the enlightened dominion of the Saracens, or Arabians, the Christian pilgrim was also unmolested in his journey to and from the Holy Sepulcher. But when the Seljuk Turks, a race of fierce barbarians from the plains of Tartary, took Jerusalem in 1076, and obtained full possession of the Holy Land in 1094, the native Christians and the pilgrims from Europe were ill-treated, and many of them became martyrs to their religion. Those who returned to Europe from their pilgrimages gave a melancholy account of the cruelties and oppressions suffered by the Christians in Palestine at the hands of the Moslem Turks, and thus excited the greatest indignation in Christian Europe.

Among others who had been witnesses of the cruelties and oppressions suffered by the Christians in Palestine was the zealous and fanatical monk, Peter the Hermit, of Amiens, in the French province of Picardy. On his return to Europe from a pilgrimage to the Holy Land, Peter the Hermit resolved to arouse the Christian nations of Europe to a gigantic effort to wrest the Holy Land from the hands of the Moslems. Peter went from town to town, and from castle to castle, preaching of the duty of Christian Europe to expel the barbarian Turks from the Holy City. Wherever he went, numerous crowds assembled to hear him; and very soon all France and Italy were aroused to the wildest enthusiasm for an expedition against the Moslem desecrators of the shrine of the Savior.

Pope Urban II., who zealously abetted the design for an expedition for the redemption of the Holy Land, assembled a Council of the Church at Clermont, in Southern France. This Council was attended by numerous bishops and an immense concourse of people. When the Pope, addressing the clergy and the multitude, said, "It is the duty of every one to deny himself and take up the cross, that he may win Christ," there arose a simultaneous shout, "It is the will of God!" and great numbers demanded to be enlisted in the sacred army. As the symbol of enlistment in the cause of God was a red cross to be worn on the right shoulder, the expedition was called a *Crusade*, and those who engaged in it were called *Crusaders*. All who engaged in the enterprise received from the Church the promise of a remission of sins and an eternal heavenly reward after death.

The enthusiasm for the Crusade was so great throughout Christian Europe that

FIRST CRUSADE.

PRAYING FOR THE SUCCESS OF THE CRUSADERS.

Norman Ladies (11th Century).

Godfrey de Bouillon.

Knight and Squire during the First Crusade (11th Century).

French Knight and Squire.

THE 11TH CENTURY. THE FIRST CRUSADE.

BATTLE OF DORYLAEUM.

THE FIRST CRUSADE.

many became impatient at what they considered the slowness of the preparations of princes; and accordingly, in 1096, numerous bands, consisting of thousands of the lowest classes of society, set out for the Holy Land without order or discipline. They were led by Peter the Hermit and a French knight called "Walter the Penniless." They proceeded through Germany and Hungary toward Constantinople, but very few of them ever reached Asia. Having attempted to obtain the necessaries of life by forcible means in the countries through which they passed, and having carried robbery and desolation through Bulgaria and stormed Belgrade, the inhabitants of those countries valiant Godfrey of Bouillon, Duke of Lorraine, led a powerful and disciplined army toward the Holy Land. The principal leaders of the Crusaders next to Godfrey of Bouillon were Count Hugh of Vermandois, brother of King Philip I. of France; Duke Robert the Devil of Normandy, son of William the Conqueror of England; Count Stephen of Blois, father of King Stephen of England; the chivalrous Count Raymond of Toulouse; Earl Robert of Flanders; and Bohemond, brother of Robert Guiscard, the Norman prince of Southern Italy. This great army of Crusaders set off for Palestine in six divisions, which took different routes to Constantinople, where all

CRUSADERS STARTING FOR THE HOLY LAND.

rose against them and destroyed nearly the entire band of Crusaders; and Peter the Hermit and Walter the Penniless had very few followers when they reached Constantinople, where they waited to join the great army of the First Crusade under Godfrey of Bouillon.

Other disorderly and undisciplined bands, which violently persecuted and even murdered Jews and others who rejected Christ, followed those of Peter the Hermit and Walter the Penniless; but they were totally destroyed before they reached Constantinople by the people whom they had robbed and plundered.

Nearly three hundred thousand of the Crusaders had already perished when the were united before passing over into Asia. When the Crusaders arrived in Asia their army consisted of six hundred thousand men, of whom one hundred thousand were cavalry.

The Crusaders captured Nice, in Asia Minor, in 1097, after a siege of two months, and defeated the Turks in the battle of Dorylæum. Proceeding in their victorious career, the Christians next laid siege to Antioch. That city was finally taken by the strategy of Prince Bohemond and the treachery of one of the Turks, who left a gate open to the besieging Crusaders. The greatest cruelties were perpetrated upon the unfortunate inhabitants of Antioch, by the victorious Christians, after taking the city.

CRUSADERS STORMING ANTIOCH.

A few days after the Crusaders had taken Antioch, an army of three hundred thousand Turks and Persians appeared before that city. The finding of a "holy lance" in the Church of St. Peter raised the courage of the Christians, who sallied out of the city, and, after a desperate battle, totally defeated the Moslems and forced them to a precipitate flight.

Onward the Crusaders proceeded. When they came in sight of Jerusalem they shouted and wept for joy, and fell down on their knees and offered thanks to God; but their joy was succeeded by rage at beholding the Holy City in the possession of the Mohammedans. The Crusaders therefore laid siege to the city, which they finally took by storm, in July, 1099, after a siege of nearly six months. The streets of the captured city were soon filled with the bodies of seventy thousand slaughtered Mohammedans. The conquering Christians believed that they were doing God good service by slaughtering all who rejected the Savior; and both Jews and Mohammedans were massacred. After this most shocking atrocity, the Crusaders proceeded with hymns of praise to the Hill of Calvary, and kissed the stone which had covered the body of the Savior; and then offered thanks to the God of Peace for the signal success of their undertaking.

After the capture of the Holy City, the Crusaders established the Christian Kingdom of Jerusalem, which lasted nearly a century. Their gallant leader, Godfrey of Bouillon, was made ruler of the new state He was too pious to assume the title of "King;" but called himself "Defender of the Holy Sepulcher," and wore a crown of thorns instead of one of gold. Godfrey gained a great victory over the Sultan of Egypt, at Ascalon, in August, 1099. He died in the following year (A. D. 1100), and was succeeded at the head of the new state by his heroic brother Baldwin.

Some time after the First Crusade, two celebrated orders of knighthood arose at Jerusalem. These were the Knights of St. John, or Hospitallers, and the Knights Templars, or Red Cross Knights. Both these orders became famous for their military exploits against the Moslems.

SECTION II.—SECOND AND THIRD CRUSADES.

HE Christian Kingdom of Jerusalem suffered many attacks from the Moslems, and some of the principal Christian fortresses in Palestine were lost. Under these circumstances, Christian Europe undertook a Second Crusade. The pious and eloquent St. Bernard, Abbot of Clairvaux, in Burgundy, preached the cross in France and Germany (A. D. 1147).

Powerful expeditions were led toward the Holy Land by Conrad III., King of Germany, and Louis VII., King of France. The army under Conrad marched by way of Constantinople into Asia Minor, where it was decoyed by the treacherous Greek generals into a waterless desert, where the Turkish cavalry suddenly attacked and thoroughly annihilated the army of German Crusaders, only a tenth part of whom succeeded in escaping to Constantinople. The French army, led by King Louis VII., marched along the coast; but the greater portion perished from famine and fatigue, and by the swords of the Moslems, before reaching Jerusalem. The shattered remnants of the immense hosts of French and Germans, led by the two sovereigns, after reaching the Holy Land, engaged in an unsuccessful siege of Damascus, which was the termination of the Second Crusade.

The situation of the Christian Kingdom of Jerusalem became more and more perilous after the Second Crusade; and at length the valiant Saladin, Sultan of Egypt, reduced a part of Palestine under his scepter. The magnanimous Saladin finally granted the Christians of Palestine a truce; but when a

RICHARD THE LION-HEARTED AT THE BATTLE OF ASCALON.

RICHARD COEUR DE LION AND THE HOSTAGES.

Christian knight interrupted the passage of Saladin's mother, seized her treasures and slew her attendants, the exasperated Sultan of Egypt recommenced hostilities, defeated the Christians in the battle of Tiberias, took Joppa, Sidon, Acre and other towns, and in 1187 Jerusalem also fell into the possession of the conquering Sultan. Saladin, who surpassed his Christian foes in virtue, generosity and nobleness of heart, treated the inhabitants of the Holy City with mildness, but caused the crosses to be torn down and the furniture of the Christian churches to be destroyed.

Upon the arrival of intelligence of the capture of Jerusalem by Saladin, great alarm prevailed throughout the whole West of Europe; and from the shores of the Mediterranean to the coasts of the Baltic, armed bands set off for the Holy Land. The three leading sovereigns of Europe—Frederick Barbarossa of Germany, Philip Augustus of France, and Richard the Lion-hearted of England—led powerful armies against the Moslems (A. D. 1189).

The Emperor Frederick Barbarossa with the German army marched by land to Asia Minor, and defeated the Sultan of Iconium in a great battle near the walls of his chief city; but the noble-hearted German Emperor lost his life in a stream which he had attempted to cross. His second son, Frederick, with a part of the expedition, proceeded to Palestine, and took part in the siege of Acre.

Kings Richard the Lion-hearted and Philip Augustus, with the English and French armies, after reaching the Holy Land by sea, laid siege to Acre, which fell into their hands in 1192, after a siege of nearly two years, during which nine great battles were fought before the city. Richard the Lion-hearted was noted for his energy, ability and valor, as well as for his pride, severity and cruelty.

By the orders of Richard the Lion-hearted, the German banner, which Duke Leopold VI. of Austria had caused to be erected on the battlements of Acre, was torn down and trampled under foot by the English. When the Moslems failed to fulfil the stipulations for the payment of a ransom for the captive Saracens, three thousand five hundred of them fell victims to the fiery temper of the English king. Richard's courage made him feared and respected by the Moslems; but notwithstanding his military skill and bravery, his efforts for the recapture of Jerusalem were unavailing.

The King of France was jealous of the superior military ability of the King of England. The two monarchs soon quarreled, and Philip Augustus returned to France. After gaining a great victory over Sultan Saladin near Ascalon, and concluding a truce with the Sultan, Richard the Lion-hearted set out on his return, by sea, to his kingdom (A. D. 1192). His vessel, having been driven by a storm to the coast of Italy, Richard proceeded on his way to England, by land, through Germany; but he was seized and imprisoned in the castle of Trifels, by order of the Emperor, Henry VI. of Germany, in revenge for the insult to the German flag after the capture of Acre; and only obtained his release upon the payment of a heavy ransom by the English.

SECTION III.—THE LAST FOUR CRUSADES.

IN THE year A. D. 1202, the Fourth Crusade was undertaken by French and Italian knights, under Count Baldwin of Flanders, at the instigation of Pope Innocent III. After assembling at Venice for the purpose of being conveyed to Palestine, the Crusaders captured Zara, in Dalmatia, for the Venetians; but instead of sailing to the Holy Land, they proceeded against Constantinople for the purpose of restoring to the throne of the Byzantine Empire, Isaac Angelus, who had been dethroned and imprisoned by his own brother.

THE BLIND DOGE DANDOLO OF VENICE HEADING THE FOURTH CRUSADE.

THE CHILDREN'S CRUSADE.

THE LAST FOUR CRUSADES.

Headed by the blind old Dandolo, Doge of Venice, the Crusaders appeared before Constantinople, took the city, and restored Isaac Angelus to the Greek throne; but when the French Crusaders demanded the rewards which had been promised to them, the inhabitants of Constantinople raised an insurrection in which the Emperor Isaac Angelus and his son Alexius perished. Thereupon the French Crusaders stormed and took the Byzantine capital, plundered the churches, palaces and dwellings, destroyed many valuable monuments of art, and filled the whole city with terror and desolation.

After plundering Constantinople, the French Crusaders subverted the Byzantine, or Greek Empire, and established in its stead a new Roman, or Latin Empire, with Constantinople for its capital, and Count Baldwin of Flanders for its sovereign. This Latin kingdom lasted fifty-six years, after which it was overthrown, and the old Byzantine dynasty was restored to the throne of Constantinople in the person of Michael Palæólogus.

The Fourth Crusade was without results, concerning Jerusalem; and at times after its conclusion separate bands of Crusaders, without chiefs or without discipline, made journeys to the Holy Land, and ventured upon the hazardous undertaking of restoring the Christian kingdom of Jerusalem and defending the Latin kingdom of Constantinople. On one occasion twenty-thousand children left their homes in Europe on a journey to the Holy Sepulcher, but they perished from hunger and fatigue, or were sold into slavery. In 1218 King Andrew II. of Hungary began the Fifth Crusade; but his expedition to Egypt had a disastrous result.

In 1228 the excommunicated Emperor, Frederick II., of Germany, led an expedition into Palestine, at a time when the Sultan of Egypt was at war with the governor of Damascus respecting the possession of Syria and Palestine. The Pope forbade all Christian warriors from joining the expedition until the Emperor Frederick II. should be relieved from the curse of the Church. In 1229 Frederick II. concluded a treaty with Sultan Malek Kamel of Egypt, by which Jerusalem and the greater part of the Holy Land were surrendered to the Christians; but the Pope excommunicated the Holy City, and Frederick II. was crowned at Jerusalem without being consecrated by the Church. The abandoned Emperor soon returned to Germany.

In the year A. D. 1243, fourteen years after the Fifth Crusade, the Korasmians, a fierce tribe of barbarians from the plains of Tartary, overran Palestine, carrying slaughter and desolation wherever they appeared, took Jerusalem, massacred its inhabitants, destroyed the Holy Sepulcher, and wasted the flower of the Christian chivalry in a desperate battle at Gaza; but they were finally defeated by the Christian and Turkish armies, which, for the moment, united against the common enemy.

The horrible deeds of the Korasmians in Palestine led to the Sixth Crusade, which was conducted by the French king, Louis IX., or St. Louis, who, in 1250, accompanied by many of his nobles, sailed at the head of a powerful expedition to Egypt. After taking the town of Damietta, the French fleet was destroyed in the Nile by means of Greek fire; and St. Louis was taken prisoner by the Sultan of Egypt, and only obtained his freedom by the payment of a heavy ransom (A. D. 1250). At length the Mamelukes, a race of Circassians who had been held as slaves in Egypt, obtained control of the government of that country.

In 1270 St. Louis undertook the Seventh Crusade—the last of those great expeditions of the Christians against the Moslems. The French fleet, having been driven by a storm upon the coast of Sardinia, St. Louis resolved to attack the piratical Moors of Northern Africa. The valiant French monarch landed near Tunis, and besieged that city; but soon a pestilential disease carried St. Louis and the greater number of his followers to their graves. The surviving French leaders concluded a treaty of peace with the Moors, and returned to France.

Prince Edward of England—afterward King Edward I.—who participated in the Seventh Crusade, went to the Holy Land, where he performed many gallant exploits, and struck such terror into the hearts of the Saracens that they hired an assassin to murder him. Prince Edward wrenched a poisoned dagger from the hand of the assassin; but in the scuffle the prince received a wound in the arm which might have proved fatal had not his affectionate wife, Eleanor, who had accompanied him to Palestine, sucked the poison from the wound.

The Moslems gradually recovered their lost power in Palestine; and in 1291 a Turkish army of two hundred thousand men appeared before Acre, and, after a vigorous siege, took the city by storm. The remaining Christians voluntarily retired from Syria, which for two centuries had been drenched with the blood of millions of Christian and Mohammedan warriors.

SECTION IV.—RESULTS OF THE CRUSADES.

THE Crusades ennobled the knightly class by furnishing a higher aim to their efforts, and gave rise to the establishment of new orders, which presented a model of Chivalry and were presumed to possess all the knightly virtues. Of these new orders were the Knights of St. John, the Knights Templars and the Teutonic Knights, which combined the spirit of the knight and the monk, their vows being chastity, poverty, obedience, and war against the Moslems.

After the reconquest of the Holy Land by the Turks, the Knights of St. John established themselves in the Island of Rhodes, which was finally wrested from them by the Ottoman Turks, in 1522, when they received the island of Malta from the celebrated Charles V., Emperor of Germany and King of Spain.

The Knights Templars acquired great wealth by donations and legacies. After the loss of their possessions in Palestine, the greater number of them returned to France, where they abandoned themselves to infidelity and corruption, the consequence of which was the final dissolution of their order during the reign of King Philip the Fair (A. D. 1285-1314), the Grand Master, Jacques de Molay, and many others being burned alive, protesting their innocence to the last. Their wealth in gold went into the coffers of the king, while their fortresses and lands were bestowed on the Knights of St. John.

The Teutonic Knights were celebrated for their services in the civilization of the countries on the shores of the Baltic sea. They defended Christianity against the heathen Prussians in the region of the Vistula, and converted the inhabitants of the territory between the Vistula and the Niemen to Christianity, and established there the German language, customs and civilization. The cities of Culm, Thorn, Elbing, Königsburg and others arose; bishoprics and monasteries sprung up; and German industry and civilization produced a complete change.

The Crusades gave rise to a free peasantry and tended to break up the Feudal System, as by their means great numbers of serfs received their freedom, and extended the power and influence of the burgher class and of the towns. The rich barons were compelled to sell their possessions, for the purpose of raising money to equip troops and to transport them to the Holy Land.

The Crusades promoted the diffusion of knowledge and the advancement of science and literature. Those who engaged in them were at first deplorably ignorant and illiterate; but when they came in contact with the Greek and Arabian civilization, they acquired a fondness for science and literature, and after returning to Europe they imparted the same spirit to their countrymen. The Crusades gave great encouragement each other; and the advantage of a mutual exchange of products was soon perceived. In consequence, great progress was made in

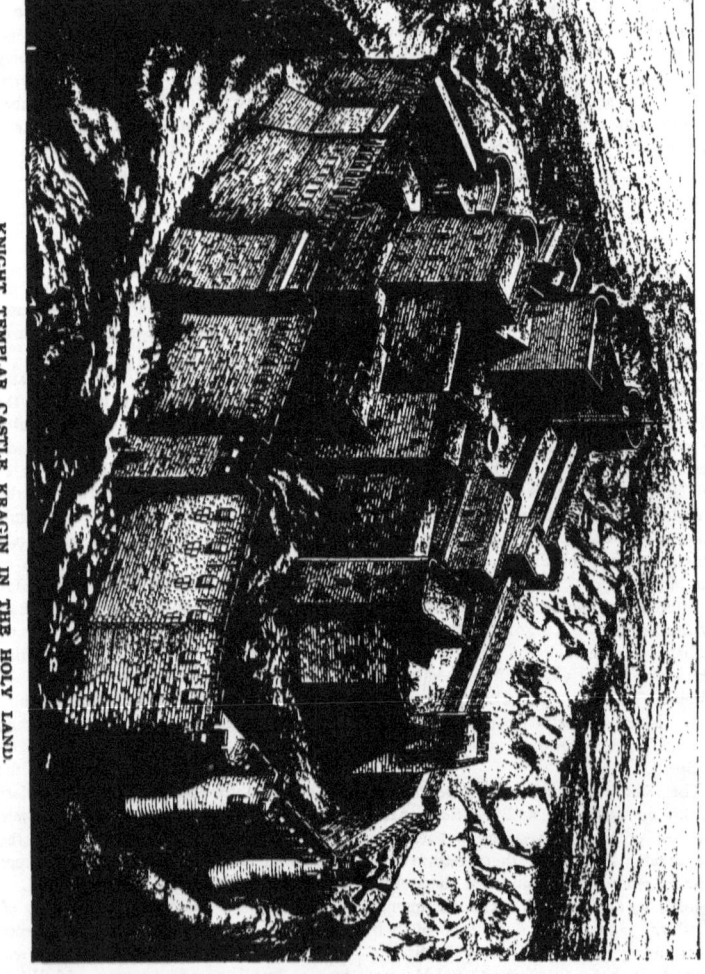

KNIGHT TEMPLAR CASTLE KRAGIN IN THE HOLY LAND.

to commerce, as by their means different countries were brought into communication and more intimate commercial relations with the arts of navigation and ship-building; and many flourishing cities, such as Venice, Pisa and Genoa, acquired immense wealth and attained to vast commercial importance. The great Venetian traveler, Marco Polo, visited China and the far East.

About the time of the First Crusade, the Mohammedan prophet, Hassan, founded the fanatical sect of the *Assassins*, who dwelt in the mountains of Syria, and who became the terror alike of Christians, Jews and Turks. These assassins were blindly devoted to their chief, "The Old Man of the Mountain," and paid the most implicit obedience to his commands; and they believed that if they sacrificed their lives for his sake, they would certainly be rewarded with the highest joys of paradise. Whenever the Old Man of the Mountain

BIRD'S-EYE VIEW OF RHODES IN THE TIME OF THE CRUSADES.

considered himself injured by any one, he dispatched some of his Assassins secretly to murder the aggressor. Thus was derived the common name of *assassin*, which has ever since been applied to a secret murderer.

SECTION V.—CRUSADE AGAINST THE ALBIGENSES.

THE Crusades gave greater power and influence to the clergy, and multiplied the riches of the Church. They also tended to exalt the religious enthusiasm produced by them into a spirit of fanatical intolerance. This intolerance was soon manifested in a Crusade against the *Albigenses*, a new religious sect which arose in the South of France, and which were a branch of the *Waldenses*, or *Vaudois*, which arose in the valleys of Piedmont, in the twelfth century, and whose leader was Peter Waldo, a rich merchant of Lyons, who resigned all his wealth from motives of piety.

The growth of heresy had already alarmed the advocates of papal supremacy during the reign of Pope Alexander III., and a general council of the Church had pronounced a solemn decree against the Albigenses. But the feudal lords of France and Italy did not readily adopt an edict which would have deprived them of their best vassals, and the new opinions were secretly preached throughout most of Europe.

Many of the preachers of this new reformation revived many of the doctrines of the Manichæans and Paulicians. A few enthusiasts ascribed the Old Testament to the principle of Evil, asserting that "God is there described as a homicide, destroying the world by water, Sodom and Gomorrah by fire, and the Egyptians by the overflow of the Red Sea."

These were, however, the sentiments of a very small portion of the Albigenses; the great bulk of the reformers protesting only against the doctrine of transubstantiation, the sacraments of confirmation, confession and marriage, the invocation of saints, the worship of images, and the temporal power of the prelates. Their enemies acknowledged their moral character in its external purity; but invented the most outrageous calumnies regarding their secret practices, without ever producing a shadow of evidence to sustain the charges, and therefore without incurring any hazard of refutation.

The reform made silent progress; as the efforts of the *paterins*, or Albigensian teachers, were directed rather to forming a moral and pure society within the Church than to establishing a new sect. They appeared desirious of holding the same relation to the Romish Church that John Wesley designed the Methodists to keep towards the Church of England. Their labors produced an independence of spirit and freedom of judgment which would probably have caused an open revolt had not Pope Innocent III. perceived the peril which menaced the papal system, and determined to crush freedom of thought before its exercise would overthrow his despotism.

As a first step in his work of suppression, Pope Innocent III. appealed to cupidity and self-interest. He relinquished the confiscated properties of heretics to the barons, and ordered that the enemies of the Church should be forever banished from the lands of which they were deprived, after which he sent commissioners into the South of France to examine and punish those who were suspected of holding heretical opinions, thus laying the first foundation of the Inquisition. The arrogance and violence of these papal emissaries disgusted all classes of society. When the commissioners discovered that their persecutions were unpopular they determined to uphold their power by armed force, and soon succeeded in collecting an army

Raymond VI., Count of Toulouse, was engaged in a war with the neighboring barons; and the papal legate, Peter de Castelnau, offered to act as mediator. He went to the barons, from whom he obtained a promise that, if Count Raymond VI. would consent to their demands, they would use all their forces to extirpate heresy. Castelnau drew up a treaty on these conditions, and offered it to Raymond VI. for his signature. The Count of Toulouse was naturally reluctant to purchase the slaughter of his best subjects by the sacrifice of his dominions and the admission of a hostile army into his territories. He peremptorily refused his consent; whereupon Castelnau excommunicated Raymond VI., placed his dominions under an interdict, and wrote to the Pope for a confirmation of the sentence.

Pope Innocent III. confirmed his legate's sentence, and commenced preaching a Crusade; but his violence exceeded all bounds, when he was informed that Castelnau had been slain by a gentleman of Toulouse whom he had personally insulted (A. D. 1208). Though Count Raymond VI. seems to have had no share in this murder, the papal vengeance was chiefly directed against him. He was excommunicated, his subjects were absolved from their oath of allegiance to him, and King Philip Augustus of France was invited to deprive him of his estates.

The French king was too busily engaged in wars with King John of England and King Otho IV. of Germany to turn his attention to the extirpation of heresy; but he permitted a Crusade against the Albigenses to be preached throughout his kingdom, and the monks of Citeaux became the principal missionaries of this war. These monks promised to those who lost their lives in the struggle the pardon of all sins committed from the day of birth to that of death; and to those who survived they promised unlimited indulgence, the protection of the Church, and a large share of spoil.

While the monks were enlisting bands of fierce wretches, who believed that they might expiate their former crimes by the perpetration of new atrocities, Pope Innocent III. was preparing a new mission to Languedoc, the savage brutalities of which surpassed even those of the Crusaders. The new monastic order of the Dominicans was founded with the Spaniard Dominicus at its head, whose special object was the extirpation of heresy by preaching against the doctrines of those who dissented from the Church and punishing with death those who could not be convinced by argument. This institution was the dreaded Inquisition, which seems to have been originally planned by the Bishop of Toulouse, who introduced it into his diocese about seven years before it was formally sanctioned by Pope Innocent III. at the council of the Lateran.

Count Raymond VI. of Toulouse and his nephew Raymond Roger, Viscount of Albi, alarmed at the coming danger, appeared before the papal legate, Arnold, Abbot of Citeaux, to avert the approaching storm by explanations and submissions. They protested that they had never sanctioned heresy and that they were entirely innocent of the murder of Castelnau. The severity with which the legate treated them convinced the young Viscount Raymond Roger that nothing could be hoped for from negotiation, and he returned to his estates, determined to defend himself to the last extremity. The Count of Toulouse displayed less fortitude, and promised to submit to any terms which the Pope would impose.

The Pope received Count Raymond's ambassadors with seeming indulgence, but offered absolution only on the most severe terms. He demanded that the count should make common cause with the Crusaders, to assist them to extirpate heretics—his own subjects—and to surrender seven of his best castles as a pledge of his intentions. Pope Innocent III. declared that if Count Raymond VI. performed these conditions he would be absolved, and even taken into special favor; but at the very same moment the Pope was inflexibly resolved on the count's destruction.

In the spring of A. D. 1209 all the fanat-

CRUSADE AGAINST THE ALBIGENSES.

ics who had taken up arms at the preaching of the monks of Citeaux commenced assembling on the frontiers of Languedoc. The land spread in beauty before them was soon to be a howling wilderness. Raymond VI. sank into abject cowardice. He surrendered his castles; he promised implicit submission to the papal legate; he even permitted himself to be publicly beaten with rods before the altar, as a penance for his errors. He was rewarded for his humiliation by being allowed to serve in the ranks of the Crusaders and to act as their guide in the war against his nephew.

Viscount Raymond Roger exhibited a bolder spirit. As he found the papal legate implacable, he summoned his barons, and, after stating all his exertions to maintain peace, he made a stirring appeal to their generosity and their patriotism. All determined on an obstinate defense. Even those who adhered to the Romish Church rightly feared the excesses of a fanatical horde eager for shedding blood and for gratifying a ruffian thirst for plunder. As the Crusaders advanced, some castles and fortified towns were abandoned to them, while others not subject to the charge of heresy were permitted to ransom themselves. Villemur was burned, and Chasseneuil capitulated after a vigorous defense. The garrison was allowed to retire, but all the inhabitants of both sexes suspected of heresy were cast into the flames amid the ferocious shouts of the victors, and their property was abandoned to the soldiery.

Beziers was the next town attacked. The citizens determined to offer a vigorous resistance, but in a sally which they made they were routed by the advanced guard of the Crusaders, and were so vigorously pursued that victors and vanquished entered the gates together. Before taking advantage of their unexpected success, the victorious leaders asked the Abbot of Citeaux how they should distinguish Catholics from heretics. The legate replied: "Kill all; God will distinguish those who belong to himself." His words were obeyed only too well. All the inhabitants of Beziers were atrociously massacred, and when the town was thus one vast slaughter-house it was fired, so that its ashes and ruins might serve as a monument of papal vengeance.

The last stronghold of Viscount Raymond Roger was Carcassonne, which was heroically defended by the valiant young viscount. Simon de Montfort, the leader of the Crusaders, found himself thwarted by a mere youth, and was detained for eight days before he obtained possession of the suburbs and was able to invest the town.

Peter II., King of Aragon, whom the Viscount of Albi and Beziers recognized as his suzerain, took advantage of this delay to interfere in behalf of his young vassal, who was also his nephew. The papal legate, unwilling to offend so powerful a sovereign, accepted Peter's mediation; but when he was asked what terms he would grant to the besieged, he demanded that two-thirds of Carcassonne should be abandoned to plunder. Viscount Raymond Roger spurned these conditions. Peter applauded his courage and personally addressed the garrison, saying: "You know the fate that awaits you; make a bold defense, for that is the best means of finally obtaining favorable terms."

The prudence of Peter's advice was demonstrated by the conduct of the papal legate in consenting to a capitulation; but when the Viscount Raymond Roger, trusting to the faith of the treaty, appeared in the camp of the Crusaders, he was treacherously arrested and cast into prison with his attendants. Warned by their leader's fate, the citizens of Carcassonne evacuated the town during the night, but some of the fugitives were overtaken by the cavalry of the Crusaders. The papal legate selected a supply of victims from his prisoners, and four hundred of them were burned alive, while about fifty were hanged.

The objects of the Crusade appeared to have been obtained. Count Raymond VI. of Toulouse submitted to all the humiliating conditions demanded of him. The Viscount of Narbonne abandoned all intentions of resistance, and the gallant lord of Beziers was a prisoner. The Crusaders also were beginning to become weary of the war; the French lords were ashamed of the cruelties which they had sanctioned and the faith which they had violated; and the knights and common soldiers were anxious to revisit their homes, after completing their term of service.

But the papal legate, Arnold, Abbot of Citeaux, was not yet satisfied. He summoned a council of the Crusaders, and tried to induce them to remain, for the purpose of protecting their conquests of Beziers and Carcassonne, the investiture of which he conferred on Simon de Montfort, the leader of the Crusaders. But most of the French nobles refused to remain any longer, and Simon de Montfort was obliged to defend his new acquisitions with the vassals from his own estates. The gallant Viscount Raymond Roger was detained a close prisoner in his own baronial hall at Carcassonne, where he soon died of an illness produced by grief, or, as was generally suspected, by poison.

The armies of the Crusaders retired, leaving the country a desert and calling it peace; but the sufferings of the Albigenses were not exhausted. The monks of the Inquisition, attended by trains of executioners, proceeded through the country at their pleasure, torturing and slaughtering all who were suspected of heresy; while the monks of Citeaux, who had found honor and profit in preaching a Crusade against heretics, were not disposed to relinquish the lucrative employment. This new Crusade was preached when there was no animosity to encounter, and new bands of fanatical warriors invaded Languedoc. They compelled their leaders to renew the war with the heretics, so that the exertions of those who profited by preaching extermination should not be lost, and that the bigotry of those who hoped to obtain their salvation by murder should be gratified.

Strengthened by such reinforcements, Simon de Montfort threw off the mask of moderation, and declared war against the unfortunate Count Raymond VI. of Toulouse. The count was again excommunicated and his dominions were laid under an interdict; but Simon de Montfort soon discovered that he had been premature in his hostilities. King Peter II. of Aragon refused to receive his homage for the viscounties of Beziers and Carcassonne, declaring that he would uphold the claims of the legitimate heir, Raymond Trencanel, the only son of the unfortunate Viscount Raymond Roger, a child about two years old, who was safe under the guardianship of the Count de Foix. A formidable rebellion broke out in the territories so recently assigned to Simon de Montfort; and only eight towns and castles remained in his possession, out of the two hundred that had been granted to him.

Count Raymond VI. of Toulouse was too much afraid of ecclesiastical vengeance to defend himself by force of arms. He sought the protection of his sovereign, the King of France, and he personally went to Rome to implore absolution. Pope Innocent III. promised him pardon on condition that he cleared himself from the charge of heresy and of participation in the murder of Castelnau; but when he appeared before the council he found that his judges had been won over by his inexorable enemy, Arnold, Abbot of Citeaux; and, instead of being allowed to enter on his defense, he was confronted by a series of new and unexpected charges. His remonstrances were in vain, his tears were met with mockery and insult, and the sentence of excommunication was formally ratified.

In the meantime the Crusaders, under the leadership of Simon de Montfort, pursued their career of extermination. Those spared by the sword perished by the hands of the executioner, and the ministers of a God of peace were found to be more cruel and vindictive than a licentious soldiery. Even King Peter II. of Aragon became alarmed, and sought the friendship of the Pope's favorite by affiancing his infant son to a daughter of Simon de Montfort. The King of Aragon perhaps expected that by this concession he would obtain more favorable terms for the Count of Toulouse, whom he accompanied to Arles, where a provincial council was convened. The terms of peace proposed by the papal legate were so extravagant that even Count Raymond VI. rejected them and secretly retired from Arles in company with the King of Aragon. For the third time the unfortunate count was excommunicated, pronounced an enemy of the Church and an apostate from the faith, and declared to have forfeited his title and estates.

The war against the Albigenses was now renewed with vigor. After a long siege, Simon de Montfort took the strong castle of Lavaur by assault, hanged its heroic governor, the lord of Montreal, and massacred the entire garrison. Says the Romish historian: "The lady of the castle, who was an execrable heretic, was by the earl's orders thrown into a well, and stones were heaped over her. Afterward the pilgrims collected the numberless heretics that were in the fortress, and burned them alive with great joy."

The same cruelties were perpetrated at all other places through which the Crusaders passed, and the friends of the victims took revenge by intercepting convoys and murdering stragglers. Simon de Montfort only laid siege to Toulouse when he had received a large reinforcement of pilgrims from Germany. In this extremity, Count Raymond VI. displayed a vigor and courage which would probably have saved him from ruin if he had manifested it in the earlier part of the war. He made so vigorous a defense that the Crusaders were obliged to raise the siege and to retire precipitately.

The ambition of the monks of Citeaux soon weakened the friendship between them and the Crusaders. Under the pretense of reforming the ecclesiastical condition of Languedoc, the monks expelled the leading prelates and seized the richest sees and benefices for themselves. The papal legate, Arnold, Abbot of Citeaux, took the archbishopric of Narbonne for his share; after which he abandoned Simon de Montfort and went to lead an expedition against the Moors in Spain. Pope Innocent III. himself paused for a moment in his career of vengeance, and, at the request of King Peter II. of Aragon, he promised Count Raymond VI. a fair trial; but the Pope found it not so easy a matter to allay the spirit of fanaticism which he had aroused. He was disobeyed by his legates and reproached by the Crusaders, so that he was obliged to retrace his conciliatory steps and to abandon the Count of Toulouse to the fury of his enemies.

King Peter II. of Aragon came to the assistance of his unfortunate relative, and encountered the formidable army of the Crusaders at Muret, but he was killed in the beginning of the conflict. Disheartened by the loss of their leader, the Spanish chivalry took to flight, and the infantry of Toulouse could offer no effective resistance single-handed. Trampled under foot by the pilgrim-knights, the citizens of Toulouse who followed their monarch to the fatal field were either cut to pieces or drowned in the Garonne.

Just when the Crusaders' victory at Muret appeared to have confirmed the power of Simon de Montfort, King Philip Augustus of France triumphed over his enemies, King John of England and King Otho IV. of Germany. But the ambitious leader of the Crusaders gained very little from his success, as the court of Rome commenced to grow jealous of his power (A. D. 1215). His influence with the papal legates and the prelates who had directed the Crusades was still very great, however, and the council of Montpellier granted him the investiture of Toulouse and all the conquests made by "the Christian pilgrims."

The King of France was not disposed to acquiesce in this arrangement, and sent his son Louis into the South of France, under the pretense of joining in the Crusade, but really to watch the proceedings of Simon de Montfort. Louis afterwards returned to accept the crown of England, and the quarrel in which this proceeding involved him with the Pope diverted his attention from Languedoc.

Arnold, Abbot of Citeaux, after returning from his expedition against the Moors in

Spain, took possession of his archbishopric of Narbonne, where he commenced exercising the rights of a sovereign prince. Simon de Montfort, who had assumed the title of Duke of Narbonne, in addition to that of Count of Toulouse, denying that Arnold had any right to temporal jurisdiction, entered the city of Narbonne by force, and erected there the ducal standard. Arnold fulminated an excommunication against Simon de Montfort, and placed the city of Narbonne under an interdict while he remained therein; but he found, to his great surprise and mortification, that these spiritual weapons were scorned by the leader of the Crusade.

Simon de Montfort was confronted by a more formidable enemy in the person of Raymond VII., son of Count Raymond VI. of Toulouse, who aided his father in a determined effort to recover the ancient inheritance of his race. Contrary to his own better judgment, Simon de Montfort was induced by Foulke, Bishop of Toulouse, to treat the citizens with treacherous cruelty because they manifested some symptoms of affection for their former lord. The result was that the people of Toulouse profited by Simon de Montfort's absence to invite Count Raymond VI. to resume his authority, and the count was publicly received into his old capital amid universal acclamations of joy, September 13, A. D. 1217.

By the assistance of the papal legate and the clergy, Simon de Montfort collected a large army; but the bravest of the Crusaders had perished in the preceding wars, or had returned to their homes in disgust. It was now universally known that heresy was extinguished in Languedoc, and that the war was maintained merely to gratify private revenge and individual ambition. Simon de Montfort laid siege to Toulouse, but was slain in a sally of the inhabitants; and after a vain effort to revenge his death, his son Almeric retired to Carcassonne.

The death of Simon de Montfort did not end the war against the Albigenses. Almeric de Montfort sold his claims over Languedoc to King Louis VIII. of France, the son and successor of Philip Augustus. Louis VIII. undertook a campaign to obtain possession of Toulouse; and with a powerful army he besieged Avignon, but only obtained possession of the town after a heroic defense on the part of the inhabitants, and after twenty thousand of his troops had perished miserably from disease and famine.

Louis VIII. died in A. D. 1226, soon after the fall of Avignon, after a short reign of three years; but the queen-regent, Blanche, prosecuted the war with such vigor that Count Raymond VII. was reduced to submission, and his dominions were united to the French crown, A. D. 1229. The Inquisition was at once established in Languedoc, and this unhappy territory in the South of France has not yet fully recovered from the calamities which it suffered at the hands of the instruments of papal vengeance.

www.ingramcontent.com/pod-product-compliance
Lightning Source LLC
Chambersburg PA
CBHW022112300426
44117CB00007B/688